THE GAA COVERED

THE GAA COVERED

THE HISTORY OF THE GAA IN MATCH PROGRAMMES

JOHN KELLY

GILL BOOKS

Gill Books
Hume Avenue
Park West
Dublin 12
www.gillbooks.ie
Gill Books is an imprint of M.H. Gill and Co.

9781804583388
Designed by Graham Thew Design © Gill Books
Typeset by Padraig McCormack
Edited by Noel O'Regan
Proofread by Jane Rogers
Printed and bound by Printer Trento, Italy.
This book is typeset in 9.5pt on 14pt, Calluna.
The paper used in this book comes from the wood pulp of sustainably managed forests.

To the best of our knowledge, this book complies in full with the requirements of the General Product Safety Regulation (GPSR). For further information and help with any safety queries, please contact us at productsafety@gill.ie.
A CIP catalogue record for this book is available from the British Library.
5 4 3 2 1
FSC www.fsc.org MIX Paper | Supporting responsible forestry FSC® C015829

To Maria, Pádraic and Lorcan, for the love, fun and support that has always been in our home; and to Mam and Dad.

AUTHOR'S NOTE

The motivation behind this book was to compile as comprehensive a collection of All-Ireland and provincial Gaelic Athletic Association (GAA) match programme covers as possible. I realised from the outset that this might be difficult to accomplish. There are several reasons for this. Some programmes may never have been printed for certain matches. Others are lost to the archive – i.e. they were printed, but copies of them are no longer in existence. Other programmes are retained privately, in all probability by relatives or descendants of those who played in the matches. They are now treasured family heirlooms and reminders of a proud achievement by a family member, but therefore difficult to source.

The lack of a single complete archive or collection is probably why this work has not been undertaken before now. Most of the programmes contained in this book are held in private collections and are owned by collectors who have assiduously collated and cared for these documents over many years, often at great expense. For them, it is a hobby and a labour of love, and I am eternally grateful to them for their cooperation in compiling this book.

In all cases every attempt has been made to locate the original document. The vast majority of the images in this book are scans of an original programme. In a small number of cases, it has not been possible to locate an original programme. Where a high-quality photocopy of the original programme has been available, it has been used as an alternative. Where this has been done, it will be indicated. The programmes for the All-Ireland finals of 1913 are the earliest surviving All-Ireland final programmes known to exist and therefore are the starting point for this project.

INTRODUCTION

Like many people, my first experience of the GAA was being brought to matches by my father. This took place in stages: first, to our local club, Palatine, then to Dr Cullen Park, the county grounds in Carlow, and, finally, to my first All-Ireland final in Croke Park in 1979. There I witnessed one of the contests between the great Dublin and Kerry teams of the 1970s. In time-honoured tradition, my father's ticket allowed me to be lifted over the turnstile. Once inside, my father bought the official match programme and gave it to me to mind. Thus began a lifelong pastime of buying the programme of every match I went to and keeping it as a souvenir of the event.

The primary purpose of the match programme is to name the players on each team. It should also include the match officials, the date, time and venue of the match. Most of the early GAA programmes merely fulfil this basic requirement. As programmes evolved, they also began to include photographs, match reports, season and all-time statistics, player profiles and advertisements. These features are what now make them invaluable local, social and sports history documents. Team and action photographs have preserved players in the vigour of their athletic youth. Contemporaneous match reports provide us with an idea of how the games were played and perceived at the time. Advertisements reflect how attitudes have changed regarding alcohol and tobacco consumption and, in some cases, gender roles. Player profiles and statistics have increased our awareness of the people who play our games and further our interest in the GAA.

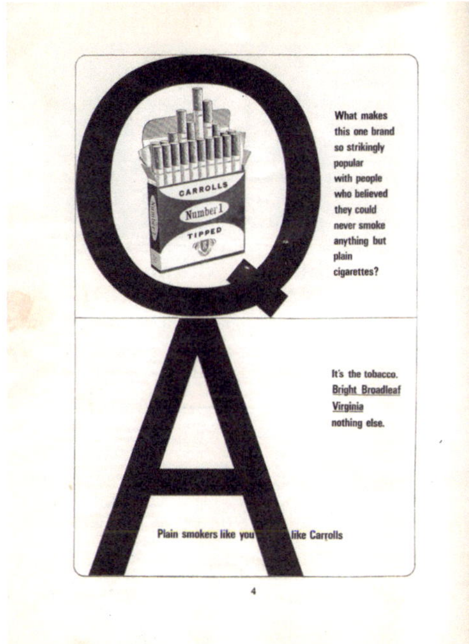

EARLY MATCH PROGRAMMES

The earliest known GAA programme was produced on 31 August 1886 for the 'First Grand Inter-County Contest' between Wicklow and Wexford at Avondale, the home of Charles Stewart Parnell. The contest consisted of six matches featuring various clubs from the respective counties. This programme listed the teams, players, match officials and also provided details of the trains on which spectators could travel to and from the venue.

The first programmes produced were never intended to be kept or indeed collected. They were ephemeral, for use on the day of the event to provide the spectators with information about the match. The programmes for the 1913 and 1914 All-Ireland finals were small and designed to fit into a coat pocket. In fact, some programmes advised spectators to dispose of the programme carefully after the match. This caused programmes to become scarce, and many are no longer in existence. Trying to source the material for this book therefore became an exercise in finding those programmes that have endured.

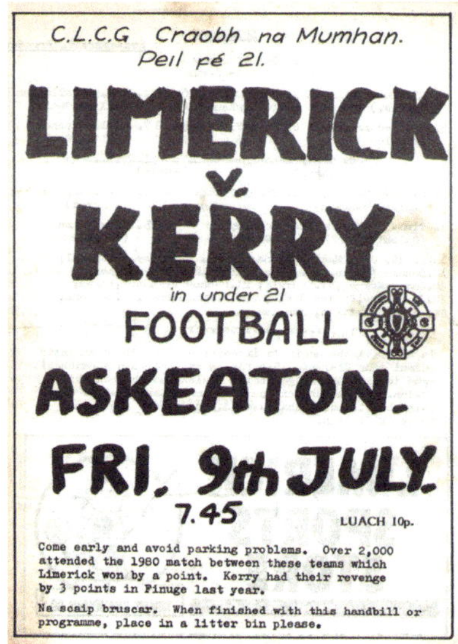
C.L.C.G Craobh na Mumhan.
Peil fé 21.

LIMERICK
v.
KERRY
in under 21
FOOTBALL
ASKEATON.
FRI. 9th JULY.
7.45

LUACH 10p.

Come early and avoid parking problems. Over 2,000 attended the 1980 match between these teams which Limerick won by a point. Kerry had their revenge by 3 points in Finuge last year.

Na scaip bruscar. When finished with this handbill or programme, place in a litter bin please.

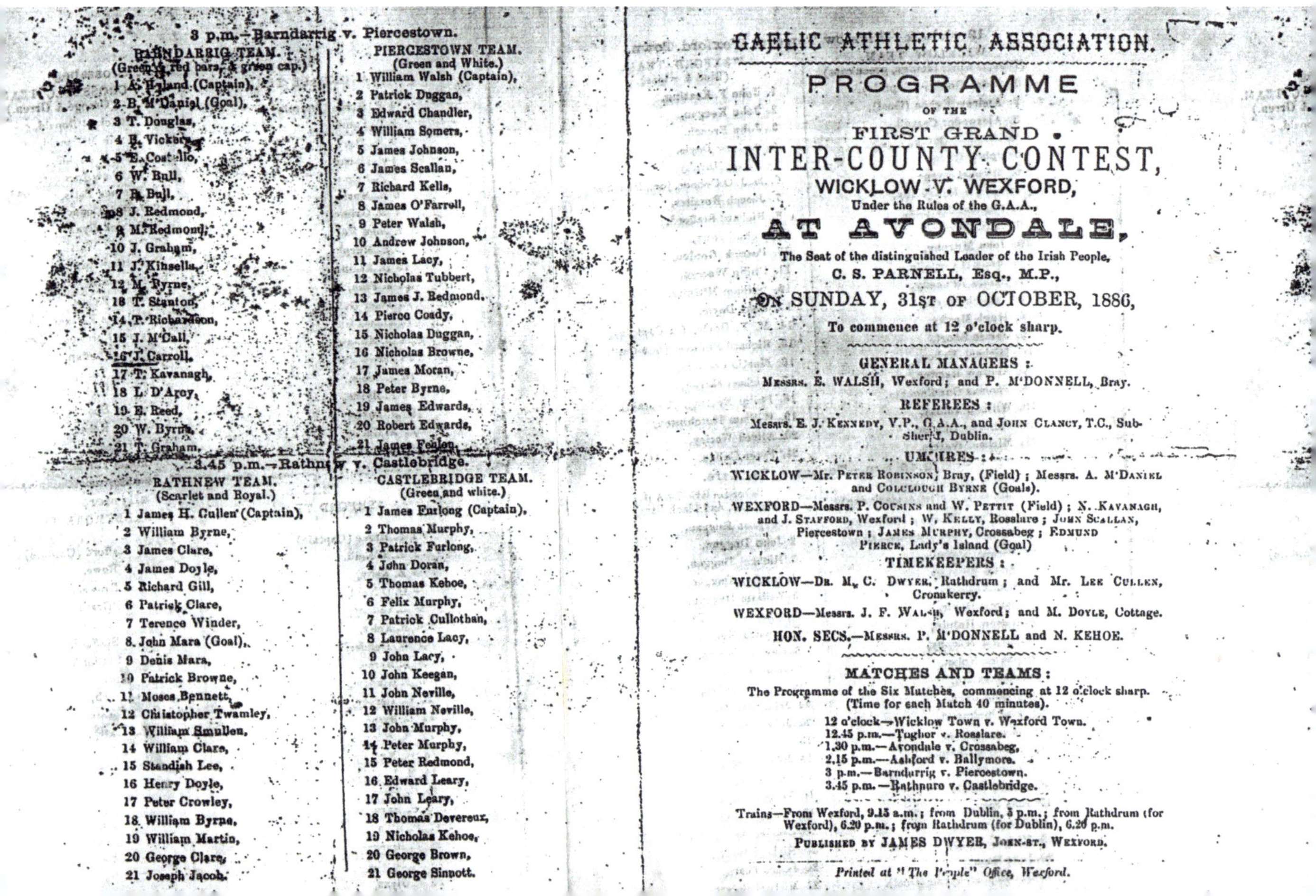
3 p.m.—Barndarrig v. Piercestown.

BARNDARRIG TEAM.
(Green & red bars, & green cap.)
1 A. Hyland (Captain),
2 B. M'Daniel (Goal),
3 T. Douglas,
4 B. Vickery,
5 E. Costello,
6 W. Bull,
7 R. Bull,
8 J. Redmond,
9 M. Redmond,
10 J. Graham,
11 J. Kinsella,
12 M. Byrne,
13 T. Stanton,
14 P. Richardson,
15 J. M'Call,
16 J. Carroll,
17 T. Kavanagh,
18 L. D'Arcy,
19 E. Reed,
20 W. Byrne,
21 T. Graham.

PIERCESTOWN TEAM.
(Green and White.)
1 William Walsh (Captain),
2 Patrick Duggan,
3 Edward Chandler,
4 William Somers,
5 James Johnson,
6 James Scallan,
7 Richard Kells,
8 James O'Farrell,
9 Peter Walsh,
10 Andrew Johnson,
11 James Lacy,
12 Nicholas Tubbert,
13 James J. Redmond,
14 Pierce Coady,
15 Nicholas Duggan,
16 Nicholas Browne,
17 James Moran,
18 Peter Byrne,
19 James Edwards,
20 Robert Edwards,
21 James Fenlon.

3.45 p.m.—Rathnew v. Castlebridge.

RATHNEW TEAM.
(Scarlet and Royal.)
1 James H. Cullen (Captain),
2 William Byrne,
3 James Clare,
4 James Doyle,
5 Richard Gill,
6 Patrick Clare,
7 Terence Winder,
8 John Mara (Goal),
9 Denis Mara,
10 Patrick Browne,
11 Moses Bennett,
12 Christopher Twamley,
13 William Smullen,
14 William Clare,
15 Standish Lee,
16 Henry Doyle,
17 Peter Crowley,
18 William Byrne,
19 William Martin,
20 George Clare,
21 Joseph Jacob.

CASTLEBRIDGE TEAM.
(Green and white.)
1 James Furlong (Captain),
2 Thomas Murphy,
3 Patrick Furlong,
4 John Doran,
5 Thomas Kehoe,
6 Felix Murphy,
7 Patrick Cullothan,
8 Laurence Lacy,
9 John Lacy,
10 John Keegan,
11 John Neville,
12 William Neville,
13 John Murphy,
14 Peter Murphy,
15 Peter Redmond,
16 Edward Leary,
17 John Leary,
18 Thomas Devereux,
19 Nicholas Kehoe,
20 George Brown,
21 George Sinnott.

GAELIC ATHLETIC ASSOCIATION.

PROGRAMME
OF THE
FIRST GRAND
INTER-COUNTY CONTEST,
WICKLOW V. WEXFORD,
Under the Rules of the G.A.A.,
AT AVONDALE,
The Seat of the distinguished Leader of the Irish People,
C. S. PARNELL, Esq., M.P.,
ON SUNDAY, 31ST OF OCTOBER, 1886,
To commence at 12 o'clock sharp.

GENERAL MANAGERS:
Messrs. E. WALSH, Wexford; and P. M'DONNELL, Bray.

REFEREES:
Messrs. E. J. Kennedy, V.P., G.A.A., and John Clancy, T.C., Sub-Sheriff, Dublin.

UMPIRES:
WICKLOW—Mr. Peter Robinson, Bray, (Field); Messrs. A. M'Daniel and Colclough Byrne (Goals).
WEXFORD—Messrs. P. Cousins and W. Pettit (Field); N. Kavanagh, and J. Stafford, Wexford; W. Kelly, Rosslare; John Scallan, Piercestown; James Murphy, Crossabeg; Edmund Pierce, Lady's Island (Goal)

TIMEKEEPERS:
WICKLOW—Dr. M. C. Dwyer, Rathdrum; and Mr. Lee Cullen, Cronakerry.
WEXFORD—Messrs. J. F. Walsh, Wexford; and M. Doyle, Cottage.

HON. SECS.—Messrs. P. M'DONNELL and N. KEHOE.

MATCHES AND TEAMS:
The Programme of the Six Matches, commencing at 12 o'clock sharp.
(Time for each Match 40 minutes).
12 o'clock—Wicklow Town v. Wexford Town.
12.45 p.m.—Tughor v. Rosslare.
1.30 p.m.—Avondale v. Crossabeg.
2.15 p.m.—Ashford v. Ballymore.
3 p.m.—Barndarrig v. Piercestown.
3.45 p.m.—Rathnew v. Castlebridge.

Trains—From Wexford, 9.15 a.m.; from Dublin, 3 p.m.; from Rathdrum (for Wexford), 6.20 p.m.; from Rathdrum (for Dublin), 6.20 p.m.

Published by JAMES DWYER, John-st., Wexford.

Printed at "The People" Office, Wexford.

ALL-IRELAND FINAL PROGRAMMES

The earliest surviving All-Ireland final programmes are those from the 1913 finals. Programmes from All-Ireland finals in 1914 and 1915 also survive, but from then until the mid-1920s, few remain. This may be attributed to the political situation in the country during those years when censorship and the breaking of printing presses made the production of programmes extremely difficult. The All-Ireland final programmes of the 1920s and 1930s were simple documents, usually an A4 page folded over and printed in black and white on delicate paper. They remained in this format up to 1942. In 1943, a coloured cover was added, and the programme took the form of a booklet. By 1945, black and white action and team photographs had been added to the booklet. The covers of the 1940s programmes are identifiable by their orange-coloured covers, which show an image of Michael Cusack accompanied by the national flag and GAA crest.

After a brief return to a plainer cover in 1951 and 1952, from 1953 the covers took on a more colourful appearance. They comprised a map of Ireland with the GAA crest in the centre and the crests of the four provinces placed in the corners of the cover. Further improvements in quality were made to the All-Ireland final programmes of the 1960s. This was largely due to the influence of Breandán Mac Lua from Co. Clare, who had been appointed to a full-time clerical position in Croke Park in 1964. The 1965 All-Ireland final programmes were larger in size and colour was added to black and white action photos on the cover. In 1976, the All-Ireland hurling final programme had a colour photograph on the front cover and on an inside page, but black and white photographs and advertisements remained in place until the end of the 1980s. By the end of that decade, the All-Ireland final programmes were predominantly colour productions printed on glossy A5 size paper and had grown in volume to 80 pages.

In 1995, the programme for the All-Ireland football final increased in size to an A4 full colour glossy publication. This format remained in place up to 2007 when the programmes returned to a smaller, more manageable size.

PROVINCIAL FINALS PROGRAMMES

Programmes for provincial finals were produced as early as the 1910s but due to the fleeting nature of their existence, they are now very rare. Provincial finals programmes for the post-war years are relatively easier to obtain. They too were usually single-page, fold-over sheets up until the early 1970s. The former Galway player and writer Jack

Mahon introduced the official souvenir programme for the 1971 Connacht football final and, inspired by this innovation, Paddy Flanagan, the Westmeath and Leinster GAA administrator, introduced a coloured cover booklet for the 1974 Leinster finals. The Munster Council provided a similar type of booklet in that year, while it was 1977 before the Ulster Council added colour to the cover of their provincial final programme, having used a standard cover for many years.

COST OF PROGRAMMES

In 1920, the cost of an All-Ireland final programme was a penny (1d). By 1930 it had risen to two pence. The 'Emergency' years (1939–46) saw rationing introduced to the country. Petrol and paper shortages meant that attendances and programme production decreased over the period. An outbreak of foot-and-mouth disease in 1941 affected both the ability of teams to enter the provincial and All-Ireland championships and of spectators to travel to matches. The price of the programme produced for the 1947 All-Ireland football final, played in New York's Polo Grounds, was 50 cents. By 1950, the cost of an All-Ireland final programme was three pence. The introduction of colour and an improvement in quality of the match programme in the 1960s saw the cost rise from six pence in 1960 to one shilling (6.25 cent approx.) in 1966.

Traditionally, VIP spectators seated in the Ard Chomhairle section of the Hogan Stand have received complimentary copies of the match programme. In the 1950s and 1960s, the covers of such programmes were made from embossed card rather than paper and did not have the cost of the programme printed on the cover. In 1984, when the GAA celebrated its centenary year, large commemorative programmes with a glossy card cover were produced, costing IR£1. Publication of the All-Ireland final programmes was taken over by the Dublin-based printing company DBA in 1988. Production quality improved, as did the content and volume of the programmes. By the turn of the century, the All-Ireland programme was £3 and with the changeover to the euro in 2002, the cover price became €4. In 2019 the All-Ireland hurling final programme contained 128 pages and the cover artwork paid homage to the cover of the 1913 final played at Jones's Road and featured a painting by George Fagan. The cost of that programme was €7. By 2024 this had further increased by one euro to €8.

UNOFFICIAL PROGRAMMES

G.A.A.

ALL-IRELAND FOOTBALL CHAMPIONSHIP.

CROKE PARK, SUNDAY NEXT.

MONAGHAN v. KERRY at 3 p.m.

OFFICIAL PROGRAMMES ON SALE ONLY WITHIN THE GROUNDS.

MINOR HURLING FINAL.

KILKENNY v. TIPPERARY, at 1.30.

JUNIOR HURLING REPLAY.

ANTRIM v. KILKENNY, at 4.15.

44,000 PEOPLE SAW LAST YEAR'S FINAL.

One of the difficulties in compiling this book is the existence of unofficial programmes, sometimes known as 'pirate programmes'. In the 1920s and 1930s, local printers often produced unofficial programmes to give people information about their teams and to provide reading and discussion material on the long train journeys to matches. From 1930, the signature of the then Ard Stiúrthóir, Pádraig Ó Caoimh, was added to the cover of the All-Ireland final programme and, along with the words 'Clár Oifigiúil', this identified the programme as the official GAA version. In most cases, the official match programmes were sold at turnstiles or inside the grounds but, in later years, spurious programmes were sold slightly further away from the stadium. These were usually of inferior quality to the genuine article and, with increased awareness around intellectual property rights, all but disappeared by the mid-1990s. When the official programme only became available inside the grounds, people soon stopped buying the pirate copies.

COLLECTORS AND COLLECTIONS

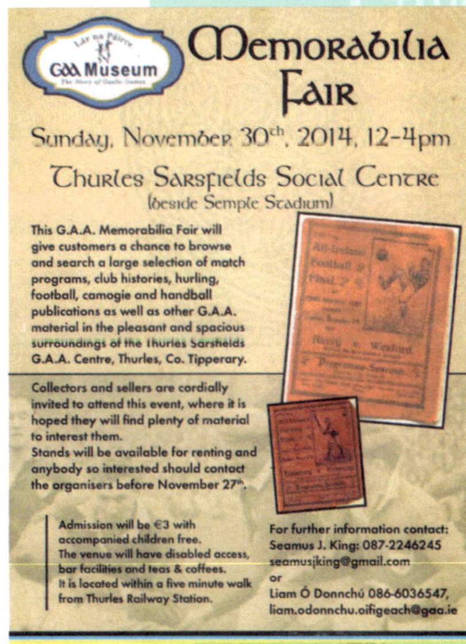

While some archives, such as those in the Croke Park Museum, the Cardinal Ó Fiaich Memorial Library and Muckross House Library contain GAA programmes in their catalogue, it is primarily the dedication of private collectors that has ensured that these documents are safely preserved for future generations. The concept of the souvenir programme only gained traction in the 1950s for All-Ireland final programmes and in the 1970s for provincial final programmes. Prior to that, the programme was a disposable commodity regarded as useless once the match was over. That so many of those items have survived is a credit to the people who recognised the value in keeping them. A committed network of programme collectors exists throughout the country. Programmes are exchanged by swapping and buying and selling at various fairs which take place annually in Thurles, Co. Tipperary and Graiguenamanagh, Co. Kilkenny. Lately there has been increased interest in collecting GAA programmes and memorabilia. As a result, many items are now attracting significant sums of money when they come up for sale at auction houses around the country or on internet sites such as eBay.

MacNAMEE AWARDS AND DIGITAL PROGRAMMES

To reward the coverage and promotion of GAA activities, the GAA MacNamee Awards are held annually 'to honour excellence in the area of communications, public relations and journalism, specifically related to the activities of the Association'. These awards are named after the late Pádraig MacNamee, a former president of the GAA. One of the awards presented is for 'Best Programme – To cater for all match day programmes produced for any level of the GAA'. The award is not limited to national publications but can be won by local public relations officers for work within their counties. Modern intercounty programmes have very high production standards, but they have become homogenous. Where previously, local printers published the provincial final match programmes, most are now printed by the same company. In contrast, local county final programmes are more attractive to collectors due to their variety of style and content.

Just as design and production values were reaching new heights, the integrity of the GAA match programme suffered from the advent of the 'dummy team' in the 1990s. In an attempt to frustrate opponents, the team printed in the programme often bore little resemblance to the team that took the field. A further setback occurred during the Covid-19 pandemic. Spectators were unable to attend matches and therefore physical programmes were not necessary. Many county boards and provincial councils, as well as DBA, made match programmes available to download via websites and social media. As well as adapting to a modern environment where much content is accessed digitally, boards and councils recognised that there is a considerable cost saving to be had by not printing large numbers of programmes for each match. Similar cost-cutting has in recent years sometimes seen a single programme represent several games. Some county boards continue to make their programmes available online.

However, for many spectators – and some managers – the programme is a working document where scores, wides and substitutions are recorded during a match. Mick O'Dwyer and, more recently, Kieran McGeeney regularly patrolled the sidelines with their programme for reference. For these people, nothing beats having the match programme in their hands and it remains an essential accessory to the match day experience.

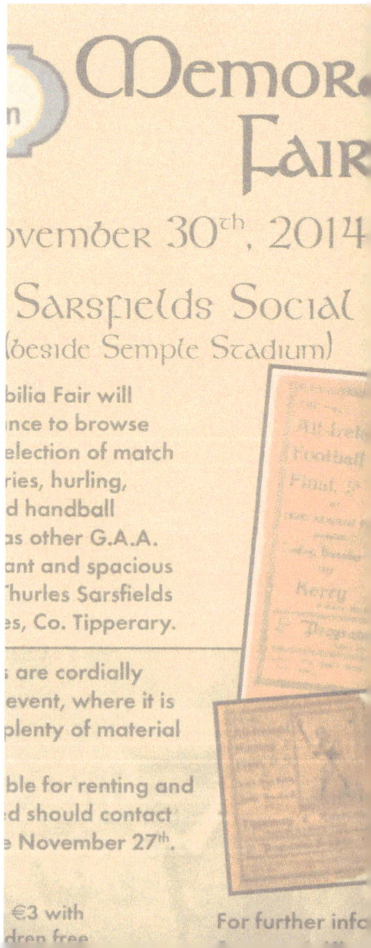

ᴀ b c ᴅ e ꝼ ᵹ h ı l m n o p ʀ s ᴛ u
ᴀ b c ᴅ e ꝼ ᵹ h ı l m n o p ꞃ ꞅ ᴛ u
a b c d e f g h i l m n o p r s t u

USE OF IRISH LANGUAGE FONT STYLE AND ORTHOGRAPHY

As a cultural organisation, the GAA was widely recognised as the sporting element of the Gaelic revival and the promotion of the Irish language was an inherent part of its mission. The most visible demonstration of the GAA's commitment to the native tongue was its match programmes, where *an Ghaeilge* was used on the covers and to name players and officials. Until the late 1950s, the orthography of the Irish language and style of print was different from what is used today. The old style of print, *an cló Gaelach* or *seanchló*, was first used on All-Ireland final programmes in 1930. Within this style, the particular font used appears to be the Newman font, first introduced in 1858. Also used was the old Gaelic alphabet – *an aibítir* – which comprised 18 letters.

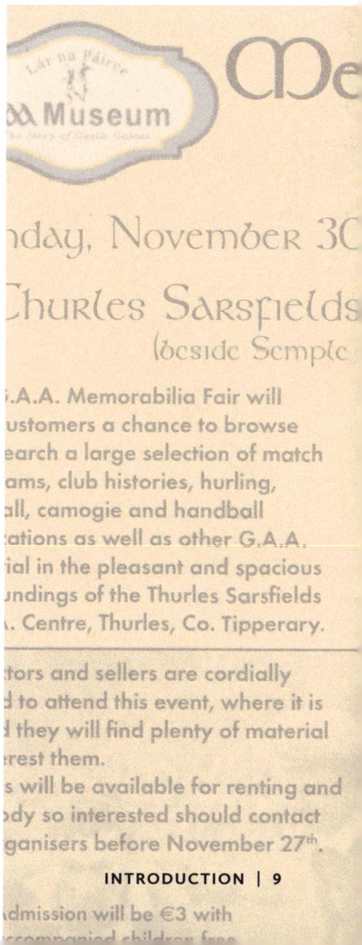

A dot, or *séimhiú*, above a consonant meant that the sound was 'softened'. The *séimhiú* is no longer in use today, and the letter 'h' is used instead, e.g. Coꞃcaiġ (*seancló*) – Corcaigh.

The *cló Gaelach* went out of fashion in 1958 when the language was standardised, and the English alphabet came into use. The font was no longer used on All-Ireland final programmes from 1966 but remained in use on Leinster final programmes up to 1970. The manner in which county names were spelled also changed after standardisation and the new versions became the norm. For example An Luġḃaiḋ became An Lú (Louth), An Ṁiḋe became An Mhí (Meath) and Ciaꞃꞃaiḋe became Ciarraí (Kerry).

The *seanchló* endured, however, mostly being used for ornamental design purposes. In 2016, for the 100th anniversary commemorations of the 1916 Easter Rising, the old font, if not the spelling, was used on the covers of the All-Ireland final programmes. It has remained in use on the covers of All-Ireland final programmes since.

All-Ireland Football Final,

AT

CROKE MEMORIAL PARK

DUBLIN,

Sunday, December 14

1913–15

1913

The covers of the 1913 All-Ireland final programmes tell the story of the acquisition of Croke Park by the GAA. Frank Dineen purchased the Jones's Road sports grounds in 1908 and established it as the main venue for Gaelic games in Dublin. In 1913, the GAA bought the site from Dineen. That year's All-Ireland hurling final between Kilkenny and Tipperary on 2 November took place at Jones's Road. Two weeks later the football final between Kerry and Wexford took place at the same grounds, now renamed Croke Memorial Park according to the match programme cover. Formal ownership of the site didn't transfer to the GAA until 22 December 1913. The number of players on football and hurling teams was reduced from 17 to 15 for this year's championship and, in the hurling final, Kilkenny defeated Tipperary. In the football final, Kerry, captained by Dick Fitzgerald, the author of *How To Play Gaelic Football*, accounted for Wexford.

1

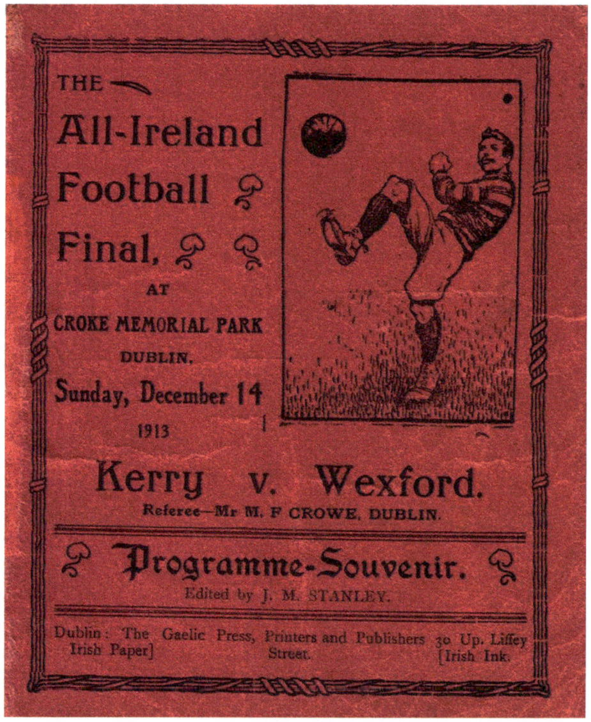

2

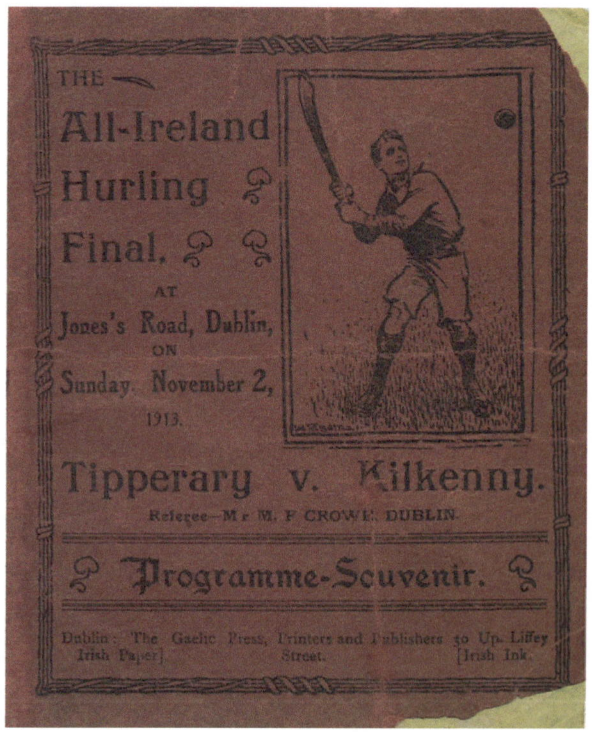

1 All-Ireland Football Final
Kerry 2-02 Wexford 0-03
Attendance – 20,000

2 All-Ireland Hurling Final
Kilkenny 2-04 Tipperary 1-02
Attendance – 15,000

3 Leinster Football Final
Wexford 2-03 Louth 2-02

3

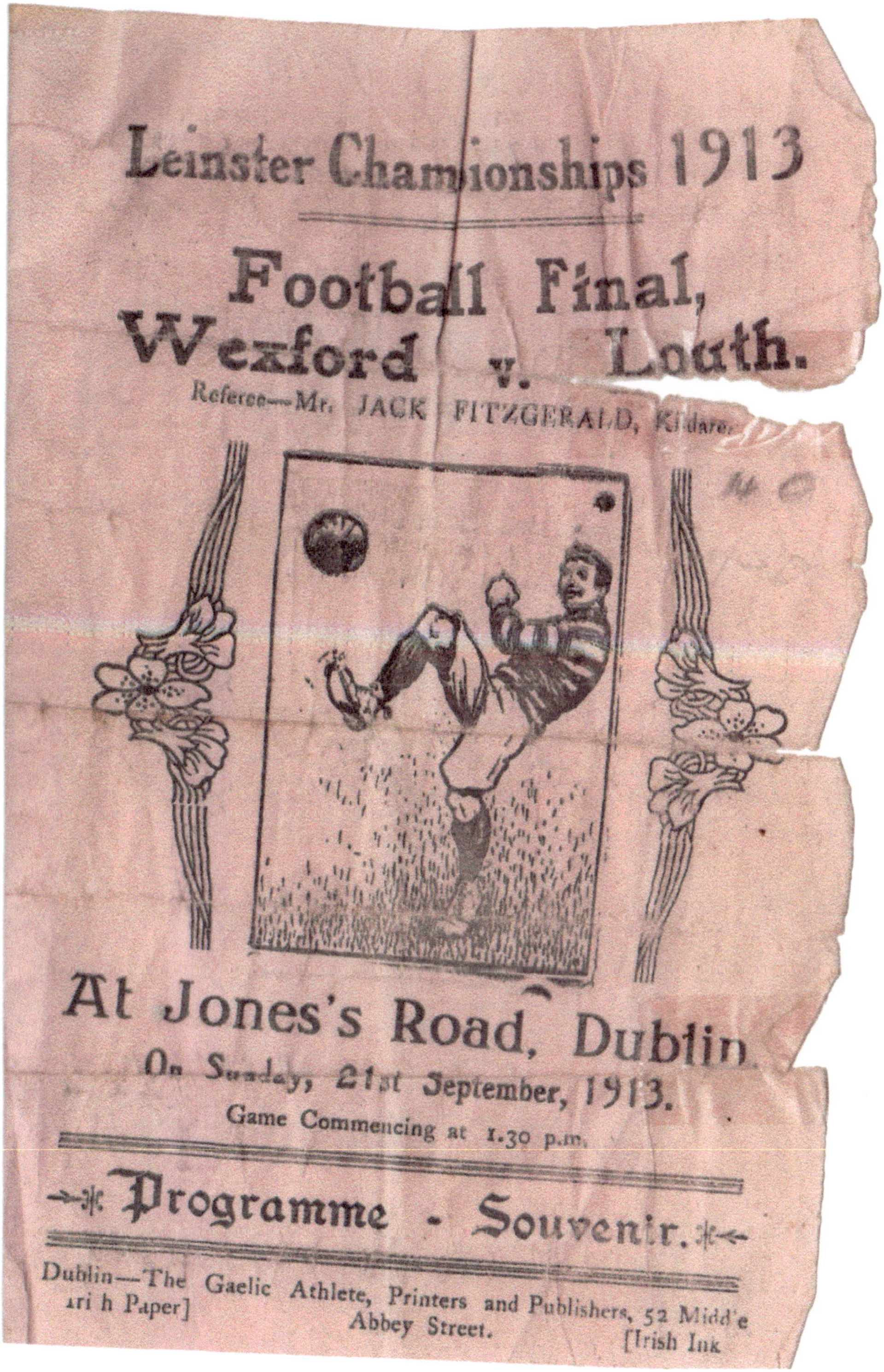

Leinster Championships 1913

Football Final,
Wexford v. Louth.

Referee—Mr. JACK FITZGERALD, Kildare.

At Jones's Road, Dublin.
On Sunday, 21st September, 1913.
Game Commencing at 1.30 p.m.

Programme - Souvenir.

Dublin—The Gaelic Athlete, Printers and Publishers, 52 Midd'e Abbey Street.
iri h Paper] [Irish Ink

1914

The programmes for the 1913, 1914 and 1915 All-Ireland finals feature depictions of a footballer and a hurler on their front covers. These illustrations were the work of artist George Fagan (1879–1907) and show the players in action poses, about to kick or strike the ball. The illustrations were again used for the covers of the 2019 All-Ireland hurling and football finals. Wexford and Kerry met for the second year in a row in the 1914 All-Ireland football final. The match ended in a draw, with Kerry going on to win the replay by three points. A match programme for the replay does not appear to exist. Both matches were refereed by the chairman of the Dublin County Board, Harry Boland. In the hurling final, Clare defeated Leix (Laois) to win their first All-Ireland title.

1

THE : : :
All-Ireland :
Football : :
Final : : :
AT
CROKE PARK,
DUBLIN
On Sunday, November 29, 1914
KERRY V. WEXFORD
Referee—MR. HAR[illegible] BOLAND, DUBLIN.
Programme Souvenir
DUBLIN:
The Gaelic Athlete, Printers and Publishers, 30 Upper Liffey Street
Irish Paper] [Irish Ink

1 All-Ireland Football Final
Kerry 1-03 Wexford 2-00
Attendance – 15,000

2 All-Ireland Hurling Final
Clare 5-01 Laois 1-00
Attendance – 12,127

THE

All-Ireland : Hurling : Final : :

AT

CROKE PARK,

DUBLIN

Sunday, October 18th, 1914

LEIX v. CLARE.

Referee—Mr. JOHN LALOR, KILKENNY.

Programme Souvenir

DUBLIN:
The Gaelic Athlete, Printers and Publishers, 30 Upper Liffey Street
Irish Paper] [Irish Ink

1915

Wexford were eventually crowned All-Ireland football champions at the third time of asking in 1915. Having been beaten in the previous two finals by Kerry, victory over the same opposition in this year's final allowed Wexford some satisfaction in having atoned for those defeats. In the years before the Sam Maguire Cup was awarded to the All-Ireland football winners, the Wexford captain, Seán Kennedy, was presented with the new Railway Cup. Kerry were allowed to keep the previous version of the cup, having won it in 1913 and 1914. This was the beginning of a remarkable run for the Wexford football team, winning four titles in a row and going undefeated in the championship until the 1919 Leinster semi-final.

Leix (Laois) returned to the All-Ireland hurling final in 1915 and avenged their defeat to Clare 12 months previously by beating Cork to win their first and only All-Ireland hurling title. As with Kennedy, the Wexford football captain, the Leix captain John (Jack) Finlay was also the team's goalkeeper.

1

1 All-Ireland Football Final
Wexford 2-04 Kerry 2-01
Attendance – 25,000

2 All-Ireland Hurling Final (photocopy)
Laois 6-02 Cork 4-01
Attendance – 11,000

ALL-IRELAND HURLING FINAL

1915

2

CORK v. LEIX

Croke Park, Jones' Road, Dublin

On Sunday, 24th October, 1915

Game Commencing at 2.45 p.m.

Referee .. Mr. WILLIAM WALSH, Waterford

Programme & Souvenir

The Gaelic Athlete, Printers and Publishers, 30 Upper Liffey Street, Dublin.

1920–29

1920

The 1920 All-Ireland football final programme is extremely rare, with only one copy known to exist. It is also quite small in comparison to today's programmes, being slightly larger than a playing card. With the War of Independence raging across the country since the previous year, only Leinster and Connacht managed to complete their provincial championships this year. With the disruption to the championship, Tipperary challenged Dublin to a match to determine the superior team. The match, played in Croke Park on 21 November 1920, was in progress when British forces opened fire on spectators and players, killing 14 people in what became known as Bloody Sunday. The 1920 All-Ireland final was not played until 11 June 1922 and it brought together again the two teams who had played in Croke Park on that infamous day, with several survivors on both teams still playing. Dan Breen, the IRA volunteer who had been on the run from the British Army in 1920, threw in the ball to start the final, which Tipperary won by four points.

1

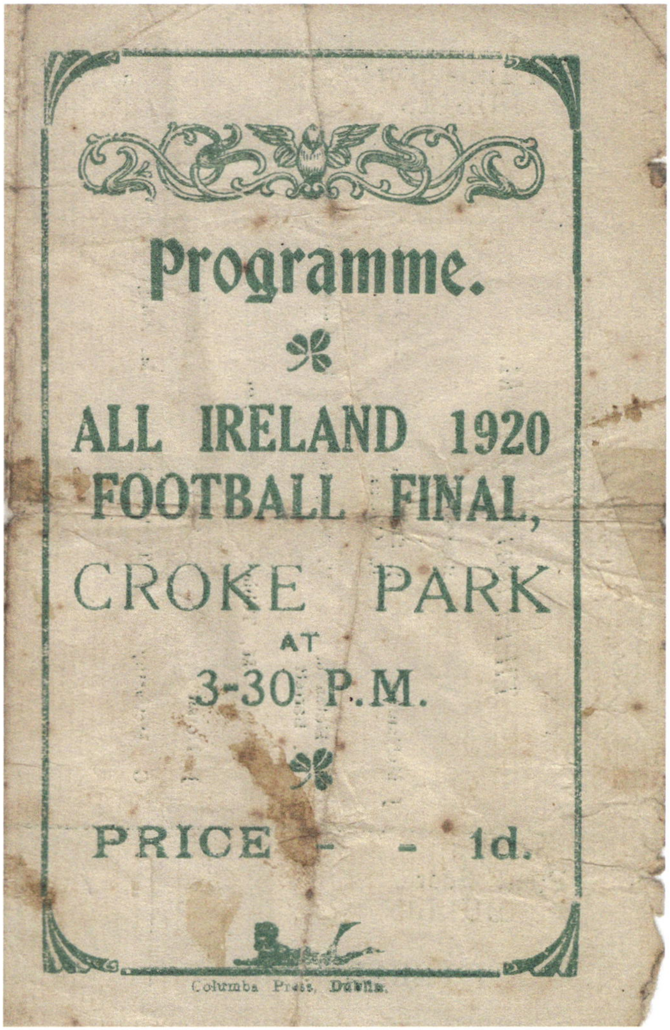

1 All-Ireland Final
Tipperary 1-06 Dublin 1-02
Attendance – 25,000

1924

With political tensions following the Civil War still causing difficulties in Munster, the 1924 All-Ireland football final did not take place until 26 April 1925. For five shillings, spectators could sit in the new 1,400-seat stand that had been erected in Croke Park for the 1924 Tailteann Games. Two weeks before the final, the GAA's Central Council agreed that the stand should be named after Michael Hogan, the Tipperary footballer who had lost his life on Bloody Sunday. In the final, Dublin came up against Kerry for the second year in a row, hoping to retain the title they had won just seven months previously. This time, however, Kerry won a low-scoring affair by a single point scored by their star player, Con Brosnan. A new scoreboard installed at the Railway end was also in use for the first time and at the final whistle it showed Kerry 0-04 Dublin 0-03.

1

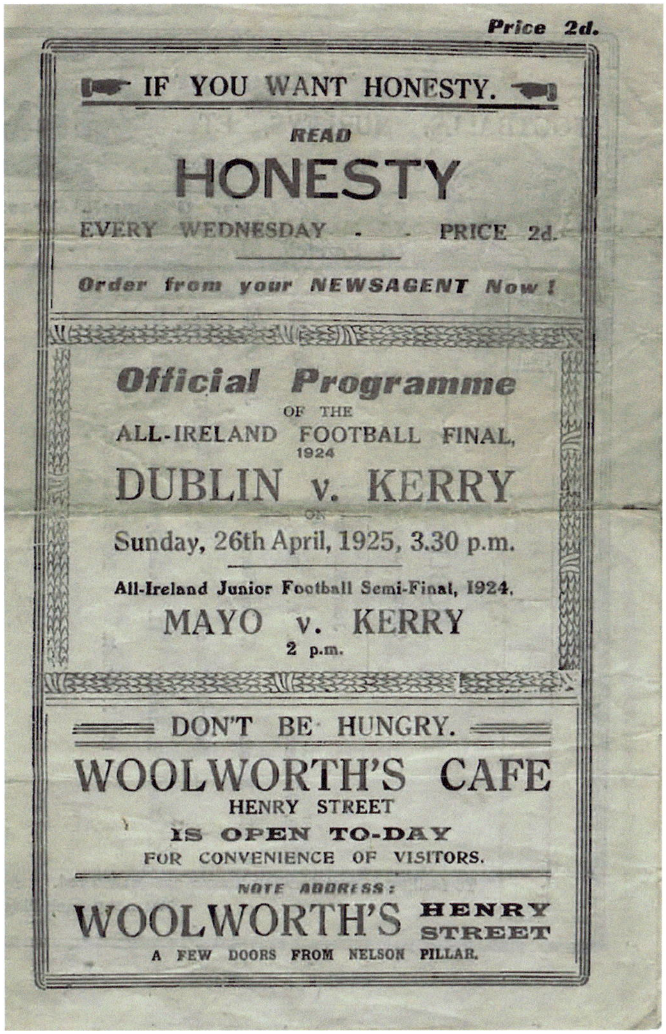

1 All-Ireland Final
Kerry 0-04 Dublin 0-03
Attendance – 28,844

1926

After several years without programmes for some provincial or All-Ireland finals and indeed without an All-Ireland football final in 1925, this year marked the re-emergence of the GAA match programme. The Munster hurling final between Cork and Tipperary took three matches to decide a winner. The first match had to be abandoned when the large crowd encroached on the pitch. The re-fixture in Thurles ended in a draw and Cork eventually had the better of the replay. The delay in Munster meant that the All-Ireland football final was played earlier than the hurling final in 1926, with Kerry defeating Kildare after a replay. In the All-Ireland hurling final, Cork easily defeated Kilkenny to take home the Liam MacCarthy Cup (named after the Irish nationalist businessman and chairman of London County Board who donated the cup to the GAA Central Council) for the first time. 1926 also saw the introduction of the National League competitions, and the All-Ireland hurling semi-final between Kilkenny and Galway was the first match to be broadcast live on Irish radio.

1

Cumann na gCleas Lúṫ nGaeḋealaċ

LEINSTER CHAMPIONSHIP, 1926

OFFICIAL PROGRAMME

SENIOR FOOTBALL FINAL

KILDARE v. WEXFORD

AT 3.15 P.M.

REFEREE—TOM BURKE (LOUTH).

JUNIOR HURLING SEMI-FINAL AT 2 P.M.

LEIX v. DUBLIN

Referee—P. McCullagh (Wexford).

AT

CROKE PARK

ON

Sunday, 1st August, 1926

This programme is officially issued by the Leinster Council, G.A.A., and the

PRICE IS - - ONE PENNY

1 Leinster Football Final
Kildare 2-08 Wexford 1-05

2 All-Ireland Football Final
Kerry 1-03 Kildare 0-06
Attendance – 37,500

2

Cumann na gCleas Lúṫ nGaeḋealaċ.

GAELIC ATHLETIC ASSOCIATION

ALL-IRELAND FOOTBALL FINAL

KERRY

v.

KILDARE

AT

CROKE PARK

5th SEPTEMBER, 1926

Match 3.[illegible] p.m.

Mr. T. Shevlin, Roscommon, Referee.

Wood Printing Works, Ltd., F[illegible] Street, Dublin.—4846

3

Cumann na gCleas Lúth nGaedhealach.
GAELIC ATHLETIC ASSOCIATION
ALL-IRELAND FOOTBALL FINAL
REPLAY.
KERRY
v.
KILDARE
3 P.M.
Junior Football Semi-Final:
Armagh v. Sligo,
1.30 P.M.,
AT CROKE PARK,
OCTOBER 17th, 1926.
MR. T. SHEVLIN, ROSCOMMON, REFEREE.
Wood Printing Works, Ltd., Fleet Street, Dublin.—4969

5

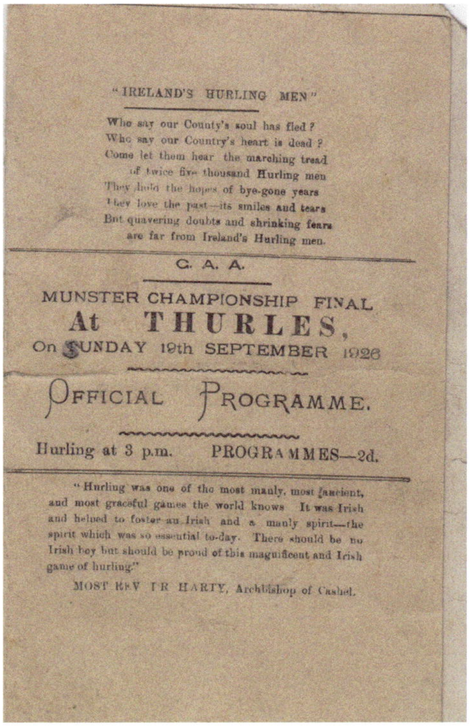

"IRELAND'S HURLING MEN"
Who say our County's soul has fled?
Who say our Country's heart is dead?
Come let them hear the marching tread
of twice five thousand Hurling men
They hold the hopes of bye-gone years
They love the past—its smiles and tears
But quavering doubts and shrinking fears
are far from Ireland's Hurling men.
G. A. A.
MUNSTER CHAMPIONSHIP FINAL
At THURLES,
On SUNDAY 19th SEPTEMBER 1926
OFFICIAL PROGRAMME.
Hurling at 3 p.m. PROGRAMMES—2d.
"Hurling was one of the most manly, most ancient, and most graceful games the world knows It was Irish and helped to foster an Irish and a manly spirit—the spirit which was so essential to-day. There should be no Irish boy but should be proud of this magnificent and Irish game of hurling."
MOST REV DR HARTY, Archbishop of Cashel.

4

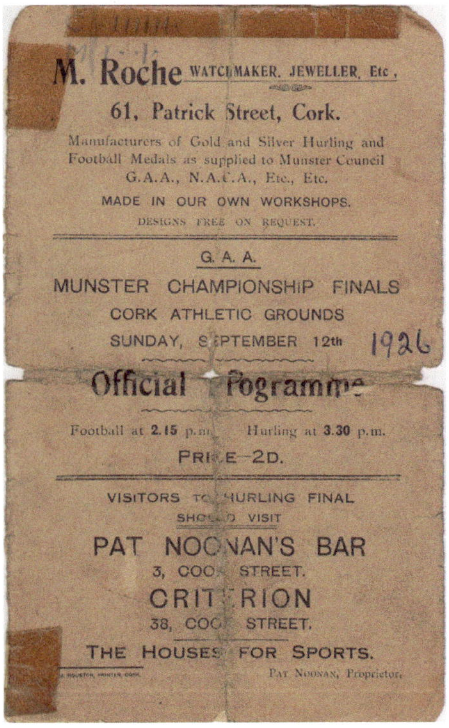

M. Roche WATCHMAKER, JEWELLER, Etc.,
61, Patrick Street, Cork.
Manufacturers of Gold and Silver Hurling and Football Medals as supplied to Munster Council G.A.A., N.A.C.A., Etc., Etc.
MADE IN OUR OWN WORKSHOPS.
DESIGNS FREE ON REQUEST.
G. A. A.
MUNSTER CHAMPIONSHIP FINALS
CORK ATHLETIC GROUNDS
SUNDAY, SEPTEMBER 12th 1926
Official Programme
Football at 2.15 p.m. Hurling at 3.30 p.m.
PRICE—2D.
VISITORS TO HURLING FINAL
SHOULD VISIT
PAT NOONAN'S BAR
3, COOK STREET.
CRITERION
38, COOK STREET.
THE HOUSES FOR SPORTS.
PAT NOONAN, Proprietor.

6

OFFICIAL PROGRAMME]
[PRICE—TWO PENCE.
JOHN LEAHY.
Referee—D. LANIGAN.
SEAN MURPHY.
C. A. A.
MUNSTER CHAMPIONSHIP FINAL
At THURLES,
On SUNDAY, 3rd OCTOBER, 1926, at 3 p.m.
Liberty Printing Works, Thurles.

7

Cumann na gCleas Lúċ nGaeḋealaċ.
GAELIC ATHLETIC ASSOCIATION

Official Programme.

HURLING FINAL

CORK

V.

KILKENNY

P.M.

AT CROKE PARK,

OCTOBER 24th, 1926.

MR. P. McCULLAGH, WEXFORD, REFEREE.

Musical Programme

The Irish Transport and General Workers' Union Band will perform the following selections:

MARCH	"Kelly the Boy from Killann"	J. Mullins
OVERTURE	"Light Cavalry"	Suppé
VALSE	"Casino Tango"	J. Gungl
SELECTION	"H.M.S. Pinafore"	F. Godfrey
SERENADE	"La Paloma"	[illegible]
SELECTION	"Humours of Donnybrook"	Carl Volti
INTERMEZZO	"After Sunset"	S. C. Jones
FINALE	National Anthem	P. Heaney

CONDUCTOR—MR. A. BURKE, B.M.T.S.M.

Wood Printing Works, Ltd. Fleet Street Dublin.—5000

3 Replay
Kerry 1-04 Kildare 0-04
Attendance – 35,500

4 Munster Hurling Final
Tipperary 1-02 Cork 0-00
(Match abandoned)

5 Re-fixture
Cork 4-01 Tipperary 3-04

6 Replay (photocopy)
Cork 3-06 Tipperary 2-04

7 All-Ireland Hurling Final
Cork 4-06 Kilkenny 2-00
Attendance – 26,829

1927

Music has traditionally been part of the pre-match entertainment on All-Ireland final day, whether by the Artane Band or other musicians, such as Liam O'Connor and Sharon Shannon in recent years. In 1927, the Irish Transport and General Workers' Union Band played for the spectators before both All-Ireland finals. The match programme cover lists the various musical pieces, finishing with the national anthem. Kerry and Kildare were back in the All-Ireland football final, with Kerry hoping to retain their title and claim a three in a row of sorts, given that there had been no final in 1925. Kildare, however, were in no mood to lose consecutive finals and beat Kerry by 0-05 to 0-03, coincidentally the same scoreline as in their defeat of Dublin in the Leinster final. In the All-Ireland hurling final, Dublin, availing of a new player residence rule that allowed players to play for an adopted county they lived in, were surprise winners over a fancied Cork team who were the reigning champions.

1

Cumann na gCleaṡ Lúṫ nGaeḋealaċ.

Souvenir Programme

OF

Leinster Football Final

KILDARE

v.

DUBLIN

At 3.30 p.m.

AT CROKE PARK

ON

Sunday, 14th August, 1927.

REFEREE—T. BURKE (Louth).

This Programme is officially issued by the Leinster Council, G.A.A.

Máirtín Ó Néill, Rúnaiḋe

2

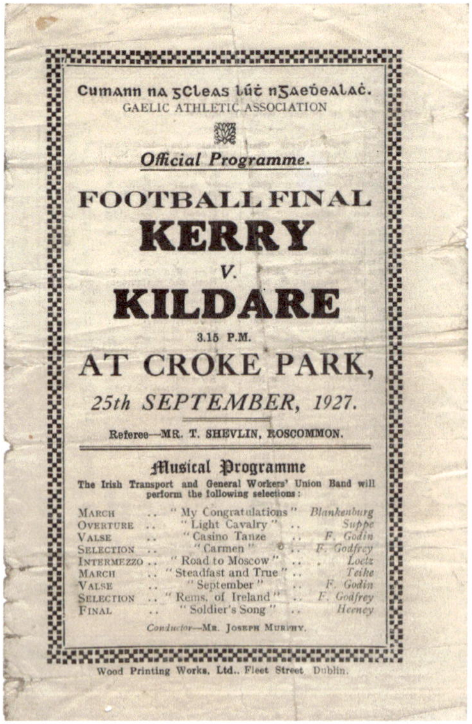

Cumann na gCleas Lúṫ nGaeḋealaċ.

GAELIC ATHLETIC ASSOCIATION

Official Programme.

FOOTBALL FINAL

KERRY

V.

KILDARE

3.15 P.M.

AT CROKE PARK,

25th SEPTEMBER, 1927.

Referee—MR. T. SHEVLIN, ROSCOMMON.

Musical Programme

The Irish Transport and General Workers' Union Band will perform the following selections:

MARCH ..	"My Congratulations"	*Blankenburg*
OVERTURE ..	"Light Cavalry" ..	*Suppe*
VALSE ..	"Casino Tanze ..	*F. Godin*
SELECTION ..	"Carmen" ..	*F. Godfrey*
INTERMEZZO ..	"Road to Moscow" ..	*Loetz*
MARCH ..	"Steadfast and True" ..	*Teike*
VALSE ..	"September" ..	*F. Godin*
SELECTION ..	"Rems. of Ireland" ..	*F. Godfrey*
FINAL ..	"Soldier's Song" ..	*Heeney*

Conductor—MR. JOSEPH MURPHY.

Wood Printing Works, Ltd., Fleet Street, Dublin.

1 Leinster Football Final
Kildare 0-05 Dublin 0-03

2 All-Ireland Football Final
Kildare 0-05 Kerry 0-03
Attendance – 36,529

3 Leinster Hurling Final
Dublin 7-07 Kilkenny 4-06

Cumann na gCleas Lúċ

nGaeḋealaċ.

Souvenir Programme

OF

Leinster Hurling Final:

KILKENNY

v.

DUBLIN

At 2.45 p.m.

AT CROKE PARK

ON

Sunday, 17th July, 1927.

REFEREE—P. McCULLAGH (Wexford)

This Programme is officially issued
by the Leinster Council, G.A.A.

Máirtín Ó Néill, Rúnaiḋe

HANRAHAN, PRINTER, WEXFORD.

4

Cumann na gCleas Lúṫ nGaeḋealaċ.

GAELIC ATHLETIC ASSOCIATION

Official Programme.

HURLING FINAL

CORK

v.

DUBLIN

3.30 P.M.

AT CROKE PARK,

4th SEPTEMBER, 1927.

MR. D. LANIGAN, LIMERICK, REFEREE.

Musical Programme

The Irish Transport and General Workers' Union Band will perform the following selections:

MARCH	..	" Colonel J. Ward "	.. *J. Cheeseman*
OVERTURE	..	" La Villagiose "	.. *A. Morelli*
VALSE ..	..	" Smiles and Kisses "	.. *C. Ancliffe*
SELECTION	..	" H.M.S. Pianofore "	.. *F. Godfrey*
DESCRIPTIVE	..	" Husking Bee "	.. *T. Thurban*
		INTERVAL.	
MARCH ..	..	" The Contemptibles "	.. *R. Stanley*
SELECTION	..	" Rems of Plantations "	.. *Chambers*
VALSE ..	..	" Flower Maiden "	.. *D. Godfrey*
SERENADE	..	" La Palonna "	.. *J. Hartman*
MARCH ..	..	" Kwang Hsu "	.. *P. Linke*
FINAL ..	..	" Soldier's Song "	.. *Heeney*

Conductor—MR. JOSEPH MURPHY.

Wood Printing Works, Ltd., Fleet Street, Dublin.

4 All-Ireland Hurling Final
Dublin 4-08 Cork 1-03
Attendance – 23,824

1928

The new Liam MacCarthy Cup was first presented in 1923 to the winners of the 1921 All-Ireland hurling final, Limerick. In 1928, it was lifted by Cork captain Seán Óg Murphy following a comprehensive win over Galway. For the years since 1917, though, no cup had been presented to the All-Ireland football champions as Wexford were allowed to keep the second Railway Cup, having won it in 1915 and 1916. In 1928, the new Sam Maguire Cup (named after the prominent republican and GAA administrator in London) was first presented to the captain of the All-Ireland-winning football team. Contesting their third final in a row, Kildare were the firm favourites to win the final and this expectation had the effect of diminishing the crowd, which was down by 12,000 on the 1927 final. The result was much closer than expected, however, and Kildare only had a point to spare over Cavan before Bill 'Squires' Gannon had the honour of lifting the new cup.

1

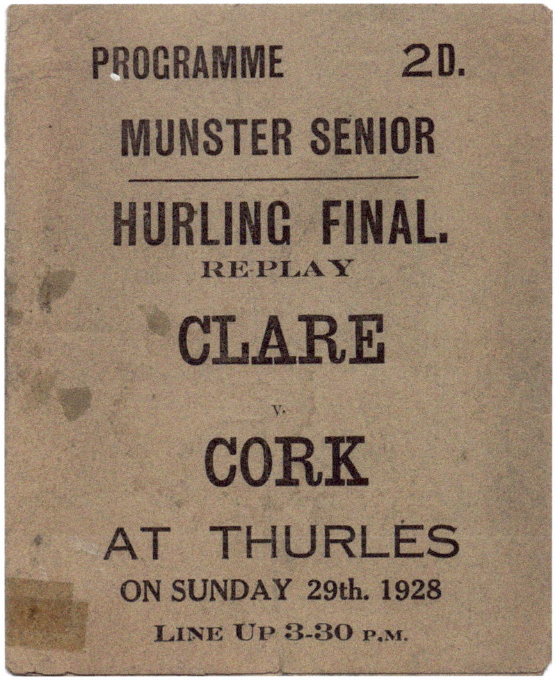
PROGRAMME 2D.
MUNSTER SENIOR
HURLING FINAL.
REPLAY
CLARE
v.
CORK
AT THURLES
ON SUNDAY 29th. 1928
LINE UP 3-30 P.M.

2

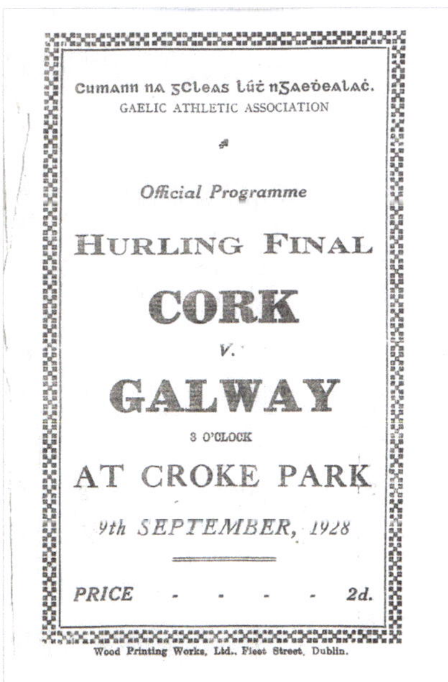
Cumann na gCleas Lúth nGaedhealach.
GAELIC ATHLETIC ASSOCIATION
Official Programme
HURLING FINAL
CORK
v.
GALWAY
3 O'CLOCK
AT CROKE PARK
9th SEPTEMBER, 1928
PRICE - - - - 2d.
Wood Printing Works, Ltd., Fleet Street, Dublin.

3

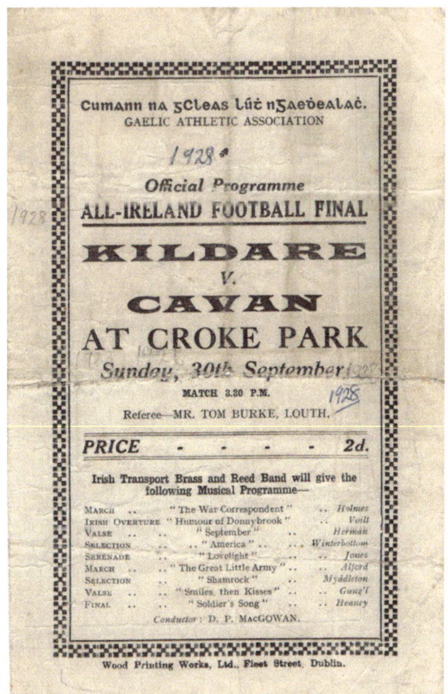
Cumann na gCleas Lúth nGaedhealach.
GAELIC ATHLETIC ASSOCIATION
Official Programme
ALL-IRELAND FOOTBALL FINAL
KILDARE
v.
CAVAN
AT CROKE PARK
Sunday, 30th September
MATCH 3.30 P.M.
Referee—MR. TOM BURKE, LOUTH.
PRICE - - - - 2d.
Irish Transport Brass and Reed Band will give the following Musical Programme—
MARCH .. "The War Correspondent" .. Holmes
IRISH OVERTURE "Humour of Donnybrook" .. Voill
VALSE .. .. "September" .. Herman
SELECTION .. .. "America" .. ... Winterbottom
SERENADE .. "Lovelight" .. .. Jones
MARCH .. .. "The Great Little Army" .. .. Alford
SELECTION .. "Shamrock" .. Myddleton
VALSE .. .. "Smiles, then Kisses" .. .. Gung'l
FINAL .. .. "Soldier's Song" .. .. Heaney
Conductor: D. P. MACGOWAN.
Wood Printing Works, Ltd., Fleet Street, Dublin.

1 Munster Hurling Final Replay
Cork 6-04 Clare 2-02

2 All-Ireland Hurling Final (photocopy)
Cork 6-12 Galway 1-00
Attendance – 15,259

3 All-Ireland Football Final
Kildare 2-06 Cavan 2-05
Attendance – 24,700

1929

The sudden death of the GAA Central Council secretary, Luke O'Toole, in July 1929 left the association without an administrator. His replacement, Pádraig Ó Caoimh, was appointed at the end of August of that year. This is also the most likely reason why 1929 is the last year without a known existing copy of an All-Ireland hurling final programme. No programme appears to be available for the hurling final played on 1 September, as Ó Caoimh had yet to take up his new position. The name of the new GAA Ard Stiúrthóir first appeared on the cover of this year's All-Ireland football final programme. Cork won the All-Ireland hurling final for the third time in four years and became the first county to retain the MacCarthy Cup. Kildare and Kerry renewed their rivalry in the football final with Kerry winning by three points.

1

Cumann Lúit Cleas Gaedeal.

Comairle Laigean.

Official Souvenir Programme

of

LEINSTER

SENIOR HURLING FINAL

AT

NEW ROSS (Barrett's Park)

On SUNDAY, 28th JULY, 1929.

Baile-Atha-Cliath agus Cill Cainnigh

(DUBLIN) (KILKENNY)

3.45 p.m.

Referee: Mr. P. McCULLAGH, WEXFORD.

N.B.—PROGRAMMES ARE FREE.

2

Cumann Lúit-Cleas Gaedeal.

OFFICIAL PROGRAMME

Dungarvan, August 11th, 1929.

Munster Hurling Final, 1929.

WATERFORD

v.

CORK

At 3.45 p.m. Referee—W. Gleeson, Limerick

MINOR CHAMPIONSHIP—

Waterford v. Limerick,

At 2.30 p.m.

PRICE - 2d.

1 Leinster Hurling Final
Kilkenny 3-05 Dublin 2-06
(Declared void – both teams disqualified for being late)

2 Munster Hurling Final
Cork 4-06 Waterford 2-03

3 Leinster Football Final
Kildare 2-03 Laois 0-06

4 Ulster Football Final (photocopy)
Monaghan 1-04 Cavan 1-04

5 All-Ireland Football Final
Kerry 1-08 Kildare 1-05
Attendance – 43,839

3

Cumann Lúit Cleas Gaeḋeal.

Comairle Laiġean.

Official Souvenir Programme

of

LEINSTER SENIOR FOOTBALL FINAL

Cill Dara agus Laoiġis

(KILDARE) 2-3 (LAOIGHISE) 0-6

3.15 p.m.

Referee: Mr. T. BURKE (Louth)

AT CROKE PARK

On SUNDAY, JULY 21st, 1929.

N.B.—PROGRAMMES ARE FREE.

5

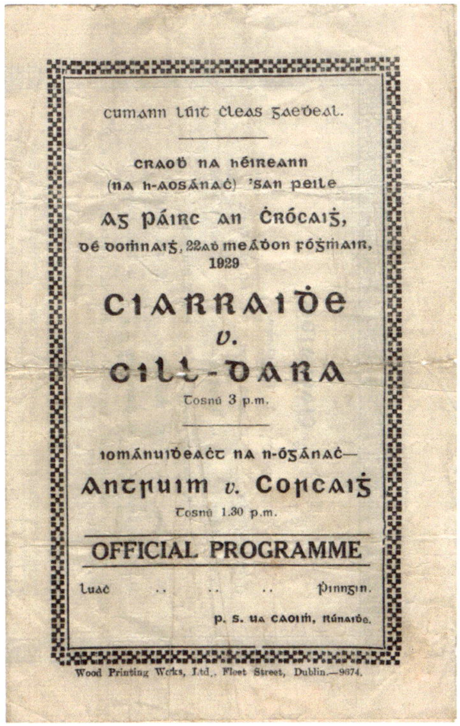
Cumann Lúit Cleas Gaeḋeal.

Craoḃ na hÉireann

(na h-Aosánaċ) 'san Peile

Ag Páirc an Ċrócaiġ,

Dé Domnaiġ, 22aḋ Meaḋon Fóġṁair,

1929

Ciarraiḋe

v.

Cill-Dara

Tosnú 3 p.m.

Iománuiḋeaċt na n-Óġánaċ—

Antruim v. Corcaiġ

Tosnú 1.30 p.m.

OFFICIAL PROGRAMME

Luaċ .. .. .. Pinngin.

P. S. Ua Caoiṁ, Rúnaiḋe.

Wood Printing Works, Ltd., Fleet Street, Dublin.—9674.

4

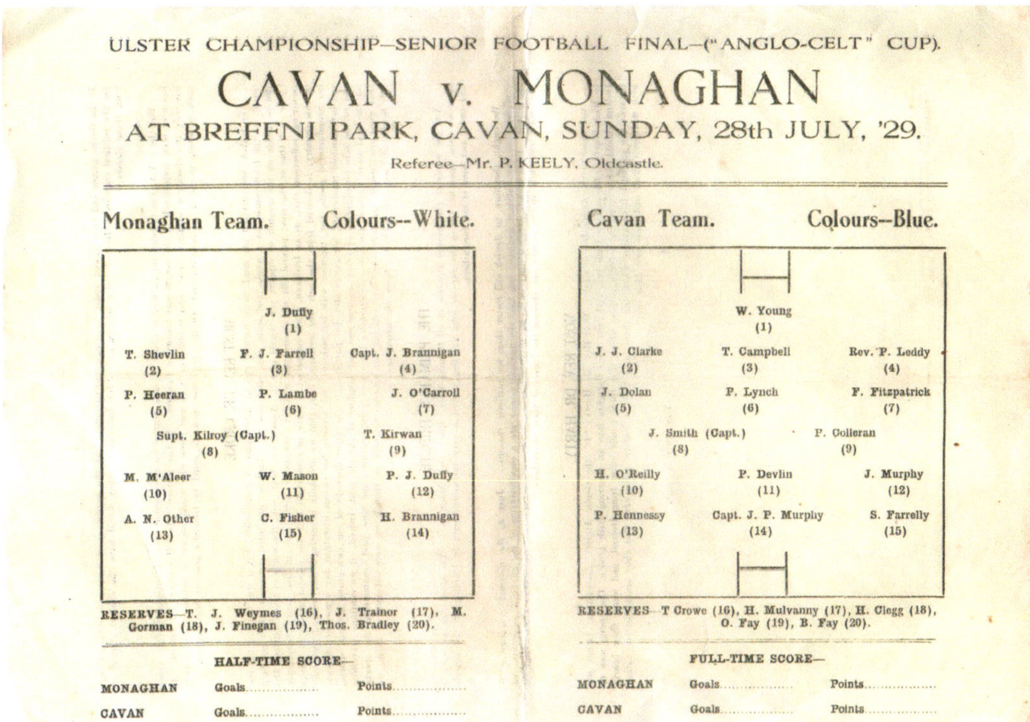
ULSTER CHAMPIONSHIP—SENIOR FOOTBALL FINAL—("ANGLO-CELT" CUP).

CAVAN v. MONAGHAN

AT BREFFNI PARK, CAVAN, SUNDAY, 28th JULY, '29.

Referee—Mr. P. KEELY, Oldcastle.

Monaghan Team. Colours--White.

J. Duffy (1)

T. Shevlin (2) — F. J. Farrell (3) — Capt. J. Brannigan (4)

P. Heeran (5) — P. Lambe (6) — J. O'Carroll (7)

Supt. Kilroy (Capt.) (8) — T. Kirwan (9)

M. M'Aleer (10) — W. Mason (11) — P. J. Duffy (12)

A. N. Other (13) — C. Fisher (15) — H. Brannigan (14)

RESERVES—T. J. Weymes (16), J. Trainor (17), M. Gorman (18), J. Finegan (19), Thos. Bradley (20).

Cavan Team. Colours--Blue.

W. Young (1)

J. J. Clarke (2) — T. Campbell (3) — Rev. P. Leddy (4)

J. Dolan (5) — P. Lynch (6) — F. Fitzpatrick (7)

J. Smith (Capt.) (8) — P. Colleran (9)

H. O'Reilly (10) — P. Devlin (11) — J. Murphy (12)

P. Hennessy (13) — Capt. J. P. Murphy (14) — S. Farrelly (15)

RESERVES—T Crowe (16), H. Mulvanny (17), H. Clegg (18), O. Fay (19), B. Fay (20).

HALF-TIME SCORE—

MONAGHAN Goals............ Points............

CAVAN Goals............ Points............

FULL-TIME SCORE—

MONAGHAN Goals............ Points............

CAVAN Goals............ Points............

OFFICIAL PR

Cumann Luith-

MUNSTER CHAM

Senior and Mino

At TH

On Sunday,

1930–39

-RAMME 2d

eas Gaedheal

IONSHIPS 1939.

Hurling Finals

RLES

h July, 1939.

1930

Monaghan's defeat of Kildare in the All-Ireland football semi-final was an enormous shock, so it was perhaps understandable that Kerry weren't caught out in a similar fashion in the final. The match was extremely one-sided and Monaghan suffered a heavy defeat in this, their first and only final to date. Such was Kerry's dominance in the match that their goalkeeper did not touch the ball, this being a time when kick-outs were usually taken by one of the full-back line. In hurling, Cork's dominance in Munster came to an end when they were beaten by Clare in the Munster semi-final. Tipperary went on to win the Munster final and defeated Dublin in the All-Ireland hurling final. By also winning the All-Ireland minor and junior finals that year, Tipperary became the first team to achieve the 'triple crown'.

1

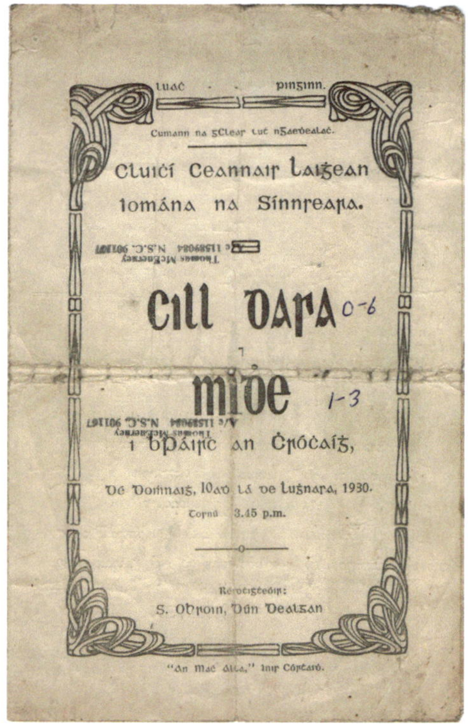

Luaċ . . pingin.

Cumann na gCleas Lúṫ nGaeḋealaċ.

Cluiċí Ceannais Laiġean
Iomána na Sinnsearaċ.

Cill Dara 0-6

mide 1-3

i bPáirc an Ċróċaiġ,

Dé Doṁnaiġ, 10aḋ Lá de Luġnasa, 1930.
Tosnú 3.45 p.m.

Reroċigteoir:
S. O'Broin, Dún Dealgan

"An Mac Alla," Inis Córṫaiḋ.

2

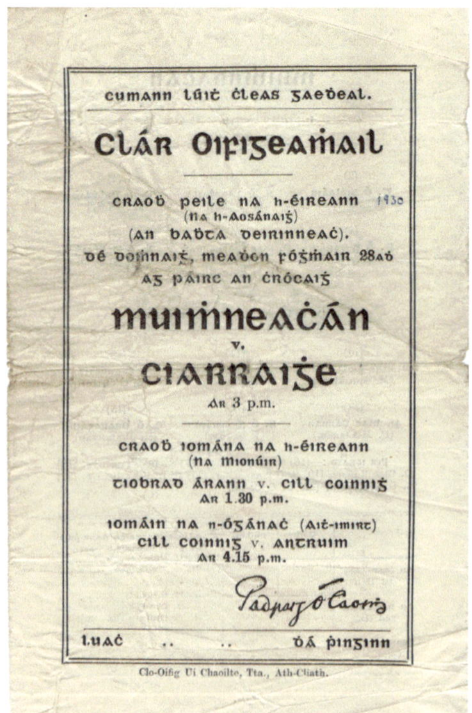

Cumann Lúiṫ Cleas Gaeḋeal.

Clár Oifigeaṁail

Craoḃ Peile na h-Éireann 1930
(na h-Aosánaiġ)
(an Babta Deirinneaċ).
Dé Doṁnaiġ, Meaḋon Fóġṁair 28aḋ
ag Páirc an Ċróċaiġ

Muiṁneaċán
v.
Ciarraiġe
an 3 p.m.

Craoḃ Iomána na h-Éireann
(na Mionúir)
Tiobrad Árann v. Cill Coinniġ
an 1.30 p.m.

Iomáin na n-Óglánaċ (Ait-imirt)
Cill Coinniġ v. Antruim
an 4.15 p.m.

Pádraig Ó Caoimh

Luaċ .. .. Dá Pingin

Clo-Oifig Ui Chaoilte, Tta., Ath-Cliath.

1 Leinster Football Final
Kildare 0-06 Meath 1-03

2 All-Ireland Football Final
Kerry 3-11 Monaghan 0-02
Attendance – 33,280

3 Munster Hurling Final
Tipperary 6-04 Clare 2-08

3

Cumann Luit-Cleas Gaedeal (G.A.A.)

Munster Senior Hurling Final.

Junior Football Semi-Final (Replay).

AT

CORK ATHLETIC GROUNDS,

SUNDAY, JULY 27th, 1930.

Junior Football, 2.30 p.m.

KERRY v. WATERFORD

REFEREE—MR. T. KEATING

Senior Hurling, 3.45 p.m.

CLARE v. TIPPERARY

REFEREE—SEAN (OG) MURPHY, Cork

ADMISSION TO GROUNDS	... ...	**1/-**
ADMISSION TO STAND ENCLOSURE	...	**2/-**
ADMISSION TO SIDE LINE, Extra	... ...	**1/-**

The following Hotels and Restaurants will be open :—

HOTELS.—Victoria; Wren's; Desmond's; Imperial; Hibernian; Metropole; Windsor; Corrigans; Munster; Station; Queen's; Thomond, Oliver Plunkett St.; Hoskins, Prince's Street; Moore's, Morrison's Island.

RESTAURANTS.—Continental, Patrick Street; Pavilion Cafe, Patrick Street; Avoca, Marlboro Street; Cosy, South Mall.; Rendevous, Oliver Plunket Street; Kincora and Buffet, Cook Street; Central, Prince's Street; Mackesy's, Oliver Plunkett Street; Cafe Cuinne, Oliver Plunkett Street.

LIGHT REFRESHMANTS.—Mullany's, Lower Road; Henchy's, Lower Road P. O'Gorman, McCurtain Street; A. Crean, McCurtain Street; J. J. Long, McCurtain Street; P. J. Noonan, Cook Street; La Cave, Cook Street; M. Twomey, Warrens Place; Murphy's, Warren's Place, Mackesy, The Vineyard; J. Hoare, Faulkner's Lane; Clancy Bros., Oliver Plunket St.; Chateau, Patrick St.; Oak, Prince's St.

OFFICIAL PROGRAMME - 2D.

EAGLE PRINTING WORKS, CORK

4

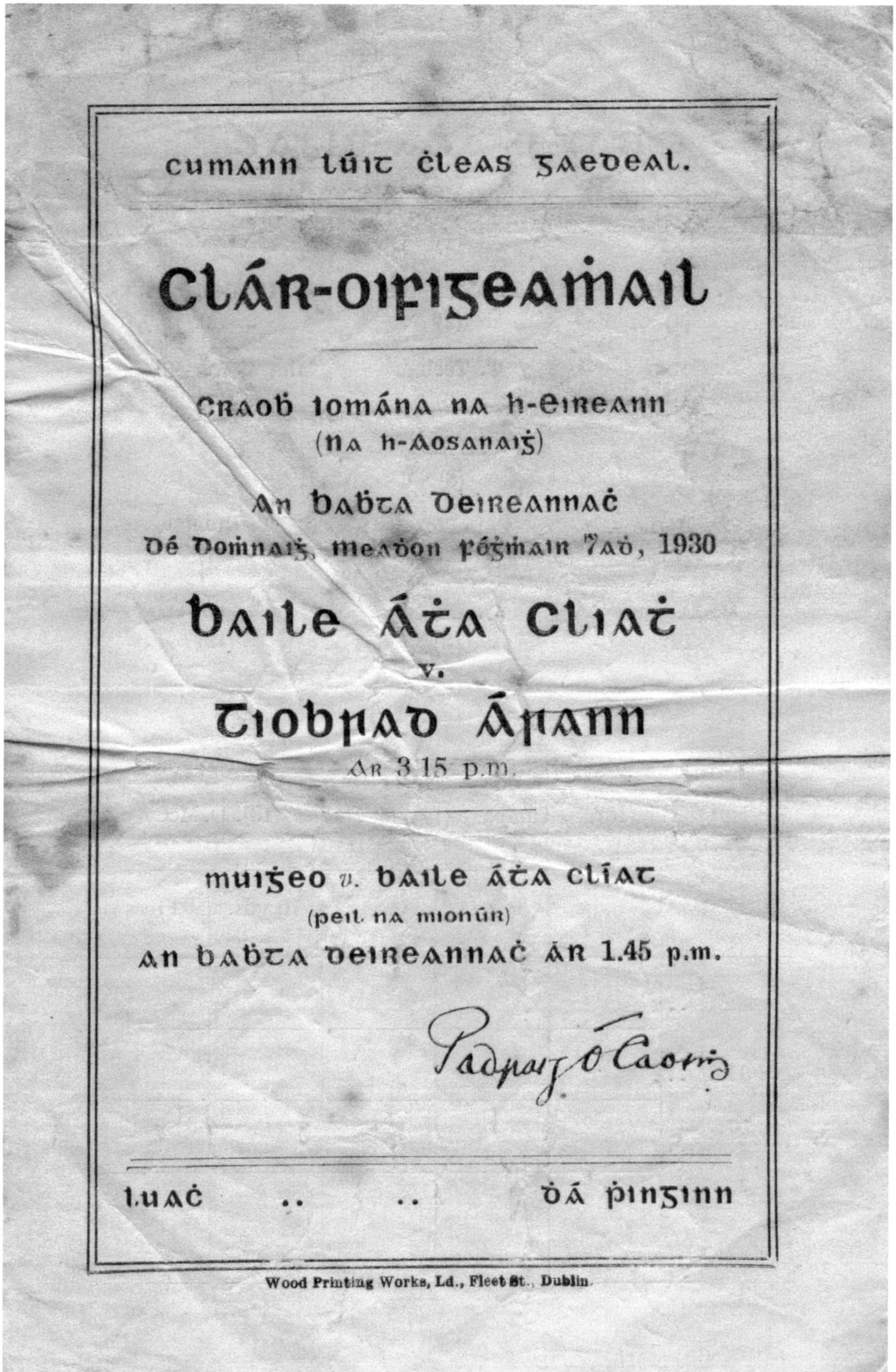

4 All-Ireland Hurling Final
Tipperary 2-07 Dublin 1-03
Attendance – 21,730

1931

Cork regained the Munster hurling championship in 1931, and the trilogy of matches with Kilkenny in the All-Ireland hurling final later that year grabbed the attention of the country. The drawn match on 6 September was a hugely exciting affair with a last-minute point snatching a draw for Cork. The replay on 11 October broke the record for the largest attendance at an All-Ireland hurling final, as 33,124 spectators paid in to watch what was then widely believed to be one of the greatest hurling matches of all time. Another draw meant that a second replay on 1 November was needed to break the deadlock. Kilkenny's talisman and captain, Lory Meagher, was unable to play, having been injured in the previous match. As a result, Cork ran out easy winners. The three programmes for this All-Ireland final are extremely rare.

1

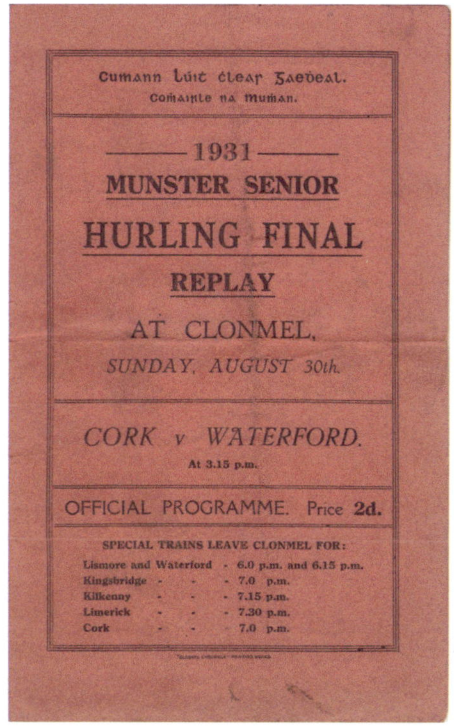

2

1 Munster Hurling Final Replay
Cork 5-04 Waterford 1-02

2 All-Ireland Hurling Final
Cork 1-06 Kilkenny 1-06
Attendance – 26,460

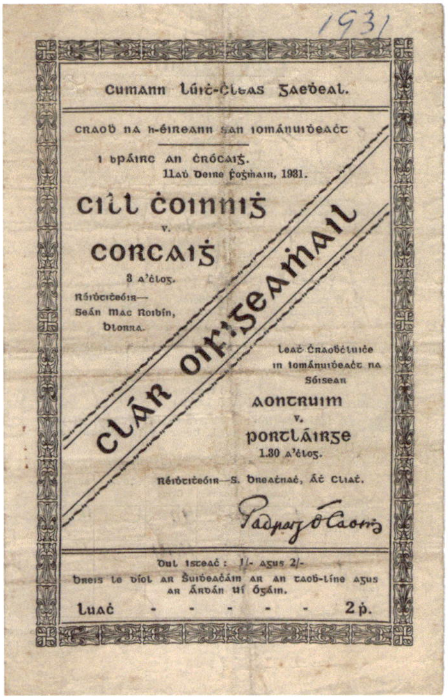
1931

Cumann Lúiṫ-Ċleas Gaeḋeal.

Craoḃ na h-Éireann san Iománuiḋeaċt

i bPáirc an Ċrócaiġ.
11aḋ Deire Foġṁair, 1931.

Cill Ċoinniġ
v.
Corcaiġ
3 a'ċloġ.

Réiḋtiġeóir—
Seán Mac Roibín,
Blarna.

Clár Oifigeamail

Leaṫ Ċraoḃċluiċe
in Iománuiḋeaċt na
Sóisear

Aontruim
v.
Portláirge
1.30 a'ċloġ.

Réiḋtiġeóir—S. Breaṫnaċ, Áṫ Cliaṫ.

Padraig Ó Caoimh

Dul isteaċ: 1/- agus 2/-
Breis le díol ar Śuiḋeaċáin ar an taoḃ-líne agus an Árdán Uí Ógáin.

Luaċ - - - - - 2p.

Cumann Lúiṫ-Ċleas Gaeḋeal.

Craoḃ na h-Éireann san Iománuiḋeaċt

i bPáirc an Ċrócaiġ.
Lá Samhna, 1931.

Cill Ċoinniġ
v.
Corcaiġ
2.30 p.m.

Réiḋtiġeóir—
Liam Breaṫnaċ,
Portlairge.

Clár Oifigeamail

Cluiċe-Ceannais
in Iománuiḋeaċt na
Sóisear

Léinpoll
v.
Portláirge
1 p.m.

Réiḋtiġeóir—S. Breaṫnaċ, Áṫ Cliaṫ.

Padraig Ó Caoimh

Dul isteaċ: 1/- agus 2/-
Breis le díol ar Śuiḋeaċáin ar an taoḃ-líne agus ar Árdán Uí Ógáin.

Luaċ - - - - - 2p.

3 Replay
Cork 2-05 Kilkenny 2-05
Attendance – 33,124

4 Second Replay
Cork 5-08 Kilkenny 3-04
Attendance – 31,935

5 All-Ireland Football Final
Kerry 1-11 Kildare 0-08
Attendance – 42,350

5

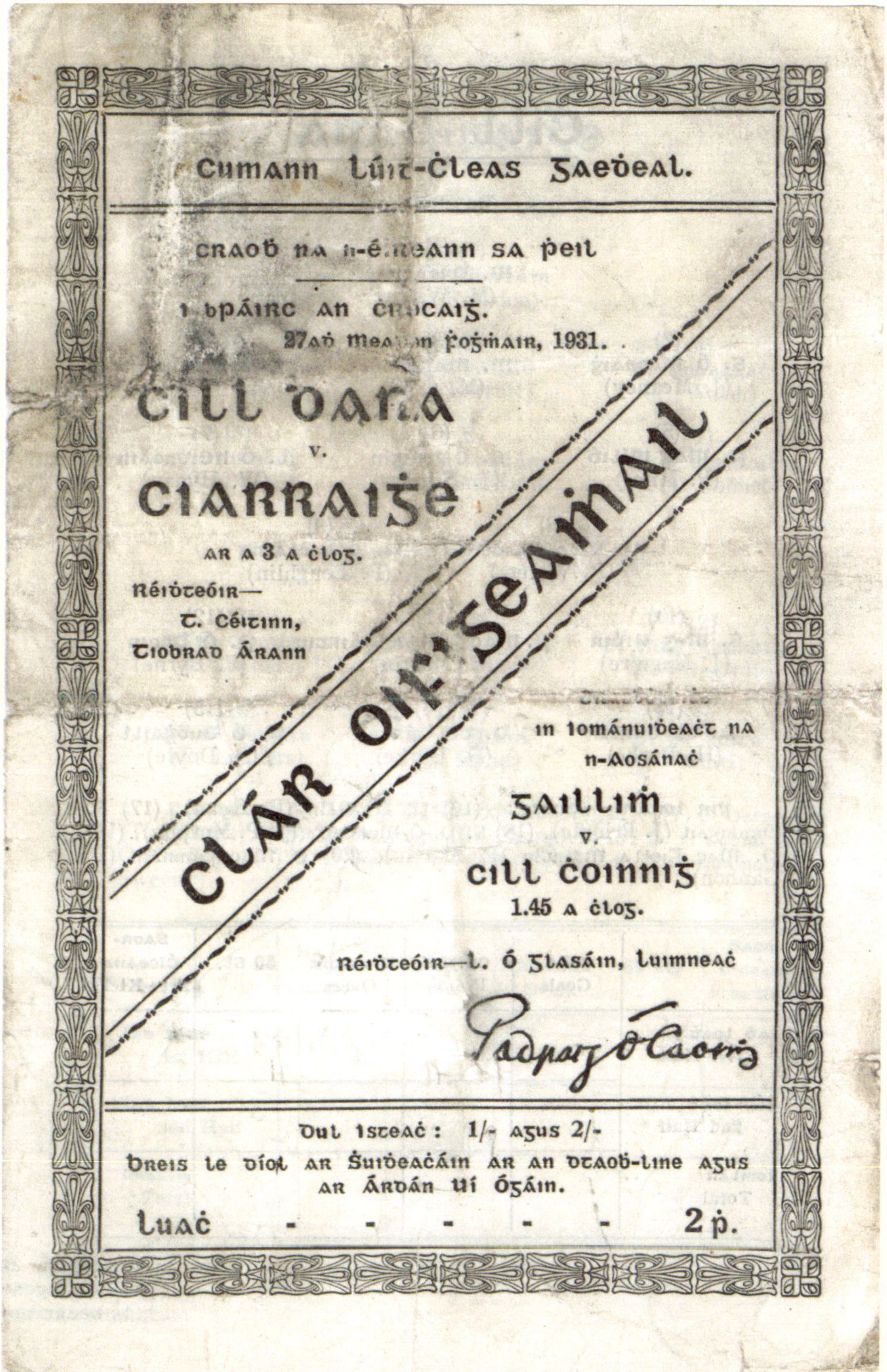
Cumann Lúṫ-Ċleas Gaeḋeal.

Craoḃ na h-Éireann sa Ṗeil

i bPáirc an Ċrócaiġ.

27aḋ Meaḋon Ḟoġmair, 1931.

Cill Dara

v.

Ciarraiġe

ar a 3 a ċlog.

Réiḋteóir—
T. Céitinn,
Tiobrad Árann

Clár Oif'geaṁail

in Iománuiḋeaċt na n-Aosánaċ

Gailliṁ

v.

Cill Ċoinniġ

1.45 a ċlog.

Réiḋteóir—L. Ó Glasáin, Luimneaċ

Padraig Ó Caoimh

Dul isteaċ: 1/- agus 2/-

Breis le díol ar Śuiḋeaċáin ar an dtaoḃ-líne agus ar Árdán Uí Ógáin.

Luaċ - - - - - 2ṗ.

1932

Kerry were back in the All-Ireland final in 1932, trying to become the second team after Wexford to win four All-Ireland football finals in a row. Standing in their way were Mayo, who had defeated Sligo in the Connacht final and then proved too strong for Cavan in the All-Ireland semi-final. Kerry, however, were without Éamonn Fitzgerald, who had been on the team for their previous victories in 1930 and 1931. Fitzgerald was representing Ireland at the Olympic Games in Los Angeles, where he was participating in the triple jump. Despite his absence and being three points down at half-time, Kerry rallied to claim the cup for the fourth time in as many years. Kerry's Mick Doyle, who had played in all four of the victories, had not yet reached 21 years of age.

1

1 Leinster Football Final Replay
Dublin 4-06 Wexford 1-05

2 All-Ireland Football Final
Kerry 2-07 Mayo 2-04
Attendance – 25,816

3 Munster Hurling Final
Clare 5-02 Cork 4-01

4 Leinster Hurling Final
Kilkenny 4-06 Dublin 3-05

5 All-Ireland Hurling Final
Kilkenny 3-03 Clare 2-03
Attendance – 34,372

2

Cumann Lúit-Ċleas Gaeḋeal.

Craoḃ na h-Éireann sa Peil.

i bPáirc an Ċrócaiġ.
Meaḋon-Foġmhair a 25, 1932

Ciarraiġe
v.
Muiġeó
ar a 3 a ċlog.

Réiḋtiḋeoir—
Máirtín Ó Néill.

Clár Oifigeamail

Leaṫ-Ċraoḃ na hÉireann Peil na nÓgánaċ.

Corcaiġ
v.
Roscomáin
1.45 p.m.

Réiḋtiḋeoir—Seán Ó Conċubair.

Pádraig Ó Caoimh

Luaċ - - - - - 2p.

Wood Printing Works Ltd., Fleet St., Dublin.

3

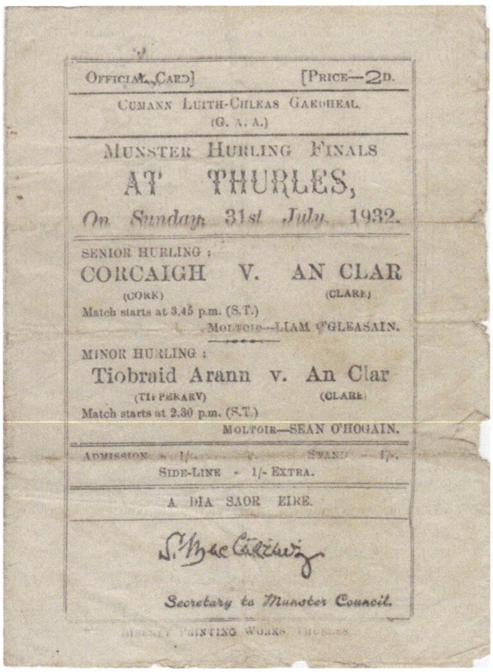

Official Card] [Price—2d.

Cumann Luith-Chleas Gaedheal
(G. A. A.)

Munster Hurling Finals
AT THURLES,
On Sunday, 31st July, 1932.

Senior Hurling:
Corcaigh v. An Clar
(Cork) (Clare)
Match starts at 3.45 p.m. (S.T.)
Moltoir—Liam O'Gleasain.

Minor Hurling:
Tiobraid Arann v. An Clar
(Tipperary) (Clare)
Match starts at 2.30 p.m. (S.T.)
Moltoir—Sean O'Hogain.

Admission - 1/- . Stand - 1/-.
Side-Line - 1/- Extra.

A Dia Saor Eire.

S. Mac Cárthaigh

Secretary to Munster Council.

Printing Works Thurles

4

Luaċ - - Pinginn

Cumann Lúit Ċleas Gaeḋeal

Cluiċí Ceannair Laiġean
Iomána na Sinnsear

Cill Ċoinniġ
v.
Baile-Áṫa-Cliaṫ

i bPáirc Ó Mórḋa
(Portlaoiġise)

Dé Domhnaiġ 24aḋ Lá de Iúl, 1932
Tosnú 3.45 p.m.

Réiḋtiḋeoir:
S. MacRoibín, Ua bFáilġe

5

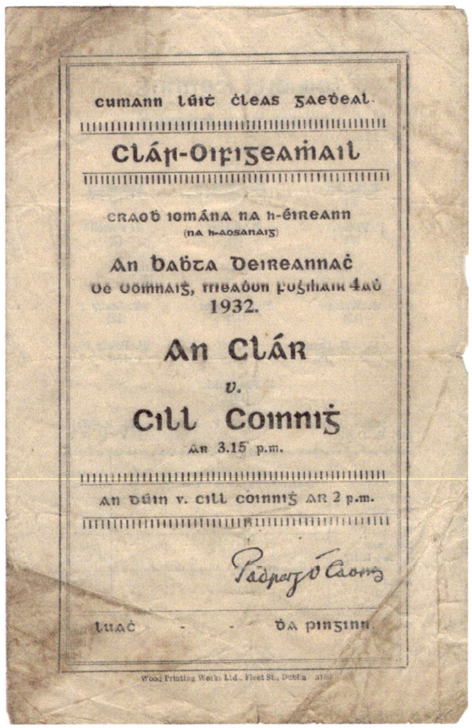

Cumann Lúit Ċleas Gaeḋeal.

Clár-Oifigeamail

Craoḃ Iomána na h-Éireann
(na h-Aosánaiġ)

An Baḃta Deireannaċ
Dé Domhnaiġ, Meaḋon Foġmhair 4aḋ
1932.

An Clár
v.
Cill Coinniġ
ar 3.15 p.m.

An Dún v. Cill Coinniġ ar 2 p.m.

Pádraig Ó Caoimh

Luaċ - - Dá Pinginn

Wood Printing Works Ltd., Fleet St., Dublin

1933

Cavan had dominated the Ulster football championship since 1920 but were yet to capitalise on that success at the All-Ireland stage. With only five surviving members of the team that were defeated by Kildare in the 1928 All-Ireland final, Cavan faced a Kerry team chasing their fifth title in a row, in the All-Ireland semi-final played in Breffni Park. A three-point victory saw Cavan progress to the final against Galway, and 45,188 spectators witnessed Cavan's first All-Ireland football victory, as Jim Smith became the first man from the county to lift the Sam Maguire Cup. This was the last time Galway wore their green and white jerseys before switching to the now familiar maroon and white.

1 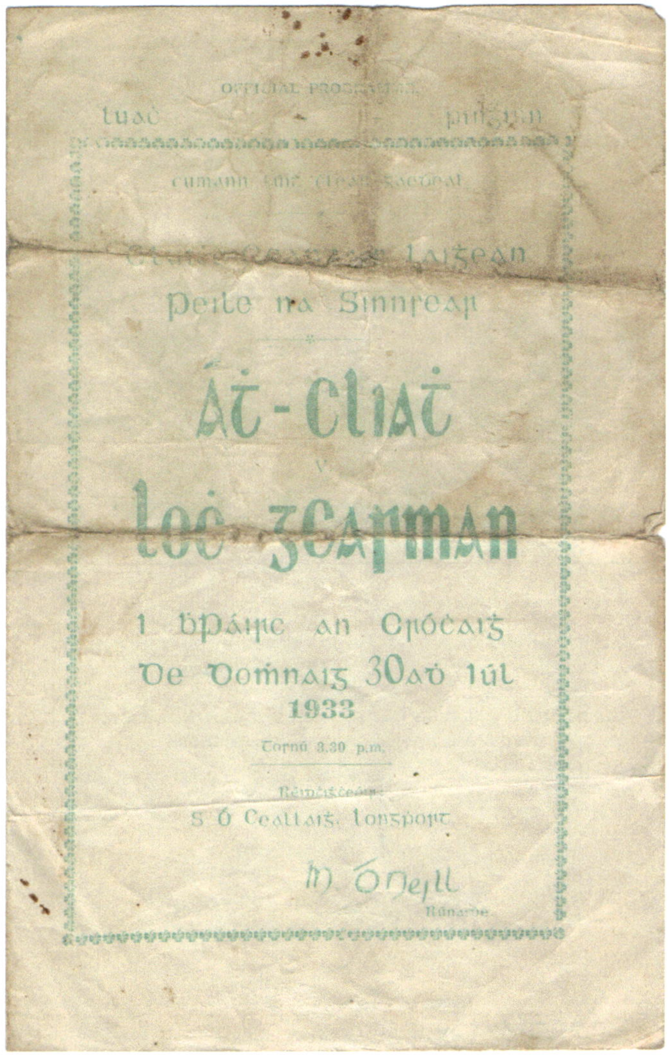

1 Leinster Football Final
Dublin 0-09 Wexford 1-04

2 Munster Football Final
Kerry 2-08 Tipperary 1-04

3 All-Ireland Football Final
Cavan 2-05 Galway 1-04
Attendance – 45,188

4 Munster Hurling Final
Limerick 3-07 Waterford 1-02
(Match unfinished, Limerick awarded title)

5 All-Ireland Hurling Final
Kilkenny 1-07 Limerick 0-06
Attendance – 45,176

2

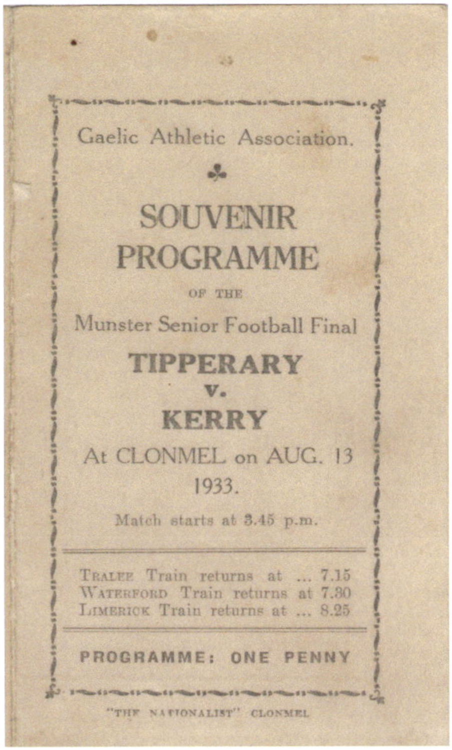
Gaelic Athletic Association.
SOUVENIR PROGRAMME
OF THE
Munster Senior Football Final
TIPPERARY
v.
KERRY
At CLONMEL on AUG. 13
1933.
Match starts at 3.45 p.m.
TRALEE Train returns at ... 7.15
WATERFORD Train returns at 7.30
LIMERICK Train returns at ... 8.25
PROGRAMME: ONE PENNY
"THE NATIONALIST" CLONMEL

4

Cumann Lúit Cleas Gaedeal
Luimneac v. Port Láirge
Corcaig v. Tiobraid-Árann
Clár Oifigeamail
2D.
JACK DOYLE
SHOULD CONSULT
THE RING SPECIALIST
The RING SHOP for MUNSTER
JAMES A. O'CONNELL
"THE JEWEL CASKET"
Phone 1489. Contractor for G.A.A. Medals to Munster Council, 1932
New Illustrated Catalogue of Rings and Hand Made Medals sent free
Jeweller & Watchmaker, 52 OLIVER PLUNKET ST., CORK

3

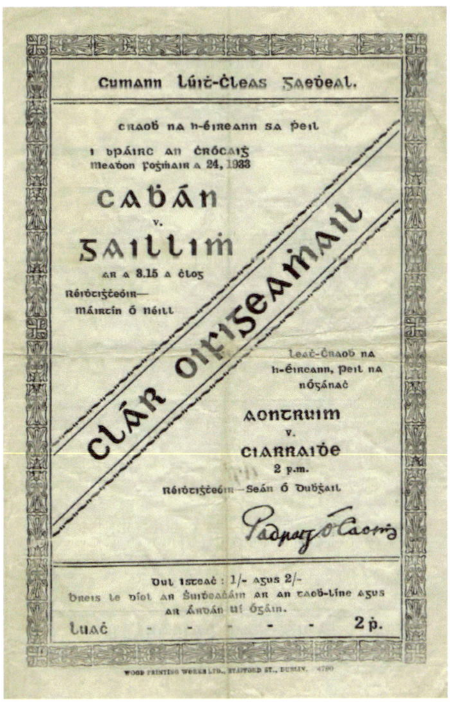
Cumann Lúit-Cleas Gaedeal.
Meadon Fogmair a 24, 1933
Cabán
v.
Gaillim
ar a 3.15 a clog
Clár Oifigeamail
Aontruim
v.
Ciarraide
2 p.m.
Dul isteac: 1/- agus 2/-
Luac 2p.

5

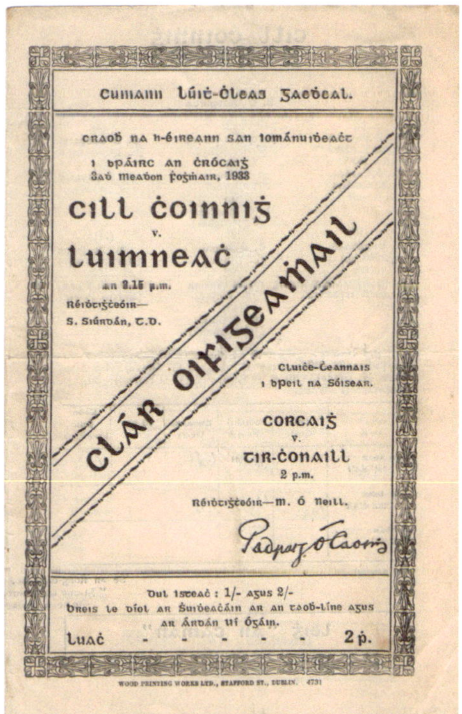
Cumann Lúit-Cleas Gaedeal.
Cill Coinnig
v.
Luimneac
an 3.15 p.m.
Clár Oifigeamail
Corcaig
v.
Tir-Conaill
2 p.m.
Dul isteac: 1/- agus 2/-
Luac 2p.

1934

In 1934, the GAA celebrated the fiftieth anniversary of its founding. The Leinster football final took three matches to find a winner with Dublin finally getting the better of Louth in Drogheda. The Leinster hurling final also went to a replay and Dublin completed a provincial double with victory in front of a large crowd in Portlaoise. Having beaten Kilkenny, Dublin faced Limerick in the All-Ireland hurling final. The two teams had met earlier in the year in the National League final, which Limerick had won. In the championship final, the first game was a draw, but thanks to an impressive display by Dave Clohessy, who scored four goals, Limerick took the honours again in the replay.

1

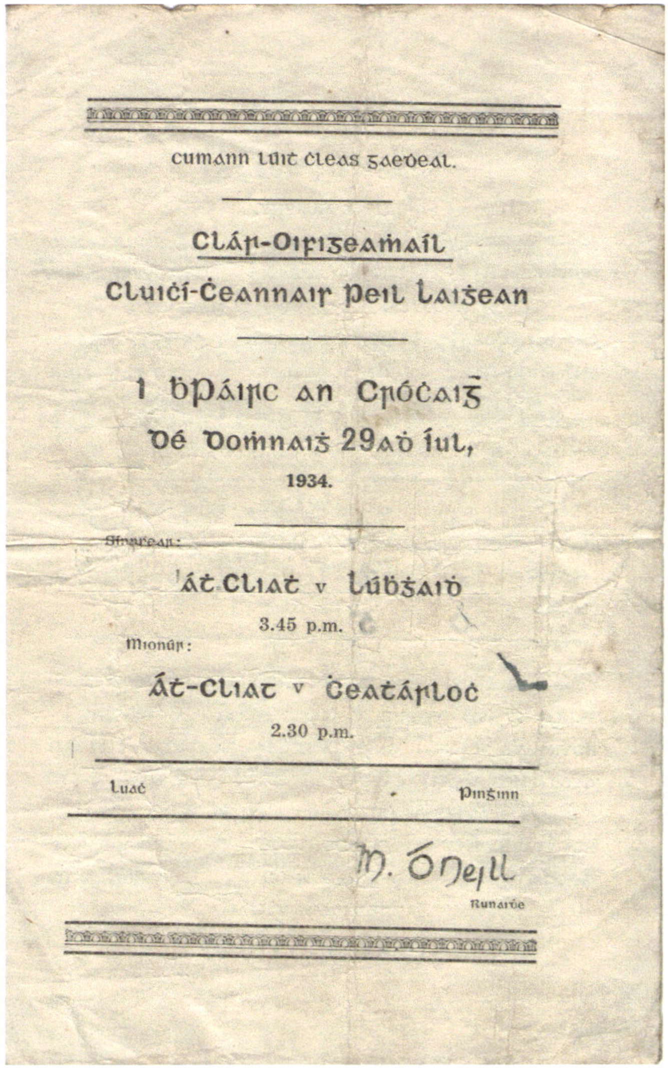

Cumann Lúiṫ Cleas Gaeḋeal.

Clár-Oifigeaṁaíl

Cluiċí-Ċeannais Peil Laiġean

I bPáirc an Ċróċaiġ

Dé Doṁnaiġ 29aḋ Iúl,

1934.

Sinnsear:

Áṫ Cliaṫ v Lúġbaiḋ

3.45 p.m.

Mionúr:

Áṫ-Cliaṫ v Ceaṫarloċ

2.30 p.m.

Luaċ Pingin

M. Ó Néill

Rúnaiḋe

1 Leinster Football Final
Dublin 1-02 Louth 0-05

2 Second Replay
Dublin 2-09 Louth 1-10

Luaċ pinġinn

Cumann Lúit Ċleas Gaedeal.

Clár-Oifigeaṁail

Cluiċí-Ċeannair Peil Laiġean

I Droiċead Áṫa

Dé Doṁnaiġ, 19aḋ Luġnasa,

1934.

Sinnsear:

Aṫ-imirt

Áṫ-Cliaṫ

v.

Luḃġaiḋ

3.45 p.m.

M. Ó Neill

Rúnaiḋe

3

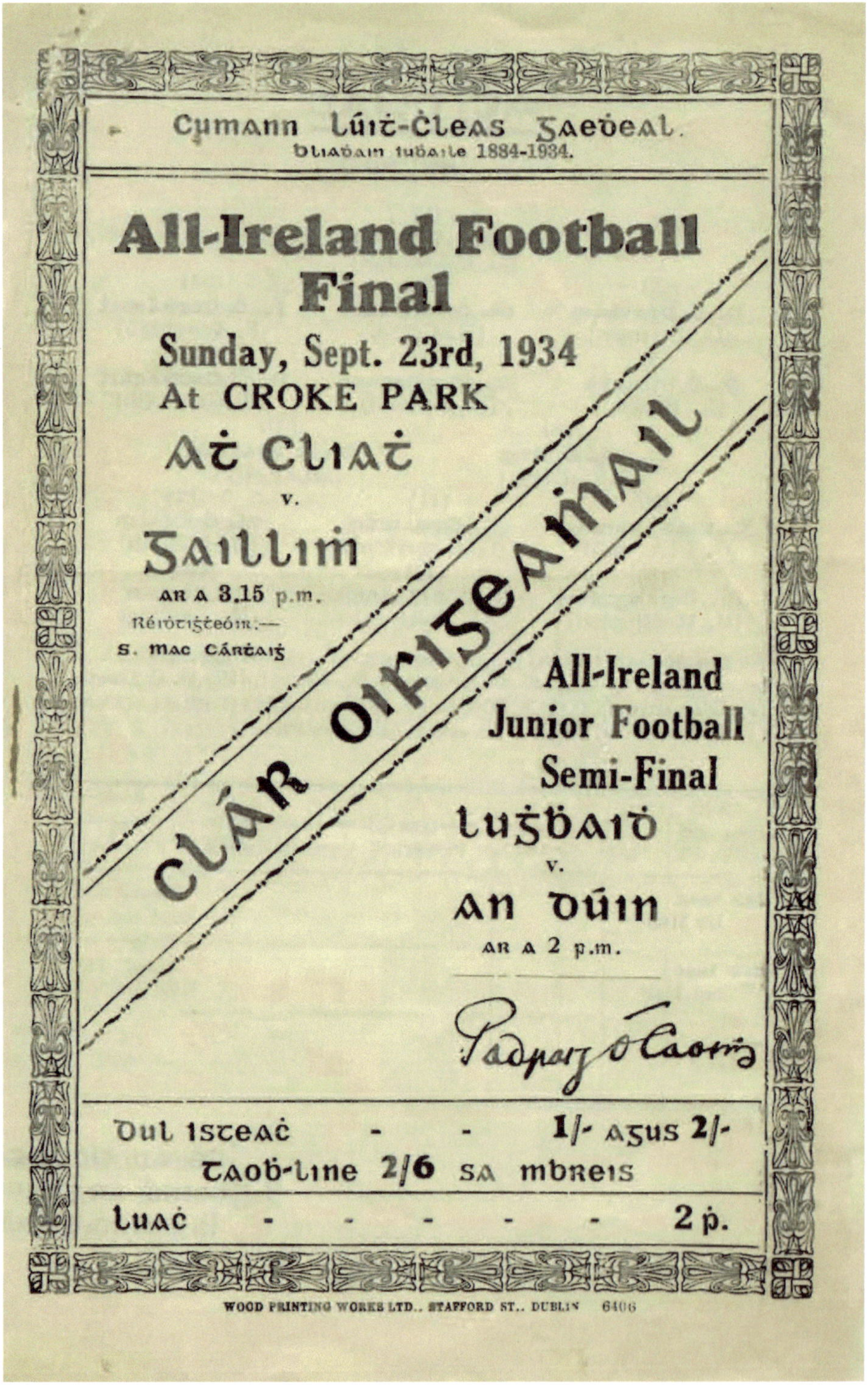
Cumann Lúṫ-Ċleas Gaeḋeal.
Bliaḋain Iubaile 1884-1934.

All-Ireland Football Final

Sunday, Sept. 23rd, 1934
At CROKE PARK

Áṫ Cliaṫ
v.
Gaillim
ar a 3.15 p.m.
Réiḋtiġṫeóir:—
S. Mac Cárṫaiġ

CLÁR OIFIGEAMAIL

All-Ireland
Junior Football
Semi-Final
Luġbaiḋ
v.
An Dúin
ar a 2 p.m.

Padraig Ó Caoimh

Dul isteaċ - - 1/- agus 2/-
Taoḃ-líne 2/6 sa mbreis

Luaċ - - - - - 2p.

WOOD PRINTING WORKS LTD., STAFFORD ST., DUBLIN 6406

3 All-Ireland Football Final
Galway 3-05 Dublin 1-09
Attendance – 36,143

4 Leinster Hurling Final Replay
Dublin 3-05 Kilkenny 2-02

5 Munster Hurling Final
Limerick 4-08 Waterford 2 05

6 All-Ireland Hurling Final
Limerick 2-07 Dublin 3-04
Attendance – 34,867

7 Replay
Limerick 5-02 Dublin 2-06
Attendance – 30,250

4

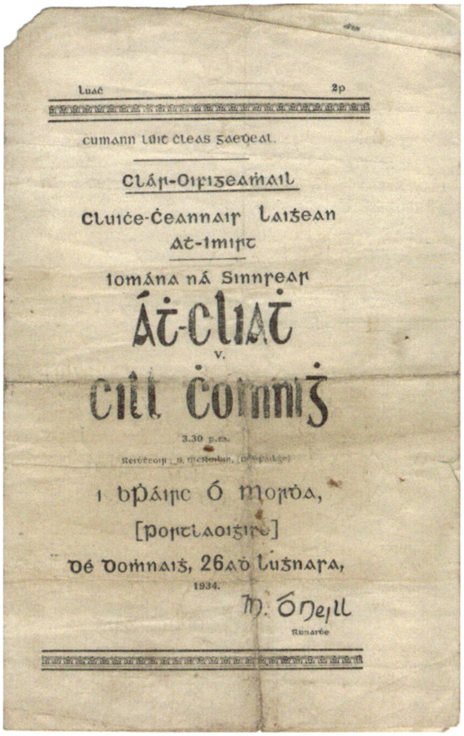

Luaċ 2p
Cumann Lúit Cleas Gaedheal.
Clár-Oifigeaṁail
Cluiċe-Ċeannair Laiġean
Aṫ-imirt
Iomána ná Sinnsear
Áṫ-Cliaṫ
v.
Cill Ċoinniġ
3.30 p.m.
i bPáirc Ó Mórḋa,
[Portlaoiġise]
Dé Domhnaiġ, 26aḋ Lúġnasa,
1934.
M. Ó Neill
Rúnaiḋe

5

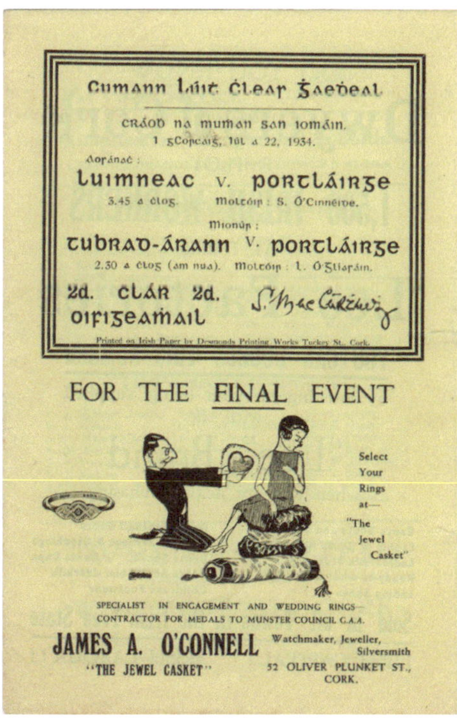

Cumann Lúit Cleas Gaedheal
Craob na Mumhan san Iomáin.
i gCorcaiġ, Iúl a 22, 1934.
Aosánaċ:
Luimneaċ v. Portláirge
3.45 a ċlog. Moltóir: S. Ó'Cinnéide.
Mionúr:
Tiobrad-Árann v. Portláirge
2.30 a ċlog (am nua). Moltóir: L. Ó Sliaḃáin.
2d. Clár 2d.
Oifigeaṁail
Printed on Irish Paper by Desmonds Printing Works Tuckey St., Cork.
FOR THE FINAL EVENT
Select Your Rings at— "The Jewel Casket"
SPECIALIST IN ENGAGEMENT AND WEDDING RINGS—
CONTRACTOR FOR MEDALS TO MUNSTER COUNCIL G.A.A.
JAMES A. O'CONNELL
"THE JEWEL CASKET"
Watchmaker, Jeweller, Silversmith
52 OLIVER PLUNKET ST., CORK.

6

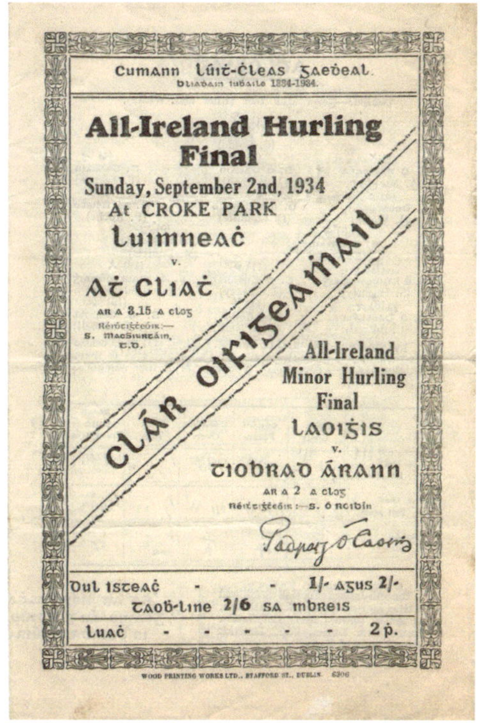

Cumann Lúit-Ċleas Gaedheal.
Bliadain Iubaile 1884-1934.
All-Ireland Hurling Final
Sunday, September 2nd, 1934
At CROKE PARK
Luimneaċ
v.
Aṫ Cliaṫ
ar a 3.15 a ċlog
Réiteoir:— S. MacSiurtáin, T.D.
Clár Oifigeaṁail
All-Ireland Minor Hurling Final
Laoiġis
v.
Tiobrad Árann
ar a 2 a ċlog
Réiteoir:—S. Ó Roibín
Dul isteaċ - - 1/- agus 2/-
Taob-líne 2/6 sa mbreis
Luaċ - - - - - - 2p.
WOOD PRINTING WORKS LTD., STAFFORD ST., DUBLIN. 6306

7

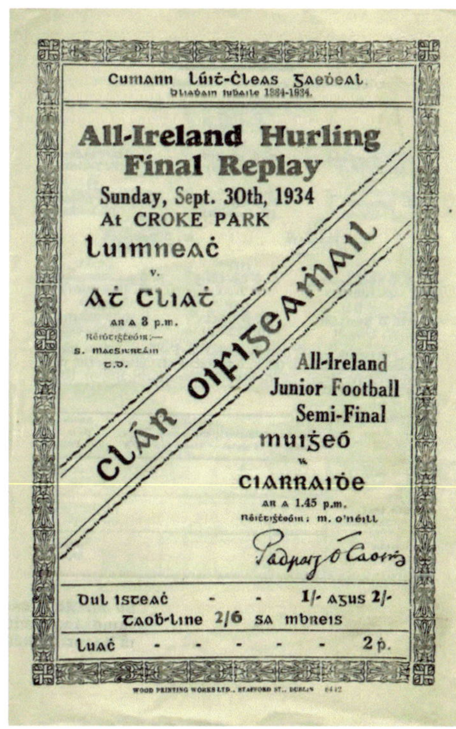

Cumann Lúit-Ċleas Gaedheal.
Bliadain Iubaile 1884-1934.
All-Ireland Hurling Final Replay
Sunday, Sept. 30th, 1934
At CROKE PARK
Luimneaċ
v.
Aṫ Cliaṫ
ar a 3 p.m.
Réiteoir:— S. MacSiurtáin T.D.
Clár Oifigeaṁail
All-Ireland Junior Football Semi-Final
Muiġeó
v.
Ciarraiḋe
ar a 1.45 p.m.
Réiteoir: M. O'Néill
Dul isteaċ - - 1/- agus 2/-
Taob-líne 2/6 sa mbreis
Luaċ - - - - - - 2p.
WOOD PRINTING WORKS LTD., STAFFORD ST., DUBLIN. 6412

1935

Kerry opted not to play in the 1935 football championship as a protest against the treatment of republican prisoners in the Curragh. In their absence, Tipperary defeated Cork in the Munster final. Kildare were the winners in Leinster, but Cavan were too strong for both teams, defeating Tipperary in the All-Ireland semi-final and Kildare in the final. The programme for the 1935 All-Ireland final is unusual among all the other programmes from the 1930s, being square in shape and a booklet rather than the usual A5 size fold-over. In the 1935 All-Ireland hurling final, two legendary hurlers, Lory Meagher and Mick Mackey, came face to face as Limerick sought to defend their title against Kilkenny. Both men were influential in the game, but it was Kilkenny who ran out winners.

1

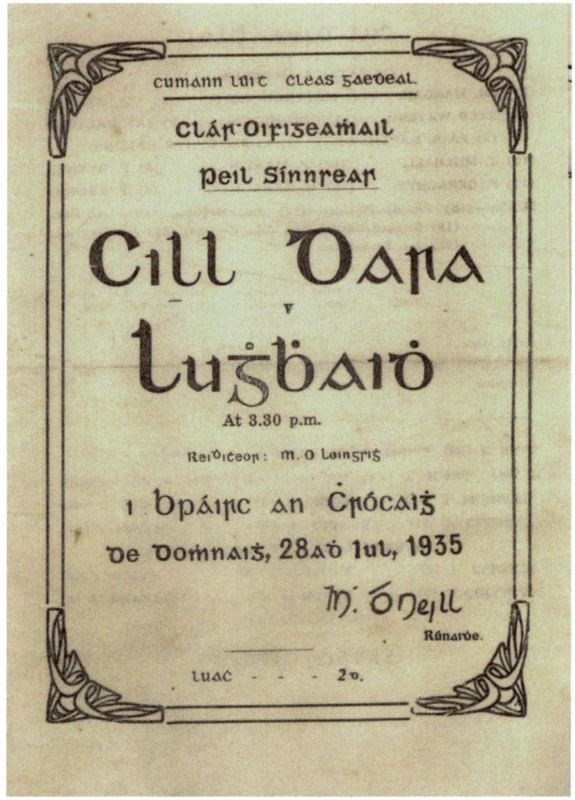

2

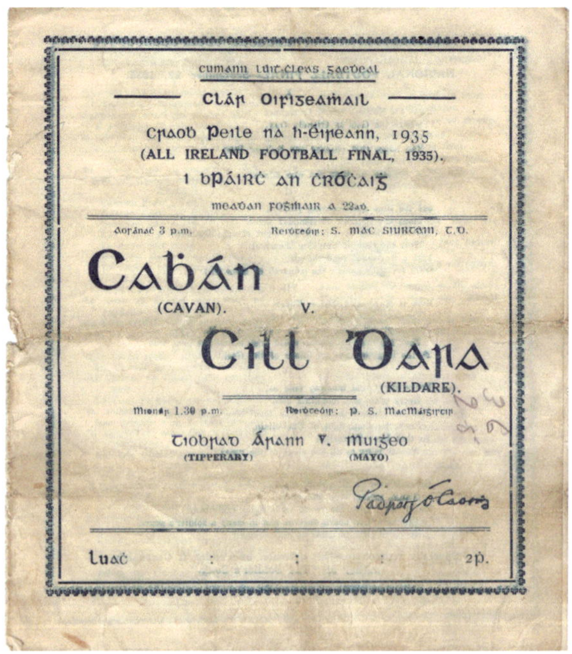

1 **Leinster Football Final**
Kildare 0-08 Louth 0-06

2 **All-Ireland Football Final**
Cavan 3-06 Kildare 2-05
Attendance – 50,380

3 **Munster Hurling Final**
Limerick 5-05 Tipperary 1-04

3

Cumann Lúiṫ Ċleas Gaeḋeal

MUNSTER CHAMPIONSHIPS, 1935
CORK ATHLETIC GROUNDS, SUNDAY, AUGUST 11

Minor Hurling Final at 2.30 p.m. (S.T.)
Tiobraid-Árann v Corcaiġ

Senior Hurling Final at 3.45 p.m. (S.T.)
Luimneaċ v Tiobrad-Árann

2d. Clár 2d.
Oifigeaṁail

Desmond's Printing Works, Cork.—Irish Paper

4

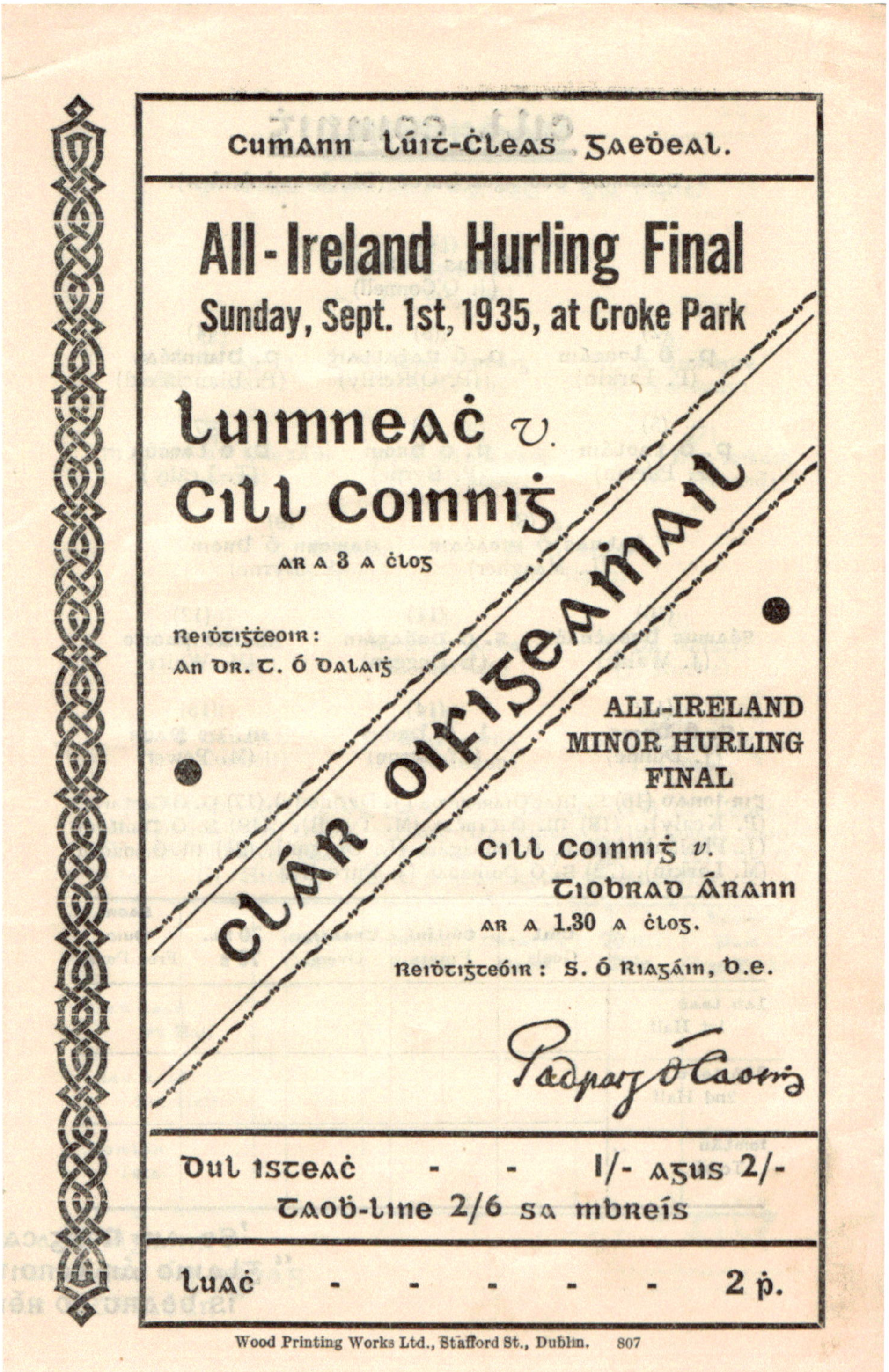

Cumann Lúit-Cleas Gaedeal.

All-Ireland Hurling Final

Sunday, Sept. 1st, 1935, at Croke Park

Luimneaċ v. Cill Coinniġ

ar a 3 a ċlog

Reiḋtiġṫeoir:

An Dr. T. Ó Dalaiġ

Clár Oifigeamail

ALL-IRELAND MINOR HURLING FINAL

Cill Coinniġ v. Tiobrad Árann

ar a 1.30 a ċlog.

Reiḋtiġṫeoir: S. Ó Riagáin, b.e.

Dul isteaċ - - 1/- agus 2/-

Taob-line 2/6 sa mbreis

Luaċ - - - - - - 2 ṗ.

Wood Printing Works Ltd., Stafford St., Dublin. 807

4 All-Ireland Hurling Final
Kilkenny 2-05 Limerick 2-04
Attendance – 46,591

1936

Mick Mackey produced one of the great Munster hurling final performances, scoring five goals and three points while captaining Limerick against Tipperary in 1936. For the second year in a row, Limerick faced Kilkenny in the All-Ireland final. On this occasion, Limerick had the better of the exchanges and avenged the defeat of 12 months earlier. Limerick's ability to score goals was the difference between the teams and Dave Clohessy again demonstrated his prowess in the forward line.

The All-Ireland football final this year brought two unfamiliar counties together to decide who would take home the Sam Maguire Cup. Mayo and Laois overcame stern challenges from Kerry and Cavan to reach the final. Playing in their fourth final, Mayo won the title in impressive fashion, captained by Séamus O'Malley, who accepted the cup on behalf of his team.

1

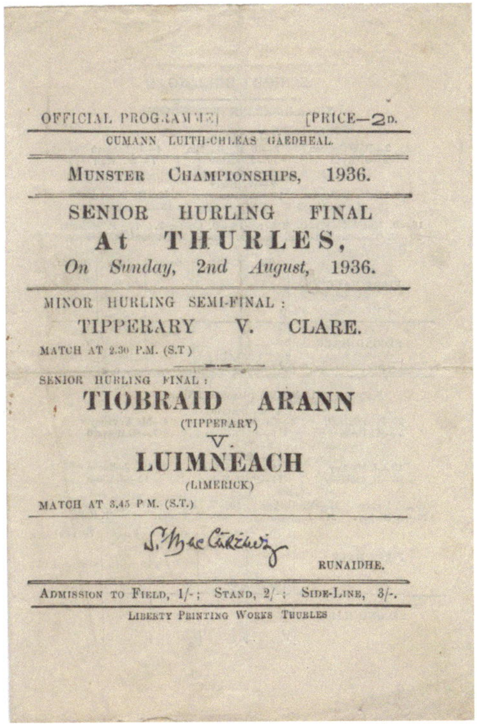

OFFICIAL PROGRAMME [PRICE—2D.
CUMANN LUITH-CHLEAS GAEDHEAL.
MUNSTER CHAMPIONSHIPS, 1936.
SENIOR HURLING FINAL
At THURLES,
On Sunday, 2nd August, 1936.
MINOR HURLING SEMI-FINAL:
TIPPERARY V. CLARE.
MATCH AT 2.30 P.M. (S.T)
SENIOR HURLING FINAL:
TIOBRAID ARANN
(TIPPERARY)
V.
LUIMNEACH
(LIMERICK)
MATCH AT 3.45 P.M. (S.T.)
RUNAIDHE.
ADMISSION TO FIELD, 1/-; STAND, 2/-; SIDE-LINE, 3/-.
LIBERTY PRINTING WORKS THURLES

2

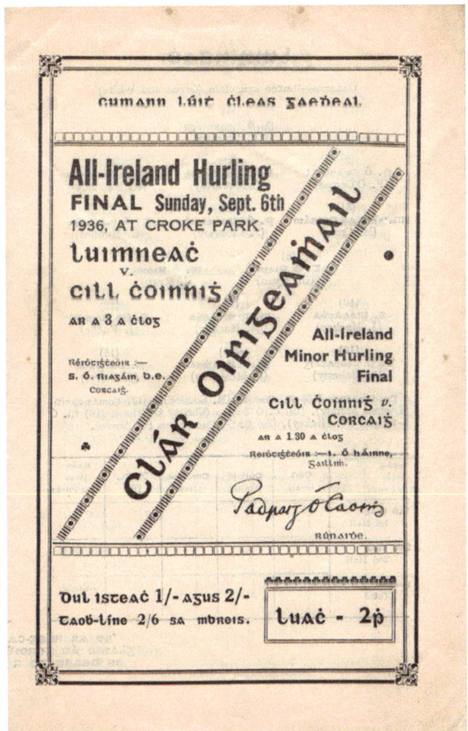

Cumann Lúiṫ Ċleas Gaeḋeal
All-Ireland Hurling
FINAL Sunday, Sept. 6th
1936, AT CROKE PARK
Luimneaċ
v.
Cill Ċoinniġ
ar a 3 a ċloġ
Réiḋtiġṫeoir :—
S. Ó. Riagáin, D.e.
Corcaiġ.
Clár Oifigeamail
All-Ireland
Minor Hurling
Final
Cill Ċoinniġ v.
Corcaiġ
ar a 1.30 a ċloġ
Réiḋtiġṫeoir :— I. Ó hÁinne,
Gaillimh.
Rúnaiḋe.
Dul isteaċ 1/- agus 2/-
Taoḃ-líne 2/6 sa mbreis.
Luaċ - 2p

1 Munster Hurling Final
Limerick 8-05 Tipperary 4-06

2 All-Ireland Hurling Final
Limerick 5-06 Kilkenny 1-05
Attendance – 51,235

3

Cumann Lúith Chleas Gaedheal.

Clár Oifigeamhail

Cluiche Ceannais Laighean

Peil Sinnsear

Cill Dára 0-8

v.

Laoighis 3-3

At 3 p.m.

Reitiṫeoir: M. Ó Lúinnigh, Ceatharloch

i bPáirc an Chrócaigh

ar an

De Domhnaigh 19adh Mí Iúil, 1936

Luach - - 2p

M. Ó Néill
Rúnaidhe

4

Cumann Lúith-Chleas Gaedheal.

1936 Munster Championship Finals

AT LIMERICK GAELIC GROUNDS,

SUNDAY, JULY 26th,

Minor Football Final

2.30 p.m. (S.T.)

Ciarraidhe v. Tiobraid Árann

Clár Oifigeamhail

Senior Football Final

3.45 p.m.

Ciarraidhe v. Cláir

S. Mac Cárthaigh (Rúnaidhe).

Dul isteach ... 1/-. Taobh Líne ... 1/- bhreis.

Buachaillí Sgoile, 6p.

Luach ... ... 2p.

Limerick Leader Ltd., Printers

3 Leinster Football Final
Laois 3-03 Kildare 0-08

4 Munster Football Final
Kerry 1-11 Clare 2-02

5 All-Ireland Football Final
Mayo 4-11 Laois 0-05
Attendance – 50,168

5

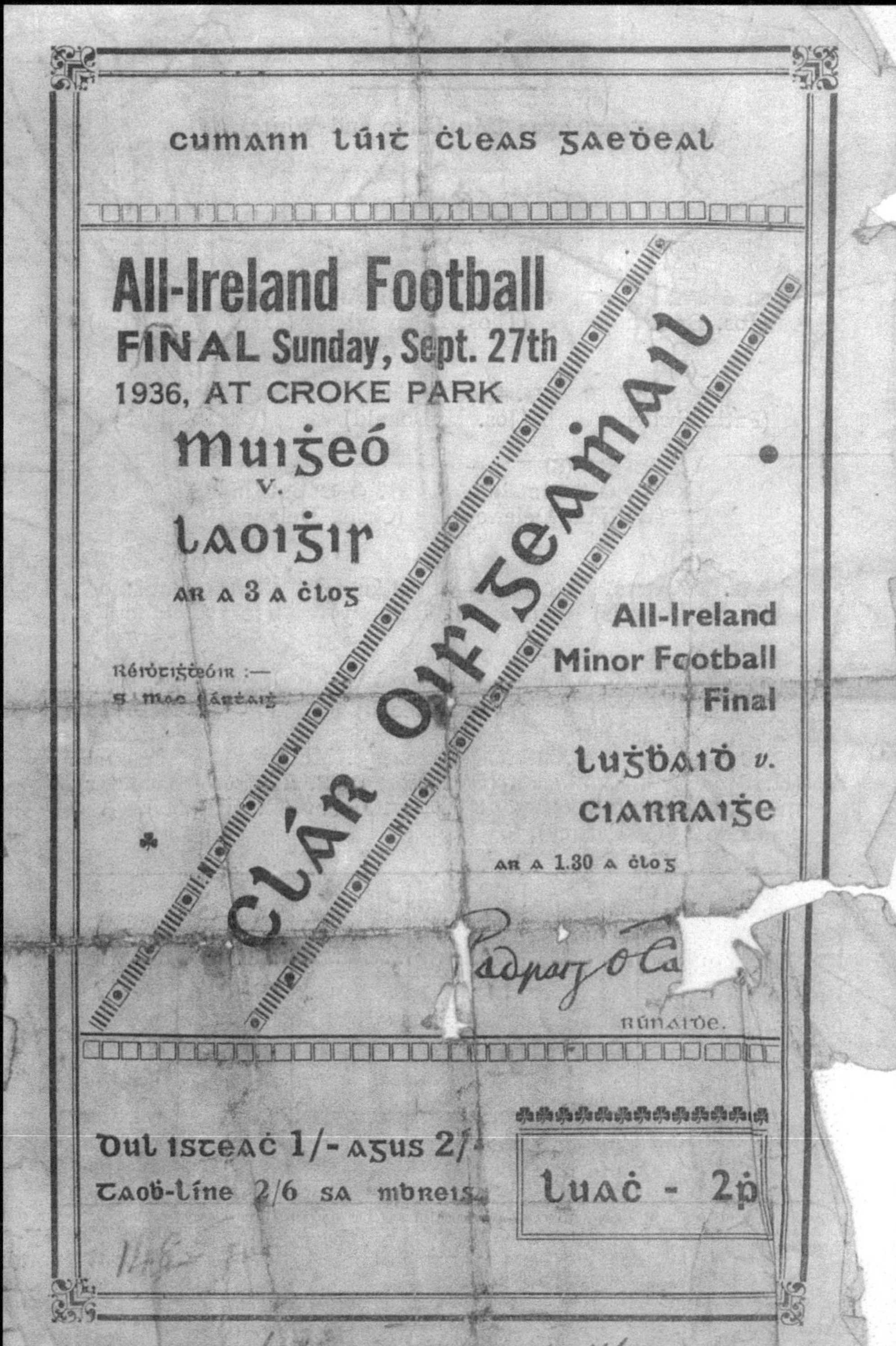

Cumann Lúiṫ Ċleas Gaeḋeal

All-Ireland Football FINAL Sunday, Sept. 27th 1936, AT CROKE PARK

Muiġeó
v.
Laoiġis

ar a 3 a ċloġ

Réiḋtiġṫeóir :—
S. Mac Cárṫaiġ

CLÁR OIFIĠEAṀAIL

All-Ireland Minor Football Final

Luġḃaiḋ v.
Ciarraiġe

ar a 1.30 a ċloġ

Rúnaiḋe.

Dul isteaċ 1/- agus 2/-
Taoḃ-líne 2/6 sa mbreis.

Luaċ - 2ṗ

1937

Having missed the early rounds of the Ulster championship because he was sitting his Leaving Certificate, John Joe O'Reilly made his championship debut for the Cavan senior football team in the Ulster football final of 1937 against Armagh. Just short of his nineteenth birthday, O'Reilly picked up his first Ulster medal and kept his place as Cavan defeated the reigning All-Ireland champions Mayo in the All-Ireland semi-final. O'Reilly took up his position in the Cavan half-back line alongside his brother and captain of the team, Tom, for the All-Ireland final against Kerry. The final, which was widely regarded as a classic, ended in a draw. The replay did not live up to the previous match in terms of excitement – not that it mattered to Kerry, who won for the twelfth time.

A builders' strike during construction of the Cusack Stand meant that Croke Park was not available to hold the All-Ireland hurling final. Instead it was played in Fitzgerald Stadium in Killarney, the first time an All-Ireland final had been played outside of Croke Park since the GAA purchased the site in 1913.

1

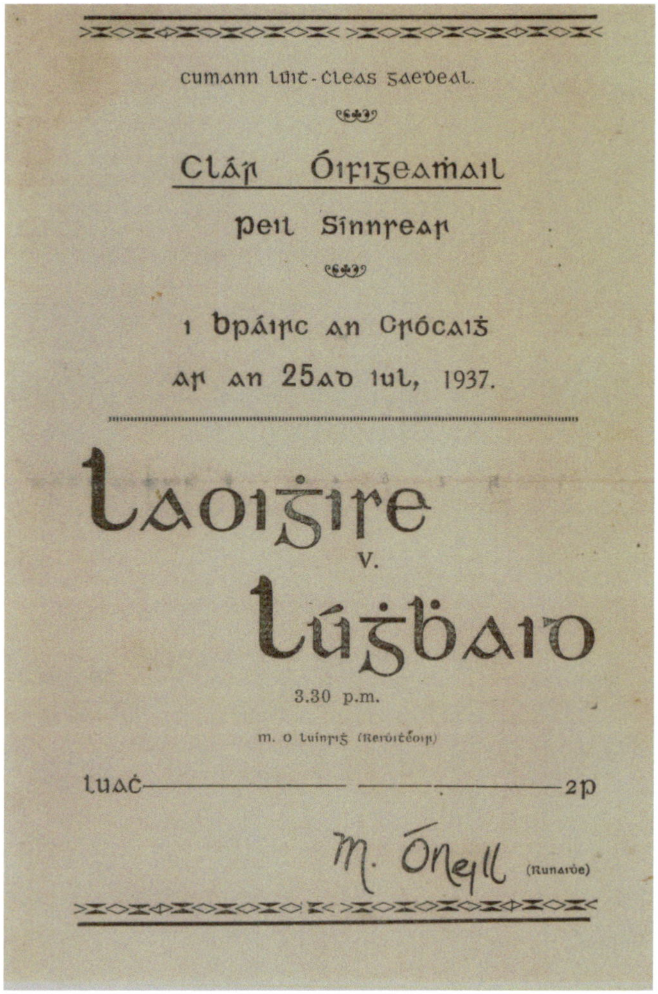

Cumann Lúit-Cleas Gaedeal.

Clár Oifigeaṁail

Peil Sinnsear

i bPáirc an Crócaiġ

ar an 25aḋ Iul, 1937.

Laoiġire

v.

Lúġḃaiḋ

3.30 p.m.

M. O Loinsiġ (Reiḋiteoir)

Luaċ — 2p

M. Ó Néill (Runaiḋe)

1 Leinster Football Final (photocopy)
Laois 0-12 Louth 0-04

2 All-Ireland Football Final
Kerry 2-05 Cavan 1-08
Attendance – 52,325

3 Replay
Kerry 4-04 Cavan 1-07
Attendance – 51,234

4 Munster Hurling Final
Tipperary 6-03 Limerick 4-03

5 All-Ireland Hurling Final
Tipperary 3-11 Kilkenny 0-03
Attendance – 43,638

2

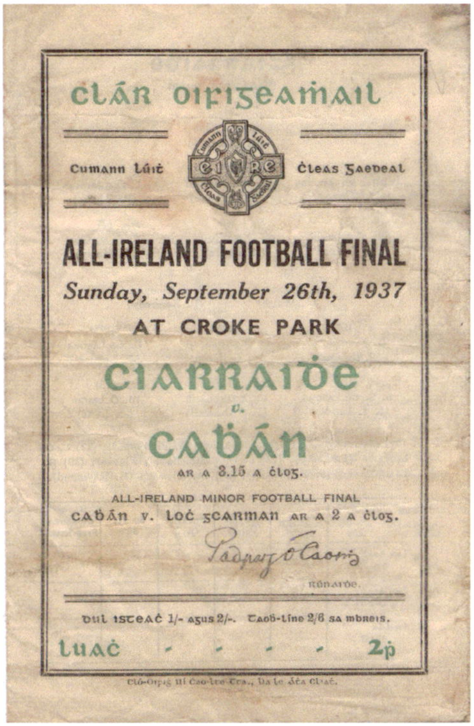
Clár Oifigeaṁail
Cumann Lúit Ċleas Gaeḋeal
ALL-IRELAND FOOTBALL FINAL
Sunday, September 26th, 1937
AT CROKE PARK
Ciarraiḋe
v.
Caḃán
ar a 3.15 a ċlog.
ALL-IRELAND MINOR FOOTBALL FINAL
Caḃán v. Loċ gCarman ar a 2 a ċlog.
Rúnaiḋe.
Dul isteaċ 1/- agus 2/-. Taoḃ-líne 2/6 sa mbreis.
Luaċ - - - - 2p

3

1937
Cumann Lúit-Ċleas Gaeḋeal
Aṫċluiċe Ceannais na h-Éireann i bPeil
i bPáirc an Ċrócaiġ
17/10/37 - ar a 3 a ċlog.
Caḃán
v.
Ciarraiḋe
Réiḋteóir: M. O'h-Aonġusa, Át Cliat.
Comórtas Báire 'na Mionúr ar 1.30 p.m.
Dul isteaċ - 1/- agus 2/-
Taoḃ-líne 2/6 sa mbreis
Luaċ 2p
Rúnaiḋe.
Clár Oifigeaṁail

4

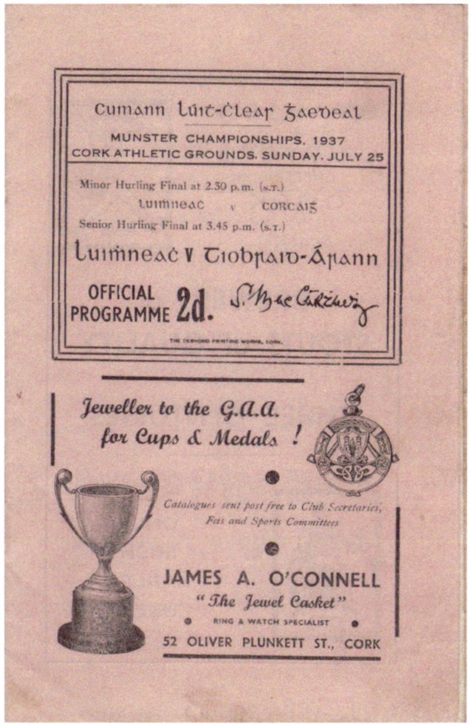
Cumann Lúit-Ċleas Gaeḋeal
MUNSTER CHAMPIONSHIPS, 1937
CORK ATHLETIC GROUNDS, SUNDAY, JULY 25
Minor Hurling Final at 2.30 p.m. (s.t.)
Luimneaċ v Corcaiġ
Senior Hurling Final at 3.45 p.m. (s.t.)
Luimneaċ v Tiobraid-Árann
OFFICIAL PROGRAMME 2d.
Jeweller to the G.A.A. for Cups & Medals!
Catalogues sent post free to Club Secretaries, Feis and Sports Committees
JAMES A. O'CONNELL
"The Jewel Casket"
RING & WATCH SPECIALIST
52 OLIVER PLUNKETT ST., CORK

5

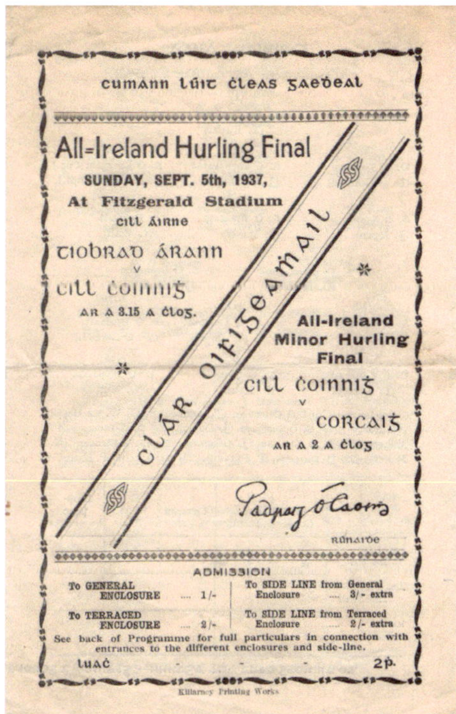
Cumann Lúit Ċleas Gaeḋeal
All-Ireland Hurling Final
SUNDAY, SEPT. 5th, 1937,
At Fitzgerald Stadium
Cill Áirne
Tiobrad Árann
v
Cill Coinniġ
ar a 3.15 a ċlog.
Clár Oifigeaṁail
All-Ireland Minor Hurling Final
Cill Coinniġ
v
Corcaiġ
ar a 2 a ċlog
Rúnaiḋe
ADMISSION
To GENERAL ENCLOSURE ... 1/-
To SIDE LINE from General Enclosure ... 3/- extra
To TERRACED ENCLOSURE ... 2/-
To SIDE LINE from Terraced Enclosure ... 2/- extra
See back of Programme for full particulars in connection with entrances to the different enclosures and side-line.
Luaċ - - - 2p.
Killarney Printing Works

1938

In a Munster hurling championship riven with controversy, Waterford broke through to become champions for the first time, defeating Clare in the final. After beating Galway in the All-Ireland semi-final, they qualified to meet Dublin in the final. The Dublin team comprised mainly country players who were based in the city and playing with local clubs, a notable exception being Jim Byrne from the Eoghan Ruadh club. Dublin defeated Waterford to win the 1938 All-Ireland hurling final by two points, which remains to date the last time that the Liam MacCarthy Cup was presented to the Dublin hurling captain. In the All-Ireland football final, a replay was needed for the second consecutive year. Galway's path to the final was simplified when only two other teams, Sligo and Mayo, took part in the Connacht championship. In the All-Ireland final, Galway accounted for Kerry at the second attempt.

1

Craoḃ Iomáint
Sinnsear Laiġean.

Clár Oifiġeamail.

i bPáirc Uí Ċonċubair,
Tualaċ Mór.

31 Iúl 1938 at 3.30 p.m.

Cill Ċoinniġ

v.

Áṫ-Cliaṫ

Reidhiteoir: L. Ó Laighléis (Ua bFháilghe).

Luaċ ...... 2p | M. Ó Neill
Rúnaiḋe.

1 Leinster Hurling Final Replay (photocopy)
Dublin 4-9 Kilkenny 3-5

2 Munster Hurling Final
Waterford 3-05 Clare 2-05

2

Cumann Lúṫ-Ċleas Ġaeḋeal

MUNSTER CHAMPIONSHIPS, 1938—FINAL

CORK ATHLETIC GROUNDS, SUNDAY, JULY 31

Minor Hurling at 2.30 p.m. (S.T.)

Ciarraiḋe v Corcaiġ

Senior Hurling at 3.45 p.m. (S.T.)

Clár v Port Láirge

OFFICIAL PROGRAMME 2d.

THE DESMOND PRINTING WORKS, CORK.

3

clár oifigeaṁail
i bPáirc an Ċrócaiġ
4/9/38 - ar a 3·15 p.m.
Craoḃ Iomána na h-Éireann
Portláirge
(WATERFORD)
v.
Áṫ Cliaṫ
(DUBLIN)
Craoḃ Iomána na Mionúr
Áṫ Cliaṫ v. Corcaiġ
(Dublin) (Cork)
Luaċ 2ṗ
Ar aġaiḋ linn

4

cumann lúṫ cleas gaeḋeal.
OFFICIAL PROGRAMME.
Connacht Senior Football Championship Final—
Galway v Mayo,
Referee---P. J. Masterson, Cavan.
At 4.30.
Preceded by Junior Hurling Final :
Roscommon v. Galway.
Referee--S. Bracken, Arigna.
At 3 o'clock.
AT ROSCOMMON,
On SUNDAY, 17th JULY, 1938.
Admission, 1/- Side Line, 1/- extra. Grand Stand, 2/- extra.
Admission to Sports Field from Market Square.
Further Fixtures—Leitrim v Galway, Junior and Minor Football Finals, July 24th, at Carrick-on-Shannon.
PRICE - - - - - 2d.
CHAMPION OFFICE, ROSCOMMON.

5

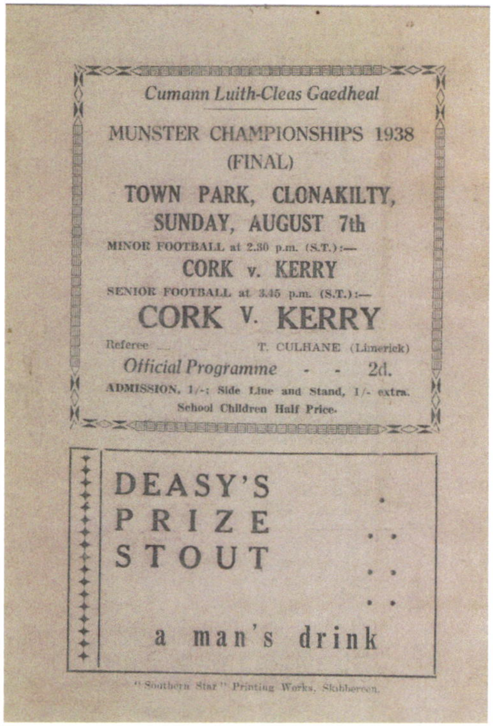
Cumann Luith-Cleas Gaedheal
MUNSTER CHAMPIONSHIPS 1938
(FINAL)
TOWN PARK, CLONAKILTY,
SUNDAY, AUGUST 7th
MINOR FOOTBALL at 2.30 p.m. (S.T.):—
CORK v. KERRY
SENIOR FOOTBALL at 3.45 p.m. (S.T.):—
CORK v. KERRY
Referee T. CULHANE (Limerick)
Official Programme - - 2d.
ADMISSION, 1/-; Side Line and Stand, 1/- extra.
School Children Half Price.
DEASY'S
PRIZE
STOUT
a man's drink
"Southern Star" Printing Works, Skibbereen.

6

clár oifigeaṁail
Craoḃ Peile na h-Éireann
Ciarraiḋe
(KERRY)
v.
Gaillim
(GALWAY)
i bPáirc an Ċrócaiġ, 25-9-38
Craoḃ Peile na Mionúr
Caḃán v. Ciarraiḋe
Luaċ 2ṗ.

7

3 All-Ireland Hurling Final
Dublin 2-05 Waterford 1-06
Attendance – 37,129

4 Connacht Football Final
Galway 0-08 Mayo 0-05

5 Munster Football Final
Kerry 4-14 Cork 0-06

6 All-Ireland Football Final
Galway 3-03 Kerry 2-06
Attendance – 68,950

7 Replay
Galway 2-04 Kerry 0-07
Attendance – 47,851

1939

On 1 September 1939, Germany invaded Poland and, two days later, Britain and France declared war on Germany. Events of such international significance took a back seat to hurling for the day, however, when Cork and Kilkenny met in the All-Ireland hurling final for the first time since the famous trilogy in 1931. Heavy rain swept across Dublin the night before the match. With 10 minutes of the second half gone, the heavens opened again, this time accompanied by thunder and lightning. The terrible weather conditions did not impact upon the excitement of the play. Down by six points at half-time, Cork drew level near the end of the game, only for Terry Leahy to snatch a late winner for Kilkenny. The game went down in history as 'The Thunder and Lightning Final'.

A pitch invasion caused the Ulster football final to be abandoned. The re-fixture, played in Croke Park, was won by Cavan – though it would ultimately be Kerry who went on to lift the Sam Maguire Cup later that year in the same venue.

1 Munster Hurling Final
Cork 4-03 Limerick 3-04

2 All-Ireland Hurling Final
Kilkenny 2-07 Cork 3-03
Attendance – 39,302

3 Leinster Football Final
Meath 2-07 Wexford 2-03

4 Munster Football Final
Kerry 2-11 Tipperary 0-04

5 Ulster Football Final Re-fixture
Cavan 2-03 Armagh 1-04

6 All-Ireland Football Final
Kerry 2-05 Meath 2-03
Attendance – 46,828

1

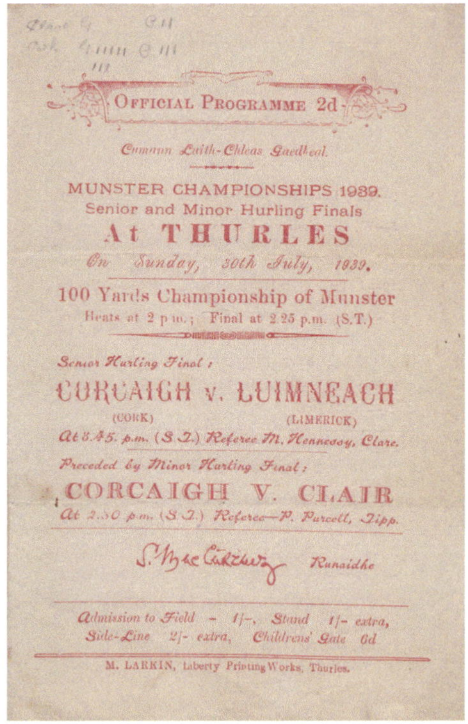

OFFICIAL PROGRAMME 2d

Cumann Lúith-Chleas Gaedheal.

MUNSTER CHAMPIONSHIPS 1939.
Senior and Minor Hurling Finals
At THURLES
On Sunday, 30th July, 1939.

100 Yards Championship of Munster
Heats at 2 p.m.; Final at 2.25 p.m. (S.T.)

Senior Hurling Final:
CORCAIGH v. LUIMNEACH
(CORK) (LIMERICK)
At 3.45 p.m. (S.T.) Referee M. Hennessy, Clare.

Preceded by Minor Hurling Final:
CORCAIGH V. CLAIR
At 2.30 p.m. (S.T.) Referee—P. Purcell, Tipp.

Runaidhe

Admission to Field – 1/-, Stand 1/- extra,
Side-Line 2/- extra, Childrens' Gate 6d

M. LARKIN, Liberty Printing Works, Thurles.

2

CLÁR OIFIGEAMAIL 1939

i bPáirc an Ċróċaiġ

3/9/39 – ar a 3.15 p.m.

Craoḃ Iomána na h-Éireann

Cill Ċoinniġ
(KILKENNY)
v.
Corcaiġ
(CORK)

Reiṫeoir: S. Ó Flaiṫbeartaiġ

Craoḃ Iomána na Mionúr

Cill Ċoinniġ v Corcaiġ
(KILKENNY) (CORK)

Reiṫeoir: M. Ó hAonġusa
ar a 2 a ċlog

Luaċ 2p.

Rúnaiḋe.

Ar aġaiḋ linn

3

1939
Luac 2p.
Clár Oifigeamail

Cumann Lúit-Cleas Gaedeal.

Craob Peil Laigean.
(Comórtas na n-Aonac).

I bPáirc an Ċrócaiġ,
30-7-'39 Ar a 3.45 a clog.

Loċ Garman
v
Miḋe

Reiḋiteoir - - P. Ó Duinn [Át-cliat]

M. Ó Neill

4

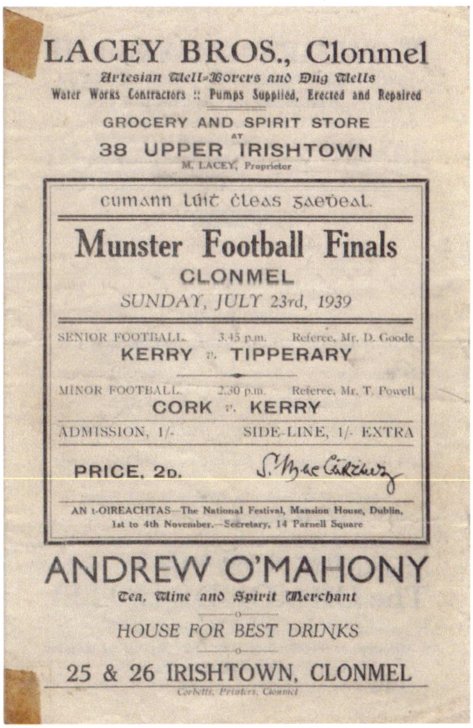

LACEY BROS., Clonmel
Artesian Well-Borers and Dug Wells
Water Works Contractors :: Pumps Supplied, Erected and Repaired
GROCERY AND SPIRIT STORE
AT
38 UPPER IRISHTOWN
M. LACEY, Proprietor

Cumann Lúit Ċleas Gaedeal.

Munster Football Finals
CLONMEL
SUNDAY, JULY 23rd, 1939

SENIOR FOOTBALL 3.45 p.m. Referee, Mr. D. Goode
KERRY v. TIPPERARY

MINOR FOOTBALL 2.30 p.m. Referee, Mr. T. Powell
CORK v. KERRY

ADMISSION, 1/- SIDE-LINE, 1/- EXTRA

PRICE, 2D. S. Mac Cárthaigh

AN t-OIREACHTAS—The National Festival, Mansion House, Dublin, 1st to 4th November.—Secretary, 14 Parnell Square

ANDREW O'MAHONY
Tea, Wine and Spirit Merchant
HOUSE FOR BEST DRINKS
25 & 26 IRISHTOWN, CLONMEL
Corbetts, Printers, Clonmel

5

Cumann Lúit-Ċleas Gaedeal

Official Programme
13-8-39

Páirc an Cróċaig

Minor Football Championship Semi-Final
Córcaig v. Roscomain
Ar 1.30

Senior Football Championship Semi-Final
Múigeo v. Ciarraiḋe
Ar 3.15

Ulster Football Championship Final
Caḃán v. Ard Maċa
Ar 4.30

Luaċ 2p. Padraig Ó Caoimh
Rúnaiḋe.

6

Cumann Lúit Ċleas Gaedeal

Official Programme
24-9-39

Páirc an Cróċaiġ

Senior Football Championship Final
Miḋe
v.
Ciarraiḋe
Ar 2.30

Minor Football Championship Final
Muineaċáin v. Roscomáin
Ar 1.15

Luaċ 2p. Padraig Ó Caoimh
Rúnaiḋe.

LEINSTER MINO
’Áṫ Cliaṫ v. Cill

1940–49

1940

In 1940, Kerry had a facile Munster campaign, defeating Waterford in a Munster football final attended by a paltry 2,000 spectators. Cavan, utterly dominant in Ulster, made little of Down's challenge in the provincial final. In Leinster, Meath retained their title, defeating Laois in a bad-tempered final. In Connacht, Galway had five points to spare over Mayo. The All-Ireland football final in 1940 was a much-anticipated clash of the winners from the previous two years, Kerry and Galway, but the match did not live up to expectations, Kerry winning a low-scoring and tempestuous match played in poor conditions.

In the All-Ireland hurling final, Mick Mackey captained Limerick to success over Kilkenny. Kilkenny began the match strongly but by switching Mackey to midfield the tide turned in favour of Limerick and they had two goals to spare at the end of the game.

1

Cumann Lúiṫ Ċleas Gaeḋeal.
G.A.A.

OFFICIAL PROGRAMME.

Connacht Senior Football
And Junior Hurling Finals
At Roscommon,
On SUNDAY, 21st JULY, 1940.

Junior Hurling—
Galway v Roscommon
At 3 o'clock.
Referee—Mr. P. Fahey.

Senior Football—
GALWAY V. MAYO.
Referee—Mr. P. J. Masterson (Cavan).
At 4 30 o'clock.

Admission, 1/- Side Line, 1/- extra. Grand Stand, 2/- extra.
Admission to Sports Field from Market Square.

Further Fixtures—Junior All-Ireland Semi-Final, at Castlerea, August 4th: Roscommon v. Cavan.

PRICE - - - - 2d.

CHAMPION OFFICE, ROSCOMMON.

2

Clár Oifigeaṁail

Craoḃ Peile na h-Éireann

Ciarraiḋe
(KERRY)
v. Gailliṁ
(GALWAY)

i bPáirc an Ċrócaiġ
22 - 9 - 40 ar a 3 p.m.
Réiḋteóir: S. de Burca

Craoḃ Peile na Mionúir
Luġbaḋ v. Muiġeo
ar a 1.30 a ċloġ

Luaċ — 2ṗ.

Rúnaiḋe

1 Connacht Football Final
Galway 1-07 Mayo 0-05

2 All-Ireland Football Final
Kerry 0-07 Galway 1-03
Attendance – 60,821

3 Leinster Hurling Final (photocopy)
Kilkenny 3-06 Dublin 2-05

4 Munster Hurling Final
Limerick 4-03 Cork 3-06

5 Replay
Limerick 3-03 Cork 2-04

6 All-Ireland Hurling Final
Limerick 3-07 Kilkenny 1-07
Attendance – 49,260

3

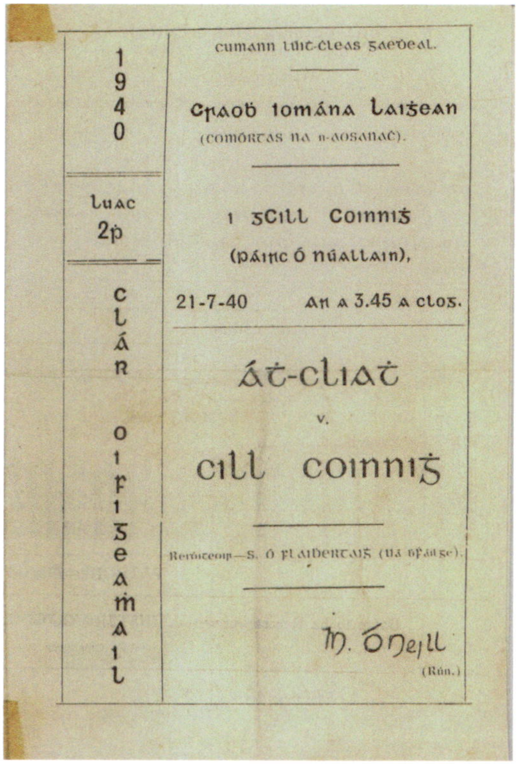
cumann lúit-cleas gaedeal.
craob iomána laigean
(comórtas na n-aosanac).
1940
luac 2p
i gCill Coinnig
(páirc ó núallain),
21-7-40 ar a 3.45 a clog.
clár oifigeamail
át-cliat
v.
cill coinnig
Reiticeoir—S. Ó Flaidbertaig (Ua bFailge).
M. Ó Neill
(Rún.)

4

cumann lúit clear gaedeal
Clár Oifigeamail (Official Programme) - Luac 3d.
What a pride and glory it is to witness the stirring scenes associated with a well-played, cleanly and keenly contested Gaelic match, especially in Hurling; to feel the thrills coursing through one's veins as the springy ash Camans crash in the air above and on the sod below; and to realise that here is being enacted before our excited and admiring gaze, a vivid symbol of the long ago; a sure reminder that Knocknagow is not dead; and a striking and soul-stirring guarantee that by Shannon, Suir and Lee, and by hillside and glenside throughout the province, the virile manhood and traditions of our race are keeping a firm hold on their hard-won inheritance.
Seán mac Cártaig, b.e., Chairman, at Munster Convention, 1940.
1940
munster championships
SENIOR AND MINOR HURLING FINALS
AT THURLES
SUNDAY, JULY 28th, 1940
SENIOR HURLING FINAL
corcaig (CORK) v. luimneac (LIMERICK)
3.45 p.m., Summer Time. Referee—D. Ryan, Kerry.
MINOR HURLING—Luimneac v. Clár
2.00 p.m., Summer Time. Referee—W. O'Donnell, Tipperary.
Admission to Field - 1s.; Stand (1s.), Sideline (2s.) extra
S. Mac Cártaig
Rúnaire

5

cumann lúit clear gaedeal
Clár Oifigeamail (Official Programme) - Luac 2d.
What a pride and glory it is to witness the stirring scenes associated with a well-played, cleanly and keenly contested Gaelic match, especially in Hurling; to feel the thrills coursing through one's veins as the springy ash Camans crash in the air above and on the sod below; and to realise that here is being enacted before our excited and admiring gaze, a vivid symbol of the long ago; a sure reminder that Knocknagow is not dead; and a striking and soul-stirring guarantee that by Shannon, Suir and Lee, and by hillside and glenside throughout the province, the virile manhood and traditions of our race are keeping a firm hold on their hard-won inheritance.
Seán mac Cártaig, b.e., Chairman, at Munster Convention, 1940.
1940
munster championship
REPLAY
SENIOR HURLING
AT THURLES
SUNDAY, AUGUST 4th, 1940
SENIOR HURLING FINAL REPLAY
corcaig (CORK) v. luimneac (LIMERICK)
3.45 p.m., Summer Time. Referee—D. Ryan, Kerry.
ALL-IRELAND JUNIOR FOOTBALL SEMI-FINAL—WESTMEATH v. CORK
2.30 p.m., Summer Time. Referee—T. Powel, Tipperary.
Admission to Field - 1s.; Stand (1s.), Sideline (2s.) extra
S. Mac Cártaig
Rúnaire
Leinster Leader, Ltd., Naas

6

clár oifigeamail
i bPáirc an Cróćaig, 1-9-40
Ar a 3.15 p.m.
Craob Iomána na h-Éireann
Cill Coinnig
(KILKENNY)
v.
Luimneać
(LIMERICK)
Reiteoir:—S. S. Callanain
Craob Iomána na Mionúr
Luimneać v. Aontruim
(LIMERICK) (ANTRIM)
Reiteoir:—An Doctúir S. Scrubaire ar a 1.45 a ćlog
Luać 2p.
Padraig Ó Caoimh
Rúnaire
Ar Agaid Linn
Cló-Oifig Uí Caoilte, Tta., Baile Átha Cliath

1941

An outbreak of foot-and-mouth disease in 1941 led to the disruption of the provincial championships. The Munster and Leinster championships were particularly affected, with the Munster hurling and Leinster football finals only being played after the conclusion of the All-Ireland finals. Carlow reached the provincial football final for the first time ever, only for the match to be postponed as a result of the outbreak. Dublin were nominated as Leinster's representatives in the All-Ireland semi-final. (Counties needed to be free of foot-and-mouth for some weeks before travel was allowed.) When the Leinster final was eventually played in November, Carlow's momentum, and the match, were lost.

Similarly, Tipperary and Kilkenny were ruled out of their provincial hurling championships due to foot-and-mouth disease. Cork and Dublin were nominated to play in the All-Ireland series, with Cork winning the final. However, when the Munster hurling final was played on 26 October, it was Tipperary who won out. In the delayed Leinster hurling final, Dublin defeated Kilkenny by a goal.

1

2

1 All-Ireland Football Final
Kerry 1-08 Galway 0-07
Attendance – 45,512

2 Munster Hurling Final
Tipperary 5-04 Cork 2-05

3 All-Ireland Hurling Final
Cork 5-11 Dublin 0-06
Attendance – 26,150

3

Clár Oifigeamail

Craoḃ Iomána na h-Éireann

Áṫ Cliaṫ
(DUBLIN)

v. Corcaiġ
(CORK)

i bPáirc an Ċrócaiġ

28 - 9 - 41 ar a 3.30 p.m.

Réiḋteóir: L. Ó Doṁnaill, Tioḃrad Árann

Craoḃ Iomána na Mionúir

Corcaiġ *v.* Gailliṁ

ar a 2.15 a ċlog

Luaċ — 2ṗ.

Pádraig Ó Caoiṁ

Rúnaiḋe

Cló-Oifig Uí Ċaoilte, Tta., Sráid Stafford, Baile Áṫa Cliaṫ

1942

Cork and Dublin met for the second year in a row in the 1942 All-Ireland hurling final, this time both teams progressing to the decider by the more conventional route of winning their provincial finals. Cork defeated Limerick and Tipperary to claim the Munster title, while Dublin accounted for Offaly in the Leinster semi-final before proving too strong for Kilkenny in the final. Dublin had a bye to the All-Ireland final, while Cork easily overcame Galway in the semi-final. Although Dublin put in a more spirited performance than the previous year, they were still no match for a Cork team captained by Jack Lynch and also featuring Christy Ring. 1942 marks the final year when the All-Ireland final programmes were fully black and white productions. Colour covers were introduced the following year.

1

2

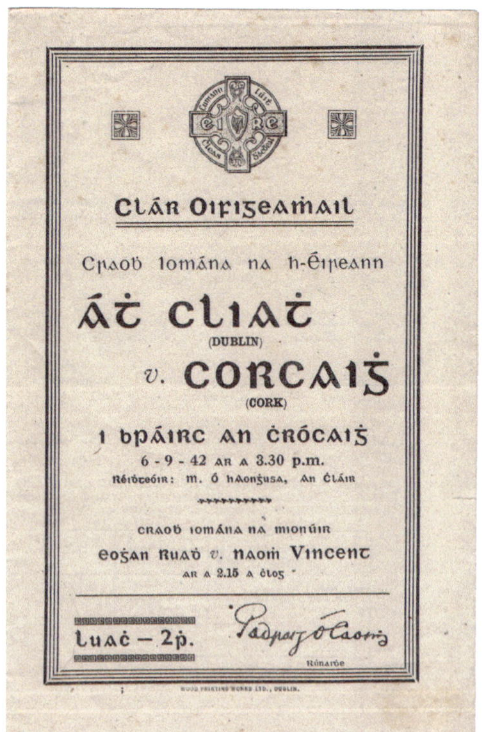

1 Munster Hurling Final
Cork 4-15 Tipperary 4-01

2 All-Ireland Hurling Final
Cork 2-14 Dublin 3-04
Attendance – 27,313

3 All-Ireland Football Final
Dublin 1-10 Galway 1-08
Attendance – 37,105

3

Clár Oifigeamail

Craoḃ Peile na h-Éireann

Áṫ Cliaṫ
(DUBLIN)

v. **Gaillim̐**
(GALWAY)

i bPáirc an Ċrócaiġ

20 - 9 - 42 ar a 3.15 p.m.

Réiḋteóir: S. Ó Cinnéide

Boḃta Deirid Sreaṫ Cluiċe Áṫ Cliaṫ
Peile na Mionúir

Naoṁ Uinnsion *v.* C. Ciċeam

ar a 2 a ċloġ.

Luaċ — 2ṗ.

Pádraig Ó Caoimh
Rúnaiḋe

WOOD PRINTING WORKS LTD., DUBLIN.

1943

The 1943 provincial hurling championships went as predicted in Munster and Leinster, with Cork and Kilkenny emerging to contest the All-Ireland series. Galway, as was customary at this time, represented Connacht. In the absence of junior and minor competitions due to the 'Emergency', Antrim were allowed to play an All-Ireland quarter-final against Galway. It was a shock when they defeated Galway by a point, but an even bigger upset came when Kilkenny went to Belfast for the semi-final and suffered the same fate. Antrim were unable to maintain their momentum, alas, and suffered a heavy defeat to Cork in the All-Ireland final.

Roscommon, so often the bridesmaid to Galway and Mayo, won the Connacht football championship by beating Galway in the final. Playing in their first All-Ireland final, Roscommon needed a replay to defeat Cavan. Although the match ended in controversy, the joy of the Roscommon supporters couldn't be suppressed, as Jimmy Murray collected the Sam Maguire Cup.

1 Munster Hurling Final
Cork 2-13 Waterford 3-08

2 All-Ireland Hurling Final
Cork 5-16 Antrim 0-04
Attendance – 48,843

3 Munster Football Final
Cork 1-07 Tipperary 1-04

4 Ulster Football Final
Cavan 2-03 Monaghan 0-05

5 All-Ireland Football Final
Roscommon 1-06 Cavan 1-06
Attendance – 68,023

6 Replay
Roscommon 2-07 Cavan 2-02
Attendance – 47,193

1

2

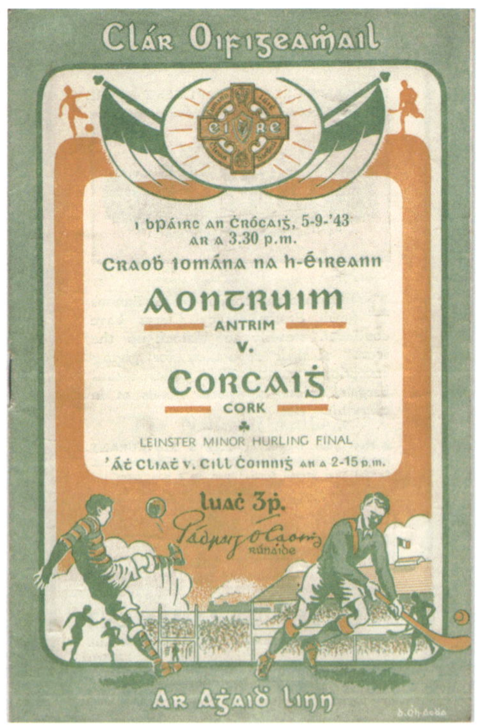

3

Cumann Luit-Cleas Gaedeal
MUNSTER CHAMPIONSHIP, 1943
FINAL
Corcaig V Tiobraid-Árann
(CORK) (TIPPERARY)
At FERMOY, SUNDAY, 25th JULY
At 3.45 p.m.
Official Programme 3d.
Admission - 1/- 2/- 3/- Schoolboys 6d.
DORAN'S GARAGE
RATHEALY ROAD,
FERMOY.
COMPLETE FUNERAL FURNISHERS
CARS FOR HIRE
After Closing Hours Apply at :
5 Newmarket Street, Fermoy
Grams "Doran" Phone 48.
DESMOND, CORK

4

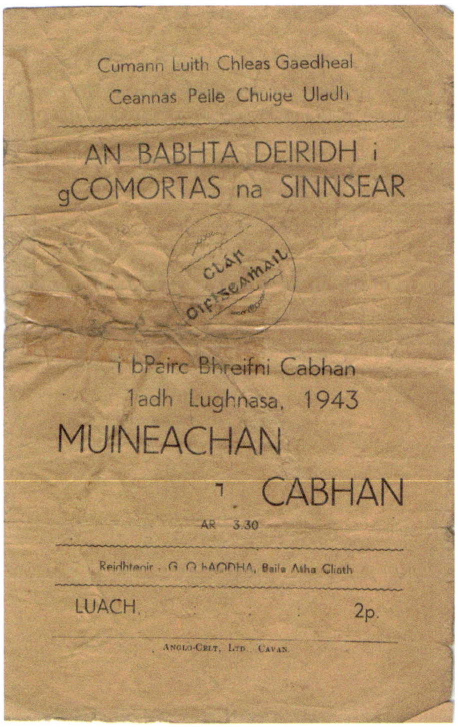
Cumann Luith Chleas Gaedheal
Ceannas Peile Chuige Uladh
AN BABHTA DEIRIDH i
gCOMORTAS na SINNSEAR
Clár Oifigeamail
i bPairc Bhreifni Cabhan
1adh Lughnasa, 1943
MUINEACHAN
CABHAN
AR 3.30
LUACH 2p.
ANGLO-CELT, LTD., CAVAN.

5

Clár Oifigeamail
Éire
i bPáirc an Chrócaig, 26-9-'43
ar a 3.15 p.m.
Craob Peile na h-Éireann
Cabán
CAVAN
v.
Roscomáin
ROSCOMMON
LEINSTER MINOR FOOTBALL FINAL
Cill Dara v. Lughbad ar a 1.45 p.m.
luach 3p.
Rúnaide
Ar Aghaidh Linn

6

Clár Oifigeamail
Éire
i bPáirc an Chrócaig, 10-10-'43
ar a 3 p.m.
Craob Peile na h-Éireann
Cabán
CAVAN
v.
Roscomáin
ROSCOMMON
Dublin Junior Football Championship Final
SKERRIES HARPS v. G.S.R. at 1.30 p.m.
luach 2p.
Rúnaide
Ar Aghaidh Linn

1944

Having been thwarted in their efforts to win a first Leinster senior football championship by foot-and-mouth disease in 1941, Carlow eventually claimed the elusive provincial title by defeating Dublin at Geraldine Park in Athy in 1944. Carlow were narrowly defeated by Kerry in the All-Ireland semi-final, who, in turn, were beaten by Roscommon in the final. Unfortunately, it was Carlow's last Leinster win and Roscommon's last All-Ireland title to date.

Wexford and Kerry had won four consecutive All-Ireland football titles by this point, but no hurling team had yet managed four (although several teams had managed three All-Ireland hurling titles in a row). By defeating Dublin in the 1944 All-Ireland final, however, Cork became the first team to do so. It was Dublin's misfortune to lose three of those finals and, while the Rebels' team is synonymous with Ring and Lynch, Joe Kelly's tally of two goals and three points was the difference in the All-Ireland final of 1944.

1

2

1 All-Ireland Football Final
Roscommon 1-09 Kerry 2-04
Attendance – 79,245

2 Munster Hurling Final
Limerick 4-13 Cork 6-07

3 Replay
Cork 4-06 Limerick 3-06

OFFICIAL PROGRAMME 2d.

Cumann Luith-Chleas Gaedheal.

Munster Senior Hurling Final, Replay, 1944.

AT THURLES,

On Sunday, July 30th, 1944

Corcaigh (CORK)

v.

Luimneach (LIMERICK)

At 3 p.m. (S.T.) ∴ Referee J. Carroll. Laoighis.

Preceded by Mid. Tipp. Senior Football Championship 1944.

Templemore v. Templetuohy

At 1.45 p.m. (S.T.) ∴ Referee S. O'Malley.

S. Mac Cuthbert, *Runaidhe.*

Admission 1/-; Stand 1/- extra; Side-Line 2/- extra.

Liberty Press Thurles

4

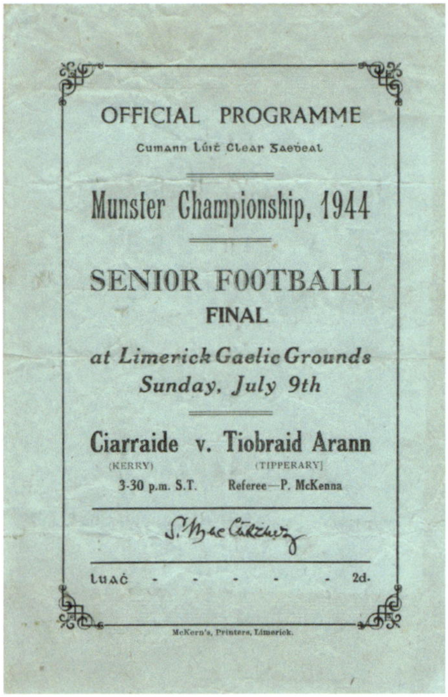

5

4 Munster Football Final
Kerry 1-06 Tipperary 0-05

5 All-Ireland Hurling Final
Cork 2-13 Dublin 1-02
Attendance – 26,896

1945

Cork's attempt to win five All-Ireland hurling finals in a row fell at the first hurdle when they were defeated by Tipperary in the 1945 Munster hurling semi-final, the Premier County going on to win this year's All-Ireland. One Cork player, however, did complete five consecutive All-Ireland wins in 1945. Jack Lynch had played in midfield for all Cork's hurling victories from 1941 to 1944, even captaining the team in 1942. Lynch also played on the county's football team for several years throughout this period and in 1945 was selected as a corner forward. Cork beat Kerry in the Munster football final and, after overcoming Galway in the All-Ireland semi-final, faced Cavan in the final. Cork proved too strong for the Ulster champions, giving the county their third All-Ireland football title and an unprecedented fifth All-Ireland medal in a row for Lynch.

1

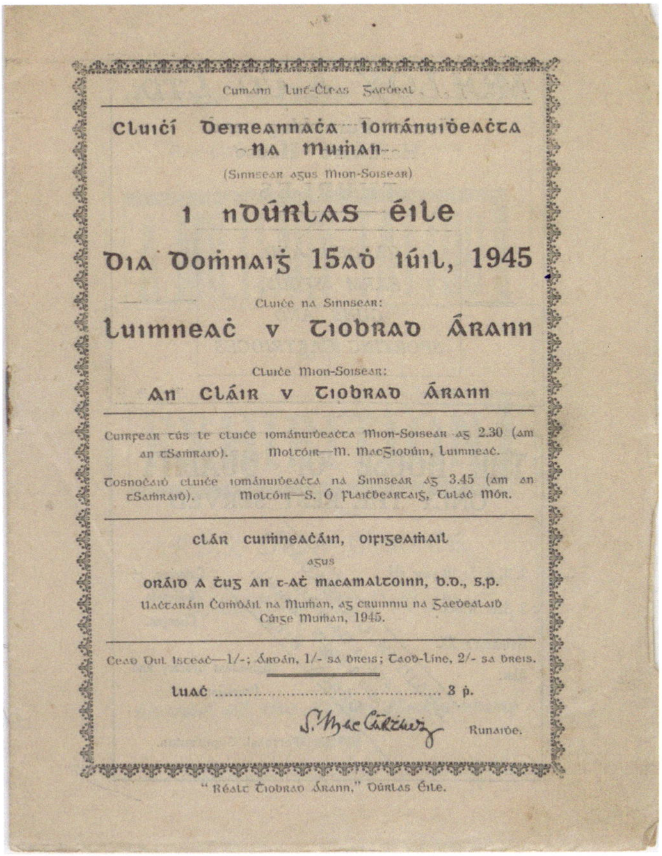

Cumann Luṫ-Ċleas Gaeḋeal

Cluiċí Deireannaċa Iománuiḋeaċta na Muṁan

(Sinnsear agus Mion-Soisear)

I nDúrlas Éile

Dia Domhnaiġ 15aḋ Iúil, 1945

Cluiċe na Sinnsear:

Luimneaċ v Tiobrad Árann

Cluiċe Mion-Soisear:

An Cláir v Tiobrad Árann

Cuirfear tús le cluiċe iománuiḋeaċta Mion-Soisear ag 2.30 (am an tSaṁraiḋ). Moltóir—M. MacGiobúin, Luimneaċ.

Tosnoċaiḋ cluiċe iománuiḋeaċta na Sinnsear ag 3.45 (am an tSaṁraiḋ). Moltóir—S. Ó Flaiṫbeartaiġ, Tulaċ Mór.

Clár Cuiṁneaċáin, Oifigeaṁail

agus

Oráid a ṫug an t-Aṫ MacAmalToinn, D.D., S.P.

Uaċtarán Ċoṁḋáil na Muṁan, ag cruinniu na Gaeḋealaiḋ Cúige Muṁan, 1945.

Cead Dul Isteaċ—1/-; Árdán, 1/- sa breis; Taoḃ-Líne, 2/- sa breis.

Luaċ .... 3 p.

Runaiḋe.

"Réalt Ṫiobrad Árann," Dúrlas Éile.

1 Munster Hurling Final
Tipperary 4-03 Limerick 2-06

2

2 All-Ireland Hurling Final
Tipperary 5-06 Kilkenny 3-06
Attendance – 69,459

3 Leinster Football Final
Wexford 1-09 Offaly 1-04

4 Munster Football Final (photocopy)
Cork 1-11 Kerry 1-06

5 Ulster Football Final
Cavan 4-10 Fermanagh 1-04

6 All-Ireland Football Final
Cork 2-05 Cavan 0-07
Attendance – 67,329

3

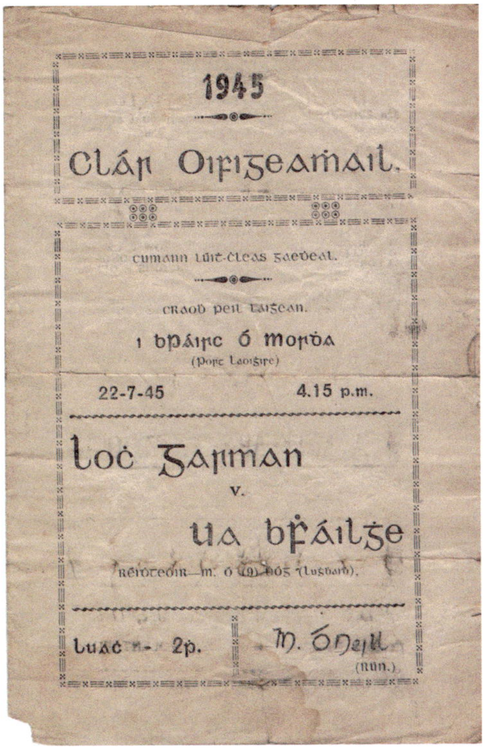
1945
Clár Oifigeamail.
Cumann Lúit-Cleas Gaedeal.
Craob Peil Laigean.
i bPáirc Ó Mórda
(Port Laoighise)
22-7-45
4.15 p.m.
Loc Garman
v.
Ua bFáilge
Luac — 2p.
M. Ó Néill
(Rún.)

4

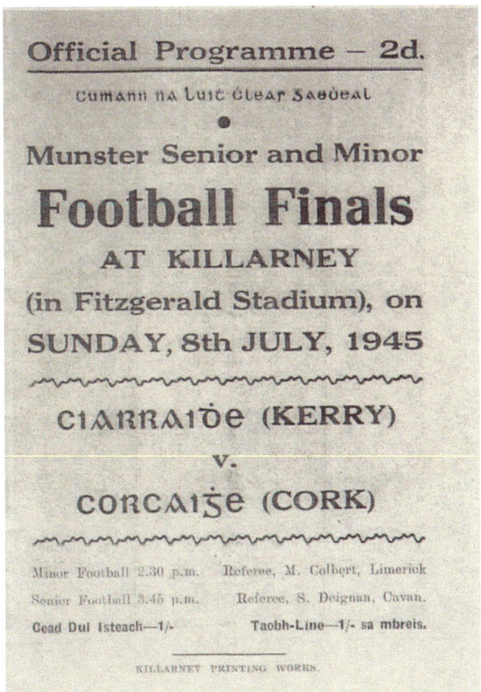
Official Programme – 2d.
Cumann na Luit Cleas Gaedeal
Munster Senior and Minor
Football Finals
AT KILLARNEY
(in Fitzgerald Stadium), on
SUNDAY, 8th JULY, 1945
Ciarraide (KERRY)
v.
Corcaige (CORK)
Minor Football 2.30 p.m.
Referee, M. Colbert, Limerick
Senior Football 3.45 p.m.
Referee, S. Deignan, Cavan.
Cead Dul Isteach—1/-
Taobh-Line—1/- sa mbreis.
KILLARNEY PRINTING WORKS.

5

Cumann Luith Chleas Gaedheal.
ULSTER SENIOR
AND MINOR
FOOTBALL FINALS
—AT—
ST. TIERNACH'S PARK, CLONES,
SUNDAY, 29th JULY, 1945.
MINOR GAME:
MONAGHAN
v.
DOWN
At 2.45 p.m.
Referee: P. Lynch (Cavan).
SENIOR GAME:
CAVAN
v.
FERMANAGH
At 4.15 p.m.
Referee: J. Murtagh (Down).
PROGRAMME : : 2d. each.
C. MURRAY, PRINTER, CLONES.

6

Clár Oifigeamail
Michael Cusack
FOUNDER OF THE G.A.A.
Luac 3p.
Craob Peile na h-Éireann
i bPáirc an Crócaig, 23-9-'45, ar 3.15 p.m.
Corcaig
v.
Cabán
Craob Peile na Mionúr
'Át Cliat v. Liatdruim
ar 1.45 p.m.
Ar Agaid Linn

1946

The Connacht football final in 1946, played between Mayo and Roscommon, sparked controversy when a goal by Roscommon captain, Jimmy Murray, was called into question. After some deliberation, the goal was awarded and Roscommon emerged with a one-point victory. Amid allegations that in the build-up to the goal, the ball had struck an umpire and rebounded back into play, there were objections and counter-objections to the Connacht Council. Eventually, a replay was ordered, which Roscommon won convincingly. In the Leinster football final, Tommy 'The Boy Wonder' Murphy was inspirational in propelling Laois to victory over Kildare and while he was prominent again in the All-Ireland semi-final, Roscommon progressed to the final. The All-Ireland final was delayed due to the 'Save the Harvest' scheme after a poor summer. In the final, Kerry staged a late rally to recoup a six-point deficit and three weeks later claimed the title for the sixteenth time.

1
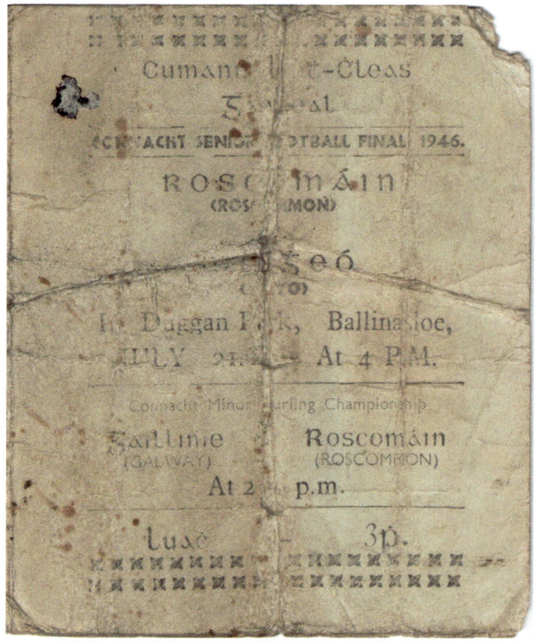

2
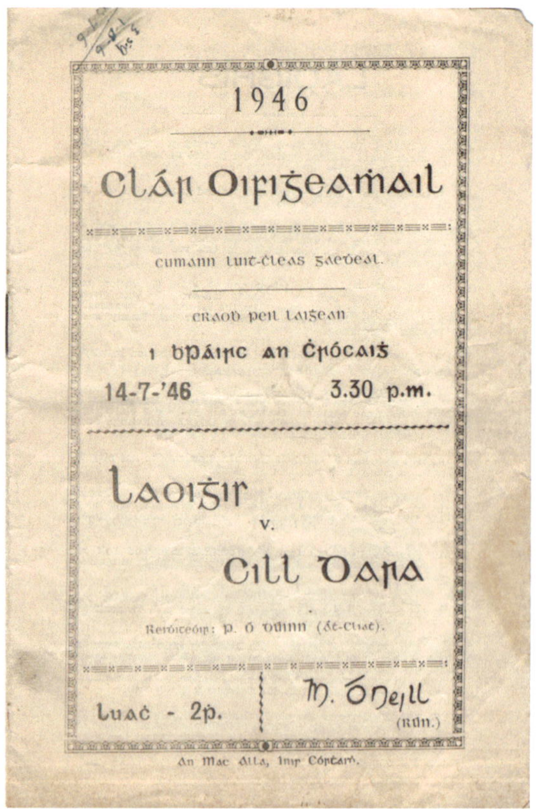

1 Connacht Football Final
Roscommon 1-04 Mayo 0-06

2 Leinster Football Final
Laois 0-11 Kildare 1-06

3 Ulster Football Final
Antrim 2-08 Cavan 1-07

3

Cumann Luith Chleas Gaedheal.
(Comhairle Uladh).

OFFICIAL PROGRAMME : : 2d.

ULSTER SENIOR

—AND—

: MINOR :

FOOTBALL CHAMPIONSHIP

— FINALS —

: AT CLONES, :

ON SUNDAY, 28th JULY, 1946.

MINOR FINAL:

MONAGHAN

v.

: TYRONE :

At 2.30 p.m. Referee: Mr. J. Kelly (FERMANAGH).

SENIOR FINAL:

: ANTRIM :

v.

: CAVAN :

At 3.45 p.m. Referee: Mr. P. Ratty (Meath).

C. MURRAY, PRINTER, CLONES.

4

Clár Oifigeamail
Michael Cusack
Founder of the G.A.A.
Luać 4ṗ.
Craoḃ Peile na h-Éireann
i bPáirc an Ċrócaiġ, 22-9-'46, ar 3.15 p.m.
Ciarraiḋe
v.
Ros Comáin
Craoḃ Peile na Mionúr
'Áṫ Cliaṫ v. Ciarraiḋe
ar 1.45 p.m.
Ar Aġaiḋ Linn

5

Clár Oifigeamail
Michael Cusack
Founder of the G.A.A.
Luać 3ṗ.
Craoḃ Peile na h-Éireann
i bPáirc an Ċrócaiġ, 27-10-'46.
Aṫ-imirt - - 2-45 p.m.
Ciarraiḋe
v.
Ros Comáin
Craoḃ Peile na Sóisear
An Dúin v. Warwickshire
ar 1.15 p.m.
Ar Aġaiḋ Linn

6

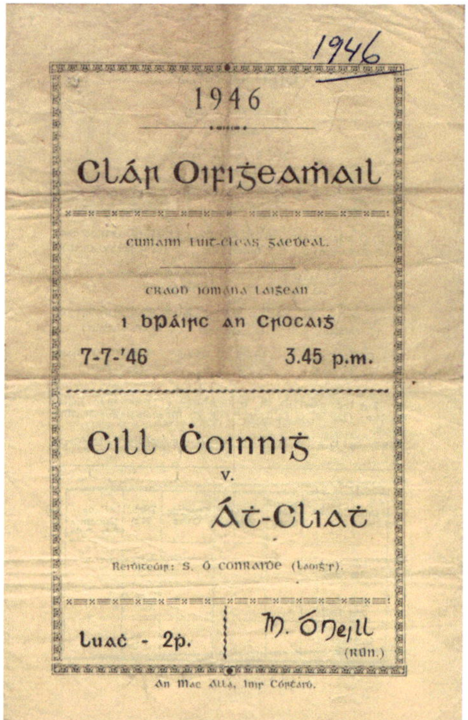
1946
1946
Clár Oifigeamail
Cumann Lúit-Cleas Gaeḋeal.
Craoḃ Iomána Laiġean
i bPáirc an Ċrócaiġ
7-7-'46
3.45 p.m.
Cill Ċoinniġ
v.
Áṫ-Cliaṫ
Luać - 2ṗ.
M. Ó Neill
(Rún.)

7

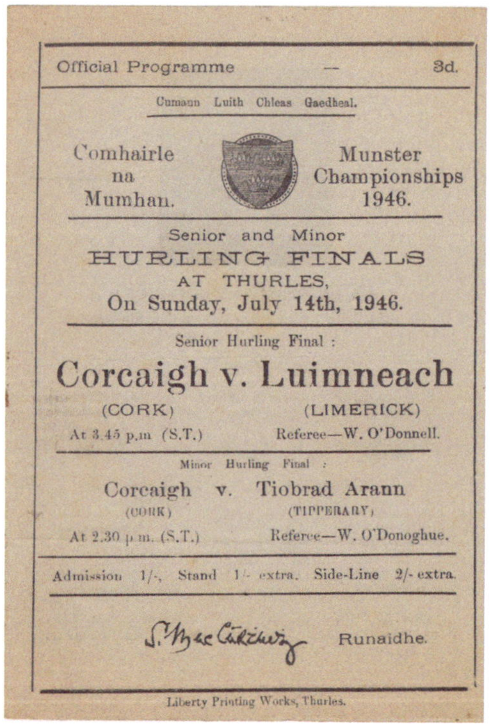
Official Programme — 3d.
Cumann Luith Chleas Gaedheal.
Comhairle na Mumhan.
Munster Championships 1946.
Senior and Minor
HURLING FINALS
AT THURLES,
On Sunday, July 14th, 1946.
Senior Hurling Final :
Corcaigh v. Luimneach
(CORK)
(LIMERICK)
At 3.45 p.m (S.T.)
Referee—W. O'Donnell.
Minor Hurling Final :
Corcaigh v. Tiobrad Arann
(CORK)
(TIPPERARY)
At 2.30 p.m. (S.T.)
Referee—W. O'Donoghue.
Admission 1/-, Stand 1/- extra. Side-Line 2/- extra.
Runaidhe.
Liberty Printing Works, Thurles.

8

4 All-Ireland Football Final
Kerry 2-04 Roscommon 1-07
Attendance – 75,771

5 Replay
Kerry 2-08 Roscommon 0-10
Attendance – 65,661

6 Leinster Hurling Final
Kilkenny 3-08 Dublin 1-12

7 Munster Hurling Final
Cork 3-08 Limerick 1-03

8 All-Ireland Hurling Final
Cork 7-05 Kilkenny 3-08
Attendance – 64,415

1947

The year 1947 will forever be remembered as the year when the All-Ireland football final was played in the Polo Grounds in New York between Cavan and Kerry. Cavan won the only All-Ireland final played outside the country and were presented with the Sam Maguire Cup on their return to Ireland. The programme for the final is unique among the other finals programmes of the 1940s. It is larger in size and contains 64 pages, including black and white photographs of players and officials. The referee for the final was Martin O'Neill from Wexford, who, as Leinster secretary, had his signature on the cover of Leinster final programmes from 1927 to 1969.

The 1947 All-Ireland hurling final is often recalled as one of the greatest ever, with 61,510 spectators attending this clash of hurling's titans, Cork and Kilkenny. Cork, having won five of the last six hurling finals, were obvious favourites, but players such as Paddy Grace, Jim Langton and Terry Leahy – who scored six points – helped Kilkenny take the title by a single point.

1

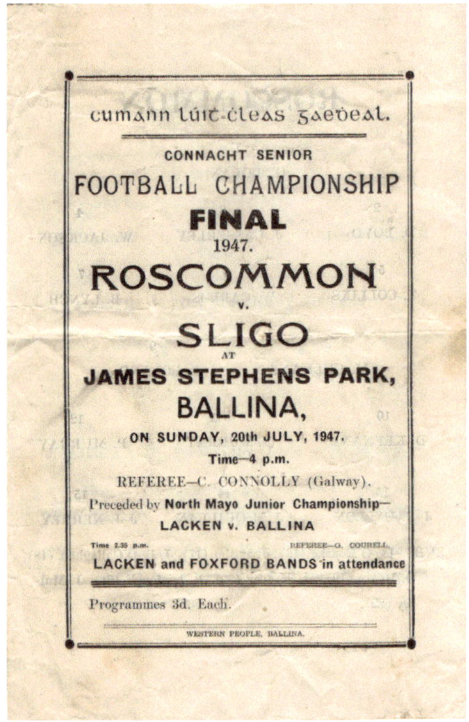

2

1 Connacht Football Final
Roscommon 2-12 Sligo 1-08

2 Leinster Football Final
Meath 3-07 Laois 1-07

3 All-Ireland Football Final
Cavan 2-11 Kerry 2-07
Attendance – 34,491

GAELIC ATHLETIC ASSOCIATION

FOUNDED 1884

OFFICIAL SOUVENIR PROGRAMME

ALL IRELAND FOOTBALL CHAMPIONSHIP FINAL

at

POLO GROUNDS, NEW YORK

SEPTEMBER 14th, 1947

SUBSCRIPTION 50c

4

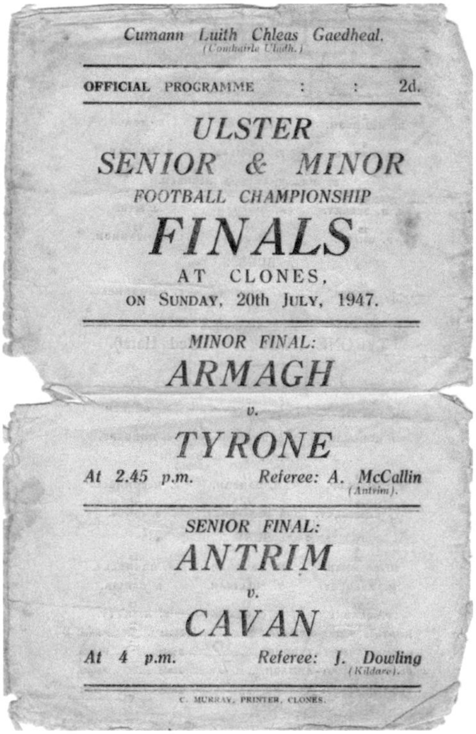
Cumann Luith Chleas Gaedheal.
(Comhairle Uladh.)

OFFICIAL PROGRAMME : : 2d.

ULSTER
SENIOR & MINOR
FOOTBALL CHAMPIONSHIP
FINALS
AT CLONES,
ON SUNDAY, 20th JULY, 1947.

MINOR FINAL:
ARMAGH
v.
TYRONE
At 2.45 p.m. Referee: A. McCallin (Antrim).

SENIOR FINAL:
ANTRIM
v.
CAVAN
At 4 p.m. Referee: J. Dowling (Kildare).

C. MURRAY, PRINTER, CLONES.

5

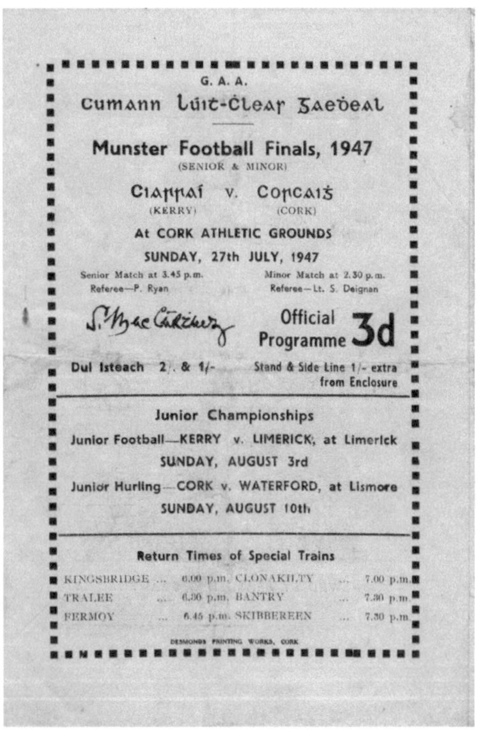
G. A. A.
Cumann Lúit-Ċleas Gaeḋeal

Munster Football Finals, 1947
(SENIOR & MINOR)

Ciarraí v. Corcaiġ
(KERRY) (CORK)

At CORK ATHLETIC GROUNDS
SUNDAY, 27th JULY, 1947
Senior Match at 3.45 p.m. Referee—P. Ryan
Minor Match at 2.30 p.m. Referee—Lt. S. Deignan

S. Mac Cárthaigh
Official Programme 3d

Dul Isteach 2/. & 1/-
Stand & Side Line 1/- extra from Enclosure

Junior Championships
Junior Football—KERRY v. LIMERICK, at Limerick
SUNDAY, AUGUST 3rd
Junior Hurling—CORK v. WATERFORD, at Lismore
SUNDAY, AUGUST 10th

Return Times of Special Trains

KINGSBRIDGE ...	6.00 p.m.	CLONAKILTY ...	7.00 p.m.
TRALEE ...	6.30 p.m.	BANTRY ...	7.30 p.m.
FERMOY ...	6.45 p.m.	SKIBBEREEN ...	7.30 p.m.

DESMONDS PRINTING WORKS, CORK

6

1947

Cumann Lúit-Ċleas Gaeḋeal.

1947

Clár Oifiġeaṁail

Craoḃ Iomána Laiġean
i bPáirc Ó Mórḋa, Portlaoiġise
13/7/'45——3.45 p.m.

Ċill Ċoinniġ
v.
Át-Ċliat

Reiteoir—S. Ó Flaiṫbeartaiġ (Uí bFailġe).

Luaċ 3p.
M. Ó Neill
Runaidhe.

7

Comhairle na Mumhan

3d. Official Programme 3d.

Munster Hurling Finals 1947
AT THURLES, JULY 20th

CORCAIGH v. LUIMNEACH
SENIOR FINAL 3.30 P.M. (S.T.) :: REFEREE V. BASTON

Tiobrad-Árann v. Portláirge
MINOR FINAL 2.15 P.M. (S.T.) :: REFEREE—M. QUAIN.

ADMISSION—1/-. SCHOOLBOYS—6d.
STAND—1/- Extra. SIDELINE—2/- Extra
NO TRANSFER FROM STAND TO SIDELINE.

S. Mac Cárthaigh Rúnaí

3d. Official Programme 3d.

"LEADER" PRINTING WORKS, DUNGARVAN

8

4 Ulster Football Final
Cavan 3-04 Antrim 1-06

5 Munster Football Final
Kerry 3-08 Cork 2-06

6 Leinster Hurling Final
Kilkenny 7-10 Dublin 3-06

7 Munster Hurling Final
Cork 2-06 Limerick 2-03

8 All-Ireland Hurling Final
Kilkenny 0-14 Cork 2-07
Attendance – 61,510

1948

Ten years after reaching their first All-Ireland hurling final, Waterford made it back to Croke Park for another attempt to win the Liam MacCarthy Cup for the first time. In the 1938 final they had faced Dublin and, a decade later, Dublin were the opposition again. Waterford had come through the Munster championship by defeating Clare in the semi-final and, in front of a large crowd in Thurles, overcame Cork by a single point to win the provincial title for only the second time. They had a more straightforward win over Galway in the All-Ireland semi-final and were installed as favourites for the final. Waterford's star player was John Keane, who scored three goals and two points to help his side to their first victory. Jim Ware, who had a fine game in goal, had the honour of being the first man from Waterford to lift the MacCarthy Cup.

1

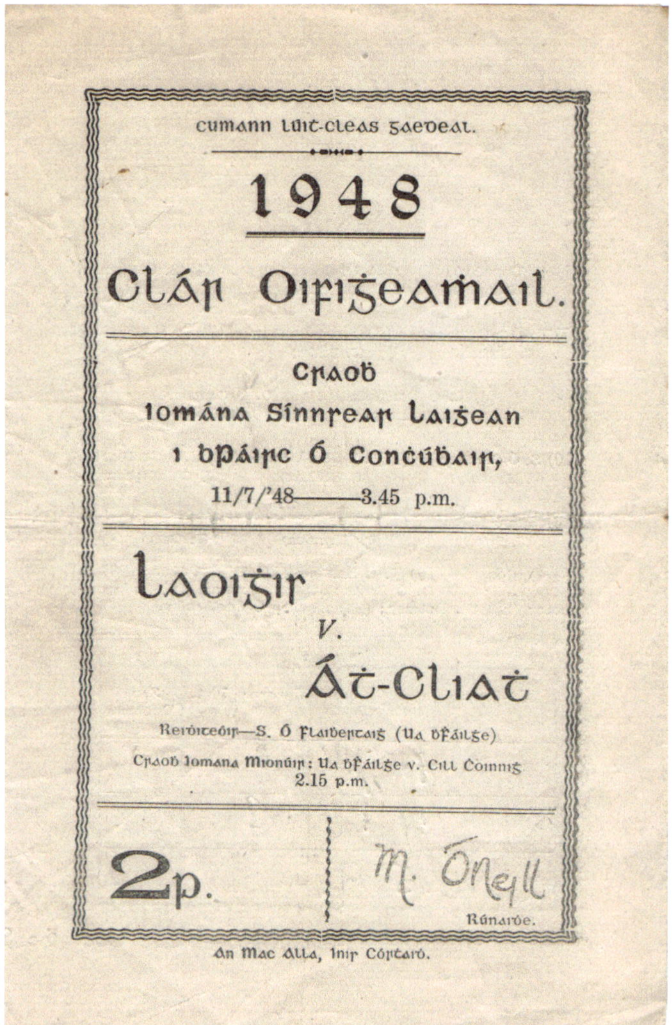

Cumann Lúṫ-Cleas Gaeḋeal.

1948

Clár Oifigeaṁail.

Craoḃ
Iomána Sinnsear Laiġean
i bPáirc Ó Concúḃair,
11/7/'48——3.45 p.m.

Laoiġis
v.
Áṫ-Cliaṫ

Reiḋiteóir—S. Ó Flaiḃeartaiġ (Ua bFáilġe)

Craoḃ Iomána Mionúir: Ua bFáilġe v. Cill Coinniġ
2.15 p.m.

2p.

M. Ó Néill
Rúnaiḋe.

An Mac Alla, Inis Córtaiḋ.

1 Leinster Hurling Final
Dublin 5-09 Laois 3-03

2 Munster Hurling Final
Waterford 4-07 Cork 3-09

Coṁairle

Official Programme 3d 3d

Muṁan

SENIOR and MINOR

Hurling Finals

1948

AT THURLES, AUG 1st

Corcaiġ v Portláirge

AT 3.30 p.m. (S.T.). REFEREE—M. QUANE.

Tiobrad-Árann v Portláirge

AT 2 P.M. (S.T.' :: REFEREE—J. ROCHE.

ADMISSION—1/-. SCHOOLBOYS—6d.

STAND—1/- Extra. SIDELINE—2/- Extra.

NO TRANSFER FROM STAND TO SIDELINE.

Rúnaí.

("The Tipperary Star," Thurles.)

3

3 All-Ireland Hurling Final
Waterford 6-07 Dublin 4-02
Attendance – 61,430

4 Leinster Football Final
Louth 2-10 Wexford 2-05

5 Munster Football Final
Kerry 2-09 Cork 2-06

6 Ulster Football Final
Cavan 2-12 Antrim 2-04

7 All-Ireland Football Final
Cavan 4-05 Mayo 4-04
Attendance – 74,645

4

Cumann Lúit-Cleas Gaedeal.
1948
Clár Oifigeamail.
Craob
Peil Sinnsear Laigean
i bPáirc an Crócaig,
25/7/'48—3.30 p.m.
Lúgbaid
v.
Loc Garman
Reidhiteoir: S. O Flaibhertaigh (Ua bFhailghe).
Peil Mionuir (2 p.m.) : Ua bFailghe v. Cill Manntain
2p.
Rúnaide.

5

Cumann Lúit-Clear Gaedeal
MUNSTER CHAMPIONSHIP
FOOTBALL FINALS
Comairle
Mumhan
FITZGERALD STADIUM, KILLARNEY
SUNDAY, 25th JULY, '48
Ciarraide v. Corcaig
Minor Final at 2 p.m. Referee: S. Boyle, Tipp.
Senior Final at 3.30. Referee: W. Delaney, Leix.
Admission to Field 1/-. Terrace (direct) 2/-
Sideline (from Field) 2/- extra.
OFFICIAL PROGRAMME
Price 3d.
Killarney Printing Works.

6

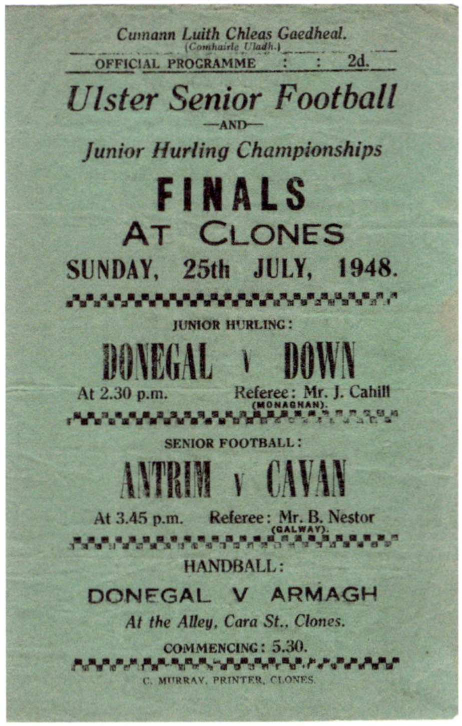
Cumann Luith Chleas Gaedheal.
(Comhairle Uladh.)
OFFICIAL PROGRAMME : : 2d.
Ulster Senior Football
—AND—
Junior Hurling Championships
FINALS
AT CLONES
SUNDAY, 25th JULY, 1948.
JUNIOR HURLING:
DONEGAL v DOWN
At 2.30 p.m. Referee: Mr. J. Cahill (MONAGHAN).
SENIOR FOOTBALL:
ANTRIM v CAVAN
At 3.45 p.m. Referee: Mr. B. Nestor (GALWAY).
HANDBALL:
DONEGAL V ARMAGH
At the Alley, Cara St., Clones.
COMMENCING: 5.30.
C. MURRAY, PRINTER, CLONES.

7

Clár Oifigeamail
Michael Cusack
Founder of the G.A.A.
Luac 4P.
Craob Peile na h-Éireann
i bPáirc an Crócaig, 26-9-48, ar 3.15 p.m.
Cabán
v.
Muigeó
Craob Peile na Mionúr
'Át Cliat v. Tír Eogain
ar 1.45 p.m.
Ar Agaid Linn

1949

Although Meath had contested the first All-Ireland football final to be played at the Jones's Road site in 1895, the title had yet to be won by a team from the county. Their first victory did not come easily, though. It took Meath six matches to win the Leinster championship, including three matches against Louth in the semi-final. With Clare having a shock win over Kerry in Munster, it looked likely that Cavan would go on to win three All-Ireland titles in a row. However, the intensity of the local rivalry with Cavan ensured that Meath rose to the challenge and, with their captain Brian Smyth scoring three points, Meath finally got their hands on the Sam Maguire Cup for the first time.

Laois defeated Offaly, Dublin, Kilkenny and Galway to take their place in the All-Ireland hurling final for the third time this year. Once there, however, they came up against a superior Tipperary team who claimed an easy victory, giving John Doyle the first of his eight All-Ireland medals.

1 Leinster Football Final
Meath 4-05 Westmeath 0-06

2 Munster Football Final
Cork 3-06 Clare 0-07

3 Ulster Football Final
Cavan 1-07 Armagh 1-06

4 All-Ireland Football Final
Meath 1-10 Cavan 1-06
Attendance – 79,460

5 Munster Hurling Final
Tipperary 1-16 Limerick 2-10

6 All-Ireland Hurling Final
Tipperary 3-11 Laois 0-03
Attendance – 67,168

1

2

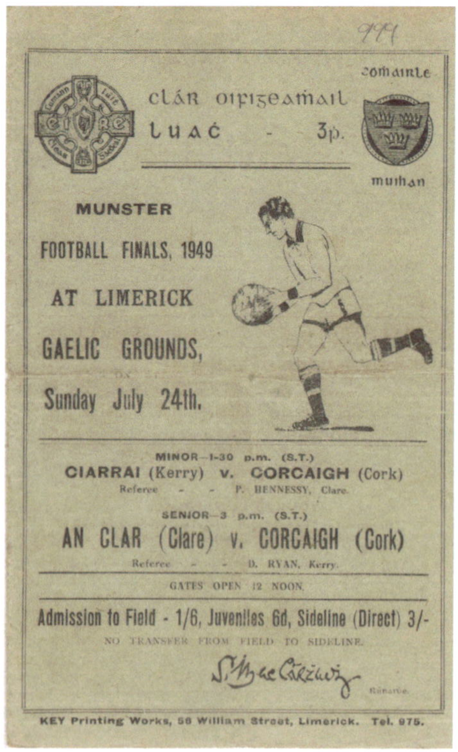

3

Cumann Luith Chleas Gaedheal.
(Comhairle Uladh.)
OFFICIAL PROGRAMME : : 2d.
ULSTER
SENIOR & MINOR
FOOTBALL CHAMPIONSHIP
FINALS
AT CLONES,
ON Sunday, 31st July, 1949.
MINOR FINAL:
ARMAGH
v.
DONEGAL
At 2.15 p.m.
Referee: J. Monaghan
(Fermanagh).
SENIOR FINAL:
CAVAN
v.
ARMAGH
At 3.45 p.m.
Referee: J. P. O'Callaghan
(Roscommon).
C. MURRAY, PRINTER, CLONES.

5

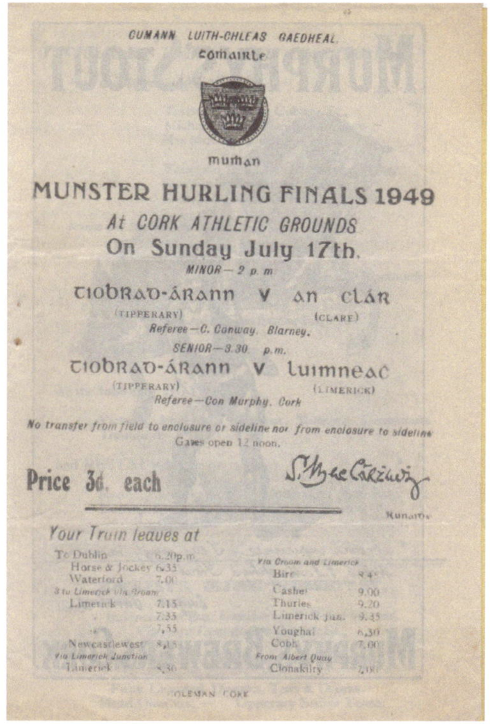
CUMANN LUITH-CHLEAS GAEDHEAL
Comhairle
Mumhan
MUNSTER HURLING FINALS 1949
At CORK ATHLETIC GROUNDS
On Sunday July 17th.
MINOR—2 p.m.
Tiobrad-Árann v An Clár
(TIPPERARY)
(CLARE)
Referee—C. Conway, Blarney.
SENIOR—3.30 p.m.
Tiobrad-Árann v Luimneach
(TIPPERARY)
(LIMERICK)
Referee—Con Murphy, Cork
No transfer from field to enclosure or sideline nor from enclosure to sideline
Gates open 12 noon.
Price 3d. each
Your Train leaves at
COLEMAN CORK

4

Clár Oifigeamhail
Michael Cusack
FOUNDER OF THE G.A.A.
Luach 4P.
Craobh Peile na h-Éireann
i bPáirc an Chrócaigh, 25-9-49, ar 3.15 p.m.
An Mhidhe
v.
Cabhán
Craobh Peile na Mionúr
Árd Mhacha v. Ciarraidhe
ar 1.45 p.m.
Ar Aghaidh Linn

6

Clár Oifigeamhail
Michael Cusack
FOUNDER OF THE G.A.A.
Luach 4P.
Craobh Iomána na h-Éireann
i bPáirc an Chrócaigh, 4-9-49, ar 3.15 p.m.
Laoighis
v.
Tiobrad Árann
Craobh Iomána na Mionúr
Cill Chainnigh v. Tiobrad Árann
ar 1.45 p.m.
Ar Aghaidh Linn

Áṫ C

Ciar

Craoḃ Peile na Mio

Áṫ Cliaṫ v. Tiobrad

1950–59

1950

Louth had come close to reaching the Leinster football final in 1949 and a year later they not only reached the final but won the title for the second time in three years when they defeated Meath in the final after a replay. A famous win over Kerry followed in the All-Ireland semi-final to qualify Louth for the final for the first time since their victory in 1912. In Connacht, Mayo were given a bye to the provincial final while Roscommon had to take a circuitous route by beating Galway and then Sligo. Mayo had six points to spare in the final and an even more comprehensive victory over Armagh followed in the semi-final to set up the meeting with Louth in the All-Ireland final. Although Louth led at half-time, a late goal by Mick Flanagan allowed his namesake, Seán, to lift the Sam Maguire Cup for Mayo.

1

Cumann Lúit-Chleas Gaedheal.
1950
Clár Oifigiúil
Craobh Peile Laighean, 23-7-'50
i bPáirc an Chrócaigh
Craobh Sinnsear:
Lughbhaidh v. Midhe
Seán Ó Conraoi (Laoighis).
3.30 p.m.
Craobh Mionúir:
Loch Garman v. Áth-Cliath
2 p.m.
3p.
M. Ó Néill (Rún.)
An Mac Alla, Inis Córthaidh.

2

Cumann Lúit-Chleas Gaedheal.
1950
Clár Oifigiúil
Craobh Peile Laighean, 6-8-'50
i bPáirc an Chrócaigh
Craobh Sinnsear:
Lughbhaidh v. Midhe
3.30 p.m.
P. Ó Miodhacháin (Loch Garman).
Leath-Chraobh Iomána Corn Ó Beolláin.
2 p.m.
3p.
M. Ó Néill (Rún.)
An Mac Alla, Inis Córthaidh.

1 Leinster Football Final
Louth 1-03 Meath 1-03

2 Replay
Louth 3-05 Meath 0-13

3 Munster Football Final
Kerry 2-05 Cork 1-05

3

cumann lúiṫ-ċleas gaeḋeal
coṁairle muṁan

Munster Championship

1950

Football Finals

CORK ATHLETIC GROUNDS
SUNDAY, 30th JULY, 1950

SENIOR 4 p.m.

CIARRAI v CORCAIGH
(Kerry) (Cork)

Referee—J. Flaherty, Offaly

MINOR 2.30 p.m.

CIARRAI v LUIMNEACH
(Kerry) (Limerick)

Referee—T. Cotter, Cork

No transfer from Field to Enclosure or Sideline nor from Enclosure to Sideline. Gates open at 12 noon.

clár oifiġeaṁail

OFFICIAL PROGRAMME

6ṗ

Rúnaiḋe

Duncan & O'Brien, Broad Street, Cork.

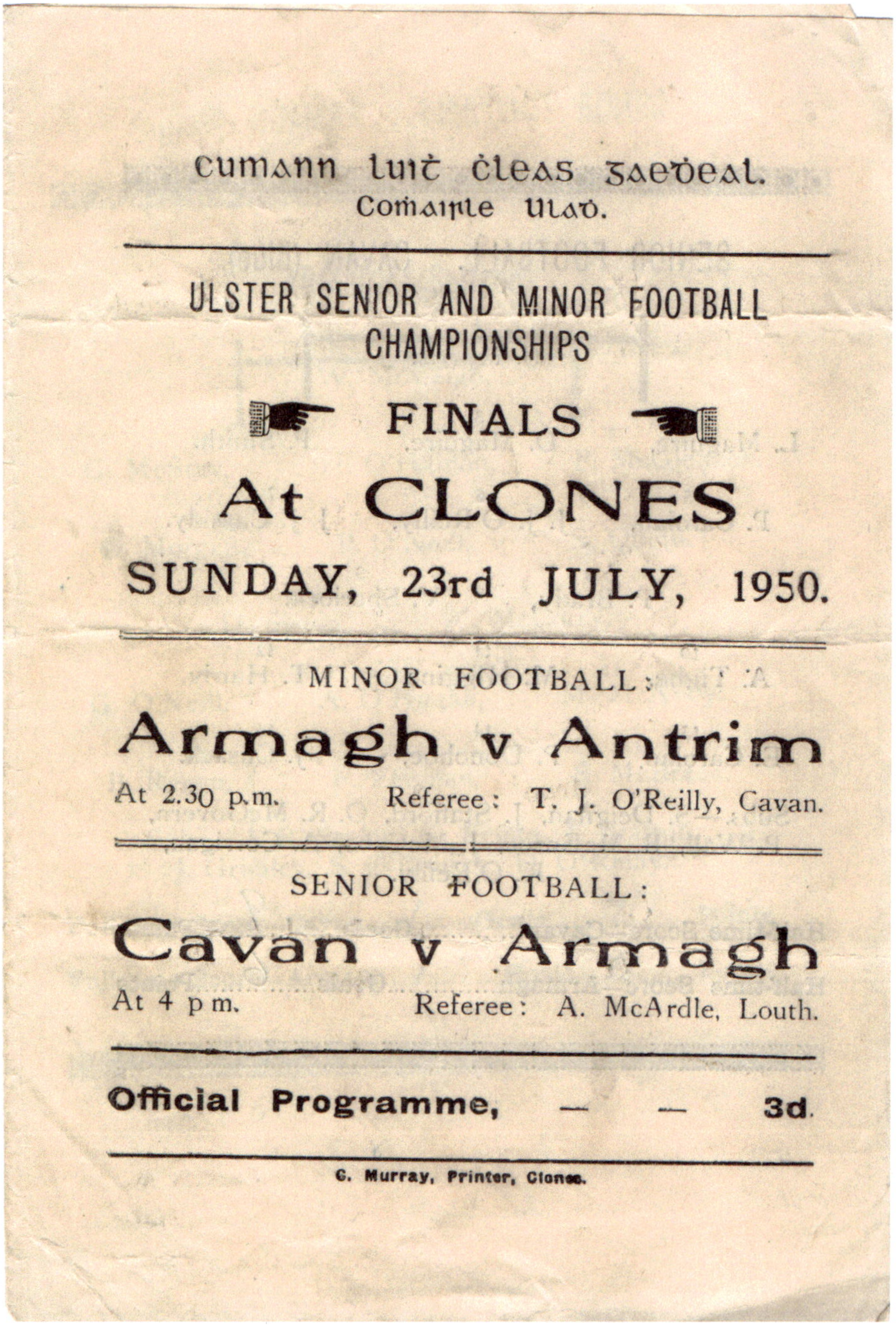

4

Cumann Luiċ Ċleas Gaeḋeal.
Coṁairle Ulaḋ.

ULSTER SENIOR AND MINOR FOOTBALL CHAMPIONSHIPS

FINALS

At CLONES

SUNDAY, 23rd JULY, 1950.

MINOR FOOTBALL:

Armagh v Antrim

At 2.30 p.m. Referee: T. J. O'Reilly, Cavan.

SENIOR FOOTBALL:

Cavan v Armagh

At 4 p.m. Referee: A. McArdle, Louth.

Official Programme, — — 3d.

G. Murray, Printer, Clones.

4 Ulster Football Final
Armagh 1-11 Cavan 1-07

5 All-Ireland Football Final
Mayo 2-05 Louth 1-06
Attendance – 76,174

6 Leinster Hurling Final
Kilkenny 3-11 Wexford 2-11

7 Munster Hurling Final
Tipperary 2-17 Cork 3-11

8 All-Ireland Hurling Final
Tipperary 1-09 Kilkenny 1-08
Attendance – 67,629

5

Clár Oifigeamail
Michael Cusack
FOUNDER OF THE G.A.A.
Luać 4P.
Craob peile na h-Éireann
Luġbaiḋ
v.
Muiġeo
craob peile na mionúr
Ciarraiḋe v. Loć gCarmain
ar 1.30 p.m.
Ar Aġaiḋ Linn

7

cumann lúit ċleas gaeḋeal
1950
MUNSTER
HURLING
FINALS
comairle
mumhan
FITZGERALD STADIUM
KILLARNEY
SUNDAY,
23RD JULY.
MAIN ENTRANCE TO FITZGERALD STADIUM
MINOR HURLING AT 2 P.M.
SENIOR HURLING AT 3.30 P.M.
Admission to Field 1/- Terraced Enclosure 2/- Sideline (from Terraced Enc.) 1/- extra
clár oifigeamail
OFFICIAL PROGRAMME 6p

6

cumann lúit-cleas gaeḋeal.
1950
Clár Oifigiúil
Cluiċí Iománíoċta Laiġean,
16-7-'50
i gCill Ċoinniġ (Páirc Ó Nualláin)
craob sinnsear:
Loċ Garman
v.
Cill Ċoinniġ
3.30 p.m.
craob mionúr:
Ua bFáilġe v. Cill Ċoinniġ
2 p.m.
3p.
M. Ó Néill
(Rún.)
An Mac Alla, Inis Córthaidh

8

Clár Oifigeamail
Michael Cusack
FOUNDER OF THE G.A.A.
Luać 4P.
Craob iomána na h-Éireann
1 bPáirc an Cróċaiġ, 3-9-50, ar 3.15 p.m.
Cill Ċainniġ
v.
Tiobrad Árann
craob iomána na mionúr
cill ċainniġ v. tiobrad árann
ar 1.30 p.m.
Ar Aġaiḋ Linn

1951

A new cover design for the All-Ireland final match programme was used for the first time in 1951. The crests of the four provinces were situated in each corner. The Celtic cross GAA crest, on a white background, replaced the image of Michael Cusack that had adorned the cover of the All-Ireland final match programme since 1945. This year, Mayo retained their All-Ireland football title by beating Meath in the final. Despite reaching the final on 11 further occasions from this point up until 2024, they have yet to add to their tally of victories.

Tipperary were now dominant in both the Munster and All-Ireland hurling championships. In 1951, they defeated Cork in an epic Munster final and progressed straight to the All-Ireland final where a resurgent Wexford awaited. With Tipperary wearing the blue of Munster and Wexford in the green of Leinster, not even the magic of Nicky Rackard's three goals and two points could prevent an emphatic Tipperary victory and a third title in a row.

1

2

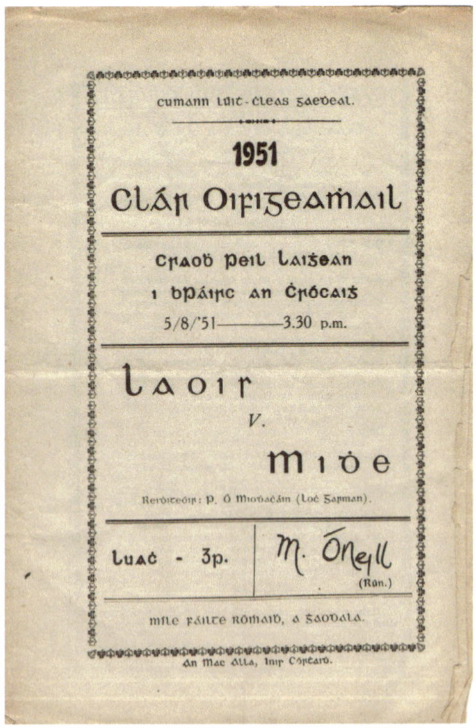

1 Connacht Football Final
Mayo 4-13 Galway 2-03

2 Leinster Football Final
Meath 4-09 Laois 0-03

3 Munster Football Final
Kerry 1-06 Cork 0-04

3

coṁairle

muṁan

Cumann Lúiṫ-Ċleas Gaeḋeal

CLÁR OIFIGIÚIL

1951

MUNSTER FOOTBALL FINALS

AT FITZGERALD STADIUM, KILLARNEY

ON SUNDAY, 15th JULY, 1951

•

CIARRAÍ v CORCAIĠ

MINOR 2.30 P.M. (S.T.).

Referee: P. DALTON, WATERFORD.

•

SENIOR 3.45 P.M. (S.T.).

Referee: S. HAYES, TIPPERARY.

ADMISSION TO FIELD - - - - 2/-.

TERRACED ENCLOSURE, 3/-; JUVENILES, 1/-.
SIDELINE, 1/6d. EXTRA FROM ENCLOSURE.
NO TRANSFER FROM FIELD TO ENCLOSURE.

Luaċ - - - - - 6 p.

Rúnaí

Kerry Champion, Ltd., The Square, Tralee

4

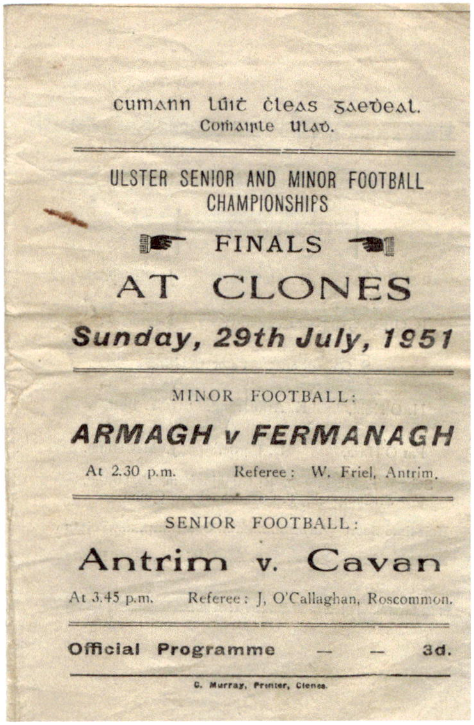
Cumann Lúiṫ Ċleas Gaeḋeal.
Comhairle Uladh.

ULSTER SENIOR AND MINOR FOOTBALL CHAMPIONSHIPS

FINALS

AT CLONES

Sunday, 29th July, 1951

MINOR FOOTBALL:

ARMAGH v FERMANAGH

At 2.30 p.m. Referee: W. Friel, Antrim.

SENIOR FOOTBALL:

Antrim v. Cavan

At 3.45 p.m. Referee: J. O'Callaghan, Roscommon.

Official Programme — — 3d.

C. Murray, Printer, Clones.

5

Clár Oifigiúil

Ceannas Peile na hÉireann
i bPáirc an Ċrócaiġ
ar 3.15 p.m. — 23 - 9 - 1951

An Míḋe
v.
Muiġeo

* * * * *

Leaṫ-Ċeannas Peile na Mionúr:
Árd Maċa v. Ciarraiḋe ar 1:30 p.m.

Luaċ 4p.

6

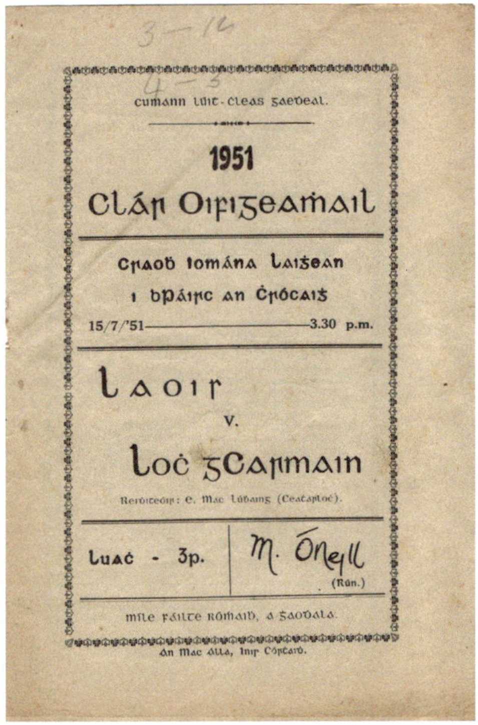
Cumann Lúiṫ-Ċleas Gaeḋeal.

1951

Clár Oifigeamail

Craoḃ Iomána Laiġean
i bPáirc an Ċrócaiġ
15/7/'51 —— 3.30 p.m.

Laoiṡ
v.
Loċ Garman

Luaċ - 3p. M. Ó Néill (Rún.)

Míle Fáilte Rómhaiḃ, a Ġaeḋala.

An Mac Alla, Inis Córṫaiḋ.

7

Clár Oifigeamail

Luaċ - 6p.

What a pride and glory it is to witness the stirring scenes associated with a well-played, cleanly and keenly contested Hurling Match, to feel the thrills coursing through one's veins as the springy ash Camens crash in the air above and on the sod below; and to realise that here is being enacted before our excited and admiring gaze, a vivid symbol of the long ago; a sure reminder that Knocknagow is not dead; and a striking and soul-stirring guarantee that by Shannon, Suir, and Lee, and by hillside and glenside throughout the province, the virile manhood and traditions of our race are keeping a firm hold on their hard-won inheritance.

Seán Mac Cárṫaiġ, U.C., *Chairman, at Munster Convention, 1940.*

Craoḃ Iomána na Muman

Corcaiġ
— v. —
Tiobrad Árann

i Luimneaċ, 29-7-1951,
ar a 3-45 a ċlog
Réiḋteoir - S. Ó Saoṫéir.

Craoḃ Iomána na Mionúir

Corcaiġ v. Luimneaċ
ar a 2-30 a ċlog.
Réiḋteoir - S. Ó Mocáin.

IMPORTANT

SPECTATORS MUST NOT ENTER THE PLAYING PITCH.
PLEASE OBEY THE STEWARDS.

Admission to Field - 2/-, Juveniles 1/-, Sideline (Direct) 4/6
— NO TRANSFER FROM FIELD TO SIDELINE. —
GATES OPEN 12 NOON.

Rúnaiḋe.

KEY Printing Works, 56 William Street, Limerick. Tel. 975.

8

4 Ulster Football Final
Antrim 1-07 Cavan 2-03

5 All-Ireland Football Final
Mayo 2-08 Meath 0-09
Attendance – 78,201

6 Leinster Hurling Final
Wexford 3-12 Laois 4-03

7 Munster Hurling Final
Tipperary 2-11 Cork 2-09

8 All-Ireland Hurling Final
Tipperary 7-07 Wexford 3-09
Attendance – 68,515

1952

Torrential rain fell in Dublin from the early hours of the morning of the All-Ireland football final until just before the throw-in, making conditions for the players of Cavan and Meath extremely difficult. Indeed, such was the effect of the rain that at 1.15p.m., 15 minutes before the scheduled throw-in, the authorities decided not to play the All-Ireland minor final between Galway and Cavan in order to protect the pitch. Despite the weather, the match is primarily remembered for the extraordinary equaliser scored by Cavan's Ed Carolan in the fifty-ninth minute. Chasing a ball that appeared to be going wide, Carolan's shot from the endline struck an upright and dropped over the bar for a point. Cavan made sure of the victory in the replay, which was received with mixed emotions in the Maguire family, originally of Cornafean (Cavan) but now living in Oldcastle (Meath). Two brothers, Des and Liam, were members of the Cavan team while their younger brother, Brendan, was midfield for Meath.

1

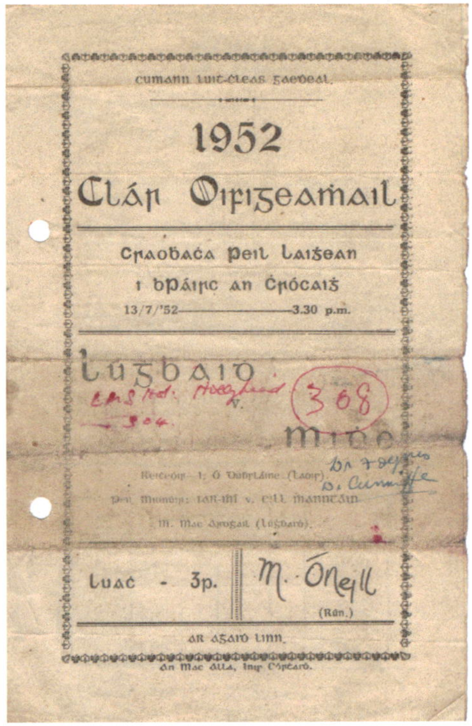

Cumann Lúit-Chleas Gaedheal.

1952

Clár Oifigeamhail

Craobhacha Peil Laighean

i bPáirc an Chrócaigh

13/7/'52——3.30 p.m.

Lughbhaidh

v.

Midhe

Luach - 3p.

M. Ó Néill (Rún.)

Ar agaidh linn.

2

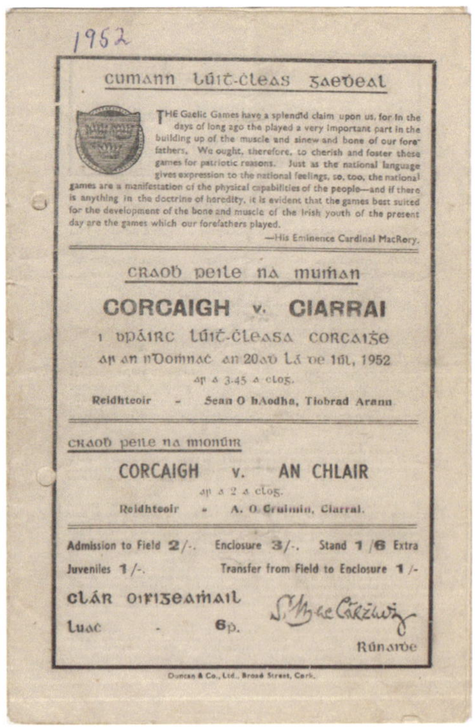

Cumann Lúit-Chleas Gaedheal

THE Gaelic Games have a splendid claim upon us, for in the days of long ago the played a very important part in the building up of the muscle and sinew and bone of our forefathers. We ought, therefore, to cherish and foster these games for patriotic reasons. Just as the national language gives expression to the national feelings, so, too, the national games are a manifestation of the physical capabilities of the people—and if there is anything in the doctrine of heredity, it is evident that the games best suited for the development of the bone and muscle of the Irish youth of the present day are the games which our forefathers played.

—His Eminence Cardinal MacRory.

Craobh Peile na Mumhan

CORCAIGH v. CIARRAI

i bPáirc Lúit-Chleasa Corcaighe

ar an nDomhnach an 20adh Lá de Iúil, 1952

ar a 3.45 a clog.

Reidhteoir - Sean O hAodha, Tiobrad Arann

Craobh Peile na Mionúr

CORCAIGH v. AN CHLAIR

ar a 2 a clog.

Reidhteoir - A. O Cruimin, Ciarrai.

Admission to Field 2/-. Enclosure 3/-. Stand 1/6 Extra

Juveniles 1/-. Transfer from Field to Enclosure 1/-

Clár Oifigeamhail

Luach - 6p.

Rúnaidhe

Duncan & Co., Ltd., Broad Street, Cork.

1 Leinster Football Final
Meath 1-06 Louth 0-08

2 Munster Football Final
Cork 0-11 Kerry 0-02

3 Ulster Football Final
Cavan 1-08 Monaghan 0-08

3 Cumann Luiṫ Ċleas Gaeḋeal

(Coṁairle Ulaḋ)

Official Programme

Ulster Senior & Minor Football Championships

AT BREFFNI PARK, CAVAN

Sunday, 27th July, 1952

MINOR FOOTBALL—SEMI-FINAL

FERMANAGH v. CAVAN

At 2.30 p.m. **Referee—J. McGUIGAN, Antrim.**

SENIOR FOOTBALL—FINAL

MONAGHAN v. CAVAN

At 3.45 p.m.

Referee—SEAN OG O'CALLAGHAN, Dublin.

Luaċ - - - 3p

The Anglo-Celt, Ltd., Cavan.

4

4 All-Ireland Football Final
Cavan 2–04 Meath 1–07
Attendance – 62,020

5 Replay
Cavan 0-09 Meath 0-05
Attendance – 62,515

6 Leinster Hurling Final
Dublin 7-02 Wexford 3-06

7 Munster Hurling Final
Cork 1-11 Tipperary 2-06

8 All-Ireland Hurling Final
Cork 2-14 Dublin 0-07
Attendance – 64,332

5

Clár Oifigiúil
Aṫ-imirt
Craoḃ Peile na hÉireann
An Mide v. Caḃán
i bPáirc an Ċrócaiġ : 12-10-1952
ar 3 p.m.
Craoḃ peile na mionúr
Caḃán v. Gaillim
ar 1.15 p.m.
Luaċ 4p

6

Cumann Luit-Ċleas Gaeḋeal.
1952
Clár Oifigeamail
Craoḃaċa Iomána Laiġean
i bPáirc Ó Nuallám
6/7/52 3.45 p.m.
Loċ Garman
v.
Át-Cliaṫ
Reiteóir—P. Ó Conaill (Ua bFáilġe).
Mionúir—Cill Coinnig v. Át Cliaṫ, 2.15 p.m.
Luaċ - 3p.
M. Ó Neill
(Rún.)
Ar agaiḋ linn.
An Mac Alla, Inir Córṫaiḋ.

7

Clár Oifigeamail
Luaċ - 6p.
THE Gaelic Games have a splendid claim upon us, for in the days of long ago they played a very important part in the building up of the muscle and sinew and bone of our forefathers. We ought, therefore, to cherish and foster these games for patriotic reasons. Just as the national language gives expression to the national feelings, so, too, the national games are a manifestation of the physical capabilities of the people—and if there is anything in the doctrine of heredity, it is evident that the games best suited for the development of the bone and muscle of the Irish youth of the present day are the games which our forefathers played.
—His Eminence Cardinal MacRory.
Craoḃ Iomána na Mumhan
Corcaiġ
v.
Tiobrad Árann
i Luimneaċ, 13-7-1952
Ar a 3.45 a Clog
Reiteóir - S. Ó Muċáin
Craoḃ Iomána na Mionúir
An Clár v. Tiobrad Árann
Ar a 2 a Clog.
Reiteóir - T. Ó Suilleaḃáin
IMPORTANT
SPECTATORS MUST NOT ENTER THE PLAYING PITCH.
PLEASE OBEY THE STEWARDS
ADMISSION TO FIELD 2/- SIDELINE (Direct) 4/6
JUVENILES 1/-
NO TRANSFER FROM FIELD TO SIDELINE.
GATES OPEN 11-30 A.M.
KEY Printing Works, 56 William Street, Limerick. Tel. 878.

8

Clár Oifigiúil
Craoḃ Iomána na hÉireann
i bPáirc an Ċrócaiġ
ar 3.15 p.m. — 7-9-1952
Át Cliaṫ
v
Corcaiġ
Craoḃ Iomána na Mionúr, ar 1.30 p.m.
Át Cliaṫ v. Tiobrad Árann
Luaċ 4p.

1953

The 1953 Ulster football final between Cavan and Armagh was the first provincial final to be played in the newly opened Casement Park in Belfast. Cavan were the undeniable kingpins of Ulster football at this time – then, the only county from the province to lift the Sam Maguire Cup, doing so on five occasions. They qualified for the Ulster final with a decisive win over Monaghan in the first round, followed by victory over Tyrone in the semi-final. In the final they faced Armagh, who had accounted for Antrim and Derry en route. Armagh pulled off a shock win over the reigning All-Ireland champions and progressed to play Roscommon in the All-Ireland semi-final. A one-point victory was enough for Armagh to reach their first All-Ireland final, where Kerry awaited them. A then-record crowd of 85,155 paid in to see Kerry take the title with an estimated 7,000 more spectators gaining free entry in a surge at the gates.

1

cumann lúit cleas gaedeal
G.A.A.

OFFICIAL PROGRAMME.

Connaught Minor & Senior Football Finals.

AT

St. Coman's Park, Roscommon.

ON

Sunday, July 19, 1953.

ROSCOMMON v MAYO (Minor)
At 2 o'clock. Referee—B. Oates, Sligo.

MAYO v ROSCOMMON (Senior)
At 4 p.m. Referee—P. McDermott, Meath.

PRICE - - - - 3d

CHAMPION OFFICE, ROSCOMMON.

2

cumann lúit-cleas gaedeal.

1953.

Clár Oifigeamail

Craob Peile Laigean
i bPáirc an Crócaig
26/7/'53—3.30 p.m.

SENIOR FOOTBALL FINAL:

Lúgbaid
v.
Loc gCarmain

Luac - 3p

M. Ó Neill

ar agaid linn.

1 Connacht Football Final
Roscommon 1-06 Mayo 0-06

2 Leinster Football Final
Louth 1-07 Wexford 0-07

3 Munster Football Final
Kerry 2-07 Cork 2-03

Coṁairle Muṁan

Cumann Lúiṫ-Ċleas Gaeḋeal

Clár Oifigiúil
1953

Munster Football Finals

AT FITZGERALD STADIUM, KILLARNEY

On Sunday, 19th July, 1953

SENIOR 3.30 P.M. (S.T.).

Corcaiġ v. Ciarraí

Referee——S. HAYES (Tipperary).

MINOR 2.0 P.M. S.T.).

Corcaiġ v. An Clár

Referee: SEAN CLERY (Clonmel).

ADMISSION TO FIELD : : : : 2/-.

TERRACED ENCLOSURE, 3/-; JUVENILES, 1/-.

SIDELINE, 1/6d. EXTRA FROM ENCLOSURE.

Proceeds of this Programme go to the Fitzgerald Stadium Fund.

Luaċ : : 3p

Rúnaiḋe.

Kerry Champion, Ltd.

4

Cumann Lúṫ-Ċleas Gaeḋeal
Clár Oifigeaṁail
I bPáirc Ruaiḋrí Ṁic Easmuinn,
Béal Feirsde
26 - 7 - 1953
Cabán v.
Árd Maċa
ar 3.45 p.m.
Craoḃ Peile na Mionúr
Árd Maċa v. Tír Eoġain
ar 2.30 p.m.
Luaċ 3p
Ar aġaiḋ linn
G. McGOURAN, BANK ST., BELFAST.

5

Clár Oifigiúil
Craoḃ Peile na hÉireann
i bPáirc an Ċróċaiġ
ar 3.15 p.m.
27ú Meán Foṁair, '53
Cumann Lúṫ Ċleas Gaeḋeal
Éire
Árd Ṁaċa
v.
Ciarraiḋe
Craoḃ Peile na Mionúr, ar 1.30 p.m.
An Clár v. Muiġeo
Luaċ 4p.

6

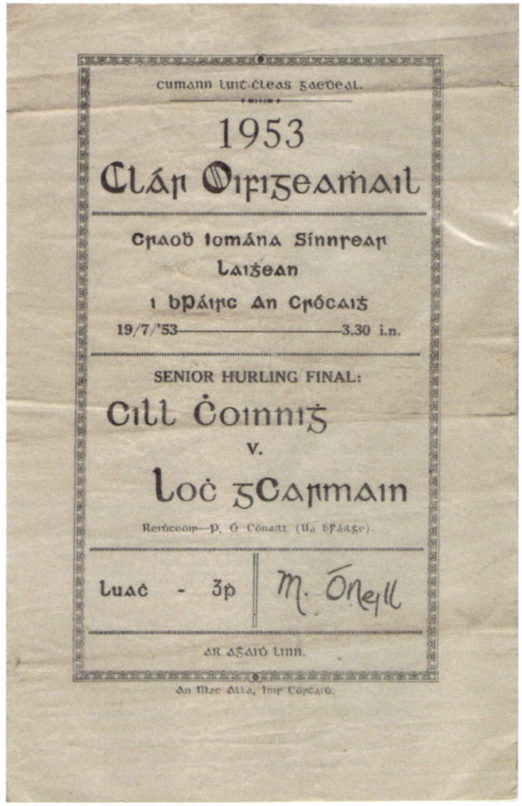
Cumann Lúṫ-Ċleas Gaeḋeal.
1953
Clár Oifigeaṁail
Craoḃ Iomána Sinnsear
Laiġean
i bPáirc an Cróċaiġ
19/7/'53—3.30 i.n.
SENIOR HURLING FINAL:
Cill Ċoinniġ
v.
Loċ gCarman
Reiḋteóir—P. Ó Conaill (Uí Ḟáilġe).
Luaċ - 3p
M. Ó Néill
Ar aġaiḋ linn.
An Mac Alla, Inis Córṫaiḋ.

7

Clár Oifigeaṁail
Craoḃ Iomána na Muṁan
i Luimneaċ
26-7-1953 ar 3-30 p.m.
Corcaiġ
v.
Tiobrad Árann
Réiṫeoir - L. Ó Donnċaḋa, Luimneaċ.
Craoḃ Iomána na Mionúr
Luimneaċ v. Tiobrad-Árann
ar a 2 a clog.
Luaċ 6p
Ar aġaiḋ linn.
KEY Printing Works, 50 William Street, Limerick. Tel. 975.

8

4 Ulster Football Final
Armagh 1-06 Cavan 0-05

5 All-Ireland Football Final
Kerry 0-13 Armagh 1-06
Attendance – 86,155

6 Leinster Hurling Final
Kilkenny 1-13 Wexford 3-05

7 Munster Hurling Final
Cork 3-10 Tipperary 1-11

8 All-Ireland Hurling Final
Cork 3-03 Galway 0-08
Attendance – 71,195

1954

The Cork–Tipperary rivalry of the early 1950s reached a climax in 1954 when the counties met in the Munster hurling final for the fifth consecutive year. The series was level at two wins each when, in a very close game, a late Cork goal gave them their third Munster championship in a row. In Leinster, Wexford were making progress. Inspired by the prolific Nicky Rackard, they accounted for Kilkenny in the semi-final and easily defeated Dublin in the final. Rackard finished the Leinster final with a tally of five goals and four points and in the All-Ireland semi-final he accumulated seven goals and seven points against Antrim. There was huge interest in the 1954 All-Ireland final and the match attracted 84,856, a record attendance for a final. Christy Ring was instrumental in Cork's victory as he claimed his eighth All-Ireland medal, also a record at the time.

1

2

1 Leinster Hurling Final
Wexford 8-05 Dublin 1-04

2 Munster Hurling Final
Cork 2-08 Tipperary 1-08

3 All-Ireland Hurling Final
Cork 1-09 Wexford 1-06
Attendance – 84,856

Clár Oifigiúil
Craoḃ Iomána na hÉireann
i bPáirc an Ċrócaiġ
ar 3.15 p.m.
5ú Meán Fómair, '54
Cumann Lúiṫ Ċleas Gaeḋeal
Éire
Corcaiġ
v.
Loċ gCarmain
Craoḃ Iomána na Mionúr, ar 1.30 p.m.
Áṫ Cliaṫ v. Tiobrad Árann
Luaċ
6ṗ.

4

Cumann Lúith - Chleas Gaedheal.

CONNACHT SENIOR FOOTBALL CHAMPIONSHIP FINAL

SLIGO

v.

GALWAY

AT 4.30 P.M.

Referee: T. J. O'REILLY (Cavan).

MINOR FOOTBALL FINAL

MAYO v. SLIGO

AT 3 P.M.

Referee: J. J. NERNEY (Roscommon)

TUAM STADIUM

Sunday, July 18,'54

OFFICIAL PROGRAMME

3d.

4 Connacht Football Final
Galway 2-10 Sligo 3-04

5 Leinster Football Final
Meath 4-07 Offaly 2-10

6 Munster Football Final
Kerry 4-09 Cork 2-03

7 Ulster Football Final
Cavan 2-10 Armagh 2-05

8 All-Ireland Football Final
Meath 1-13 Kerry 1-07
Attendance – 75,276

5

Clár Oifigiúil.
Craoḃ Peile Sinnsear Laiġean
i bPáirc an Ċrócaiġ, 25-7-'54
Ua bḞailġe
v.
Miḋe
Réiteoir: L. Mac Guid (Loċ Garmán)
ar 3.30 p.m.
Peil Mionúir Laiġean
Miḋe v. Át-Cliat
Réiteoir: L. Ó Concubair
ar 2 p.m.
Luaċ - 3p.
M. Ó Néill
(Rún.)
An Mac Alla, Inis Córtaid.

7

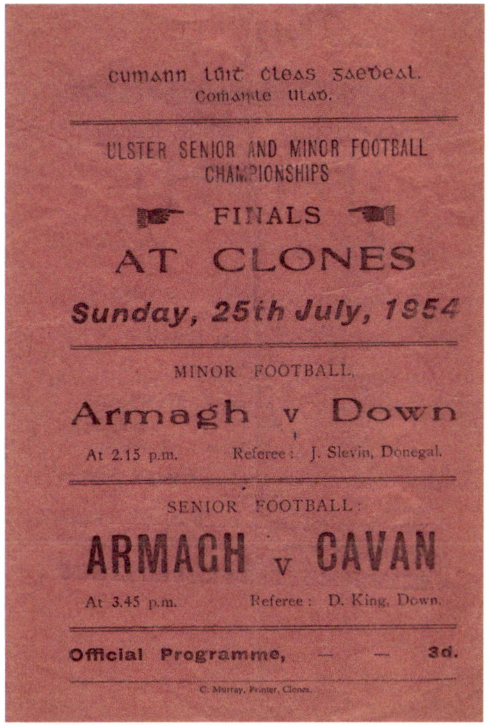

Cumann Lúit Cleas Gaeḋeal.
Comairle Ulaḋ.
ULSTER SENIOR AND MINOR FOOTBALL CHAMPIONSHIPS
FINALS
AT CLONES
Sunday, 25th July, 1954
MINOR FOOTBALL.
Armagh v Down
At 2.15 p.m.
Referee: J. Slevin, Donegal.
SENIOR FOOTBALL:
ARMAGH v CAVAN
At 3.45 p.m.
Referee: D. King, Down.
Official Programme, — — 3d.
C. Murray, Printer, Clones.

6

Cumann Lúit-Cleas Gaeḋeal
Munster Football Championship
CORK ATHLETIC GROUNDS
SUNDAY, 25th JULY at 3.30 p.m. 1954
(Blocks by Courtesy "Cork Examiner")
T. Lyne, Kerry
C. Duggan, Cork
CIARRAI v. CORCAIGH
Réiḋteoir—R. Stailcliuim, Tiobrad-Árann.
Minor Football Ċhampionship
CIARRAI v. CORCAIGH
Réiḋteoir—P. Ó Naoiṁeáin, Luimneaċ.
at 2 p.m.
Clár Oifigeaṁail
OFFICIAL PROGRAMME
6p.
Rúnaí
BLAIR, DUNCAN & CO. LTD

8

Clár Oifigiúil
Craoḃ Peile na hÉireann
i bPáirc an Ċrócaiġ
ar 3.15 p.m.
26ú Meán Fómair, '54
Cumann Lúit Cleas Gaeḋeal
Éire
An Miḋe
v.
Ciarraiḋe
Craoḃ Peile na Mionúr, ar 1.30 p.m.
Át Cliaṫ v. Ciarraiḋe
Luaċ
6p.

1955

Having fallen at the final hurdle in 1954, Wexford were determined to make it back to the All-Ireland hurling final the following year. A replay was required before they eventually saw off Kilkenny in the Leinster final. With the Rackard brothers, Nick O'Donnell and Ned Wheeler exciting spectators and inspiring the team, Wexford then faced Limerick in the All-Ireland semi-final. Limerick made a brave fight of it, but Wexford's experience saw them home. In the All-Ireland final, Galway were no match for Wexford. Nicky Rackard led the scoring as Wexford won their first All-Ireland title since 1910 and Nick O'Donnell became the first man to lift the Liam MacCarthy Cup for the county.

In the All-Ireland football final, the seeds of a famous rivalry were sown as Kerry defeated a Dublin team containing 12 players from the St Vincent's club, among them Kevin Heffernan, the future manager, and Pádraig 'Jock' Haughey, brother of future taoiseach, Charlie.

1

2

1 Leinster Hurling Final
Wexford 2-07 Kilkenny 2-07

2 Replay
Wexford 5-06 Kilkenny 3-09

3 Munster Hurling Final
Limerick 2-16 Clare 2-06

Craoḃ Iomána na Muṁan

An Clár

— v. —

Luimneaċ

i Luimneaċ

Dia Doṁnaiġ 10aḋ Iúil, 1955.

Clár Oifiġeaṁail

Luaċ - - - 6p.

KEY PRINTING WORKS, WILLIAM ST., LIMERICK

4

Clár Oifigiúil
Craob Iomána na hÉireann
i bPáirc an Ċrócaiġ
ar 3.15 p.m.
4ú Meán Ḟomair,'55
Cumann Lúiṫ Ċleas Gaeḋeal
Éire
Gaillim
v.
Loċ gCarmain
Craob Iomána na Mionúr, ar 1.30 p.m.
Gaillim v. Tiobrad Árann
Luaċ
6p.

5

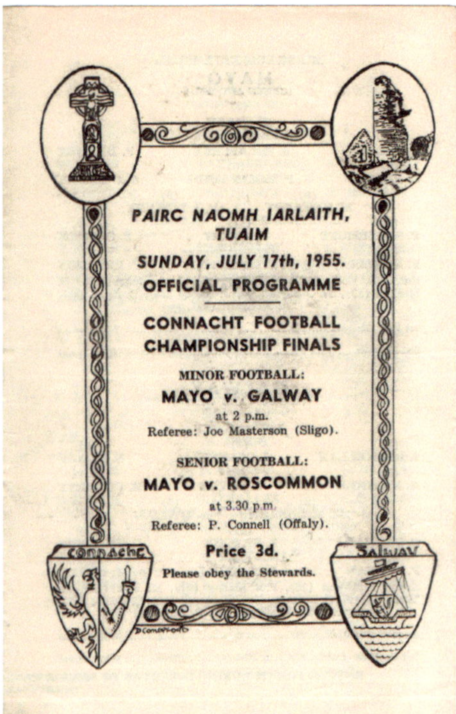
PAIRC NAOMH IARLAITH,
TUAIM
SUNDAY, JULY 17th, 1955.
OFFICIAL PROGRAMME
CONNACHT FOOTBALL
CHAMPIONSHIP FINALS
MINOR FOOTBALL:
MAYO v. GALWAY
at 2 p.m.
Referee: Joe Masterson (Sligo).
SENIOR FOOTBALL:
MAYO v. ROSCOMMON
at 3.30 p.m.
Referee: P. Connell (Offaly).
Price 3d.
Please obey the Stewards.
CONNACHT
GALWAY

6

Comairle Laiġean.
1955.
Clár Oifigiúil
Peil Laiġean
i bPáirc an Crócaiġ
24/7/'55.
An Míḋe
v.
Át Cliat
Luaċ - 3p.
Rúnaiḋe.

7

comairle
mumhan
Cumann Lúit-Cleas Gaeḋeal
CLÁR OIFIGIÚIL
1955
Munster Football Finals
At Fitzgerald Stadium, Killarney,
On Sunday, 24th July, 1955
MINOR 2 P.M. (S.T.)
CIARRAÍ V. TIOBRAD ÁRANN
Referee: TIM COTTER (Cork)
SENIOR 3.30 P.M. (S.T.)
CIARRAÍ V. CORCAIĠ
Referee: BOB STAKELUM (Tipperary)
ADMISSION — — — — — — — — — — — — 2/-
TERRACED ENCLOSURE 3/-; JUVENILES 1/-; SIDELINE
1/6d. EXTRA FROM TERRACED ENCLOSURE
Luaċ : : : 4p.
Proceeds of this Programme go to Fitzgerald Stadium Fund
Rúnaiḋe.
KERRY CHAMPION LTD.

8

9

4 All-Ireland Hurling Final
Wexford 3-13 Galway 2-08
Attendance – 72,854

5 Connacht Football Final
Mayo 3-11 Roscommon 1-03

6 Leinster Football Final
Dublin 5-12 Meath 0-07

7 Munster Football Final
Kerry 0-14 Cork 2-06

8 Ulster Football Final
Cavan 0-11 Derry 0-08

9 All-Ireland Football Final
Kerry 0-12 Dublin 1-06
Attendance – 87,102

1956

If 1954 had set the record for the highest attendance at an All-Ireland hurling final, the same two teams meeting again in the final of 1956 was bound to grab the imagination of the sporting public. Cork were back in the final after defeating the reigning Munster champions Limerick in the provincial final. Wexford, the defending All-Ireland champions, had beaten Kilkenny in the Leinster final, with only a point to spare. The All-Ireland finals were delayed by two weeks due to an outbreak of polio. In the hurling final, Wexford avenged their defeat of 1954 by beating Cork by six points. Late in the match, the Wexford goalkeeper, Art Foley, made a famous save from Christy Ring. After the final whistle, Ring was carried shoulder-high from the field by Wexford's Nick O'Donnell and Bobby Rackard in tribute to both his performance in the final and his status in the game of hurling. It was a double defeat for Cork in 1956, as they also suffered a football final defeat to Galway. Cork's Éamonn Goulding played in both finals.

1

2

1 Leinster Hurling Final
Wexford 4-08 Kilkenny 3-10

2 Munster Hurling Final
Cork 5-05 Limerick 3-05

3 All-Ireland Hurling Final
Wexford 2-14 Cork 2-08
Attendance – 83,096

3

Clár Oifigiúil
Craoḃ Iomána na hÉireann
i bPáirc an Ċrócaiġ
ar 3.15 p.m.
23 Meán Fómair, '56
Cumann Lúiṫ Ċleas Gaeḋeal
Éire
Corcaiġ
v.
Loċ gCarmain
Craoḃ Iomána na Mionúr, ar 1.30 p.m.
Cill Ċoinniġ v. Tiobrad Árann
Luaċ
6ṗ.

4

CUMANN LUITH-CHLEAS GAEDHEAL.

Clar Oifigiuil. № 4220

COUNTESS MARKIEVICZ PARK, SLIGO

ON SUNDAY, 15th JULY, 1956

Connaught Football Championship Finals

MINOR FOOTBALL:
ROSCOMMON v. LEITRIM
AT 3 P.M.
REFEREE—MR. P. HENEGAN (MAYO).

SENIOR FOOTBALL:
SLIGO v. GALWAY.
AT 4.30 P.M.
REFEREE—MR. P. CONNELL (OFFALY).

Keep this Programme for Free Raffle for £1.

PROGRAMME - - - - - - 3d.

5

Coṁairle Laiġean.

1956

Clár Oifiġeaṁail

Craoḃaċa Peil Laiġean
i bPáirc an Ċrócaiġ
(22/7/'56)

Mionúir 2 p.m. — An Miḋe v. Át-Cliat
Reiṫeóir: E. De Moulte (Cill Manntain)

Sinnsear:
Loċ gCarmain
v.
Cill Dara
3.30 p.m. Reiṫeóir: M. Mac Arogail (Lúġbaiḋ)

Luaċ - 3p.

M. Ó Neill
(Rúnaiḋe).

An Mac Alla, Imp Córċaiḋ.

4 Connacht Football Final
Galway 3-12 Sligo 1-05

5 Leinster Football Final
Kildare 2-11 Wexford 1-08

6 Munster Football Final
Cork 0-08 Kerry 2-02

7 Replay
Cork 1-08 Kerry 1-07

8 Ulster Football Final
Tyrone 3-05 Cavan 0-04

9 All-Ireland Football Final
Galway 2-13 Cork 3-07
Attendance – 70,772

6

Cumann Lúiṫ-Ċleas Gaeḋeal
MUNSTER FOOTBALL FINAL
CORK ATHLETIC GROUNDS
SUNDAY, 15th JULY, 1956
at 3.30 p.m.
CORCAIGH
v.
CIARRAI
MINOR FOOTBALL FINAL
CIARRAI v. LUIMNEACH
OFFICIAL PROGRAMME
6p.
Rúnaí
BLAIR DUNCAN, CORK.

7

comairle
muṁan
Cumann Lúiṫ-Ċleas Gaeḋeal
CLÁR OIFIGIÚIL
1956
MUNSTER FINALS
At Fitzgerald Stadium, Killarney
On Sunday, 29th July, 1956
Ciarraí V. Portláirge
Junior Hurling 1 p.m. (S.T.). Referee T. O'Sullivan
Junior Football 2.15 p.m. Referee P. O'Grady (Cork)
SENIOR FOOTBALL FINAL REPLAY
CIARRAÍ V. CORCAIĠ
3.45 p.m. Referee S. Cleary (Tipperary)
ADMISSION 2/-. JUVENILES 1/-.
TERRACES 1/-. and SIDELINE 2/6 extra.
Luaċ - - - 6p.
Proceeds of this Programme go to the Fitzgerald Stadium Fund
(Rúnaiḋe)
Kerry Champion, Ltd., Tralee.

8

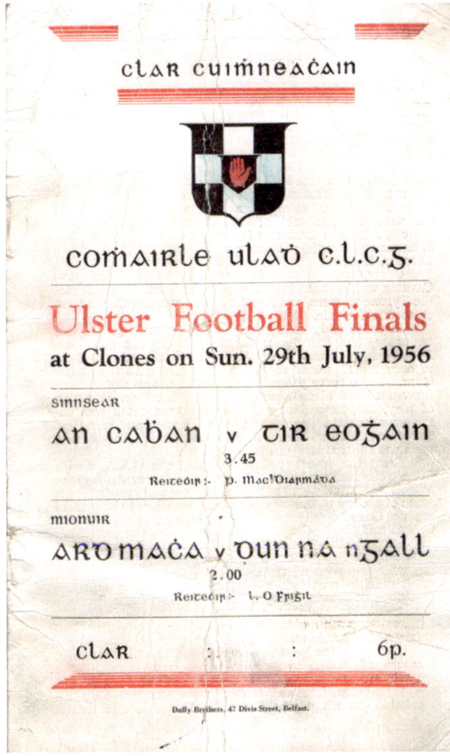
clar cuimneaċain
comairle ulaḋ c.l.c.g.
Ulster Football Finals
at Clones on Sun. 29th July, 1956
sinnsear
an caḃan v tir eoġain
3.45
minuir
ardmaċa v dun na ngall
2.00
clar : : 6p.
Duffy Brothers, 47 Divis Street, Belfast.

9

Clár Oifigiúil
Craoḃ Peile na hÉireann
i bPáirc an Ċrócaigh
ar 3.15 p.m.
7 Deire Fóṁair, '56
Cumann Lúiṫ Cleas Gaeḋeal
éire
Corcaiġ
v.
Gailliṁ
Craoḃ Peile na Mionúr, ar 1.30 p.m.
Áṫ Cliaṫ v. Liaṫdruim
Luaċ
6p.

1957

In a season of shocks, the biggest was the defeat of Kerry at the hands of Waterford in the 1957 Munster football semi-final. Meanwhile, in Ulster, Cavan failed to reach the final for the first time since 1938. The 1950s, however, were proving fruitful years for the footballers of Louth. Having reached the Leinster final on three occasions – winning in 1950 and 1953 – Louth were back in the provincial final in 1957, having dispatched the reigning Leinster champions Kildare in the semi-final. Jim McDonnell scored two goals as Dublin fell victim to Louth in the final. Tyrone's challenge faltered at the semi-final stage and Louth advanced to meet Cork in the final. Although trailing at half-time, Louth recovered to win by two points, adding to their victories in 1910 and 1912, and allowing their captain, and well-known musician, Dermot O'Brien to pick up the Sam Maguire Cup for the first time.

1

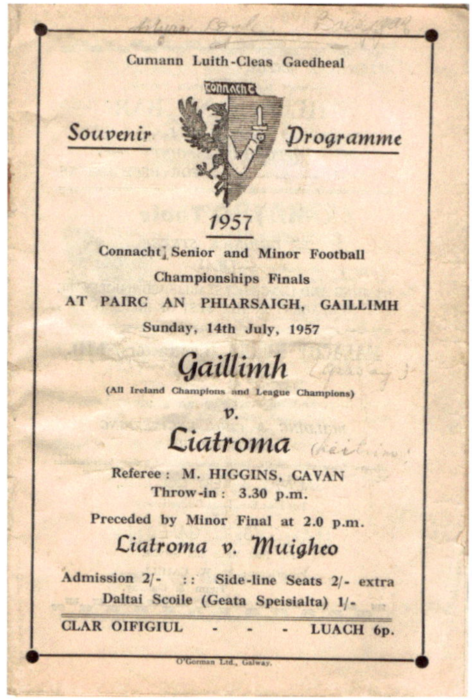

Cumann Luith-Cleas Gaedheal

Souvenir Programme

1957

Connacht Senior and Minor Football Championships Finals

AT PAIRC AN PHIARSAIGH, GAILLIMH

Sunday, 14th July, 1957

Gaillimh

(All Ireland Champions and League Champions)

v.

Liatroma

Referee: M. HIGGINS, CAVAN

Throw-in: 3.30 p.m.

Preceded by Minor Final at 2.0 p.m.

Liatroma v. Muigheo

Admission 2/- :: Side-line Seats 2/- extra

Daltai Scoile (Geata Speisialta) 1/-

CLAR OIFIGIUL - - - LUACH 6p.

O'Gorman Ltd., Galway.

2

Clár Oifigiúil

Peil Laiġean

i bPáirc an Ċrócaiġ

7/7/57.

Comhairle Laiġean 1957

An Craoḃ

Dublin Junior Hurling Semi-final—2 p.m.:

Naoṁ Uinsionn v Naoṁ Fionnbarr

Áṫ Ċliaṫ

v.

Luġḃaiḋ

E. de Moilte (Cill Mannċáin). 3.30 p.m.

(Runaiḋe). Luaċ - 3p.

An Mac Alla, Inir Corcaiḋ.

1 Connacht Football Final
Galway 4-08 Leitrim 0-04

2 Leinster Football Final
Louth 2-09 Dublin 1-07

3 Munster Football Final
Cork 0-16 Waterford 1-02

3

Clár - - - - 3ṗ.

Cumann Lúiṫ-Ċleas Gael.

Clár Oifigiúil

1957

Craoḃ Ċluiċí Peile na Muṁan

Dúrlas Éile

21ú Iúil, 1957

SENIOR FOOTBALL:

CORCAIĠ

v.

PORT LÁIRGE

At 3.45 p.m. (S.T.).

MINOR FOOTBALL:

CORCAIĠ v. CIARRAÍ

At 2.30 p.m. (S.T.).

Réalt Tiobraid Árann, Dúrlas Éile do ċlóḃuail.

4

Clar Oifigiúil
Coṁairle Ulaḋ C.L.C.G.
ULSTER FOOTBALL FINALS
at Clones on Sunday, 28th July, '57
Sinnsear
Doire v Tir Eoġain
at 3.45 p.m.
Reiteoir:- M. Ó hUiginn
Mionuir
Ard Maċa v Dún na nGall
at 2.15 p.m.
Reiteoir:- T. P. Ó Ragallaiġ
Luaċ : : 6p.

5

Clár Oifigiúil
Craoḃ Peile na hÉireann
i bPáirc an Ċrócaiġ
ar 3.15 p.m.
22 Meán Fóṁair, '57
Corcaiġ
v.
Luġbaiḋ
Craoḃ Peile na Mionúr, ar 1.30 p.m.
An Ṁiḋe v. Árd Ṁaċa
Luaċ 6p.

6

Clar Oifigiúil
Iomána Laiġean
i bPáirc an Ċrócaiġ
4/8/'57.
Comairle Laiġean
1957
Loċ gCarmáin
v.
Cill Ċoinniġ
3.30 p.m.
M. Ó Néill
Luaċ - 3p.

7

Clár 3p.
Cumann Lúṫ-Ċleas Gael.
Clár Oifigiúil
1957
Craoḃ Ċluiċí Iomána na Muṁan
Dúrlas Éile
14ú Iúil, 1957
SENIOR HURLING:
Corcaiġ v. Port Láirge
At 3.45 p.m. (S.T.)
Moltóir: S. Gleeson, Limerick.
MINOR HURLING:
Tiobrad Árann v. Luimneaċ
At 2.30 p.m. (S.T.)
Moltóir: M. Pollard, Waterford.

8

4 Ulster Football Final
Tyrone 1-09 Derry 0-10

5 All-Ireland Football Final
Louth 1-09 Cork 1-07
Attendance – 72,732

6 Leinster Hurling Final
Kilkenny 6-09 Wexford 1-05

7 Munster Hurling Final
Waterford 1-11 Cork 1-06

8 All-Ireland Hurling Final
Kilkenny 4-10 Waterford 3-12
Attendance – 70,594

1958

Derry made great strides in the Ulster football championship in the 1950s, contesting the finals in 1955 and 1957. In 1958, they reached the final again, where they faced Down. A new winner was guaranteed, as neither side had won the Anglo-Celt Cup before. Jim McKeever played a central role as Derry brushed aside the Down challenge that day, qualifying to meet Kerry in the All-Ireland semi-final. Against all expectations, Derry beat Kerry by a point to reach their first All-Ireland final.

There they met a Dublin team who had lost their way since the 1955 All-Ireland final, failing to even win their own province in the intervening years – until this year, at least. Dublin were in no mood to spurn another opportunity, however, and with eight veterans of the 1955 final still playing, they proved too strong for the Derry challenge.

1

cumann lúit cleas gaedeal

Official Programme

Connacht Senior & Minor Football Finals

AT

St. Coman's Park, Roscommon

ON

Sunday, July 13th 1958.

LEITRIM

v

GALWAY

Referee —J. MULVEY

4. P.M.

Preceded by Minor Championship

MAYO

v

ROSCOMMON

Referee P GERAGHTY 2 30 p.m.

Luach - - - 3d.

TOMAS MacGIOLLA CADHAIN, Runai.

CHAMPION, Roscommon.

2

Comairle Laigean

Clár Oifigiúil

1958.

An Uaim

(Páirc Tailtean)

20/7/58

Át Cliat

v.

Lúgbáid

Craob Mionúir 2 p.m. (S. Ó Fearg, Cill Dara).

Craob Sinnsear 3.30 p.m. (S. Ó Dubtaing, Ua bFáilge).

Luac - 3p. | M. Ó Neill

Runaidhe.

An Mac Alla, Imp Corcaid.

1 Connacht Football Final
Galway 2-10 Leitrim 1-11

2 Leinster Football Final
Dublin 1-11 Louth 1-06

3 Munster Football Final
Kerry 2-07 Cork 0-03

Cumann Lúiṫ-Ċleas Gael

Munster Football Finals

Cork Athletic Grounds, Sunday, 13th July, 1958

Senior—3.30 p.m. Réiḋteoir—P. Silke, Luimneaċ

Corcaiġ

v.

Ciarraí

Minor—2.15 p.m. Réiḋteoir—A. Ó Scanaill, Corcaiġ.

Portlairge

v.

Ciarraí

Clár Oifigiúil - 6p.

BLAIR DUNCAN, CORK.

4

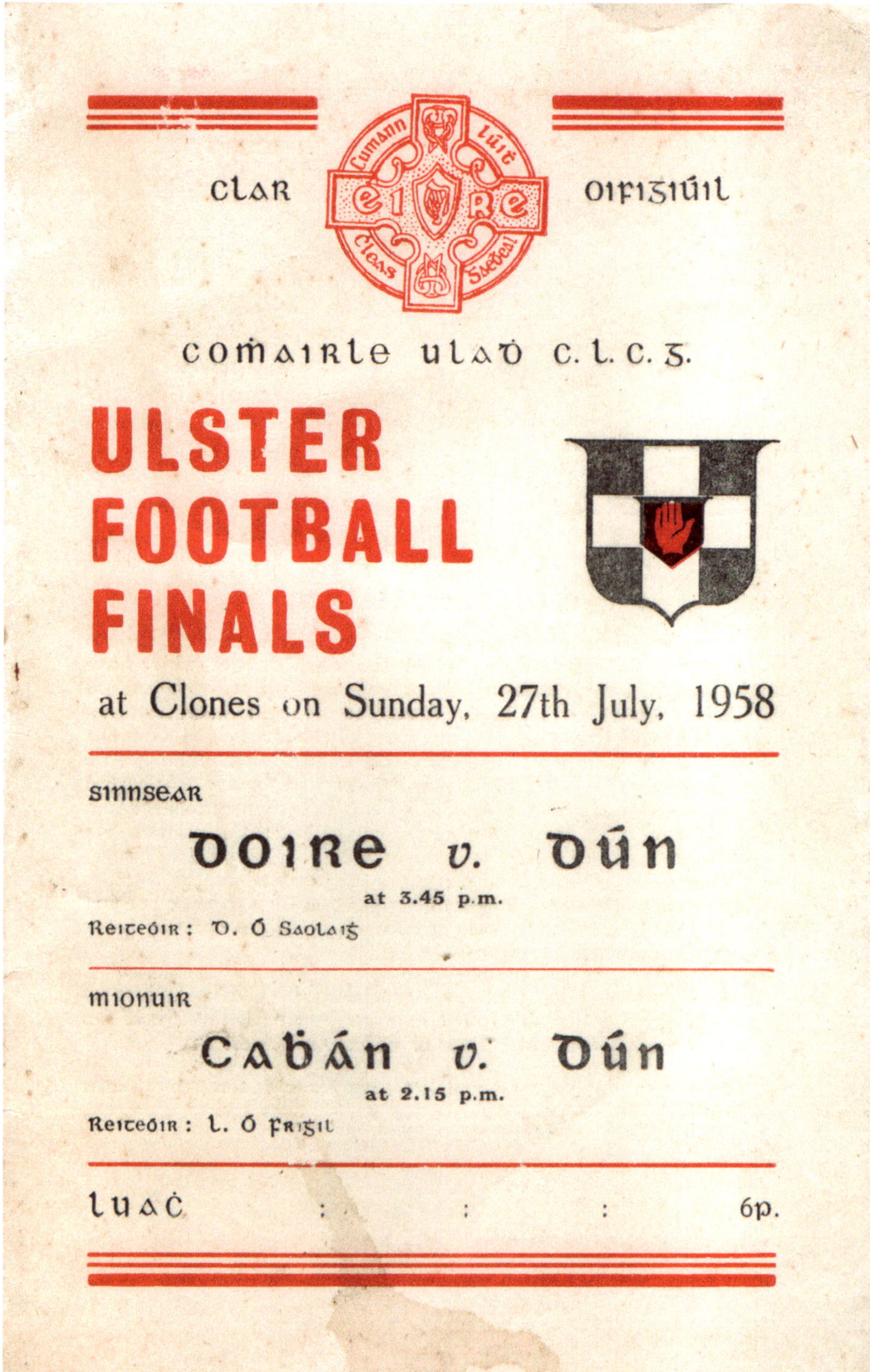

Clar Oifiziúil

Coṁairle Ulaḋ C.L.C.G.

ULSTER FOOTBALL FINALS

at Clones on Sunday, 27th July, 1958

Sinnsear

Doire v. Dún

at 3.45 p.m.

Reiteóir: D. Ó Saolaiʒ

Mionuir

Caḃán v. Dún

at 2.15 p.m.

Reiteóir: L. Ó Friʒil

Luaċ : : : 6p.

4 Ulster Football Final
Derry 1-11 Down 2-04

5 All-Ireland Football Final
Dublin 2-12 Derry 1-09
Attendance – 73,371

6 Leinster Hurling Final
Kilkenny 5-12 Wexford 4-09

7 Munster Hurling Final
Tipperary 4-12 Waterford 1-05

8 All-Ireland Hurling Final
Tipperary 4-09 Galway 2-05
Attendance – 47,276

5

Clár Oifigiúil
Craoḃ Peile na hÉireann
i bPáirc an Ċrócaiġ
ar 3.15 p.m.
28 Meán Fóṁair, '58
Cumann Lúiṫ Cleas Gaeḋeal
Éire
Áṫ Cliaṫ
v.
Doire
Craoḃ Peile na Mionúr, ar 1.30 p.m.
Áṫ Cliaṫ v. Muiġeo
Luaċ
6ṗ.

7

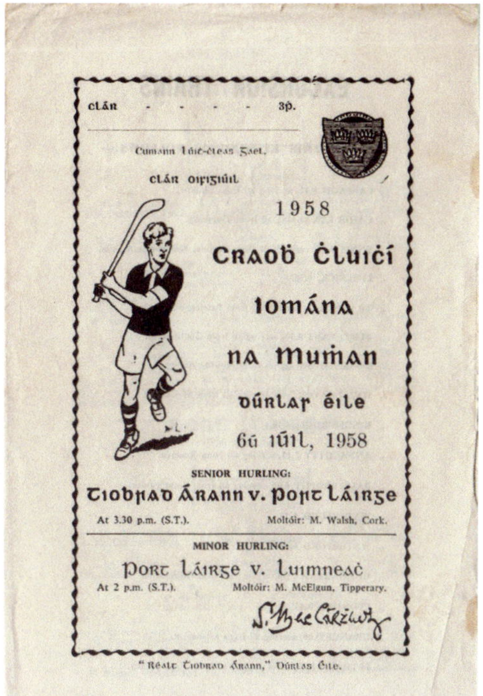
Clár - - - - 3ṗ.
Clár Oifigiúil
1958
Craoḃ Ċluiċí Iomána na Muṁan
Dúrlas Éile
6ú Iúil, 1958
SENIOR HURLING:
Tiobrad Árann v. Port Láirge
At 3.30 p.m. (S.T.). Moltóir: M. Walsh, Cork.
MINOR HURLING:
Port Láirge v. Luimneaċ
At 2 p.m. (S.T.). Moltóir: M. McElgun, Tipperary.
"Réalt Tiobrad Árann," Dúrlas Éile.

6

Comhairle Laiġean
Clár Oifigiúil
1958.
Craoḃ Iomána Laiġean
i bPáirc an Crócaiġ
27/7/58.
Loċ Garmán
v.
Cill Ċoinniġ
Luaċ - 3p.
Runaidhe.

8

Clár Oifigiúil
Craoḃ Iomána na hÉireann
i bPáirc an Ċrócaiġ
ar 3.15 p.m.
7 Meán Fóṁair, '58
Cumann Lúiṫ Cleas Gaeḋeal
Éire
Gailliṁ
v.
Tiobrad Árann
Craoḃ Iomána na Mionúr, ar 1.30 p.m.
Gailliṁ v. Luimneaċ
Luaċ
6ṗ.

1959

This was the last year that the distinctive All-Ireland final match programme covers of the 1950s were used. A colour background had been introduced in 1953 to enhance the programmes used in the previous two years. The programmes for the two All-Ireland final replays of the decade had a different design: slightly larger and with less colour, apparently in an attempt to distinguish them from the unofficial versions.

The 1959 All-Ireland hurling final was the first to be played in front of the new Hogan Stand. The game between Waterford and Kilkenny ended in a draw with the unusual scoreline of 1-17 to 5-05. Waterford won the replay to claim their second All-Ireland title. Kilkenny's Eddie Keher came on as a substitute in the replay to earn the distinction of playing in both the minor and senior All-Ireland finals in the same year. Unfortunately for him, he won neither.

1

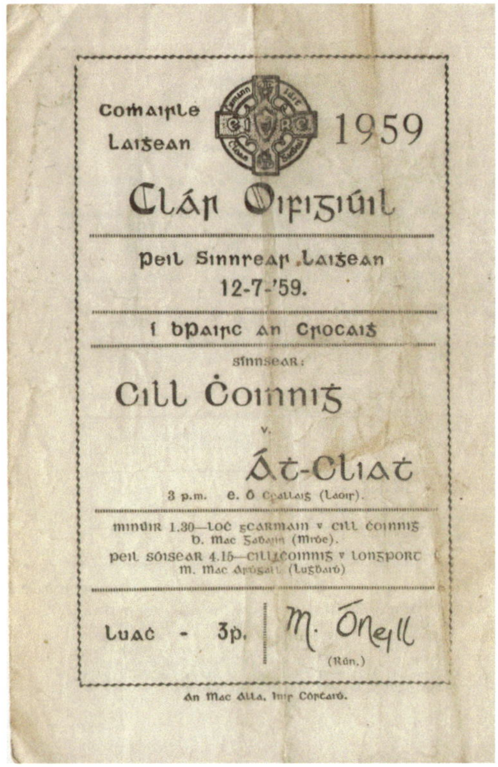

2

1 Leinster Hurling Final
Kilkenny 2-09 Dublin 1-11

2 Munster Hurling Final
Waterford 3-09 Cork 2-09

3 All-Ireland Hurling Final
Waterford 1-17 Kilkenny 5-05
Attendance – 73,707

3

Clár Oifigiúil
Craoḃ Iomána na hÉireann
i bPáirc an Ċrócaiġ
ar 3.15 p.m.
6aḋ Meán Fómair, '59
Cumann Lúiṫ Ċleas Gaeḋeal
Éire
Cill Ċoinniġ
v.
Port Láirge
Craoḃ Iomána na Mionúr, ar 1.45 p.m.
Cill Ċoinniġ v. Tiobrad Árann
Luaċ
6p.

4

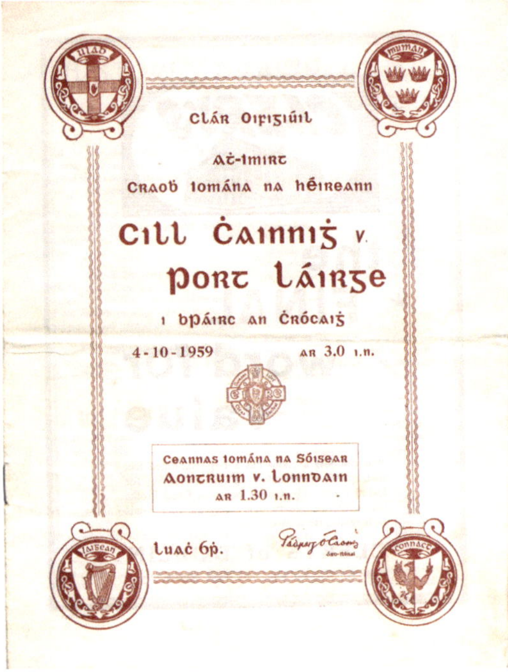
Clár Oifigiúil

Aṫ-imirt

Craoḃ Iomána na hÉireann

Cill Ċainniġ v.

Port Láirge

i bPáirc an Ċrócaiġ

4-10-1959 ar 3.0 i.n.

Ceannas Iomána na Sóisear

Aontruim v. Londain

ar 1.30 i.n.

Luaċ 6p.

5

CUMANN LUITH-CHLEAS GAEDHEAL

CLAR OIFIGIUIL № 774

CONNACHT FOOTBALL CHAMPIONSHIP FINALS

Senior Football Final:

GALWAY v. LEITRIM

AT 3.30 P.M.

REFEREE—MR. J. DOWLING, TULLAMORE.

Minor Football Final:

MAYO v. GALWAY

AT 2 P.M.

REFEREE—MR. J. P. CALLAGHAN, ROSCOMMON.

AT MARKIEVICZ PARK, SLIGO

On Sunday, 9th August, 1959

Luach - - - - - 6d.

TOMAS Mac GIOLLA CADHAIN, RUNAI.

6

Comhairle Laiġean 1959

Clár Oifigiúil

Craobaċa Peil Laiġean, 2-8-'59.

Tulach Mór

Sinnsear:

Áṫ-Cliaṫ

v.

Laoiṡ

3.30 p.m. S. Ó Dubhlaine (Ua bFáilge).

Peil Mionúir—Ua bFáilge v Áṫ Cliaṫ (2 p.m.).

D. Mac Gabhann (Miḋe).

Luaċ - 3p.

M. Ó Néill (Rún.)

An Mac Alla, Inis Corṫaiḋ.

7

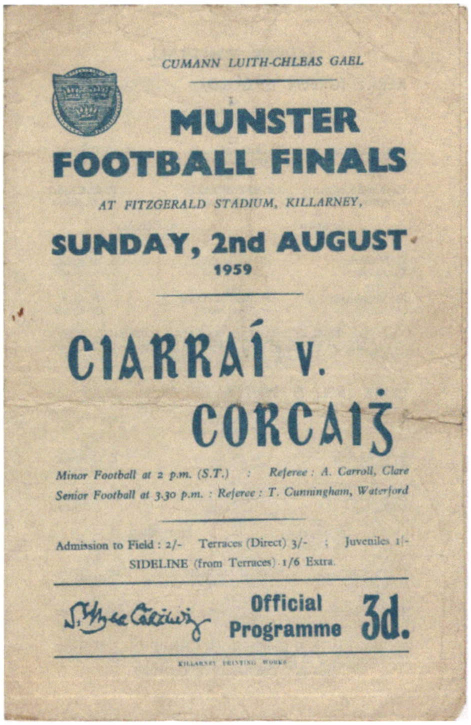
CUMANN LUITH-CHLEAS GAEL

MUNSTER FOOTBALL FINALS

AT FITZGERALD STADIUM, KILLARNEY,

SUNDAY, 2nd AUGUST 1959

CIARRAÍ v. CORCAIĠ

Minor Football at 2 p.m. (S.T.) : Referee : A. Carroll, Clare

Senior Football at 3.30 p.m. : Referee : T. Cunningham, Waterford

Admission to Field : 2/- Terraces (Direct) 3/- ; Juveniles 1/-

SIDELINE (from Terraces) 1/6 Extra.

Official Programme 3d.

KILLARNEY PRINTING WORKS

8

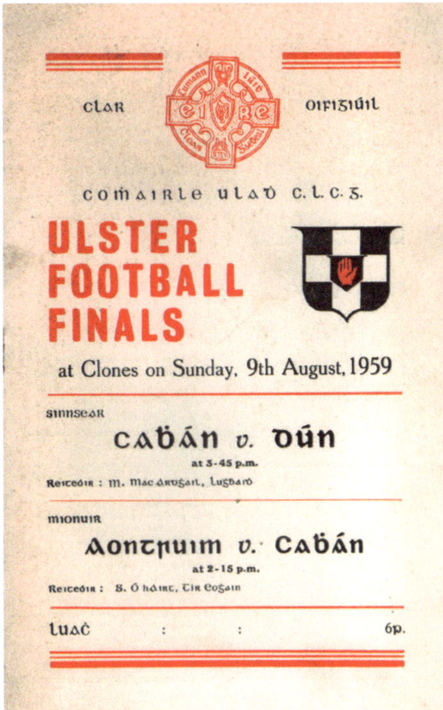

9

4 Replay
Waterford 3-12 Kilkenny 1-10
Attendance – 77,285

5 Connacht Football Final
Galway 5-08 Leitrim 0-12

6 Leinster Football Final
Dublin 1-18 Laois 2-08

7 Munster Football Final
Kerry 2-15 Cork 2-08

8 Ulster Football Final
Down 2-16 Cavan 0-07

9 All-Ireland Football Final
Kerry 3-07 Galway 1-04
Attendance – 85,897

1960–69

1960

Archbishop Thomas Croke and Michael Cusack, two influential figures in the foundation of the GAA, feature on the covers of the 1960 All-Ireland final match programmes. The publications contained 20 pages of articles, photographs, advertisements and team information. The introduction on page one was written entirely *as Gaeilge* and printed in the cló Gaelach.

Down won their first Ulster football title in 1959 and repeated the feat 12 months later, brushing aside Cavan's challenge in Clones. The All-Ireland semi-final pairing of Down and Offaly meant that at least one of the teams would qualify for their first final. A replay was needed for Down to advance to the final, where Kerry awaited. With the superb James McCartan scoring 1-01, Down handed Kerry their heaviest defeat in a final so far. This year was the first time that the Sam Maguire Cup was won by a team from north of the border, with Kevin Mussen the first Down captain to receive it.

1

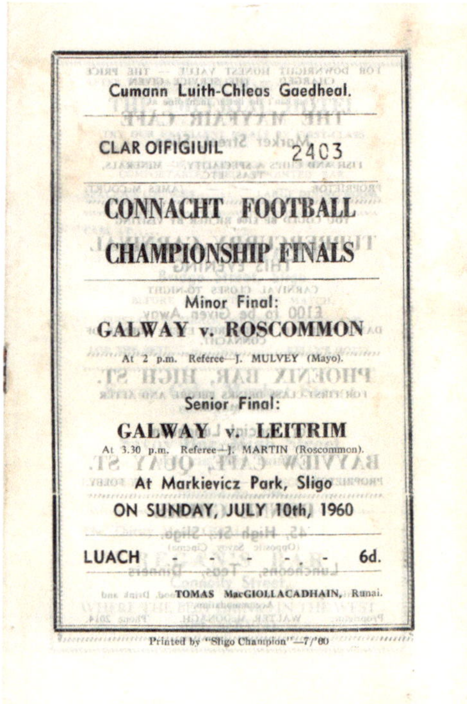

2

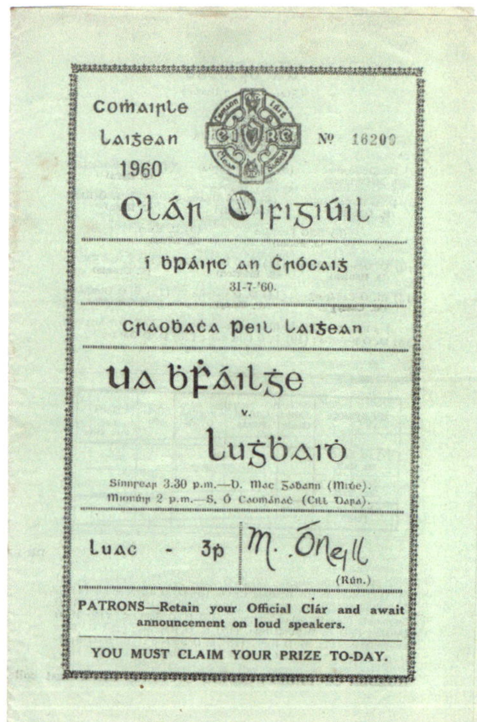

1 Connacht Football Final
Galway 2-05 Leitrim 0-05

2 Leinster Football Final
Offaly 0-10 Louth 1-06

3 Munster Football Final
Kerry 3-15 Waterford 0-08

CUMANN LÚIṪ-ĊLEAS GAEḊEAL

MUNSTER FOOTBALL FINALS

Cork Athletic Grounds, Sunday, 24th July, 1960

Senior—3.30 p.m. Réiteóir—A. Ó Cearúil, An Ċláir

PORTLAIRGE

v.

CIARRAÍ

Minor—2 p.m. Réiteóir—S. Ó Siocáin, Luimneac

3-8 CORCAIĠ v. CIARRAÍ

CLÁR OIFIGIÚIL - 6p.

BLAIR DUNCAN. CORK.

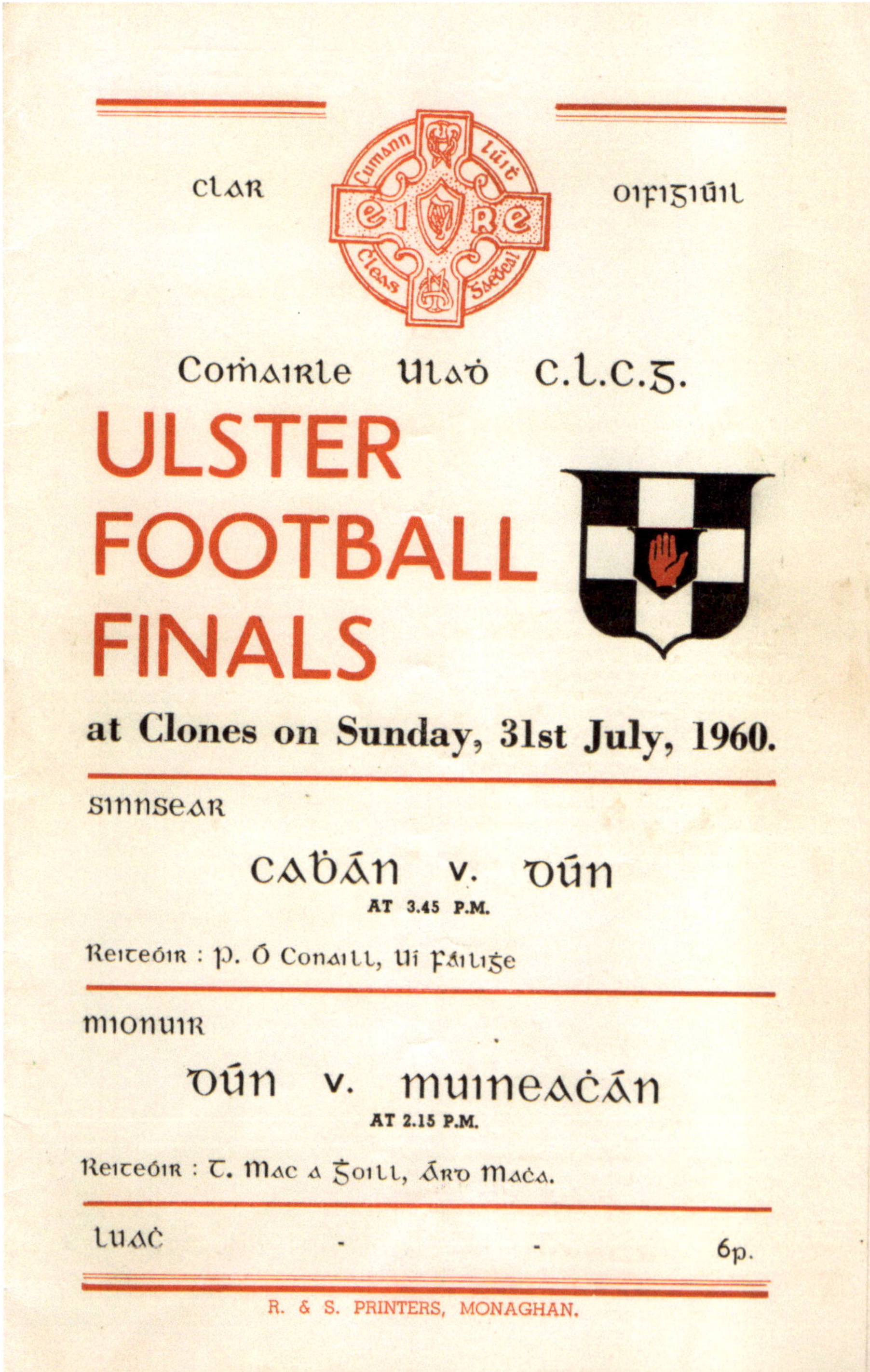
4

Clár Oifigiúil

Coṁairle Ulaḋ C.L.C.G.

ULSTER FOOTBALL FINALS

at Clones on Sunday, 31st July, 1960.

Sinnsear

Caḃán v. Dún

AT 3.45 P.M.

Reiteóir : P. Ó Conaill, Uí Fáilge

Mionúir

Dún v. Muineaċán

AT 2.15 P.M.

Reiteóir : T. Mac a Goill, Árd Maċa.

Luaċ - - 6p.

R. & S. PRINTERS, MONAGHAN.

4 Ulster Football Final
Down 3-07 Cavan 1-08

5 All-Ireland Football Final
Down 2-10 Kerry 0-08
Attendance – 87,768

6 Leinster Hurling Final
Wexford 3-10 Kilkenny 2-11

7 Munster Hurling Final
Tipperary 4-13 Cork 4-11

8 All-Ireland Hurling Final
Wexford 2-15 Tipperary 0-11
Attendance – 77,154

5

Clár Oifigiúil
Craob Peile na hÉireann
i bPáirc an Ċrócaiġ
25 Meán Fómair, 1960
MOST REV. DR. CROKE
ARCHBISHOP of Cashel & Emly and first PATRON of the Association
An Dún
v.
Ciarraí
ar 3.15 p.m.
Craob Peile na Mionúr ar 1.45 p.m.
Corcaiġ v. Gaillim
Luaċ 6ṗ.

6

Comairle Laiġean
1960
Clár Oifiġiúil
i bPáirc an Ċrócaiġ
24/7/'60
Craobaċa Iomáint Laiġean
Loċ Garmán
v.
Cill Ċoinniġ
Luaċ - 3p
M. Ó Néill
(Rún.)
PATRONS NOTE.—Your Official Programme to-day may win you a 10-year Ticket to All-Ireland Finals. Hold your Programme. Watch the number on it. Listen for Announcement at Interval in senior game.
[SEE BACK PAGE]

7

Clár - - - 3ṗ.
Cumann Lúiṫ-Ċleas Gael.
Clár Oifigiúil
1960
Craob-Ċluiċí na Mumhan
Dúrlas Éile
31 Iúil, 1960
SENIOR HURLING:
Corcaiġ v. Tiobrad Árann
At 3.30 p.m. (S.T.).
Moltóir: G. Fitzgerald, Limerick.
MINOR HURLING:—
Gaillim v. Tiobrad Árann
At 2 p.m. (S.T.).
Moltóir: G. Browne, Clare.

8

Clár Oifigiúil
Craob Iomána na hÉireann
i bPáirc an Ċrócaiġ
4 Meán Fómair, 1960
Mícheál Cíosóg,
Founder and First Secretary of the Association
Loċ Garman
v.
Tiobraid Árann
ar 3.15 p.m.
Craob Iomána na Mionúr ar 1.45 p.m.
Tiobraid Árann v. Cill Ċainniġ
Luaċ 6ṗ.

1961

For the third time in as many years, the GAA used a new format for the cover of the All-Ireland final match programme. The distinctive new covers featured the match information written in Celtic script and illustrations of players in action poses. As was common at the time, advertisements for both alcohol and cigarettes were included in the programmes.

In football, Down and Offaly came through their provinces and All-Ireland semi-finals to meet in the All-Ireland final. The meeting of the two counties renewed the rivalry of the previous year's semi-final and was much anticipated. This was reflected in the huge crowd that gained access to Croke Park for the final: 90,566 remains the record attendance for an All-Ireland football final and those present witnessed Down retain the championship by the narrowest of margins.

1

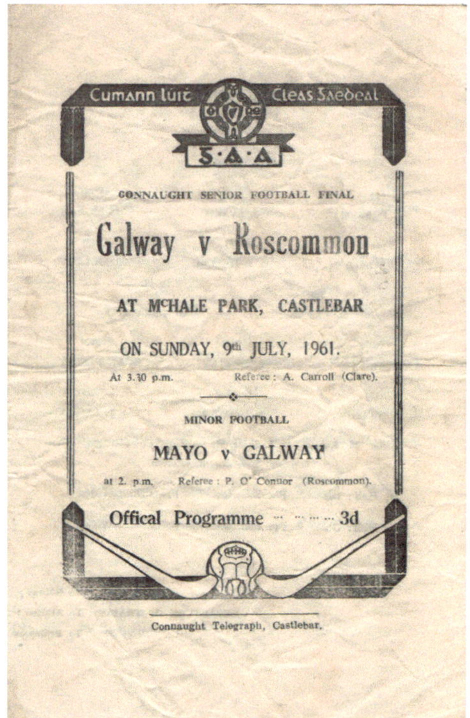

2

1 Connacht Football Final
Roscommon 1-11 Galway 2-07

2 Leinster Football Final
Offaly 1-13 Dublin 1-08

3 Munster Football Final
Kerry 0-10 Cork 1-07

3

Cumann Lúiṫ-Ċleas Gaeḋeal

Munster Football Finals

Cork Athletic Grounds, Sunday, 16th July, 1961

Senior—3.30 p.m. Réiteóir—A. Ó Cearúil, An Ċláir

CORCAIĠ

v.

CIARRAÍ

Minor—2 p.m. Réiteóir—S. Ó Céirín

CORCAIĠ v. CLÁIR

CLÁR OIFIGIÚIL

6p.

BLAIR DUNCAN. CORK.

4

Clar Oifigiul
S. Mac Cárthaigh
Rúnaí
MUNSTER CHAMPIONSHIP 1961
SENIOR FOOTBALL FINAL REPLAY
Ciarrai v. Corcaig
REITEOIR — A. O CEARUIL, CO. AN CHLAIR
I STAID AN GEARALTAIGH, CILL AIRNE
23 IUIL, 1961 TOSNU 3.30
Luach 3p.
PROCEEDS OF OFFICIAL PROGRAMME
GO TO FITZGERALD STADIUM FUNDS

5

CLAR OIFIGIÚIL
Comairle Ulaḋ C.L.C.G.
ULSTER FOOTBALL FINALS
at Casement Park, Belfast, on Sun., 23rd July, 1961.
SINNSEAR
DÚN V ÁRD MAĊA
AT 3.45 P.M.
Reiteóir : L. Mag Uróin, Muineaċán
MIONUIR
ÁRD MAĊA V MUINEAĊÁN
AT 2.15 P.M.
Reiteóir : S. Ó Loinn, Doire.
LUAĊ - 6p

6

Cluiċí Ceannais Peile na hÉireann
24 Meán Fómair 1961
SINSIR 3.15 P.M.
An Dún v. Ua bFáilí
Clár Oifigiúil
MIONÚIR 1.45 P.M.
Corcaiġ v. Muiġeo
Pádraig Ó Caoimh
Árd-Rúnaí
luaċ 6p

7

Comairle Laiġean
Iomáint 1961
Clár Oifigiúil
CRAOḂ IOMÁNA SINNSIR
16-7-'61.
i gCill Ċoinniġ
(PAIRC UI NUALLÁIN)
ÁṪ CLIAṪ
v.
LOĊ GARMÁN
S. Ó Dubláing (Ua bFáilge). 3.30 p.m.
MIONÚR 2 p.m.: Áṫ Cliaṫ v Ua bFáilge.
Luaċ - 3p
M. Ó Néill
(Rún.)
Patrons, Please Obey the Stewards and Enjoy the Games.

8

9

4 Replay
Kerry 2-13 Cork 1-04

5 Ulster Football Final
Down 2-10 Armagh 1-10

6 All-Ireland Football Final
Down 3-06 Offaly 2-08
Attendance – 90,556

7 Leinster Hurling Final
Dublin 7-05 Wexford 4-08

8 Munster Hurling Final
Tipperary 3-06 Cork 0-07

9 All-Ireland Hurling Final
Tipperary 0-16 Dublin 1-12
Attendance – 67,866

1962

Tipperary and Wexford played each other in the All-Ireland hurling final four times over the course of the 1960s, with each team winning twice. The second instalment, the 1962 final, was a wonderful game as both teams served up a classic. Wexford went two goals down within 80 seconds of the throw-in but, despite that setback, rallied and were level coming up to half-time. However, Tipperary finished stronger and claimed the Liam MacCarthy Cup for the nineteenth time.

If the All-Ireland hurling final was a classic, the football final was the opposite, which was unfortunate as it was the first to be shown live on television. The newspaper headlines proclaimed it a 'dismal' final and, as predicted, Kerry won easily in the face of a disappointing Roscommon. Kerry's captain, Seán Óg Sheehy, in picking up the Sam Maguire Cup, emulated his father, who had also captained Kerry, in 1926 and 1930.

1

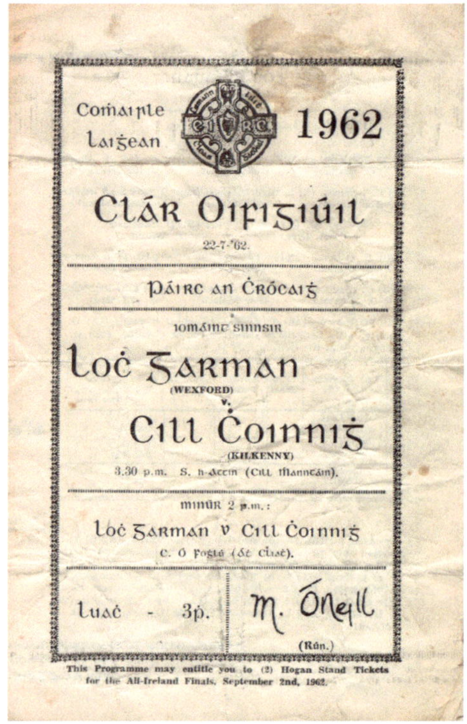

2

1 Leinster Hurling Final
Wexford 3-09 Kilkenny 2-10

2 Munster Hurling Final
Tipperary 5-14 Waterford 2-03

3 All-Ireland Hurling Final
Tipperary 3-10 Wexford 2-11
Attendance – 75,039

3

Cluiċí Ceannais
Iomána na hÉireann
2 Meán Fóṁair 1962
Sinsir 3.15 p.m.
Loċ Garman
v.
Tiobraid Árann
Clár
Oifigiúil
Mionúir 1.45 p.m.
Tiobraid Árann
v.
Cill Ċainniġ
Pádraiġ Ó Caoiṁ
Árd-Rúnaí

4

Cumann Lúit Cleas Gaedeal

G·A·A

Connacht Senior Football Championship Final

GAILLIMH

v.

ROSCOMAIN

IN McHALE PARK, CASTLEBAR

SUNDAY, JULY 22, 1962

Commencing: 4 p.m. :: Referee: M. HIGGINS (Cavan)

PRECEDED BY CONNACHT MINOR FINAL

MHUIGHEO v GAILLIMH

at 2.30 p.m. :: Referee: J. O'CONNOR (Roscommon)

Offical Programme 3d

TELEGRAPH, CASTLEBAR.

4 Connacht Football Final
Roscommon 3-07 Galway 2-09

5 Leinster Football Final
Dublin 2-08 Offaly 1-07

6 Munster Football Final
Kerry 4-08 Cork 0-04

7 Ulster Football Final
Cavan 3-06 Down 0-05

8 All-Ireland Football Final
Kerry 1-12 Roscommon 1-06
Attendance – 75,771

5

Comhairle Laighean
1962
Clár Oifigiúil
15-7-'62.
Páirc an Chrócaigh
Peil Sinnsir:
Ua bhFailí
(OFFALY)
v.
Áth Cliath
(DUBLIN)
Peil Mionúir:
Ua bhFailí v Áth Cliath
Luach - 3p.
(Rún.)

7

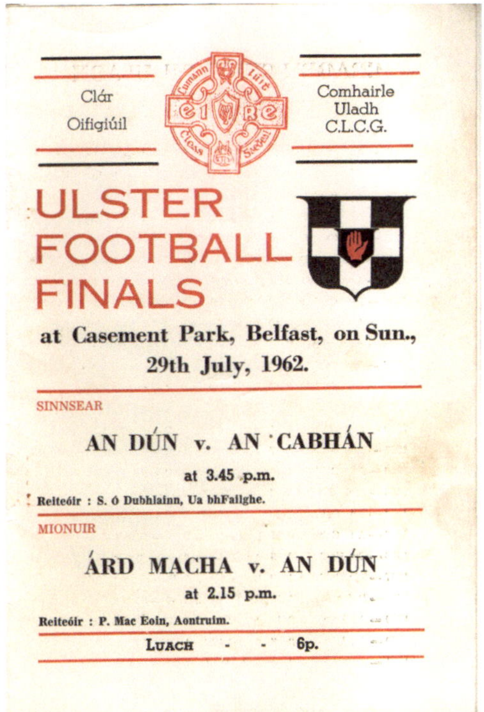

Clár
Oifigiúil
Comhairle
Uladh
C.L.C.G.
ULSTER
FOOTBALL
FINALS
at Casement Park, Belfast, on Sun.,
29th July, 1962.
SINNSEAR
AN DÚN v. AN CABHÁN
at 3.45 p.m.
Reiteóir : S. ó Dubhlainn, Ua bhFailghe.
MIONUIR
ÁRD MACHA v. AN DÚN
at 2.15 p.m.
Reiteóir : P. Mac Eoin, Aontruim.
LUACH - - 6p.

6

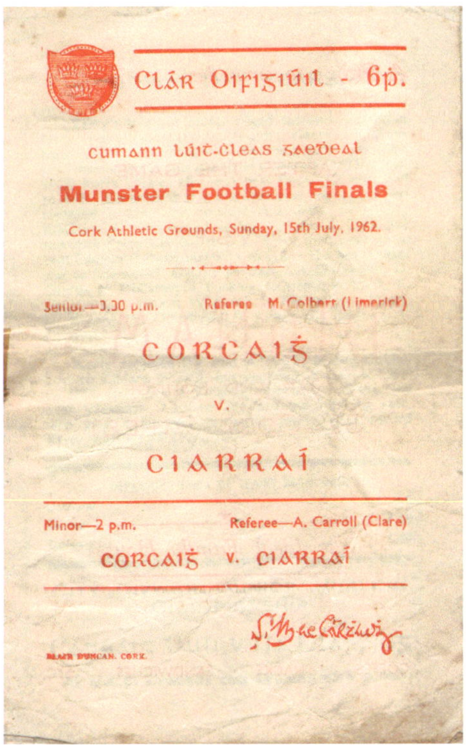

Clár Oifigiúil - 6p.
Cumann Lúith-Chleas Gaedheal
Munster Football Finals
Cork Athletic Grounds, Sunday, 15th July, 1962.
Senior—3.30 p.m.
Referee M. Colbert (Limerick)
CORCAIGH
v.
CIARRAÍ
Minor—2 p.m.
Referee—A. Carroll (Clare)
CORCAIGH v. CIARRAÍ

8

Cluichí Ceannais
Peile na hÉireann
23 Meán Fómhair 1962
Sinsir 3.15 p.m.
Ciarraí
v.
Ros Comáin
Clár
Oifigiúil
Mionúir 1.45 p.m.
Ciarraí
v.
Muigheo
Árd-Rúnaí

1963

The Tipperary–Wexford tussles of the 1960s captured the public's imagination but another local rivalry also sparked intense interest. The 1963 All-Ireland hurling final brought Waterford and Kilkenny together again for the third time in seven years. Kilkenny had taken the honours in 1957, while Waterford avenged that defeat in the 1959 final. This year, a high-scoring and entertaining final produced 35 scores in all. Out of that total, Kilkenny's Eddie Keher amassed 14 points to help propel his county to victory. Waterford's appearance in the final was to be their last until 2008, when they would again meet a Kilkenny team at the height of its powers.

Dublin defeated Galway in the All-Ireland football final of 1963. The team was captained by Des Foley, who five years previously had captained the Dublin minor team when they defeated Mayo in the final.

1

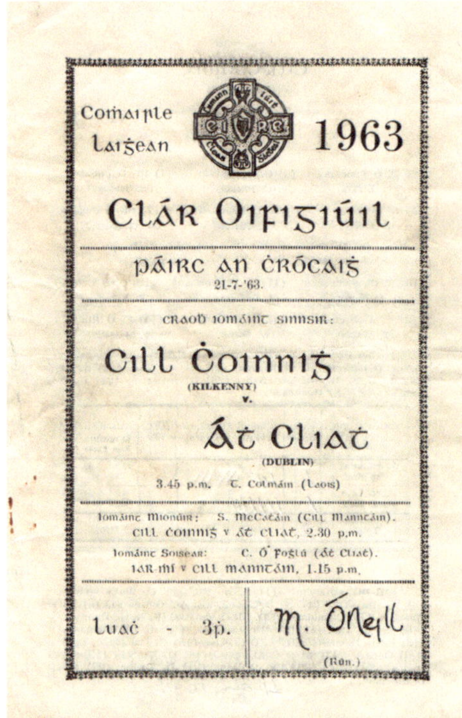

2

1 Leinster Hurling Final
Kilkenny 2-10 Dublin 0-09

2 Munster Hurling Final
Waterford 0-11 Tipperary 0-08

3 All-Ireland Hurling Final
Kilkenny 4-17 Waterford 6-08
Attendance – 73,123

Cluiċí Ceannais Iomána na hÉireann

1 Meán Fóṁair 1963

SINSIR 3.15 P.M.

Cill Ċainniġ
v.
Port Láirge

Clár Oifigiúil

MIONÚIR 1.45 P.M.

Loċ Garman
v.
Luimneaċ

Luaċ 6p

Pádraig Ó Caoimh
Árd-Rúnaí

4

Cumann Lúit Cleas Gaedeal

G.A.A.

Clár Oifigiúil

Minor Football Semi-Final

Roscomáin v Liathdruim

2.45 :: Referee: P. Geraghty (Galway)

Connaught Senior Football Championship Final

Liaṫdruim v Gaillim

4 p.m. :: Referee: Dr. M. Loftus (Mayo)

Junior Hurling Semi-Final

Roscomáin v Muigheo

5.30 :: Referee: J. Duggan (Galway)

— at —

McHALE PARK, CASTLEBAR

Sunday, July 14th, 1963

LUACH : : : : 3d.

CONNAUGHT TELEGRAPH, PRINTERS, CASTLEBAR

5

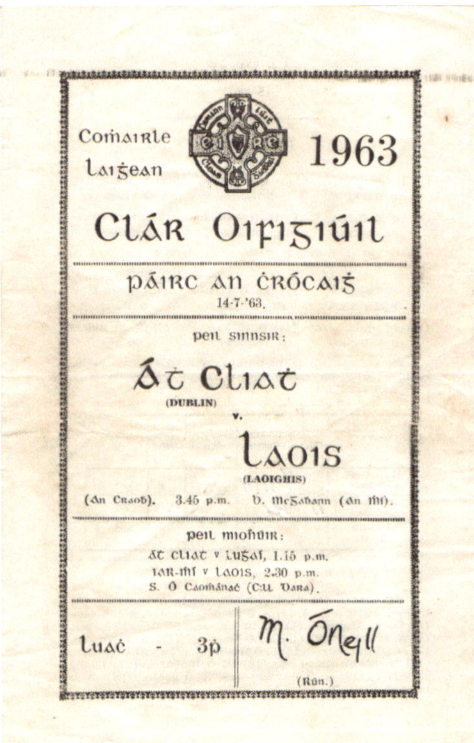
Coṁairle Laiġean 1963

Clár Oifiġiúil

Páirc an Ċrócaiġ

14-7-'63.

Peil Sinnsir:

Át Cliat (DUBLIN)

v.

Laois (LAOIGHIS)

(An Craob). 3.45 p.m. D. McGabann (An Mí).

Peil Mionúir:

Át Cliat v Luġaí, 1.15 p.m.

Iar-Mí v Laois, 2.30 p.m.

S. Ó Caoṁánaċ (Cill Dara).

Luaċ - 3p

(Rún.)

6

C.L.C.G.

Clár

MUNSTER FOOTBALL FINAL

at Fitzgerald Stadium, Killarney

on Sunday, 14th July, 1963

SENIOR

KERRY v. CORK

TOSNU 3.30 p.m. MOLTOIR: J. MARTIN (Roscommon)

A Nation mutilated;
A People's will defied;

A puppet State created
And Democracy denied!

LEST WE FORGET

MINOR

CORK v. KERRY

TOSNU 2 p.m. MOLTOIR: D. WHITE (Clare)

LUACH - - - - - - - - - - - - - 6p.

7

Clár Oifigiúil

Comhairle Uladh C.L.C.G.

ULSTER FOOTBALL FINALS

BREFFNI PARK, CAVAN

ON SUNDAY, 28th JULY, 1963

SINNSEAR:

Dún na nGall v. an Dún

at 3.45 p.m.

Reiteóir: S. O Mairtin, Tír Eoghain.

MIONUIR:

An Dún v. Dún na nGall

at 2.15 p.m.

Reiteóir: L. Mag Uidhir, Muineachan.

LUACH - - 6p.

The Anglo-Celt Ltd., Cavan

8

4 Connacht Football Final
Galway 4-11 Leitrim 1-06

5 Leinster Football Final
Dublin 2-11 Laois 2-09

6 Munster Football Final
Kerry 1-18 Cork 3-07

7 Ulster Football Final
Down 2-11 Donegal 1-04

8 All-Ireland Football Final
Dublin 1-09 Galway 0-10
Attendance – 87,106

1964

The All-Ireland hurling final programme cover of 1964 is unusual in that it does not feature the signature of the Ard Stiúrthóir of the GAA. Seán Ó Síocháin replaced Pádraig Ó Caoimh as Ard Stiúrthóir following Ó Caoimh's death in May 1964. His appointment on 28 August 1964 came too late for his signature to be added to the All-Ireland hurling final programme. However, his signature appears on the cover of the All-Ireland football final programme of that year.

In 1964, the Galway football team were on the cusp of achieving a feat which only a few counties before them had managed – winning three All-Ireland titles in a row. In 1964, they defeated Mayo in the Connacht final to retain the title that they had won the previous year and, meeting Kerry in the All-Ireland final, were determined to atone for their defeat to Dublin in the 1963 final. Galway enjoyed a five-point victory over Kerry, but the joy of captain John Donnellan was short-lived as he discovered that his father Mick had died while watching the match in the stand. Mick had captained Galway in the 1933 final.

1

2

1 Connacht Football Final
Galway 2-12 Mayo 1-05

2 Leinster Football Final
Meath 2-12 Dublin 1-07

3 Munster Football Final
Kerry 2-11 Cork 1-08

3

Clár Oifigiúil - 6p.

Cumann Lúiṫ-Ċleas Gaeḋeal

Munster Football Finals

Cork Athletic Grounds, Sunday, 19th July, 1964.

Senior—3.30 p.m. Referee—J. Martin (Roscommon)

CORCAIĠ

v.

CIARRAÍ

Minor—2 p.m. Referee—J. Kerins (Tralee)

CORCAIĠ v. AN ĊLÁR

BLAIR DUNCAN, CORK.

4

Clár Oifigiúil

Comhairle Uladh C.L.C.G.

ULSTER FOOTBALL FINALS

CASEMENT PARK, BELFAST

ON SUNDAY, 19th JULY, 1964

SINNSEAR:

An Dún v. An Cabán

at 3.45 p.m.

Reiteóir: Liam MagUidhir, Múineachán

MIONUIR:

Aontruim v. An Cabán

at 2.15 p.m.

Reiteóir: S. O Mairtin, Tír Eoghain

LUACH - 6p.

4 Ulster Football Final
Cavan 2-10 Down 1-10

5 All-Ireland Football Final
Galway 0-15 Kerry 0-10
Attendance – 76,498

6 Leinster Hurling Final
Kilkenny 4-11 Dublin 1-08

7 Munster Hurling Final
Tipperary 3-13 Cork 1-05

8 All-Ireland Hurling Final
Tipperary 5-13 Kilkenny 2-08
Attendance – 71,282

5

Cluiċí Ceannais
Peile na hÉireann
27 Meán Fómhair 1964
Sinsir 3.15 p.m.
Ciarraí
v.
Gaillimh
Clár
Oifigiúil
Mionúir 1.45 p.m.
Corcaiġ
v.
Ua bFáilí
Seán Ó Síocháin
Ard-Rúnaí
Luaċ
6p

6

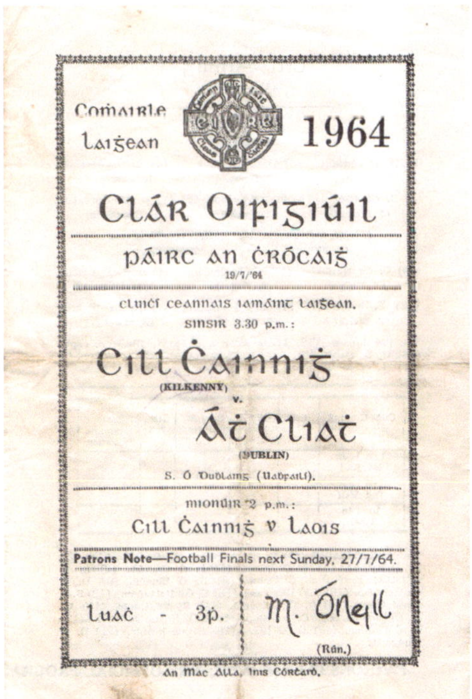
Comhairle
Laiġean
1964
Clár Oifiġiúil
Páirc an Ċrócaiġ
19/7/'64
Cluiċí Ceannais Iomáint Laiġean.
Sinsir 3.30 p.m.:
Cill Ċainniġ
(KILKENNY)
v.
Áṫ Cliaṫ
(DUBLIN)
S. Ó Dubláing (Uabfailí).
Mionúir 2 p.m.:
Cill Ċainniġ v Laois
Patrons Note—Football Finals next Sunday, 27/7/64.
Luaċ - 3p.
M. Ó Néill
(Rún.)
An Mac Alla, Inis Córṫaiḋ.

7

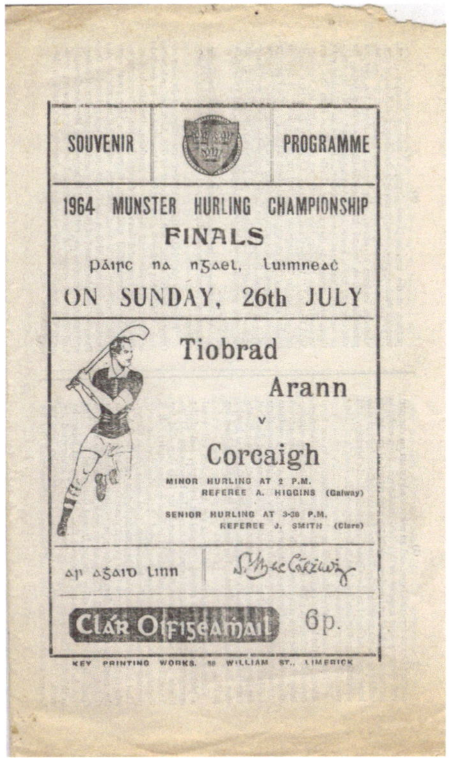
SOUVENIR
PROGRAMME
1964 MUNSTER HURLING CHAMPIONSHIP
FINALS
Páirc na nGael, Luimneaċ
ON SUNDAY, 26th JULY
Tiobrad
Arann
v
Corcaigh
MINOR HURLING AT 2 P.M.
REFEREE A. HIGGINS (Galway)
SENIOR HURLING AT 3-30 P.M.
REFEREE J. SMITH (Clare)
Ar agaiḋ linn
Clár Oifiseamail
6p.
KEY PRINTING WORKS, 38 WILLIAM ST., LIMERICK

8

Cluiċí Ceannais
Iomána na hÉireann
6 Meán Fómhair 1964
Sinsir 3.15 p.m.
Cill Ċainniġ
v.
Tiobraid Árann
Clár
Oifigiúil
Mionúir 1.45 p.m.
Corcaiġ
v.
Laois
Luaċ
6p

1965

The All-Ireland final match programmes for 1965 saw a larger format publication with colour photographs on the cover. They also began an era of noticeable improvements in the production quality of the programme.

In the All-Ireland football final, Galway and Kerry met for the second year in a row and, with Galway also having beaten Kerry in the 1963 semi-final, the scene was set for an epic battle. It did not materialise, though, as the game was a disappointment. It mattered little to Galway as they lifted the cup for the second consecutive year. Tipperary played Wexford in the All-Ireland hurling final, the third instalment in the saga between the teams in the 1960s. Tipperary were the victors on this occasion, allowing John Doyle to collect his eighth All-Ireland medal, equalling the record set by Christy Ring in 1956. Jimmy Doyle picked up the Liam MacCarthy Cup, having missed out on the honour through injury in 1962.

1

2

1 Connacht Football Final
Galway 1-12 Sligo 2-06

2 Leinster Football Final
Dublin 3-06 Longford 0-09

3 Munster Football Final
Kerry 2-16 Limerick 2-07

3

Souvenir Programme

1965 MUNSTER FOOTBALL CHAMPIONSHIPS

FINALS

Pairc na nGael, Luimneach

On Sunday, 18th July, 1965

Minor Football
at 2 p.m.

Corcaiġ
v.
Ciarraí

Referee
Denis O'Connell,

Sonior Football
at 3-30 p.m.

Ciarraí
v.
Luimneaċ

John Dowling, Offaly
Referee

Clár Oifiġeaṁail 6p

Ar aġaiḋ linn

Printed by Key Printing Works, Limerick

4

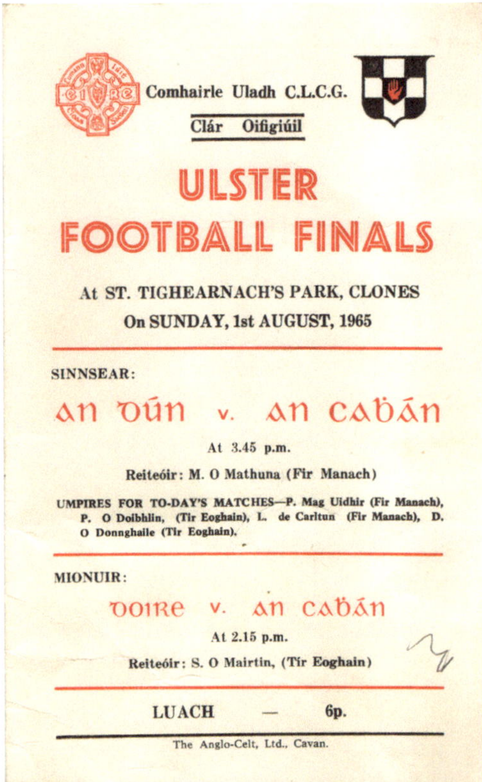

Comhairle Uladh C.L.C.G.

Clár Oifigiúil

ULSTER FOOTBALL FINALS

At ST. TIGHEARNACH'S PARK, CLONES
On SUNDAY, 1st AUGUST, 1965

SINNSEAR:

An Dún v. An Cabhán

At 3.45 p.m.

Reiteóir: M. O Mathuna (Fir Manach)

UMPIRES FOR TO-DAY'S MATCHES—P. Mag Uidhir (Fir Manach), P. O Doibhlin, (Tir Eoghain), L. de Carltun (Fir Manach), D. O Donnghaile (Tir Eoghain).

MIONUIR:

Doire v. An Cabhán

At 2.15 p.m.

Reiteóir: S. O Mairtin, (Tír Eoghain)

LUACH — 6p.

The Anglo-Celt, Ltd., Cavan.

5

Cluichí Ceannais Peile na hÉireann

26 Meán Fómhair 1965

Sinsir 3.15 p.m.

Ciarraí v. Gaillimh

OFFICIAL PROGRAMME

Mionúir 1.45 p.m.

Ciarraí v. Doire

Luach 1/-

Seán Ó Síocháin
Ard-Rúnaí

6

Comhairle Laighean 1965

Clár Oifigiúil

Páirc an Chrócaigh, 1-8-'65.

Craobh Iomána Sinsir:

Cill Choinnigh ((KILKENNY))

v.

Loch Garman (WEXFORD)

S. de Grae (Át Cliat).

Craobh Mionúir:

Át Cliat v Loch Garman

P. Ó Bogaig (Cill Coinnig)

Note—8/8/'65: Next Sunday's Fixtures Pairc an Chrócaigh—All-Ireland Senior Football Semi-final Kerry v. Dublin, Minor Football Semi-final Kerry v. Offaly.

Luach - 3p. | M. Ó Néill (Rún.)

An Mac Alla, Inis Córtaid.

7

Souvenir Programme

1965 MUNSTER HURLING CHAMPIONSHIPS FINALS

Pairc na nGael, Luimneach
On Sunday, 25th July, 1965

Minor Hurling at 2 p.m.

Tiobrad Árann
v.
Luimneach

Referee M. Hayes, Clare

Senior Hurling at 3-30 p.m.

Corcaigh
v.
Tiobrad Árann

Referee J. Smith, Clare

Clár Oifigeamhail 6p

Ar Aghaidh Linn | S. Mac Cárthaigh

Printed by Key Printing Works, Limerick

8

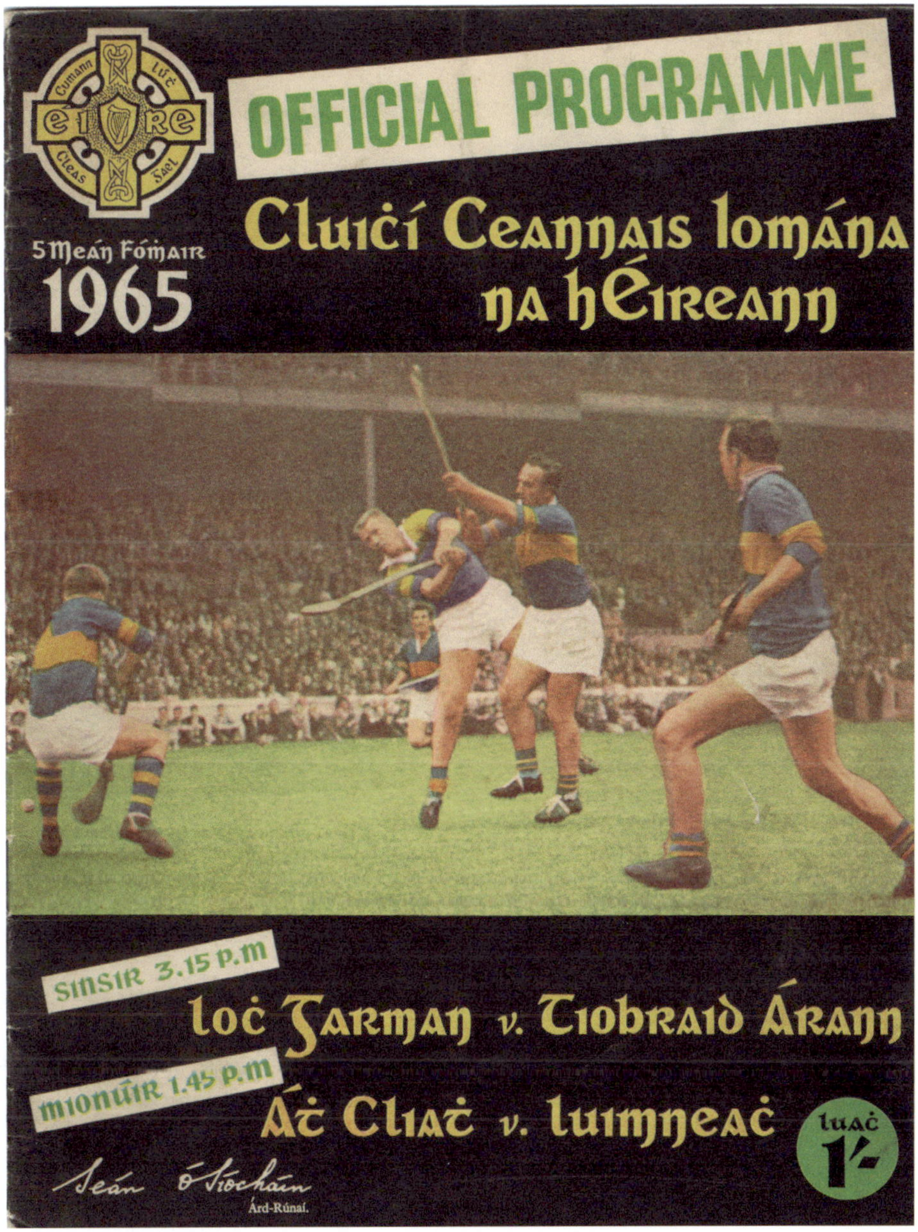

4 Ulster Football Final
Down 3-05 Cavan 1-08

5 All-Ireland Football Final
Galway 0-12 Kerry 0-09
Attendance – 77,735

6 Leinster Hurling Final
Wexford 2-11 Kilkenny 3-07

7 Munster Hurling Final
Tipperary 4-11 Cork 0-05

8 All-Ireland Hurling Final
Tipperary 2-16 Wexford 0-10
Attendance – 67,498

1966

Television coverage of matches was now more common and increased the popularity of Gaelic games by bringing them to a wider audience. The 1966 Ulster final between Down and Donegal was the first to be shown live by the BBC, with Down progressing to face the Leinster champions, Meath, in the All-Ireland semi-final. In the other semi-final, Galway, having won the Connacht championship for the fourth consecutive year, came up against Cork. A Galway victory allowed them to advance to the All-Ireland football final, in search of the three in a row, where they would face a strongly fancied Meath team. By beating Meath 1-10 to 0-07, Galway achieved a famous milestone, which was all the more impressive for not conceding a goal in any of the three finals.

The All-Ireland hurling final was contested by Cork and Kilkenny, with Cork coming out on top. 1966 was the last year when both All-Ireland finals were refereed by the same man, Jimmy Hatton from Wicklow.

1

2

1 Connacht Football Final
Galway 0-12 Mayo 1-08

2 Leinster Football Final
Meath 1-09 Kildare 1-08

3 Munster Football Final
Cork 2-07 Kerry 1-07

Cumann Luith-Chleas Gael

Clar Oifigiul

S. MacCárthaigh
Rúnaí.

MUNSTER FOOTBALL FINALS

CILL AIRNE (FITZGERALD STADIUM)

DE DOMHNAIGH, 17th JULY, 1966

MIONUIRI :

CORCAIGH v. CIARRAI

2.00 p.m. J. MOLONEY (Tipperary)

SINNSIR :

CORCAIGH v. CIARRAI

3.30 p.m. J. MARTIN (Roscommon)

Luach 6d.

PROCEEDS OF OFFICIAL PROGRAMME GO TO FITZGERALD STADIUM FUNDS

KILLARNEY PW

4

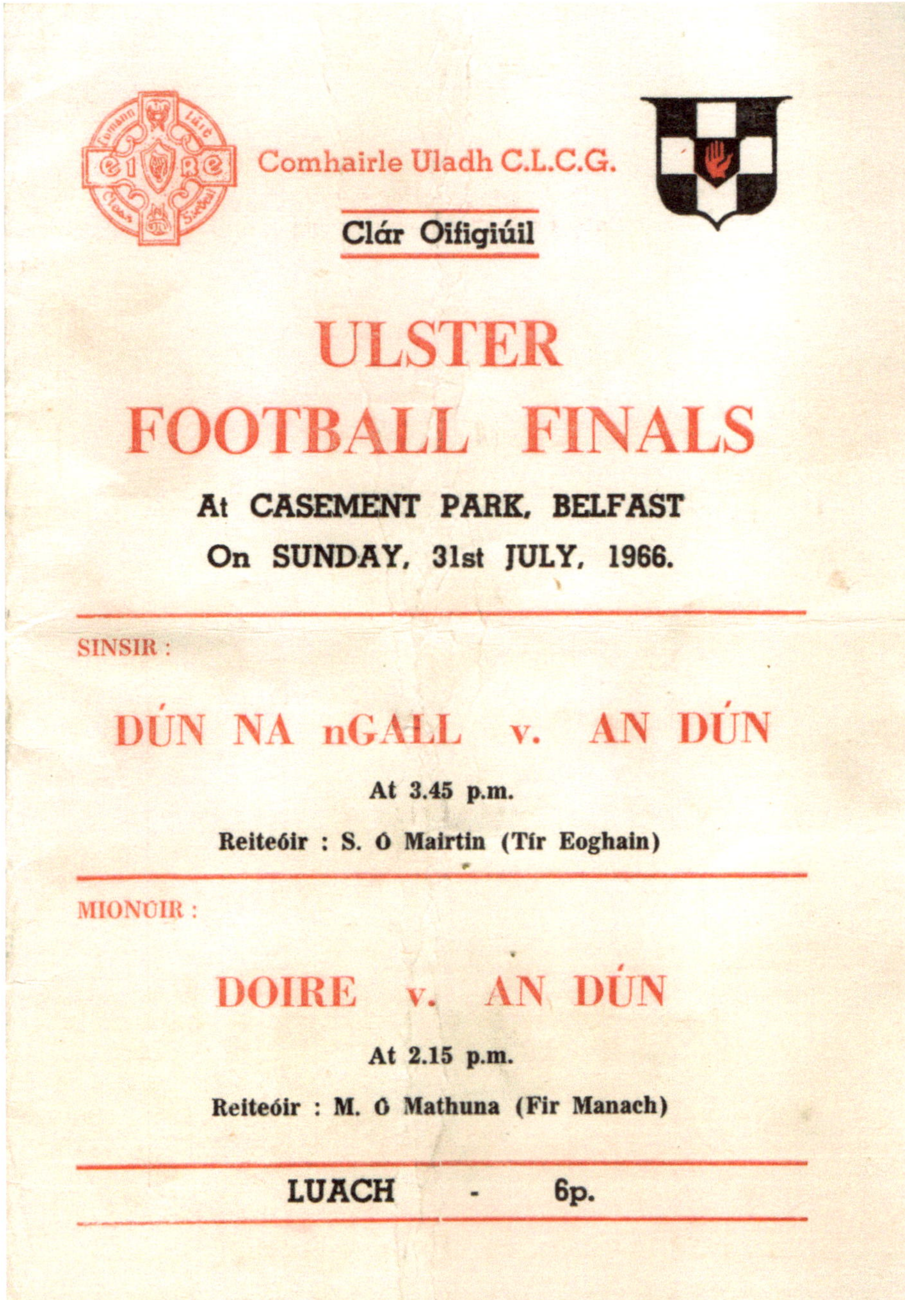

Comhairle Uladh C.L.C.G.

Clár Oifigiúil

ULSTER

FOOTBALL FINALS

At CASEMENT PARK, BELFAST

On SUNDAY, 31st JULY, 1966.

SINSIR :

DÚN NA nGALL v. AN DÚN

At 3.45 p.m.

Reiteóir : S. Ó Mairtin (Tír Eoghain)

MIONÚIR :

DOIRE v. AN DÚN

At 2.15 p.m.

Reiteóir : M. Ó Mathuna (Fir Manach)

LUACH - 6p.

4 Ulster Football Final
Down 1-07 Donegal 0-08

5 All-Ireland Football Final
Galway 1-10 Meath 0-07
Attendance – 71,569

6 Leinster Hurling Final
Kilkenny 1-15 Wexford 2-06

7 Munster Hurling Final
Cork 4-09 Waterford 2-09

8 All-Ireland Hurling Final
Cork 3-09 Kilkenny 1-10
Attendance – 68,249

5

CLUICHÍ CEANNAIS
PEILE na hÉIREANN
25 Meán Fómhair 1966
MIONÚIR 1. 45
SINSIR 3. 15
LUACH
1/-
OFFICIAL PROGRAMME
Seán Ó Síocháin

6

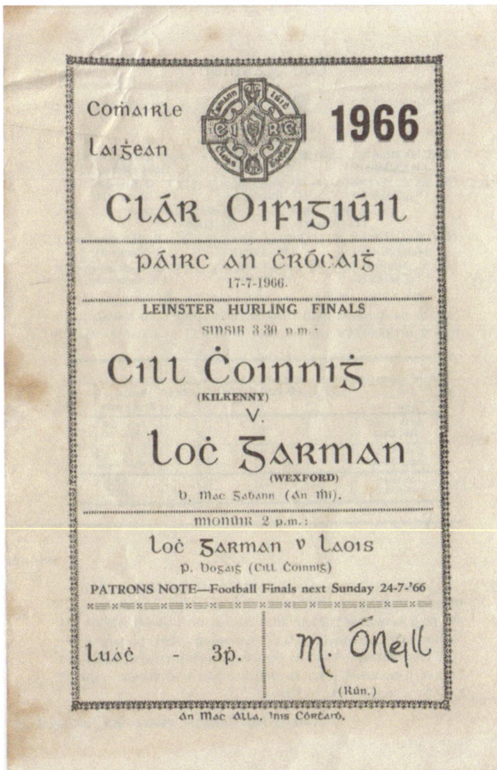
Comhairle
Laighean
1966
Clár Oifigiúil
Páirc an Chrócaigh
17-7-1966.
LEINSTER HURLING FINALS
Cill Choinnigh
(KILKENNY)
V.
Loch Garman
(WEXFORD)
Loch Garman v Laois
PATRONS NOTE—Football Finals next Sunday 24-7-'66
Luach - 3p.
M. Ó Néill
(Rún.)

7

Souvenir
Programme
MUNSTER HURLING CHAMPIONSHIP FINALS
Pairc na nGael, Luimneach
On Sunday, 24th July, 1966
Minor Hurling at 2 p.m.
CORK
v.
GALWAY
Referee M. Hayes, Clare
Senior Hurling at 3-30 p.m.
WATERFORD
v.
CORK
Referee G. Fitzgerald, Limerick
Clár Oifigeamail
6p.
KEY PRINTING WORKS, 56 WILLIAM ST., LIMERICK

8

CLUICHÍ CEANNAIS
IOMÁNA na hÉIREANN
4 Meán Fómhair 1966
MIONÚIR 1.45 P.M.
SINSIR 3.15 P.M.
LUACH
1/-
Seán Ó Síocháin
ÁRD RÚNAÍ
OFFICIAL PROGRAMME

1967

Having won the All-Ireland hurling final in 1966, Cork fancied their chances as the 1967 Munster championship approached. However, their Munster and All-Ireland titles were relinquished in the first round after a defeat by Waterford. They, in turn, were beaten by Tipperary, who went on to inflict a heavy defeat on Clare in the Munster final.

In Leinster, Kilkenny had a facile victory over Dublin and qualified to play Wexford in the Leinster final for the third year in a row – which, apart from a break in 1969, would continue to be the provincial final pairing until the end of the 1970s. Kilkenny prevailed to set up a highly anticipated All-Ireland final against Tipperary. A younger Kilkenny team proved too strong for their opponents, beating Tipperary in the final for the first time since 1922. In the process, they deprived John Doyle of a ninth All-Ireland medal in his last appearance for Tipperary.

1

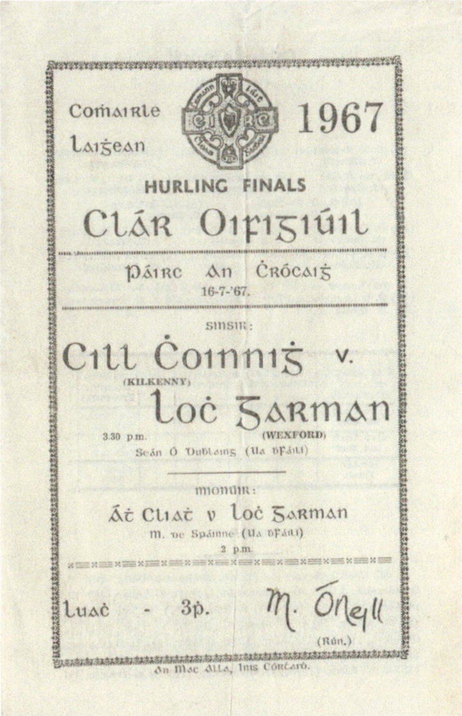

Coṁairle Laiġean 1967

HURLING FINALS

Clár Oifigiúil

Páirc An Ċrócaiġ
16-7-'67.

Sinsir:

Cill Ċoinniġ v. Loċ Garman
(KILKENNY) (WEXFORD)
3.30 p.m.
Seán Ó Dublaing (Ua bFáili)

Mionúir:

Áṫ Cliaṫ v Loċ Garman
M. de Spáinne (Ua bFáili)
2 p.m.

Luaċ - 3p. M. Ó Néill (Rún.)

An Mac Alla, Inis Córṫaidh.

2

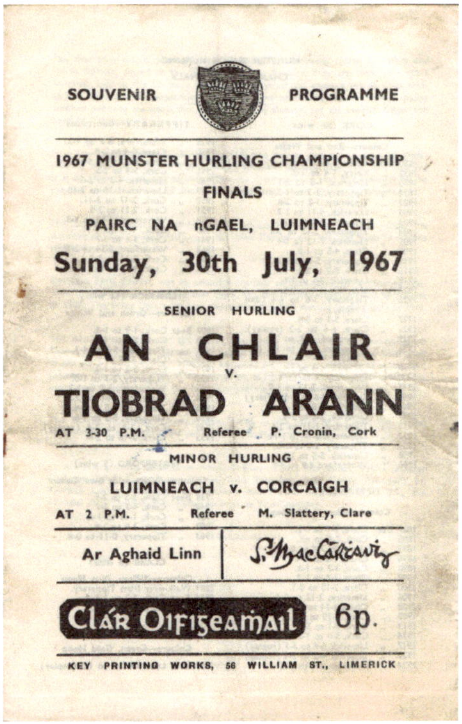

SOUVENIR PROGRAMME

1967 MUNSTER HURLING CHAMPIONSHIP FINALS

PAIRC NA nGAEL, LUIMNEACH

Sunday, 30th July, 1967

SENIOR HURLING

AN CHLAIR v. TIOBRAD ARANN

AT 3-30 P.M. Referee P. Cronin, Cork

MINOR HURLING

LUIMNEACH v. CORCAIGH

AT 2 P.M. Referee M. Slattery, Clare

Ar Aghaid Linn S. Mac Cárṫaiġ

Clár Oifigeaṁail 6p.

KEY PRINTING WORKS, 56 WILLIAM ST., LIMERICK

1 Leinster Hurling Final
Kilkenny 4-10 Wexford 1-12

2 Munster Hurling Final
Tipperary 4-12 Clare 2-06

3 All-Ireland Hurling Final
Kilkenny 3-08 Tipperary 2-07
Attendance – 64,241

CLUICHÍ CEANNAIS IOMÁNA

3

MIONÚIR
1.45

SINSIR
3.15

1/-

OFFICIAL PROGRAMME

Seán Ó Síocháin
ARD-RÚNAÍ

4

Connacht Senior Football Final
MAYO
v.
LEITRIM
at 4 p.m.
Referee: J. HATTON (Wicklow)
PRECEDED BY
Connacht Minor Football Semi-Final
MAYO v. GALWAY
at 2.30 p.m.
Ref.: P. O'CONNOR (Roscommon)
TUAM STADIUM
Sunday, July 16th, 1967
Programme
6d

6

CLAR OIFIGIUIL - 6ph.
CUMANN LUTH-CHLEAS GAEL
Munster Championships Finals
Peil Sinsir—3.30 p.m.
CORCAIGH
v
CIARRAI
Peil Mhionur—2 p.m.
CORCAIGH
v
CIARRAI
CORK ATHLETIC GROUNDS
SUNDAY, 16th JULY, 1967
Hickey & Byrne, Cork

5

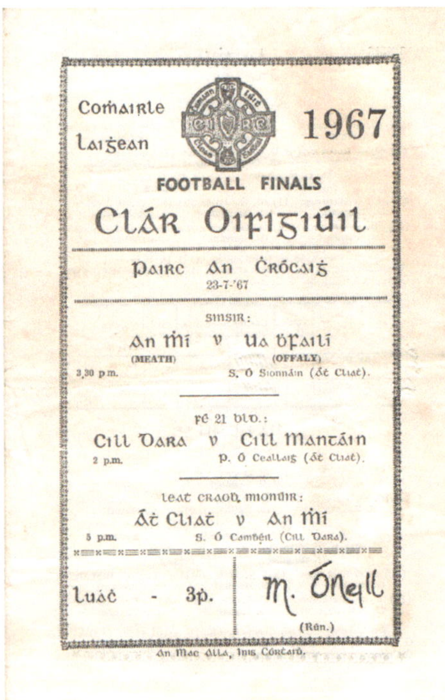
Coṁairle Laiġean
1967
FOOTBALL FINALS
Clár Oifiġiúil
Páirc An Ċrócaiġ
23-7-'67
SINSIR:
An Ṁí v Ua bFailí
(MEATH) (OFFALY)
3.30 p.m. S. Ó Sionnáin (Áṫ Cliaṫ).
FÉ 21 BLD.:
Cill Dara v Cill Mantáin
2 p.m. P. Ó Ceallaiġ (Áṫ Cliaṫ).
Leaṫ Ċraoḃ Mionúir:
Áṫ Cliaṫ v An Ṁí
5 p.m. S. Ó Caoiṁ (Cill Dara).
Luaċ - 3p.
(Rún.)
An Mac Alla, Inis Córṫaiḋ.

7

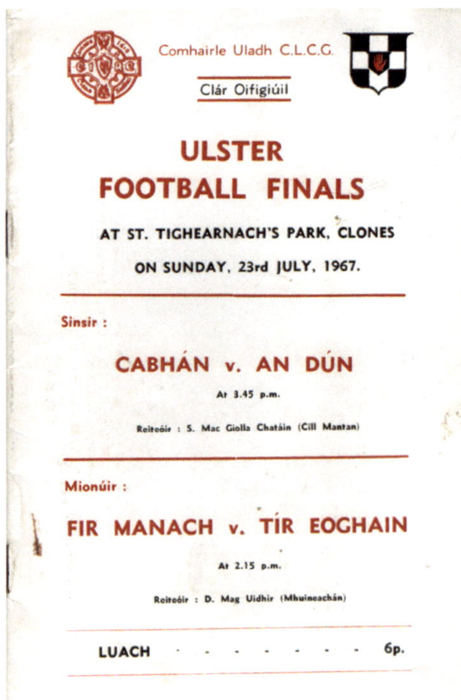
Comhairle Uladh C.L.C.G.
Clár Oifigiúil
ULSTER FOOTBALL FINALS
AT ST. TIGHEARNACH'S PARK, CLONES
ON SUNDAY, 23rd JULY, 1967.
Sinsir :
CABHÁN v. AN DÚN
At 3.45 p.m.
Reiteóir : S. Mac Giolla Chatáin (Cill Mantan)
Mionúir :
FIR MANACH v. TÍR EOGHAIN
At 2.15 p.m.
Reiteóir : D. Mag Uidhir (Mhuineachán)
LUACH - - - - - - - 6p.

8

4 Connacht Football Final
Mayo 4-15 Leitrim 0-07

5 Leinster Football Final
Meath 0-08 Offaly 0-06

6 Munster Football Final
Cork 0-08 Kerry 0-07

7 Ulster Football Final
Cavan 2-12 Down 0-08

8 All-Ireland Football Final
Meath 1-09 Cork 0-09
Attendance – 70,343

1968

The Leinster football championship of 1968 saw the novel pairing of Longford and Laois reach the provincial decider. Longford had overcome a disappointing Dublin outfit in the quarter-final before seeing off the All-Ireland champions, Meath, in the semi-final. Laois came through the other side of the draw to face Longford in the final, but they were no match for them as Longford claimed their first Leinster title. A brilliant Munster football final in Killarney saw Mick O'Connell and Mick O'Dwyer back in the Kerry team to thwart Cork's hopes of a third Munster championship in a row. In the end, though, it was the Ulster champions, Down, who ended up lifting the Sam Maguire Cup this year, defeating Kerry in the final.

The 1968 All-Ireland hurling final brought Wexford and Tipperary into opposition again. In a tremendous match, Tipperary had a commanding lead at half-time after controlling the opening 30 minutes. However, a second-half comeback, in which Wexford scored four goals and five points, was enough to give them a two-point victory and their fifth All-Ireland title.

1

2

1 Connacht Football Final
Galway 2-10 Mayo 2-09

2 Leinster Football Final
Longford 3-09 Laois 1-04

3 Munster Football Final
Kerry 1-21 Cork 3-08

3

CUMANN LUITH CHLEAS GAEL

KERRY V. CORK

THE LATE DICK FITZGERALD

MUNSTER
FOOTBALL
FINALS

FITZGERALD STADIUM, KILLARNEY

SUNDAY, 14th JULY, 1968

Senior
Cork v. Kerry
at 3.30 p.m.
Ref: J. Dowling
Offaly

Minor
Cork v. Kerry
Ref: D. O'Connell
Tipperary
at 2 p.m.

ADMISSION 4/-
SIDELINE
1/- EXTRA

CLAR OIFIGIUIL | OFFICIAL PROGRAMME 6d.

PROCEEDS IN AID OF FITZGERALD STADIUM

4

Comhairle Uladh C.L.C.G.

Clár Oifigiúil

ULSTER FOOTBALL FINALS

AT CASEMENT PARK, BELFAST
ON SUNDAY, 28th JULY, 1968

Sinsir :

CABHÁN v. AN DÚN

at 3.45 p.m.

Reiteóir : Dr. M. de Lochtus (Muigheo)

Mionúir :

ÁRD MACHA v. DOIRE

at 2.15 p.m.

Reiteóir : F. O Grianna (Aontruim)

INVITATION MILE RACE UNDER AUSPICES OF
CASEMENT ATHLETIC CLUB
(At interval — Senior Final)

Luach - - - - - - 6p.

4 Ulster Football Final
Down 0-16 Cavan 1-08

5 All-Ireland Football Final
Down 2-12 Kerry 1-13
Attendance – 71,294

6 Leinster Hurling Final
Wexford 3-13 Kilkenny 4-09

7 Munster Hurling Final
Tipperary 2-13 Cork 1-07

8 All-Ireland Hurling Final
Wexford 5-08 Tipperary 3-12
Attendance – 63,461

5

CLUICHÍ CEANNAIS
PEILE na hÉIREANN
PÁIRC AN CHRÓCAIGH
22-9-'68
MIONÚIR
1.30 p.m.
SINSIR
3.15 p.m.
S. Ó LEANNÁIN (An Dún)
P. Ó GRÍOFA (Ciarraí)
A. Mac RISTEAIRD (Sligeach)
D. Ó hEATHÍRN (Corcaigh)
LUACH 1/-
OFFICIAL PROGRAMME

6

Comhairle Laiġean
1968
Clár Oifigiúil
Páirc an Ċrócaiġ
14-7-'68.
Iomáint Sinsir 3.30 p.m.:
Cill Ċainniġ
(KILKENNY)
v
Loċ Garman
(WEXFORD)
S. Ó Dubhlaing (Ua bFáilí)
Iomáint Mionúir 2 p.m.:
Cill Ċainniġ v Loċ Garman
D. de Stáic (Laois).
Luaċ - 3p.
(Rún.)
An Mac Alla, Inis Córṫaiḋ.

7

SOUVENIR
PROGRAMME
1968 Munster Hurling Championships
PAIRC NA nGAEL, LUIMNEACH
Sunday, 21st July, 1968
SENIOR HURLING FINAL
TIOBRAD ARANN
v.
CORCAIGH
AT 3-30 P.M.
Referee M. SLATTERY, Clare
MINOR HURLING FINAL
Port Lairge v. Corcaigh
AT 2 P.M.
Referee S. O'CONNOR, Limerick
Clár Oifigeamail 6d.
AR AGHAID LINN
Key Printing Works, Limerick

8

CLUICHÍ CEANNAIS
IOMÁNA na hÉIREANN
PÁIRC AN CHRÓCAIGH
1-9-1968
MIONÚIR
1.30 p.m.
SINSIR
3.15 p.m.
M. de RÓISTE (Tiobraid Árann)
D. Ó COIGLIGH (Loch Garman)
T. Ó BROIN (Loch Garman)
D. Mac CÁRTHAIGH (Corcaigh)
LUACH 1/-
OFFICIAL PROGRAMME

1969

As the end of the decade approached, the All-Ireland final match programme covers now featured a distinctive design with the photographs of the four team captains, minor and senior, on a yellow background. Two years previously, in 1967, the names of the match referee and umpires had been added to the centre page containing the team lineouts, and the programme usually had 36 pages now.

In 1969, a new rivalry was forged between Kerry and Offaly that would grow in intensity over the coming years, culminating in the famous 1982 All-Ireland final. With Kerry having beaten Offaly by 12 points in the National League final that spring, a Kerry win was predicted in the All-Ireland final. The margin of victory was considerably less, but Kerry, with the influential Mick O'Connell at midfield, still did enough to win the county's twenty-first All-Ireland title.

1

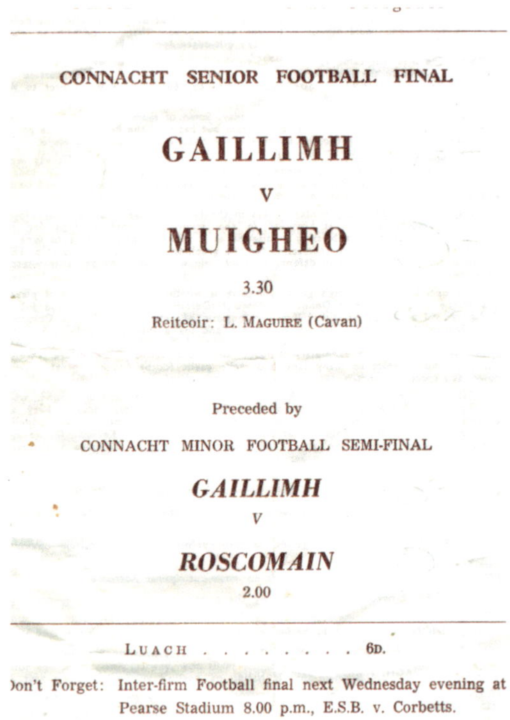

CONNACHT SENIOR FOOTBALL FINAL

GAILLIMH

v

MUIGHEO

3.30

Reiteoir: L. Maguire (Cavan)

Preceded by

CONNACHT MINOR FOOTBALL SEMI-FINAL

GAILLIMH

v

ROSCOMAIN

2.00

Luach . . . . 6d.

)on't Forget: Inter-firm Football final next Wednesday evening at Pearse Stadium 8.00 p.m., E.S.B. v. Corbetts.

2

(Official Programme)

CONNACHT SENIOR FOOTBALL FINAL

GAILLIMH

v

MHUIGHEO

Time: 4 p.m. — Referee: S. Moloney (Tipperary)

SUNDAY, AUGUST 3, 1969

at MacHALE PARK, CASTLEBAR

Preceded by

Connacht Minor Football Final

GAILLIMH

v

MHUIGHEO

Time: 2.30 p.m. — Referee: P. Lang (Sligo)

1 Connacht Football Final
Mayo 0-11 Galway 1-08

2 Replay
Mayo 1-11 Galway 1-08

3 Leinster Football Final
Offaly 3-07 Kildare 1-08

Coṁairle Laiġean

1969

Clár Oifigiúil

Páirc an Ċrócaiġ

27-7-69.

Peil Sinsir (An Craoḃ):

Ua bFáilí v.

(OFFALY) 3.15 p.m.

Cill Dara

(KILDARE)

D. Ó h-Eiḋáin (Ceaṫarlaċ)

Peil Mionúir (An Leaṫ-Craoḃ):

Ua bFáilí v. **Loċ Garman**

1.45 p.m. P. Ó Ceallaiġ (Áṫ Cliaṫ)

Iomáint Soisear (An Craoḃ):

Luḃái v. **Cill Dara**

4.30 p.m. P. Ó Coileáin (Iar Mí)

Luaċ - 3p.

M. Ó Neill
(Rún.)

An Mac Alla, Inis Córṫaiḋ

4

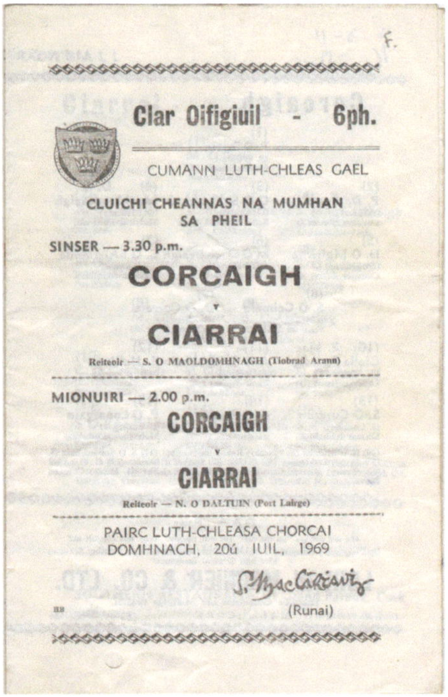

Clar Oifigiuil - 6ph.

CUMANN LUTH-CHLEAS GAEL

CLUICHI CHEANNAS NA MUMHAN SA PHEIL

SINSER — 3.30 p.m.

CORCAIGH

v

CIARRAI

Reiteoir — S. O MAOLDOMHNAGH (Tiobrad Arann)

MIONUIRI — 2.00 p.m.

CORCAIGH

v

CIARRAI

Reiteoir — N. O DALTUIN (Port Lairge)

PAIRC LUTH-CHLEASA CHORCAI
DOMHNACH, 20ú IUIL, 1969

(Runai)

5

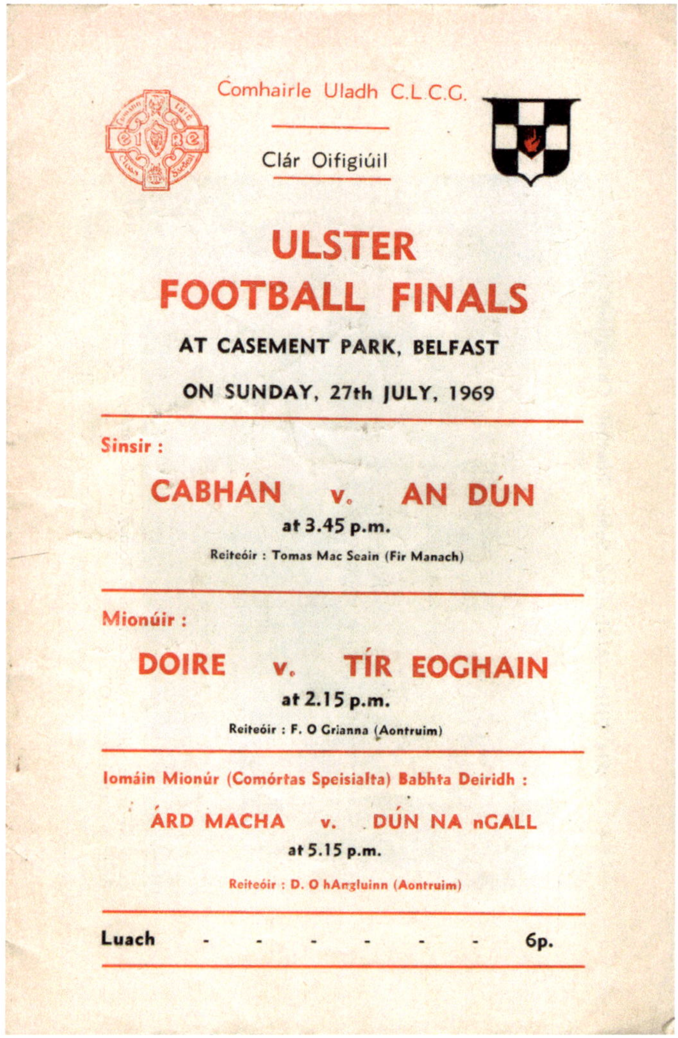

Comhairle Uladh C.L.C.G.

Clár Oifigiúil

ULSTER
FOOTBALL FINALS

AT CASEMENT PARK, BELFAST

ON SUNDAY, 27th JULY, 1969

Sinsir :

CABHÁN v. AN DÚN

at 3.45 p.m.

Reiteóir : Tomas Mac Seain (Fir Manach)

Mionúir :

DOIRE v. TÍR EOGHAIN

at 2.15 p.m.

Reiteóir : F. O Grianna (Aontruim)

Iomáin Mionúr (Comórtas Speisialta) Babhta Deiridh :

ÁRD MACHA v. DÚN NA nGALL

at 5.15 p.m.

Reiteóir : D. O hAngluinn (Aontruim)

Luach - - - - - - 6p.

4 Munster Football Final
Kerry 0-16 Cork 1-04

5 Ulster Football Final
Cavan 2-13 Down 2-06

6 All-Ireland Football Final
Kerry 0-10 Offaly 0-07
Attendance – 67,828

7 Leinster Hurling Final
Kilkenny 3-9 Offaly 0-16

8 Munster Hurling Final
Cork 4-06 Tipperary 0-09

9 All-Ireland Hurling Final
Kilkenny 2-15 Cork 2-09
Attendance – 66,844

6

CLUICHÍ CEANNAIS
PEILE NA hÉIREANN
PÁIRC AN CHRÓCAIGH 28-9-1969
SINSIR
3.15 p.m.
MIONÚIR
1.45 p.m.
S. Mac AOGAIN (Ua bhFailghe)
S. O COLLATA (Ciarraí)
E. Mac GIOLLA PHADRAIG (Corcaigh)
B. Mac an BHAIRD (Doire)
LUACH
1/-
OFFICIAL PROGRAMME
Árd-Rúnaí.

7

Comairle Laiġean
1969
Clár Oifigiúil
Páirc an Ċrócaiġ
20-7-69
Iomáint Sinsir:
Ua bFáilí v.
Cill Ċoinniġ
3.15 p.m.
S. de Grae (Áṫ Cliaṫ).
Iomáint Mionúir:
Áṫ Cliaṫ v. Cill Ċoinniġ
1.45 p.m.
D. de Stáic (Laois).
Luaċ - 3p.
(Rún.).

8

Souvenir
Programme
1969 Munster Senior & Minor Hurling
Championship Finals
Pairc na nGael, Luimneach
Sunday, 27th July, 1969
Minor Hurling 2 p.m.
Referee J. Duggan, Galway
TIOBRAD
ARANN
v
CORCAIGH
Senior Hurling 3-30 p.m.
Referee S. O'Connor, Limerick
Clár Oifigeamail
6d.
AR AGHAID LINN
KEY PRINTING WORKS, 50 WILLIAM ST., LIMERICK

9

CLUICHÍ CEANNAIS
IOMÁNA na hÉIREANN
PÁIRC AN CHRÓCAIGH 7-9-1969
SINSIR
3.15 p.m.
MIONÚIR
1.45 p.m.
D. O MURCHU (Corcaigh)
E. O CEITHIR (Cill Chainnigh)
D. Mac CORMAIC (Cill Chainnigh)
S. O COILEAIN (Corcaigh)
LUACH
1/-
OFFICIAL PROGRAMME
Árd-Rúnaí.

1970–79

1970

All GAA matches were of 60 minutes in duration until 1970, when the 80-minute match was introduced for All-Ireland semi-finals, finals and the provincial finals. The first such football match was the 1970 Connacht final between Roscommon and Galway in Pearse Stadium. It was also the first Connacht final to be televised live and resulted in a comfortable win for Galway. The first 80-minute hurling match was the Leinster final between Wexford and Kilkenny, played on the same day and with the same throw-in time. If the scoreline in Connacht wasn't unusual, the same can't be said for the hurling, which produced a total of 7 goals and 30 points. The effect of the extra 20 minutes was reflected in the scoreline of both All-Ireland finals, as Cork defeated Wexford by 6-21 to 5-10 in hurling and Kerry scored 2-19 to Meath's 0-18 in the football final.

1

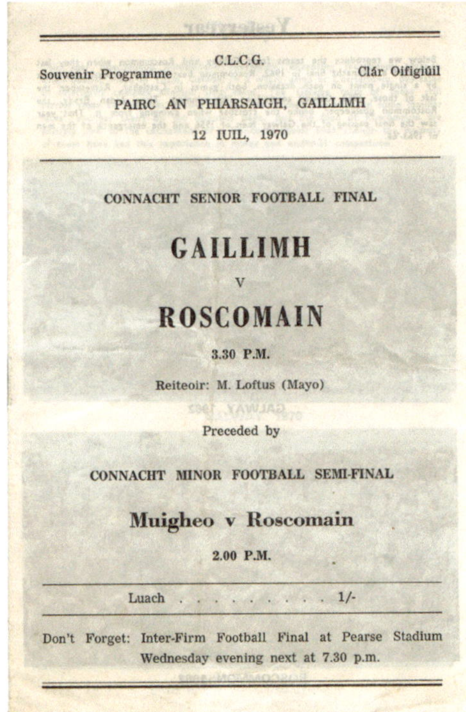

Souvenir Programme — C.L.C.G. — Clár Oifigiúil

PAIRC AN PHIARSAIGH, GAILLIMH

12 IUIL, 1970

CONNACHT SENIOR FOOTBALL FINAL

GAILLIMH

v

ROSCOMAIN

3.30 P.M.

Reiteoir: M. Loftus (Mayo)

Preceded by

CONNACHT MINOR FOOTBALL SEMI-FINAL

Muigheo v Roscomain

2.00 P.M.

Luach 1/-

Don't Forget: Inter-Firm Football Final at Pearse Stadium Wednesday evening next at 7.30 p.m.

2

Comairle Laighean — 1970

Clár Oifigiúil

Páirc an Chrócaigh

19-7-1970.

3.30 p.m. Peil Sinsear—An Chraobh.
(Forty minutes each side).

An Mí (MEATH) v. Ua bFáilí (OFFALY)

Réiteóir: B. Ó hEidín (Ceatharloch)

2.00 p.m. Peil Mionúr—An Chraobh:
(Thirty minutes each side)

An Mí (MEATH) v. Át. Cliat (DUBLIN)

Réiteóir: S. Mac Cathmhaoil (Cill Dara)

Luac - 6p. | (Rúnaí)

1 Connacht Football Final
Galway 2-15 Roscommon 1-08

2 Leinster Football Final
Meath 2-22 Offaly 5-12

3 Munster Football Final
Kerry 2-22 Cork 2-09

CUMANN LUITH CHLEAS GAEL

KERRY V. CORK

3

MUNSTER
FOOTBALL
FINALS

FITZGERALD STADIUM, KILLARNEY

SUNDAY, 26th JULY, 1970.

Senior
Cork v. Kerry
at 3.30 p.m.
Ref: S. Moloney
Tipperary.

Minor
Cork v. Kerry
Ref: N. Dalton
Waterford

ADMISSION 6/-s.
SIDELINE & TERRAC
2/-s. EXTRA.

THE LATE DICK FITZGERALD

CLAR OIFIGIUIL | OFFICIAL PROGRAMME 1/-

PROCEEDS IN AID OF FITZGERALD STADIUM

4

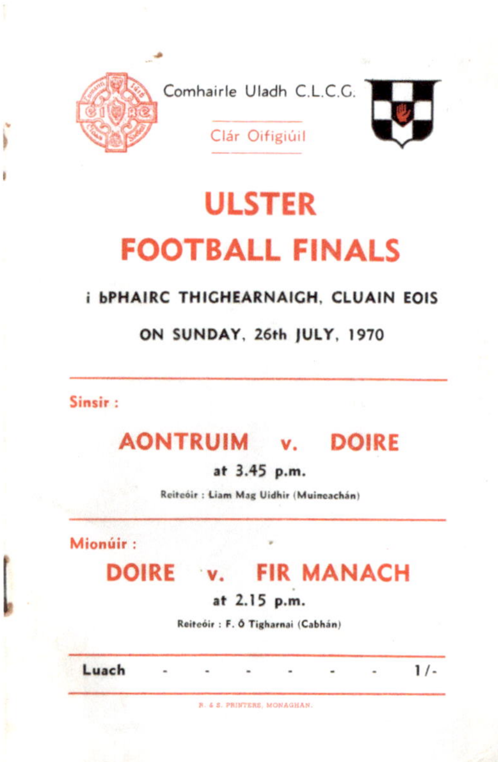
Comhairle Uladh C.L.C.G.

Clár Oifigiúil

ULSTER
FOOTBALL FINALS

i bPHAIRC THIGHEARNAIGH, CLUAIN EOIS

ON SUNDAY, 26th JULY, 1970

Sinsir :

AONTRUIM v. DOIRE

at 3.45 p.m.

Reiteóir : Liam Mag Uidhir (Muineachán)

Mionúir :

DOIRE v. FIR MANACH

at 2.15 p.m.

Reiteóir : F. Ó Tigharnai (Cabhán)

Luach - - - - - - 1/-

R. & S. PRINTERS, MONAGHAN.

5

CLUICHÍ CEANNAIS PEILE

PÁIRC AN CHRÓCAIGH 27-9-1970

MIONÚIR 1.30
SINSIR 3.15

OFFICIAL PROGRAMME

Seán Ó Síocháin
Ard-Rúnaí

1/-

6

Coṁairle Laiġean 1970

Clár Oifigiúil

Páirc an Ċrócaiġ
12-7-1970

3.30 p.m. Iomáint Sinnsear—An Craobh
(Forty minutes each side)

Cill Ċoinniġ (KILKENNY) v. Loċ Garman (WEXFORD)

Réiteóir—S. MacGiolla Chatáin (Cill Mantáin).

2.00 p.m. Iomáint Idirméanach (Replay).
(Winners meet Cill Mantáin in Final)

Cill Ċoinniġ v. Áṫ Cliaṫ
(KILKENNY) (DUBLIN)

Réiteóir—R. MacAoire (Ceatharloch).

Luaċ - 6p.

(Rúnaí)

7

Souvenir Programme

1970 Munster Senior & Minor Hurling Championship Finals

Pairc na nGael Luimneach

Sunday, 19th July, 1970

Minor Hurling 2 p.m.
Referee S. O'Connor, Limerick

TIOBRAD ARANN
v.
CORCAIGH

Senior Hurling 3 30 p.m.
Referee G. FITZGERALD, Limerick

Clár Oifigeaṁail 6d.

AR AGHAID LINN

KEY PRINTING WORKS, WILLIAM ST., LIMERICK

8

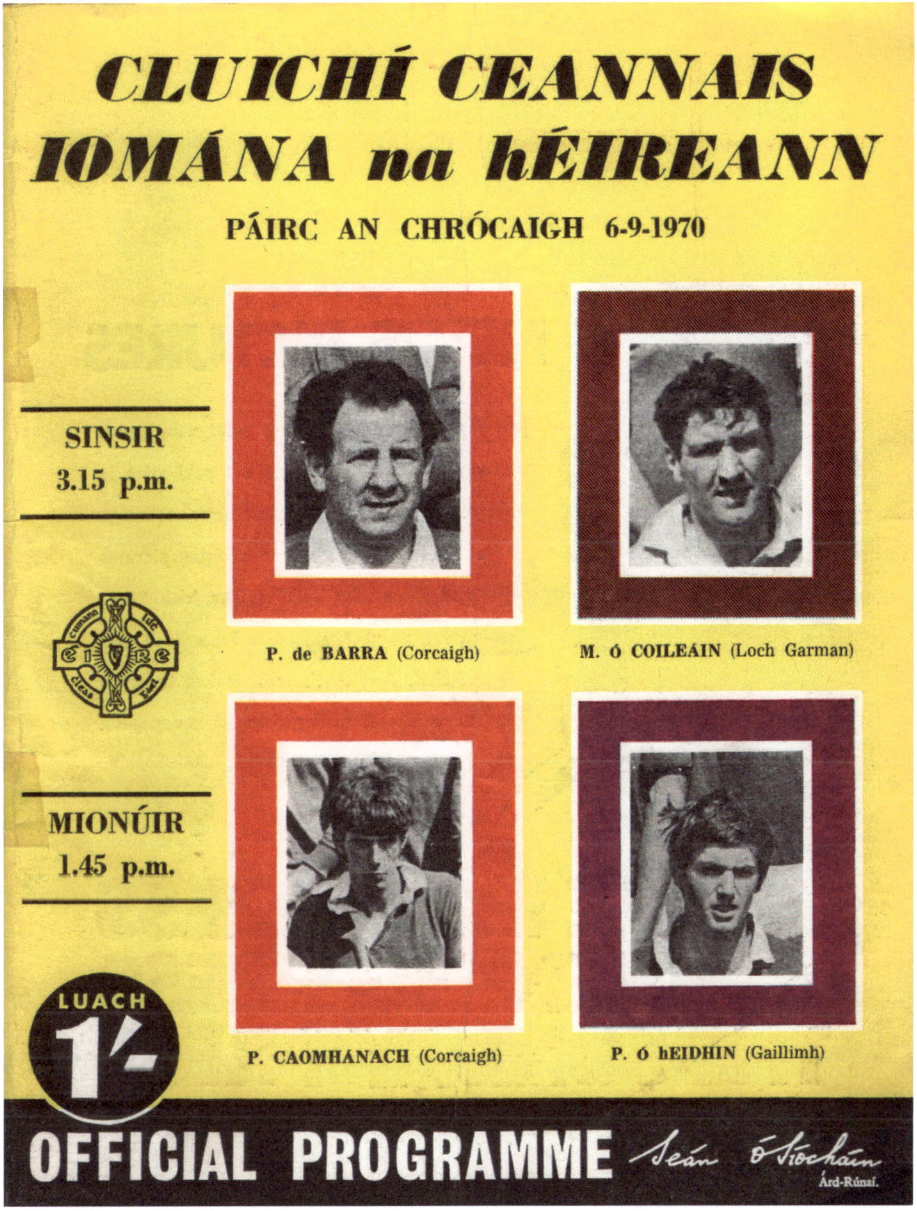

4 Ulster Football Final
Derry 2-13 Antrim 1-12

5 All-Ireland Football Final
Kerry 2-19 Meath 0-18
Attendance – 71,775

6 Leinster Hurling Final
Wexford 4-16 Kilkenny 3-14

7 Munster Hurling Final
Cork 3-10 Tipperary 3-08

8 All-Ireland Hurling Final
Cork 6-21 Wexford 5-10
Attendance – 65,062

1971

At the GAA Congress in 1971, Rule 27, or 'The Ban' on playing and attending foreign sports was abolished. The increasing popularity and televising of soccer and rugby meant that the rule was outdated and unenforceable. In terms of the GAA match programme, one of the most influential figures was Galway's Jack Mahon. Mahon, a former All-Ireland winner in 1956 and a prolific writer on GAA matters, was responsible for the introduction of the souvenir programme for the 1971 Connacht final. The booklet publication, which set the standard for the other provinces to follow, was the beginning of the end for the single-sheet fold-over programme for provincial finals.

The All-Ireland hurling final of 1971 between Tipperary and Kilkenny was the first final to be televised in colour. Tipperary won a high-scoring match in which Michael 'Babs' Keating, playing in his bare feet for part of the match, scored seven points while Kilkenny's Eddie Keher scored a then-record 2-11, only to finish on the losing side. Both players were included in the first All-Star team when the scheme was introduced this year to reward excellence in hurling and football.

1

2

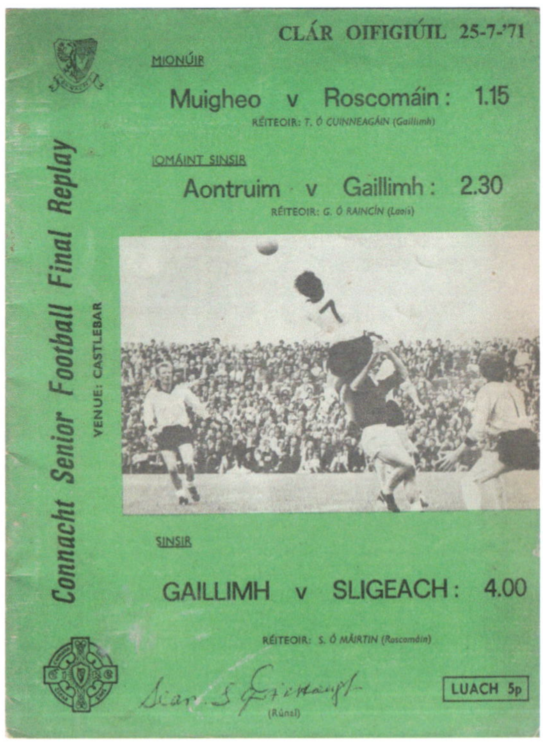

1 Connacht Football Final
Galway 2-15 Sligo 2-15

2 Replay
Galway 1-17 Sligo 3-10

3 Leinster Football Final
Offaly 2-14 Kildare 0-06

3

Comhairle Laighean 1971

CLÁR OIFIGIÚIL

Páirc an Chrócaigh, 18-7-1971

4.00 p.m.—PEIL SINSIR—(An Chraobh)
(Forty minutes each side)

CILL DARA v Ua bhFAILI
(KILDARE) (OFFALY)

Réiteoir: P. Ó Ceallaigh (Áth Cliath)

2.30 p.m.—PEIL MIONÚIR—(Leath Craobh)

ATH CLIATH v Ua bhFAILI
(DUBLIN) (OFFALY)

Réiteoir: T. Ó Clandiollúin (Cill Mantáin)

1.00 p.m.—PEIL MIONÚIR—(Leath Craobh)

An Mhí v Luí
(MEATH) (LOUTH)

Réiteoir: S. Mac Cathmhaoil (Cill Dara)

LUACH 3p

(Rúnaí)

4

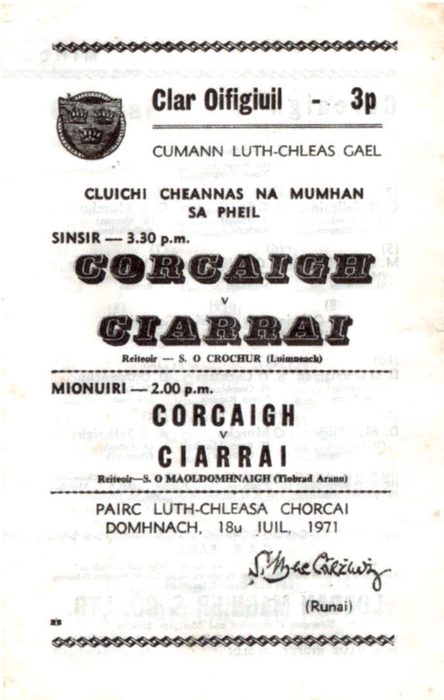

Clar Oifigiuil - 3p

CUMANN LUTH-CHLEAS GAEL

CLUICHI CHEANNAS NA MUMHAN SA PHEIL

SINSIR — 3.30 p.m.

CORCAIGH

v

CIARRAI

Reiteoir — S. O CROCHUR (Luimneach)

MIONUIRI — 2.00 p.m.

CORCAIGH

v

CIARRAI

Reiteoir—S. O MAOLDOMHNAIGH (Tiobrad Arann)

PAIRC LUTH-CHLEASA CHORCAI

DOMHNACH, 18u IUIL, 1971

(Runai)

5

Comhairle Uladh C.L.C.G.

Clár Oifigiúil

ULSTER

FOOTBALL FINALS

AT CASEMENT PARK, BELFAST

ON SUNDAY, 25th JULY, 1971

Sinsir :

DOIRE v. AN DUN

at 3.45 p.m.

Réiteoir : Pádraig Ó Doibhlin (Tír Eoin)

Mionúir :

FIR MANACH v. TIR EOIN

at 2.15 p.m.

Réiteoir : F. Ó Tigharnai (Cabhán)

Iomáin Mionúr (Comórtas Speisialta) Babhta Deiridh :

ÁRD MACHA v. DÚN NA nGALL

at 1 p.m.

Réiteoir : D. Ó hAngluinn (Aontruim)

Luach - - - - - - - 5p

4 Munster Football Final
Cork 0-25 Kerry 0-14

5 Ulster Football Final
Down 4-15 Derry 4-11

6 All-Ireland Football Final
Offaly 1-14 Galway 2-08
Attendance – 70,798

7 Leinster Hurling Final
Kilkenny 6-16 Wexford 3-16

8 Munster Hurling Final
Tipperary 4-16 Limerick 3-18

9 All-Ireland Hurling Final
Tipperary 5-17 Kilkenny 5-14
Attendance – 61,393

6

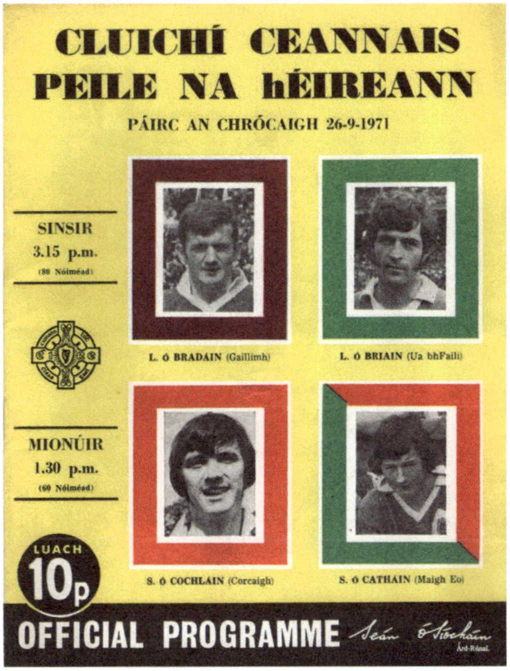
CLUICHÍ CEANNAIS
PEILE NA hÉIREANN
PÁIRC AN CHRÓCAIGH 26-9-1971
SINSIR
3.15 p.m.
(80 Nóiméad)
L. Ó BRADAIN (Gaillimh)
L. Ó BRIAIN (Ua bhFaili)
MIONÚIR
1.30 p.m.
(60 Nóiméad)
LUACH
10p
S. Ó COCHLAIN (Corcaigh)
S. Ó CATHAIN (Maigh Eo)
OFFICIAL PROGRAMME
Árd-Rúnaí.

7

Comhairle Laighean 1971
CLÁR OIFIGIÚIL
Páirc an Chrócaigh, 11-7-1971
4.00 p.m.—IOMÁINT SINSIR—(An Chraobh)
(Forty minutes each side)
Loch Garman v Cill Choinnigh
(WEXFORD) (KILKENNY)
Réiteoir: S. Ó Raincín (Laois)
2.30 p.m.—IOMÁINT MIONÚIR (Leath Craobh)
Loch Garman v Ua bhFaili
(WEXFORD) (OFFALY)
Réiteoir: S. Mac Fheorais (Áth Cliath)
1.00 p.m.—IOMÁINT MIONÚIR (Leath Craobh)
Cill Choinnigh v Laois
(KILKENNY) (LAOIS)
Réiteoir: D. Ó Dúdaigh (Áth Cliath)
LUACH 3p
(Rúnaí)

8

Cumann Luit-cleas Gaedeal
MUNSTER HURLING FINALS 1971
2.00 P.M.
Mionuir:
Clar v. Corcaigh
Moltóir: Gerry Fitzgerald
(Limerick)
3.30 P.M.
Sinnsir
Luimneach v. Tiobraid Arann
Moltóir: Frank Murphy
(Cork)
OFFICIAL PROGRAMME
(Proceeds to Fitzgerald Stadium Building Fund)
5p

9

CLUICHÍ CEANNAIS
IOMÁNA na hÉIREANN
PÁIRC AN CHRÓCAIGH 5-9-1971
SINSIR
3.15 p.m.
P. Mac AINDRÉIS (Cill Chainnigh)
T. Ó CONCHUIR (Tiobraid Árann)
MIONÚIR
1.30 p.m.
LUACH
10p
S. Ó COCHLAIN (Corcaigh)
T. de BUITLEAR (Cill Chainnigh)
OFFICIAL PROGRAMME
Árd-Rúnaí.

1972

As reigning All-Ireland football champions, Offaly faced into the 1972 Leinster campaign in the knowledge that no Leinster team had retained the Sam Maguire Cup since Kildare in 1928. Determined to buck this trend, they started their campaign with a straightforward win over Meath before comfortably retaining their provincial title against Kildare in the final. This set them up for an All-Ireland semi-final against a Donegal team who had just won their first-ever Ulster championship title. A four-point victory for Offaly was enough to see them return to the final. In the other semi-final, Kerry were easy winners over Roscommon and the scene was set for a reprise of the 1969 final.

The 1972 All-Ireland football final between Kerry and Offaly was also a meeting of the previous two years' winners and it took a replay to separate them. Powered by midfielder Willie Bryan, Offaly were stronger when the teams met again and took the title for the second year in a row.

1

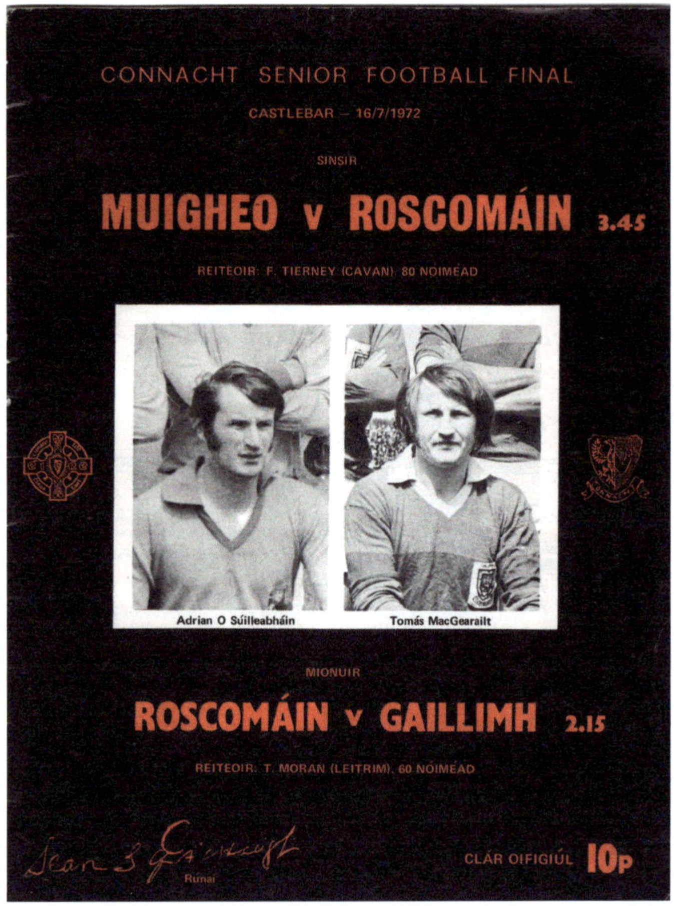

1 Connacht Football Final
Roscommon 5-08 Mayo 3-10

2 Leinster Football Final
Offaly 1-18 Kildare 2-08

3 Munster Football Final
Kerry 2-21 Cork 2-15

4 Ulster Football Final
Donegal 2-13 Tyrone 1-11

5 All-Ireland Football Final
Offaly 1-13 Kerry 1-13
Attendance – 72,032

2

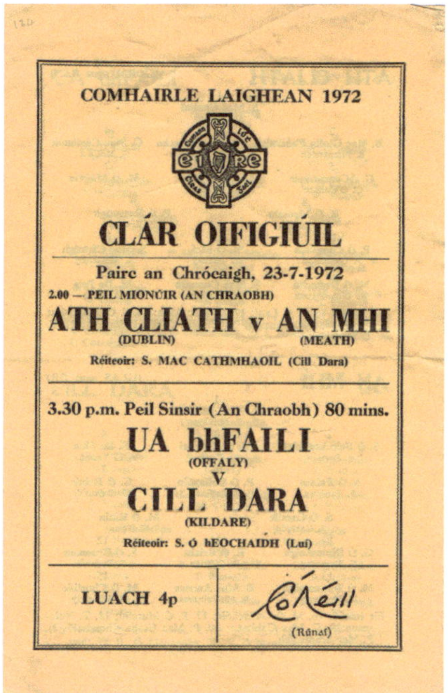
COMHAIRLE LAIGHEAN 1972
CLÁR OIFIGIÚIL
Pairc an Chrócaigh, 23-7-1972
2.00 — PEIL MIONÚIR (AN CHRAOBH)
ATH CLIATH v AN MHI
(DUBLIN) (MEATH)
Réiteoir: S. MAC CATHMHAOIL (Cill Dara)
3.30 p.m. Peil Sinsir (An Chraobh) 80 mins.
UA bhFAILI
(OFFALY)
V
CILL DARA
(KILDARE)
Réiteoir: S. Ó hEOCHAIDH (Luí)
LUACH 4p
(Rúnaí)

3

CRAOBH PEILE NA MUN C.L.G.
Official Programme
10p
PROCEEDS TO FITZGERALD STADIUM
FREE DRAW FOR TEN ALL-IRELAND TICKETS
— exciting details inside !
MUNSTER FOOTBALL FINALS 1972
MIONUIRI 2.00 PM
SINSIR 3.30 PM
Ciarrai v Corcaigh
SINSIR — MOLTOIR JOHN MALONEY, TIPPERARY
MIONUIRI — MOLTOIR SEAN O'CONNOR, LIMERICK
Donal Hunt, Cork Captain
Tom Prendergast, Kerry Capt.

4

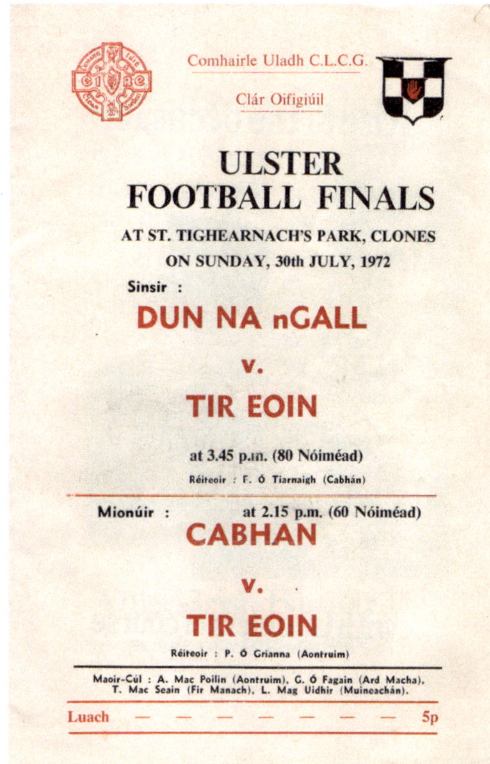
Comhairle Uladh C.L.C.G.
Clár Oifigiúil
ULSTER FOOTBALL FINALS
AT ST. TIGHEARNACH'S PARK, CLONES
ON SUNDAY, 30th JULY, 1972
Sinsir :
DUN NA nGALL
v.
TIR EOIN
at 3.45 p.m. (80 Nóiméad)
Réiteoir : F. Ó Tiarnaigh (Cabhán)
Mionúir :
at 2.15 p.m. (60 Nóiméad)
CABHAN
v.
TIR EOIN
Réiteoir : P. Ó Grianna (Aontruim)
Maoir-Cúl : A. Mac Poilin (Aontruim), G. Ó Fagain (Ard Macha), T. Mac Seain (Fir Manach), L. Mag Uidhir (Muineachán).
Luach — — — — — — — 5p

5

10p
CLUICHÍ CEANNAIS PEILE NA hÉIREANN i bPáirc an Chrócaigh
24-9-72
Sinsir
Ciarraí v Uíbh Fhailí
3·15
Réiteoir: F. Ó TIARNAIGH (An Cabhán)
Mionúir
Corcaigh v Tír Eoghain
1·30
Réiteoir: M. Ó hEIDHIN (Ros Comáin)
CLÁR OIFIGIÚIL
Ard-Rúnaí

6

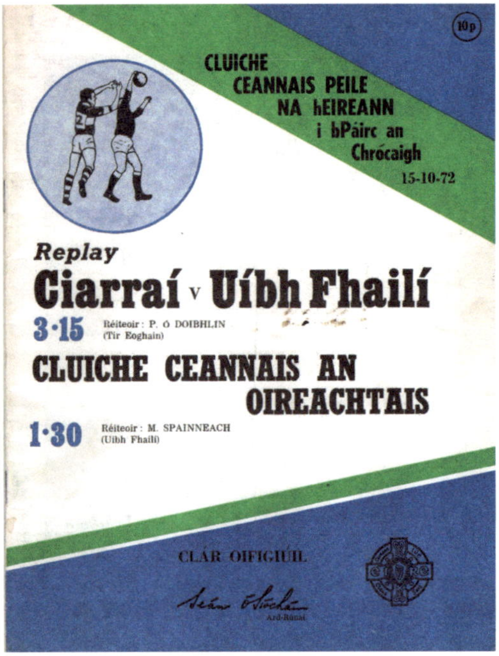
10p
CLUICHE CEANNAIS PEILE NA hEIREANN i bPáirc an Chrócaigh
15-10-72
Replay
Ciarraí v Uíbh Fhailí
3·15 Réiteoir: P. Ó DOIBHLIN (Tír Eoghain)
CLUICHE CEANNAIS AN OIREACHTAIS
1·30 Réiteoir: M. SPAINNEACH (Uíbh Fhailí)
CLÁR OIFIGIÚIL
Ard-Rúnaí

7

Comhairle Laighean C.L.G.
CLÁR OIFIGIÚIL
Páirc an Chrocaigh – 9-7-1972
12.45 p.m. — Iomáint Mionúir (Leath Craobh)
ATH CLIATH v LOCH GARMAN
(DUBLIN) (WEXFORD)
Réiteoir: D. Mac Roibín (Cill Dara)
2.00 p.m. — Iomáint Idirmheánach (An Chraobh)
LOCH GARMAN v ATH CLIATH
(WEXFORD) (DUBLIN)
Réiteoir: S. Ó Ciarubháin (Ua bhFáilí)
3.30 p.m. — Iomáint Sinsir (80 mins.) An Chraobh
CILL CHOINNIGH
(KILKENNY)
v
LOCH GARMAN
(WEXFORD)
Réiteoir: M. De Spáinne (Ua bhFáilí)
LUACH 4p
(Rúnaí)

8

COMHAIRLE LAIGHEAN 1972
CLÁR OIFIGIÚIL
Páirc an Chrócaigh, 30–7–1972
1.00 p.m.—Fé 14 bliain Iomáint (Craobh) 50 minutes
Ath Cliath v Cill Choinnigh
(Dublin) (Kilkenny)
Réitheoir: T. De Rís (Luí)
2.00 p.m.—Iomáint Mionúir (Craobh) 60 minutes
CILL CHOINNIGH
(KILKENNY)
V
LOCH GARMAN
(WEXFORD)
Réiteoir: D. Mac Roibín (Cill Dara)
3.30 p.m. — IOMÁINT SINSIR (Craobh) Replay 80 minutes
Cill Choinnigh v Loch Garman
(Kilkenny) (Wexford)
Réiteoir: M. DE SPÁINNE (Ua bhFáilí)
LUACH 4p
(Rúnaí)

9

MUNSTER HURLING CHAMPIONSHIPS
1972
Senior and Minor Finals
Semple Stadium
Thurles
ON SUNDAY, 30th JULY
SENIOR AT 3.30 P.M.
CLARE v. CORK
Referee—J. O'Grady (Limerick).
MINOR AT 2 P.M.
CORK v. LIMERICK
Referee—John Moloney (Tipperary).
OFFICIAL PROGRAMME in aid of Thurles C.B.S. and Thurles Sarsfields Club.
5p
"Tipperary Star," Thurles.

10

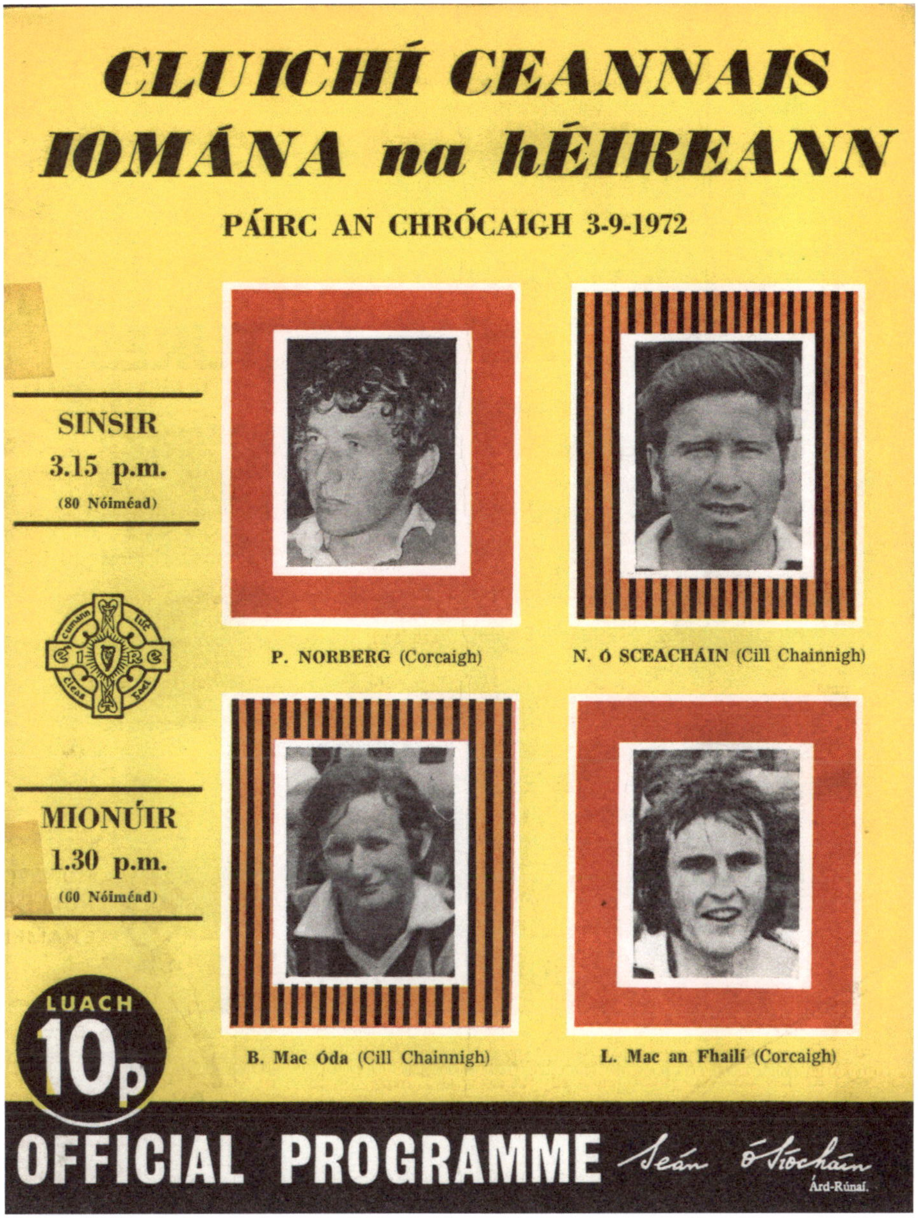

6 Replay
Offaly 1-19 Kerry 0-13
Attendance – 66,136

7 Leinster Hurling Final
Kilkenny 6-13 Wexford 6-13

8 Replay
Kilkenny 3-16 Wexford 1-14

9 Munster Hurling Final
Cork 6-18 Clare 2-08

10 All-Ireland Hurling Final
Kilkenny 3-24 Cork 5-11
Attendance – 66,137

1973

The 1973 All-Ireland hurling final was played in miserable conditions. Heavy rain made for treacherous conditions for hurling and equally so for match programmes, as many of the souvenirs were used as makeshift umbrellas. Limerick were back in the final for the first time since their victory in the 1940 final; awaiting them were the reigning All-Ireland champions, Kilkenny. An outstanding performance, inspired by relocating Éamonn Cregan to centre half-back, and ten points from Richie Bennis, gave Limerick a well-deserved victory.

Cork entered the All-Ireland football final without a win in the final since 1945. They came up against Galway who, although they put it up to Cork for a time, never really threatened to win the match. A young Jimmy Barry Murphy scored two goals and a point in a high-scoring final, allowing Cork goalkeeper and captain Billy Morgan to collect the Sam Maguire Cup.

1

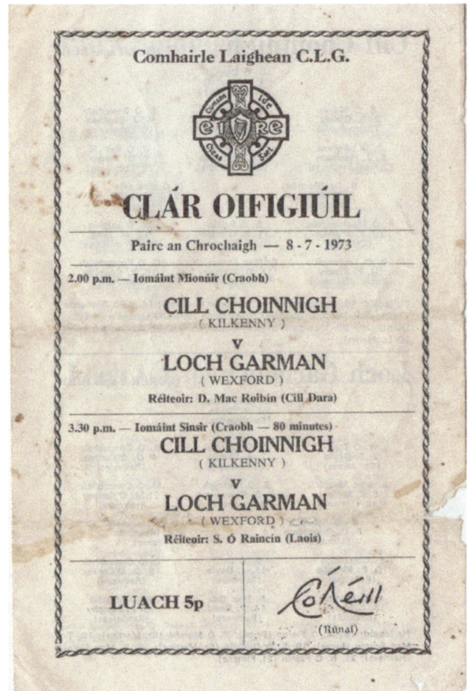

2

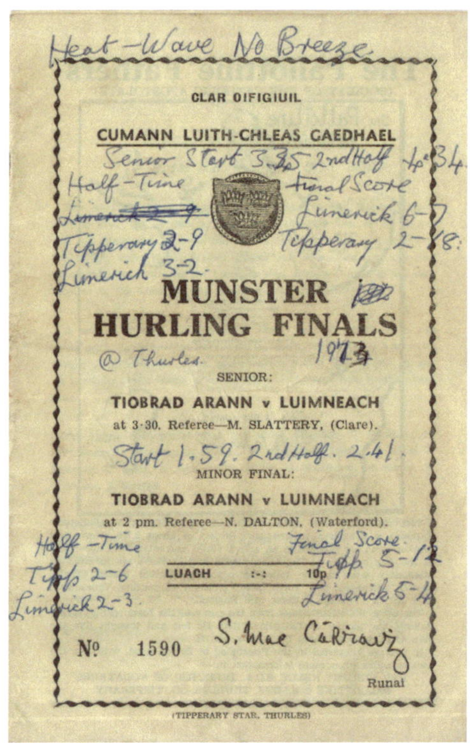

1 Leinster Hurling Final
Kilkenny 4-22 Wexford 3-15

2 Munster Hurling Final
Limerick 6-07 Tipperary 2-18

3 All-Ireland Hurling Final
Limerick 1-21 Kilkenny 1-14
Attendance – 59,009

CLUICHÍ CEANNAIS IOMÁNA na hÉIREANN

PÁIRC AN CHRÓCAIGH 2-9-1973

SINSIR
3.15 p.m.
(80 Nóiméad)

P. Ó Dúláinne (Cill Chainnigh)

E. Ó Greacháin (Luimneach)

MIONÚIR
1.30 p.m.
(60 Nóiméad)

S. Ó Doirbheáin (Gaillimh)

C. Mac Roibín (Cill Chainnigh)

LUACH 10p

OFFICIAL PROGRAMME

Seán Ó Síocháin
Ard Stiurthóir

4

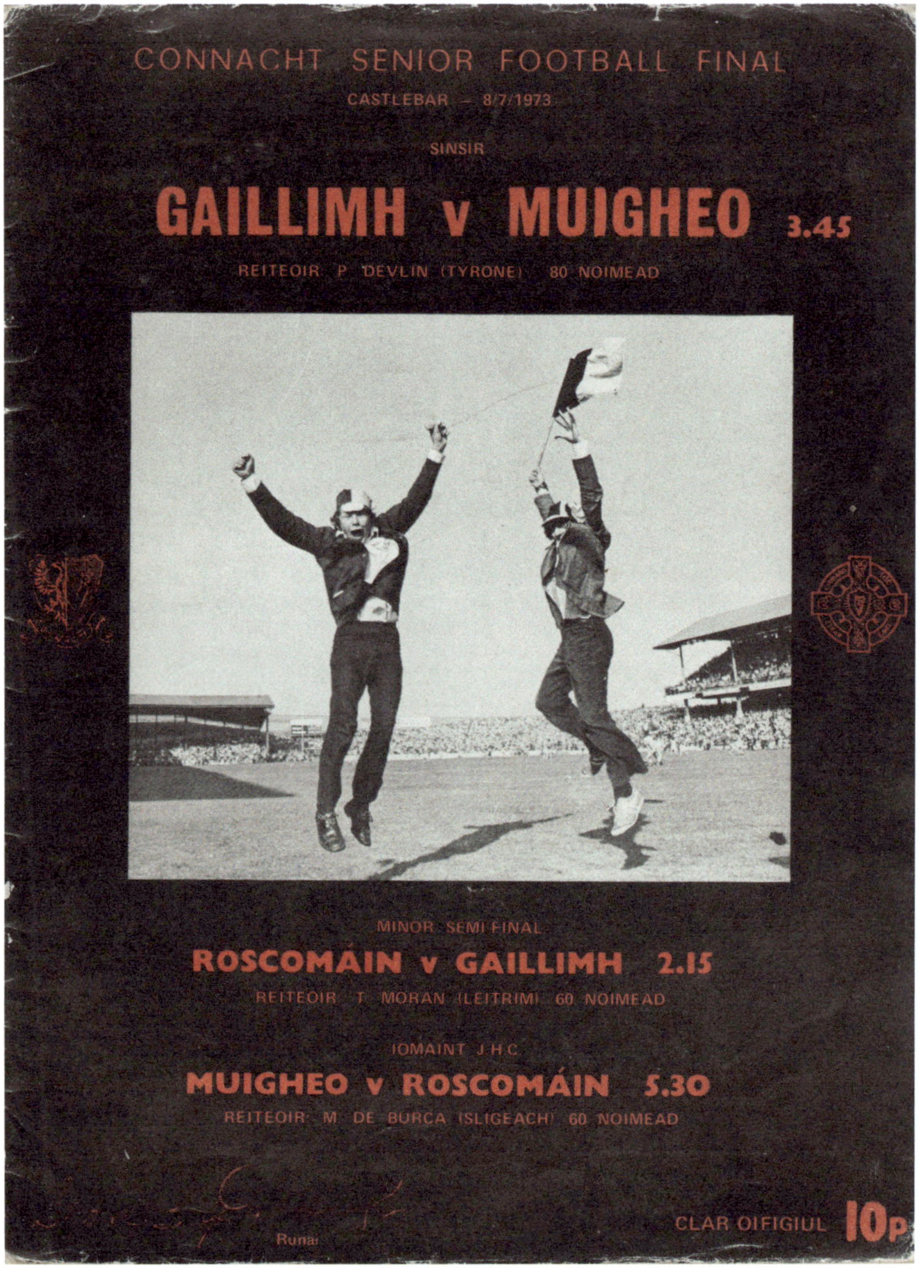

4 Connacht Football Final
Galway 1-17 Mayo 2-12

5 Leinster Football Final
Offaly 3-21 Meath 2-12

6 Munster Football Final
Cork 5-12 Kerry 1-15

7 Ulster Football Final
Tyrone 3-13 Down 1-11

8 All-Ireland Football Final
Cork 3-17 Galway 2-13
Attendance – 73,308

5

Comhairle Laighean C.L.G.

CLÁR OIFIGIÚIL

Pairc an Chrocaigh — 22-7-1973

2.00 p.m. — Peil Mionúir (Craobh)

CILL DARA v LAOIS
(KILDARE) (LAOIS)
Réiteoir : T. Ó Clandiolláin (Cill Mantáin)

3.30 p.m. — Peil Sinsir (Craobh — 80 Minutes)

UA bhFÁILÍ v AN MHÍ
(OFFALY) (MEATH)
Réiteoir : B. Ó hÉidin (Ceatharloch)

LUACH 5p

(Rúnaí)

7

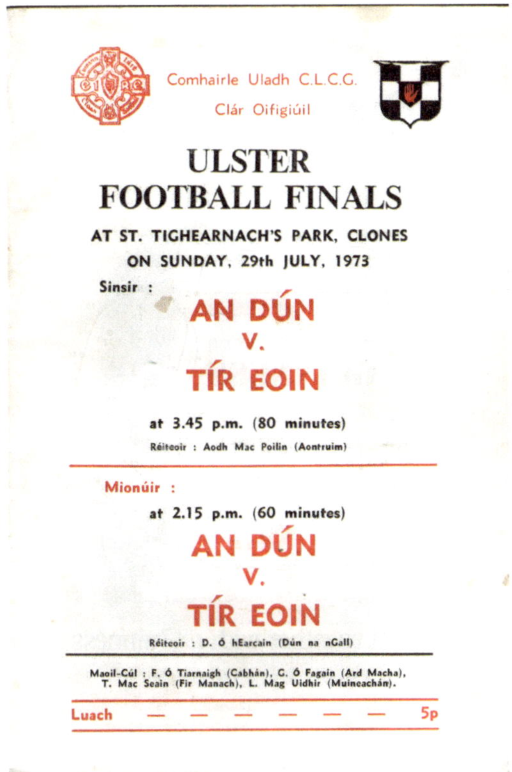

Comhairle Uladh C.L.C.G.
Clár Oifigiúil

ULSTER
FOOTBALL FINALS
AT ST. TIGHEARNACH'S PARK, CLONES
ON SUNDAY, 29th JULY, 1973

Sinsir :
AN DÚN
V.
TÍR EOIN
at 3.45 p.m. (80 minutes)
Réiteoir : Aodh Mac Poilin (Aontruim)

Mionúir :
at 2.15 p.m. (60 minutes)
AN DÚN
V.
TÍR EOIN
Réiteoir : D. Ó hEarcain (Dún na nGall)

Maoil-Cúl : F. Ó Tiarnaigh (Cabhán), G. Ó Fagain (Ard Macha), T. Mac Seain (Fir Manach), L. Mag Uidhir (Muineachán).

Luach — — — — — — 5p

6

Cumann Luith-Chleas Gael

Clar Oifigiuil - 5p

Cluichi Ceannais na Mumhan

Ciarrai
v
Corcaigh

Ar 3.30 a'chlog
Reiteoir — S: O MAOLOMHNAIGH (Tiobrad Arann)

PAIRC LUTH-CHLEAS CHORCAI
DOMHNACH, 15 IUIL, 1973

Corcaigh v Ciarraí no Tiobrad Arann
Reiteoir — P. VERDUN Mionuir 2.00

Runai

CNB PRESS

8

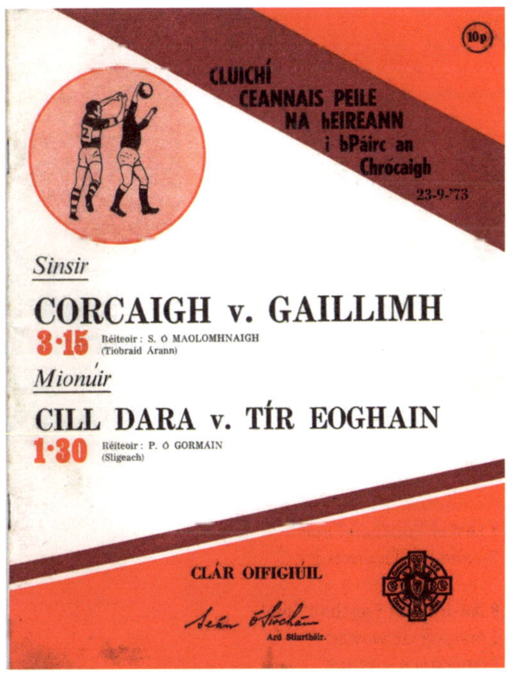

10p

CLUICHÍ CEANNAIS PEILE NA hEIREANN i bPáirc an Chrócaigh
23-9-'73

Sinsir
CORCAIGH v. GAILLIMH
3·15 Réiteoir : S. Ó MAOLOMHNAIGH (Tiobraid Árann)

Mionúir
CILL DARA v. TÍR EOGHAIN
1·30 Réiteoir : P. Ó GORMAIN (Sligeach)

CLÁR OIFIGIÚIL

Ard Stiurthóir.

1974

Somewhat belatedly, the Leinster and Munster Councils followed Connacht's lead and introduced the slightly larger, booklet-style programmes with colour covers for their 1974 provincial finals. Over the coming decades, the production quality of the GAA match programme steadily improved with advances in printing and photographic technology.

Gaelic football in the capital city was in decline. Without a Leinster final win since 1965 and an All-Ireland victory since 1963, Dublin were in division two of the National Football League and entered the Leinster championship in the preliminary round. However, Kevin Heffernan took over as manager and improvements soon followed. Bolstered by St Vincent's players such as Brian Mullins, Tony Hanahoe and Jimmy Keaveney, Dublin beat Meath in the Leinster final and reigning champions Cork in the All-Ireland semi-final. In the final against Galway, Paddy Cullen's second-half penalty save tipped the balance in Dublin's favour.

1

2

1 Connacht Football Final
Galway 2-14 Roscommon 0-08

2 Leinster Football Final
Dublin 1-14 Meath 1-09

3 Munster Football Final
Cork 1-11 Kerry 0-07

3

CLAR OIFIGIUIL

S. Mac Cárthaigh

LUACH 10p

COMHAIRLE NA MUMHAN C.L.G.

MUNSTER FOOTBALL FINALS — KILLARNEY 14-7-'74

Corcaigh v Ciarrai

Mioniur 2 p.m. **Moltoir: Jim Landers (Waterford)**

Sinsir 3.30 p.m. **Moltoir: Brendan Cross, Limerick**

Proceeds in aid of Fitzgerald Stadium

FREE DRAW FOR 10 ALL-IRELAND TICKETS

FULL DETAILS INSIDE

4

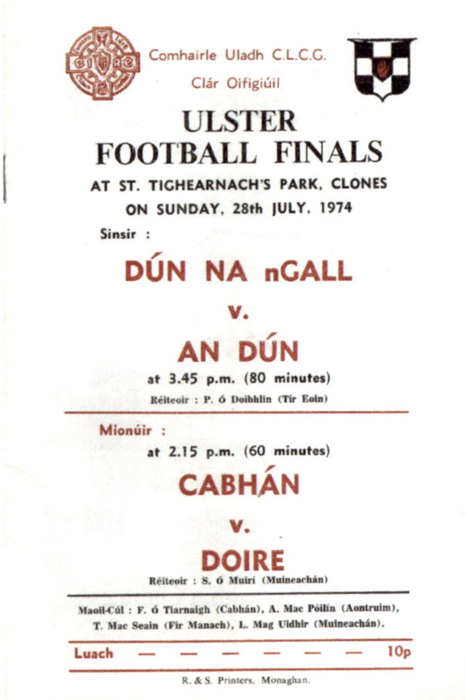

Comhairle Uladh C.L.C.G.
Clár Oifigiúil

ULSTER
FOOTBALL FINALS
AT ST. TIGHEARNACH'S PARK, CLONES
ON SUNDAY, 28th JULY, 1974

Sinsir :

DÚN NA nGALL
v.
AN DÚN
at 3.45 p.m. (80 minutes)
Réiteoir : P. Ó Doibhlin (Tír Eoin)

Mionúir :
at 2.15 p.m. (60 minutes)

CABHÁN
v.
DOIRE
Réiteoir : S. Ó Muirí (Muineachán)

Maoil-Cúl : F. Ó Tiarnaigh (Cabhán), A. Mac Póilín (Aontruim), T. Mac Seain (Fir Manach), L. Mag Uidhir (Muineachán).

Luach — — — — — — — 10p

R. & S. Printers, Monaghan.

6

CLUICHÍ CEANNAIS
PEILE na hÉIREANN
PAIRC AN CHRÓCAIGH 22-9-74

SINSIR
3.15 p.m.
(80 Nóiméad)

S. Ó DOCHARTAIGH
(Áth Cliath)

G. MISTÉIL
(Gaillimh)

MIONÚIR
1.30 p.m.
(60 Nóiméad)

LUACH
10p

OFFICIAL PROGRAMME Seán Ó Síocháin
Ard Stiúrthóir

5

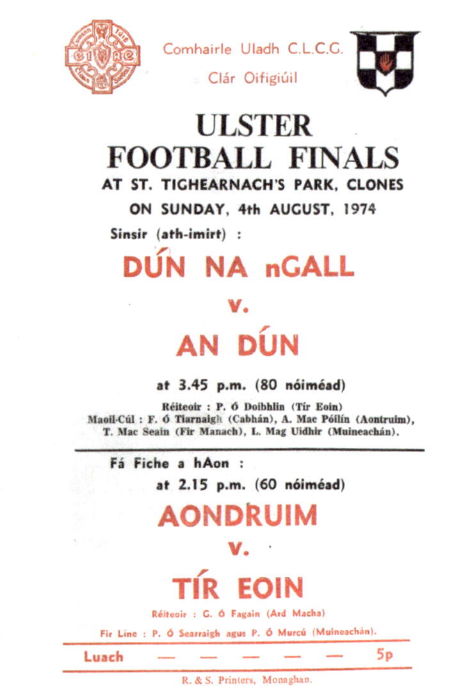

Comhairle Uladh C.L.C.G.
Clár Oifigiúil

ULSTER
FOOTBALL FINALS
AT ST. TIGHEARNACH'S PARK, CLONES
ON SUNDAY, 4th AUGUST, 1974

Sinsir (ath-imirt) :

DÚN NA nGALL
v.
AN DÚN
at 3.45 p.m. (80 nóiméad)
Réiteoir : P. Ó Doibhlin (Tír Eoin)
Maoil-Cúl : F. Ó Tiarnaigh (Cabhán), A. Mac Póilín (Aontruim), T. Mac Seain (Fir Manach), L. Mag Uidhir (Muineachán).

Fá Fiche a hAon :
at 2.15 p.m. (60 nóiméad)

AONDRUIM
v.
TÍR EOIN
Réiteoir : G. Ó Fagain (Ard Macha)
Fir Líne : P. Ó Searraigh agus P. Ó Murcú (Muineachán).

Luach — — — — — — 5p

R. & S. Printers, Monaghan.

7

clár
oifigiúil

Leinster Hurling Finals
21st July, 1974

CILL CHOINNIGH
v
LOCH GARMAN
SINSIR (3.30 p.m. - 80 minutes)
Réiteoir : M. DE SPÁINNE (Uabh Fáilí)

O'KEEFFE CUP, LEINSTER SENIOR HURLING TROPHY

MIONÚIR (2.00 p.m. - 60 minutes)
Réiteoir : S. Ó RAINCÍN (Laois)

Ath Cliath v Cill Choinnigh

LUACH 5p

Ó Néill
(Rónal)

COMHAIRLE LAIGHEAN C.L.G.

8

9

4 Ulster Football Final
Donegal 1-14 Down 2-11

5 Replay
Donegal 3-9 Down 1-12

6 All-Ireland Football Final
Dublin 0-14 Galway 1-06
Attendance – 71,898

7 Leinster Hurling Final
Kilkenny 6-13 Wexford 2-24

8 Munster Hurling Final
Limerick 6-14 Clare 3-09

9 All-Ireland Hurling Final
Kilkenny 3-19 Limerick 1-13
Attendance – 62,071

1975

In 1975, all senior intercounty matches became 70 minutes in duration. The 1975 Connacht football final saw Sligo claim only their second provincial title, and their first since 1928, after a replay against Mayo. However, their subsequent capitulation to Kerry in the All-Ireland semi-final took some of the shine off their achievement. Kerry had reasserted themselves in Munster after two years of finishing runners-up to Cork, in a game often remembered for Páidí Ó Sé and Dinny Allen's contretemps in the middle of the field. Kerry then met Dublin in the All-Ireland final for the first time since 1955, in what was the beginning of a famous rivalry in this decade. Recently retired from playing, Mick O'Dwyer was now managing Kerry and led them to All-Ireland victory at his first attempt. Pat Spillane accepted the cup in place of Kerry captain Micky 'Ned' O'Sullivan, who was unable to finish the game after a collision with Dublin's Seán Doherty.

1
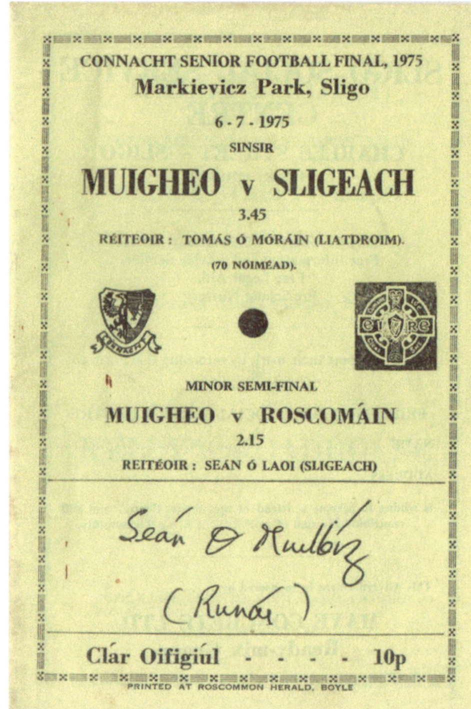

2

1 Connacht Football Final
Sligo 2-10 Mayo 1-13

2 Replay
Sligo 2-10 Mayo 0-15

3 Leinster Football Final
Dublin 3-13 Kildare 0-08

COMHAIRLE LAIGHEAN C.L.G.

LEINSTER FOOTBALL FINALS

CROKE PARK, JULY 27th, 1975

OLLY CRINNIGAN
(Kildare)

SEAN DOHERTY
(Dublin)

SENIOR: 3.30 p.m. ATH CLIATH v. CILL DARA
Reiteoir: BRENDAN HAYDEN (CARLOW).

MINOR: 2.00 p.m. AN MHI v. CILL DARA
Reiteoir: GEORGE SOMERVILLE (DUBLIN).

LUACH 10p.

OFFICIAL PROGRAMME

(Rúnaí)

4

5

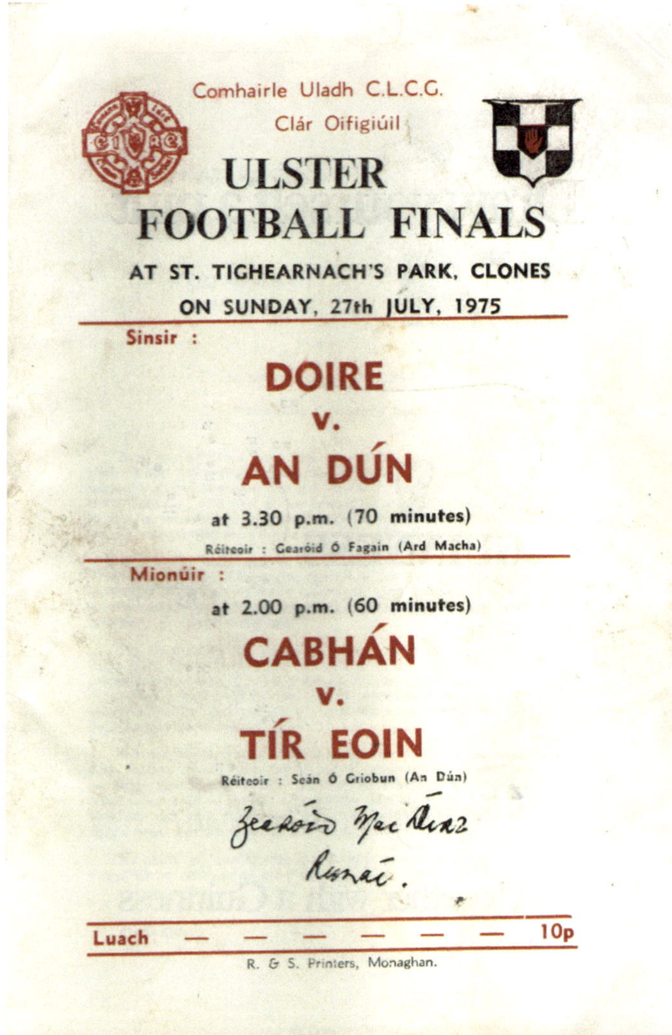

4 Munster Football Final
Kerry 1-14 Cork 0-07

5 Ulster Football Final
Derry 1-16 Down 2-06

6 All-Ireland Football Final
Kerry 2-12 Dublin 0-11
Attendance – 66,346

7 Leinster Hurling Final
Kilkenny 2-20 Wexford 2-14

8 Munster Hurling Final
Cork 3-14 Limerick 0-12

9 All-Ireland Hurling Final
Kilkenny 2-22 Galway 2-10
Attendance – 63,711

6

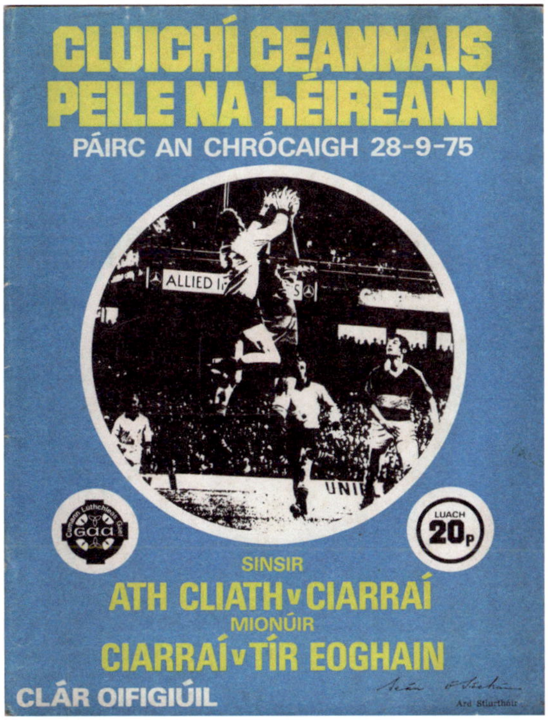
CLUICHÍ CEANNAIS
PEILE NA hÉIREANN
PÁIRC AN CHRÓCAIGH 28-9-75
LUACH 20p
SINSIR
ATH CLIATH v CIARRAÍ
MIONÚIR
CIARRAÍ v TÍR EOGHAIN
CLÁR OIFIGIÚIL

8

CLAR OIFIGIUIL
COMHAIRLE NA MUMHAN C.L.G.
MUNSTER HURLING FINALS
LIMERICK 27-7-'75
P. HARTIGAN (Limerick)
1974 Carrolls All-Star
JOHN HORGAN (Cork)
1974 Carrolls All-Star
MIONUR 1.45 p.m.
TIOBRAD ARANN v CORCAIGH
Moltóir : LIAM O CONCHUIR (Portlairge)
SINSIR : 3.15 p.m.
LUIMNEACH v CORCAIGH
Moltóir : SEAN O MALDOMHNAIGH (Tiobrad Arann)
LUACH 15P

7

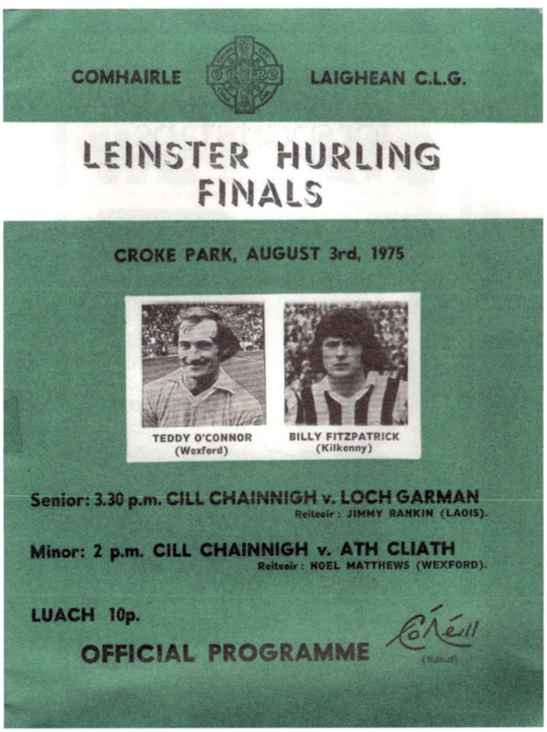
COMHAIRLE LAIGHEAN C.L.G.
LEINSTER HURLING FINALS
CROKE PARK, AUGUST 3rd, 1975
TEDDY O'CONNOR
(Wexford)
BILLY FITZPATRICK
(Kilkenny)
Senior: 3.30 p.m. CILL CHAINNIGH v. LOCH GARMAN
Reiteoir : JIMMY RANKIN (LAOIS).
Minor: 2 p.m. CILL CHAINNIGH v. ATH CLIATH
Reiteoir : NOEL MATTHEWS (WEXFORD).
LUACH 10p.
OFFICIAL PROGRAMME

9

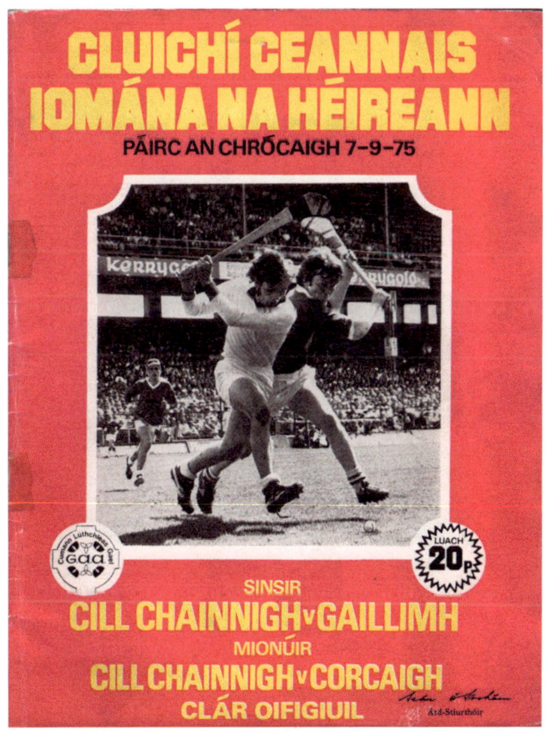
CLUICHÍ CEANNAIS
IOMÁNA NA HÉIREANN
PÁIRC AN CHRÓCAIGH 7-9-75
LUACH 20p
SINSIR
CILL CHAINNIGH v GAILLIMH
MIONÚIR
CILL CHAINNIGH v CORCAIGH
CLÁR OIFIGIUIL

1976

Cork County Board unveiled their new stadium, Páirc Uí Chaoimh, in June 1976, and both the Munster hurling and football finals were played in the new stadium some weeks later. If the Cork footballers were destined for a spell in the wilderness while Kerry's 'Golden Years' were in their pomp (although the Kingdom ended up losing this year's All-Ireland final to Dublin), the Cork hurlers kept the county colours flying for the foreseeable future. Having won the 1975 Munster hurling final, Cork retained their title this year. They narrowly defeated Tipperary in the semi-final, but the final was a different matter as they cruised past Limerick. Having received a bye to the All-Ireland final, Cork awaited the winners of Wexford and Galway, which went Wexford's way after a replay. The 1976 final between Cork and Wexford is often remembered as a classic. Despite a slow start, Cork were level at half-time and a strong second-half performance, particularly by midfielder Pat Moylan, gave Cork the victory.

1

2

1 Connacht Football Final
Galway 1-08 Roscommon 1-08

2 Replay
Galway 1-14 Roscommon 0-09

3 Leinster Football Final
Dublin 2-08 Meath 1-09

4 Munster Football Final
Kerry 0-10 Cork 0-10

5 Replay
Kerry 3-20 Cork 2-19 (aet)

6 Ulster Football Final
Derry 1-08 Cavan 1-08

3

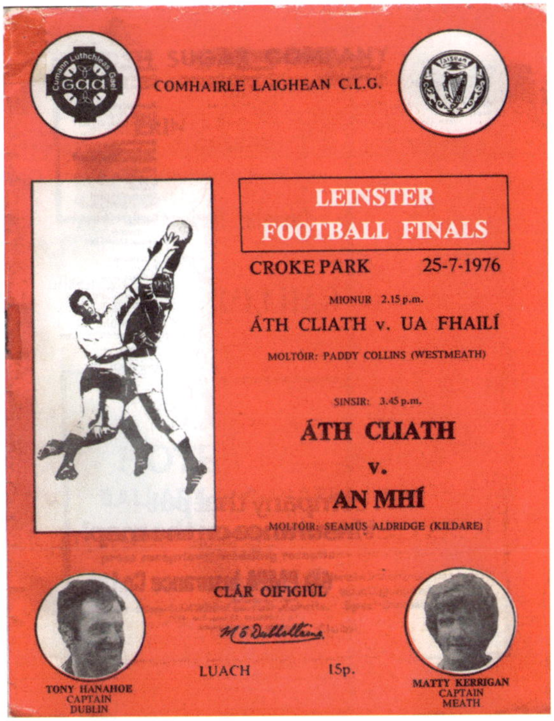
COMHAIRLE LAIGHEAN C.L.G.
LEINSTER FOOTBALL FINALS
CROKE PARK 25-7-1976
MIONUR 2.15 p.m.
ÁTH CLIATH v. UA FHAILÍ
MOLTÓIR: PADDY COLLINS (WESTMEATH)
SINSIR: 3.45 p.m.
ÁTH CLIATH
v.
AN MHÍ
MOLTÓIR: SEAMUS ALDRIDGE (KILDARE)
CLÁR OIFIGIÚL
LUACH 15p.
TONY HANAHOE
CAPTAIN
DUBLIN
MATTY KERRIGAN
CAPTAIN
MEATH

4

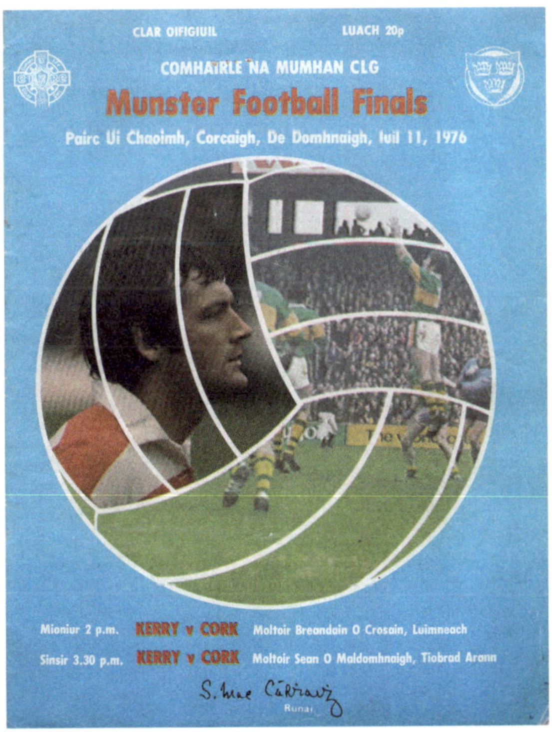
CLAR OIFIGIUIL
LUACH 20p
COMHAIRLE NA MUMHAN CLG
Munster Football Finals
Pairc Ui Chaoimh, Corcaigh, De Domhnaigh, Iuil 11, 1976
Mioniur 2 p.m. KERRY v CORK Moltoir Breandain O Crosain, Luimneach
Sinsir 3.30 p.m. KERRY v CORK Moltoir Sean O Maldomhnaigh, Tiobrad Arann
Runai

5

CLAR OIFIGIUIL
LUACH 20p
COMHAIRLE NA MUMHAN CLG
cluiche cheannais peile na mumhan (ath imirt)
Pairc Ui Chaoimh, De Domhnaigh, Iuil 25, 1976
Faoi 16 12.30 pm: Cluiche Cheannais Aonach Tailteann
CORCAIGH THUAIDH v CORCAIGH THEAS
Faoi 21 2pm: Cluiche Leathcheannais Iomana na hÉireann
CORCAIGH v GAILLIMH – Moltoir: Padraig Mac Eoin (Cill Coinnigh)
Sinsir 3.30: CIARRAI v CORCAIGH
Moltoir: Sean O Maoldomhnaigh, Tiobrad Arann
Runai

6

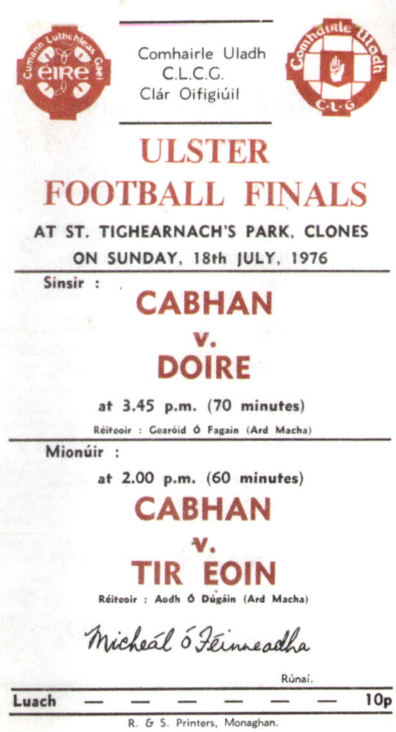
Comhairle Uladh
C.L.C.G.
Clár Oifigiúil
ULSTER
FOOTBALL FINALS
AT ST. TIGHEARNACH'S PARK, CLONES
ON SUNDAY, 18th JULY, 1976
Sinsir :
CABHAN
v.
DOIRE
at 3.45 p.m. (70 minutes)
Réiteoir : Gearóid Ó Fagain (Ard Macha)
Mionúir :
at 2.00 p.m. (60 minutes)
CABHAN
v.
TIR EOIN
Réiteoir : Aodh Ó Dúgáin (Ard Macha)
Micheál Ó Féinneadha
Rúnaí.
Luach — — — — — — 10p
R. & S. Printers, Monaghan.

7

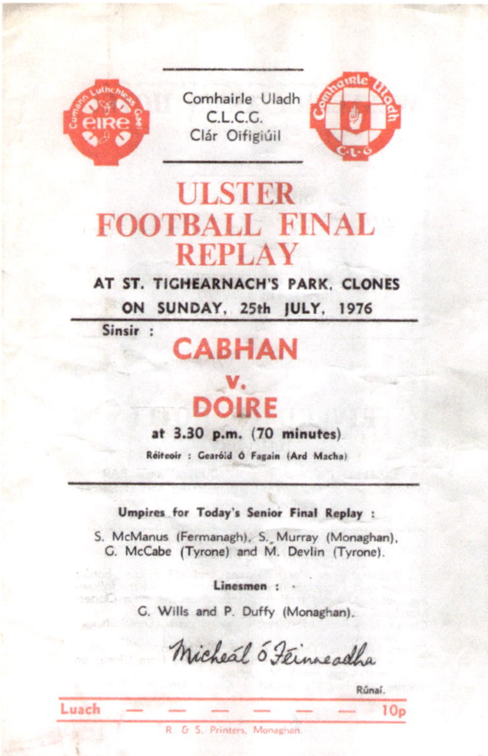
Comhairle Uladh
C.L.C.G.
Clár Oifigiúil
ULSTER
FOOTBALL FINAL
REPLAY
AT ST. TIGHEARNACH'S PARK, CLONES
ON SUNDAY, 25th JULY, 1976
Sinsir :
CABHAN
v.
DOIRE
at 3.30 p.m. (70 minutes)
Réiteoir : Gearóid Ó Fagain (Ard Macha)
Umpires for Today's Senior Final Replay :
S. McManus (Fermanagh), S. Murray (Monaghan), G. McCabe (Tyrone) and M. Devlin (Tyrone).
Linesmen :
G. Wills and P. Duffy (Monaghan).
Micheál Ó Feinneadha
Rúnaí.
Luach — — — — — — — 10p
R & S. Printers, Monaghan.

9

COMHAIRLE LAIGHEAN C.L.G.
LEINSTER
HURLING FINALS
CROKE PARK
18-7-1976
CILL CHAINNIGH V. LOCH GARMAN
CILL CHAINNIGH
V.
LOCH GARMAN
CLÁR OIFIGIÚIL
LUACH
15p.

8

CLUICHÍ CEANNAIS
PEILE NA hÉIREANN
CORCAIGH v GAILLIMH
Mionúir - 1.30 p.m.
ÁTH CLIATH v CIARRAÍ
Sinsir - 3.15 p.m.
26·9·76
Clár Oifigiúil Luach 20p

10

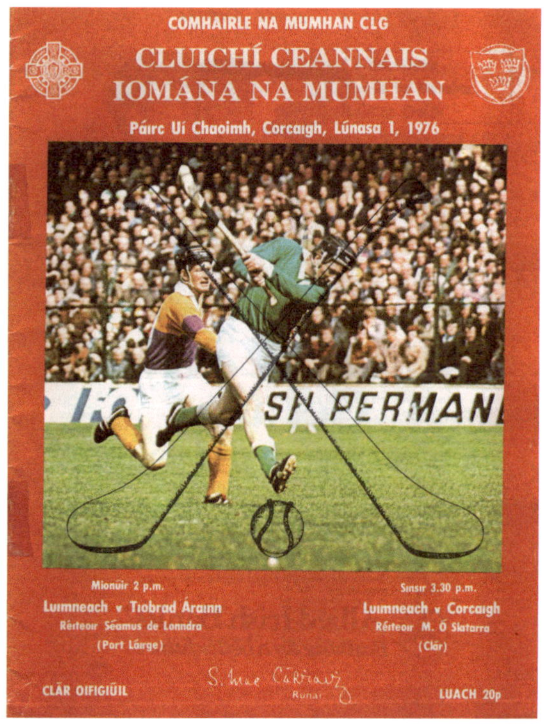
COMHAIRLE NA MUMHAN CLG
CLUICHÍ CEANNAIS
IOMÁNA NA MUMHAN
Páirc Uí Chaoimh, Corcaigh, Lúnasa 1, 1976
Mionúir 2 p.m.
Luimneach v Tiobrad Árainn
Réiteoir Séamus de Lonndra
(Port Láirge)
Sinsir 3.30 p.m.
Luimneach v Corcaigh
Réiteoir M. Ó Slatarra
(Clár)
CLÁR OIFIGIÚIL
Rúnaí
LUACH 20p

11

7 Replay
Derry 0-22 Cavan 1-16 (aet)

8 All-Ireland Football Final
Dublin 3-08 Kerry 0-10
Attendance – 73,588

9 Leinster Hurling Final
Wexford 2-20 Kilkenny 1-06

10 Munster Hurling Final
Cork 3-15 Limerick 4-05

11 All-Ireland Hurling Final
Cork 2-21 Wexford 4-11
Attendance – 62,684

1977

The All-Ireland hurling final of 1977 brought Wexford and Cork back together again for a reprise of the previous year's final. Cork had beaten Clare in a high-scoring Munster final and Wexford had got the better of Kilkenny in an equally exciting Leinster final. While this year's final did not match the spectacle of the 1976 final, the outcome was the same, with Cork withstanding a late Wexford rally to retain the Liam MacCarthy Cup.

In the Ulster football final, Armagh easily brushed aside Derry, who were looking to complete a provincial three in a row, but a replay was needed before they got the better of Roscommon in the All-Ireland semi-final. In the final, Armagh were no match for Dublin, with Jimmy Keaveney scoring 2-06 – a new record for a final. The previous October, Kevin Heffernan had shocked the Dublin GAA world by stepping down as manager a few short weeks after winning the All-Ireland football final. Tony Hanahoe, the team captain, assumed the role of player-manager and led Dublin as they retained their title.

1

2

1 Leinster Hurling Final
Wexford 3-17 Kilkenny 3-14

2 Munster Hurling Final
Cork 4-15 Clare 4-10

3 All-Ireland Hurling Final
Cork 1-17 Wexford 3-08
Attendance – 63,168

3

clár oifigiúil

Cluichí Cheannais Iomána na hÉireann 1977

Páirc an Chrócaigh
4 Mean Fomhair

SINSIR
3·15

Corcaigh

Loch garman

Réiteoir:
S. Ó Gráda

Cill Chainnigh v Corcaigh

Mionúir 1·30
Réiteoir: G. Ó Ciarubháin

LUACH
20p

Seán Ó Síocháin
Ard-Stiurthoir

4

Official Programme
Comhairle Connacht C.L.C.G.
CONNACHT SENIOR FOOTBALL FINAL
1977
Douglas Hyde Park, Roscommon
10 - 7 - '77
SINNSIR
ROSCOMÁIN v GAILLIMH
3.45.
REITEOIR: T. Ó MORÁIN (Liathdruim)
(70 NÓIMÉAD).
Cumann Lúthchleas Gael
GAA
CONNACHT MINOR FOOTBALL FINAL
Liathdruim v. Maigh Eo
2.15.
REITEOIR: P. Ó BRAONÁIN (Sligeach)
(60 NÓIMÉAD).
CLÁR OIFIGIÚL - - - - - - - 20p.
PRINTED AT ROSCOMMON HERALD, BOYLE.

6

Cluichí Ceannais Peile na Mumhan
PÁIRC AN GHEARALTAIGH, CILL ÁIRNE, 24 IÚIL 1977
12.30pm
Cluiche Ceannais Willwood Tailteann fé 16 (Ath-imirt)
CATHAIR LUIMNÍ v CATHAIR CORCAIGH THUAIDH
Mionúir 2pm:
CORCAIGH v CIARRAÍ
Réiteoir: Pádraig Ó Laighin (Luimneach)
Sinsir 3.30pm:
CIARRAÍ v CORCAIGH
Réiteoir: Breandán Mac Crosáin (Luimneach)
Clár Oifigiúil
Rúnaí
Luach 20p

5

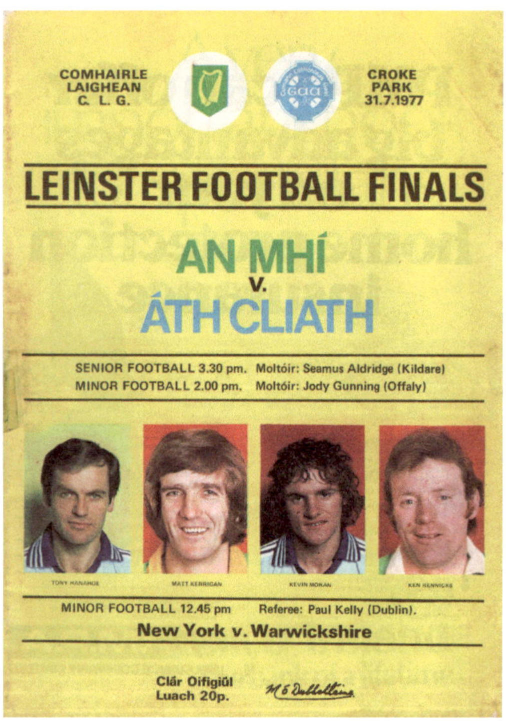
COMHAIRLE LAIGHEAN C. L. G.
CROKE PARK 31.7.1977
LEINSTER FOOTBALL FINALS
AN MHÍ
v.
ÁTH CLIATH
SENIOR FOOTBALL 3.30 pm. Moltóir: Seamus Aldridge (Kildare)
MINOR FOOTBALL 2.00 pm. Moltóir: Jody Gunning (Offaly)
MINOR FOOTBALL 12.45 pm Referee: Paul Kelly (Dublin).
New York v. Warwickshire
Clár Oifigiúl
Luach 20p.

7

Comhairle Uladh C.L.G.
ULSTER FOOTBALL FINALS
in ST. TIARNACH'S PARK, CLONES
on SUNDAY, 24th JULY, 1977
Official Programme
Rúnaí
LUACH 20p
MIONÚIR 2 p.m.
ARD MACHA
v.
AN DUN
Réiteoir:
Gearóid Mac Cába (Tír Eoin)
SINSEAR 3.45 (70 mins.)
ARD MACHA
v.
DOIRE
Réiteoir:
Séamas Ó Muirí (Muineachán)
R. & S. Printers, Monaghan.

8

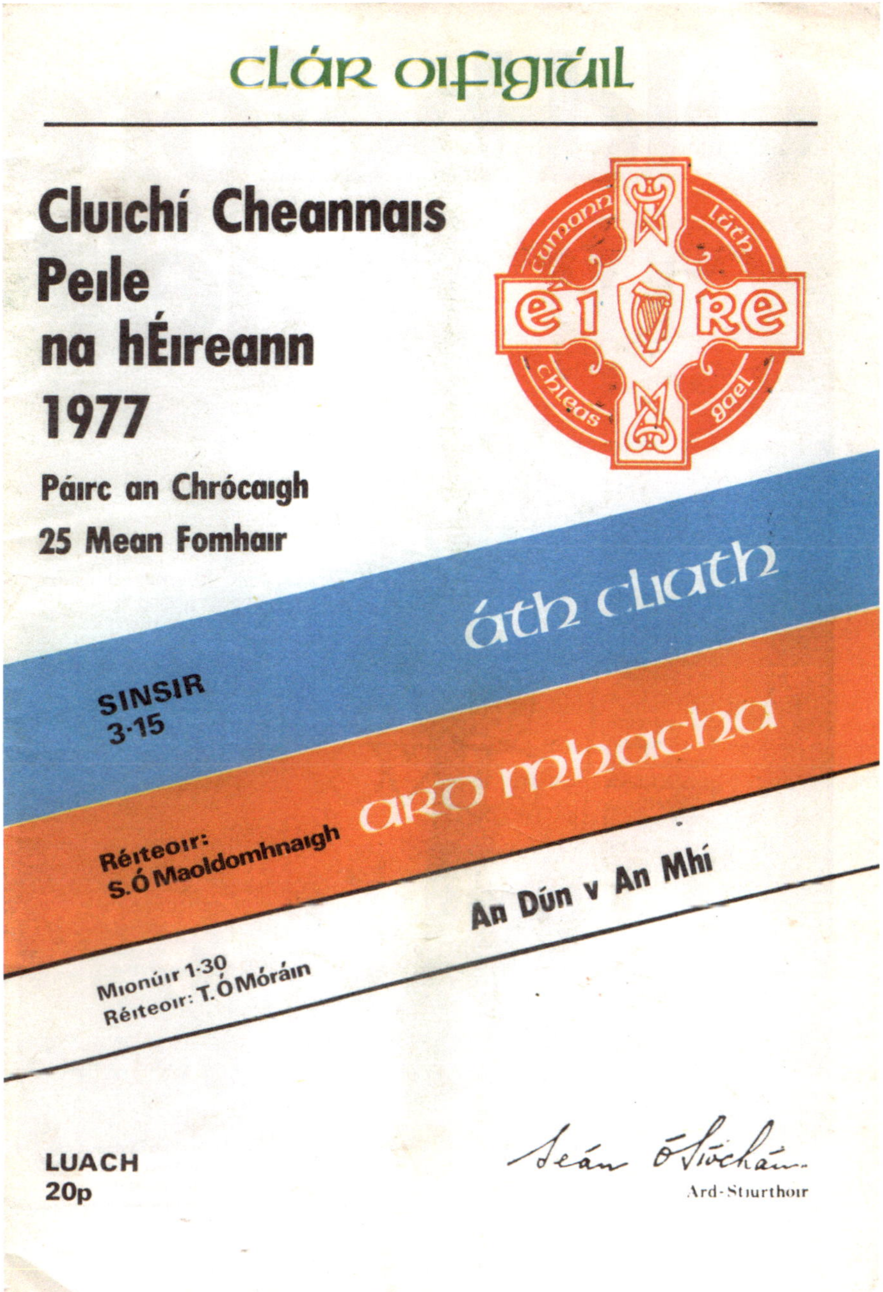

4 Connacht Football Final
Roscommon 1-12 Galway 2-08

5 Leinster Football Final
Dublin 1-09 Meath 0-08

6 Munster Football Final
Kerry 3-15 Cork 0-09

7 Ulster Football Final
Armagh 3-10 Derry 1-05

8 All-Ireland Football Final
Dublin 5-12 Armagh 3-06
Attendance – 66,542

1978

Seven years after the removal of 'the Ban', Kevin Moran, Dublin's All-Ireland-winning centre half-back, joined Manchester United in February of 1978 and went on to become the only man to win both FA Cup and All-Ireland medals. With United's permission, he returned to play in this year's All-Ireland football final against Kerry. While Kerry were comprehensive winners, Dublin felt aggrieved by the awarding of a controversial free, from which Mikey Sheehy deftly chipped the retreating Dublin goalkeeper, Paddy Cullen. Denis 'Ogie' Moran lifted the Sam Maguire Cup for what became the first of four titles in a row by Kerry.

In the hurling final, Cork defeated Kilkenny to complete their own All-Ireland three in a row, having put four Munster titles back-to-back earlier in the summer by beating Clare for the second consecutive year in the Munster final.

1

2

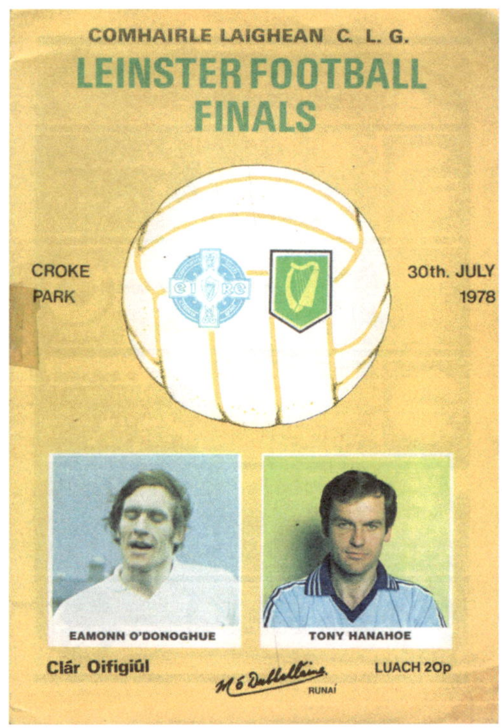

1 Connacht Football Final
Roscommon 2-07 Galway 0-09

2 Leinster Football Final
Dublin 1-17 Kildare 1-06

3 Munster Football Final
Kerry 3-14 Cork 3-07

3

Clár Oifigiúil Luach 20p

Cluichí Ceannais Peile na Mumhan

PÁIRC UÍ CHAOIMH, CORCAIGH 16ú IÚIL 1978

Mionúir 2pm:

CORCAIGH v CIARRAÍ

Réiteoir: Pádraig Ó Laighin (Luimneach)

Sinsir 3.30pm:

CIARRAÍ v CORCAIGH

Réiteoir: Seán Ó Conchúir (Luimneach)

Dónal Ó Nialláin **Rúnaí**

4

4 Ulster Football Final
Down 2-19 Cavan 2-12

5 All-Ireland Football Final
Kerry 5-11 Dublin 0-09
Attendance – 71,503

6 Leinster Hurling Final
Kilkenny 2-16 Wexford 1-16

7 Munster Hurling Final
Cork 0-13 Clare 0-11

8 All-Ireland Hurling Final
Cork 1-15 Kilkenny 2-08
Attendance – 64,155

5

clár oifigiúil
Cluichí Ceannais Peile na hÉireann 1978
Páirc an Chrócaigh
24/9/1978
SINSIR: 3.15 p.m.
Áth Cliath
Clarraí
Réiteóir: S. Alddrí
MIONUIR: 1.30 p.m.
Réiteóir: S. O Duinneagáin
Ath Cliath v Maigh Eo
LUACH 20p
Ard-Stiurthoir

6

COMHAIRLE LAIGHEAN C. L. G.
Leinster Hurling Finals
CROKE PARK
16th. JULY 1978
NOEL SKEHAN
CHRISTY KEOGH
Clár Oifigiúl
RUNAÍ
Luach 20p.

7

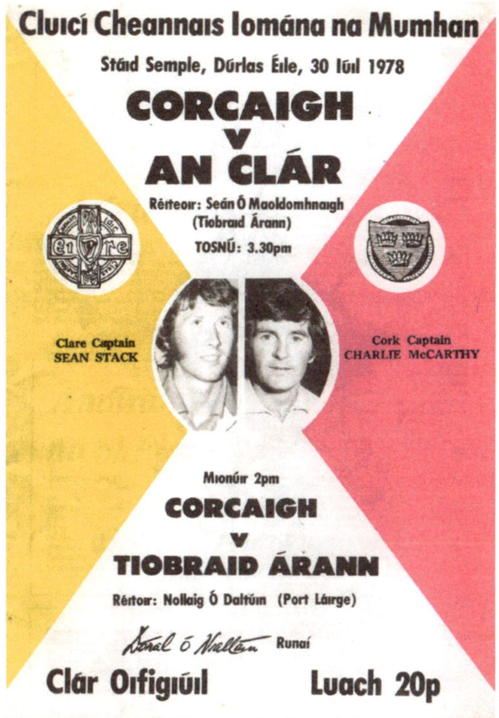
Cluicí Cheannais Iomána na Mumhan
Stáid Semple, Dúrlas Éile, 30 Iúil 1978
CORCAIGH
v
AN CLÁR
Réiteoir: Seán Ó Maoldomhnaigh (Tiobraid Árann)
TOSNÚ: 3.30pm
Clare Captain SEAN STACK
Cork Captain CHARLIE McCARTHY
Mionúir 2pm
CORCAIGH
v
TIOBRAID ÁRANN
Réitoir: Nollaig Ó Daltúin (Port Láirge)
Runaí
Clár Oifigiúil
Luach 20p

8

clár oifigiúil
Cluichí Cheannais Iomána na hÉireann 1978
Páirc an Chrócaigh
3/9/1978
SINSIR: 3.15 p.m.
cill chainnigh
corcaigh
Réiteóir: S. Ó Raincín
Cill Chainnigh v Corcaigh
MIONÚIR: 1.30 p.m.
Réiteóir: S de Londre
LUACH 20p
Ard-Stiurthoir

1979

In June 1979, Liam Mulvihill from Longford succeeded Seán Ó Síocháin as Ard Stiúrthóir of the GAA. His signature first appeared on the All-Ireland hurling final match programme later in the year. Mulvihill served until 2008 and oversaw a period of unprecedented change in the GAA, during which he oversaw the redevelopment of Croke Park and the abolition of Rules 21 and 42, as well as steering the association through the difficulties that faced the association during the IRA hunger strikes in the early 1980s.

In the absence of a Connacht hurling championship since 1923, the Galway hurling team represented the province in the All-Ireland series and had made steady progress during the 1970s, reaching the All-Ireland final in 1975. In 1979, they reached the final again, only for poor shooting, and the concession of an unfortunate goal, to allow Kilkenny to win their twenty-first title. Kerry and Dublin met again in the All-Ireland football final, and again, the result was a comfortable win for Kerry. Mikey Sheehy posted 2-06, equalling the scoring record for a final, and signalling the end of the great Dublin team of the 1970s.

1

2

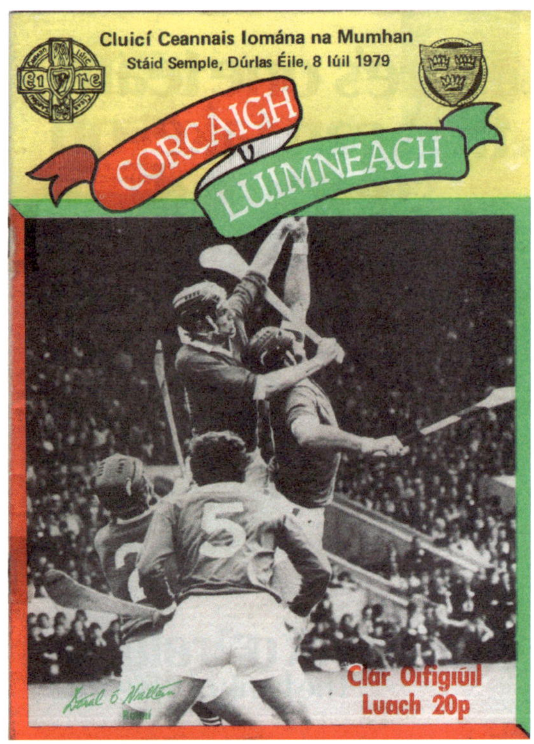

1 Leinster Hurling Final
Kilkenny 2-21 Wexford 2-17

2 Munster Hurling Final
Cork 2-14 Limerick 0-09

3 All-Ireland Hurling Final
Kilkenny 2-12 Galway 1-08
Attendance – 53,535

3

CLÁR OIFIGIÚL
Luach 25p
Cluichí Ceannais Iomána na hÉireann
Páirc an Chrócaigh
2.9.1979
Mionúir: 1.30
Corcaigh v Cill Chainnigh
Sinsir: 3.15
Cill Chainnigh v Gaillimh
—Ard-Stiúrthóir

4

Official Programme
Seán Ó Muilbhéin (Rúnaí)
Comhairle Connacht C.L.C.G.
CONNACHT SENIOR FOOTBALL FINAL 1979
MAIGH EO v ROSCOMÁIN
15 - 7 - 1979
McHale Park, Castlebar
3.30 p.m.
Reiteóir: PADHRAIC Ó GORMÁIN (Sligeach)
(70 NÓIMÉAD)
CONNACHT MINOR FOOTBALL FINAL
GAILLIMH v MAIGH EO
1.45 p.m.
Reiteóir: MICHÉAL Ó CIARÁIN (Sligeach)
(60 NÓIMÉAD)
CLÁR OIFIGIÚL - - - - - 25p
PRINTED BY ROSCOMMON HERALD BOYLE

5

COMHAIRLE LAIGHEAN C.L.G.
Leinster Football Finals
CROKE PARK
29th JULY 1979
KEVIN KILMURRAY (Uíbh Fhailí)
JIMMY KEAVENEY (Áth Cliath)
EUGENE MULLIGAN (Uíbh Fhailí)
CLÁR OIFIGIÚL
RUNAÍ
LUACH 20p

6

Cluichí Ceannais Peile na Mumhan
Páirc an Ghearaltaigh, Cill Áirne, 22 Iúil, 1979
DUNLOP
Mionúir 2 p.m.:
CORCAIGH v CIARRAÍ
Réiteoir: Seoirse Ó Riain
Sinsir 3.30 p.m.:
CIARRAÍ v CORCAIGH
Réiteoir: Pádraig Ó Laighin
Rúnaí
CLÁR OIFIGIÚIL
LUACH 20p

7

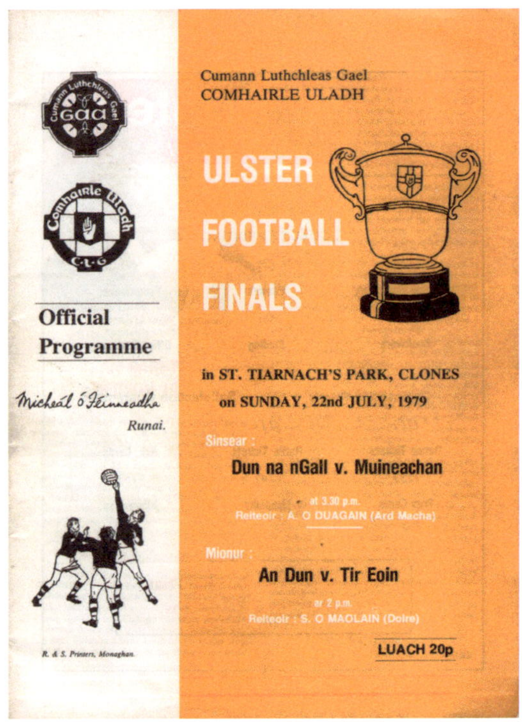
Cumann Luthchleas Gael
COMHAIRLE ULADH
ULSTER FOOTBALL FINALS
Official Programme
Micheál Ó Féinneadha
Runai.
in ST. TIARNACH'S PARK, CLONES
on SUNDAY, 22nd JULY, 1979
Sinsear:
Dun na nGall v. Muineachan
at 3.30 p.m.
Reiteoir: A. O DUAGAIN (Ard Macha)
Mionur:
An Dun v. Tir Eoin
at 2 p.m.
Reiteoir: S. O MAOLAIN (Doire)
LUACH 20p
R. & S. Printers, Monaghan.

8

4 Connacht Football Final
Roscommon 3-15 Mayo 2-10

5 Leinster Football Final
Dublin 1-08 Offaly 0-09

6 Munster Football Final
Kerry 2-14 Cork 2-04

7 Ulster Football Final
Monaghan 1-15 Donegal 0-11

8 All-Ireland Football Final
Kerry 3-13 Dublin1-08
Attendance – 72,185

1980–89

1980

In 1980, the Galway hurlers made the breakthrough they had been threatening for the previous decade. By defeating Limerick in the All-Ireland hurling final, they bridged a gap extending back to 1923* when, by a quirk of GAA history, Limerick were also the opposition. Two early goals gave Galway the lead at the break, but a spirited fightback by Limerick kept the match competitive to the end. Superb performances from Michael Conneely and Jimmy Cooney helped Galway to a victory that was greeted with wild celebrations at the final whistle. Joe Connolly, the Galway captain, gave one of the GAA's finest acceptance speeches when collecting the Liam MacCarthy Cup. Future GAA president Joe McDonagh then began the celebrations with an emotional rendition of 'The West's Awake' from the steps of the Hogan Stand.

A fortnight later, in a low-scoring All-Ireland football final, Kerry completed three wins in a row by defeating Roscommon. Having fallen five points behind early on, Kerry regrouped in time to retain the Sam Maguire Cup.

* The 1923 All-Ireland hurling final was played in 1924.

1

2

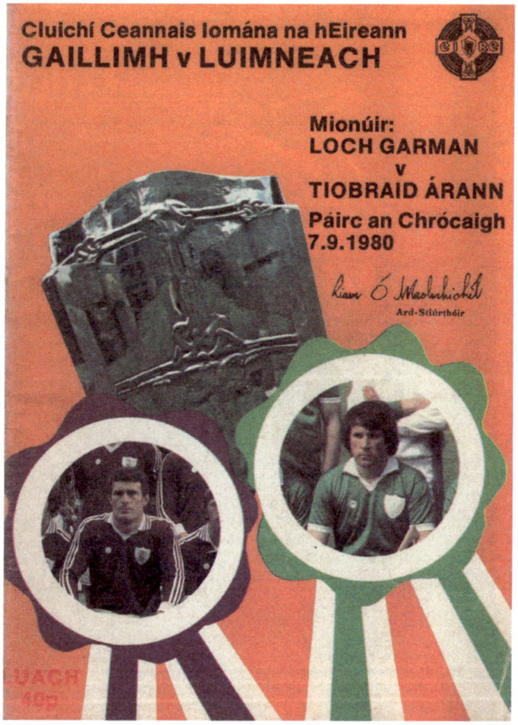

1 All-Ireland Final
Kerry 1-09 Roscommon 1-06
Attendance – 63,854

2 All-Ireland Final
Galway 2-15 Limerick 3-09
Attendance – 64,895

3 Connacht Final
Roscommon 3-13 Mayo 0-08

3

Official Programme

Comhairle Connacht
C.L.C.G.

CONNACHT SENIOR FOOTBALL FINAL 1980

MAIGH EO v ROSCOMÁIN

13 - 7 - 1980

Dr. Hyde Park, Roscommon

3.30 p.m.

Reiteóir : MICHEAL Ó CÍARAIN (Sligeach)

(70 NÓIMÉAD)

CONNACHT MINOR FOOTBALL FINAL

MAIGH EO v ROSCOMÁIN

1.45 p.m.

Reiteóir : SEÁN Ó LAOI (Sligeach)

(60 NÓIMÉAD)

CLÁR OIFIGIÚIL - - - - 25p

PRINTED AT ROSCOMMON HERALD, BOYLE.

4

COMHAIRLE LAIGHEAN C.L.G.

Leinster Football Finals

CROKE PARK, 27th JULY 1980

CLÁR OIFIGIÚIL

M. Ó Dubhshláine

RUNAÍ

Bernard Brogan (Áth Cliath

Captains Richie Connors (Uibh Fháilí) and Tony Hanahoe (Áth Cliath) shake hands before the 1979 Leinster Final. In centre is referee Paddy Collins

Seán Lowry (Uibh Fháilí)

LUACH 30p

4 Leinster Final
Offaly 1-10 Dublin 1-08

5 Leinster Final
Offaly 3-17 Kilkenny 5-10

6 Munster Final
Kerry 3-13 Cork 0-12

7 Munster Final
Limerick 2-14 Cork 2-10

8 Ulster Final
Armagh 4-10 Tyrone 4-07

5

COMHAIRLE LAIGHEAN
C.L.G.
Leinster
Hurling
Finals
Damian Martin
Uíbh Fhailí
Joe Hennessy
Cill Chainnigh
Noel Skehan Cill Chainnigh
CROKE PARK
13th JULY 1980
CLÁR OIFIGIÚIL
RUNAÍ
LUACH 30p

7

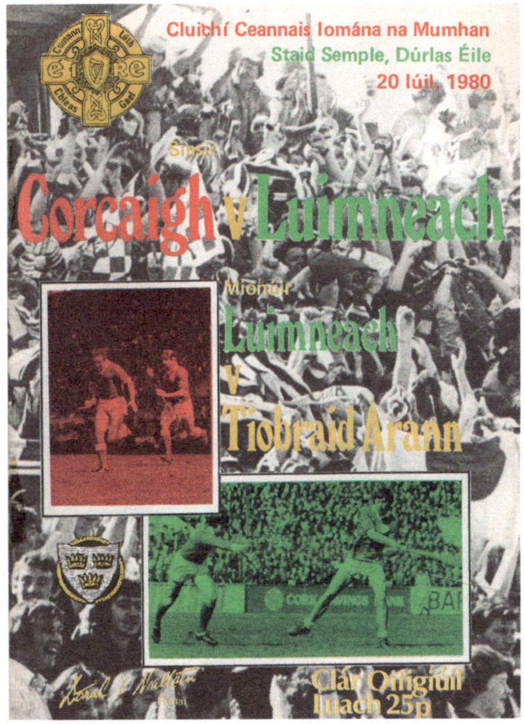
Cluichí Ceannais Iomána na Mumhan
Staid Semple, Dúrlas Éile
20 Iúil, 1980
Sinsir
Corcaigh v Luimneach
Mionúir
Luimneach
v
Tiobraid Árann
Clár Oifigiúil
Luach 25p

6

CLUICHÍ
CEANNAIS
PEILE NA
MUMHAN
Pairc Uí Chaoimh
6 Iúil 1980
Corcaigh
v
Ciarraí
3.30 p.m.
MIONUIR
2.00 p.m.
Ciarraí
v
Corcaigh
CLAR OIFIGIUIL
Luach 25p
Donal Ó Niallain

8

Ulster Football Finals
Cluain Eois
20 Iúl 1980
PADDY MORIARTY
(Ard Macha)
KEVIN McCABE
(Tír Eoin)
Micheál Ó Féinneadha
Rúnaí
Clár Oifigiúil 20p

1981

Galway returned to the All-Ireland hurling final in 1981 but this time the unconfined joy belonged to the supporters of Offaly, who witnessed their county win the Liam MacCarthy Cup for the first time. Shortly after half-time, Galway were ahead by seven points but thereafter failed to press home their advantage. With time running out, Johnny Flaherty scored the goal which gave Offaly the victory. Pádraig Horan had the honour of being the first man from the county to accept the MacCarthy Cup.

Two weeks later, it was the turn of the Offaly footballers to attempt to win the All-Ireland final. Standing in their way was one of the best football teams in the history of the GAA. A year previously, Kerry had beaten Offaly by five points in the All-Ireland semi-final and this year, though level at half-time, a superb passing movement ended with Kerry's Jack O'Shea blasting the ball to the net to give Kerry four All-Ireland titles in a row. It was a bittersweet year for Offaly's Liam Currams, who played in both finals.

1

2

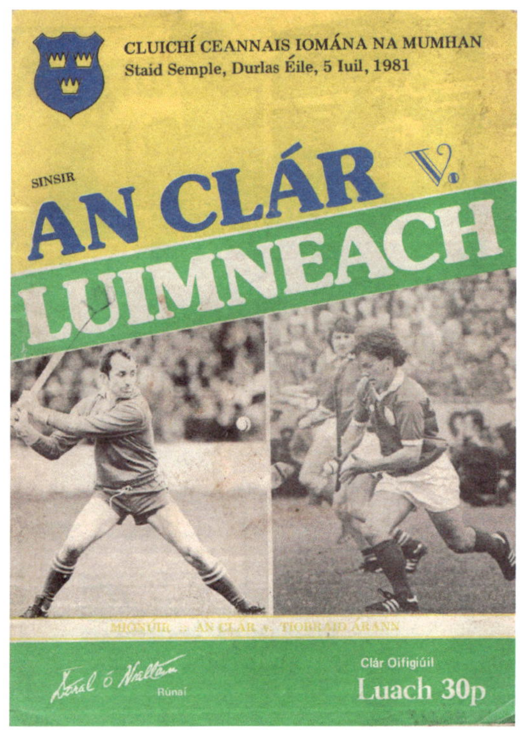

1 Leinster Hurling Final
Offaly 3-12 Wexford 2-13

2 Munster Hurling Final
Limerick 3-12 Clare 2-09

3 All-Ireland Hurling Final
Offaly 2-12 Galway 0-15
Attendance – 71,384

Clár Oifigiúl
Luach 40p
Ard-Stiúrthóir
Cluichí Ceannais Iomána na hÉireann
Sinsir: GAILLIMH v UIBH FHÁILÍ
Mionúir: Cill Chainnigh v. Gaillimh
Páirc an Chrócaigh 6.9.1981

4

Comhairle Connacht C.L.C.G.
Connacht Senior Football Final 1981
MacHALE PARK, CASTLEBAR
July 12th, 1981
Sinsear:
MAIGH EO v SLIGEACH
3.15 p.m. - (70 noimead)
Reiteoir: TOMAS O'CUINNEAGAIN (Gaillimh)
Mionuir:
MAIGH EO v ROSCOMAIN
1.45 (60 noimead)
Reiteoir: PADRAIC MacAOGAIN (Liathdroim)
Clar Oifigiul
30p
Comhairle Connacht C.L.C.G.
Design, printing, pictures by "Western People".

5

COMHAIRLE LAIGHEAN C.L.G.
LEINSTER FOOTBALL FINALS
Croke Park
July 26th
1981.
Rúnaí
LUACH
40p

6

Cluichí Ceannais Peile na Mumhan
Stáid an Ghearaltaigh, Cill Áirne
19 Iúil, 1981.
CIARRAÍ V CORCAIGH
Donal Ó Nialláin, Rúnaí.
Clár Oifigúil
Luach 30p.

7

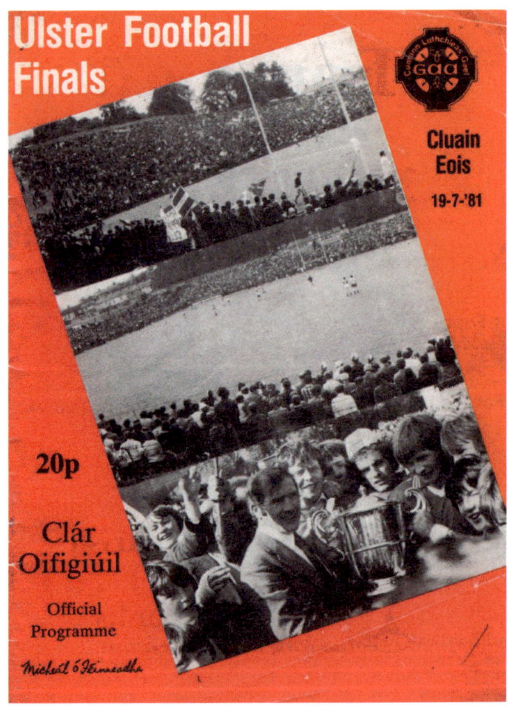

Ulster Football Finals
Cluain Eois
19-7-'81
20p
Clár Oifigiúil
Official Programme

8

4 Connacht Football Final
Mayo 0-12 Sligo 0-04

5 Leinster Football Final
Offaly 1-18 Laois 3-09

6 Munster Football Final
Kerry 1-11 Cork 0-03

7 Ulster Football Final
Down 3-12 Armagh 1-10

8 All-Ireland Football Final
Kerry 1-12 Offaly 0-08
Attendance – 61,489

1982

No team in the history of the GAA had ever won five All-Ireland senior titles in a row. In 1982, Kerry were the hottest of favourites to be the first. To do this, they had to beat an Offaly team, managed by Eugene McGee, that they had played in each of the last two seasons. All was going according to plan until: 'Two minutes left in the game, Kerry leading by two points ... it looks as if they are winning, the way the Offaly men are diddling and dawdling ... here they come, this is Liam Connor the full back ... a high lobbing, dropping ball in towards the goalmouth ... a shot, A GOAL! A goal, a goal for Offaly.'

Michael O'Hehir's classic commentary described Séamus Darby's famous winning goal as Offaly became champions and denied Kerry the elusive five in a row. Richie Connor lifted the Sam Maguire Cup, and Liam Currams had a football medal to go with the hurling medal he'd won the previous year.

Brian Cody captained Kilkenny as they inflicted a heavy defeat on Cork in the All-Ireland hurling final.

1

2

1 Connacht Football Final
Galway 3-17 Mayo 0-10

2 Leinster Football Final
Offaly 1-16 Dublin 1-07

3 All-Ireland Football Final
Offaly 1-15 Kerry 0-17
Attendance – 62,309

Clár Oifigiúl

Luach 50p

Cluichí Ceannais Peile na hÉireann

Sinsir:

Ciarraí

v

Uibh Fháilí

Mionúir:

Ath Cliath

v

Ciarraí

PAIRC AN CHRÓCAIGH

19.9.1982

Ard-Stiúrthóir

4

5

4 Munster Football Final
Kerry 0-09 Cork 0-09

5 Replay
Kerry 2-18 Cork 0-12

6 Ulster Football Final
Armagh 0-10 Fermanagh 1-04

7 Leinster Hurling Final
Kilkenny 1-11 Offaly 0-12

8 Munster Hurling Final
Cork 5-31 Waterford 3-06

9 All-Ireland Hurling Final
Kilkenny 3-18 Cork 1-13
Attendance – 59,550

6

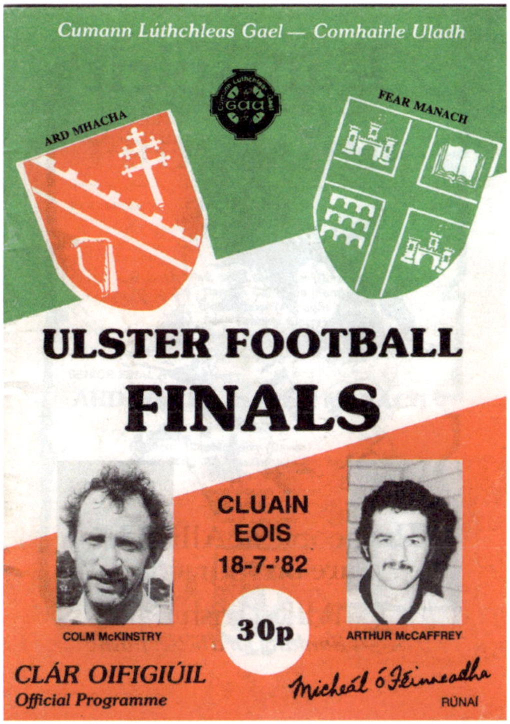
Cumann Lúthchleas Gael — Comhairle Uladh
ARD MHACHA
FEAR MANACH
ULSTER FOOTBALL
FINALS
CLUAIN
EOIS
18-7-'82
COLM McKINSTRY
30p
ARTHUR McCAFFREY
CLÁR OIFIGIÚIL
Official Programme
RÚNAÍ

7

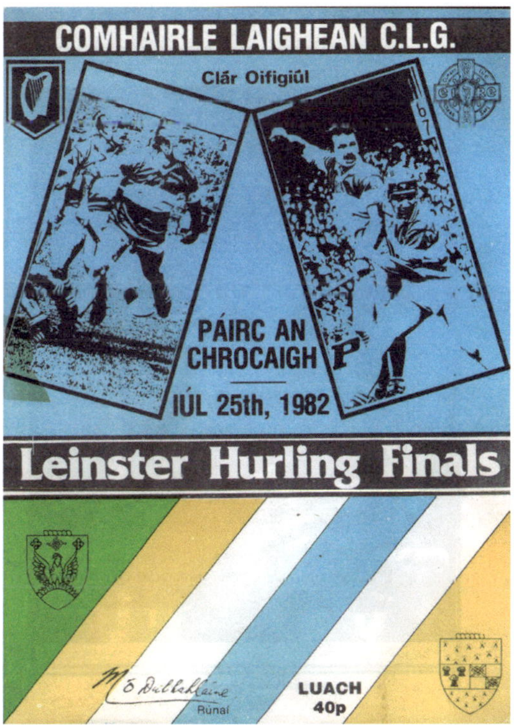
COMHAIRLE LAIGHEAN C.L.G.
Clár Oifigiúl
PÁIRC AN
CHROCAIGH
IÚL 25th, 1982
Leinster Hurling Finals
Rúnaí
LUACH
40p

8

Cluichí Ceannais Iomána na Mumhan
Stáid Semple, Dúrlas Éile
18 Iúil, 1982
Corcaigh
v.
Port Láirge
Clár Oifigiúil
Luach 40p

9

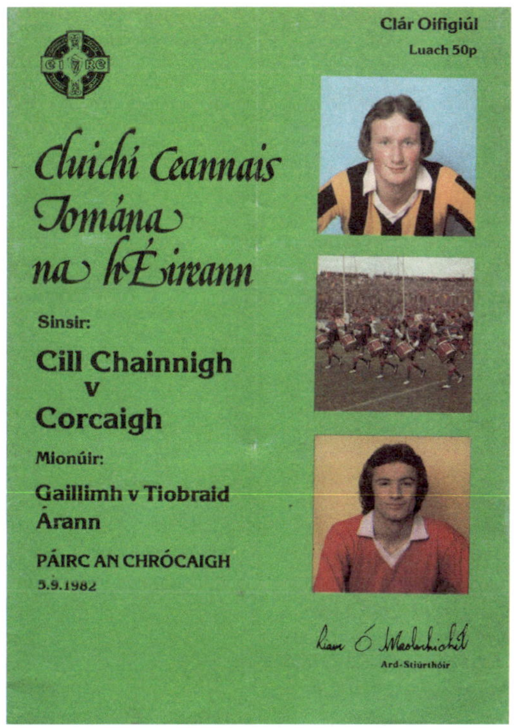
Clár Oifigiúl
Luach 50p
Cluichí Ceannais
Iomána
na hÉireann
Sinsir:
Cill Chainnigh
v
Corcaigh
Mionúir:
Gaillimh v Tiobraid
Árann
PÁIRC AN CHRÓCAIGH
5.9.1982
Ard-Stiúrthóir

1983

In the 1983 Munster football final, Kerry were once again undone by a late goal as Cork took the provincial crown for the first time since 1974. Dublin, having regained the Leinster title, beat Cork after a replay in Páirc Uí Chaoimh and advanced to play Galway in the All-Ireland final. In a highly controversial game, four players were sent off and, even though Dublin finished the match with 12 men, they also finished with the Sam Maguire Cup.

Cork and Kilkenny met in the final for a second consecutive year and Kilkenny again had the upper hand, but by a considerably smaller margin. Cork had beaten Galway in an All-Ireland semi-final, memorable for Jimmy Barry Murphy's wonder goal after he doubled on a John Fenton pass from midfield.

1

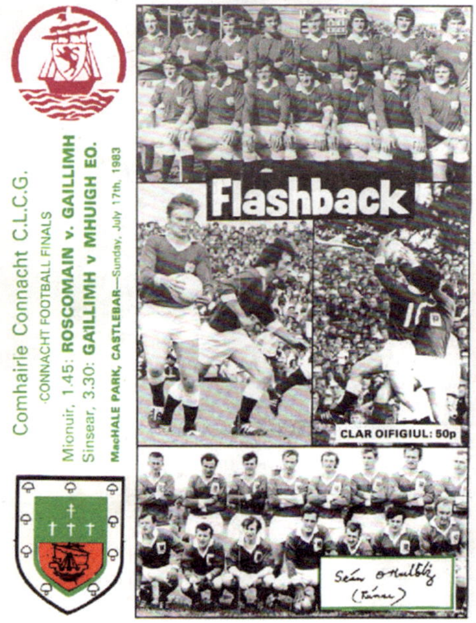

2

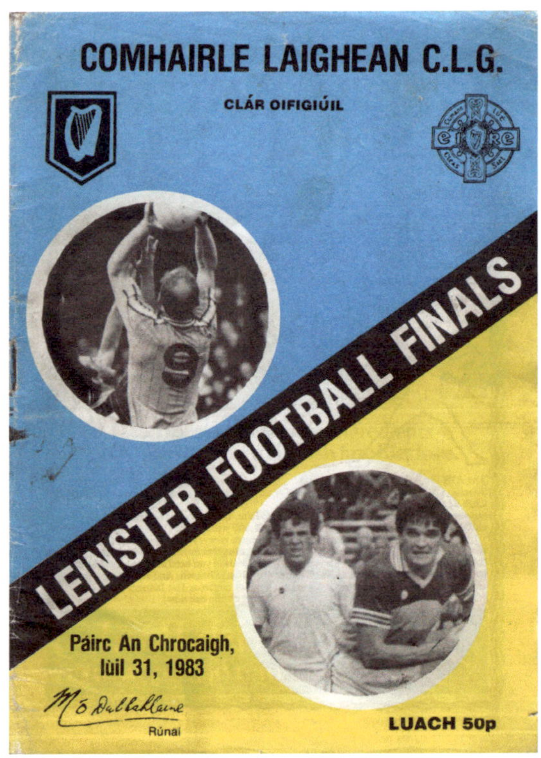

1 Connacht Football Final
Galway 1-13 Mayo 1-10

2 Leinster Football Final
Dublin 2-13 Offaly1-11

3 Munster Football Final
Cork 3-10 Kerry 3-09

Cluichí Ceannais Peile na Mumhan
Paírc Uí Chaoimh, Corcaigh, 17 Iúil, 1983

3

Corcaigh v. Ciarraí

Clár Oifigiúil

Luach 50p

4

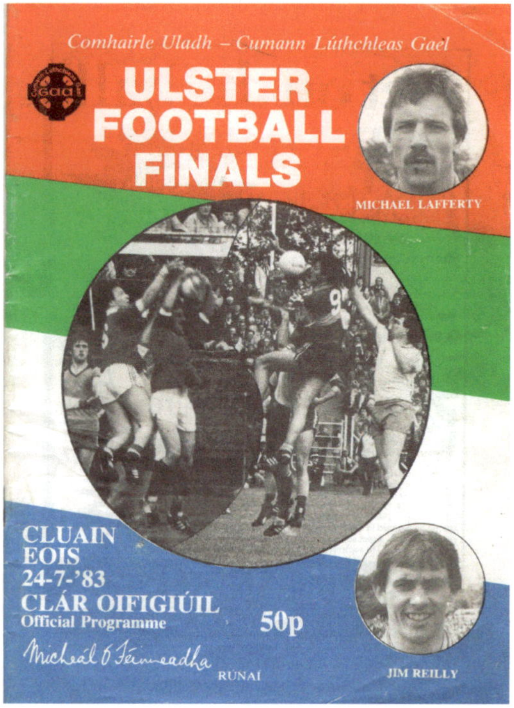
Comhairle Uladh – Cumann Lúthchleas Gael
ULSTER FOOTBALL FINALS
MICHAEL LAFFERTY
CLUAIN EOIS
24-7-'83
CLÁR OIFIGIÚIL
Official Programme
50p
RUNAÍ
JIM REILLY

5

Cluichí Ceannais Peile na hÉireann
CLÁR OIFIGIÚIL
Luach
50p
Páirc an Chrócaigh
18-9-1983
Ard-Stiurthóir

6

COMHAIRLE LAIGHEAN C.L.G.
CLÁR OIFIGIÚIL
LEINSTER HURLING FINALS
Páirc An Chrocaigh,
Iúil 10, 1983
Rúnaí
LUACH 50p

7

CLUICHÍ CHEANNAIS IOMÁNA NA MUMHAN
CORCAIGH v PORT LAIRGE
Dónal Ó Nialláin, Runaí
Clár Oifigiúil Luach 50p

4 Ulster Football Final
Donegal 1-14 Cavan 1-11

5 All-Ireland Football Final
Dublin 1-10 Galway 1-08
Attendance – 71,988

6 Leinster Hurling Final
Kilkenny 1-17 Offaly 0-13

7 Munster Hurling Final
Cork 3-22 Waterford 0-12

8 All-Ireland Hurling Final
Kilkenny 2-14 Cork 2-12
Attendance – 58,381

1984

The GAA celebrated its centenary year in 1984. To mark the milestone, a special competition – the Ford Centenary Cup – was played. In the football competition, Meath defeated Monaghan in the final and Cork beat Laois in the hurling final. Furthermore, a series of Compromise Rules football matches was played between Ireland and Australia, and, in recognition of the town's special place in the founding of the GAA, the All-Ireland hurling final was played in Semple Stadium in Thurles.

The Connacht Council produced a wonderful commemorative souvenir booklet to go with the match programme for the Connacht final. The All-Ireland final match programmes were also special souvenir productions. Cork were determined not to lose three consecutive All-Ireland hurling finals and were convincing winners over Offaly in the final in Thurles. In the football final, Kerry and Dublin resumed hostilities, but, once again, Kerry had the upper hand.

1

2

1 Leinster Hurling Final
Offaly 1-15 Wexford 2-11

2 Munster Hurling Final
Cork 4-15 Tipperary 3-14

3 All-Ireland Hurling Final
Cork 3-16 Offaly 1-12
Attendance – 59,814

3

CLÁR OIFIGIÚIL
GAA
1884–1984
Cluichí Ceannais Iomána na hÉireann
CLG
Stáid Semple,
Durlas
2 Meán Fomhair 1984
CORCAIGH v UÍBH FHAILÍ
Pascal Long (Cill Chainnigh) 3.30 i.n.
Cill Chainnigh v Luimneach
Frank Murphy (Corcaigh) 1.30 i.n.
100
Bliain Comóradh An Chéid
Ard-Stiúrthóir
Luach £1

4

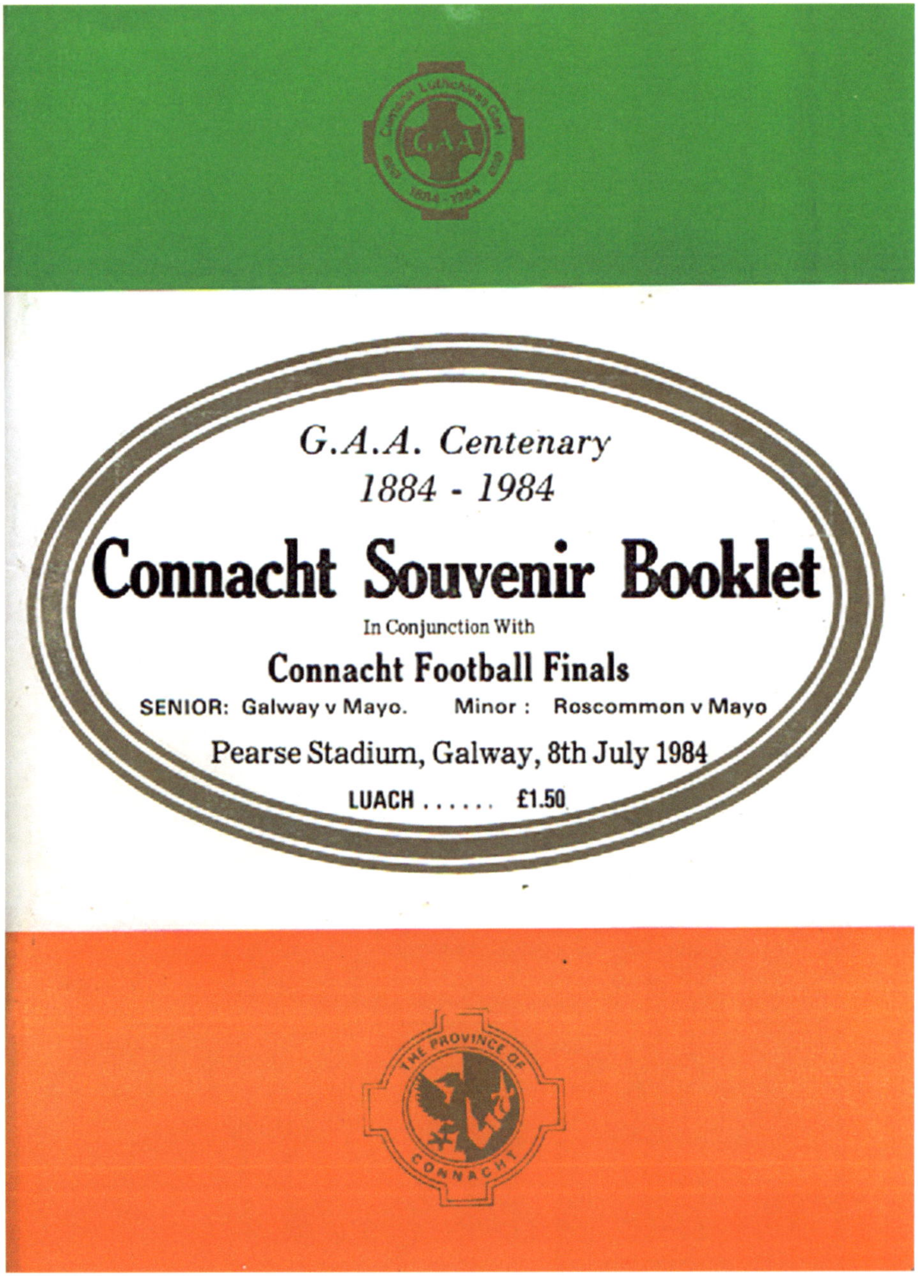

4 Connacht Football Final
Galway 2-13 Mayo 2-09

5 Leinster Football Final
Dublin 2-10 Meath 1-09

6 Munster Football Final
Kerry 3-14 Cork 2-10

7 Ulster Football Final
Tyrone 0-15 Armagh 1-07

8 All-Ireland Football Final
Kerry 0-14 Dublin 1-06
Attendance – 68,365

5

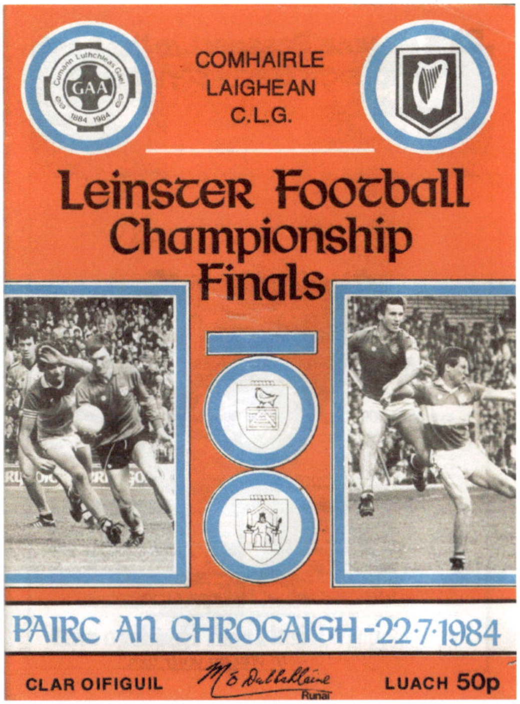
COMHAIRLE
LAIGHEAN
C.L.G.
Leinster Football
Championship
Finals
PAIRC AN CHROCAIGH - 22·7·1984
CLAR OIFIGUIL
Runai
LUACH 50p

6

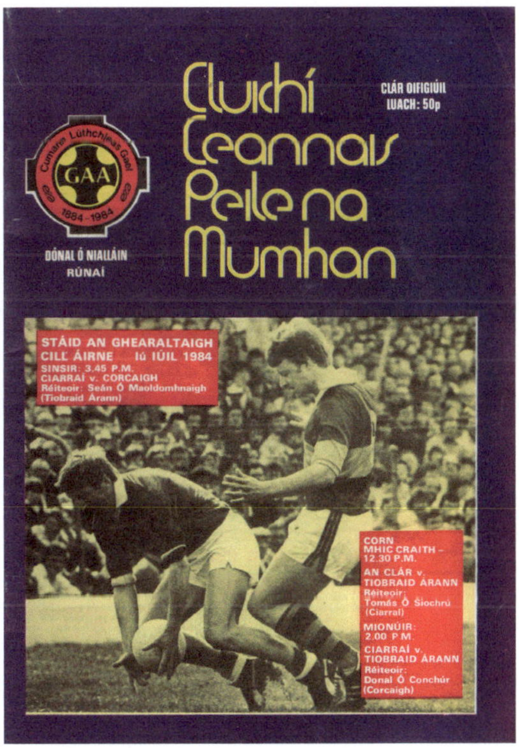
Cluichí
Ceannais
Peile na
Mumhan
CLÁR OIFIGIÚIL
LUACH: 50p
DÓNAL Ó NIALLÁIN
RÚNAÍ
STÁID AN GHEARALTAIGH
CILL ÁIRNE 15 IÚIL 1984
SINSIR: 3.45 P.M.
CIARRAÍ v. CORCAIGH
Réiteoir: Seán Ó Maoldomhnaigh
(Tiobraid Árann)
CORN
MHIC CRAITH –
12.30 P.M.
AN CLÁR v.
TIOBRAID ÁRANN
Réiteoir:
Tomás Ó Siochrú
(Ciarraí)
MIONÚIR:
2.00 P.M.
CIARRAÍ v.
TIOBRAID ÁRANN
Réiteoir:
Donal Ó Conchúr
(Corcaigh)

7

Cumann Lúthchleas Gael – Comhairle Uladh
Clár Oifigiúil
Official Programme
PADDY MORIARTY
EUGENE McKENNA
ULSTER FOOTBALL
FINALS
Cluain Eois, 15-7-1984
£1

8

Cluichí Ceannais Peile na hÉireann
baile átha cliath
tiobraid árann
ciarraí
baile átha cliath
Luach £1.00
CLÁR OIFIGIÚIL
Ard-Stiúrthóir
23 Meán Fómhair 1984
PÁIRC AN CHRÓCAIGH
Bliain Comóradh an Chéid

1985

Offaly retained their Leinster hurling title in 1985 by beating Kilkenny after a replay and easing past neighbours Laois in the final. In Munster, Cork and Tipperary met again in the provincial hurling final with Cork securing a relatively comfortable six-point victory. In the All-Ireland semi-finals, the reigning All-Ireland and Munster champions suffered a shock defeat to Galway, while Offaly swept the Antrim challenge aside. That brought Offaly and Galway, the two teams who had experienced break-out years in 1980 and 1981, together in the All-Ireland final. Veteran Pádraig Horan inspired Offaly to a narrow win as they won their second All-Ireland hurling championship.

Both All-Ireland football semi-finals needed a replay to decide who would meet in the final. Eventually, it was the familiar pairing of Dublin and Kerry that emerged – and a familiar result also ensued, as Kerry won by four points.

1

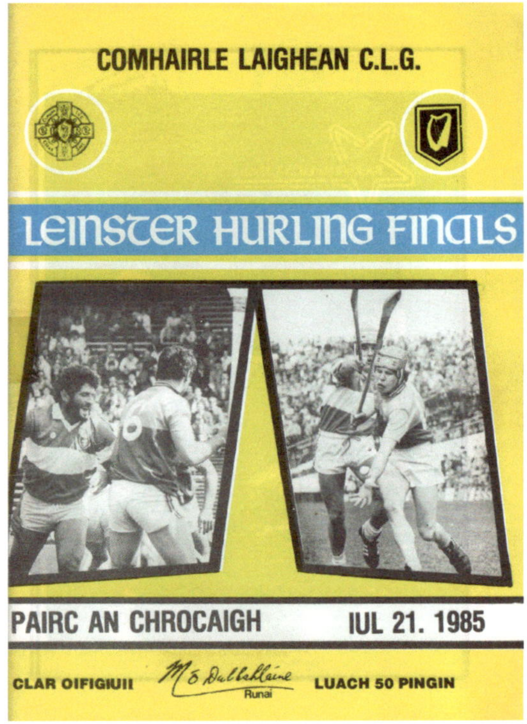

2

1 Leinster Hurling Final
Offaly 5-15 Laois 0-17

2 Munster Hurling Final
Cork 4-17 Tipperary 4-11

3 All-Ireland Hurling Final
Offaly 2-11 Galway 1-12
Attendance – 61,814

CLÁR OIFIGIÚIL
Cluichí Ceannais Iomána
na hÉireann
i bPáirc an Chrócaigh
1 Meán Fomhair 1985
Ard-stiúrthóir
Luach £1

4

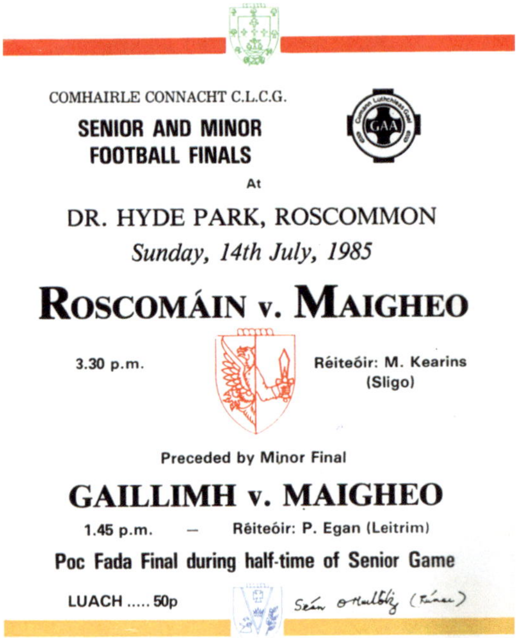
COMHAIRLE CONNACHT C.L.C.G.
SENIOR AND MINOR FOOTBALL FINALS
At
DR. HYDE PARK, ROSCOMMON
Sunday, 14th July, 1985
ROSCOMÁIN v. MAIGHEO
3.30 p.m.
Réiteóir: M. Kearins (Sligo)
Preceded by Minor Final
GAILLIMH v. MAIGHEO
1.45 p.m. — Réiteóir: P. Egan (Leitrim)
Poc Fada Final during half-time of Senior Game
LUACH 50p

5

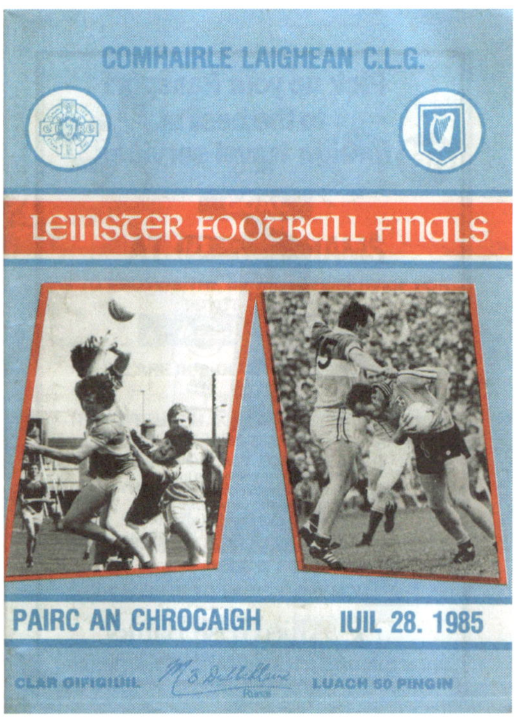
COMHAIRLE LAIGHEAN C.L.G.
LEINSTER FOOTBALL FINALS
PAIRC AN CHROCAIGH
IUIL 28. 1985
CLAR OIFIGIUIL
LUACH 50 PINGIN

6

Cluichí Ceannais Peile na Mumhan
Pairc Uí Chaoimh, 21 Iúil, 1985
Corcaigh
Ciarraí
Rúnaí
Clár Oifigiuil
Luach 50p

7

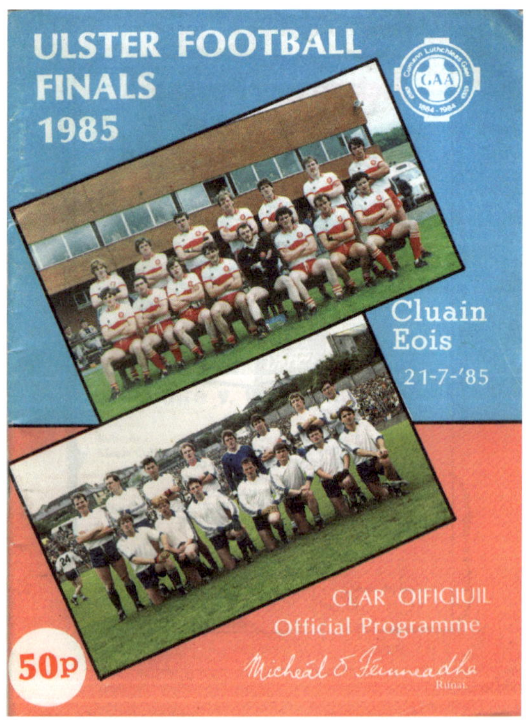
ULSTER FOOTBALL FINALS
1985
Cluain Eois
21-7-'85
CLAR OIFIGIUIL
Official Programme
50p
Rúnaí

8

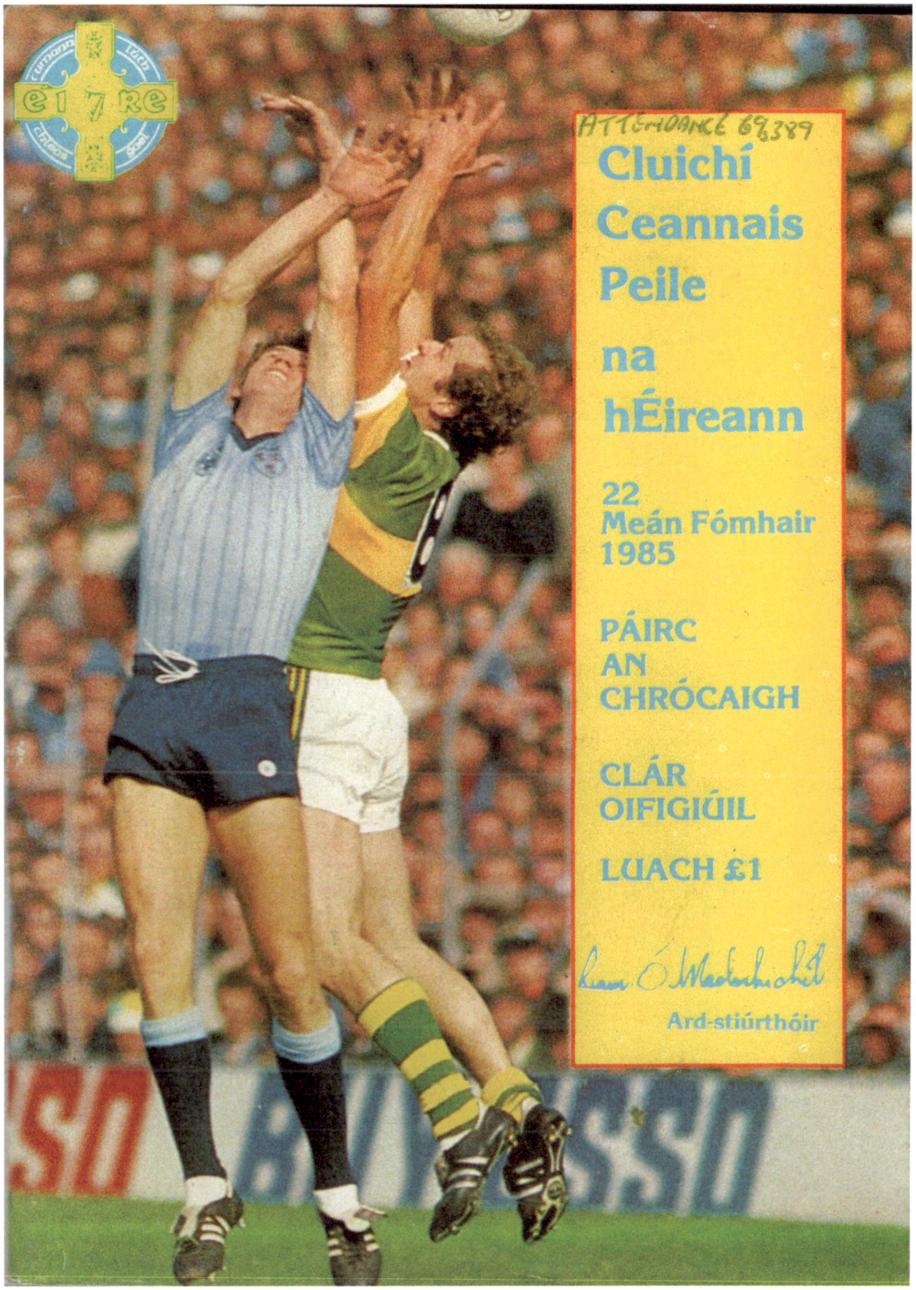

4 Connacht Football Final
Mayo 2-11 Roscommon 0-08

5 Leinster Football Final
Dublin 0-10 Laois 0-04

6 Munster Football Final
Kerry 2-11 Cork 0-11

7 Ulster Football Final
Monaghan 2-9 Derry 0-08

8 All-Ireland Football Final
Kerry 2-12 Dublin 2-08
Attendance – 69,389

1986

Two counties showed increasing improvement in the 1986 hurling championship. Galway's impressive defeat of Kilkenny in the All-Ireland semi-final set up a final meeting with Cork, who only had five points to spare over an Antrim team that were making steady progress. In the first meeting of the teams in an All-Ireland final since 1953, Cork were convincing winners over Galway. Kerry's victory in the All-Ireland football final meant that five players – Pat Spillane, Ger Power, Denis 'Ogie' Moran, Mikey Sheehy and Páidí Ó Sé – collected a then-record eighth All-Ireland football medal this year.

Political dignitaries had to source their own tickets for the 1986 All-Ireland finals. The GAA was in dispute with the government over VAT on hurleys, DIRT on development funds and rates on GAA venues; as a result, they did not invite politicians to sit in the Ard Chomhairle section as was customary. Jerry O'Sullivan, the Lord Mayor of Cork, watched his county win the hurling final from Hill 16.

1

2
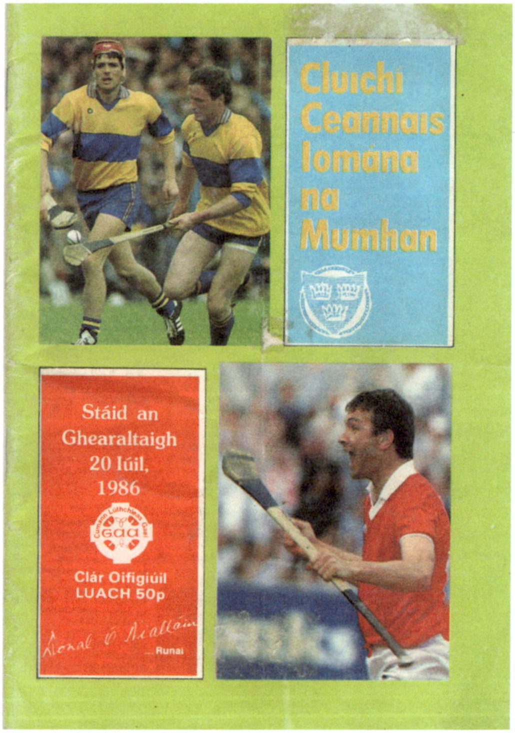

1 Leinster Hurling Final
Kilkenny 4-10 Offaly 1-11

2 Munster Hurling Final
Cork 2-18 Clare 3-12

3 All-Ireland Hurling Final
Cork 4-13 Galway 2-15
Attendance – 63,451

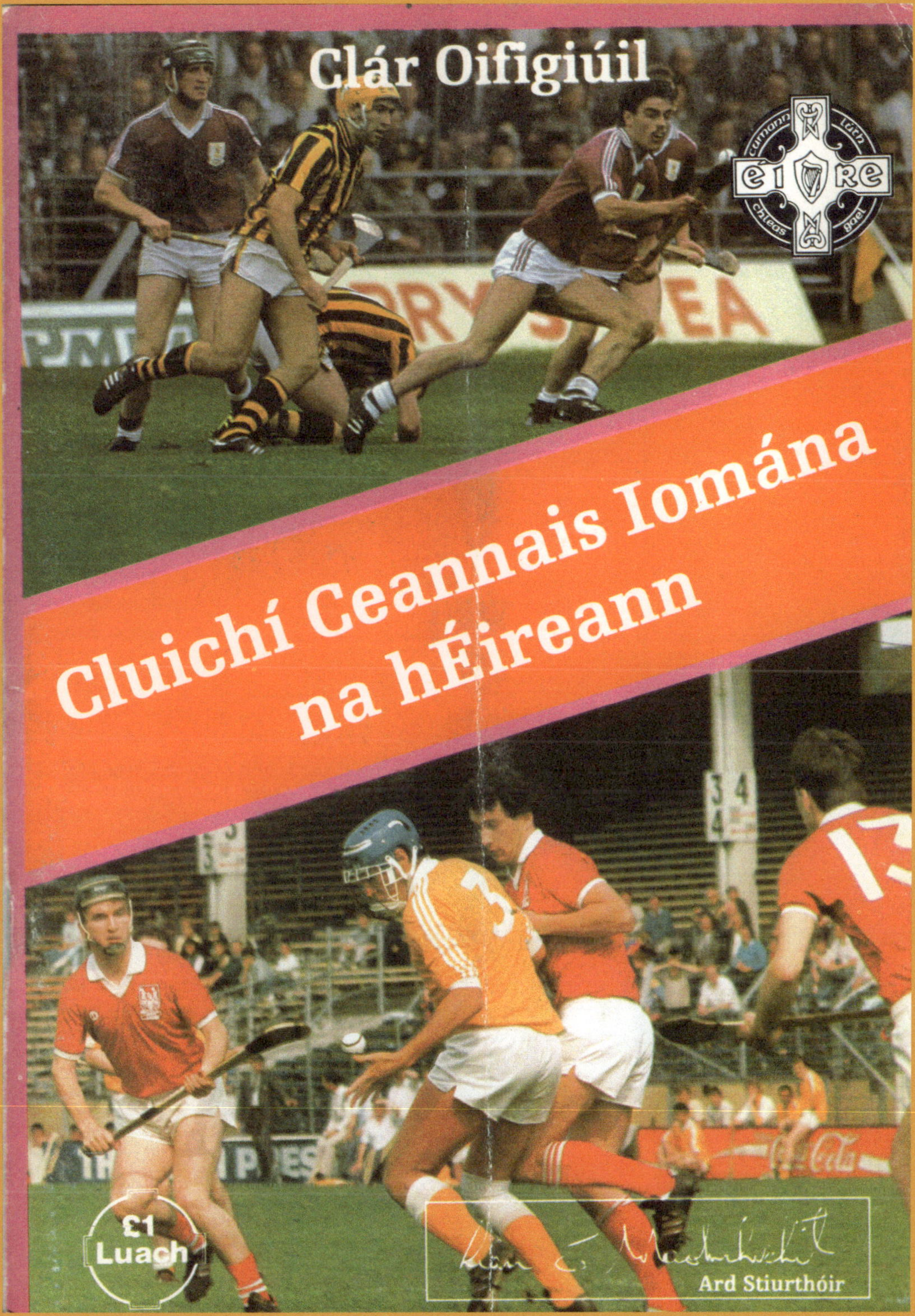

Clár Oifigiúil
Cumann Lúth Chleas Gael
éire
Cluichí Ceannais Iomána na hÉireann
£1 Luach
Ard Stiurthóir

4

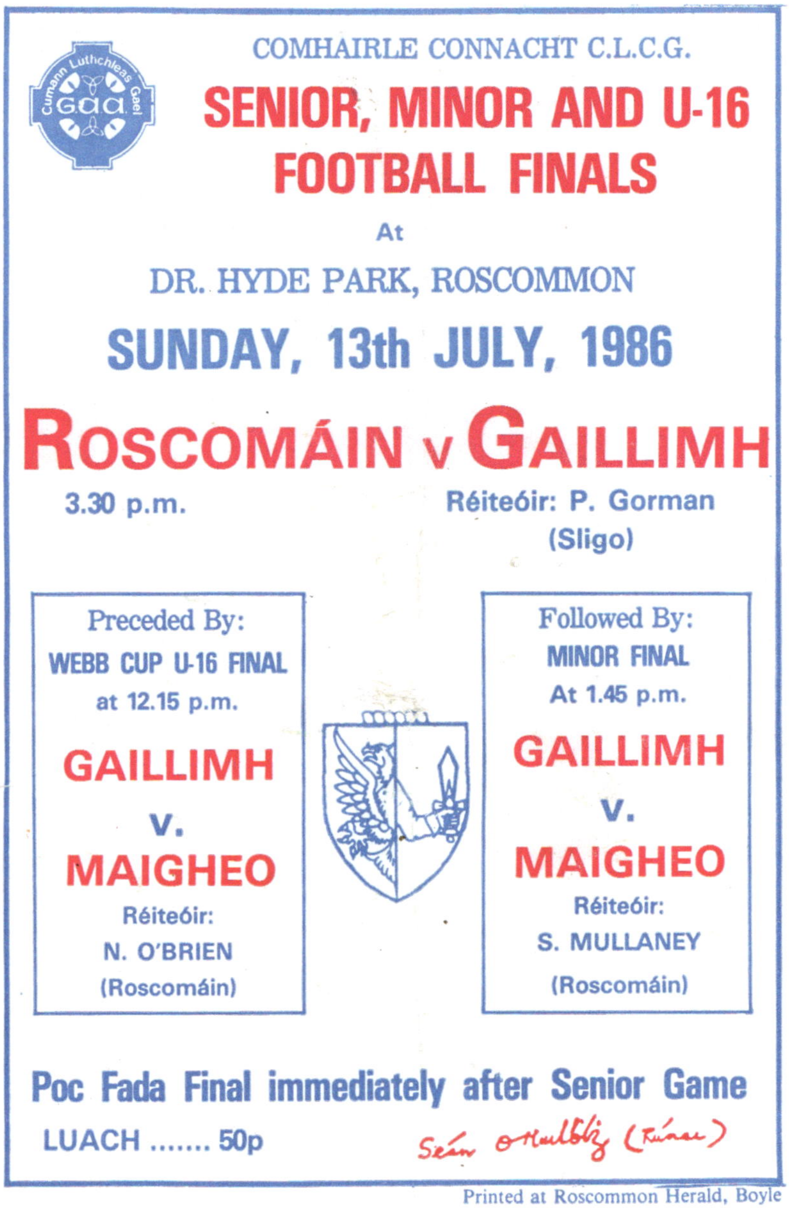

COMHAIRLE CONNACHT C.L.C.G.

SENIOR, MINOR AND U-16 FOOTBALL FINALS

At

DR. HYDE PARK, ROSCOMMON

SUNDAY, 13th JULY, 1986

ROSCOMÁIN v GAILLIMH

3.30 p.m.

Réiteóir: P. Gorman (Sligo)

Preceded By:
WEBB CUP U-16 FINAL
at 12.15 p.m.
GAILLIMH
v.
MAIGHEO
Réiteóir:
N. O'BRIEN
(Roscomáin)

Followed By:
MINOR FINAL
At 1.45 p.m.
GAILLIMH
v.
MAIGHEO
Réiteóir:
S. MULLANEY
(Roscomáin)

Poc Fada Final immediately after Senior Game

LUACH 50p

Printed at Roscommon Herald, Boyle

4 Connacht Football Final
Galway 1-08 Roscommon 1-05

5 Leinster Football Final
Meath 0-09 Dublin 0-07

6 Munster Football Final
Kerry 0-12 Cork 0-08

7 Ulster Football Final
Tyrone 1-11 Down 0-10

8 All-Ireland Football Final
Kerry 2-15 Tyrone 1-10
Attendance – 68,628

5

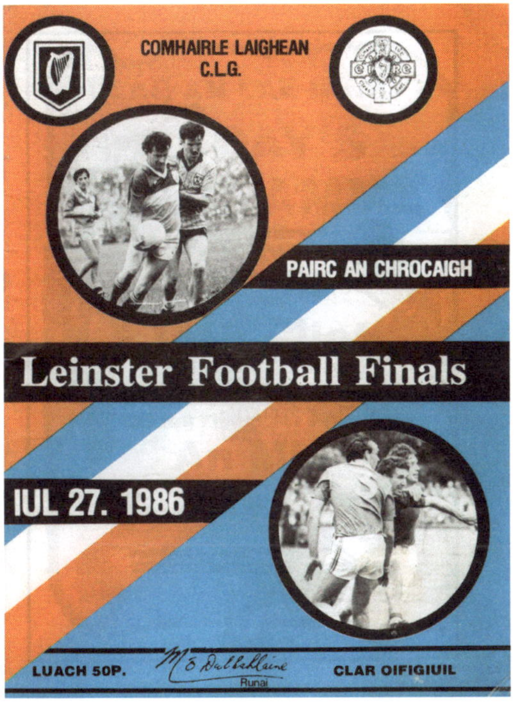
COMHAIRLE LAIGHEAN
C.L.G.
PAIRC AN CHROCAIGH
Leinster Football Finals
IUL 27. 1986
LUACH 50P.
Runai
CLAR OIFIGIUIL

7

Cumann Lúthchleas Gael
Comhairle Uladh
ULSTER FOOTBALL
FINALS
CLUAIN EOIS
20-7-'86
50p
An Dún
Tír Eoin
CLÁR OIFIGIÚIL
Official Programme
RÚNAÍ.

6

Craobh Peil
na Mumhan
1986
Clár Oifigiúil: £1
Dónal Ó Nialláin
Runai

8

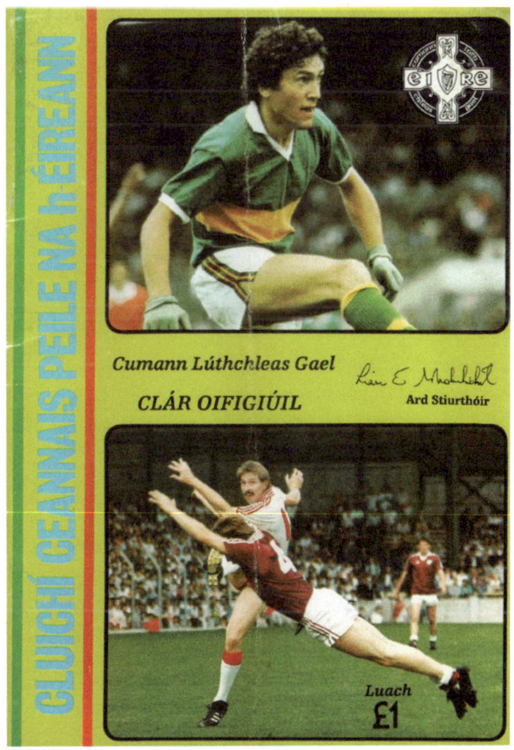
CLUICHÍ CEANNAIS PEILE NA h-ÉIREANN
Cumann Lúthchleas Gael
CLÁR OIFIGIÚIL
Ard Stiurthóir
Luach
£1

1987

In 1987, with Michael 'Babs' Keating at the helm, Tipperary met Cork in the Munster hurling final. A draw in Semple Stadium, memorable for Nicky English's kicked goal, meant a replay in Fitzgerald Stadium in Killarney a week later. The replay went to extra time before Tipperary eventually got the better of Cork. Emotional scenes ensued as Tipperary captain Richard Stakelum, when accepting the cup, declared the county's 16-year famine without a Munster championship to be over.

In the All-Ireland football final, Meath's victory over Cork meant that Meath captain Mick Lyons became the last man to receive the original Sam Maguire Cup. The cup, first played for in 1928, was retired after 60 years of service. Wear and tear had taken its toll on the cup, and it now resides in the Croke Park Museum.

1

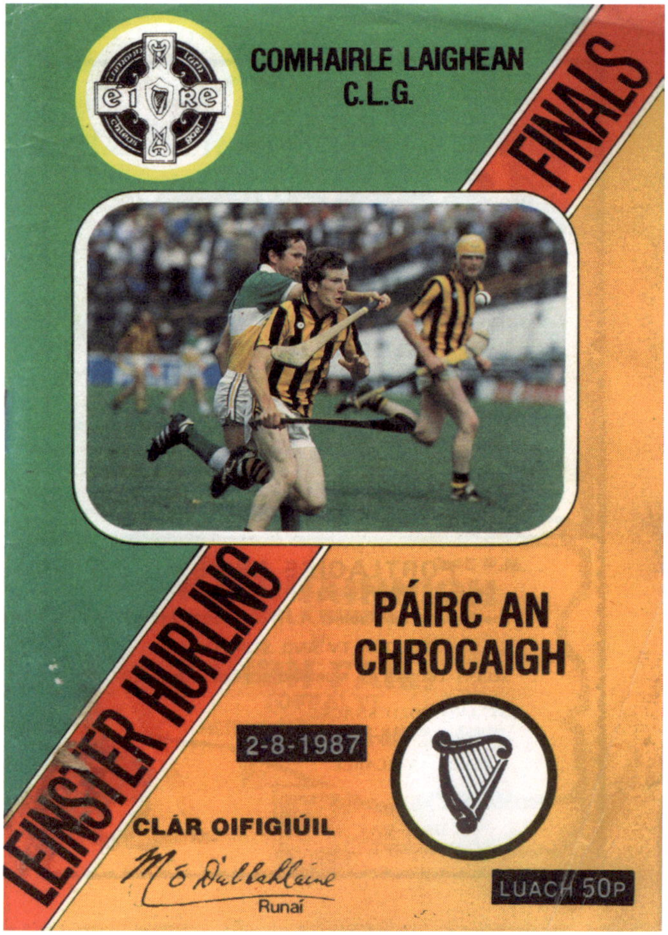

1 Leinster Hurling Final
Kilkenny 2-14 Offaly 0-17

2 Munster Hurling Final
Tipperary 1-18 Cork 1-18

3 Replay
Tipperary 4-22 Cork 1-22 (aet)

4 All-Ireland Hurling Final
Galway 1-12 Kilkenny 0-09
Attendance – 65,586

5 Connacht Football Final
Galway 0-08 Mayo 0-07

2

Cluichí Ceannais Iomána na Mumhan
STÁID SEMPLE, DÚRLAS ÉILE
12 IÚIL 1987
CORCAIGH v.
TIOBRAID ÁRANN
LUACH:
50p
Rúnaí
CLÁR OIFIGIÚIL

3

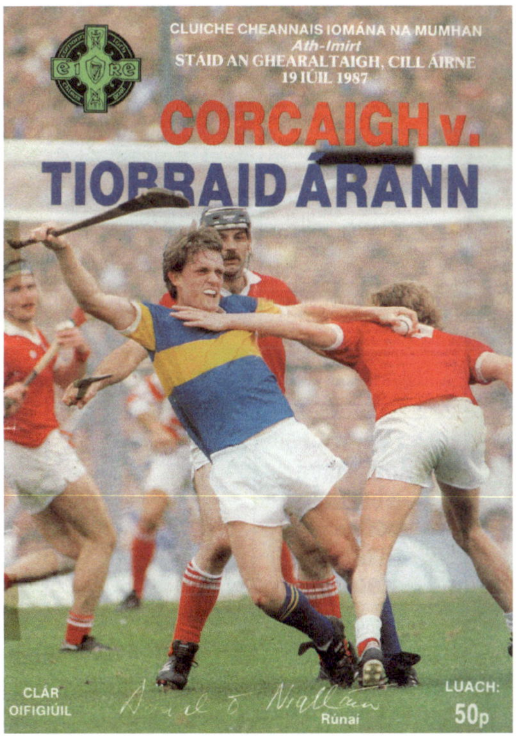
CLUICHE CHEANNAIS IOMÁNA NA MUMHAN
Ath-Imirt
STÁID AN GHEARALTAIGH, CILL ÁIRNE
19 IÚIL 1987
CORCAIGH v.
TIOBRAID ÁRANN
CLÁR
OIFIGIÚIL
Rúnaí
LUACH:
50p

4

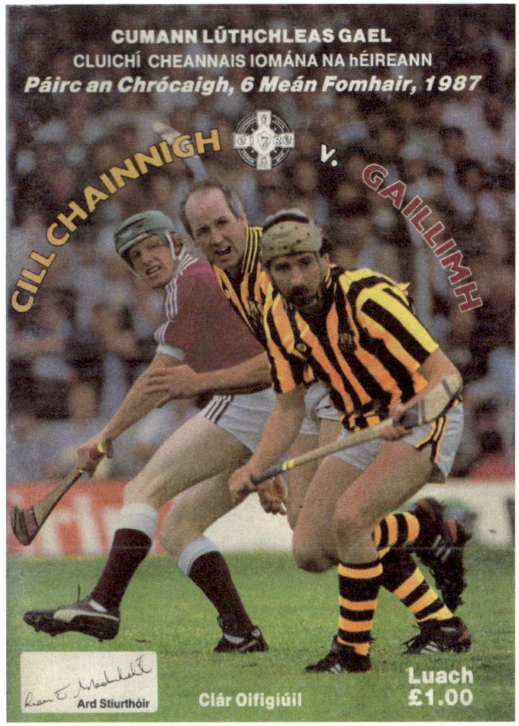
CUMANN LÚTHCHLEAS GAEL
CLUICHÍ CHEANNAIS IOMÁNA NA hÉIREANN
Páirc an Chrócaigh, 6 Meán Fomhair, 1987
CILL CHAINNIGH
v.
GAILLIMH
Ard Stiurthóir
Clár Oifigiúil
Luach
£1.00

5

COMHAIRLE CHONNACHTA
CUMANN LUTHCHLEAS GAEL
VAL DALY
12.7.87
T. J. KILGALLON
(Rúnaí)
IRIS OIFIGIÚIL
LUACH: 50p

6

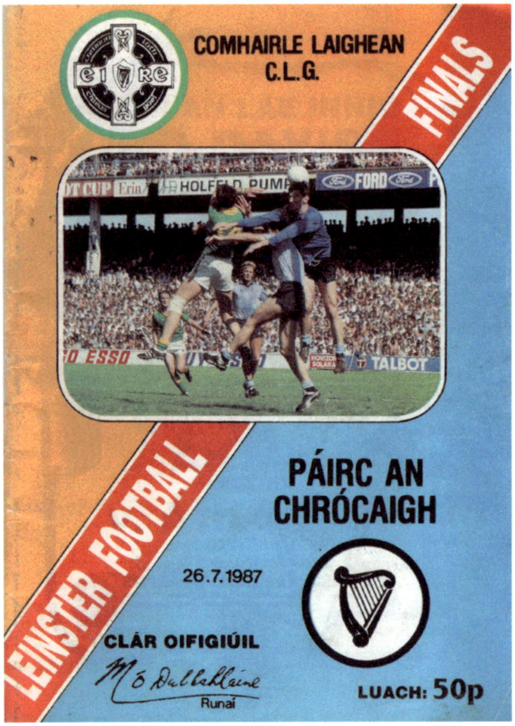
COMHAIRLE LAIGHEAN
C.L.G.
FINALS
PÁIRC AN
CHRÓCAIGH
LEINSTER FOOTBALL
26.7.1987
CLÁR OIFIGIÚIL
Runaí
LUACH: 50p

8

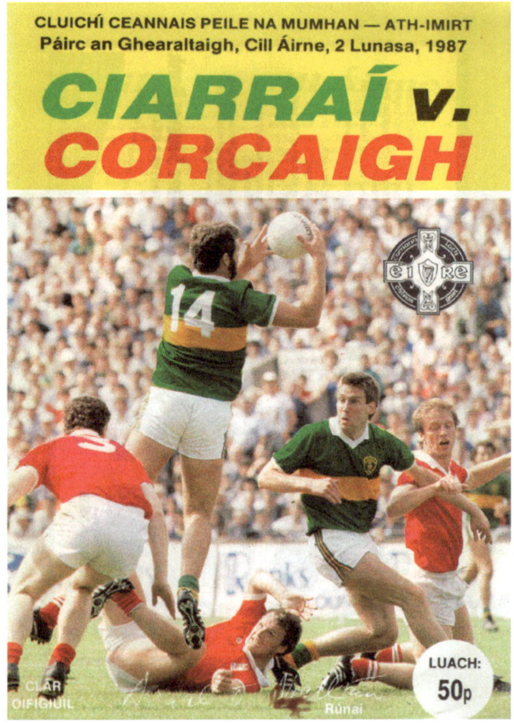
CLUICHÍ CEANNAIS PEILE NA MUMHAN — ATH-IMIRT
Páirc an Ghearaltaigh, Cill Áirne, 2 Lunasa, 1987
CIARRAÍ v.
CORCAIGH
LUACH:
50p
CLÁR
OIFIGIÚIL
Rúnaí

7

Craobh Peil na Mumhan 1987
Clár Oifigiúil
LUACH: 50p

9

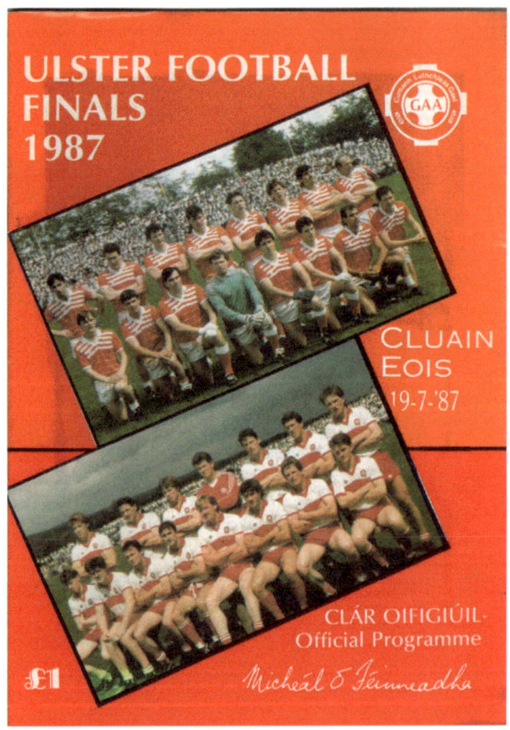
ULSTER FOOTBALL
FINALS
1987
CLUAIN
EOIS
19-7-'87
CLÁR OIFIGIÚIL·
Official Programme
£1

10

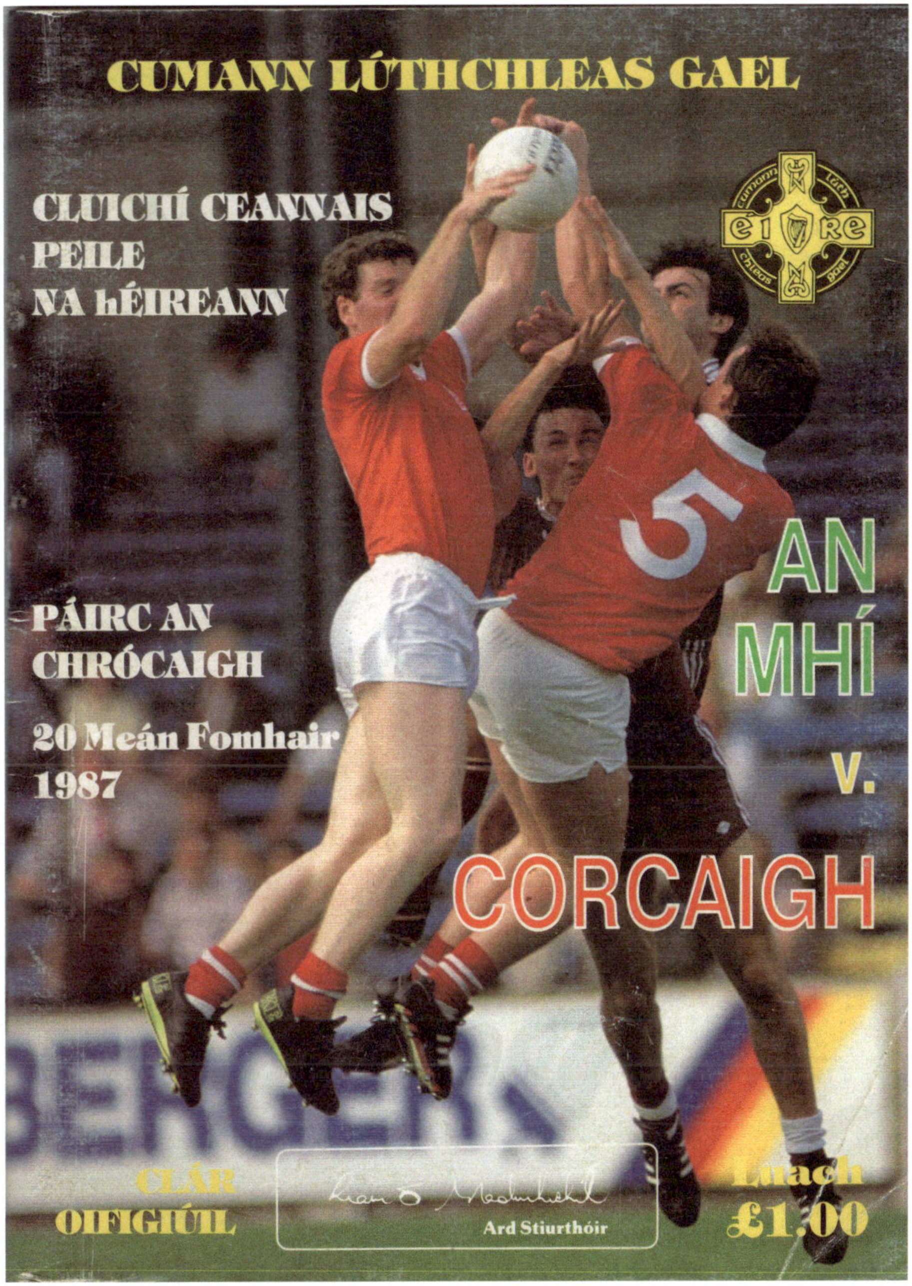

6 Leinster Football Final
Meath 1-13 Dublin 0-12

7 Munster Football Final
Cork 1-10 Kerry 2-07

8 Replay
Cork 0-13 Kerry 1-05

9 Ulster Football Final
Derry 0-11 Armagh 0-09

10 All-Ireland Football Final
Meath 1-14 Cork 0-11
Attendance – 68,431

1988

Galway were becoming a dominant force in hurling. Under Cyril Farrell, they had reached the previous three All-Ireland hurling finals and, in 1988, were back in the final hoping to retain their title. Tipperary were resurgent in Munster, and when the teams met for the second year in a row, a rivalry was developing. Galway goalkeeper John Commins kept a clean sheet in consecutive finals as Galway won by four points.

After years of Dublin and Kerry, another Munster–Leinster rivalry was developing in the shape of Cork and Meath. They met in the All-Ireland football final for the second year in a row with a late controversial free for Meath forcing a draw. In a bad-tempered replay, Meath retained their title by a point and Joe Cassells lifted the new Sam Maguire Cup for the first time. After critical comments about rough tactics perceived to be directed at Meath by the GAA president, John Dowling, some Meath players refused to accept their medals from him at the presentation function.

1

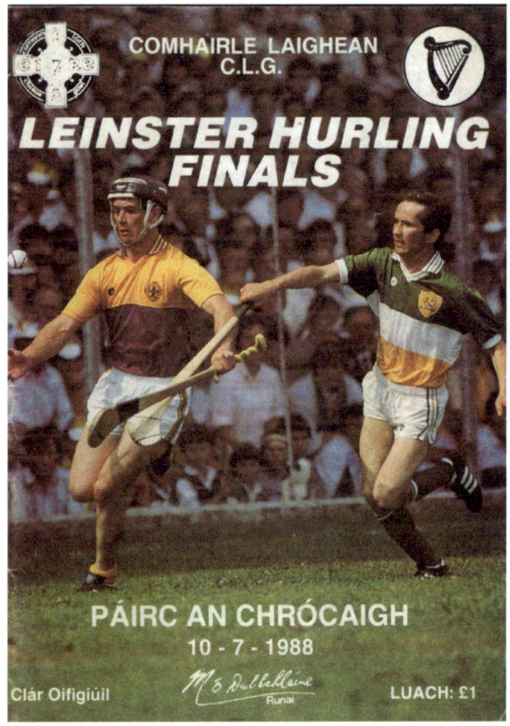

2

1 Leinster Hurling Final
Offaly 3-12 Wexford 1-14

2 Munster Hurling Final
Tipperary 2-19 Cork 1-13

3 All-Ireland Hurling Final
Galway 1-15 Tipperary 0-14
Attendance – 63,545

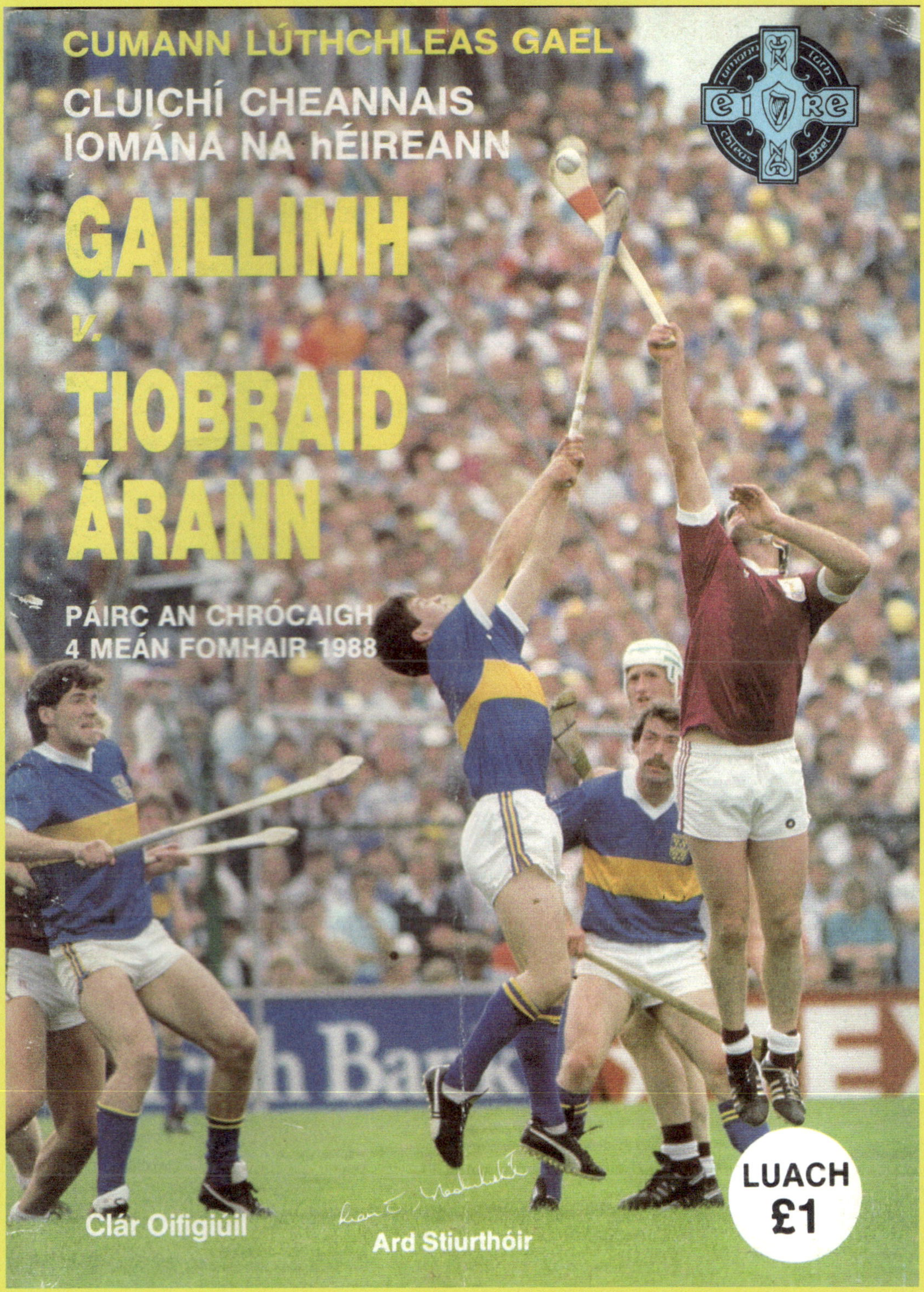
CUMANN LÚTHCHLEAS GAEL
CLUICHÍ CHEANNAIS
IOMÁNA NA hÉIREANN
GAILLIMH
v.
TIOBRAID
ÁRANN
PÁIRC AN CHRÓCAIGH
4 MEÁN FOMHAIR 1988
LUACH
£1
Clár Oifigiúil
Ard Stiurthóir

4

5

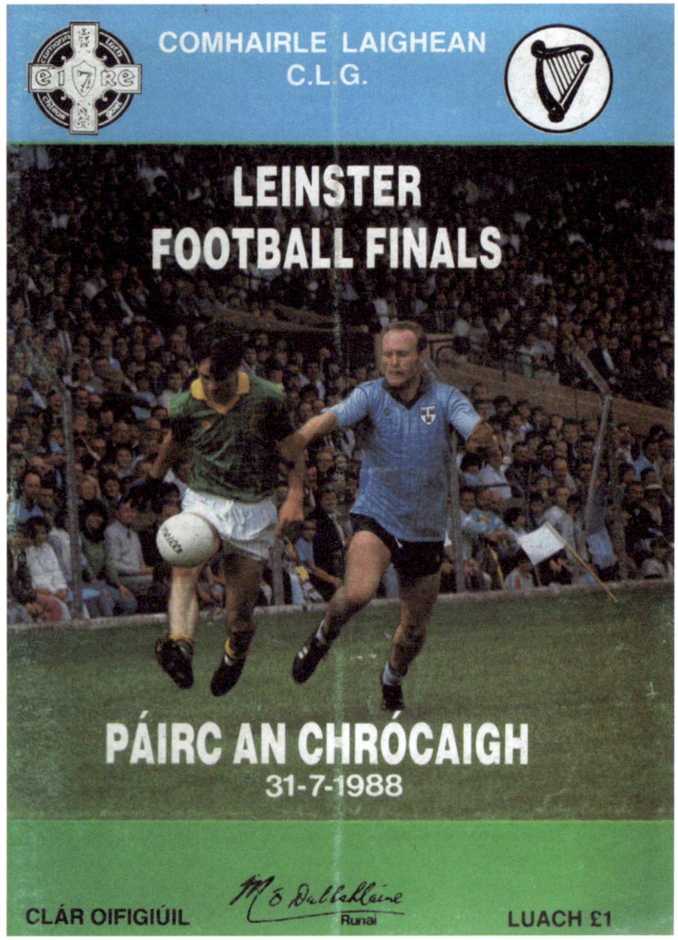

4 Connacht Football Final
Mayo 1-12 Roscommon 0-08

5 Leinster Football Final
Meath 2-05 Dublin 0-09

6 Munster Football Final
Cork 1-14 Kerry 0-16

7 Ulster Football Final
Monaghan 1-10 Tyrone 0-11

8 All-Ireland Football Final
Meath 0-12 Cork 1-09
Attendance – 63,000

9 Replay
Meath 0-13 Cork 0-12
Attendance – 64,069

6

CLUICHÍ CEANNAIS
PEILE
NA MUMHAN
PÁIRC UÍ
CHAOIMH
3 Iúil 1988
CORCAIGH
v.
CIARRAÍ
CLÁR
OIFIGIÚIL
Runai
LUACH
£1.00

7

Cumann Luthchleas Gael, Comhairle Uladh
CEANNAS PEILE ULADH 1988
CLAR OIFIGIUIL
£1
Runai

8

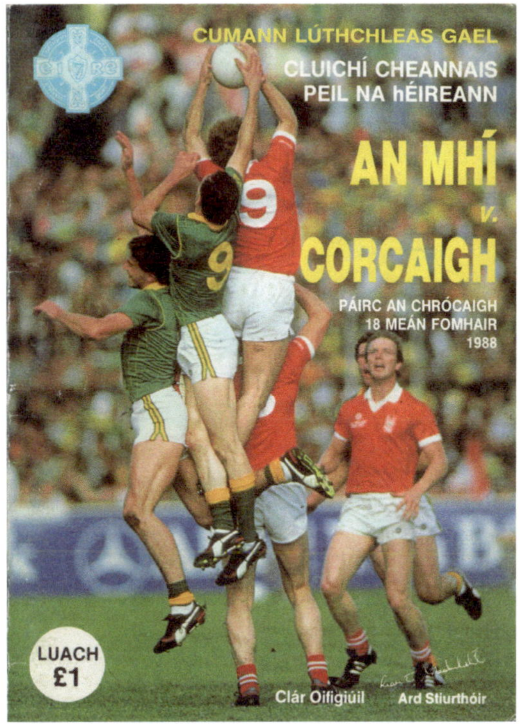
CUMANN LÚTHCHLEAS GAEL
CLUICHÍ CHEANNAIS
PEIL NA hÉIREANN
AN MHÍ
v.
CORCAIGH
PÁIRC AN CHRÓCAIGH
18 MEÁN FOMHAIR
1988
LUACH
£1
Clár Oifigiúil
Ard Stiurthóir

9

CUMANN LÚTHCHLEAS GAEL
CLUICHÍ
CEANNAIS PEILE
NA hÉIREANN
Clár Oifigiúil
ATHIMIRT
AN MHÍ
v.
CORCAIGH
PÁIRC AN
CHRÓCAIGH,
9 DEIREADH
FÓMHAIR 1988
LUACH
£1
Ard Stiurthóir

1989

Mayo reached the 1989 All-Ireland football final only to meet a Cork team determined to atone for losses in the previous two finals. With two Kildare exiles, Larry Tomkins and Shay Fahy, playing central roles, Cork's experience proved crucial as they won the championship for the first time since 1973.

Galway's Tony Keady, the 1988 Hurler of the Year, became embroiled in a controversy over playing illegally in New York. The resulting suspension ruled him out of the All-Ireland semi-final against Tipperary, which Galway lost, ending their ambitions of achieving a famous three in a row. After a long absence, the Ulster hurling championship resumed with a win for Antrim. The Antrim hurlers had improved steadily throughout the decade, but their defeat of Offaly in the All-Ireland semi-final was still a huge shock. They were no match for Tipperary in the final, however, as Nicky English racked up a record 2-12 and captain Bobby Ryan collected the Liam MacCarthy Cup to bridge an 18-year gap.

1

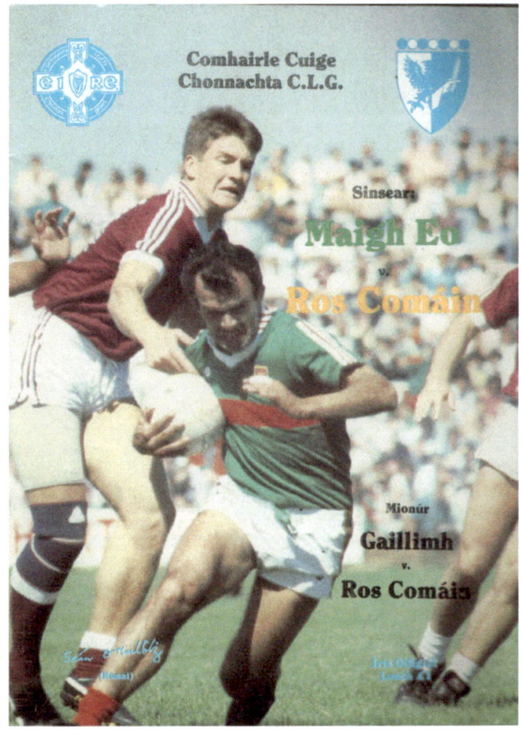

2

1 Connacht Football Final
Mayo 0-12 Roscommon 1-09

2 Replay
Mayo 3-14 Roscommon 2-13 (aet)

3 Leinster Football Final
Dublin 2-12 Meath 1-10

4 Munster Football Final
Cork 1-12 Kerry 1-09

5 Ulster Football Final
Tyrone 0-11 Donegal 0-11

6 Replay
Tyrone 2-13 Donegal 0-07

3

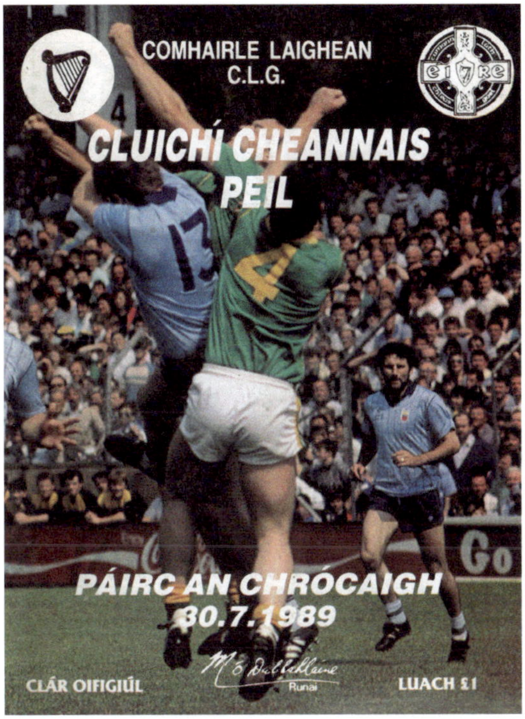
COMHAIRLE LAIGHEAN
C.L.G.
CLUICHÍ CHEANNAIS
PEIL
PÁIRC AN CHRÓCAIGH
30.7.1989
CLÁR OIFIGIÚL
LUACH £1

4

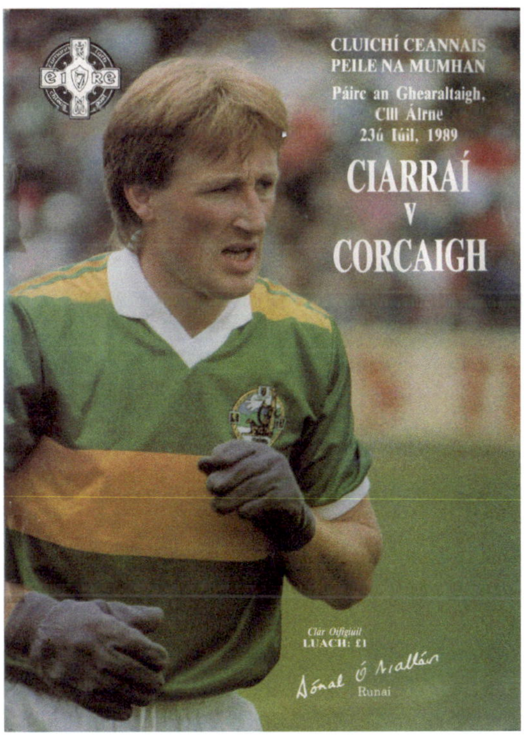
CLUICHÍ CEANNAIS
PEILE NA MUMHAN
Páirc an Ghearaltaigh,
Cill Áirne
23ú Iúil, 1989
CIARRAÍ
V
CORCAIGH
Clár Oifigiúil
LUACH: £1

5

Cumann Luthchleas Gael, Comhairle Uladh
Ceannas Peile Uladh 1989
Clár Oifigiúil
£1

6

Cumann Luthchleas Gael, Comhairle Uladh
An Cluiche
Ceannais
ÁTH-IMIRT
Clár Oifigiúil
50p

7

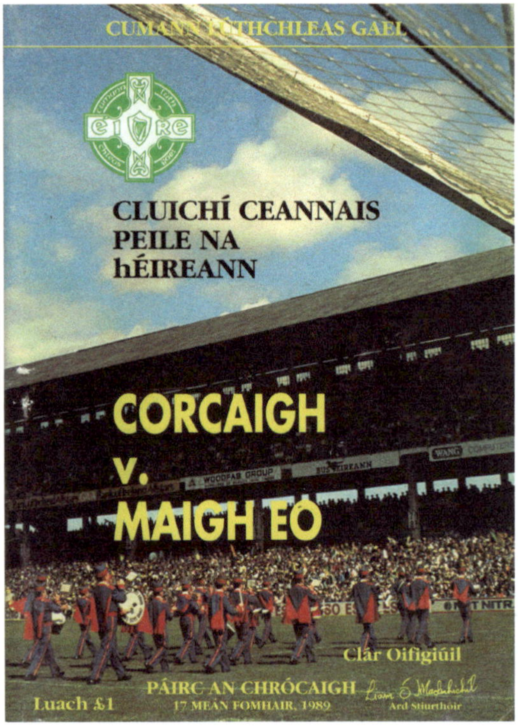
CUMANN LÚTHCHLEAS GAEL
CLUICHÍ CEANNAIS
PEILE NA
hÉIREANN
CORCAIGH
v.
MAIGH EO
Clár Oifigiúil
PÁIRC AN CHRÓCAIGH
17 MEÁN FOMHAIR, 1989
Ard Stiurthóir
Luach £1

9

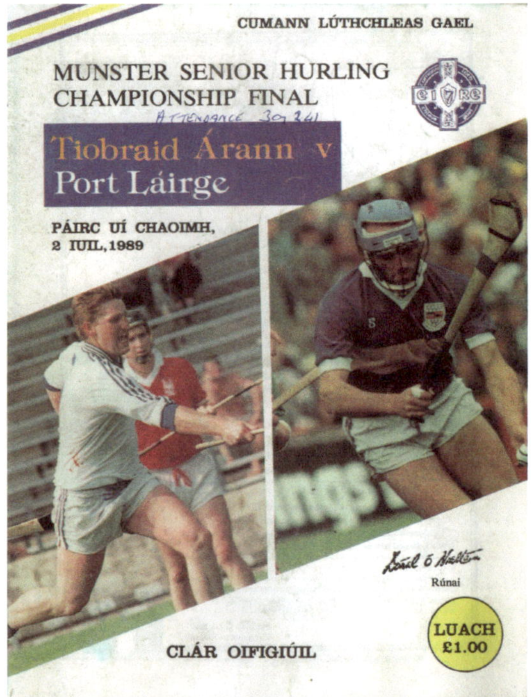
CUMANN LÚTHCHLEAS GAEL
MUNSTER SENIOR HURLING
CHAMPIONSHIP FINAL
Tiobraid Árann v
Port Láirge
PÁIRC UÍ CHAOIMH,
2 IUIL, 1989
Rúnai
CLÁR OIFIGIÚIL
LUACH
£1.00

8

COMHAIRLE LAIGHEAN
C.L.G.
CLUICHÍ CHEANNAIS
IOMÁNA
PÁIRC AN CHRÓCAIGH
9 — 7 — 1989
CLÁR OIFIGIÚL
LUACH £1

10

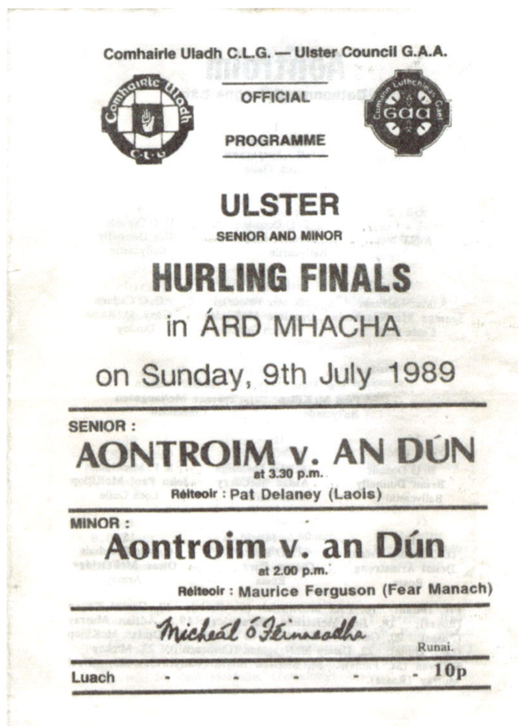
Comhairle Uladh C.L.G. — Ulster Council G.A.A.
OFFICIAL
PROGRAMME
ULSTER
SENIOR AND MINOR
HURLING FINALS
in ÁRD MHACHA
on Sunday, 9th July 1989
SENIOR :
AONTROIM v. AN DÚN
at 3.30 p.m.
Réiteoir : Pat Delaney (Laois)
MINOR :
Aontroim v. an Dún
at 2.00 p.m.
Réiteoir : Maurice Ferguson (Fear Manach)
Micheál Ó Féinneadha
Runai.
Luach - - - - - 10p

11

7 All-Ireland Football Final
Cork 0-17 Mayo 1-11
Attendance – 65,519

8 Leinster Hurling Final
Offaly 3-15 Kilkenny 4-09

9 Munster Hurling Final
Tipperary 0-26 Waterford 2-08

10 Ulster Hurling Final
Antrim 2-16 Down 0-09

11 All-Ireland Hurling Final
Tipperary 4-24 Antrim 3-09
Attendance – 65,496

1990–99

1990

In 1890 two Cork clubs, Aghabullogue (hurling) and Midleton (football), represented the county in the All-Ireland championships, winning both All-Ireland finals. One hundred years later, Cork repeated the feat and achieved what had previously proved elusive in the modern era, by winning both the Liam MacCarthy and Sam Maguire Cups in the space of a fortnight in September 1990. The All-Ireland double was preceded by a Munster double when the Cork hurlers defeated Tipperary and the footballers put Kerry to the sword in the provincial finals. Cork's defeat of Galway in the All-Ireland hurling final was something of an upset and, in the football final, they avenged the defeats by Meath in the 1987 and 1988 finals to retain the cup. Cork's Teddy McCarthy had the unique distinction of playing in both All-Ireland finals, while Denis Walsh, also a member of both panels, played in both Munster finals that year.

1

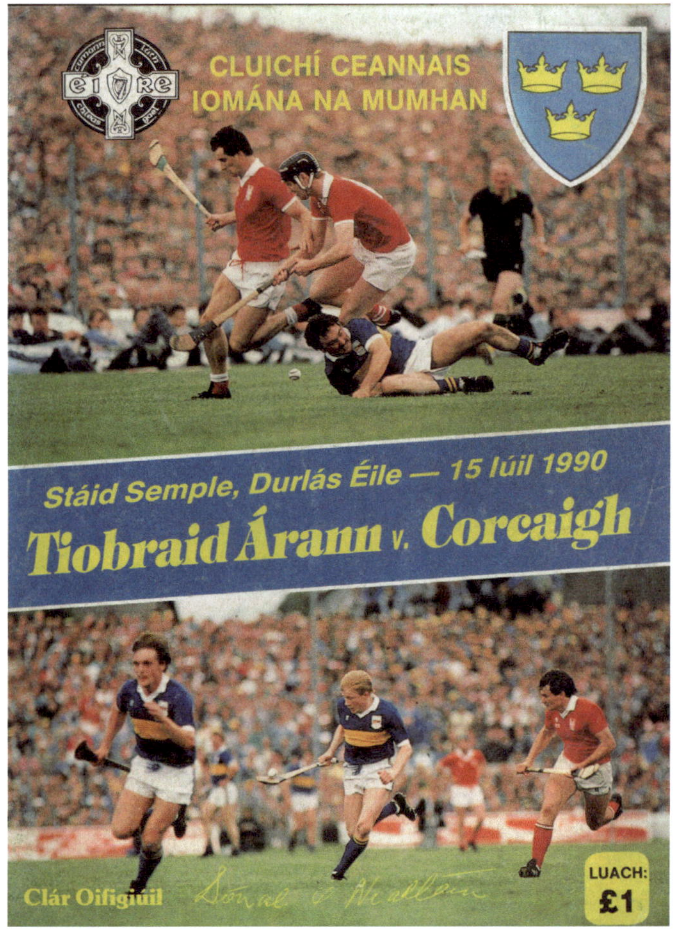

2

1 Munster Hurling Final
Cork 4-16 Tipperary 2-14

2 Leinster Hurling Final
Offaly 1-19 Dublin 2-11

3 Ulster Hurling Final
Antrim 4-11 Down 2-11

Cumann Lúthchleas Gael
COMHAIRLE ULADH
Ceannas Iomána Uladh 1990
CLÁR OIFIGIÚIL Micheál Ó Fenneadha Luach 50p

4

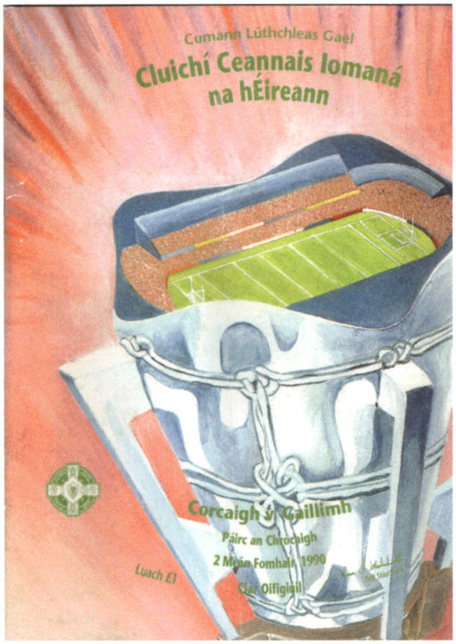

5

4 All-Ireland Hurling Final
Cork 5-15 Galway 2-21
Attendance – 63,954

5 Connacht Football Final
Roscommon 0-16 Galway 1-11

6 Munster Football Final
Cork 2-23 Kerry 1-11

7 Leinster Football Final
Meath 1-14 Dublin 0-14

8 Ulster Football Final
Donegal 0-15 Armagh 0-14

9 All-Ireland Football Final
Cork 0-11 Meath 0-09
Attendance – 65,723

6

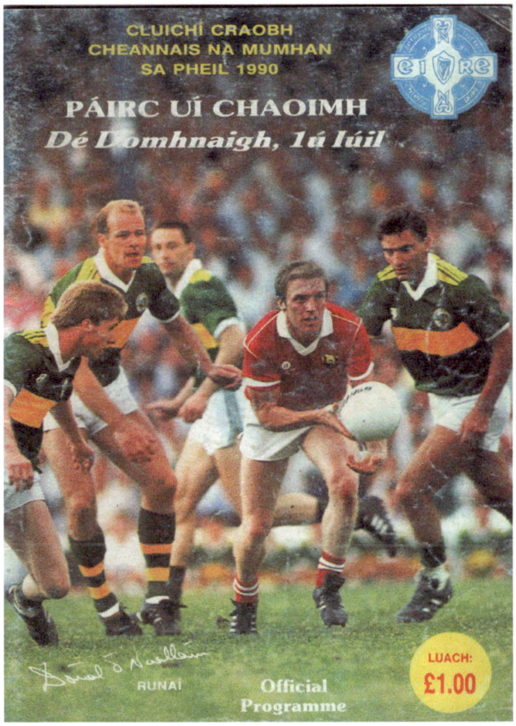
CLUICHÍ CRAOBH
CHEANNAIS NA MUMHAN
SA PHEIL 1990
PÁIRC UÍ CHAOIMH
Dé Domhnaigh, 1ú Iúil
RUNAÍ
Official Programme
LUACH: £1.00

7

COMHAIRLE LAIGHEAN
C.L.G.
CLUICHÍ CHEANNAIS PEIL
PÁIRC AN CHRÓCAIGH
29.7.1990
CLÁR OIFIGIUIL
LUACH £1

8

Cumann Lúthchleas Gael, Comhairle Uladh
Ceannas Peile Uladh 1990
Clár Oifigiúil
Rúnaí
£1

9

Cumann Lúthchleas Gael
Cluichí Ceannais Peile na hÉireann
An Mhí v. Corcaigh
Páirc an Chrócaigh
16 Meán Fómhair, 1990
Luach £1
Clár Oifigiúil

1991

By the time Meath reached the 1991 All-Ireland football final, they had already played nine matches, a number unheard of before the advent of the All-Ireland qualifiers. This included the four-match epic series against Dublin in the preliminary round of the Leinster championship. The first game of this enthralling duel was played on 2 June, and the fourth over a month later on 6 July. The series of matches had a combined attendance of 237,277 and, in the 5 hours and 40 minutes of football, 9 goals and 96 points were scored, with Meath winning by a single point. The Leinster championship itself was the lengthiest ever, taking 15 matches to complete. The 10-match odyssey eventually took its toll on Meath in the final, as Down claimed their first title since 1968. Tipperary won the All-Ireland hurling final, ensuring that their captain, Declan Carr, was the last man to lift the old Liam MacCarthy Cup.

1

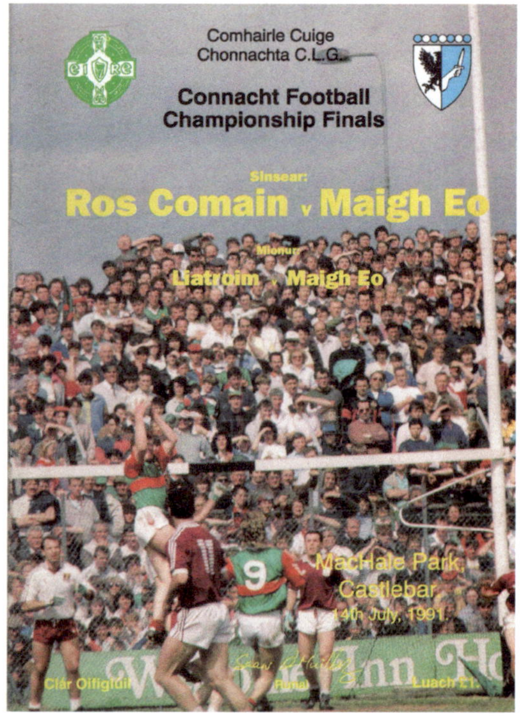

2

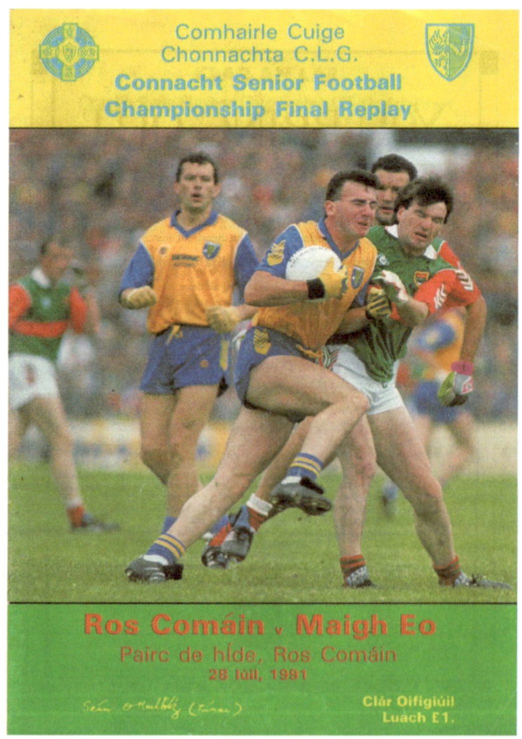

1 Connacht Football Final
Roscommon 0-14 Mayo 0-14

2 Replay
Roscommon 0-13 Mayo 1-09

3 Leinster Football Final
Meath 1-11 Laois 0-08

4 Munster Football Final
Kerry 0-23 Limerick 3-12

5 Ulster Football Final
Down 1-15 Donegal 0-10

6 All-Ireland Football Final
Down 1-16 Meath 1-14
Attendance – 64,500

3

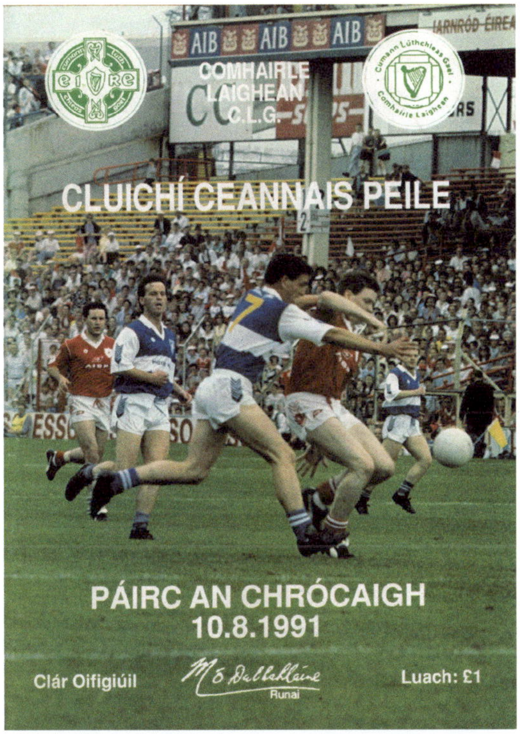
COMHAIRLE LAIGHEAN C.L.G.
CLUICHÍ CEANNAIS PEILE
PÁIRC AN CHRÓCAIGH
10.8.1991
Clár Oifigiúil
Rúnaí
Luach: £1

4

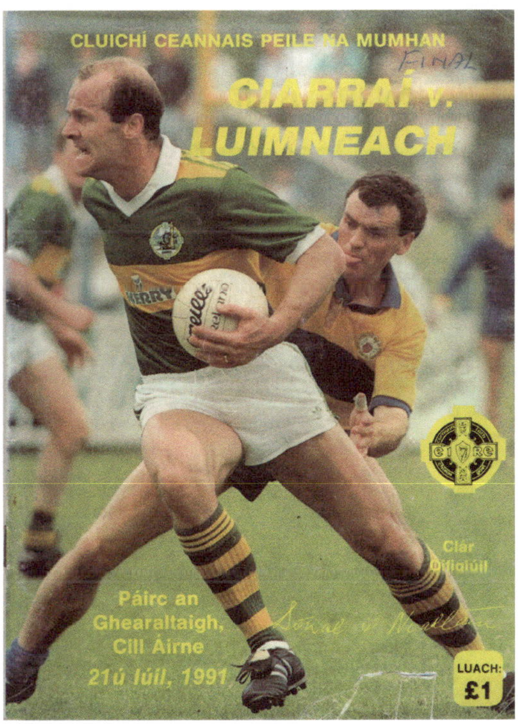
CLUICHÍ CEANNAIS PEILE NA MUMHAN
CIARRAÍ v. LUIMNEACH
Clár Oifigiúil
Páirc an Ghearaltaigh, Cill Airne
21ú Iúil, 1991
LUACH: £1

5

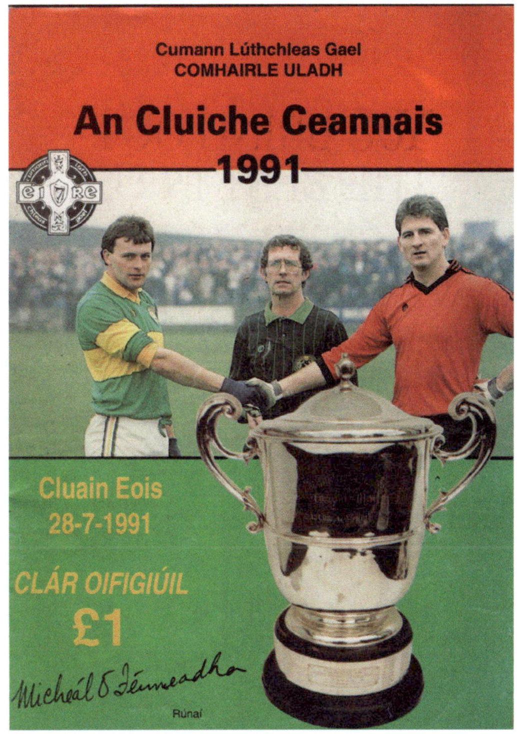
Cumann Lúthchleas Gael
COMHAIRLE ULADH
An Cluiche Ceannais
1991
Cluain Eois
28-7-1991
CLÁR OIFIGIÚIL
£1
Rúnaí

6

Cumann Lúthcleas Gael
Cluichí Ceannais Peile na hÉireann
Páirc an Chrócaigh, 15 Meán Fómhair, 1991
Clár Oifigiúil
Luach £1

7

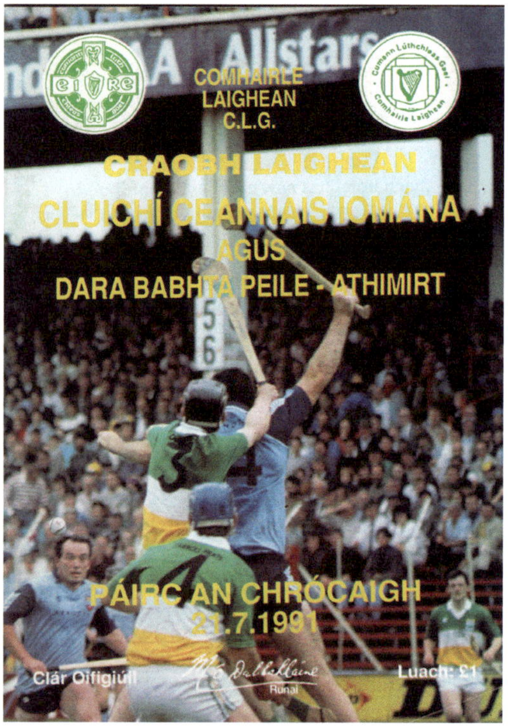
COMHAIRLE
LAIGHEAN
C.L.G.
CRAOBH LAIGHEAN
CLUICHÍ CEANNAIS IOMÁNA
AGUS
DARA BABHTA PEILE - ATHIMIRT
PÁIRC AN CHRÓCAIGH
21.7.1991
Clár Oifigiúil
Rúnaí
Luach: £1

8

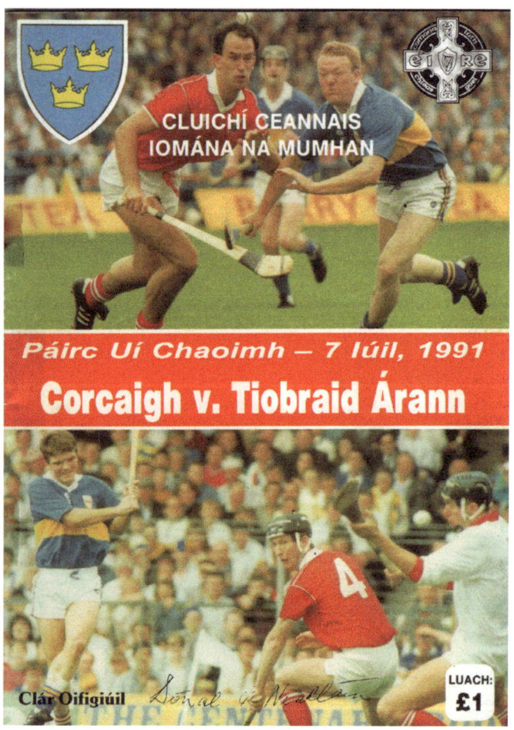
CLUICHÍ CEANNAIS
IOMÁNA NA MUMHAN
Páirc Uí Chaoimh – 7 Iúil, 1991
Corcaigh v. Tiobraid Árann
Clár Oifigiúil
LUACH:
£1

9

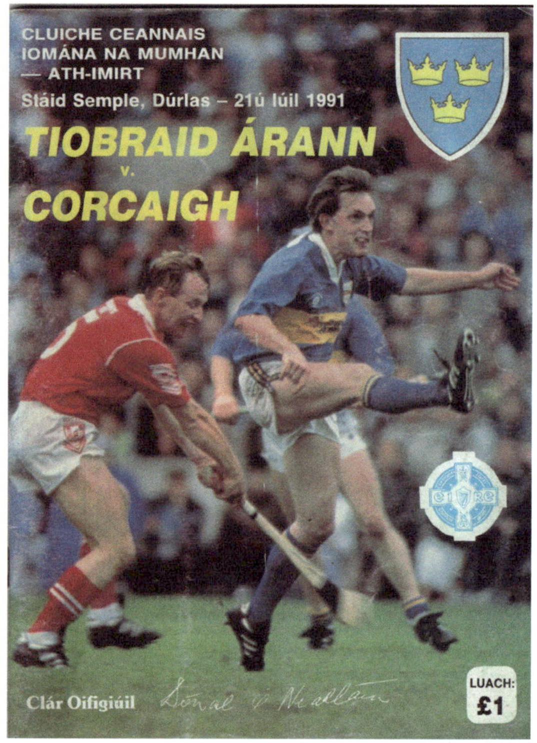
CLUICHE CEANNAIS
IOMÁNA NA MUMHAN
— ATH-IMIRT
Stáid Semple, Dúrlas – 21ú Iúil 1991
TIOBRAID ÁRANN
v.
CORCAIGH
Clár Oifigiúil
LUACH:
£1

10

Cumann Lúthchleas Gael
COMHAIRLE ULADH
Ceannas Iomána Uladh 1991
CLÁR OIFIGIÚIL
Luach 50p

11

7 Leinster Hurling Final
Kilkenny 1-13 Dublin 1-11

8 Munster Hurling Final
Tipperary 2-16 Cork 4-10

9 Replay
Tipperary 4-19 Cork 4-15

10 Ulster Hurling Final
Antrim 3-14 Down 3-10

11 All-Ireland Hurling Final
Tipperary 1-16 Kilkenny 0-15
Attendance – 64,500

1992

The defeat of Kerry in this year's Munster football final heralded one of the biggest shocks in the history of the football championship, as Clare captured their first Munster title since 1917. The match also brought down the final curtain on the career of one of Kerry's legendary midfielders, Jack O'Shea.

By winning just the county's fifth Ulster football title, and seeing off Mayo in the semi-final, Donegal qualified for their first All-Ireland football final. Managed by the stalwart Brian McEniff, and inspired by Martin McHugh and Manus Boyle, Donegal edged past Dublin to give Anthony Molloy the honour of being the first man to captain the county to All-Ireland success. In the 1992 All-Ireland hurling final, Kilkenny faced Cork, hoping to make up for the defeat to Tipperary in last year's final. Ultimately, Kilkenny had a straightforward victory and captain Liam Fennelly became the first man to receive the new Liam MacCarthy Cup. He had also lifted the original MacCarthy Cup as Kilkenny captain in 1983.

1

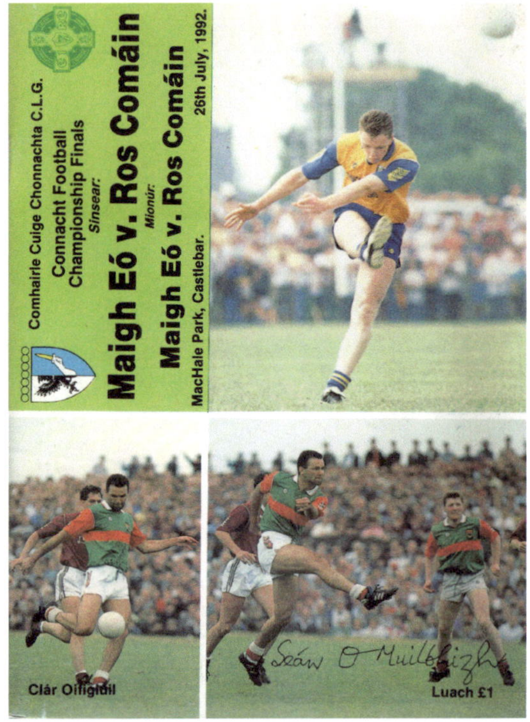

2

1 Connacht Football Final
Mayo 1-14 Roscommon 0-10

2 Leinster Football Final
Dublin 1-13 Kildare 0-10

3 Munster Football Final
Clare 2-10 Kerry 0-12

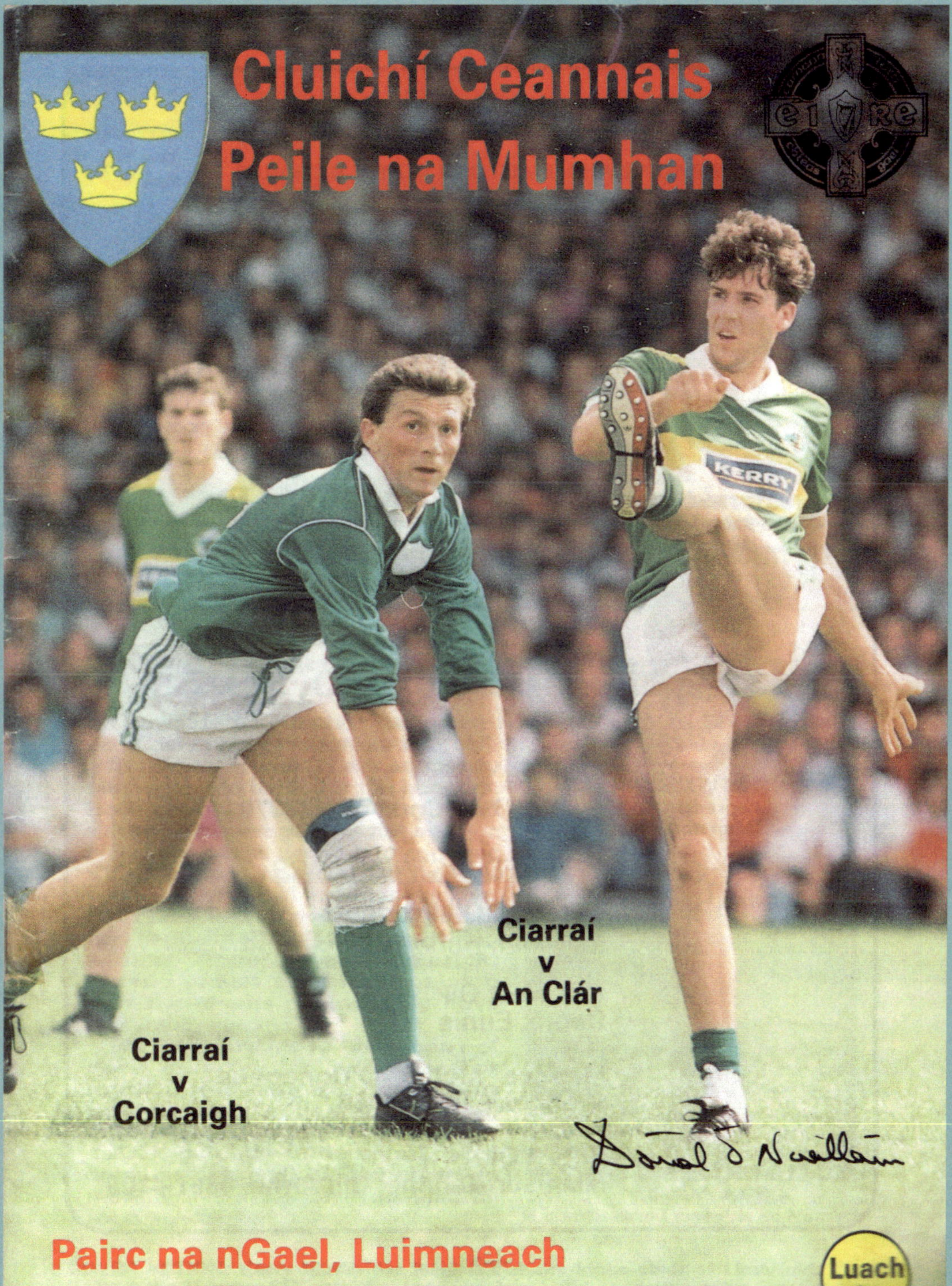
Cluichí Ceannais
Peile na Mumhan
KERRY
Ciarraí
v
An Clár
Ciarraí
v
Corcaigh
Pairc na nGael, Luimneach
19ú Lá Iúil 1992
Clár Oifigiúil
Luach
£1

4

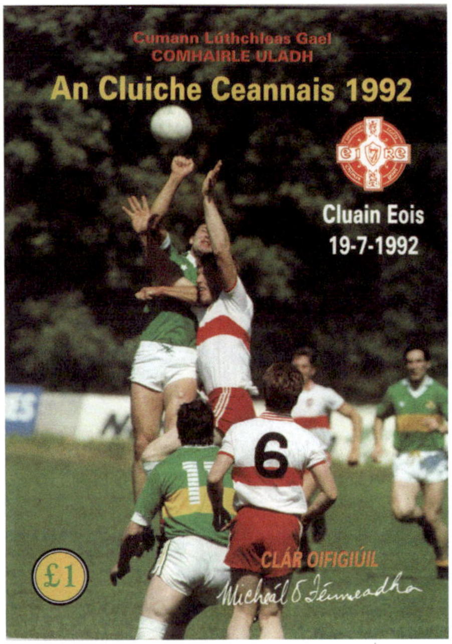

5

4 Ulster Football Final
Donegal 0-14 Derry 1-09

5 All-Ireland Football Final
Donegal 0-18 Dublin 0-14
Attendance – 64,547

6 Leinster Hurling Final
Kilkenny 3-16 Wexford 2-09

7 Munster Hurling Final
Cork 1-22 Limerick 3-11

8 Ulster Hurling Final
Down 2-16 Antrim 0-11

9 All-Ireland Hurling Final
Kilkenny 3-10 Cork 1-12
Attendance – 64,534

6

COMHAIRLE LAIGHEAN C.L.G.
Cluichí Cheannais
Iomána Laighean
PÁIRC AN CHRÓCAIGH
19.7.1992
CLÁR OIFIGIÚIL
£1
Rúnaí

7

CLUICHÍ CHEANNAIS
NA MUMHAN 1992
Páirc Uí Chaoimh – 5ú lá Iúil
Runaí
CLÁR
OIFIGIÚIL
LUACH:
£1

8

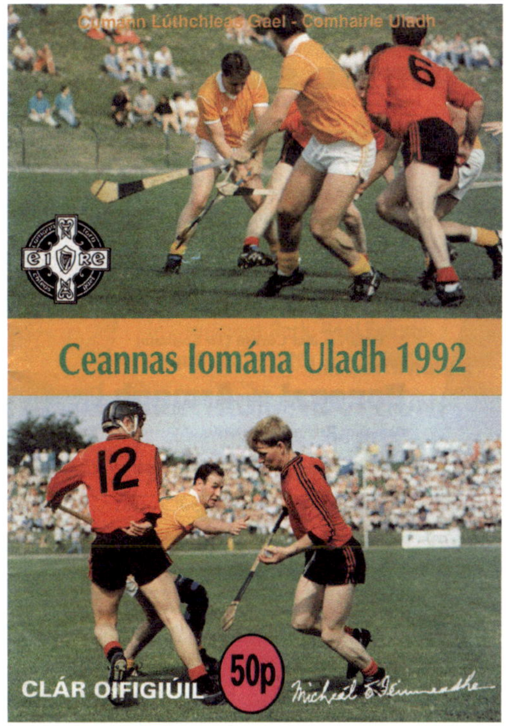
Cumann Lúthchleas Gael - Comhairle Uladh
Ceannas Iomána Uladh 1992
CLÁR OIFIGIÚIL
50p

9

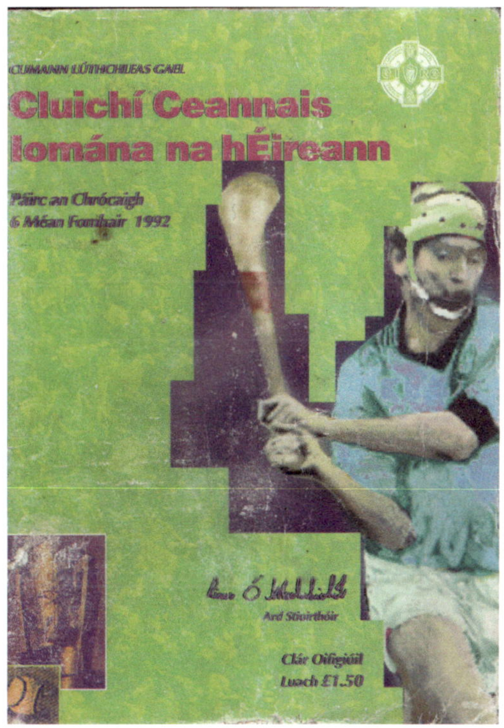
CUMANN LÚTHCHLEAS GAEL
Cluichí Ceannais
Iomána na hÉireann
Páirc an Chrócaigh
6 Méan Fómhair 1992
Ard Stiúirthóir
Clár Oifigiúil
Luach £1.50

1993

Ulster football was now experiencing a renaissance and, with the All-Ireland champions failing to defend their provincial title for the second consecutive season, Ulster was proving a difficult football championship to win. Derry won the provincial title this year, beating Donegal in a deluge in the newly renovated St Tiernach's Park in Clones. The Leinster champions, Dublin, having lost an epic to Meath in 1991, as well as the previous year's All-Ireland final, were looking to go one better in 1993. However, Derry beat them in the semi-final to set up a meeting with Cork. When Cork were controversially reduced to 14 men, Derry took full advantage and the inspirational Anthony Tohill, Johnny McGurk and Enda Gormley helped Derry to victory. Henry Downey captained Derry to their first All-Ireland football title in the last final to be played before the Cusack Stand was demolished so as to begin the development of the new Croke Park stadium.

1

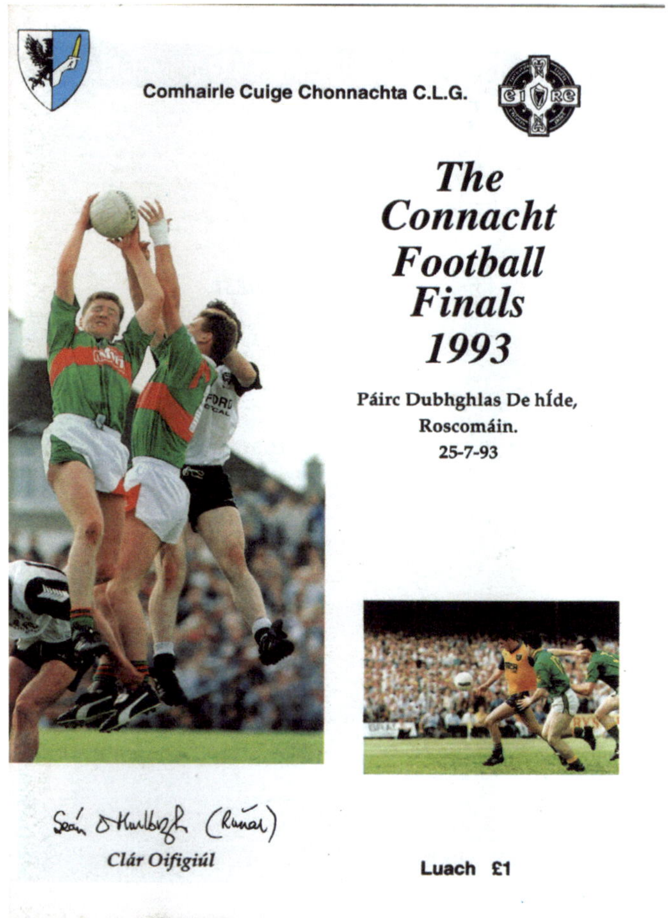

1 Connacht Football Final
Mayo 1-05 Roscommon 0-07

2 Leinster Football Final
Dublin 0-11 Kildare 0-07

3 Munster Football Final
Cork 1-16 Tipperary 1-08

4 Ulster Football Final
Derry 0-08 Donegal 0-06

5 All-Ireland Football Final
Derry 1-14 Cork 2-08
Attendance – 64,500

2

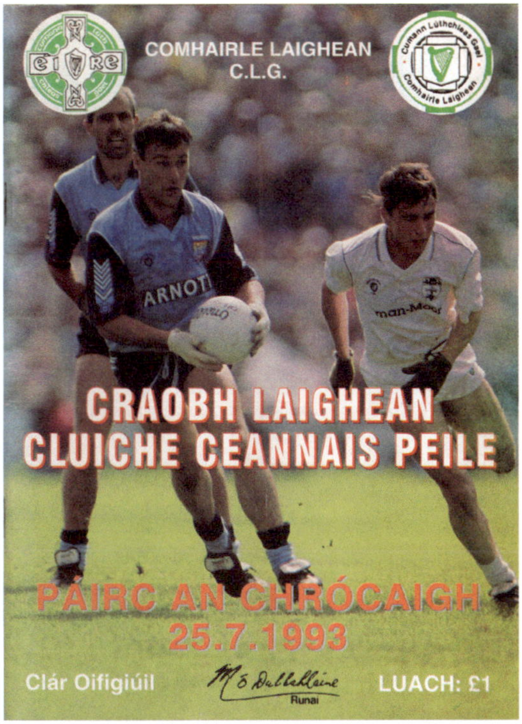
COMHAIRLE LAIGHEAN
C.L.G.
Cumann Lúthchleas Gael
Comhairle Laighean
CRAOBH LAIGHEAN
CLUICHE CEANNAIS PEILE
PÁIRC AN CHRÓCAIGH
25.7.1993
Clár Oifigiúil
Rúnaí
LUACH: £1

3

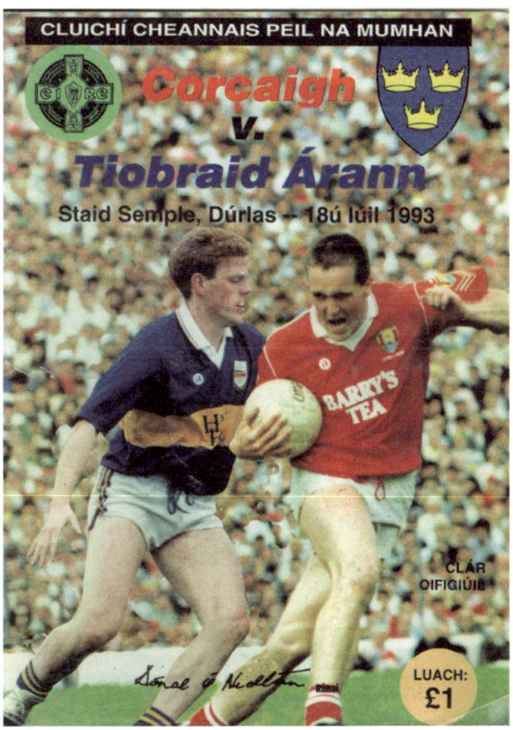
CLUICHÍ CHEANNAIS PEIL NA MUMHAN
Corcaigh
v.
Tiobraid Árann
Staid Semple, Dúrlas -- 18ú Iúil 1993
CLÁR
OIFIGIÚIL
LUACH:
£1

4

Cumann Lúthchleas Gael
COMHAIRLE ULADH
AN CLUICHE CEANNAIS 1993
i bPáirc Naomh Thighearnaigh,
CLUAIN EOIS
18ú Iúil 1993
CLÁR OIFIGIÚIL
£1
Rúnaí

5

Cumann Lúthchleas Gael
DOIRE
Cluichí Ceannais
Peile na hÉireann
Páirc an Chrócaigh 19 Meán Fómhair 1993
Ard Stiúrthóir
£1.50 CLÁR OIFIGIÚIL

6

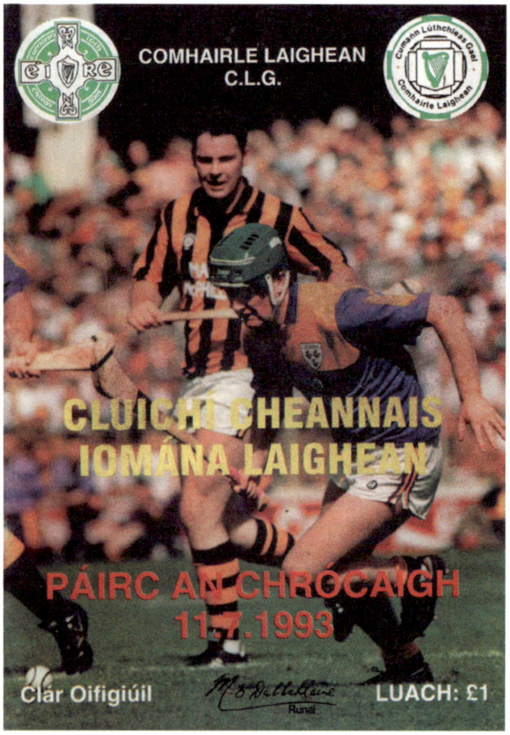
COMHAIRLE LAIGHEAN
C.L.G.
CLUICHÍ CHEANNAIS
IOMÁNA LAIGHEAN
PÁIRC AN CHRÓCAIGH
11.7.1993
Clár Oifigiúil
Runaí
LUACH: £1

8

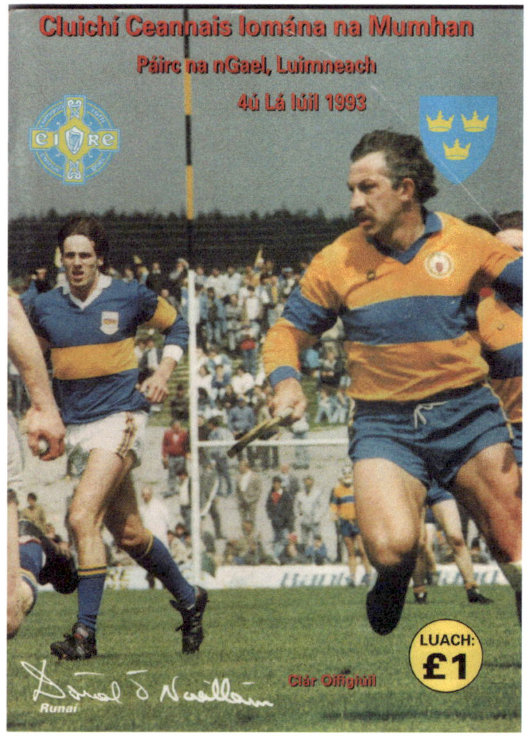
Cluichí Ceannais Iomána na Mumhan
Páirc na nGael, Luimneach
4ú Lá Iúil 1993
LUACH:
£1
Runaí
Clár Oifigiúil

7

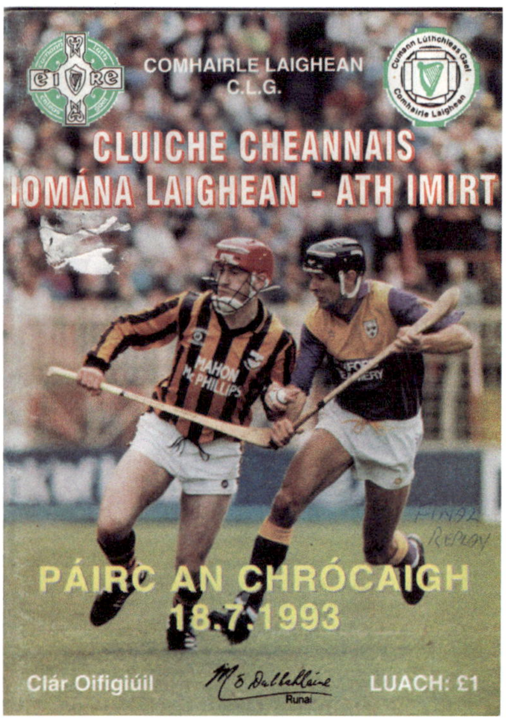
COMHAIRLE LAIGHEAN
C.L.G.
CLUICHE CHEANNAIS
IOMÁNA LAIGHEAN - ATH IMIRT
PÁIRC AN CHRÓCAIGH
18.7.1993
Clár Oifigiúil
Runaí
LUACH: £1

9

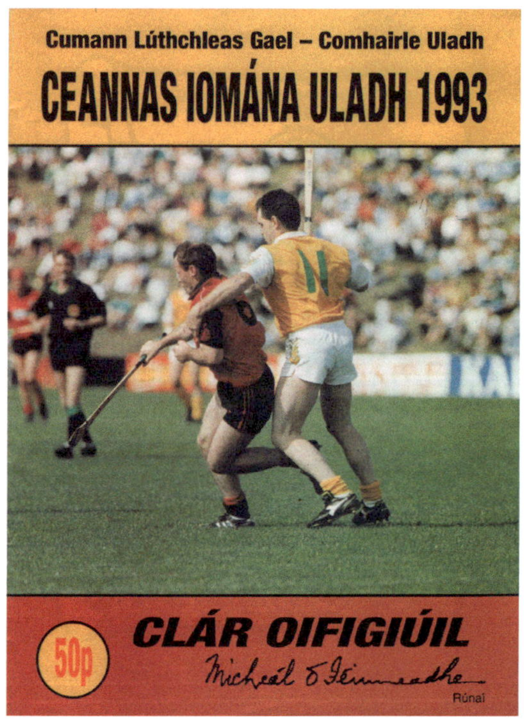
Cumann Lúthchleas Gael – Comhairle Uladh
CEANNAS IOMÁNA ULADH 1993
CLÁR OIFIGIÚIL
50p
Rúnaí

10

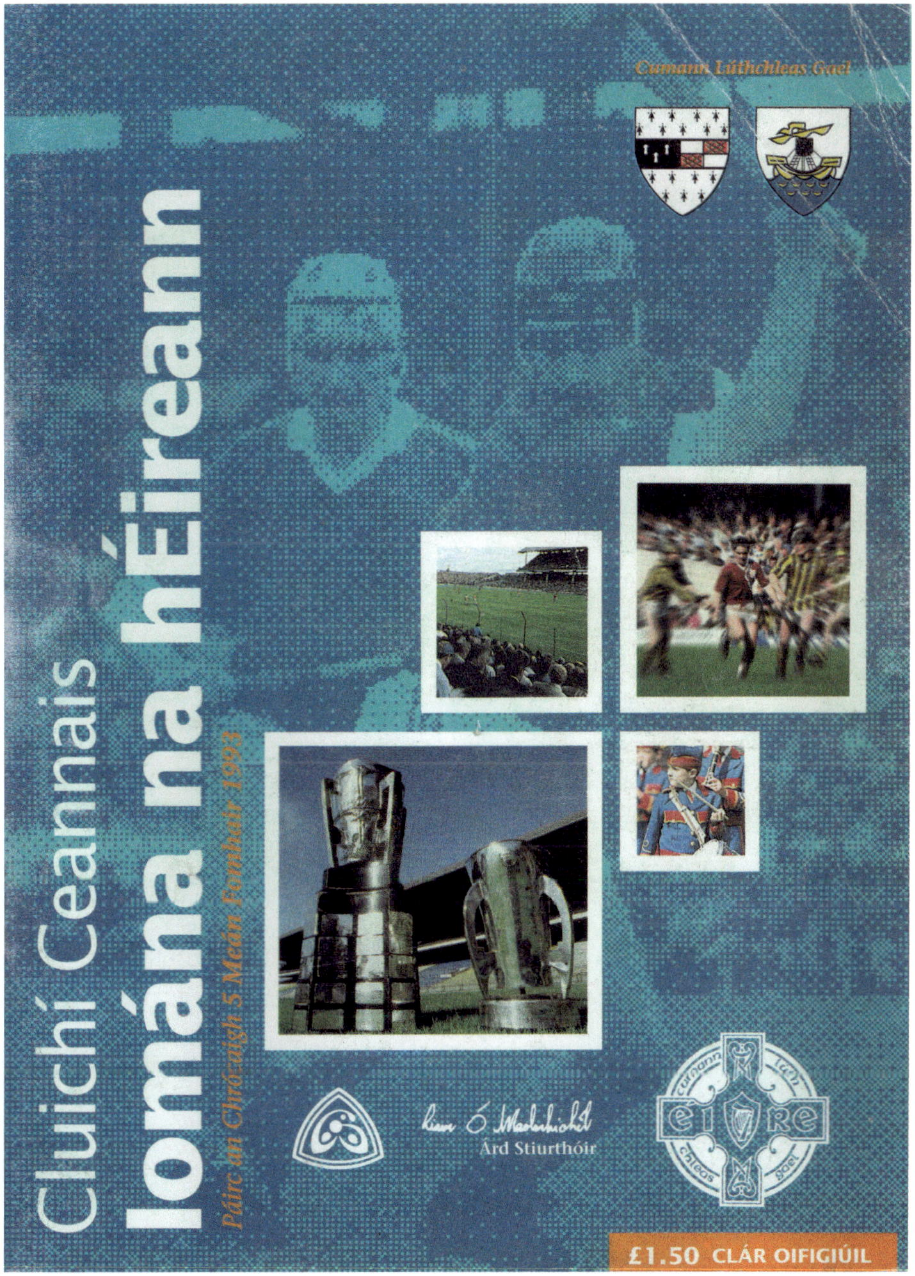

6 Leinster Hurling Final
Kilkenny 2-14 Wexford 1-17

7 Replay
Kilkenny 2-12 Wexford 0-11

8 Munster Hurling Final
Tipperary 3-27 Clare 2-12

9 Ulster Hurling Final
Antrim 0-24 Down 0-11

10 All-Ireland Hurling Final
Kilkenny 2-17 Galway 1-15
Attendance – 63,460

1994

The 1994 All-Ireland hurling final produced one of the most stunning comebacks ever witnessed in Croke Park. Limerick had produced a brilliant performance to lead Offaly by 2-13 to 1-11 with just five minutes remaining. Then, Offaly's Johnny Dooley seemed ready to take a point from a close-range free, but instead drove it low and hard to the net. Within a minute, Offaly substitute Pat O'Connor had the ball in the net again. These goals, plus a flurry of late points, gave Offaly a six-point victory at the full-time whistle. The Dooley brothers – Johnny, Joe and Billy – scored 2-12 of their team's total of 3-16 as Offaly won their third Liam MacCarthy Cup. It proved to be a bittersweet victory for the Offaly manager, Éamonn Cregan, who had been one of Limerick's greatest hurlers.

1

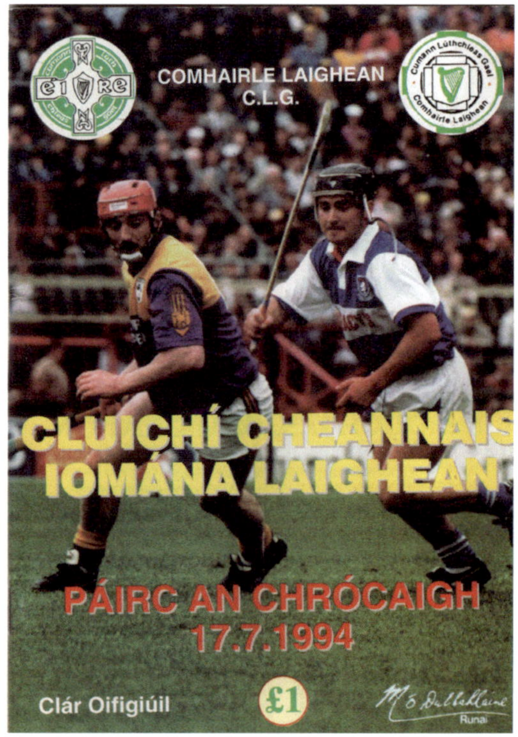

2

1 Leinster Hurling Final
Offaly 1-18 Wexford 0-14

2 Munster Hurling Final
Limerick 0-25 Clare 2-10

3 Ulster Hurling Final
Antrim 1-19 Down 1-13

Cumann Lúthchleas Gael
Comhairle Uladh
Ceannas Iomána Uladh
1994
CLÁR OIFIGIÚIL £1

4

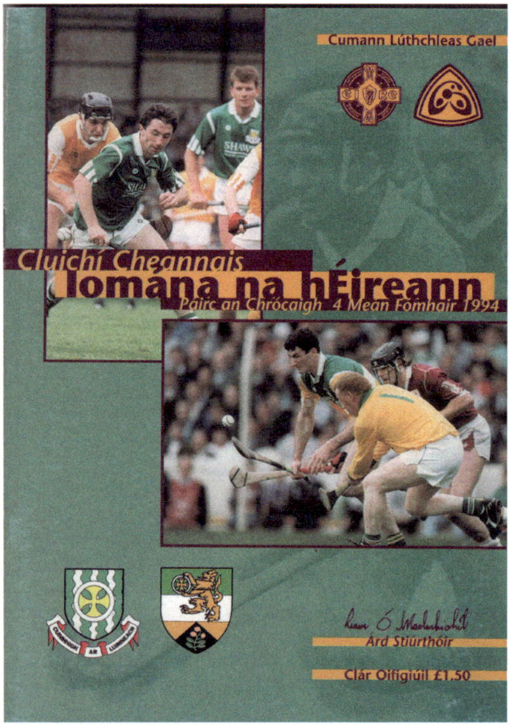
Cumann Lúthchleas Gael
Cluichí Cheannais
Iomána na hÉireann
Páirc an Chrócaigh 4 Mean Fómhair 1994
Ard Stiúrthóir
Clár Oifigiúil £1.50

5

Comhairle Connacht C.L.G.
CRAOBH
CHONNACHTA
CLUICHÍ
CEANNAIS PEILE
Páirc Dr. de hÍde
Ros Comáin
24 Iúil
1994
£1.00 Clár Oifigiúil
Runai
Bank of Ireland
Football Championship

6

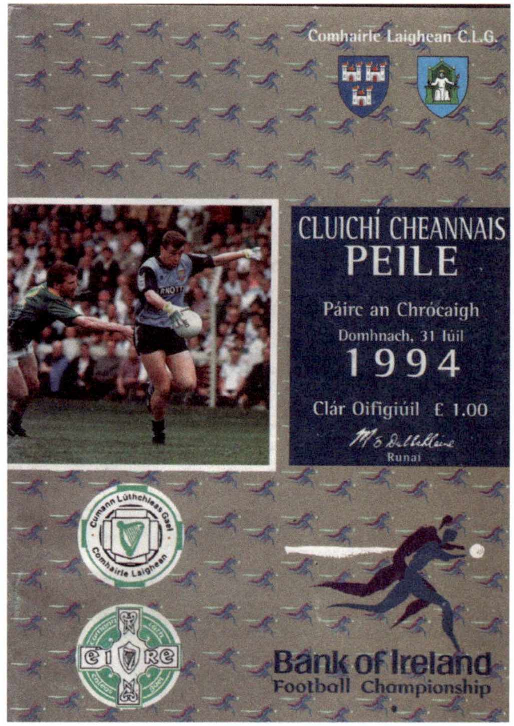
Comhairle Laighean C.L.G.
CLUICHÍ CHEANNAIS
PEILE
Páirc an Chrócaigh
Domhnach, 31 Iúil
1994
Clár Oifigiúil £ 1.00
Runai
Bank of Ireland
Football Championship

7

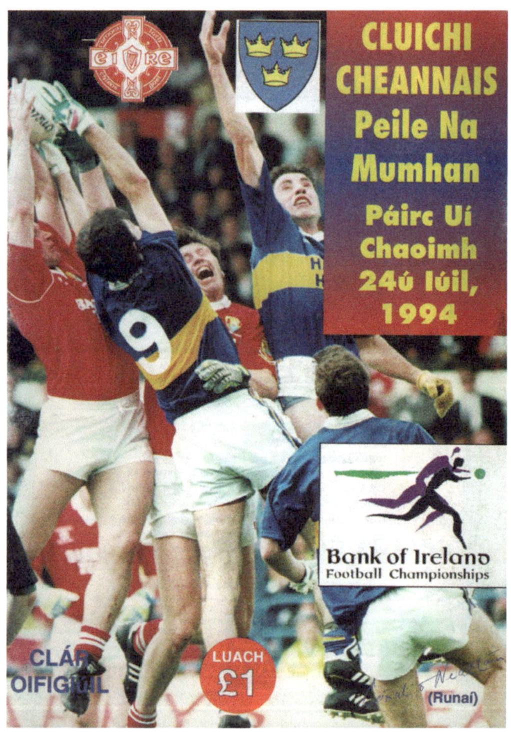
CLUICHI
CHEANNAIS
Peile Na
Mumhan
Páirc Uí
Chaoimh
24ú Iúil,
1994
Bank of Ireland
Football Championships
CLÁR
OIFIGIÚIL
LUACH
£1
(Runaí)

8

9

4 All-Ireland Hurling Final
Offaly 3-16 Limerick 2-13
Attendance 54,458

5 Connacht Football Final
Leitrim 0-12 Mayo 2-04

6 Leinster Football Final
Dublin 1-09 Meath 1-08

7 Munster Football Final
Cork 2-19 Tipperary 3-09

8 Ulster Football Final
Down 1-17 Tyrone 1-11

9 All-Ireland Football Final
Down 1-12 Dublin 0-13
Attendance – 58,684

1995

Clare's only previous success in the All-Ireland hurling championship came in 1914, when they defeated Laois in the final, and their last Munster championship title was achieved as far back as 1932. Their manager, Ger Loughnane, had played on the Clare team in the 1970s, which had come close, but ultimately couldn't surmount the hurdle of the Munster final, losing on four occasions. However, 1995 proved to be a watershed moment in the history of Clare hurling. Emotional scenes greeted the final whistle following their Munster final victory over neighbours Limerick. After defeating Galway in the All-Ireland semi-final, Clare set up a final meeting with the reigning champions, Offaly. This time it was Offaly who suffered the impact of a late comeback, as substitute Éamonn Taffe's goal put Clare on the road to victory. Clare joy was unconfined when Anthony Daly became the first man from the county to accept the Liam MacCarthy Cup after winning their second All-Ireland title.

1

2

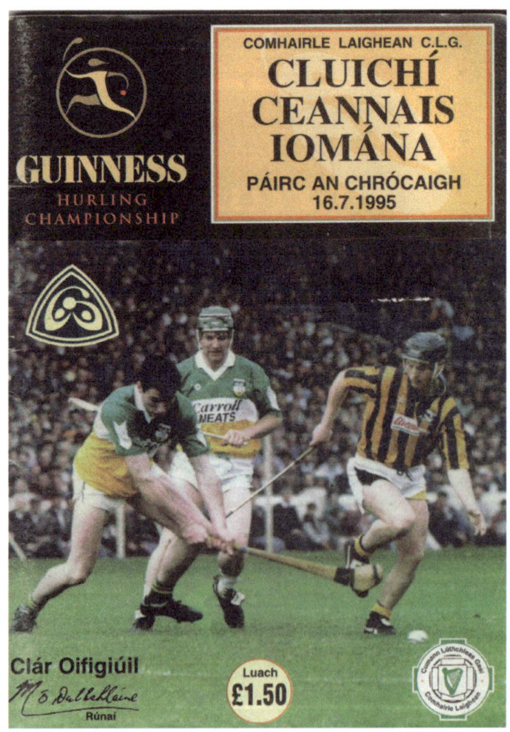

1 Connacht Hurling Final
Galway 2–21 Roscommon 2–12

2 Leinster Hurling Final
Offaly 2-16 Kilkenny 2-05

3 Munster Hurling Final
Clare 1-17 Limerick 0-11

4 Ulster Hurling Final
Down 3-7 Antrim 1-13

5 Replay
Down 1-19 Antrim 2-10

6 All-Ireland Hurling Final
Clare 1-13 Offaly 2-08
Attendance – 65,092

3

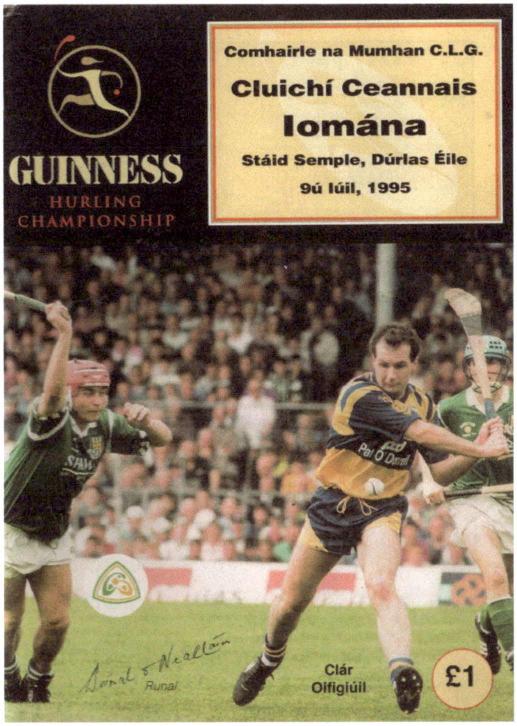
GUINNESS
HURLING
CHAMPIONSHIP
Comhairle na Mumhan C.L.G.
Cluichí Ceannais
Iomána
Stáid Semple, Dúrlas Éile
9ú Iúil, 1995
Rúnaí
Clár
Oifigiúil
£1

5

GUINNESS
HURLING
CHAMPIONSHIP
Cumann Lúthchleas Gael
-Comhairle Uladh
CEANNAS IOMÁNA ULADH
Aontroim
v. An Dún
REPLAY
PÁIRC MHIC EASMUINN, 16ú IÚIL '95
CLÁR OIFIGIÚIL
Míchéal Ó Ithmeadha
Rúnaí

4

GUINNESS
HURLING
CHAMPIONSHIP
Cumann Lúthchleas Gael
-Comhairle Uladh
CEANNAS IOMANA ULADH
Aontroim
v. An Dún
PÁIRC MHIC EASMUINN, 9 IÚIL '95
£1
CLÁR OIFIGIÚIL
Míchéal Ó Ithmeadha
Rúnaí

6

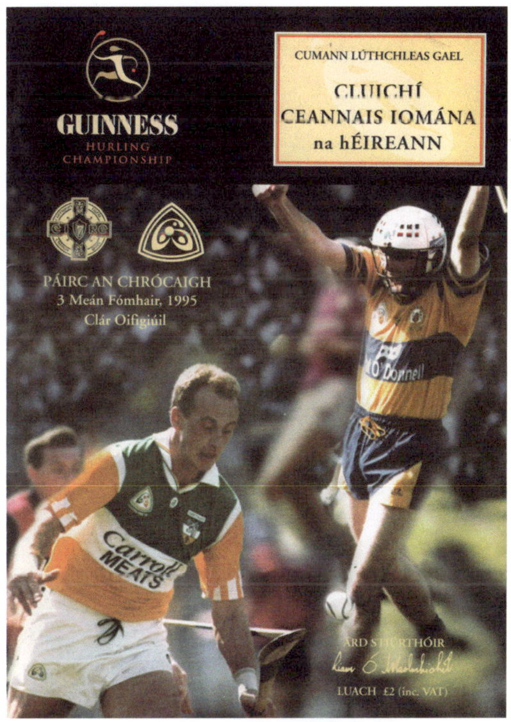
GUINNESS
HURLING
CHAMPIONSHIP
CUMANN LÚTHCHLEAS GAEL
CLUICHÍ
CEANNAIS IOMÁNA
na hÉIREANN
PÁIRC AN CHRÓCAIGH
3 Meán Fómhair, 1995
Clár Oifigiúil
ARD STIÚRTHÓIR
LUACH £2 (inc. VAT)

7

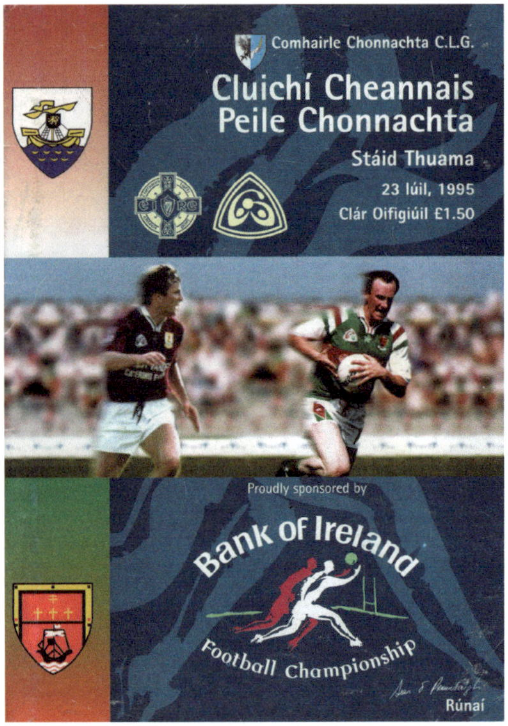
Comhairle Chonnachta C.L.G.
Cluichí Cheannais Peile Chonnachta
Stáid Thuama
23 Iúil, 1995
Clár Oifigiúil £1.50
Proudly sponsored by
Bank of Ireland
Football Championship
Rúnaí

8

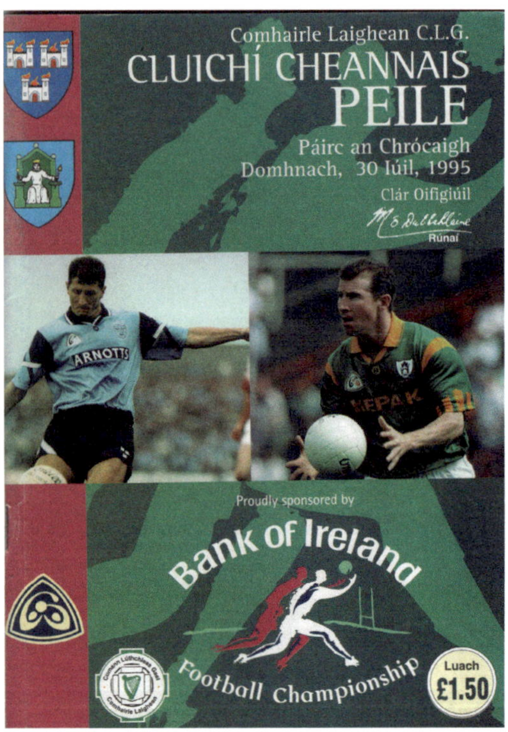
Comhairle Laighean C.L.G.
CLUICHÍ CHEANNAIS PEILE
Páirc an Chrócaigh
Domhnach, 30 Iúil, 1995
Clár Oifigiúil
Rúnaí
Proudly sponsored by
Bank of Ireland
Football Championship
Luach £1.50

9

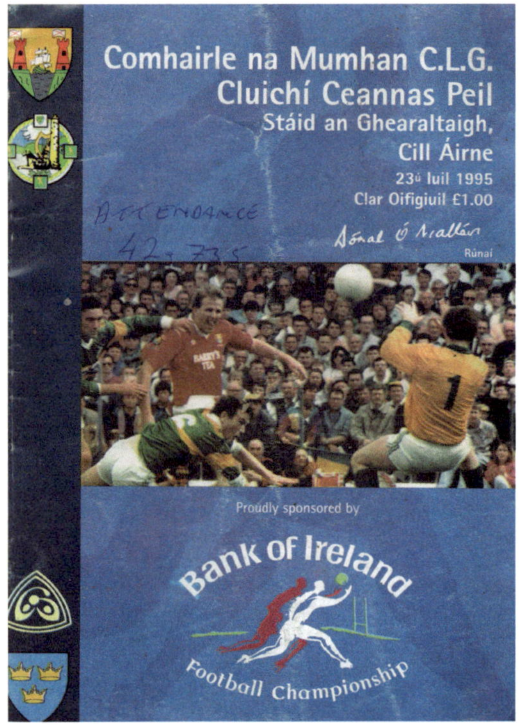
Comhairle na Mumhan C.L.G.
Cluichí Ceannas Peil
Stáid an Ghearaltaigh,
Cill Áirne
23ú Iuil 1995
Clar Oifigiuil £1.00
Rúnaí
Proudly sponsored by
Bank of Ireland
Football Championship

10

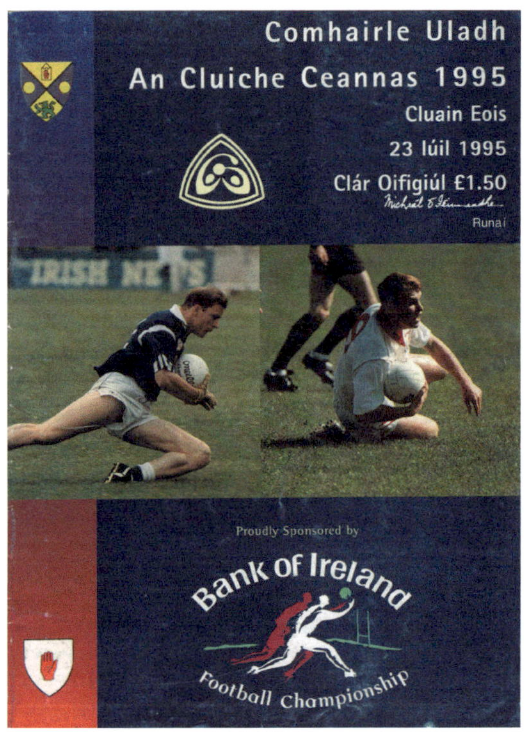
Comhairle Uladh
An Cluiche Ceannas 1995
Cluain Eois
23 Iúil 1995
Clár Oifigiúl £1.50
Runaí
Proudly Sponsored by
Bank of Ireland
Football Championship

11

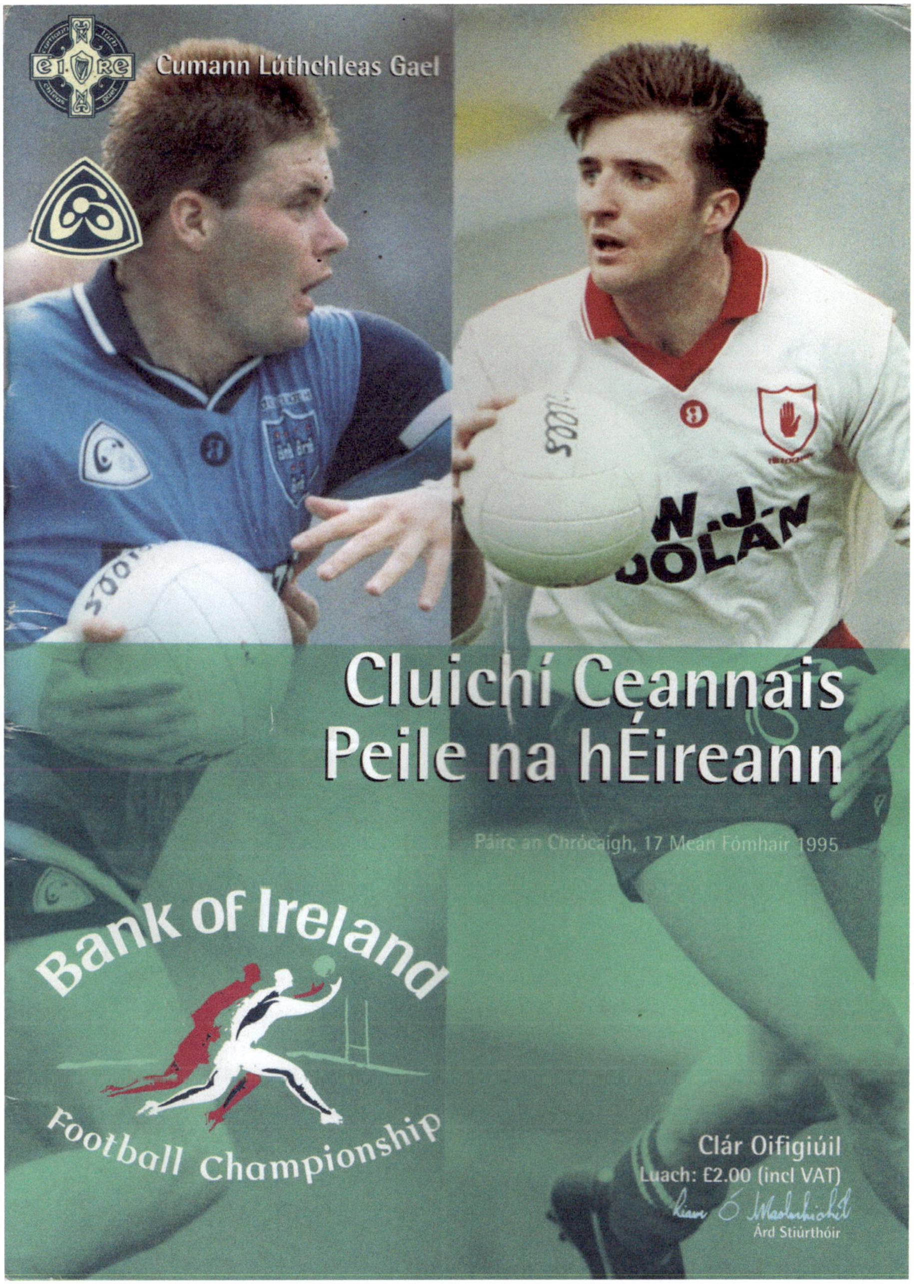

7 Connacht Football Final
Galway 0-17 Mayo 1-07

8 Leinster Football Final
Dublin 1-18 Meath 1-08

9 Munster Football Final
Cork 0-15 Kerry 1-09

10 Ulster Football Final
Tyrone 2-13 Cavan 0-10

11 All-Ireland Football Final
Dublin 1-10 Tyrone 0-12
Attendance – 65,600

1996

New York came through two preliminary rounds to set up an All-Ireland hurling quarter-final with Galway, but there the adventure ended as Galway advanced to a meeting with the Leinster champions, Wexford. Wexford had lost three of the last four Leinster finals but in 1996, led by their inspirational manager Liam Griffin, they saw off Kilkenny, Dublin and Offaly to win the title. They then bridged a 28-year gap to capture the Liam MacCarthy Cup for the sixth time in their history. Despite having a man sent off, Wexford were able to overcome Limerick's challenge, leaving the Treaty county to lick their wounds for the second time in three years.

A draw in the All-Ireland football final meant Meath and Mayo had to meet again. A 28-man brawl in the sixth minute of the replay resulted in the sending-off of Colm Coyle (Meath) and Liam McHale (Mayo). Once the football resumed, Meath prevailed, prolonging Mayo's wait for an All-Ireland victory.

1

1 Connacht Hurling Final
Galway 3–19 Roscommon 2–10

2 Leinster Hurling Final
Wexford 2-23 Offaly 2-15

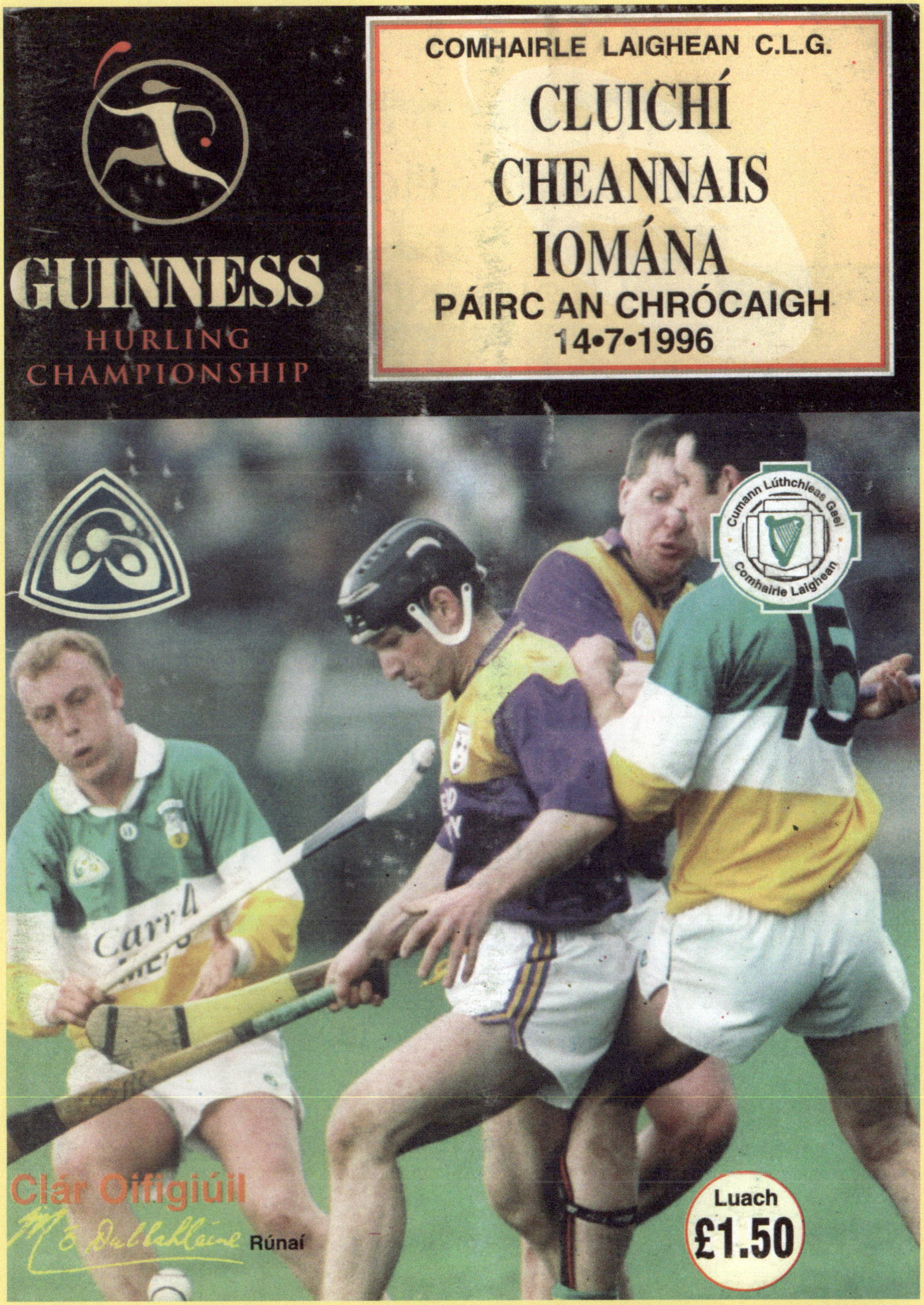
GUINNESS
HURLING
CHAMPIONSHIP
COMHAIRLE LAIGHEAN C.L.G.
CLUICHÍ
CHEANNAIS
IOMÁNA
PÁIRC AN CHRÓCAIGH
14•7•1996
Cumann Lúthchleas Gael
Comhairle Laighean
Clár Oifigiúil
Rúnaí
Luach
£1.50

3

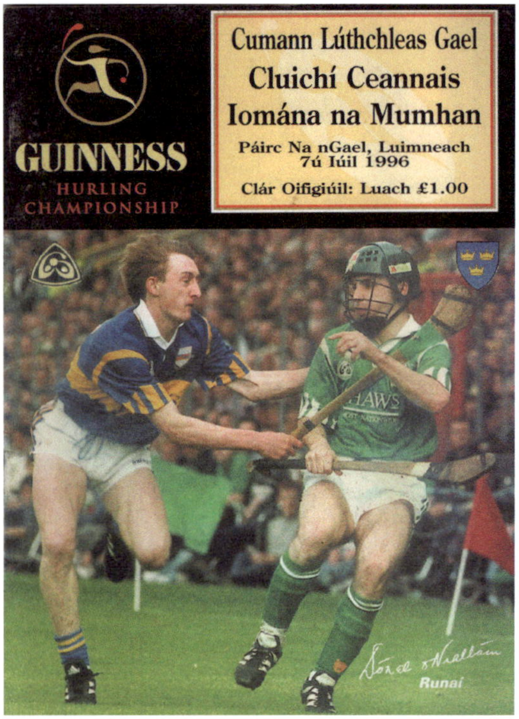
GUINNESS
HURLING
CHAMPIONSHIP
Cumann Lúthchleas Gael
Cluichí Ceannais
Iomána na Mumhan
Páirc Na nGael, Luimneach
7ú Iúil 1996
Clár Oifigiúil: Luach £1.00
Runaí

4

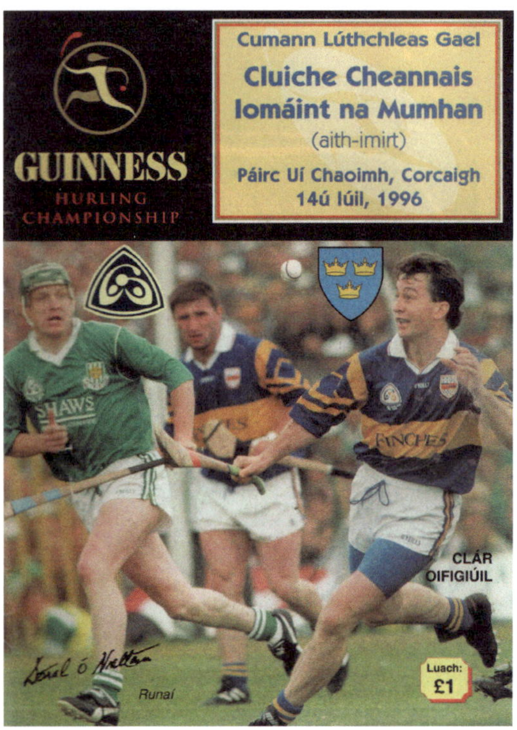
GUINNESS
HURLING
CHAMPIONSHIP
Cumann Lúthchleas Gael
Cluiche Cheannais
Iomáint na Mumhan
(aith-imirt)
Páirc Uí Chaoimh, Corcaigh
14ú Iúil, 1996
CLÁR
OIFIGIÚIL
Runaí
Luach:
£1

5

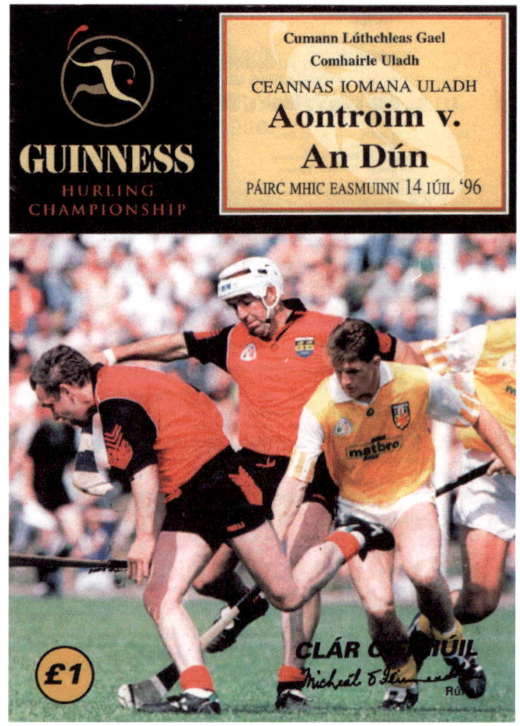
GUINNESS
HURLING
CHAMPIONSHIP
Cumann Lúthchleas Gael
Comhairle Uladh
CEANNAS IOMANA ULADH
Aontroim v.
An Dún
PÁIRC MHIC EASMUINN 14 IÚIL '96
£1

6

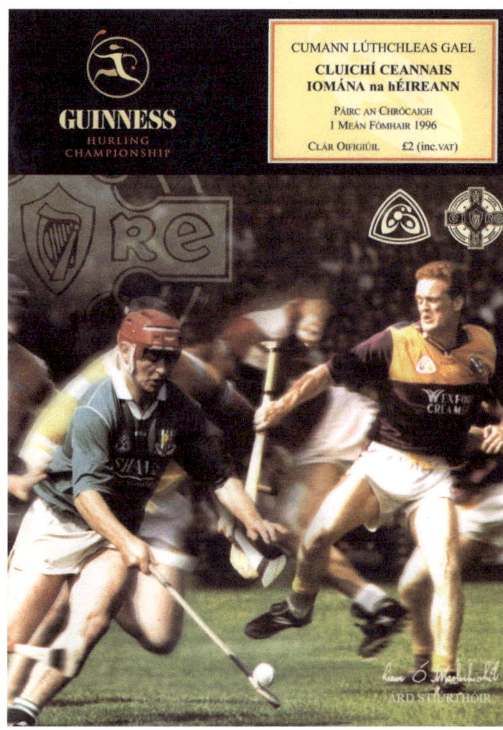
GUINNESS
HURLING
CHAMPIONSHIP
CUMANN LÚTHCHLEAS GAEL
CLUICHÍ CEANNAIS
IOMÁNA na hÉIREANN
PÁIRC AN CHRÓCAIGH
1 MEÁN FÓMHAIR 1996
CLÁR OIFIGIÚIL £2 (inc.vat)
ARD STIÚRTHÓIR

7

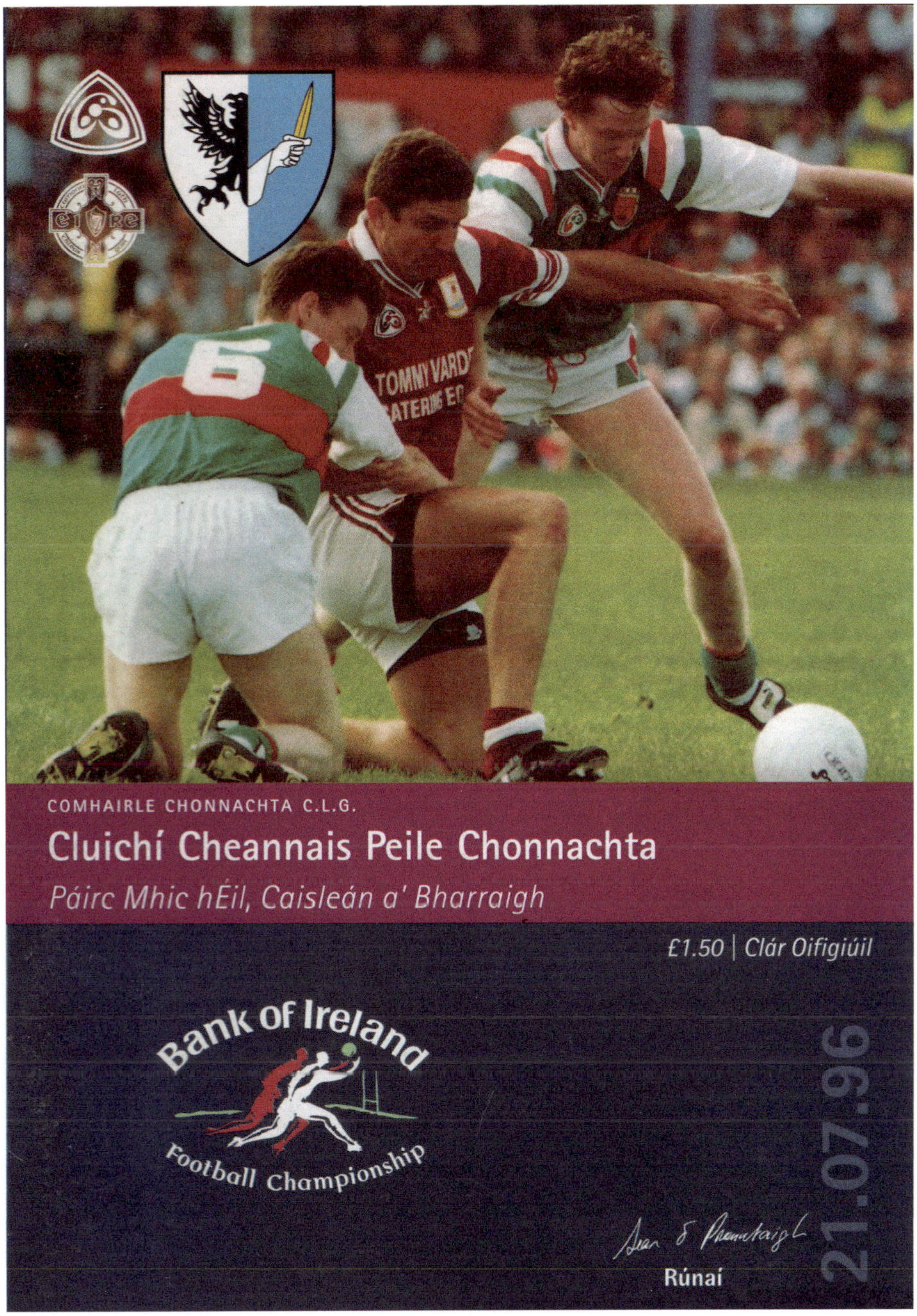

3 Munster Hurling Final
Limerick 0-19 Tipperary 1-16

4 Replay
Limerick 4-07 Tipperary 0-16

5 Ulster Hurling Final
Antrim 1-20 Down 2-12

6 All-Ireland Hurling Final
Wexford 1-13 Limerick 0-14
Attendance – 65,849

7 Connacht Football Final
Mayo 3-09 Galway 1-11

8

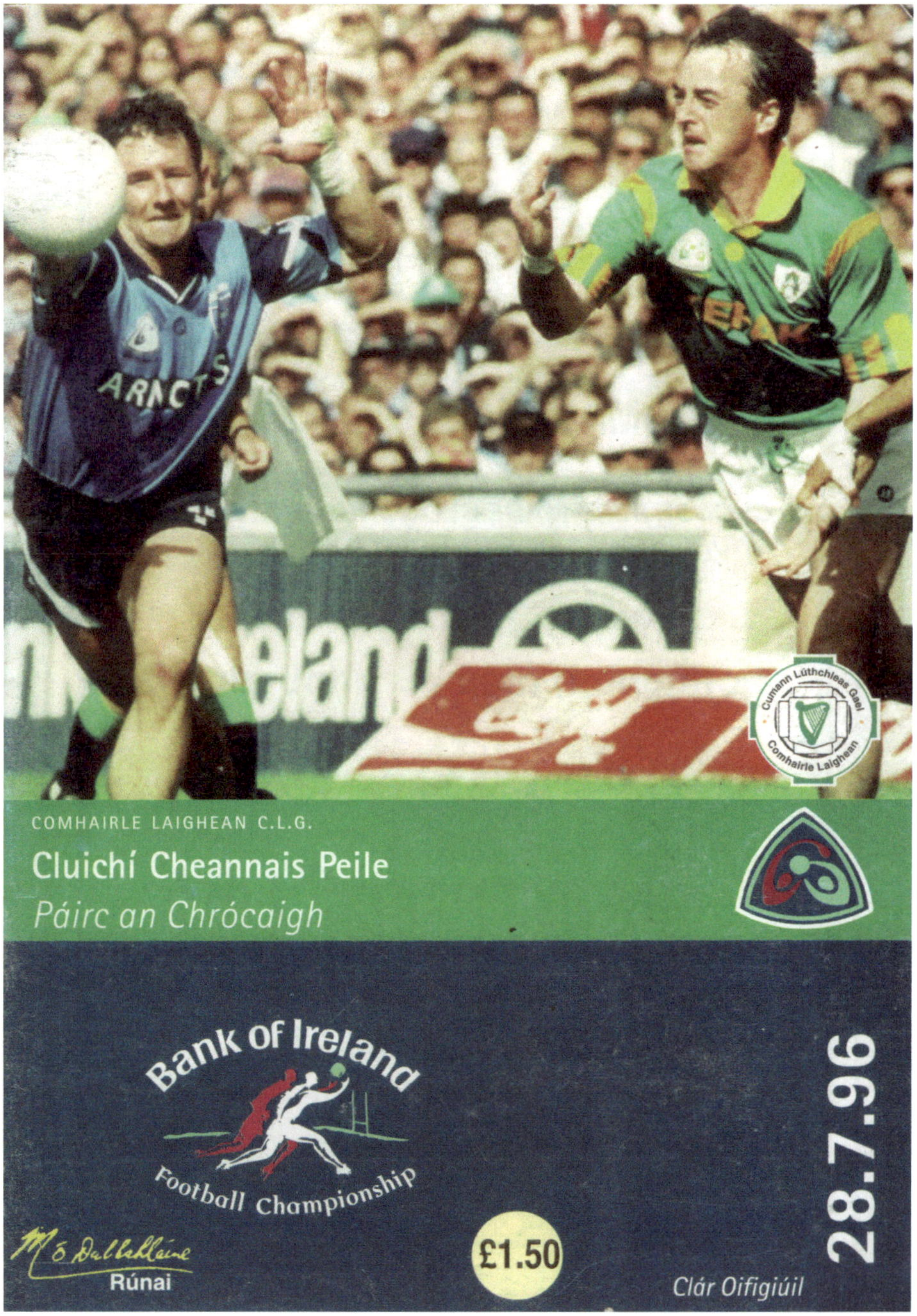

8 Leinster Football Final
Meath 0-10 Dublin 0-08

9 Munster Football Final
Kerry 0-14 Cork 0-11

10 Ulster Football Final
Tyrone 1-09 Down 0-09

11 All-Ireland Football Final
Meath 0-12 Mayo 1-09
Attendance – 65,898

12 Replay
Meath 2-09 Mayo 1-11
Attendance – 65,802

9

Bank of Ireland
Football Championship
CUMANN LÚTHCHLEAS GAEL
CLUICHÍ CHEANNAIS PEILE NA MUMHAN
Páirc Uí Chaoimh
21 Iúil, 1996
CLÁR OIFIGIÚIL
£1.00
Runaí

10

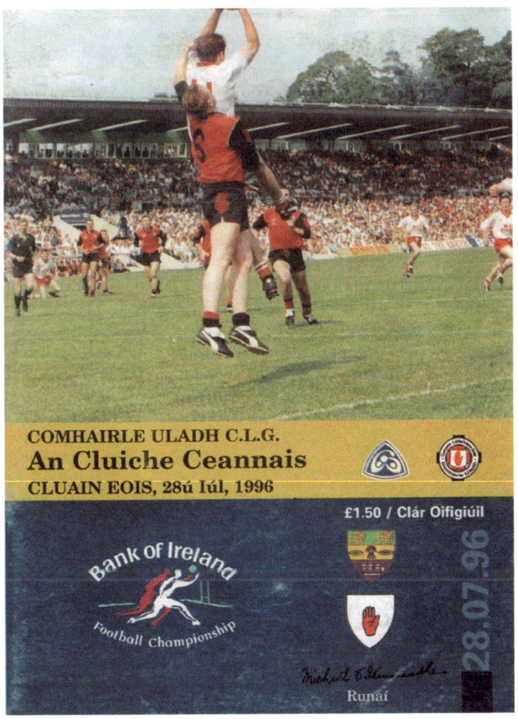
COMHAIRLE ULADH C.L.G.
An Cluiche Ceannais
CLUAIN EOIS, 28ú Iúl, 1996
£1.50 / Clár Oifigiúil
Bank of Ireland
Football Championship
28.07.96
Runaí

11

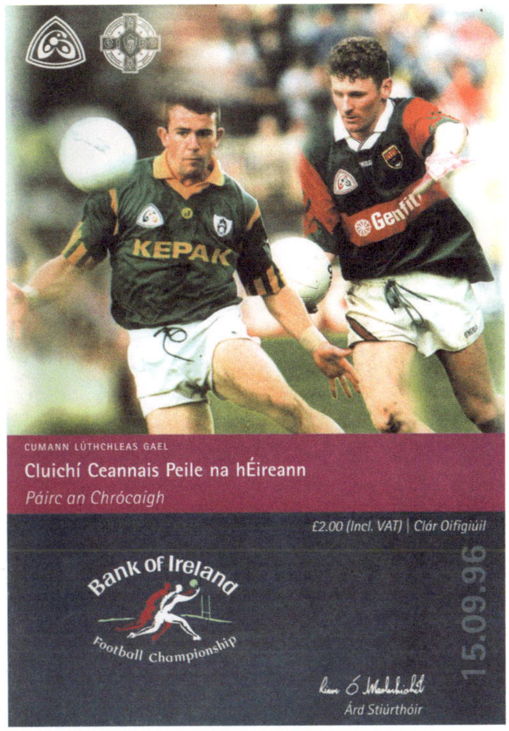
KEPAK
CUMANN LÚTHCHLEAS GAEL
Cluichí Ceannais Peile na hÉireann
Páirc an Chrócaigh
£2.00 (Incl. VAT) | Clár Oifigiúil
Bank of Ireland
Football Championship
15.09.96
Árd Stiúrthóir

12

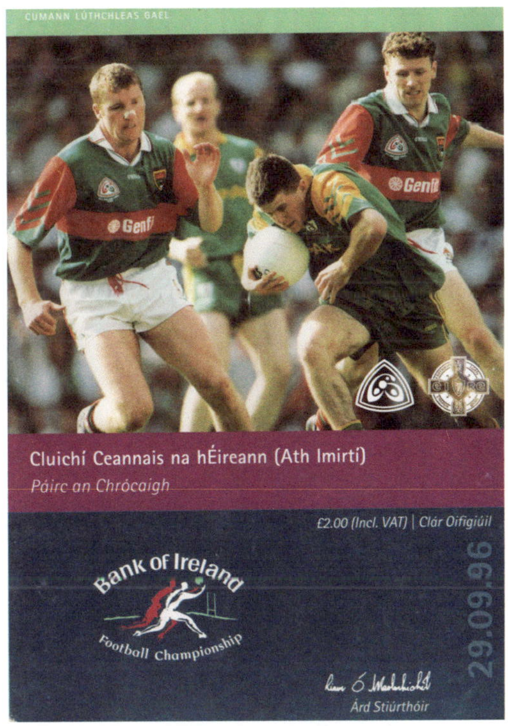
CUMANN LÚTHCHLEAS GAEL
Cluichí Ceannais na hÉireann (Ath Imirtí)
Páirc an Chrócaigh
£2.00 (Incl. VAT) | Clár Oifigiúil
Bank of Ireland
Football Championship
29.09.96
Árd Stiúrthóir

1997

For the 1997 hurling championship, the introduction of the qualifier, or so-called 'back-door' system, allowed teams who had been beaten in their provincial championship final a second chance to qualify for the All-Ireland semi-final. In the Leinster hurling final, Wexford retained their title by defeating Kilkenny while, in Munster, Clare overcame Tipperary in the final. After Tipperary overcame Down in the All-Ireland quarter-final and then Wexford in the semi-final, it became clear that there would be a first-ever all-Munster All-Ireland final. In the final, controversy surrounded an Aidan Ryan shot, which was eventually deemed wide. A late point-blank save by David Fitzgerald from John Leahy gave Clare their second victory in three years.

In the Ulster football final, the one-time superpower of the province, Cavan, regained the provincial title for the first time since 1969 with a win over Derry. However, it proved to be an isolated victory, and it was 2020 before the Anglo-Celt Cup returned to the county.

1

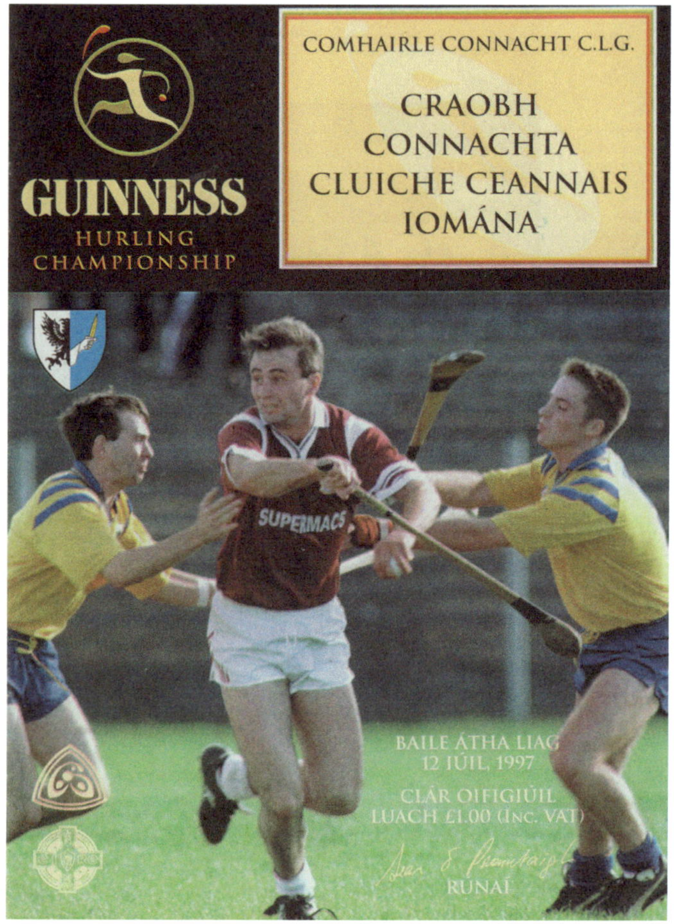

1 Connacht Hurling Final
Galway 6–24 Roscommon 0–05

2 Leinster Hurling Final
Wexford 2-14 Kilkenny 1-11

3 Munster Hurling Final
Clare 1-18 Tipperary 0-18

4 Ulster Hurling Final
Down 3-14 Antrim 0-19

5 All-Ireland Hurling Final
Clare 0-20 Tipperary 2-13
Attendance – 65,575

2

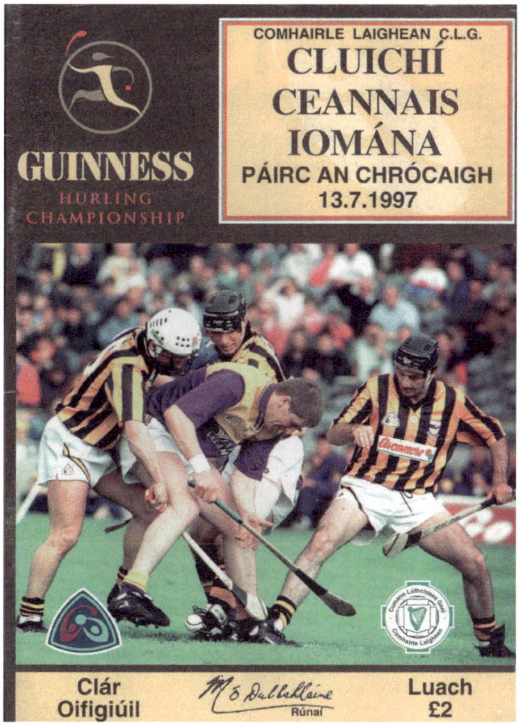
COMHAIRLE LAIGHEAN C.L.G.
CLUICHÍ CEANNAIS IOMÁNA
PÁIRC AN CHRÓCAIGH
13.7.1997
GUINNESS
HURLING CHAMPIONSHIP
Clár Oifigiúil
Rúnaí
Luach £2

4

Cumann Lúthchleas Gael
- Comhairle Uladh
CEANNAS IOMÁNA ULADH
Aontroim
v. An Dún
PÁIRC MHIC EASMUINN, 6 IÚIL '97
GUINNESS
HURLING CHAMPIONSHIP
£1
CLÁR OIFIGIÚIL
Rúnaí Gníomhach

3

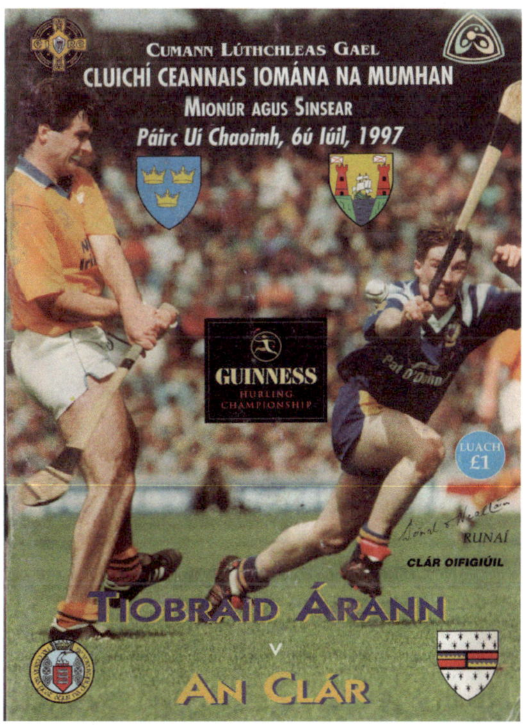
Cumann Lúthchleas Gael
CLUICHÍ CEANNAIS IOMÁNA NA MUMHAN
Mionúr agus Sinsear
Páirc Uí Chaoimh, 6ú Iúil, 1997
GUINNESS
HURLING CHAMPIONSHIP
LUACH £1
RÚNAÍ
CLÁR OIFIGIÚIL
TIOBRAID ÁRANN
v
AN CLÁR

5

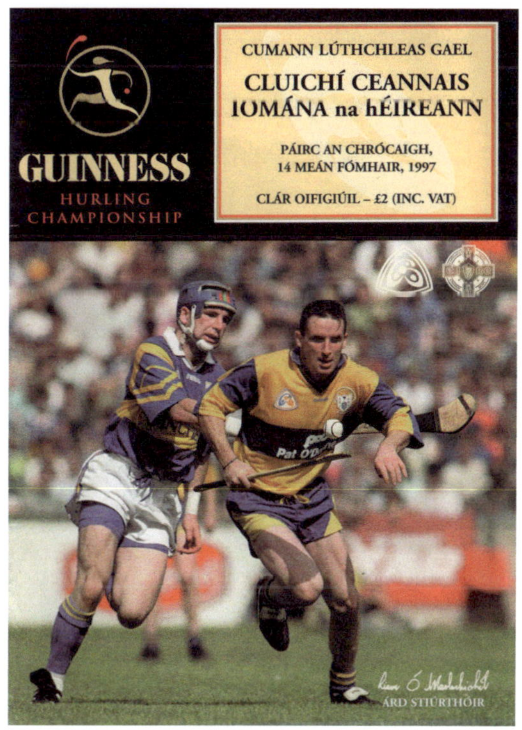
CUMANN LÚTHCHLEAS GAEL
CLUICHÍ CEANNAIS IOMÁNA na hÉIREANN
PÁIRC AN CHRÓCAIGH,
14 MEÁN FÓMHAIR, 1997
CLÁR OIFIGIÚIL – £2 (INC. VAT)
GUINNESS
HURLING CHAMPIONSHIP
ÁRD STIÚRTHÓIR

6

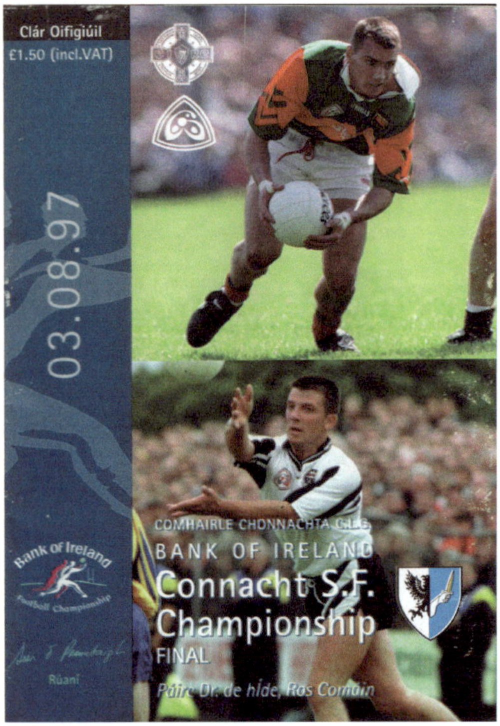
Clár Oifigiúil
£1.50 (incl.VAT)
03.08.97
COMHAIRLE CHONNACHTA C.L.G.
BANK OF IRELAND
Connacht S.F.
Championship
FINAL
Páirc Dr. de hÍde, Ros Comáin
Bank of Ireland
Football Championship
Rúaní

8

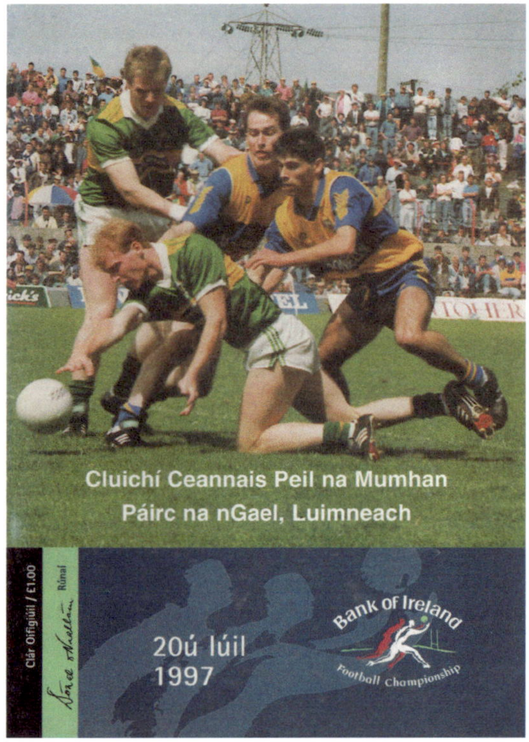
Cluichí Ceannais Peil na Mumhan
Páirc na nGael, Luimneach
Clár Oifigiúil / £1.00
Rúnaí
20ú Iúil
1997
Bank of Ireland
Football Championship

7

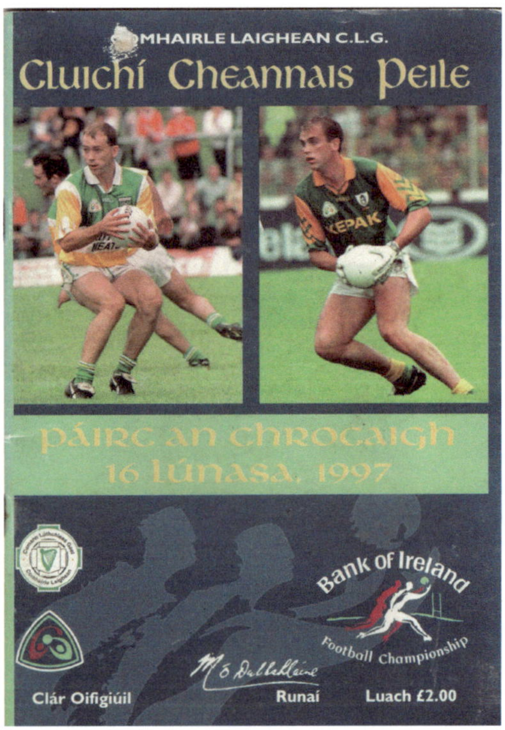
MHAIRLE LAIGHEAN C.L.G.
Cluichí Cheannais Peile
Páirc an Chrócaigh
16 Lúnasa, 1997
Bank of Ireland
Football Championship
Clár Oifigiúil
Runaí
Luach £2.00

9

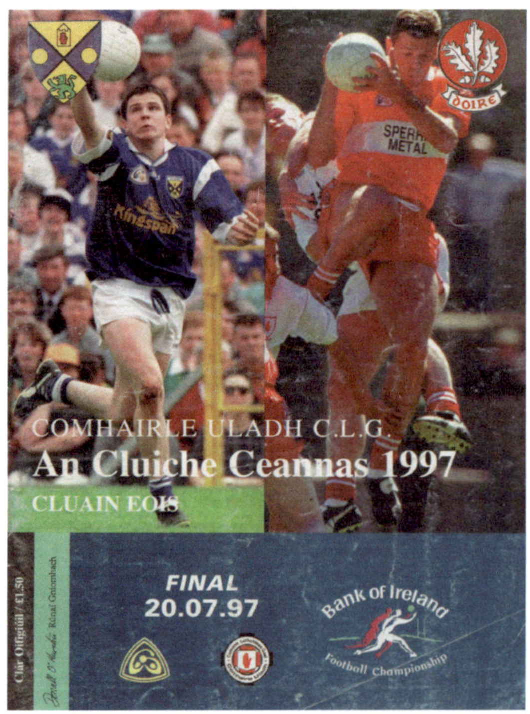
DOIRE
COMHAIRLE ULADH C.L.G.
An Cluiche Ceannas 1997
CLUAIN EOIS
FINAL
20.07.97
Bank of Ireland
Football Championship
Clár Oifigiúil / £1.50

10

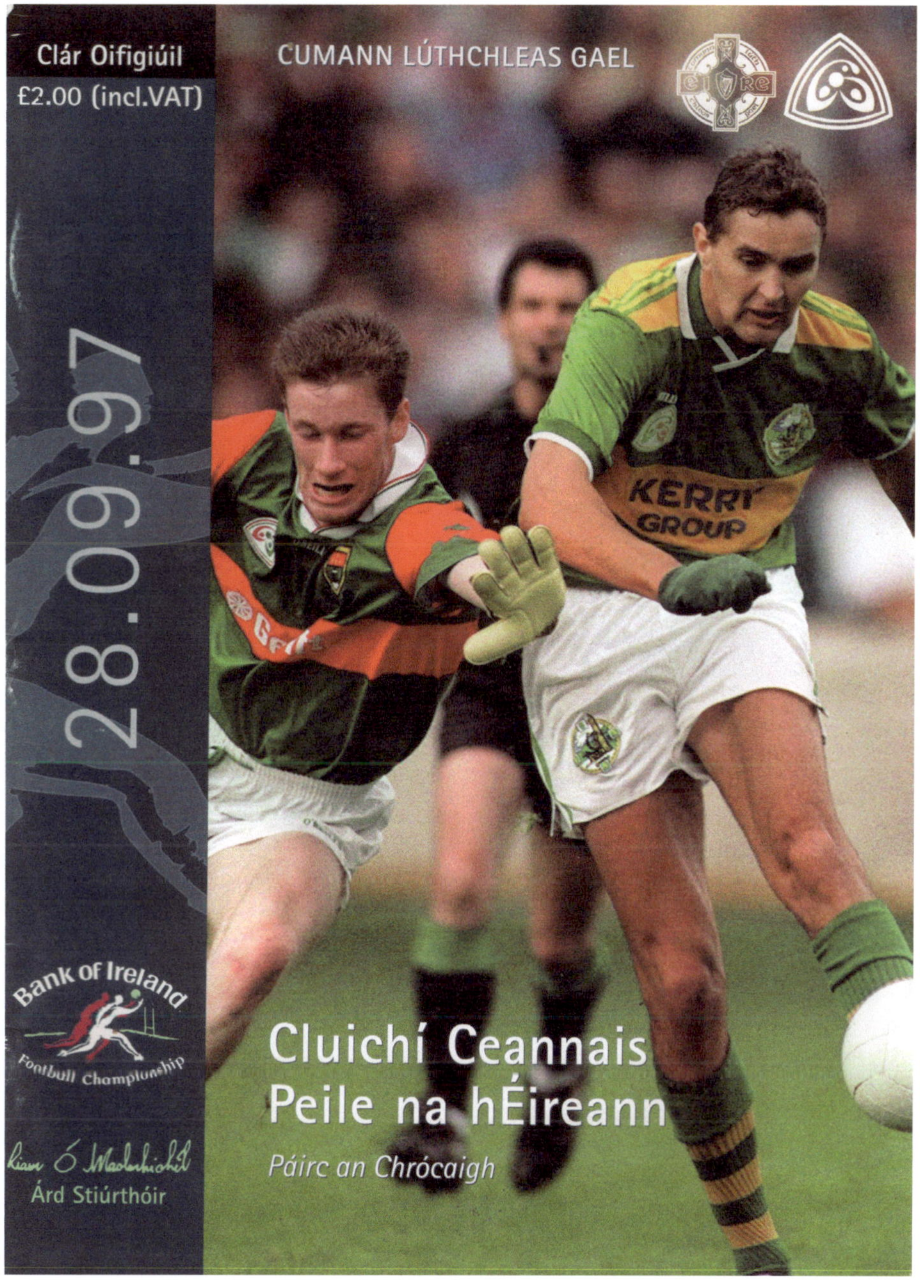

6 Connacht Football Final
Mayo 0-11 Sligo 1-07

7 Leinster Football Final
Offaly 3-17 Meath 1-15

8 Munster Football Final
Kerry 1-13 Clare 0-11

9 Ulster Football Final
Cavan 1-14 Derry 0-16

10 All-Ireland Football Final
Kerry 0-13 Mayo 1-07
Attendance – 65,601

1998

After losing to Kilkenny in the 1998 Leinster final, comments by the Offaly manager, Michael 'Babs' Keating, about his players led to his resignation. Replaced by Michael Bond, an All-Ireland quarter-final win over Antrim allowed Offaly to regroup and progress to the semi-final. The outcome of a tempestuous Munster final replay between Clare and Waterford was that Colin Lynch and Brian Lohan were both suspended when Clare met Offaly in the All-Ireland semi-final. The first match was a draw, and the replay ended in chaos when an error by the referee caused the match to finish before the full 70 minutes had elapsed. With Offaly growing in confidence with every game, and Clare looking more weary, Offaly won the re-fixture that had been ordered on the back of the error. Offaly then defeated Kilkenny in the All-Ireland final to become the first team to do so having failed to win their provincial championship.

1

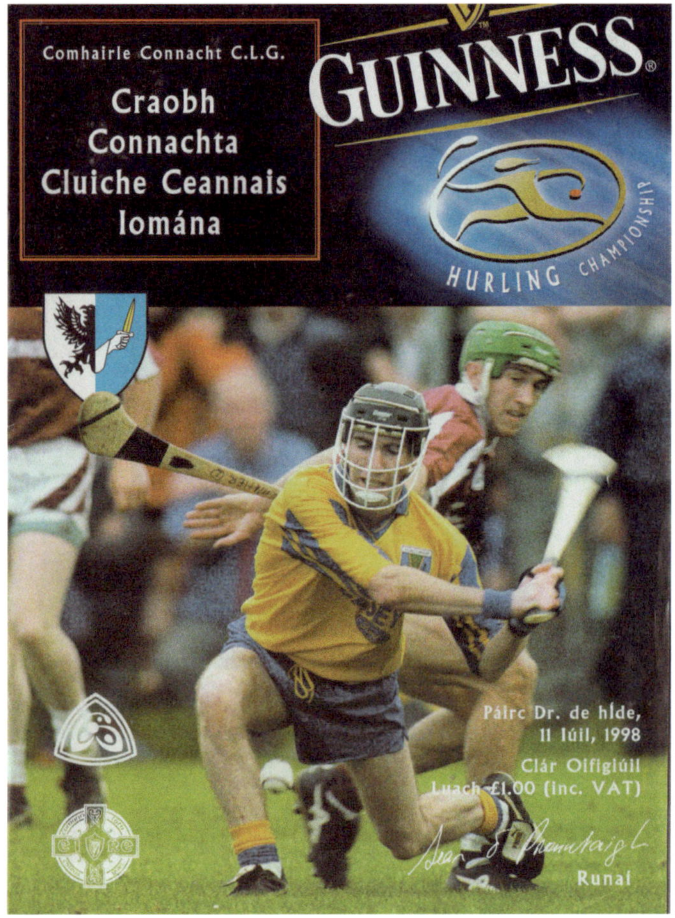

1 Connacht Hurling Final
Galway 2–27 Roscommon 3–13

2 Leinster Hurling Final
Kilkenny 3-10 Offaly 1-11

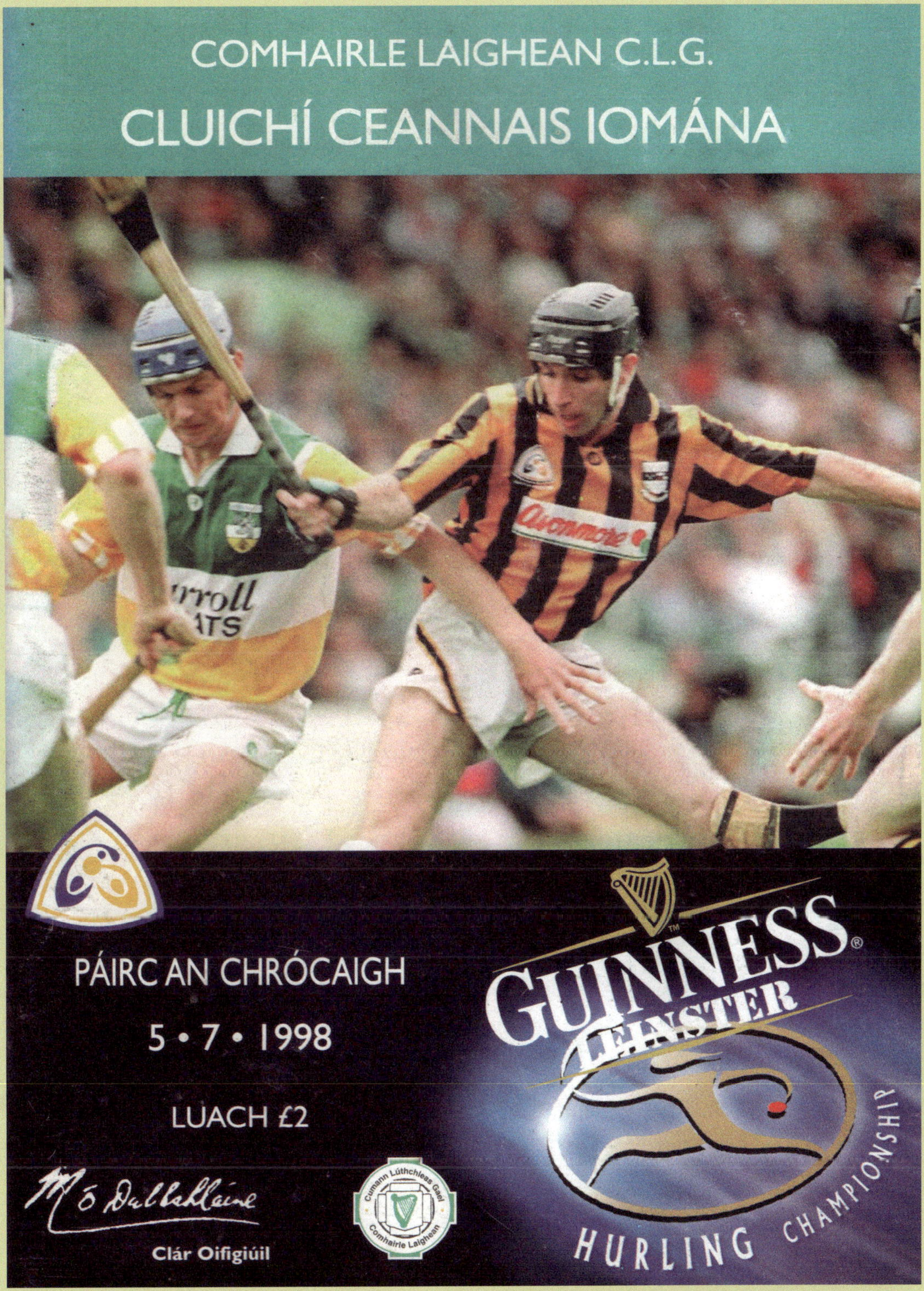
COMHAIRLE LAIGHEAN C.L.G.
CLUICHÍ CEANNAIS IOMÁNA
PÁIRC AN CHRÓCAIGH
5 • 7 • 1998
LUACH £2
Clár Oifigiúil
Cumann Lúthchleas Gael
Comhairle Laighean
GUINNESS
LEINSTER
HURLING CHAMPIONSHIP

3

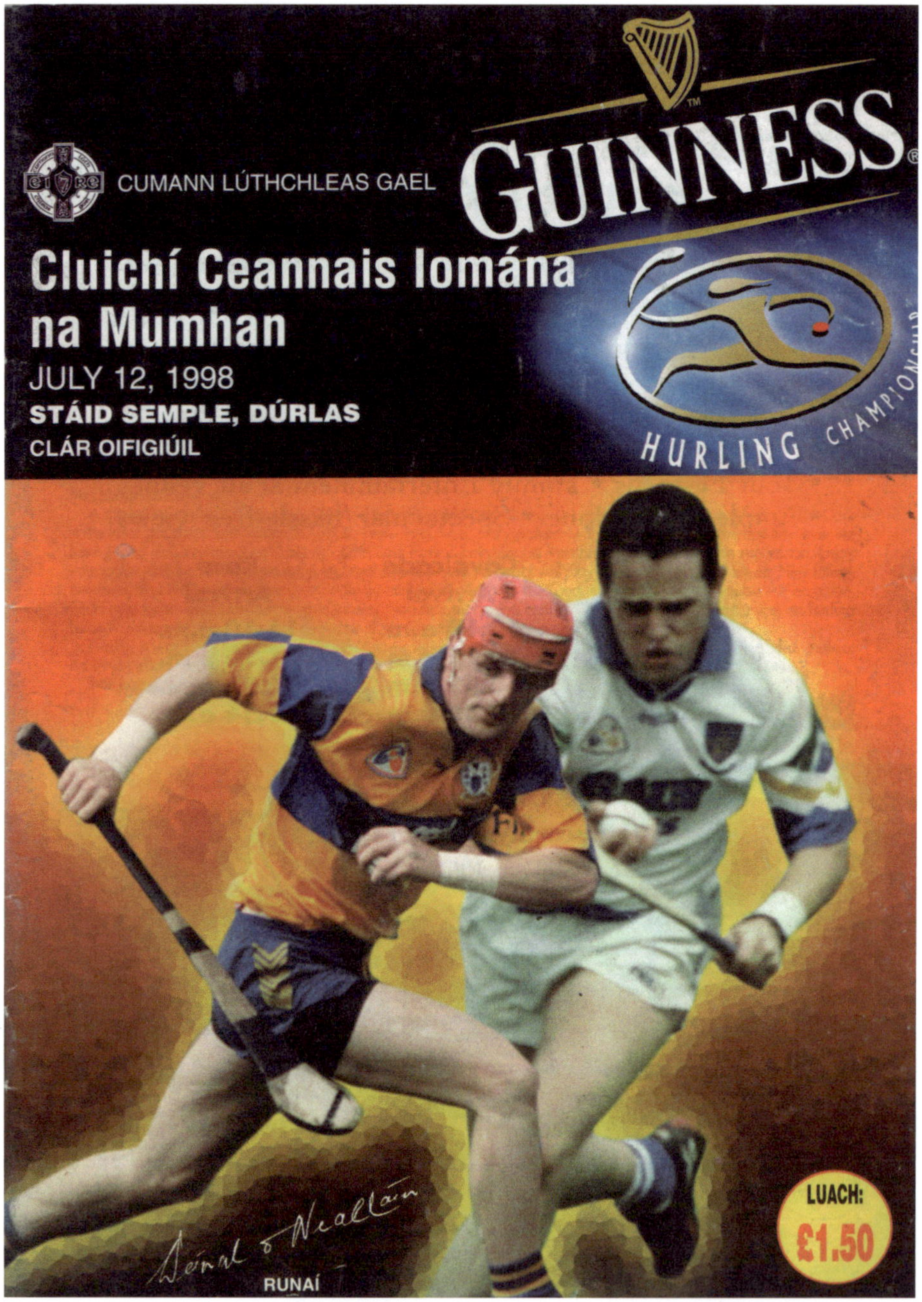

3 Munster Hurling Final
Clare 1-16 Waterford 3-10

4 Replay
Clare 2-16 Waterford 0-10

5 Ulster Hurling Final
Antrim 1-19 Derry 2-13

6 All-Ireland Hurling Final
Offaly 2-16 Kilkenny 1-13
Attendance – 65,491

7 Connacht Football Final
Galway 0-11 Roscommon 0-11

4

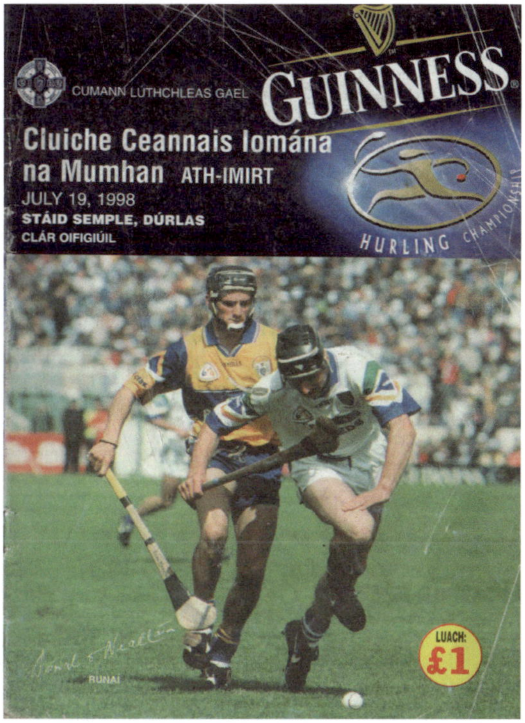
CUMANN LÚTHCHLEAS GAEL
GUINNESS
Cluiche Ceannais Iomána
na Mumhan ATH-IMIRT
JULY 19, 1998
STÁID SEMPLE, DÚRLAS
CLÁR OIFIGIÚIL
HURLING CHAMPIONSHIP
LUACH:
£1
RÚNAI

5

GUINNESS
HURLING
CHAMPIONSHIP
Cumann Lúthchleas Gael
Comhairle Uladh
CEANNAS IOMÁNA ULADH
Aontroim
v. Doire
PÁIRC MHIC EASMUINN, 5 JÚIL '98
DOIRE
Clár Oifigiúil / £1.00

6

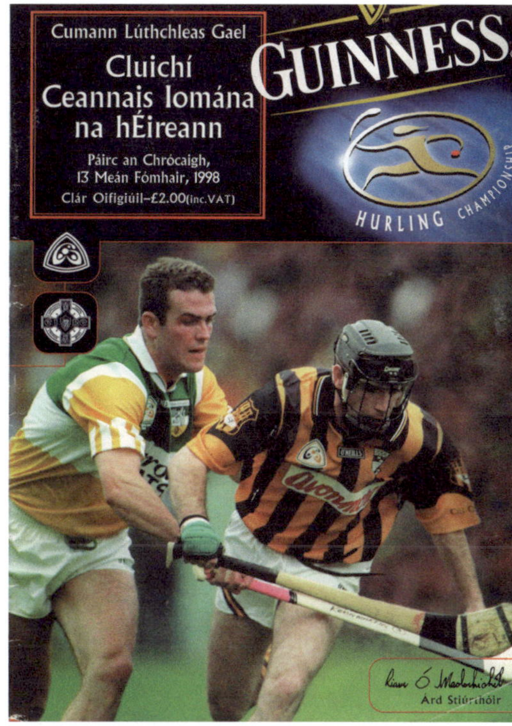
Cumann Lúthchleas Gael
Cluichí
Ceannais Iomána
na hÉireann
Páirc an Chrócaigh,
13 Meán Fómhair, 1998
Clár Oifigiúil–£2.00(inc.VAT)
GUINNESS
HURLING CHAMPIONSHIP
Ard Stiúrthóir

7

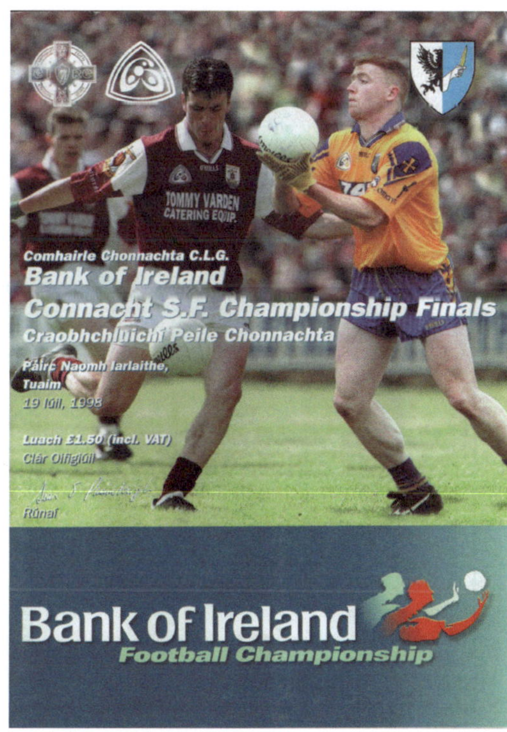
TOMMY VARDEN
CATERING EQUIP.
Comhairle Chonnachta C.L.G.
Bank of Ireland
Connacht S.F. Championship Finals
Craobhchluichí Peile Chonnachta
Páirc Naomh Iarlaithe,
Tuaim
19 Iúil, 1998
Luach £1.50 (incl. VAT)
Clár Oifigiúil
Rúnaí
Bank of Ireland
Football Championship

8

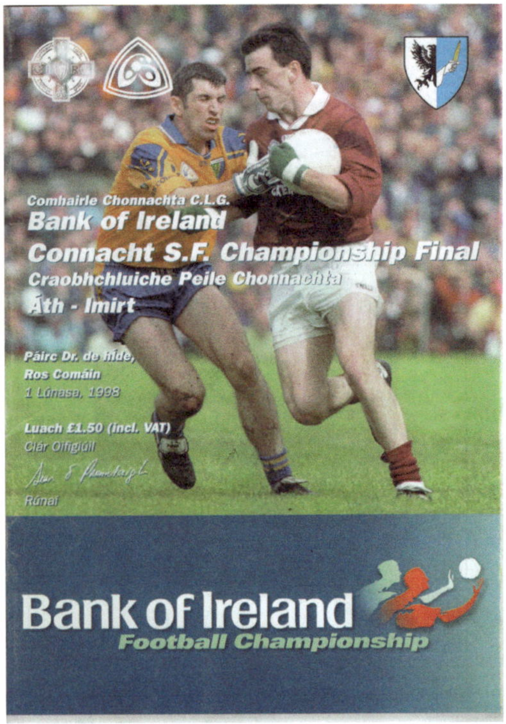
Comhairle Chonnachta C.L.G.
Bank of Ireland
Connacht S.F. Championship Final
Craobhchluiche Peile Chonnachta
Áth - Imirt
Páirc Dr. de hÍde,
Ros Comáin
1 Lúnasa, 1998
Luach £1.50 (incl. VAT)
Clár Oifigiúil
Rúnaí
Bank of Ireland
Football Championship

9

COMHAIRLE LAIGHEAN C.L.G.
CLUICHÍ
CHEANNAIS PEILE
PÁIRC AN CHRÓCAIGH
2 • 8 • 1998
LUACH £2
CLÁR OIFIGIÚIL
Bank of Ireland
Leinster Football Championship

10

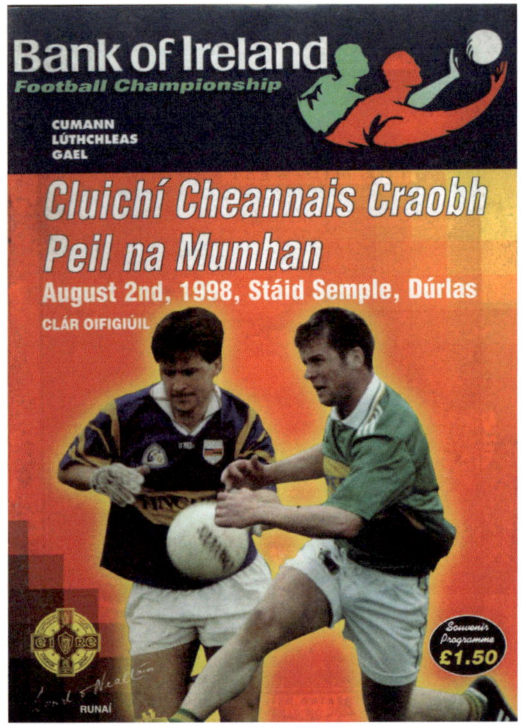
Bank of Ireland
Football Championship
CUMANN
LÚTHCHLEAS
GAEL
Cluichí Cheannais Craobh
Peil na Mumhan
August 2nd, 1998, Stáid Semple, Dúrlas
CLÁR OIFIGIÚIL
Souvenir
Programme
£1.50
RUNAÍ

11

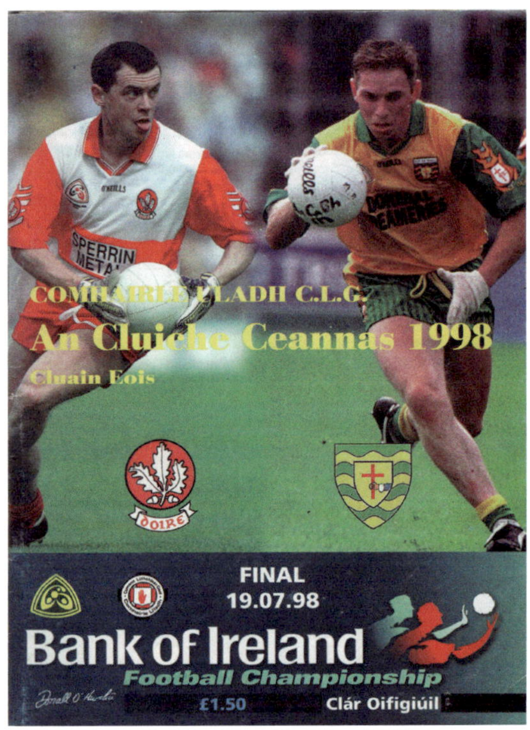
COMHAIRLE ULADH C.L.G.
An Cluiche Ceannas 1998
Cluain Eois
DOIRE
FINAL
19.07.98
Bank of Ireland
Football Championship
£1.50
Clár Oifigiúil

12

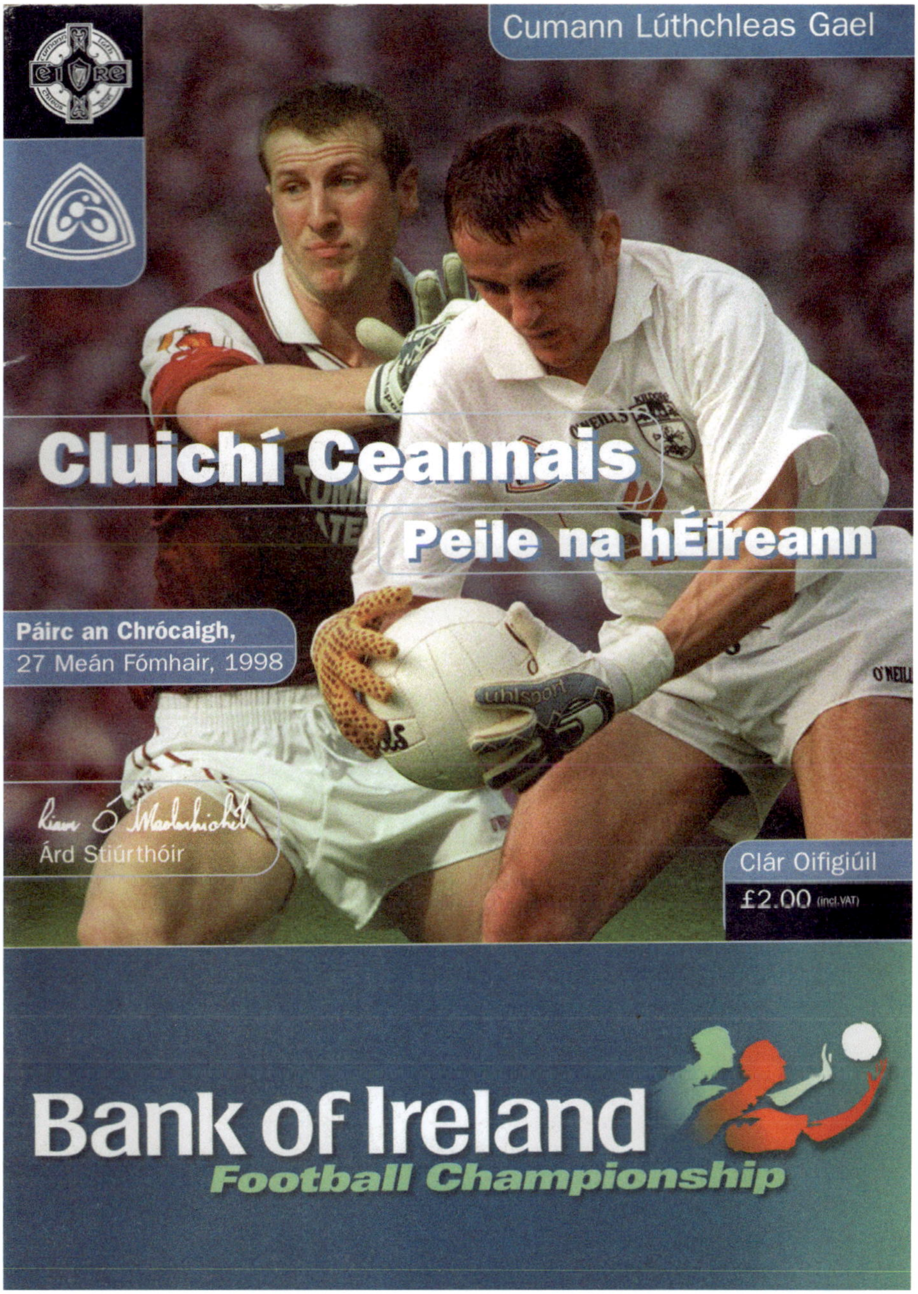

8 Replay
Galway 1-17 Roscommon 0-17 (aet)

9 Leinster Football Final
Kildare 1-12 Meath 0-10

10 Munster Football Final
Kerry 0-17 Tipperary 1-10

11 Ulster Football Final
Derry 1-07 Donegal 0-08

12 All-Ireland Football Final
Galway 1-14 Kildare 1-10
Attendance – 65,886

1999

After a five-year experiment to reintroduce the Connacht senior hurling championship, the last Connacht hurling final was played in 1999. Only two teams entered the championship from 1995 to 1999 – Galway and Roscommon – with Galway winning all five finals, often by a considerable margin. Just as they had at the beginning of the decade, Cork contested both All-Ireland finals. Managed by Jimmy Barry Murphy in 1999, the hurlers completed the first half of a possible double, defeating Kilkenny in the final. The All-Ireland football final between old rivals Meath and Cork was the last to be played in front of the old Hogan Stand. It was demolished in October to facilitate the ongoing reconstruction of the stadium. Cork were unable to complete a second double in the 1990s as Meath took the last All-Ireland of the millennium. In 1999, the Gaelic Players Association was formed to address issues of player welfare and give a voice to intercounty GAA players.

1

1 Connacht Hurling Final
Galway 4–26 Roscommon 2–08

2 Leinster Hurling Final
Kilkenny 5-14 Offaly 1-16

3 Munster Hurling Final
Cork 1-15 Clare 0-14

4 Ulster Hurling Final
Antrim 2-19 Derry 1-09

5 All-Ireland Hurling Final
Cork 0-13 Kilkenny 0-12
Attendance – 62,989

2

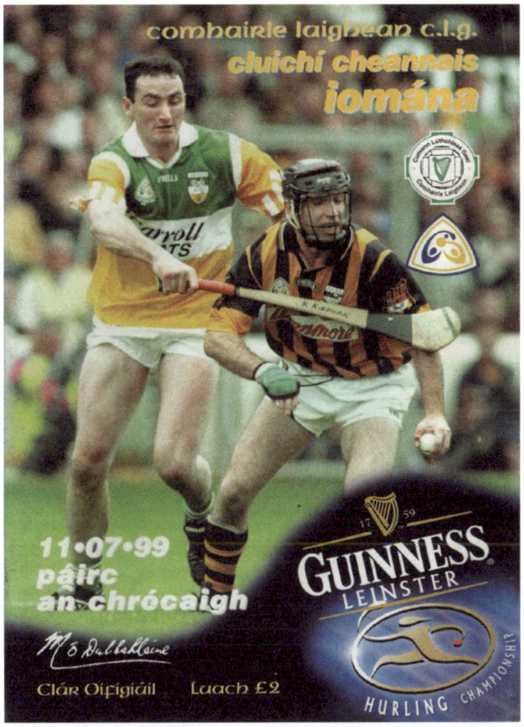
comhairle laighean c.l.g.
cluichí cheannais
iomána
11•07•99
páirc
an chrócaigh
GUINNESS
LEINSTER
HURLING CHAMPIONSHIP
Clár Oifigiúil
Luach £2

3

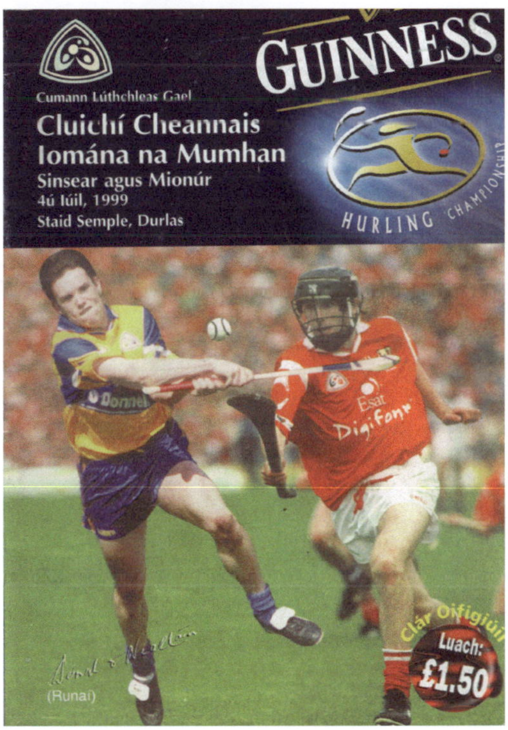
GUINNESS
Cumann Lúthchleas Gael
Cluichí Cheannais
Iomána na Mumhan
Sinsear agus Mionúr
4ú Iúil, 1999
Staid Semple, Durlas
HURLING CHAMPIONSHIP
(Runaí)
Clár Oifigiúil
Luach:
£1.50

4

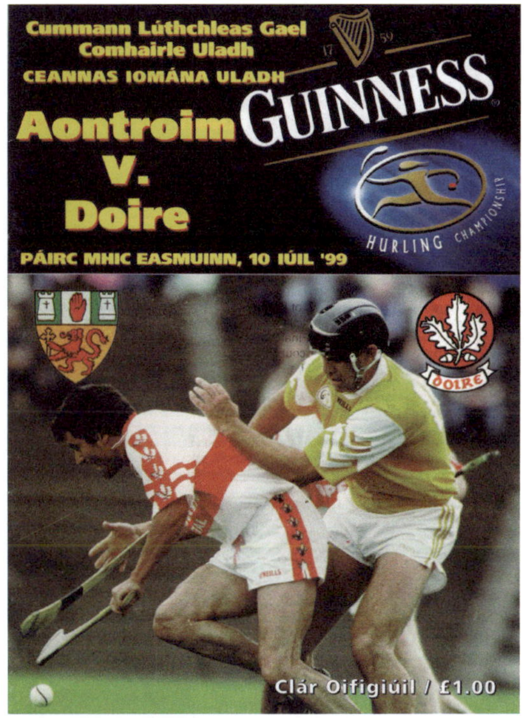
Cummann Lúthchleas Gael
Comhairle Uladh
CEANNAS IOMÁNA ULADH
Aontroim
V.
Doire
GUINNESS
HURLING CHAMPIONSHIP
PÁIRC MHIC EASMUINN, 10 IÚIL '99
DOIRE
Clár Oifigiúil / £1.00

5

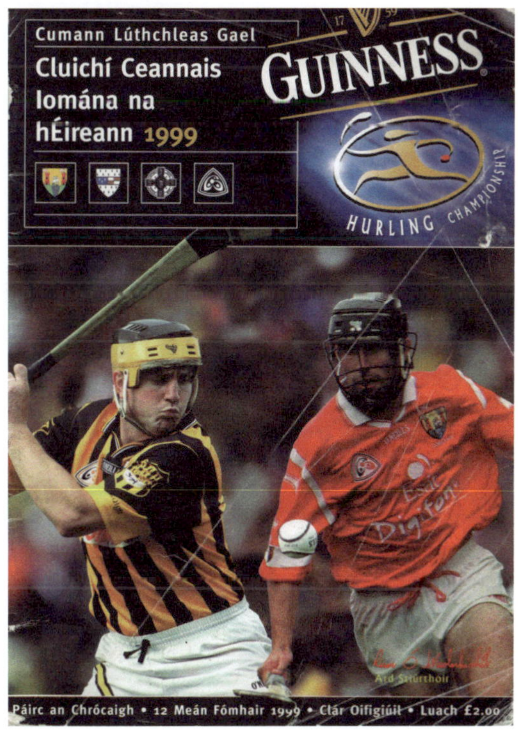
Cumann Lúthchleas Gael
Cluichí Ceannais
Iomána na
hÉireann 1999
GUINNESS
HURLING CHAMPIONSHIP
Ard Stiúrthóir
Páirc an Chrócaigh • 12 Meán Fómhair 1999 • Clár Oifigiúil • Luach £2.00

6

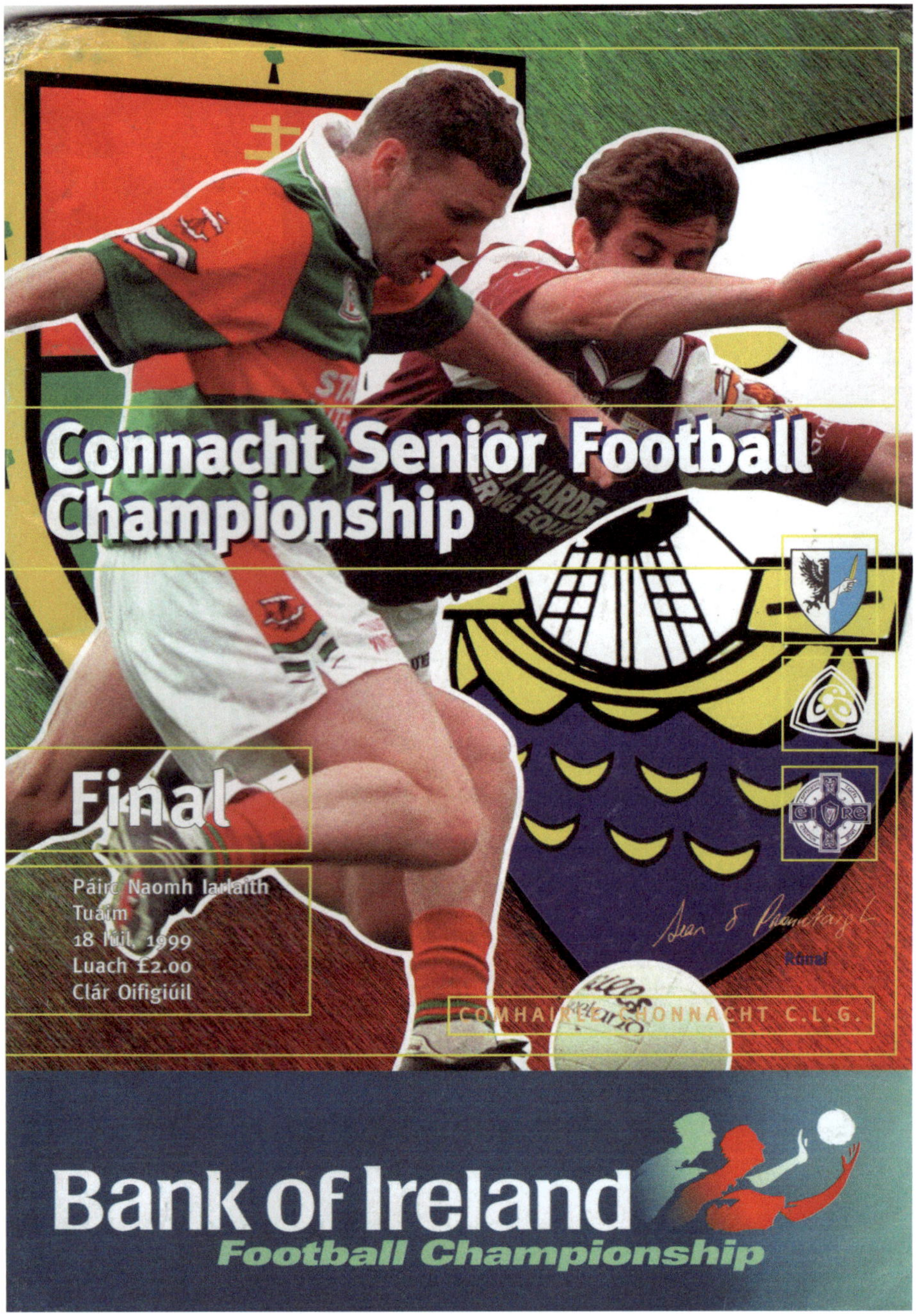

6 Connacht Football Final
Mayo 1-14 Galway 1-10

7 Leinster Football Final
Meath 1-14 Dublin 0-12

8 Munster Football Final
Cork 2-10 Kerry 2-04

9 Ulster Football Final
Armagh 3-12 Down 0-10

10 All-Ireland Football Final
Meath 1-11 Cork 1-08
Attendance – 63,276

7

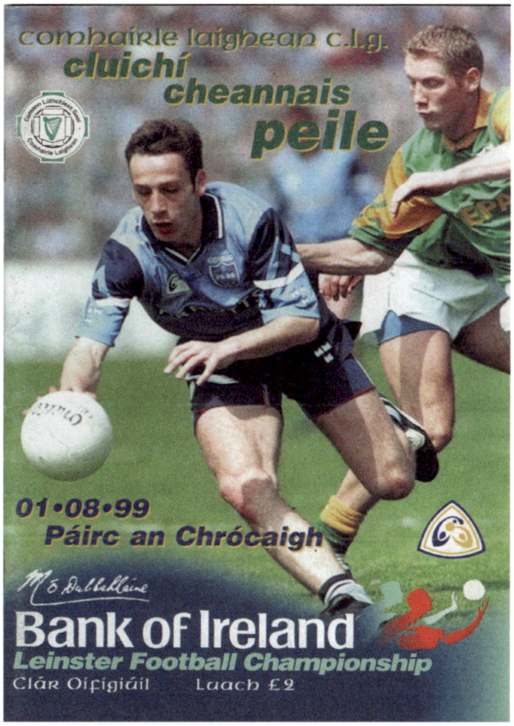
comhairle laighean c.l.g.
cluichí
cheannais
peile
01•08•99
Páirc an Chrócaigh
Bank of Ireland
Leinster Football Championship
Clár Oifigiúil Luach £2

9

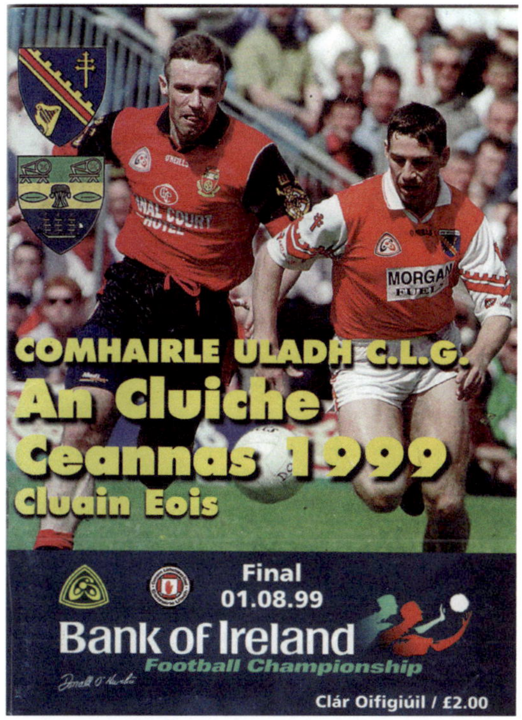
COMHAIRLE ULADH C.L.G.
An Cluiche
Ceannas 1999
Cluain Eois
Final
01.08.99
Bank of Ireland
Football Championship
Clár Oifigiúil / £2.00

8

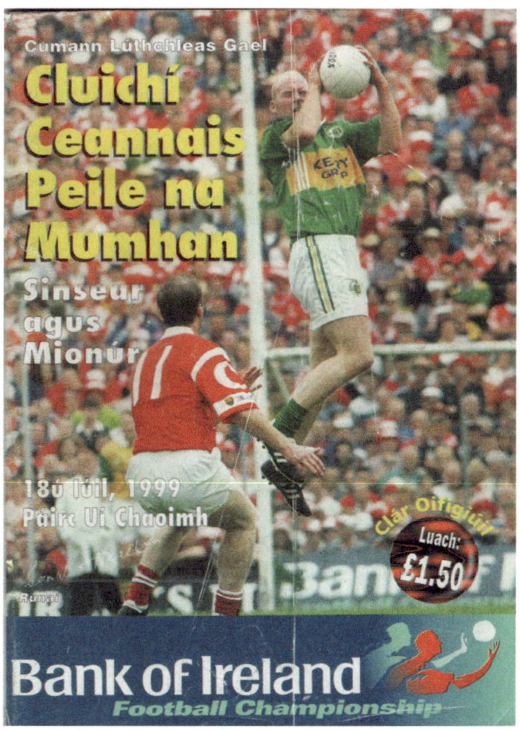
Cumann Lúthchleas Gael
Cluichí
Ceannais
Peile na
Mumhan
Sinsear
agus
Mionúr
18ú Iúil, 1999
Páirc Uí Chaoimh
Clár Oifigiúil
Luach:
£1.50
Bank of Ireland
Football Championship

10

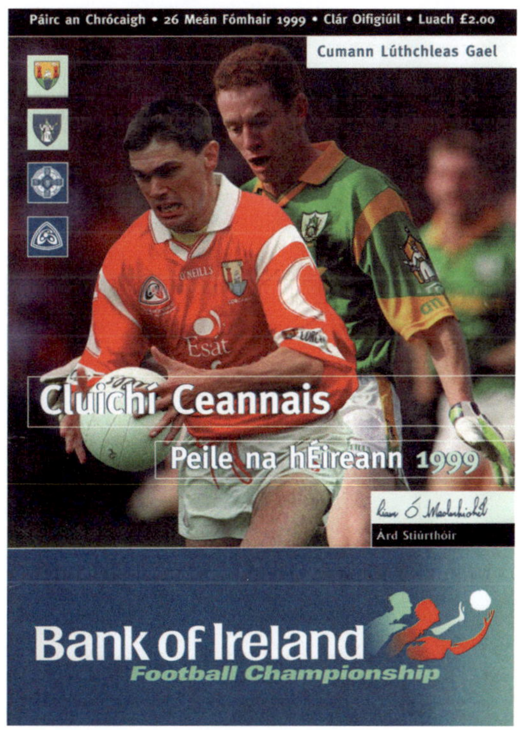
Páirc an Chrócaigh • 26 Meán Fómhair 1999 • Clár Oifigiúil • Luach £2.00
Cumann Lúthchleas Gael
Cluichí Ceannais
Peile na hÉireann 1999
Árd Stiúrthóir
Bank of Ireland
Football Championship

2000–09

2000

With the GAA having decided to change the structure of the All-Ireland football championship, 2000 was the last year that it was played as a fully knockout competition.* This season, the Leinster Council addressed the issue of more games for the so-called 'weaker' counties by introducing a round-robin preliminary section for four teams. 'Weaker' counties in the other provinces were proving more successful as Leitrim and Clare reached their provincial finals, Fermanagh and Antrim made the Ulster semi-finals and Sligo got the better of Mayo in Connacht.

However, it was the more traditional powers that contested the All-Ireland final, with Kerry needing a replay to see off Galway's challenge. In the All-Ireland hurling final, DJ Carey was the Man of the Match as Kilkenny eased past Offaly. Having tasted defeat the previous year, it was Brian Cody's first All-Ireland final win as Kilkenny manager.

* *A knockout football championship was played during the Covid pandemic in 2020 and 2021.*

1 Connacht Football Final
Galway 1-13 Leitrim 0-08

2 Leinster Football Final
Kildare 0-14 Dublin 0-14

3 Replay
Kildare 2-11 Dublin 0-12

4 Munster Football Final
Kerry 3-15 Clare 0-08

5 Ulster Football Final
Armagh 1-12 Derry 1-11

6 All-Ireland Football Final
Kerry 0-14 Galway 0-14
Attendance – 63,349

1

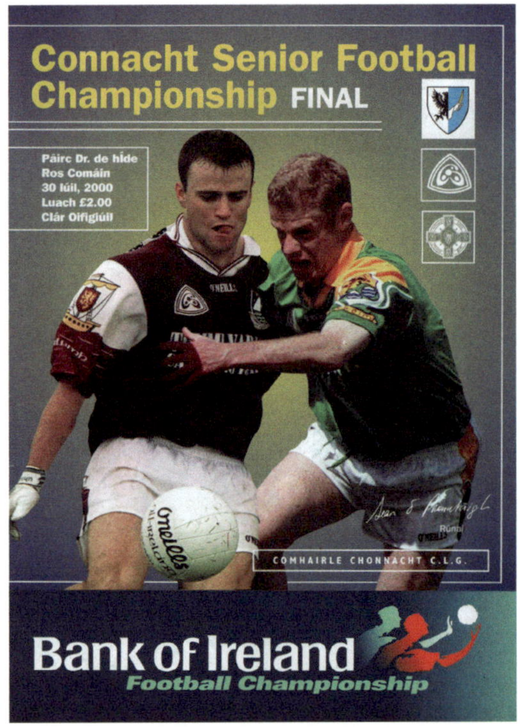

2

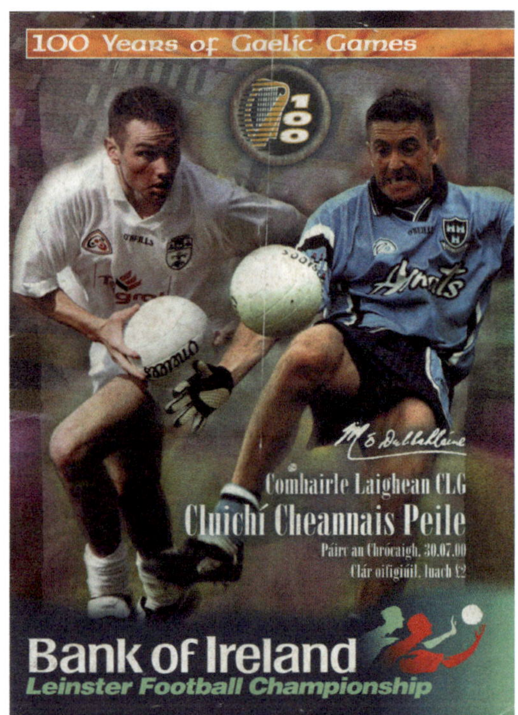

3

céad bliain de cluichí gaelacha
Comhairle Laighean CLG
Cluiche Cheannais (athimirt) Peile
Páirc an Chrócaigh 12.08.00
Clár oifigiúil, luach £2
Bank of Ireland
Leinster Football Championship

4

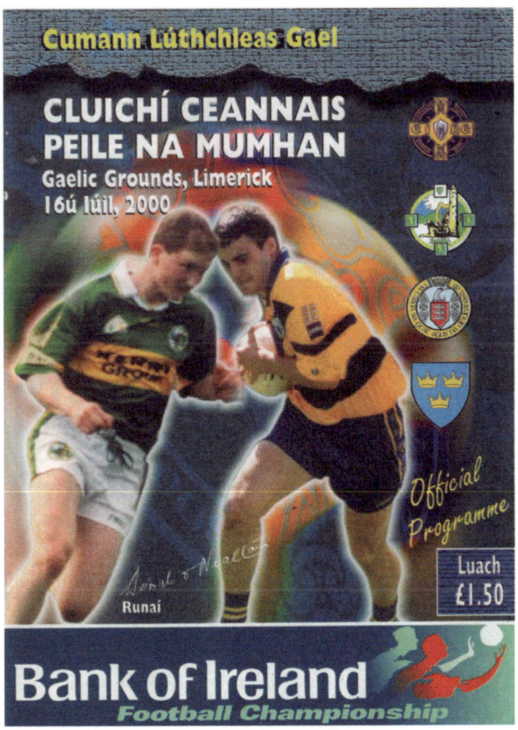

Cumann Lúthchleas Gael
CLUICHÍ CEANNAIS
PEILE NA MUMHAN
Gaelic Grounds, Limerick
16ú Iúil, 2000
Official
Programme
Luach
£1.50
Runaí
Bank of Ireland
Football Championship

5

16.07.00
Bank of Ireland
Football Championship
Final
Clár Oifigiúil / £2.00
COMHAIRLE ULADH C.L.G.
Ceannas Peil
Uladh 2000
Cluain Eois

6

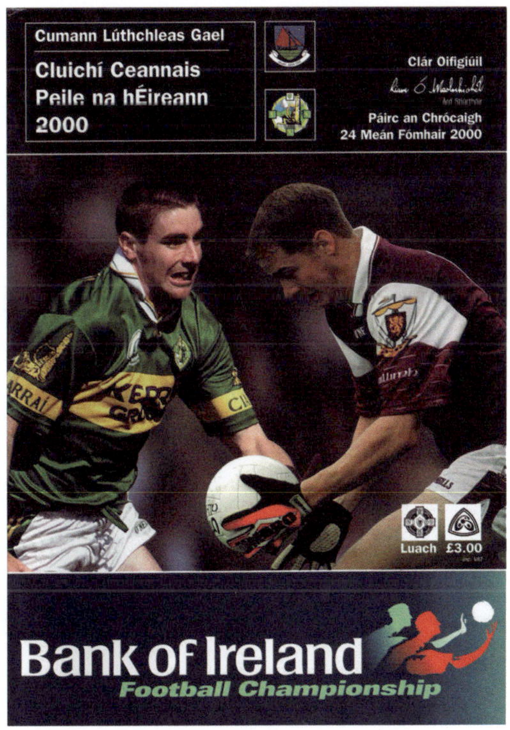

Cumann Lúthchleas Gael
Cluichí Ceannais
Peile na hÉireann
2000
Clár Oifigiúil
Páirc an Chrócaigh
24 Meán Fómhair 2000
Luach £3.00
Bank of Ireland
Football Championship

7

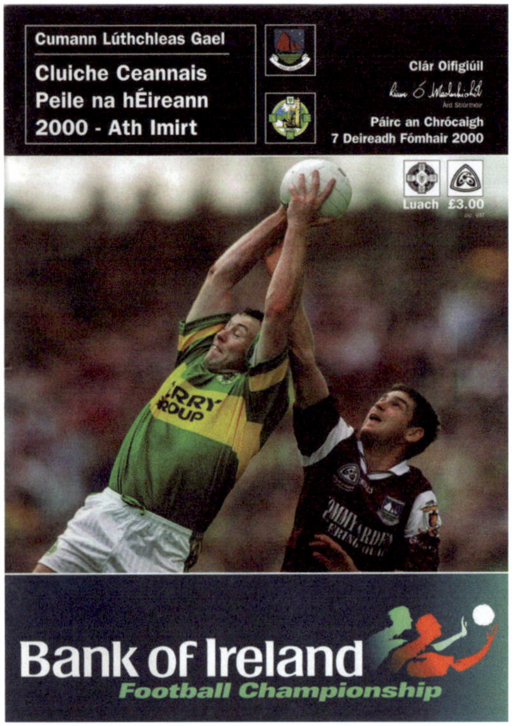
Cumann Lúthchleas Gael
Cluiche Ceannais
Peile na hÉireann
2000 - Ath Imirt
Clár Oifigiúil
Páirc an Chrócaigh
7 Deireadh Fómhair 2000
Luach £3.00
Bank of Ireland
Football Championship

8

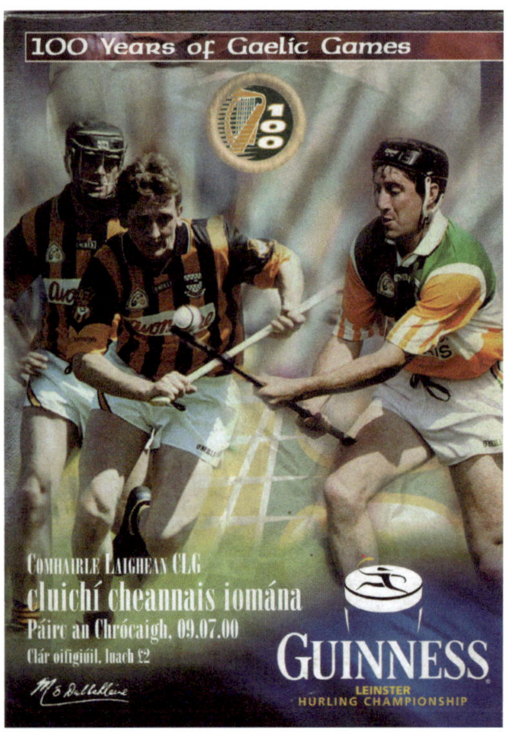
100 Years of Gaelic Games
Comhairle Laighean CLG
cluichí cheannais iomána
Páirc an Chrócaigh, 09.07.00
Clár oifigiúil, luach £2
GUINNESS
LEINSTER
HURLING CHAMPIONSHIP

9

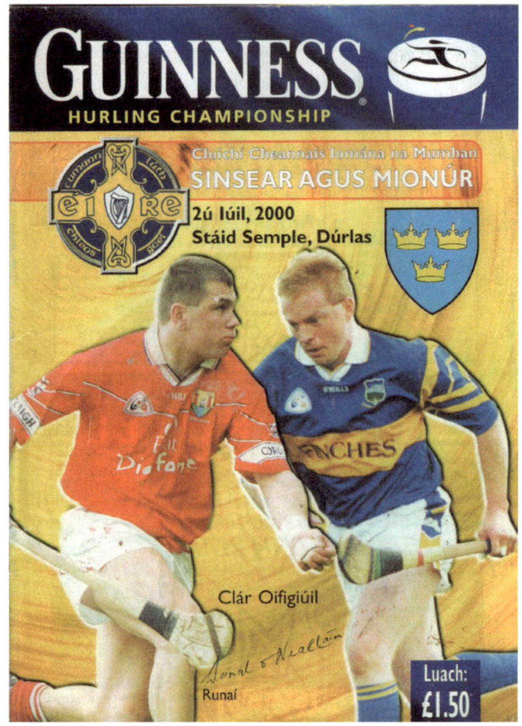
GUINNESS
HURLING CHAMPIONSHIP
Cluichí Cheannais Iomána na Mumhan
SINSEAR AGUS MIONÚR
2ú Iúil, 2000
Stáid Semple, Dúrlas
Clár Oifigiúil
Runaí
Luach:
£1.50

10

CUMANN LÚTHLEAS GAEL
Comhairle Uladh
Ceannas Iomána Uladh
GUINNESS
HURLING CHAMPIONSHIP
Senior Hurling Championship Final
AONTROIM
V
DOIRE
9ú Iúil 2000
3.30in, in bPairc Mhic Easmuinn, Beal Feirste
Luach/ £1.00
Clár Oifigiúil

11

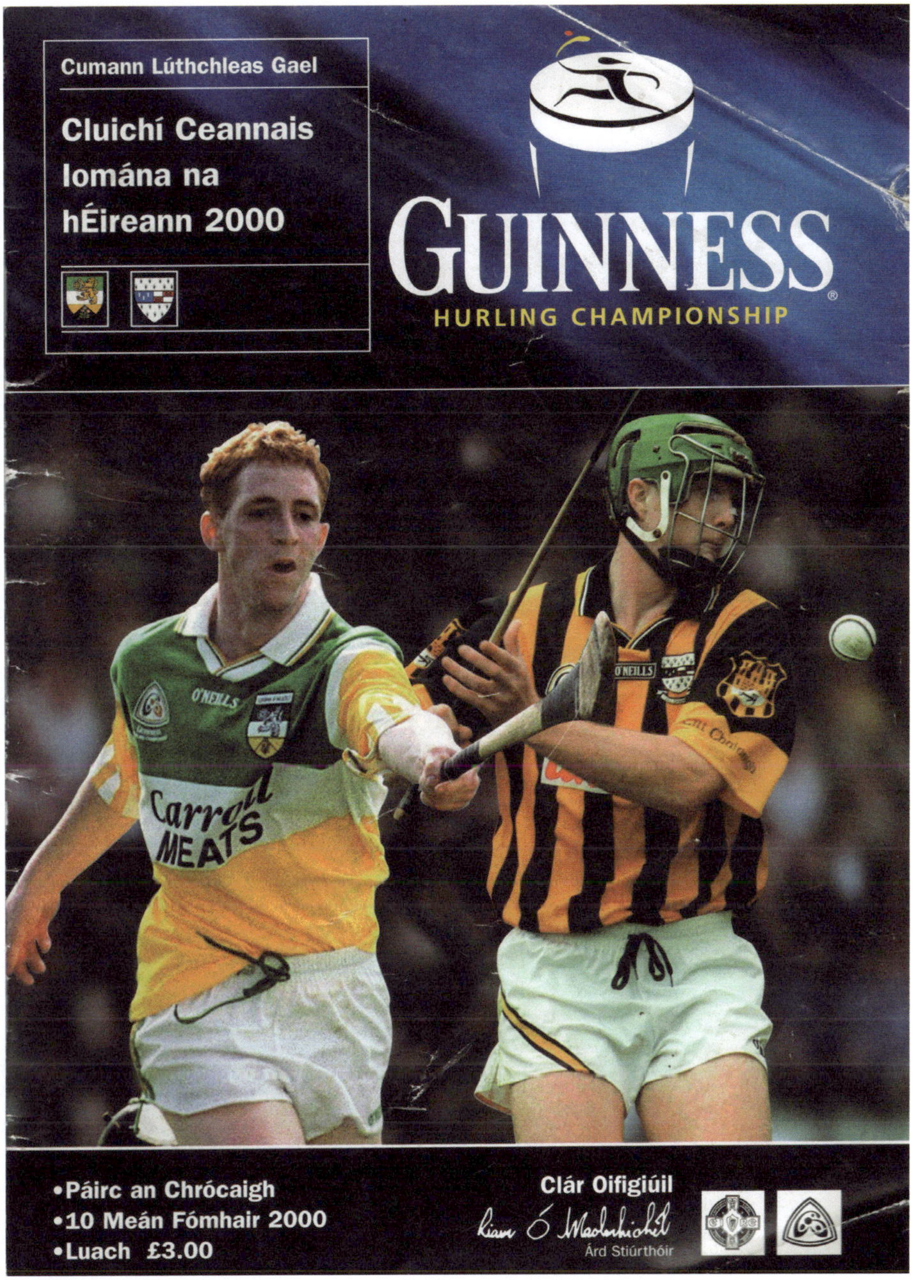

7 Replay
Kerry 0-17 Galway 1-10
Attendance – 64,094

8 Leinster Hurling Final
Kilkenny 2-21 Offaly 1-13

9 Munster Hurling Final
Cork 0-23 Tipperary 3-12

10 Ulster Hurling Final
Derry 4-8 Antrim 0-19

11 All-Ireland Hurling Final
Kilkenny 5-15 Offaly 1-14
Attendance – 61,493

2001

The introduction of the All-Ireland football championship qualifier system was designed to give teams who were defeated in their provincial championships a second chance to progress. As part of this new structure, it was the first time that All-Ireland football quarter-finals were played. The Dublin–Kerry quarter-final went to a replay after Kerry's Maurice Fitzgerald kicked a stunning point from the sideline in Semple Stadium to draw the match. The All-Ireland final was eventually won by Galway, the first team to do so having failed to reach their provincial final. The Galway hurlers were not so lucky, going down to Tipperary in the All-Ireland hurling final. Galway's Alan Kerins played in both finals.

At a special congress in November, the GAA overwhelmingly passed the abolition of Rule 21, which had prevented members of the British Army and Northern Ireland police service from becoming members of the GAA. The abolition of the rule was seen as a positive contribution by the GAA to the Northern peace process.

1

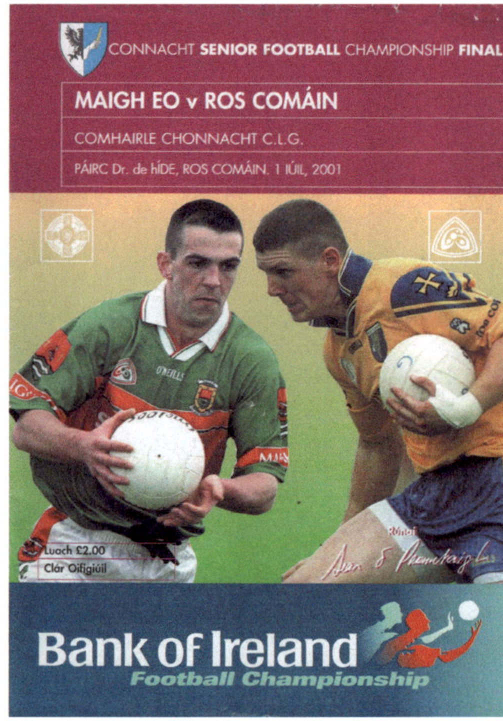

2

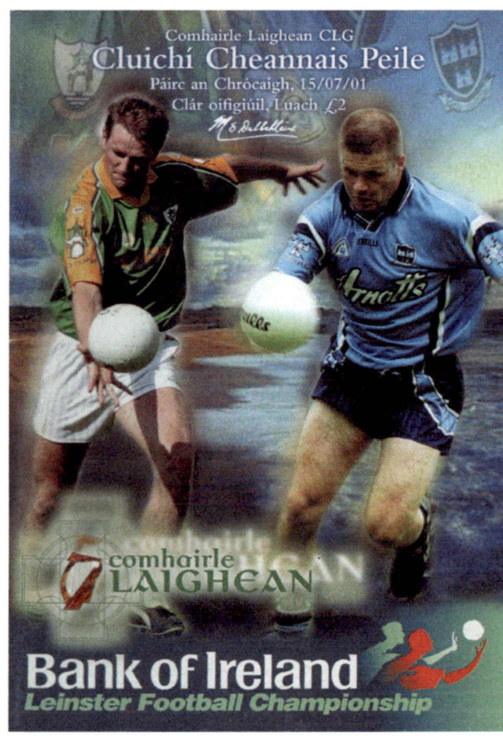

1 Connacht Football Final
Roscommon 2-10 Mayo 1-12

2 Leinster Football Final
Meath 2-11 Dublin 0-14

3 Munster Football Final
Kerry 0-19 Cork 1-13

Special Centenary Edition

Bank of Ireland
Football Championship

Céad Bliain ag Imirt

Cluichí Ceannais Peile na Mumhan 2001

(Sinsear agus Mionúr)

Páirc Uí Chaoimh
15ú Iúil, 2001

4

5

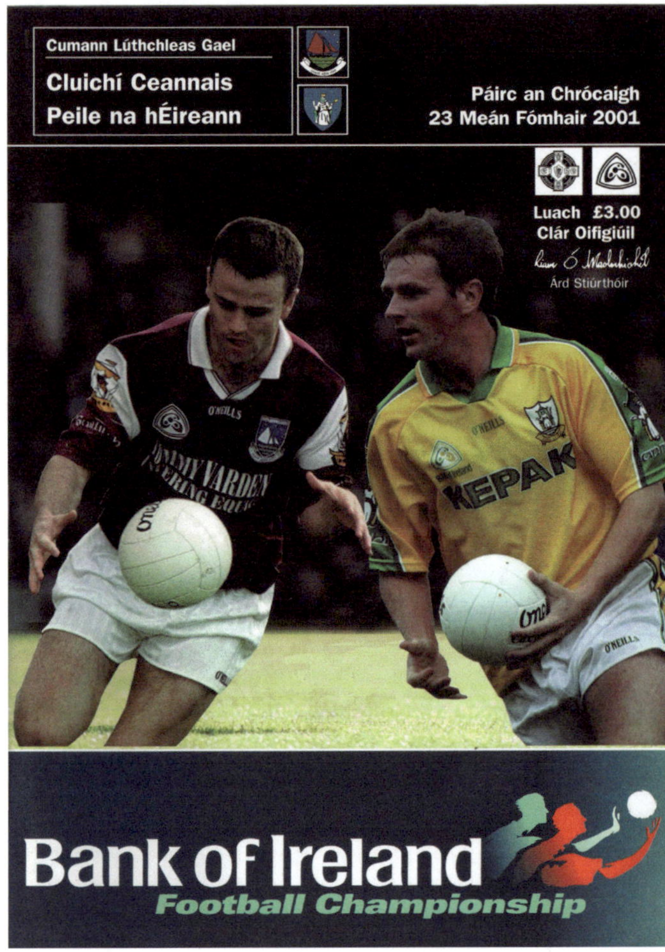

4 Ulster Football Final
Tyrone 1-13 Cavan 1-11

5 All-Ireland Football Final
Galway 0-17 Meath 0-08
Attendance – 70,482

6 Leinster Hurling Final
Kilkenny 2-19 Wexford 0-12

7 Munster Hurling Final
Tipperary 2-16 Limerick 1-17

8 Ulster Hurling Final
Derry 1-17 Down 3-10

9 All-Ireland Hurling Final
Tipperary 2-18 Galway 2-15
Attendance – 68,512

6

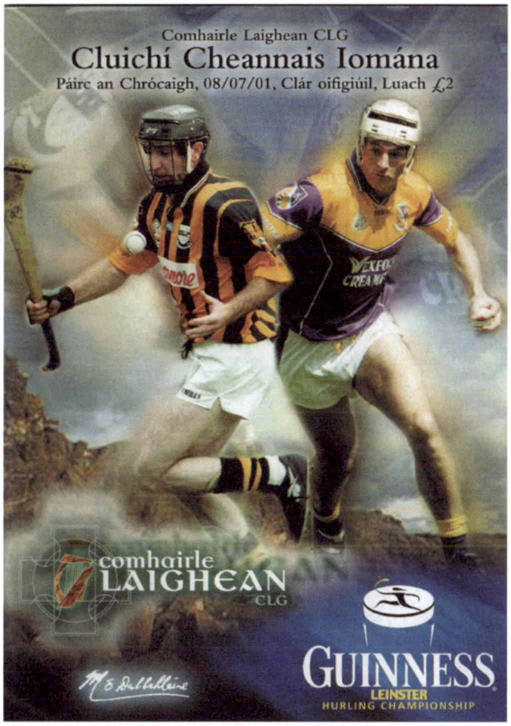
Comhairle Laighean CLG
Cluichí Cheannais Iomána
Páirc an Chrócaigh, 08/07/01, Clár oifigiúil, Luach £2
comhairle LAIGHEAN CLG
GUINNESS
LEINSTER
HURLING CHAMPIONSHIP

7

Special Centenary Edition
GUINNESS
HURLING CHAMPIONSHIP
Céad Bliain ag Imirt
Cluichí Ceannais Iomána na Mumhan
[Sinsear agus Mionúr]
1ú Iúil, 2001 - Páirc Uí Chaoimh
Donal Ó Nialláin Runaí
Luach £2

8

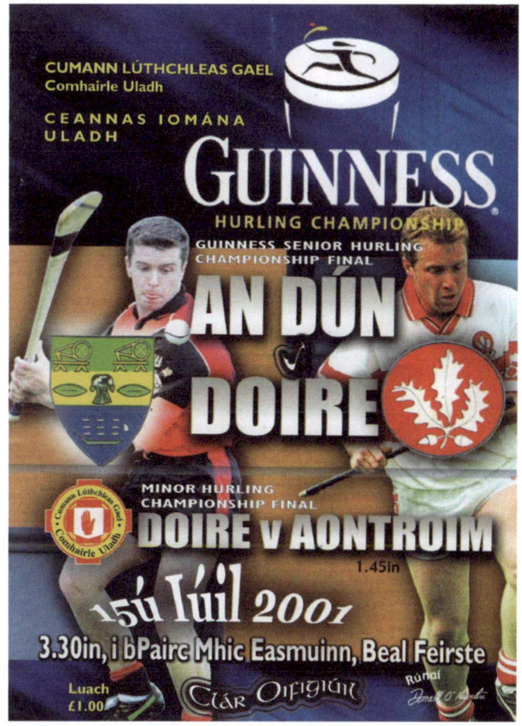
CUMANN LÚTHCHLEAS GAEL
Comhairle Uladh
CEANNAS IOMÁNA ULADH
GUINNESS
HURLING CHAMPIONSHIP
GUINNESS SENIOR HURLING CHAMPIONSHIP FINAL
AN DÚN
DOIRE
MINOR HURLING CHAMPIONSHIP FINAL
DOIRE V AONTROIM
1.45in
15ú Iúil 2001
3.30in, i bPairc Mhic Easmuinn, Beal Feirste
Luach £1.00
Clár Oifigiúil
Rúnaí

9

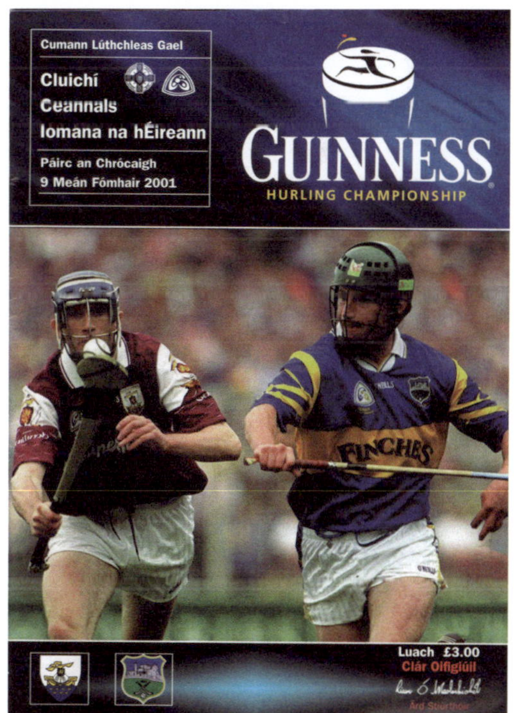
Cumann Lúthchleas Gael
Cluichí Ceannais Iomana na hÉireann
Páirc an Chrócaigh
9 Meán Fómhair 2001
GUINNESS
HURLING CHAMPIONSHIP
Luach £3.00
Clár Oifigiúil

2002

Armagh won consecutive Ulster finals in 1999 and 2000 and were unfortunate to lose the All-Ireland semi-finals in both years. After an early exit in 2001, they were back in this year's provincial final, having first avenged the previous year's defeat to Tyrone and then brushed aside Fermanagh in the semi-final. An Ulster final win over Donegal put them into the All-Ireland quarter-final where a replay was needed to see off Sligo. A nail-biting one-point victory over Dublin set up a final meeting with Kerry in a repeat of the 1953 final. Oisín McConville missed a first-half penalty, just as Bill McCorry had in the final 49 years before, but McConville later scored the winning goal, as Kerry failed to score after the 54th minute. Kieran McGeeney lifted the Sam Maguire Cup as Armagh won their first title.

1

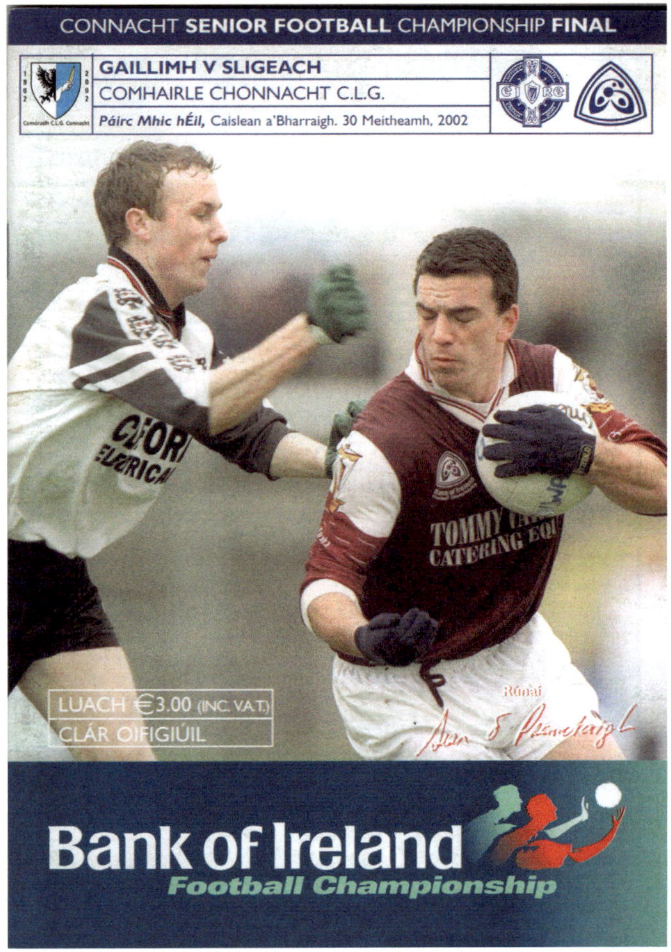

1 Connacht Football Final
Galway 1-11 Sligo 0-11

2 Leinster Football Final
Dublin 2-13 Kildare 2-11

3 Munster Football Final
Cork 2-11 Tipperary 1-14

4 Replay
Cork 1-23 Tipperary 0-07

5 Ulster Football final
Armagh 1-14 Donegal 1-10

2

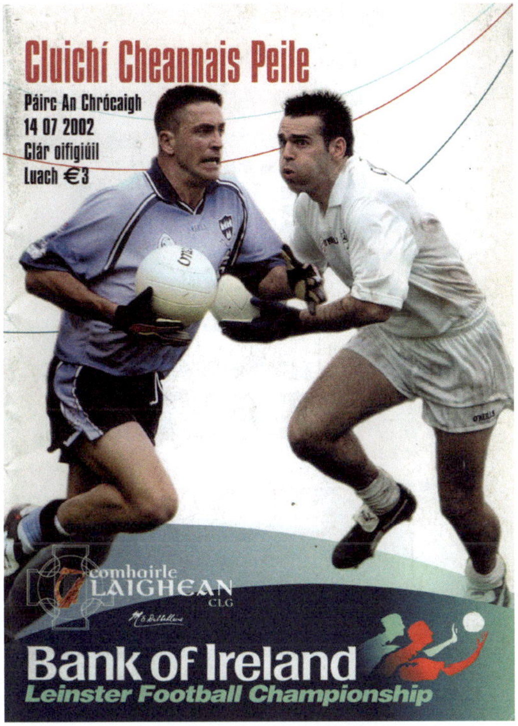
Cluichí Cheannais Peile
Páirc An Chrócaigh
14 07 2002
Clár oifigiúil
Luach €3
Comhairle LAIGHEAN CLG
Bank of Ireland
Leinster Football Championship

3

Bank of Ireland
Football Championship
Cluichí Ceannais Peil na Mumhan
(Sinsear agus Mionúr)
Staid Semple,
Durlas
14ú Iúil,
2002
Clár Oifigiúil
Runaí
Luach:
€2.50
GUINNESS
HURLING CHAMPIONSHIP

4

Cumann Lúthchleas Gael
Cluiche Ceannais Peil
Sinsear na Mumhan
(Ath-Imirt)
Páirc Uí Chaoimh, Corcaigh
21ú Iúil, 2002
Clár Oifigiúil
Luach:
€2.00
Runaí
Bank of Ireland
Football Championship

5

Comhairle Uladh C.L.G.
Ceannas Peil Uladh 2002
i bPairc Naomh Tighearnach, Cluain Eois
7ú Iúil 2002
FINAL
FINAL
Clár Oifigiúil: Luach €3.00 Stg. £2.00
Runaí

6

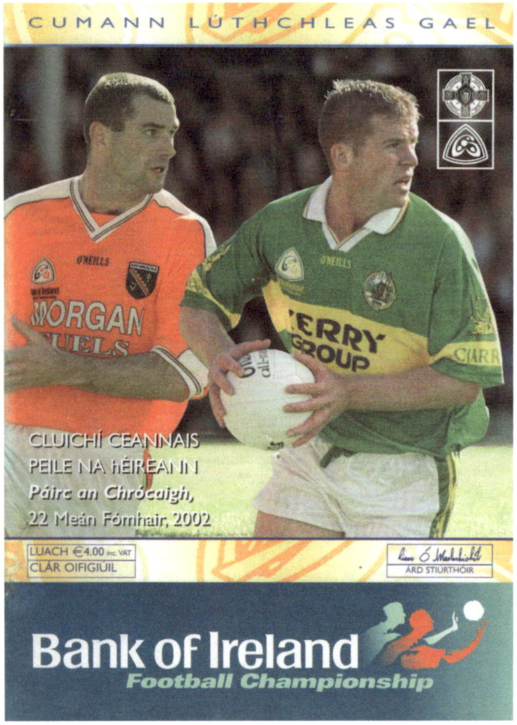

CUMANN LÚTHCHLEAS GAEL
CLUICHÍ CEANNAIS
PEILE NA hÉIREANN
Páirc an Chrócaigh,
22 Meán Fómhair, 2002
LUACH €4.00 inc. VAT
CLÁR OIFIGIUIL
ARD STIURTHOIR
Bank of Ireland
Football Championship

8

Cluichí Ceannais Iomána
na Mumhan 2002
(Sinsear agus Mionúr)
Donal Ó Nialláin
(Runai)
Clár Oifigiúil
Luach
€2.50
GUINNESS
30ú Bealtaine, Páirc Uí Chaoimh

7

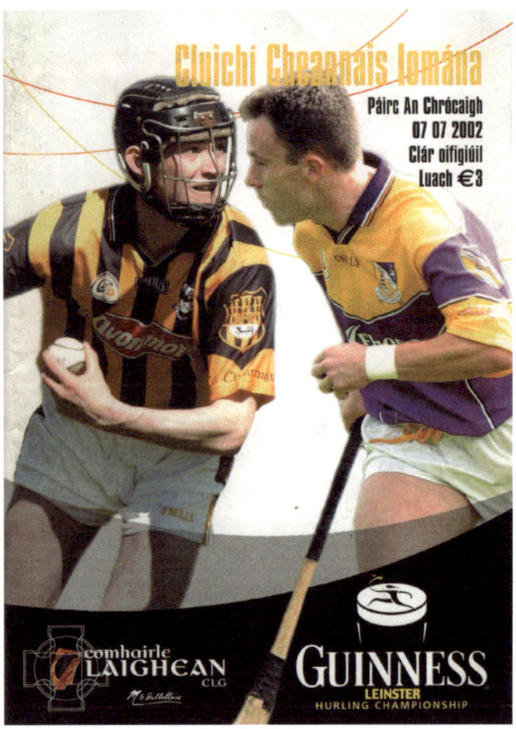

Cluichí Cheannais Iomána
Páirc An Chrócaigh
07 07 2002
Clár oifigiúil
Luach €3
Comhairle LAIGHEAN CLG
GUINNESS
LEINSTER
HURLING CHAMPIONSHIP

9

CUMANN LÚTHCHLEAS GAEL
Comhairle Uladh
CEANNAS IOMÁNA
ULADH
GUINNESS
HURLING CHAMPIONSHIP
Guinness Senior Hurling
Championship Final
Aontroim v An Dún
3.00in
I bPAIRC MHIC EASMUINN,
BEAL FEIRSTE
9ú Meitheamh 2002
Minor Hurling Championship Final
Aontroim v Doire
1.00in
Clár Oifiguil
Luach £1/€2

10

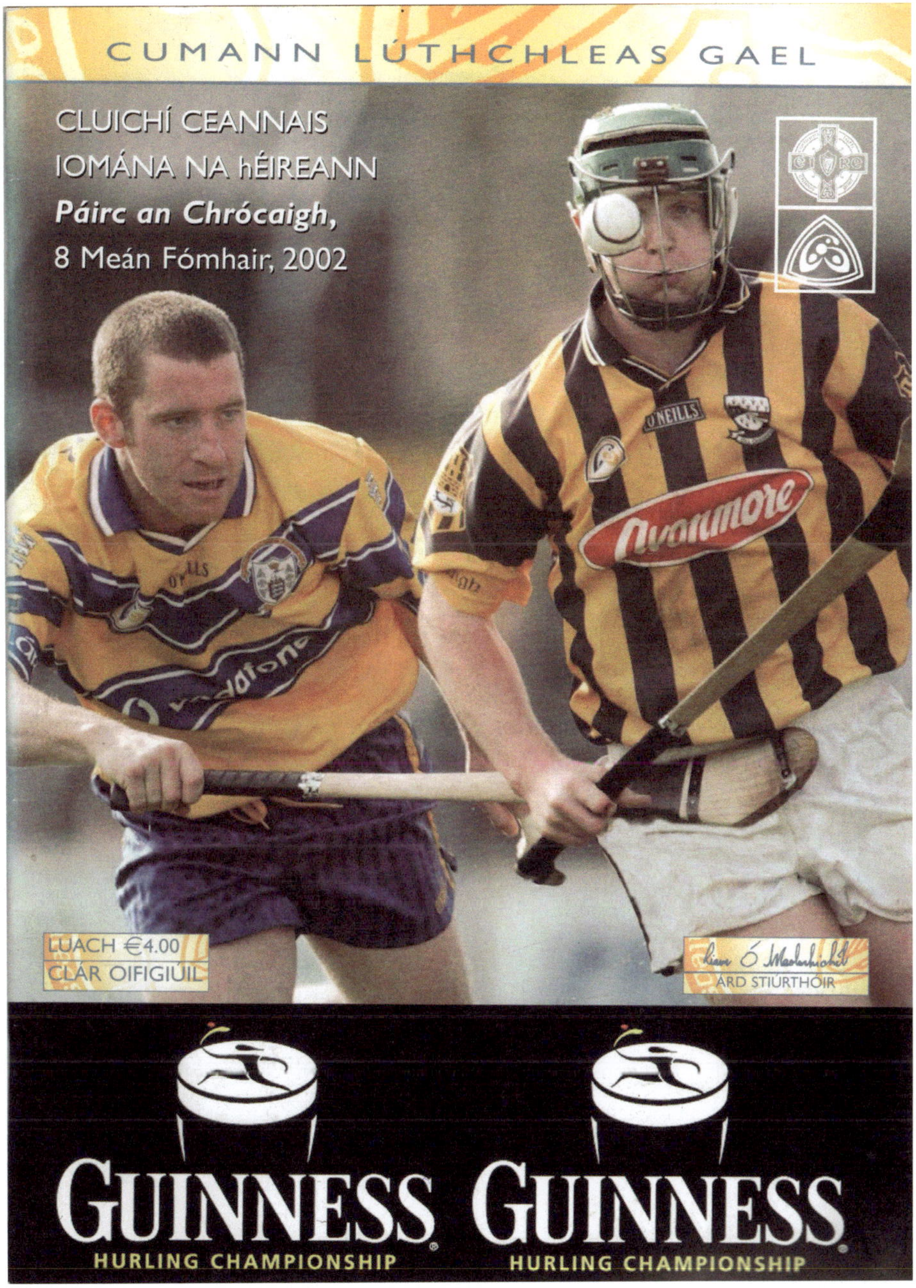

6 All-Ireland Football Final
Armagh 1-12 Kerry 0-14
Attendance – 79,500

7 Leinster Hurling Final
Kilkenny 0-19 Wexford 0-17

8 Munster Hurling Final
Waterford 2-23 Tipperary 3-12

9 Ulster Hurling Final
Antrim 3-16 Down1-18

10 All-Ireland Hurling Final
Kilkenny 2-20 Clare 0-19
Attendance – 76,254

2003

The Cork hurling team went on strike in November 2002, following a dispute with their county board over inadequate resources and poor conditions. Ultimately, the players' success in their action brought about an improvement on the field. Cork defeated Waterford in the Munster final and went down by just three points in the All-Ireland final, as Kilkenny retained their title.

Mick O'Dwyer, having failed to be reappointed as manager by Kildare, took over as manager of Laois for the 2003 season. Ironically, it was those two counties who came face to face in the Leinster final this year, with Laois winning the title for the first time since 1946. Tyrone and Armagh met in the first all-Ulster All-Ireland football final as Armagh looked to retain their title. Tyrone captain Peter Canavan retired injured in the first half only to reappear as a second-half substitute to help Tyrone win by three points and claim their first All-Ireland title.

1

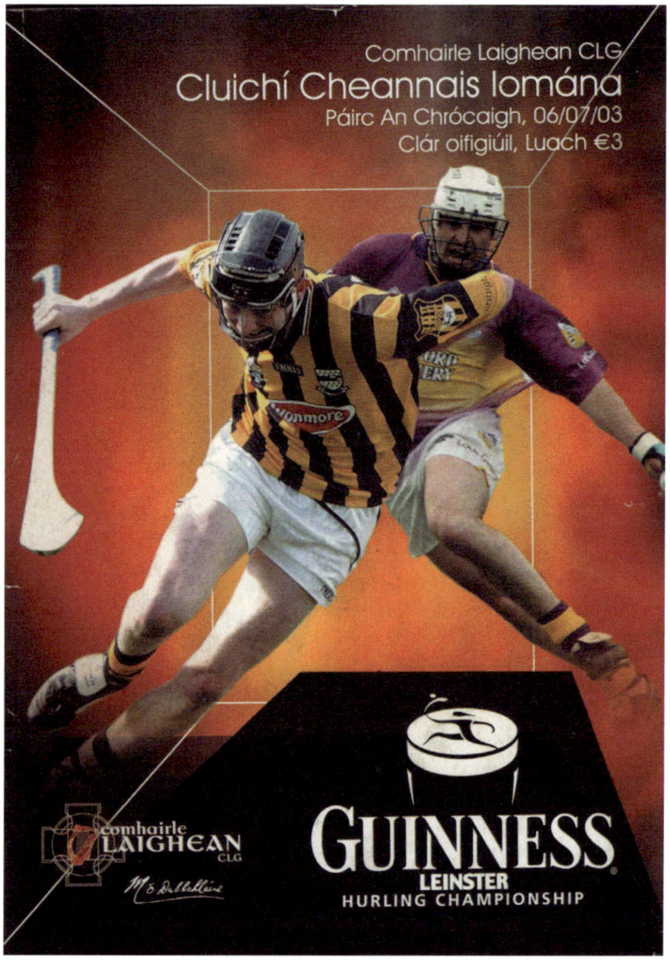

1 Leinster Hurling Final
Kilkenny 2-23 Wexford 2-12

2 Munster Hurling Final
Cork 3-16 Waterford 3-12

3 Ulster Hurling Final
Antrim 3-21 Derry 1-12

4 All-Ireland Hurling Final
Kilkenny 1-14 Cork 1-11
Attendance – 79,383

5 Connacht Football Final
Galway 1-14 Mayo 0-13

2

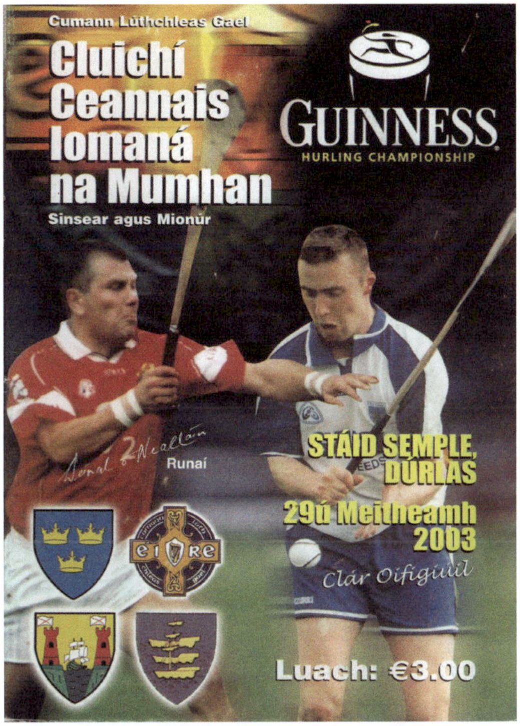
Cumann Lúthchleas Gael
Cluichí Ceannais Iomaná na Mumhan
Sinsear agus Mionúr
GUINNESS
HURLING CHAMPIONSHIP
Runaí
STÁID SEMPLE, DÚRLAS
29ú Meitheamh 2003
Clár Oifigiúil
Luach: €3.00

3

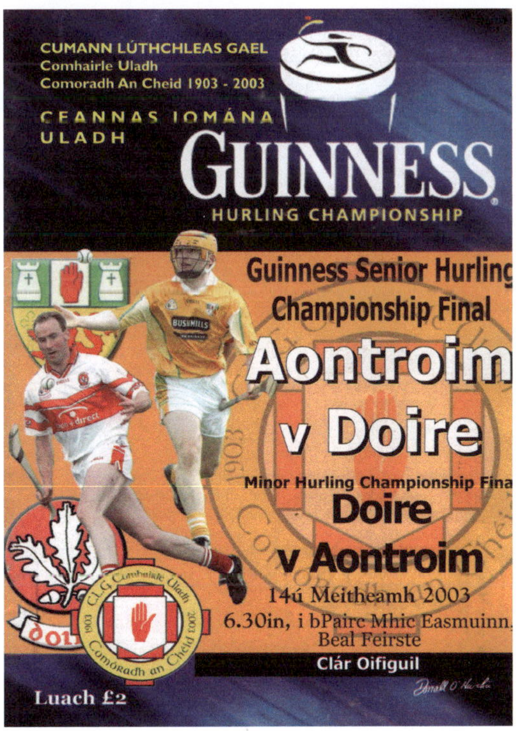
CUMANN LÚTHCHLEAS GAEL
Comhairle Uladh
Comoradh An Cheid 1903 - 2003
CEANNAS IOMÁNA ULADH
GUINNESS
HURLING CHAMPIONSHIP
Guinness Senior Hurling Championship Final
Aontroim v Doire
Minor Hurling Championship Final
Doire v Aontroim
14ú Meitheamh 2003
6.30in, i bPairc Mhic Easmuinn, Beal Feirste
Clár Oifiguil
Luach £2

4

CUMANN LÚTHCHLEAS GAEL
CLUICHÍ CEANNAIS IOMÁNA NA hÉIREANN
Páirc an Chrócaigh, Baile Átha Cliath. 14 Meán Fómhair, 2003
CLÁR OIFIGIÚIL LUACH €4.00
Ard Stiurthóir
GUINNESS
HURLING CHAMPIONSHIP

5

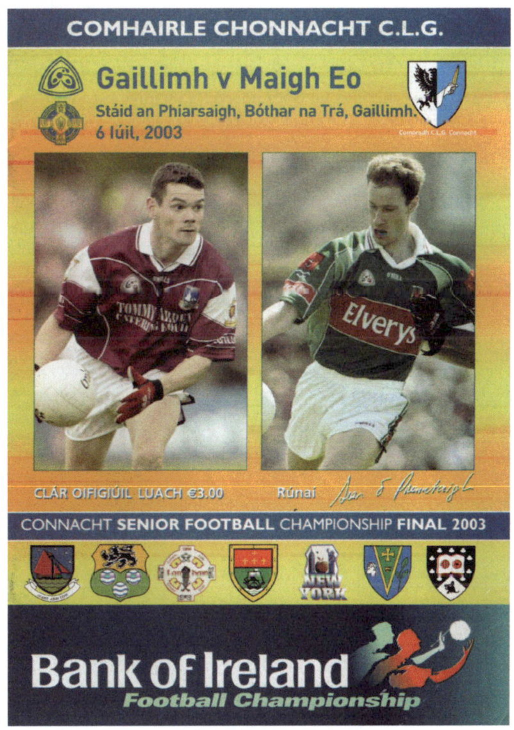
COMHAIRLE CHONNACHT C.L.G.
Gaillimh v Maigh Eo
Stáid an Phiarsaigh, Bóthar na Trá, Gaillimh.
6 Iúil, 2003
CLÁR OIFIGIÚIL LUACH €3.00
Rúnaí
CONNACHT SENIOR FOOTBALL CHAMPIONSHIP FINAL 2003
Elverys
Bank of Ireland
Football Championship

6

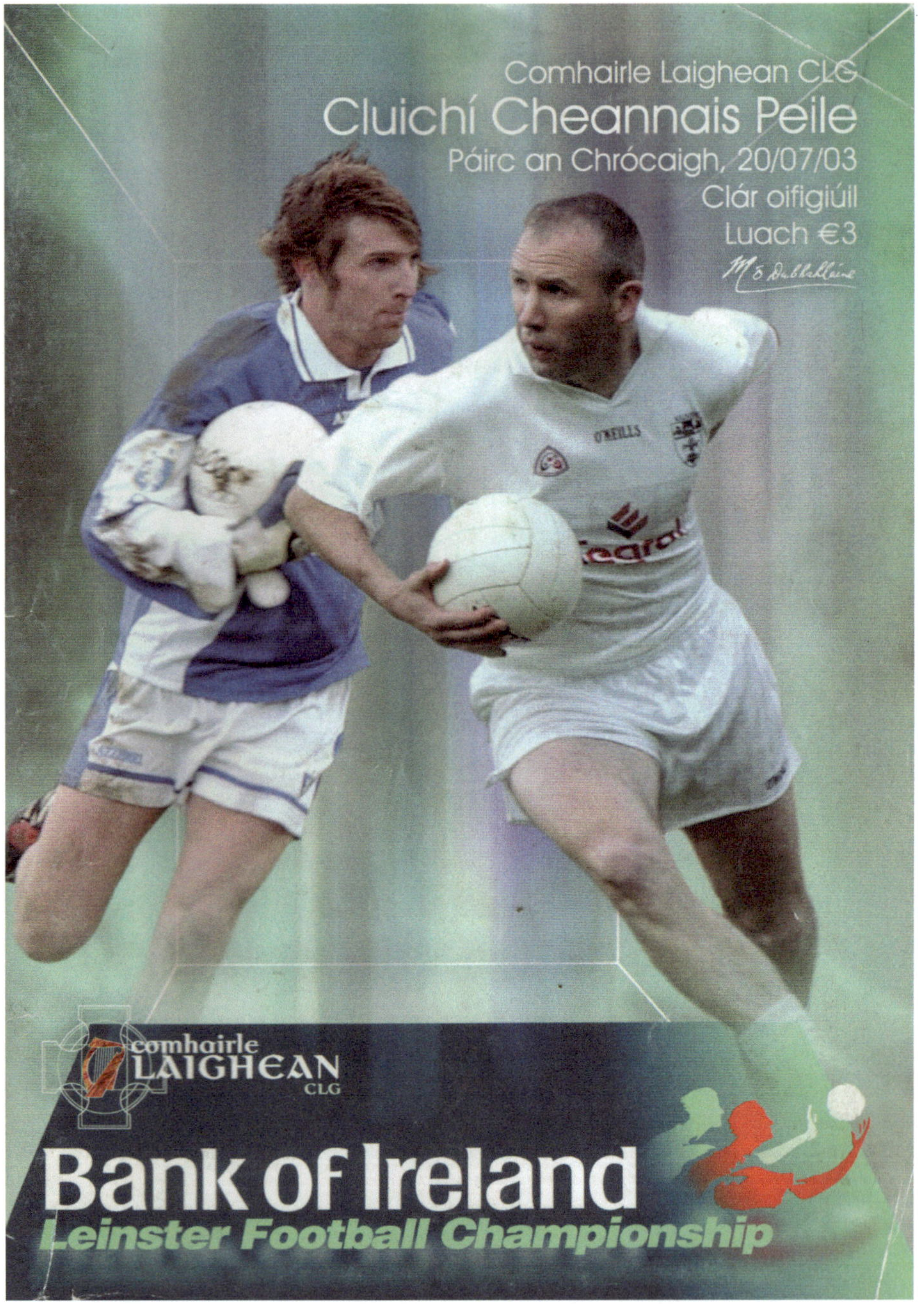

6 Leinster Football Final
Laois 2-13 Kildare 1-13

7 Munster Football Final
Kerry 1-11 Limerick 0-09

8 Ulster Football Final
Tyrone 1-17 Down 4-08

9 Replay
Tyrone 0-23 Down 1-05

10 All-Ireland Football Final
Tyrone 0-12 Armagh 0-09
Attendance – 79,391

7

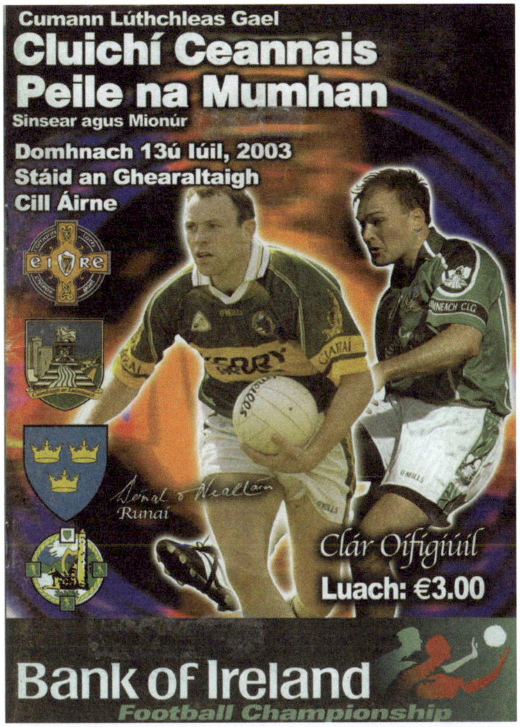
Cumann Lúthchleas Gael
Cluichí Ceannais
Peile na Mumhan
Sinsear agus Mionúr
Domhnach 13ú Iúil, 2003
Stáid an Ghearaltaigh
Cill Áirne
Rúnaí
Clár Oifigiúil
Luach: €3.00
Bank of Ireland
Football Championship

9

comoradh an cheid 1903–2003
Páirc Naomh Tighearnach, Cluain Eois
20ú Iúil 2003
Comhairle Uladh C.L.G.
Ceannas Peil Uladh 2003
CLÁR
OIFIGIÚIL
ATH IMIRT
final
comoradh an cheid 1903–2003
2003
RUNAI
Luach: €3.00 Stg£2.00
Bank of Ireland
Football Championship

8

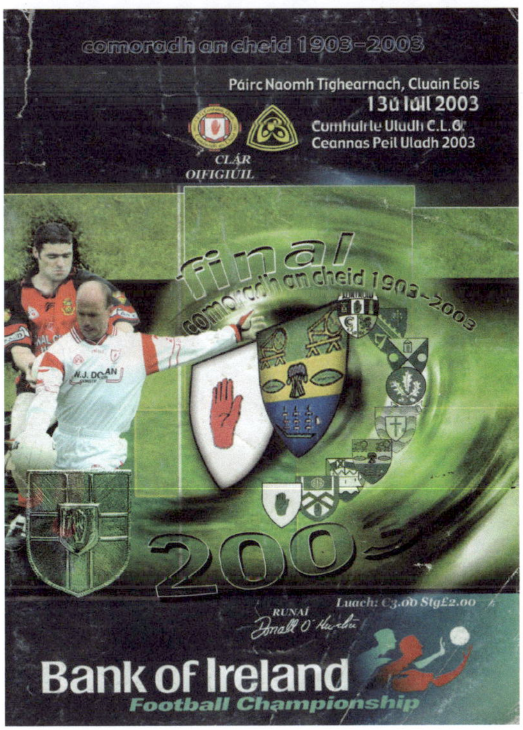
comoradh an cheid 1903–2003
Páirc Naomh Tighearnach, Cluain Eois
13ú Iúil 2003
Comhairle Uladh C.L.G.
Ceannas Peil Uladh 2003
CLÁR
OIFIGIÚIL
final
comoradh an cheid 1903–2003
2003
RUNAI
Luach: €3.00 Stg£2.00
Bank of Ireland
Football Championship

10

CUMANN LÚTHCHLEAS GAEL
CLUICHÍ CEANNAIS PEILE NA hÉIREANN
Páirc an Chrócaigh, Baile Átha Cliath.
28 Méan Fómhair, 2003
CLÁR OIFIGIÚIL LUACH €4.00
Ard Stiurthóir
Bank of Ireland
Football Championship

2004

Beaten in the 2003 provincial final, Waterford upset the odds in this year's Munster hurling final to avenge that defeat. They got the better of Cork by a point in an epic encounter in Thurles. With the Cork players' strike still a recent memory and Cork having now lost the most recent All-Ireland and provincial finals, the pressure came on the team and management to produce a victory. Cork duly obliged by returning to the All-Ireland final where they exacted revenge on their Leinster rivals, Kilkenny, by handing them an eight-point defeat.

The All-Ireland football championship included a second-tier competition to cater for teams that had lost both the provincial and first-round qualifier matches. The Tommy Murphy Cup was named after the great Laois player of the 1930s and 1940s who had been selected on the Team of the Millennium. Clare defeated Sligo in the first Tommy Murphy Cup final, while Kerry defeated Mayo to lift the Sam Maguire Cup.

1

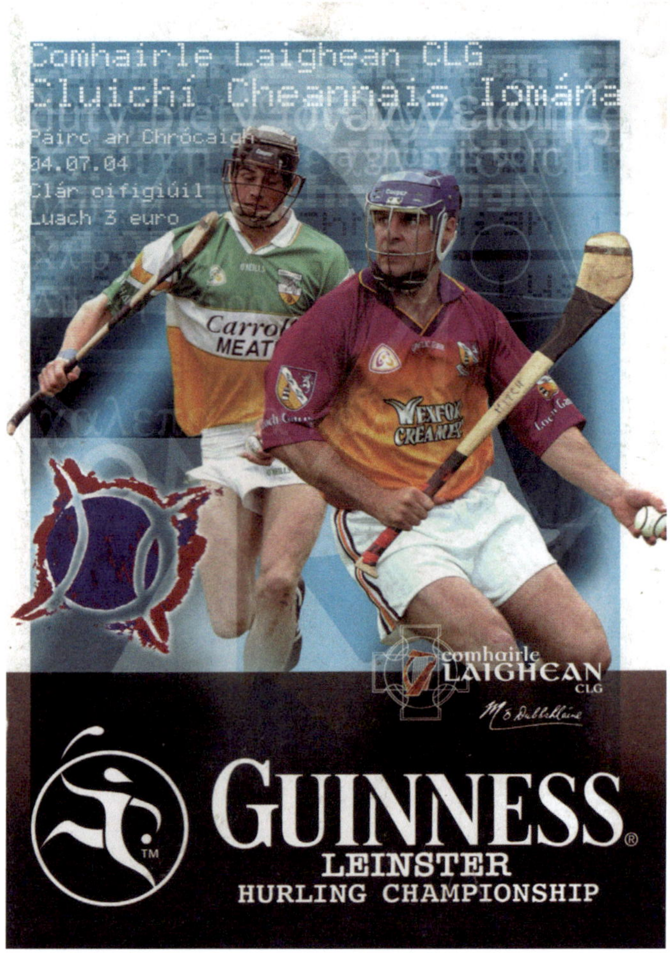

1 Leinster Hurling Final
Wexford 2-12 Offaly 1-11

2 Munster Hurling Final
Waterford 3-16 Cork 1-21

Cumann Lúthchleas Gael

Cluichí Ceannais Iomaná na Mumhan

Sinsear agus Mionúr

STÁID SEMPLE, DÚRLAS

27ú Meitheamh

2004

Clár Oifigiúil

Luach €3.00

http://munster.gaa.ie

Runaí

THE GUINNESS HURLING CHAMPIONSHIP

3

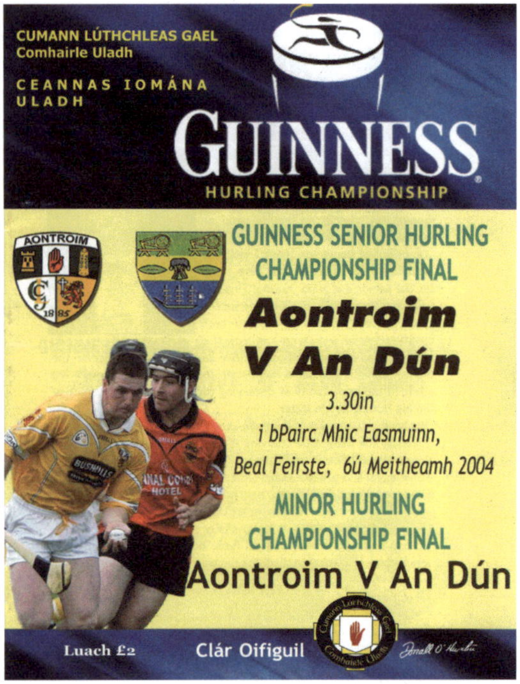
CUMANN LÚTHCHLEAS GAEL
Comhairle Uladh
CEANNAS IOMÁNA ULADH
GUINNESS
HURLING CHAMPIONSHIP
AONTROIM
GUINNESS SENIOR HURLING CHAMPIONSHIP FINAL
Aontroim
V An Dún
3.30in
i bPairc Mhic Easmuinn,
Beal Feirste, 6ú Meitheamh 2004
MINOR HURLING CHAMPIONSHIP FINAL
Aontroim V An Dún
Luach £2
Clár Oifiguil

4

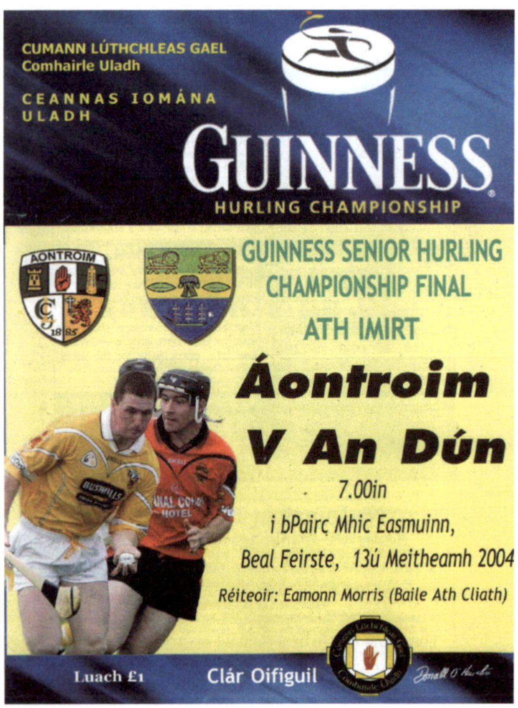
CUMANN LÚTHCHLEAS GAEL
Comhairle Uladh
CEANNAS IOMÁNA ULADH
GUINNESS
HURLING CHAMPIONSHIP
AONTROIM
GUINNESS SENIOR HURLING CHAMPIONSHIP FINAL
ATH IMIRT
Áontroim
V An Dún
7.00in
i bPairc Mhic Easmuinn,
Beal Feirste, 13ú Meitheamh 2004
Réiteoir: Eamonn Morris (Baile Ath Cliath)
Luach £1
Clár Oifiguil

5

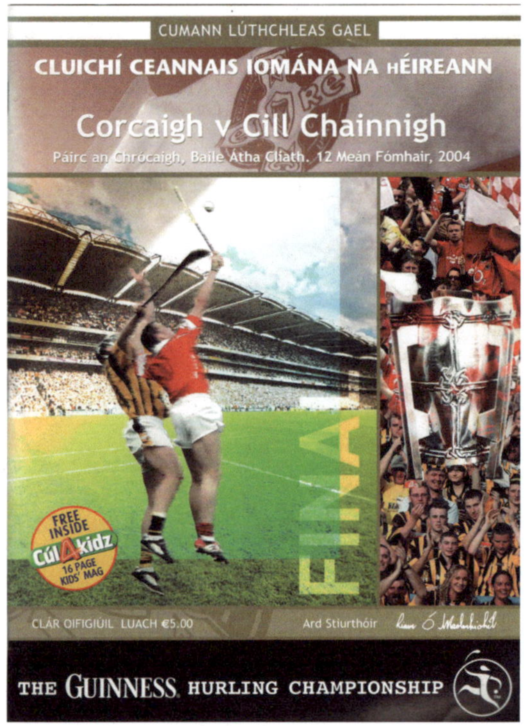
CUMANN LÚTHCHLEAS GAEL
CLUICHÍ CEANNAIS IOMÁNA NA hÉIREANN
Corcaigh v Cill Chainnigh
Páirc an Chrócaigh, Baile Átha Cliath. 12 Meán Fómhair, 2004
FREE INSIDE
Cúl 4 kidz
16 PAGE KIDS' MAG
CLÁR OIFIGIÚIL LUACH €5.00
Ard Stiurthóir
THE GUINNESS HURLING CHAMPIONSHIP

6

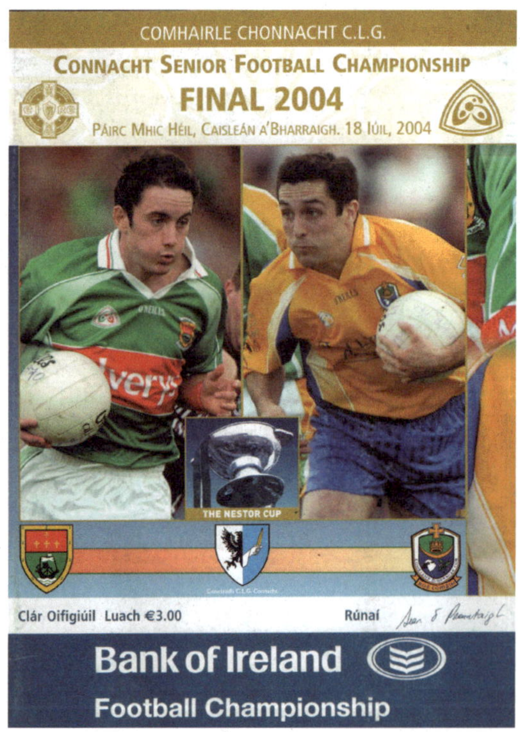
COMHAIRLE CHONNACHT C.L.G.
CONNACHT SENIOR FOOTBALL CHAMPIONSHIP
FINAL 2004
PÁIRC MHIC HÉIL, CAISLEÁN A'BHARRAIGH. 18 IÚIL, 2004
THE NESTOR CUP
Clár Oifigiúil Luach €3.00
Rúnaí
Bank of Ireland
Football Championship

7

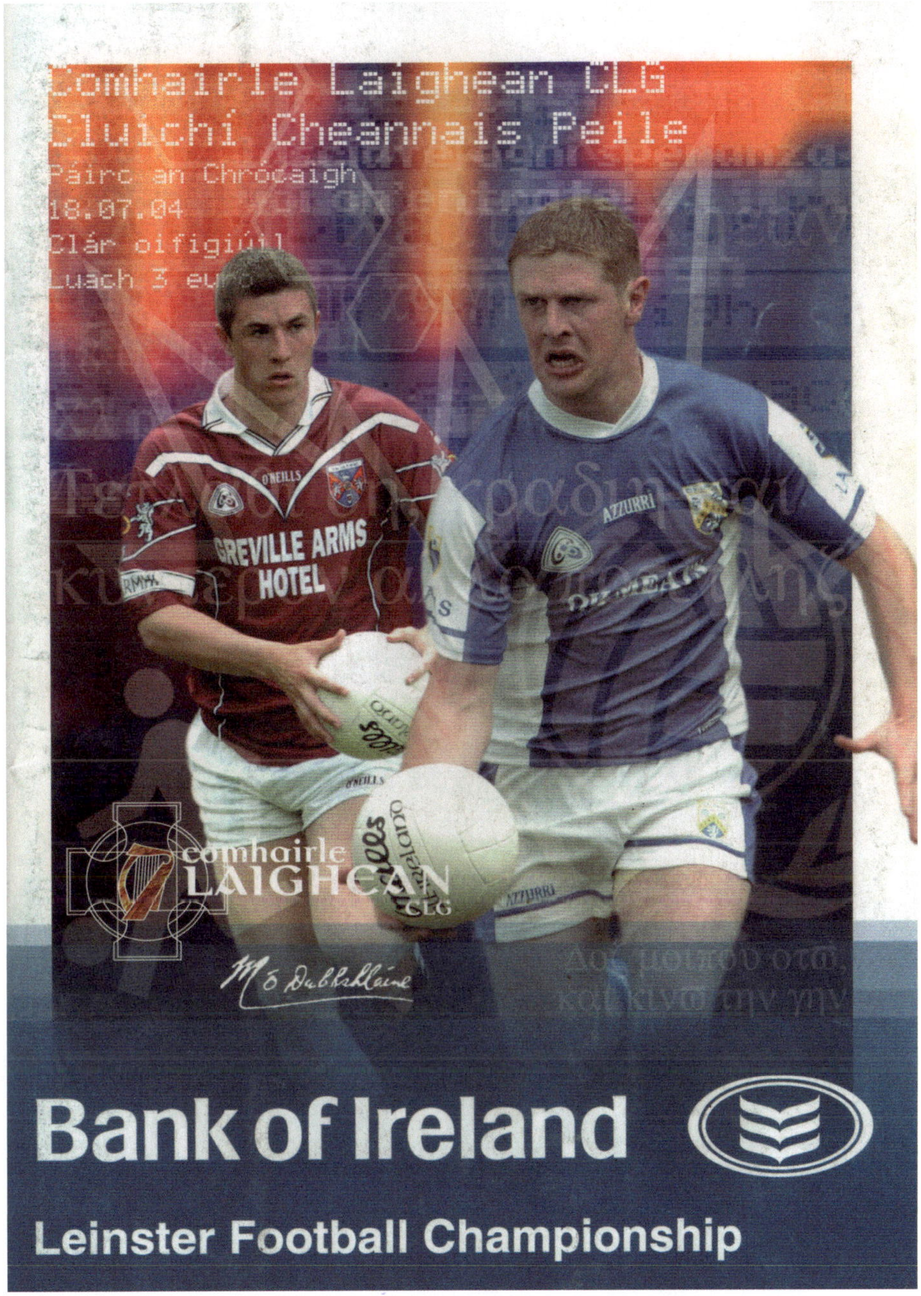

3 Ulster Hurling Final
Antrim 1-15 Down 1-15

4 Replay
Antrim 3-14 Down 0-18

5 All-Ireland Hurling Final
Cork 0-17 Kilkenny 0-09
Attendance – 78,212

6 Connacht Football Final
Mayo 2-13 Roscommon 0-09

7 Leinster Football Final
Westmeath 0-13 Laois 0-13

8

Comhairle Laighean CLG
Cluiche Cheannais Peile
ATH-IMIRT
Páirc an Chrócaigh
24.07.04
Clár oifigiúil
Luach 3 euro
comhairle LAIGHEAN CLG
Bank of Ireland
Leinster Football Championship

9

CUMANN LÚTHCHLEAS GAEL
Cluichí Ceannais Peile Na Mumhan
Sinsear agus Mionúr
11ú Lúil 2004
Pairc Na nGael, Luimneach
Clár Oifígiúil
Luach: €3.00
RUNAÍ:
Bank of Ireland
Football Championship

10

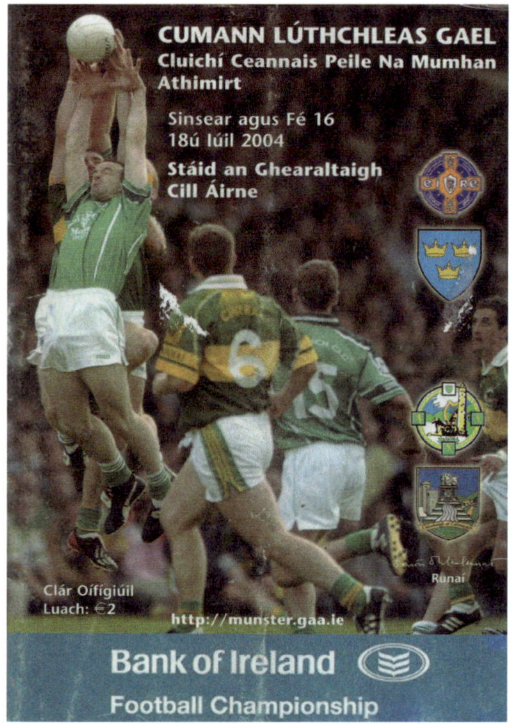
CUMANN LÚTHCHLEAS GAEL
Cluichí Ceannais Peile Na Mumhan
Athimirt
Sinsear agus Fé 16
18ú Iúil 2004
Stáid an Ghearaltaigh
Cill Áirne
Rúnaí
Clár Oifigiúil
Luach: €2
http://munster.gaa.ie
Bank of Ireland
Football Championship

11

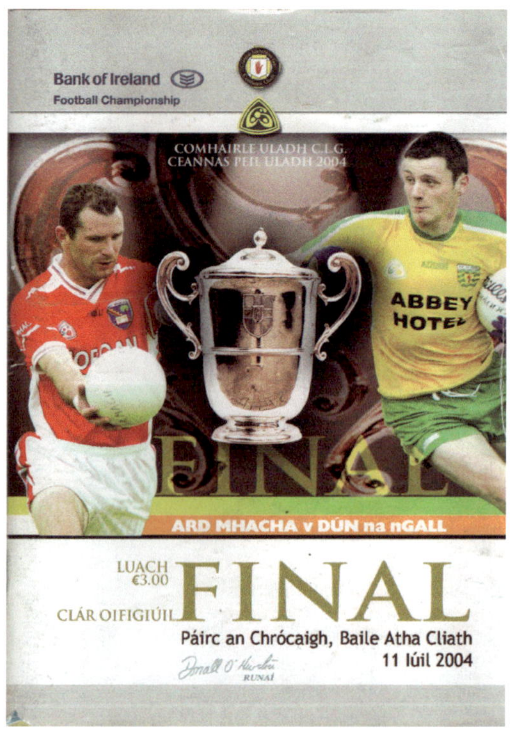
Bank of Ireland
Football Championship
COMHAIRLE ULADH C.L.G.
CEANNAS PEIL ULADH 2004
ABBEY HOTEL
FINAL
ARD MHACHA v DÚN na nGALL
LUACH €3.00
CLÁR OIFIGIÚIL
FINAL
Páirc an Chrócaigh, Baile Atha Cliath
11 Iúil 2004
RUNAÍ

12

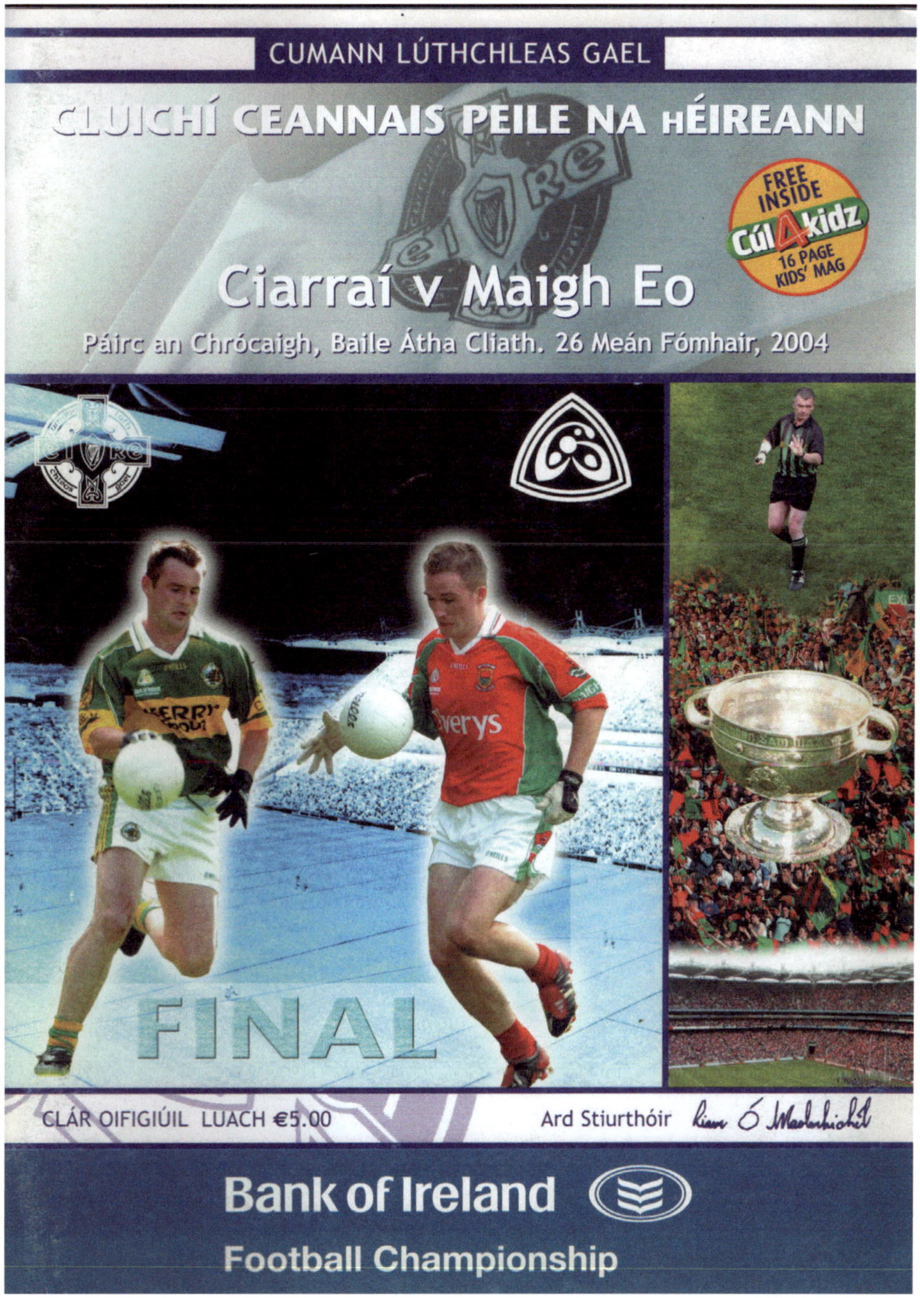

8 Replay
Westmeath 0-12 Laois 0-10

9 Munster Football Final
Kerry 1-10 Limerick 1-10

10 Replay
Kerry 3-10 Limerick 2-09

11 Ulster Football Final
Armagh 3-15 Donegal 0-11

12 All-Ireland Football Final
Kerry 1-20 Mayo 2-09
Attendance – 79,749

2005

The redevelopment of Croke Park was now complete and the new stadium was officially opened by GAA President Seán Kelly in March. Sections of the stadium were renamed – the Canal End became the Davin Stand and the new Nally Terrace occupied the place of the old Nally Stand. In recognition of the man who sold the site to the GAA, Hill 16 was officially renamed Dineen Hill 16. The GAA now had to make a decision regarding the availability of Croke Park to other sports. In April 2005, GAA Congress voted to abolish Rule 42, opening Croke Park. The motion gave the GAA Central Council the power to authorise the use of Croke Park for events other than those controlled by the association during the upcoming period when Lansdowne Road was closed for redevelopment. The 2005 All-Ireland finals were the first to be played in the new Croke Park and saw Cork retain their hurling crown, while Tyrone recaptured the title after a year's break.

1

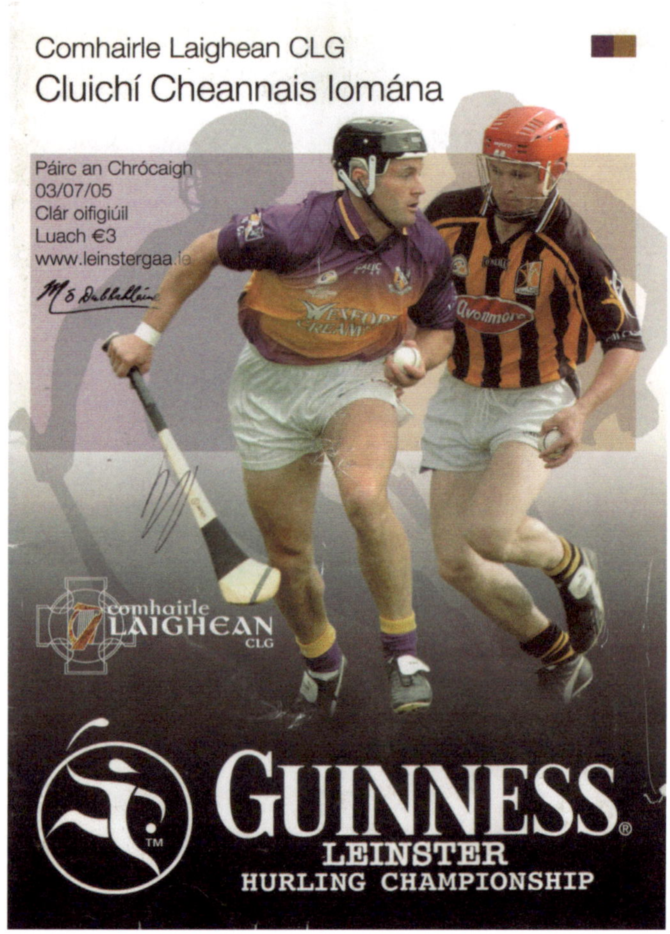

1 Leinster Hurling Final
Kilkenny 0-22 Wexford 1-16

2 Munster Hurling Final
Cork 1-21 Tipperary 1-16

3 Ulster Hurling Final
Antrim 2-22 Down 1-18

4 All-Ireland Hurling Final
Cork 1-21 Galway 1-16.
Attendance – 81,136

5 Connacht Football Final
Galway 0-10 Mayo 0-08

2

CLUICHÍ CEANNAIS IOMÁNA
na MUMHAN 2005
Sinsear agus Mionúr
Clár
Oifigiúil
http://munster.gaa.ie
Siomón Ó Maolrunaí
Runaí
LUACH
€3
Páirc Uí Chaoimh 26ú Meitheamh

3

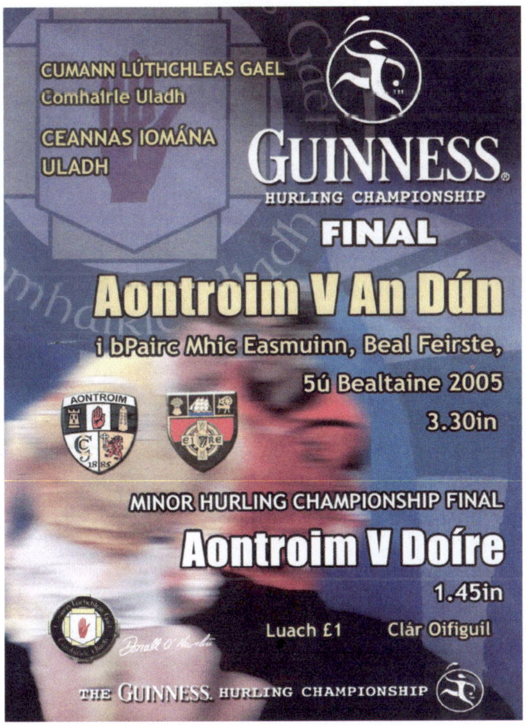
CUMANN LÚTHCHLEAS GAEL
Comhairle Uladh
CEANNAS IOMÁNA
ULADH
GUINNESS
HURLING CHAMPIONSHIP
FINAL
Aontroim V An Dún
i bPairc Mhic Easmuinn, Beal Feirste,
5ú Bealtaine 2005
3.30in
AONTROIM
MINOR HURLING CHAMPIONSHIP FINAL
Aontroim V Doíre
1.45in
Luach £1
Clár Oifiguil
THE GUINNESS HURLING CHAMPIONSHIP

4

CUMANN LÚTHCHLEAS GAEL
GUINNESS CLUICHE
CEANNAIS IOMÁNA
SINSIR NA hÉIREANN
Páirc an Chrócaigh,
Baile Átha Cliath.
11 Meán Fómhair 2005
CORCAIGH
GAILLIMH
ESB CLUICHE CEANNAIS
IOMÁNA MIONÚIR
NA hÉIREANN
GAILLIMH v LUIMNEACH
CLÁR OIFIGIÚIL
LUACH €5.00
ARD STIURTHÓIR
THE GUINNESS HURLING CHAMPIONSHIP

5

COMHAIRLE CHONNACHT C.L.G.
STÁID AN PHIARSAIGH,
BÓTHAR NA TRÁ.
10 IÚIL 2005
CONNACHT FOOTBALL CHAMPIONSHIP
FINAL 2005
CLÁR OIFIGIÚIL
LUACH €3.00
Rúnaí
Bank of Ireland
Football Championship

6

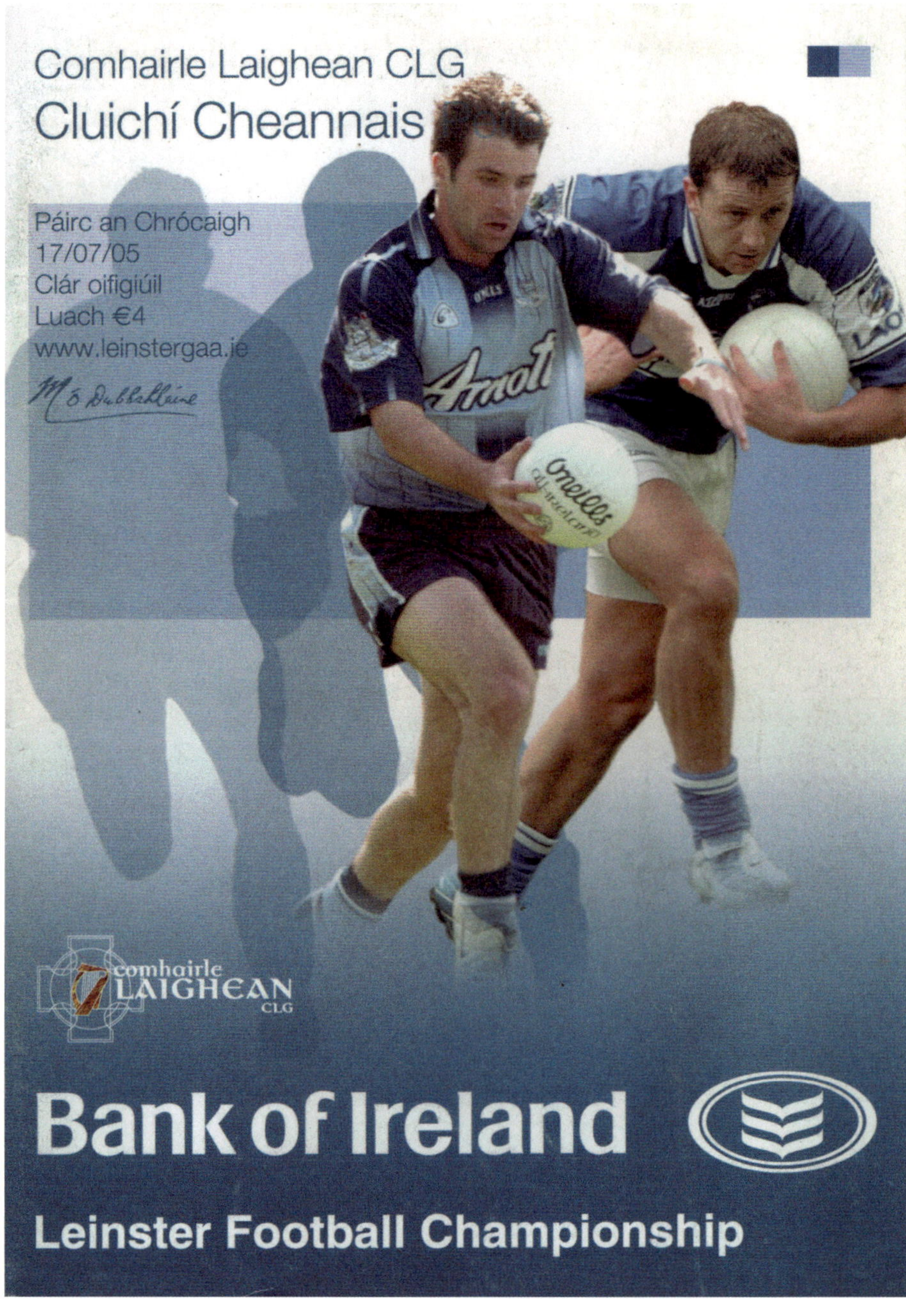

6 Leinster Football Final
Dublin 0-14 Laois 0-13

7 Munster Football Final
Kerry 1-11 Cork 0-11

8 Ulster Football Final
Armagh 2-8 Tyrone 0-14

9 Replay
Armagh 0-13 Tyrone 0-11

10 All-Ireland Football Final
Tyrone 1-16 Kerry 2-10
Attendance – 82,112

7

Cluichí Ceannais Peile
na Mumhan 2005
(Sinsear agus Mionúr)
Clár
Oifigiúil
LUACH
€3
Siomón Ó Maolrunaí
Runaí
http://munster.gaa.ie
Páirc Uí Chaoimh 10ú Iúil

8

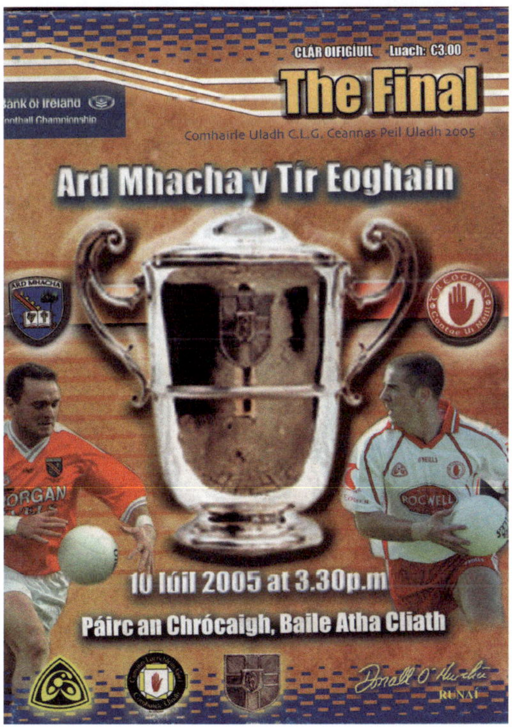
CLÁR OIFIGIUIL Luach: €3.00
The Final
Comhairle Uladh C.L.G. Ceannas Peil Uladh 2005
Ard Mhacha v Tír Eoghain
10 Iúil 2005 at 3.30p.m
Páirc an Chrócaigh, Baile Atha Cliath
RUNAÍ

9

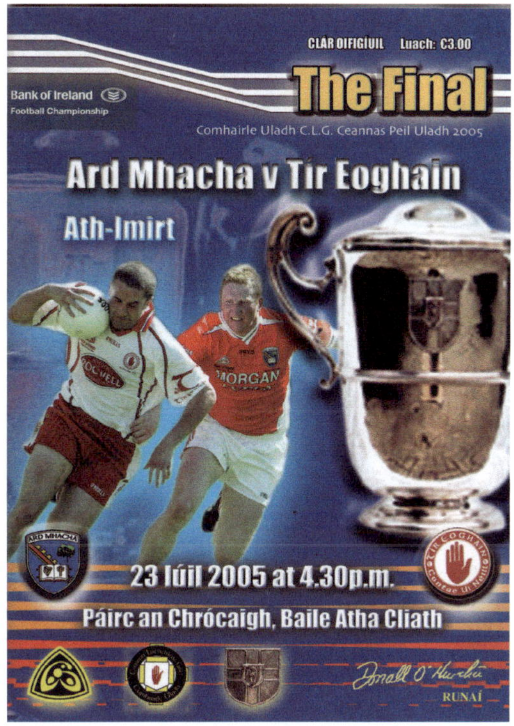
CLÁR OIFIGIUIL Luach: €3.00
Bank of Ireland
Football Championship
The Final
Comhairle Uladh C.L.G. Ceannas Peil Uladh 2005
Ard Mhacha v Tír Eoghain
Ath-Imirt
23 Iúil 2005 at 4.30p.m.
Páirc an Chrócaigh, Baile Atha Cliath
RUNAÍ

10

CUMANN LÚTHCHLEAS GAEL
BANK OF IRELAND
CLUICHE CEANNAIS PEILE
SINSIR NA hÉIREANN
Páirc an Chrócaigh,
Baile Átha Cliath.
25 Meán Fómhair 2005
CIARRAÍ
TÍR EOGHAIN
ESB CLUICHE CEANNAIS
PEILE MIONÚIR
NA hÉIREANN
AN DÚN v MAIGH EO
CLÁR OIFIGIÚIL
LUACH €5.00
ARD STIURTHÓIR
Bank of Ireland
Football Championship

2006

Since the reintroduction of the Ulster senior hurling championship in 1989, only three counties had won the Liam Harvey Cup. Antrim were by far the dominant team, winning the first championship in 1989 before playing in that year's All-Ireland final. In 2006, they had a narrow five-point win over London in the Ulster quarter-final before easing past Down in the semi-final. On the other side of the draw, New York caused a huge shock by defeating Derry, the 2000 and 2001 Ulster champions. A unique final ensued where New York played Antrim in an Ulster hurling final played in Canton Park in Boston, Massachusetts. The match was played in October as the Ulster counties were no longer competing for the Liam MacCarthy Cup following the introduction of the tiered hurling championship in 2005. New York's last Ulster championship match ended in defeat, however, as Antrim added the Ulster title to the Christy Ring Cup they had won earlier in the year. A three-tiered hurling championship comprising the Liam MacCarthy Cup, the Christy Ring Cup and the Nicky Rackard Cup was introduced this year to provide all counties with more meaningful championship fixtures.

1

1 Leinster Hurling Final
Kilkenny 1-23 Wexford 2-12

2 Munster Hurling Final
Cork 2-14 Tipperary 1-14

3 Ulster Hurling Final
Antrim 2-20 New York 1-14

4 All-Ireland Hurling Final
Kilkenny 1-16 Cork 1-13
Attendance – 82,275

5 Connacht Football Final
Mayo 0-12 Galway 1-08

2

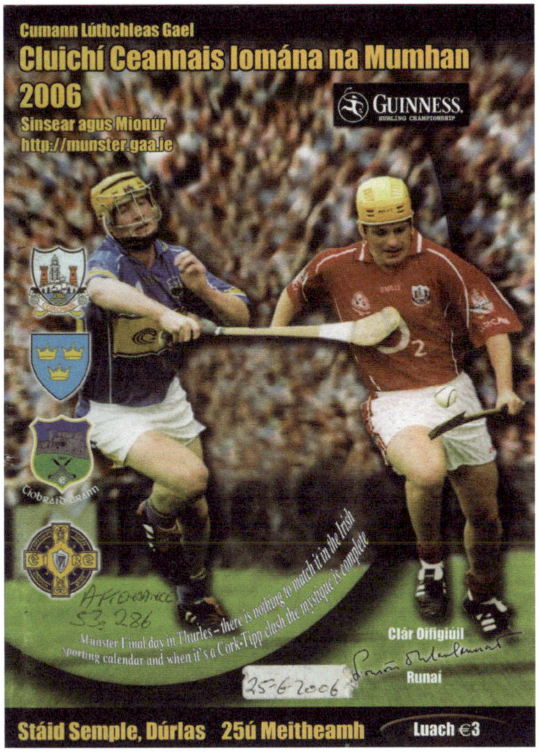
Cumann Lúthchleas Gael
Cluichí Ceannais Iomána na Mumhan
2006
Sinsear agus Mionúr
http://munster.gaa.ie
GUINNESS
Munster Final day in Thurles – there is nothing to match it in the Irish sporting calendar and when it's a Cork-Tipp clash the mystique is complete
Clár Oifigiúil
Runaí
Stáid Semple, Dúrlas 25ú Meitheamh Luach €3

3

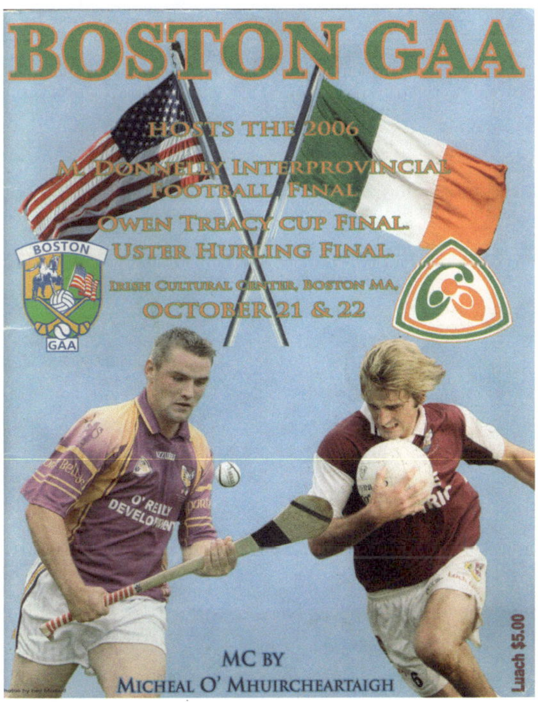
BOSTON GAA
HOSTS THE 2006
M DONNELLY INTERPROVINCIAL
FOOTBALL FINAL
OWEN TREACY CUP FINAL
ULSTER HURLING FINAL
IRISH CULTURAL CENTER, BOSTON MA
OCTOBER 21 & 22
BOSTON
GAA
MC BY
MICHEAL O' MHUIRCHEARTAIGH
Luach $5.00

4

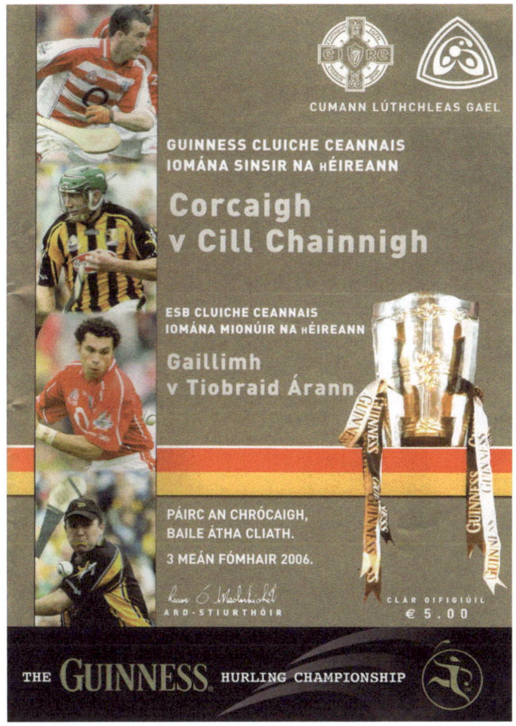
CUMANN LÚTHCHLEAS GAEL
GUINNESS CLUICHE CEANNAIS
IOMÁNA SINSIR NA hÉIREANN
Corcaigh
v Cill Chainnigh
ESB CLUICHE CEANNAIS
IOMÁNA MIONÚIR NA hÉIREANN
Gaillimh
v Tiobraid Árann
PÁIRC AN CHRÓCAIGH,
BAILE ÁTHA CLIATH.
3 MEÁN FÓMHAIR 2006.
ARD-STIURTHÓIR
CLÁR OIFIGIÚIL
€ 5.00
THE GUINNESS HURLING CHAMPIONSHIP

5

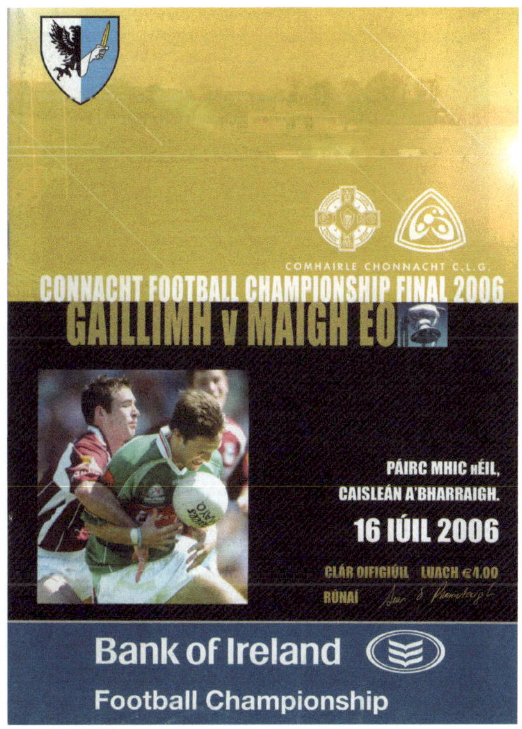
COMHAIRLE CHONNACHT C.L.G.
CONNACHT FOOTBALL CHAMPIONSHIP FINAL 2006
GAILLIMH v MAIGH EO
PÁIRC MHIC hÉIL,
CAISLEÁN A'BHARRAIGH.
16 IÚIL 2006
CLÁR OIFIGIÚIL LUACH €4.00
RÚNAÍ
Bank of Ireland
Football Championship

6

Comhairle Laighean CLG
Cluichí Cheannais Peile
Páirc an Chrócaigh
16/07/06
Clár oifigiúil
Luach €4
www.leinstergaa.ie
comhairle
LAIGHEAN
CLG
Bank of Ireland
Leinster Football Championship

7

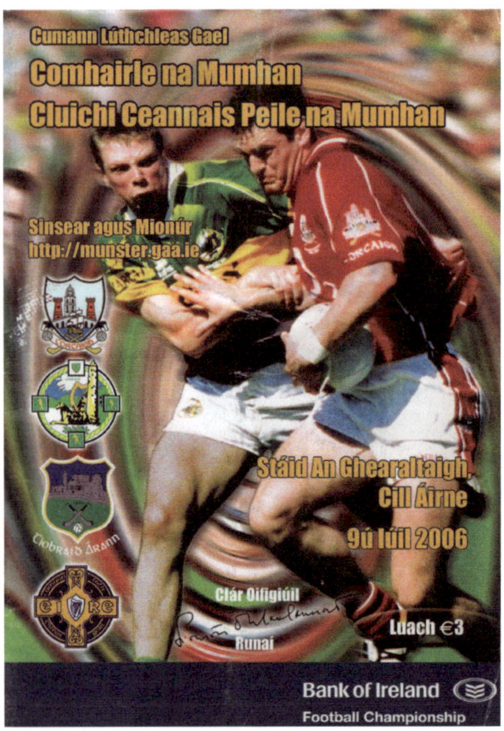
Cumann Lúthchleas Gael
Comhairle na Mumhan
Cluichí Ceannais Peile na Mumhan
Sinsear agus Mionúr
http://munster.gaa.ie
Staid An Ghearaltaigh,
Cill Áirne
9ú Iúil 2006
Clár Oifigiúil
Runaí
Luach €3
Bank of Ireland
Football Championship

8

Cumann Luthchleas Gael
Símón Ó Maolrunaí
Runaí
Clár
Oifigiúil
LUACH
€2
Bank of Ireland
Páirc Uí Chaoimh, 16ú Iúil, 2006

9

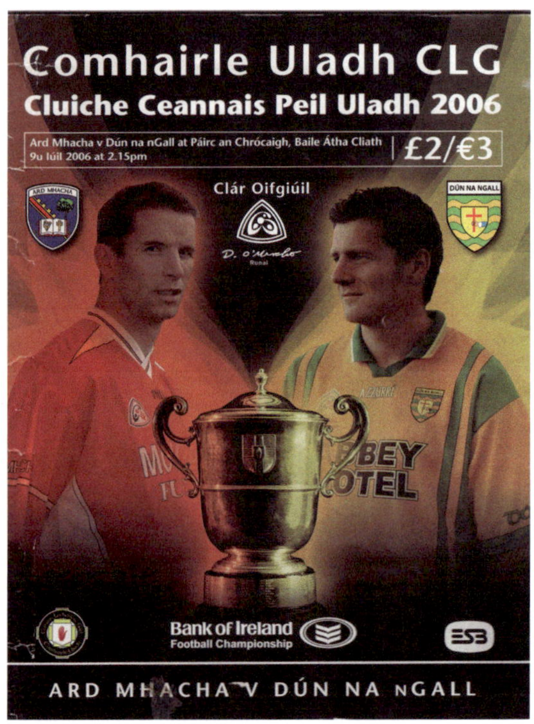
Comhairle Uladh CLG
Cluiche Ceannais Peil Uladh 2006
Ard Mhacha v Dún na nGall at Páirc an Chrócaigh, Baile Átha Cliath
9u Iúil 2006 at 2.15pm
£2/€3
Clár Oifgiúil
DÚN NA NGALL
Bank of Ireland
Football Championship
ESB
ARD MHACHA V DÚN NA NGALL

10

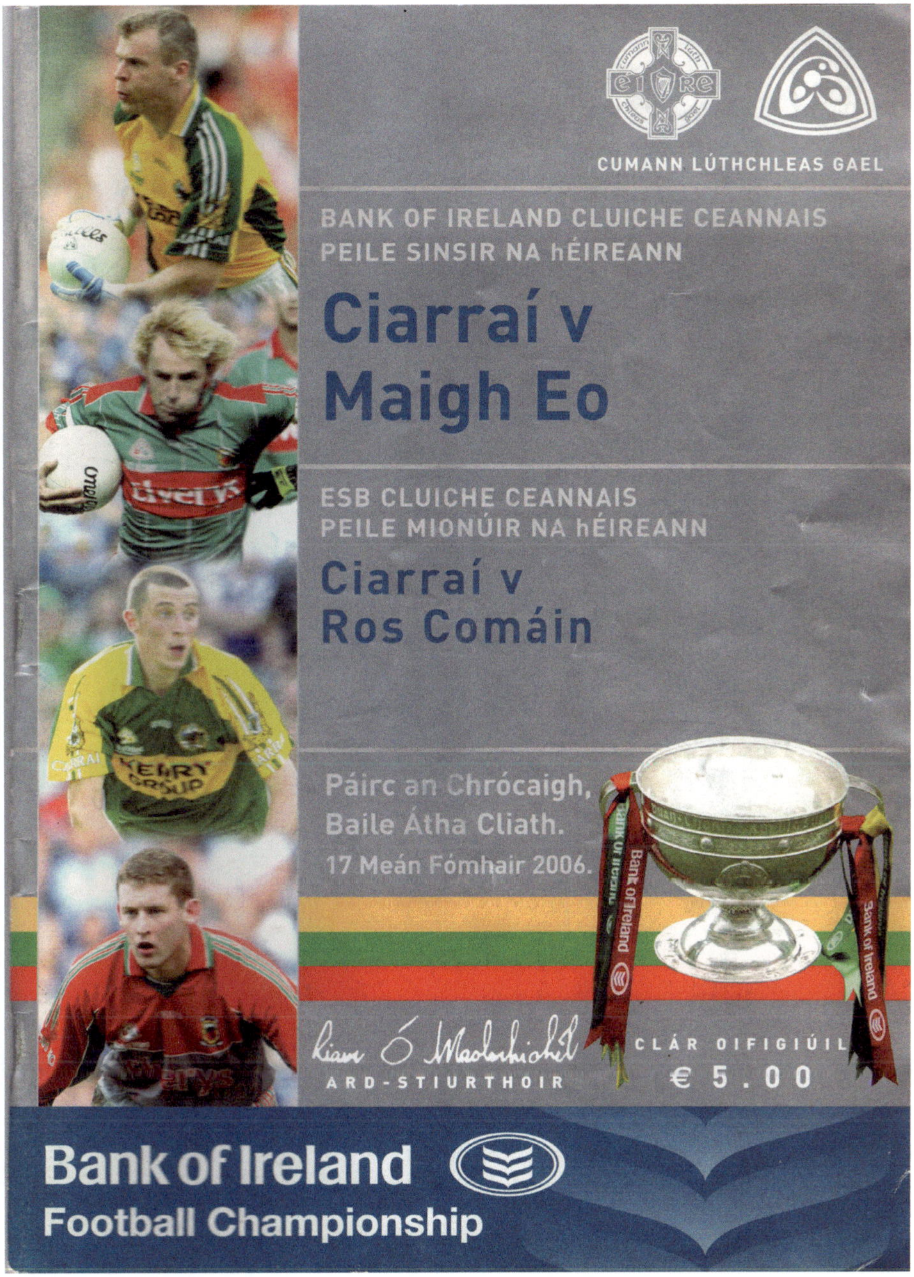

6 Leinster Football Final
Dublin 1-15 Offaly 0-09

7 Munster Football Final
Cork 0-10 Kerry 0-10

8 Replay
Cork 1-12 Kerry 0-09

9 Ulster Football Final
Armagh 1-09 Donegal 0-09

10 All-Ireland Football Final
Kerry 4-15 Mayo 3-05
Attendance – 82,289

2007

The All-Ireland championship qualifier system threw up some unique pairings in the early years of its existence. There had already been an all-Ulster pairing in the 2003 All-Ireland football final and in 2007 it was the turn of Munster as Cork and Kerry met in the final. The counties had already met in the All-Ireland semi-finals of 2002, 2005 and 2006, as well as this year's Munster football final in Killarney, which resulted in a two-point victory for the home side. However, when the teams met again in September, the Kerry margin of victory was ten points as they retained the Sam Maguire Cup.

The vagaries of the qualifier system meant that although Waterford beat Limerick in the Munster hurling final, Limerick reversed the result in the All-Ireland hurling semi-final. Limerick were unable to match the power of a Kilkenny team in their prime in the final, however, and so, like Kerry in football, Kilkenny retained the All-Ireland title. Floodlights were erected in Croke Park this year, with the first match under lights at headquarters played in February between Dublin and Tyrone. All-Ireland match programmes were reduced in size after years of the A4 format.

1

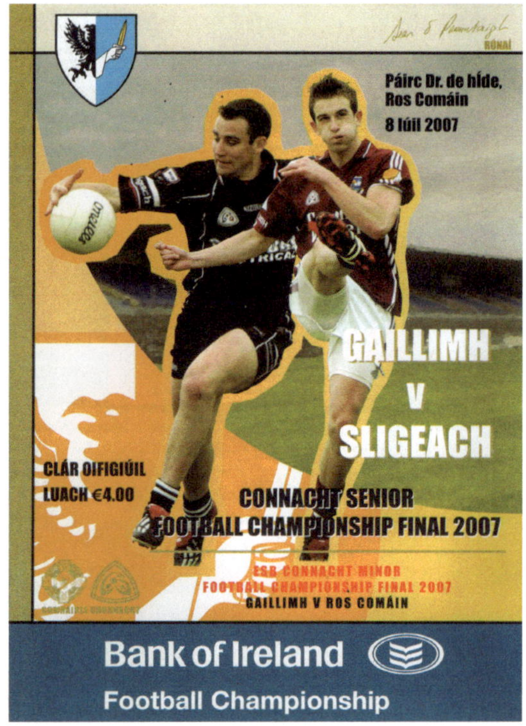

2

1 Connacht Football Final
Sligo 1-10 Galway 0-12

2 Leinster Football Final
Dublin 3-14 Laois 1-14

3 Munster Football Final
Kerry 1-15 Cork 1-13

3

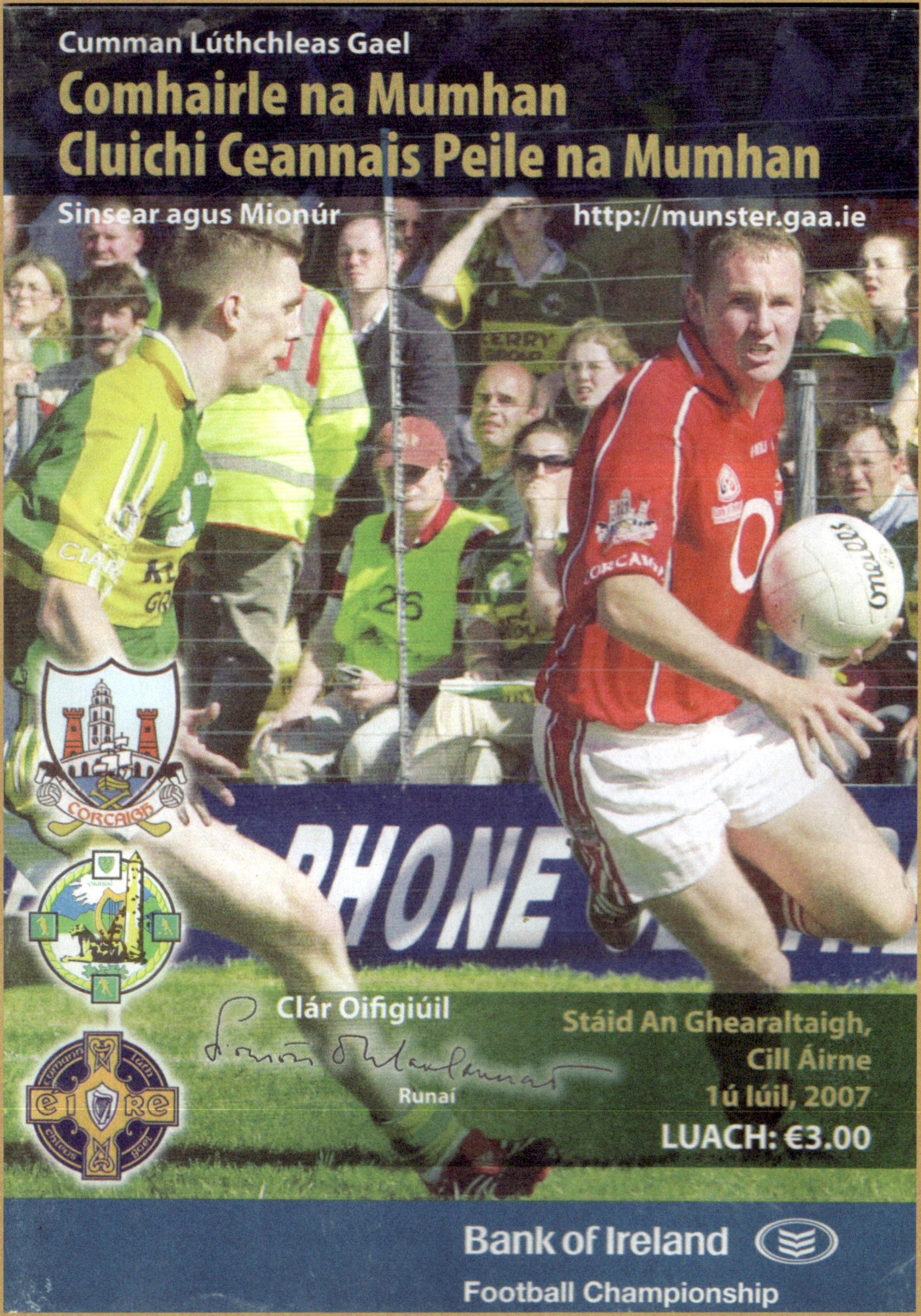

Cumman Lúthchleas Gael
Comhairle na Mumhan
Cluichi Ceannais Peile na Mumhan
Sinsear agus Mionúr
http://munster.gaa.ie
Clár Oifigiúil
Runaí
Stáid An Ghearaltaigh,
Cill Áirne
1ú Iúil, 2007
LUACH: €3.00
Bank of Ireland
Football Championship

4

5

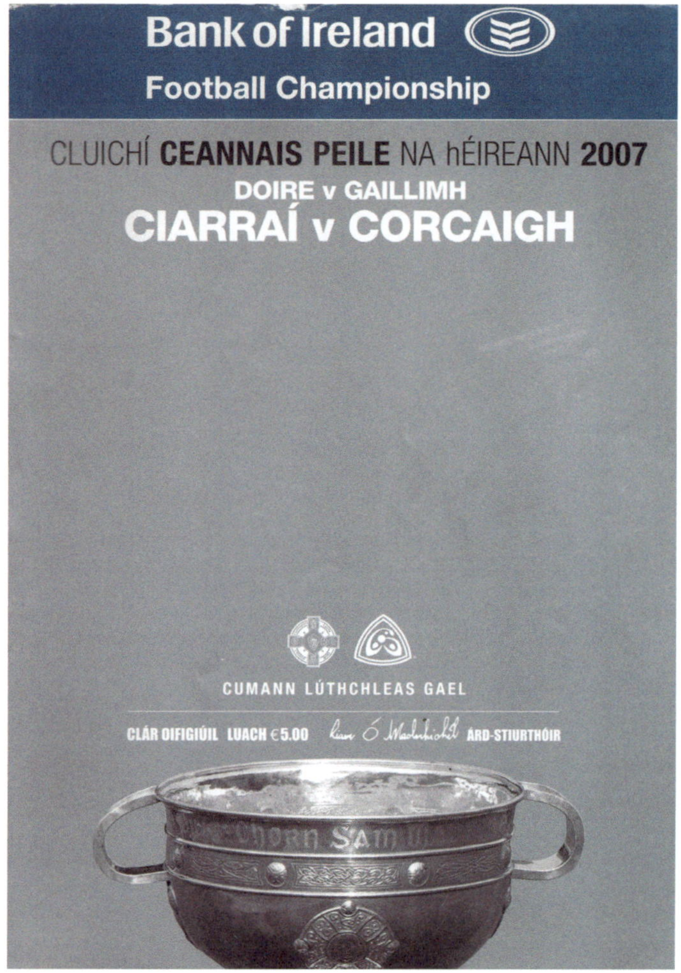

4 Ulster Football Final
Tyrone 1-15 Monaghan 1-13

5 All-Ireland Football Final
Kerry 3-13 Cork 1-09
Attendance – 82,126

6 Leinster Hurling Final
Kilkenny 2-24 Wexford 1-12

7 Munster Hurling Final
Waterford 3-17 Limerick 1-14

8 Ulster Hurling Final
Antrim 2-24 Down 0-04

9 All-Ireland Hurling Final
Kilkenny 2-19 Limerick 1-15
Attendance – 82,127

6

Comhairle Laighean CLG
Cluichí Cheannais Iomána
Páirc an Chrócaigh
01/07/07
Clár oifigiúil
Luach €5
www.leinstergaa.ie
comhairle LAIGHEAN CLG
GUINNESS
LEINSTER HURLING CHAMPIONSHIP

7

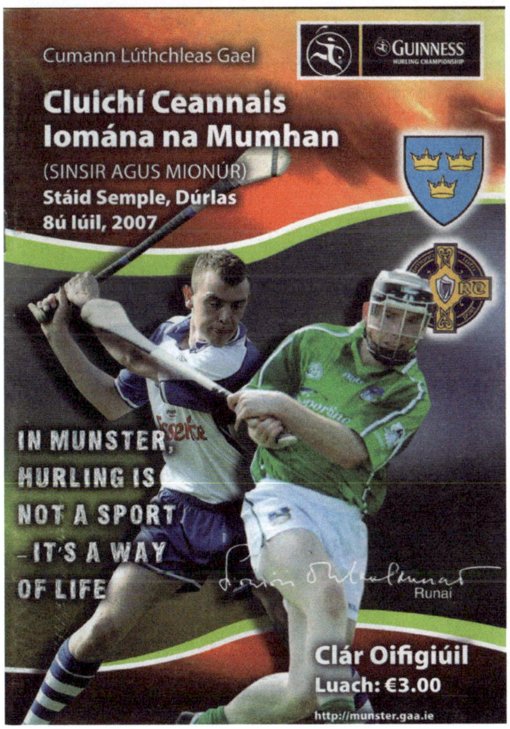
Cumann Lúthchleas Gael
GUINNESS
Cluichí Ceannais Iomána na Mumhan
(SINSIR AGUS MIONÚR)
Stáid Semple, Dúrlas
8ú Iúil, 2007
IN MUNSTER, HURLING IS NOT A SPORT - IT'S A WAY OF LIFE
Runai
Clár Oifigiúil
Luach: €3.00
http://munster.gaa.ie

8

COMHAIRLE ULADH CLG
CEANNAS IOMÁNA AGUS PEIL ULADH 2007
Aontroim V An Dún & Aontroim V Doire
Casement Park, Belfast 3ú Meitheamh 2007 at 2.15pm & 4.15pm
£2/€3
Aontroim
An Dún
Aontroim
Clár Oifgiúil
Doíre
GUINNESS
HURLING CHAMPIONSHIP
Bank of Ireland
Football Championship

9

GUINNESS
HURLING CHAMPIONSHIP
CLUICHÍ CEANNAIS IOMÁNA NA hÉIREANN 2007
CORCAIGH v TIOBRAID ÁRANN
CILL CHAINNIGH v LUIMNEACH
CUMANN LÚTHCHLEAS GAEL
CLÁR OIFIGIÚIL LUACH €5.00
ARD-STIURTHÓIR

2008

A new signature featured on the cover of the All-Ireland final match programmes this year. Páraic Duffy, a Monaghan native, assumed the role of Ard Stiúrthóir following the retirement of Liam Mulvihill in November 2007. Duffy was the eighteenth Ard Stiúrthóir/General Secretary but only the fourth to have his signature on the cover of the programme.

This year's All-Ireland football final between Kerry and Tyrone was the first to feature two teams who had failed to win their provincial title. Both had navigated the qualifier system to reach the final. Tyrone won their third title as Kerry again struggled to cope with their northern rivals. Kilkenny won their third All-Ireland hurling title in a row as they dismantled Waterford's challenge in a one-sided final. The Tommy Murphy Cup, won by Antrim, slipped into oblivion following this year's final. Lack of promotion and interest were deemed to be among the reasons for its decline.

1

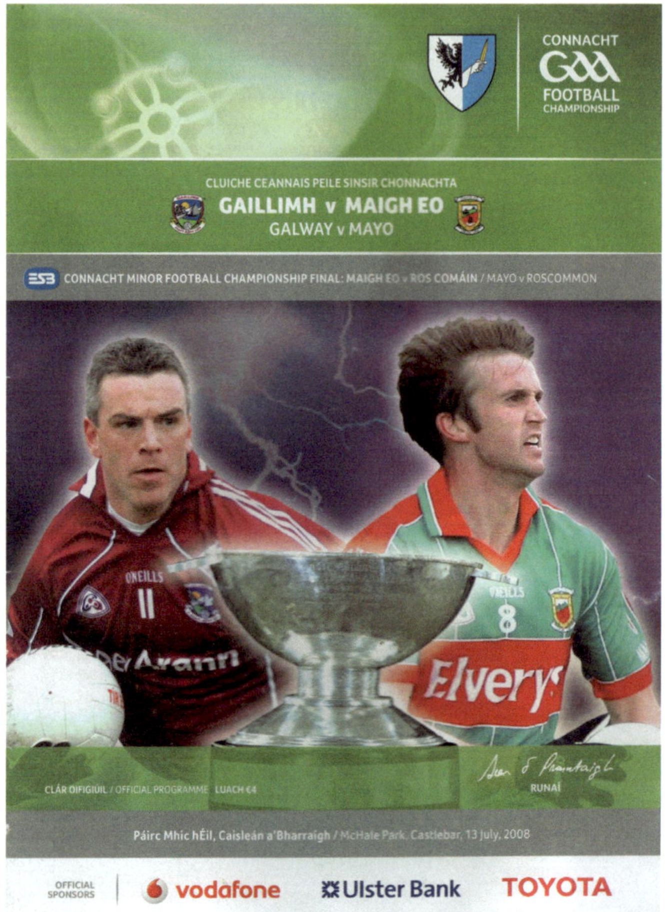

1 Connacht Football Final
Galway 2-12 Mayo 1-14

2 Leinster Football Final
Dublin 3-23 Wexford 0-09

3 Munster Football Final
Cork 1-16 Kerry 1-11

4 Ulster Football Final
Armagh 2-8 Fermanagh 1-11

5 Replay
Armagh 1-11 Fermanagh 0-08

2

LEINSTER
GAA
FOOTBALL
CHAMPIONSHIP
CLUICHE CEANNAIS PEILE SINSEAR LAIGHEAN
ÁTH CLIATH v LOCH GARMAN
DUBLIN v WEXFORD
CLUICHE CEANNAIS PEILE MIONÚIR ESB LAIGHEAN
UÍBH FHÁILÍ v AN MHÍ / OFFALY v MEATH
RÚNAÍ
Páirc an Chrócaigh, Baile Átha Cliath, 20ú Iúil, 2008 / Croke Park, Dublin, 20th July, 2008
OFFICIAL SPONSORS
vodafone
Ulster Bank
TOYOTA

3

MUNSTER
GAA
FOOTBALL
CLUICHE CHEANNAIS PEILE SINSEAR GAA NA MUMHAN
CORCAIGH V CIARRAÍ
CLUICHE CHEANNAIS PEILE MIONÚR ESB GAA NA MUMHAN
TIOBRAID ÁRANN V CIARRAÍ
CLÁR OIFIGIÚIL LUACH €3
RÚNAÍ
Páirc Uí Chaoimh, 6ú Iúil, 2008
OFFICIAL SPONSORS
vodafone
Ulster Bank
TOYOTA

4

Páirc Naofa Thiarnaigh / St Tiernachs Pk, Clones
20ú Iúil / 20th July 2008 at 2.00pm
CLUICHÍ CEANNAIS
PEIL ULADH 2008
Ard Mhacha
Armagh
Fear Manach
Fermanagh
£2/€3
ULSTER
GAA
FOOTBALL
CHAMPIONSHIP
Clár Oifigiúil
OFFICIAL SPONSORS
vodafone
Ulster Bank
TOYOTA

5

Páirc Naofa Thiarnaigh / St Tiernachs Pk, Clones
27ú Iúil / 27th July 2008 at 3.00pm
CLUICHÍ CEANNAIS
PEIL ULADH 2008
Ard Mhacha
Armagh
Fear Manach
Fermanagh
Áth Imirt
Replay
£2/€3
ULSTER
GAA
FOOTBALL
CHAMPIONSHIP
Clár Oifigiúil
OFFICIAL SPONSORS
vodafone
Ulster Bank
TOYOTA

6

GAA
FOOTBALL
ALL-IRELAND SENIOR
CHAMPIONSHIP
CRAOBH CLUICHE CEANNAIS PEILE SINSEAR NA hÉIREANN
CIARRAÍ v TÍR EOGHAIN
KERRY v TYRONE
CRAOBH CLUICHE CEANNAIS PEILE MIONÚIR ESB NA hÉIREANN
MAIGH EO v TÍR EOGHAIN / MAYO v TYRONE
CLÁR OIFIGIÚIL / OFFICIAL PROGRAMME LUACH €5
ÁRD STIURTHÓIR
Páirc an Chrócaigh, 21 Meán Fómhair / Croke Park, 21 September, 2008
OFFICIAL SPONSORS
vodafone
Ulster Bank
TOYOTA

7

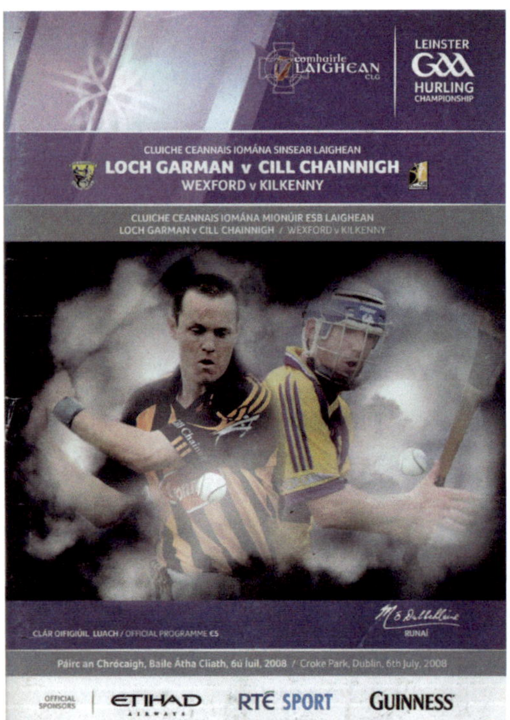

Comhairle LAIGHEAN CLG
LEINSTER
GAA
HURLING
CHAMPIONSHIP
CLUICHE CEANNAIS IOMÁNA SINSEAR LAIGHEAN
LOCH GARMAN v CILL CHAINNIGH
WEXFORD v KILKENNY
CLUICHE CEANNAIS IOMÁNA MIONÚIR ESB LAIGHEAN
LOCH GARMAN v CILL CHAINNIGH / WEXFORD v KILKENNY
CLÁR OIFIGIÚIL LUACH / OFFICIAL PROGRAMME €5
RÚNAÍ
Páirc an Chrócaigh, Baile Átha Cliath, 6ú Iúil, 2008 / Croke Park, Dublin, 6th July, 2008
OFFICIAL SPONSORS
ETIHAD
RTÉ SPORT
GUINNESS

8

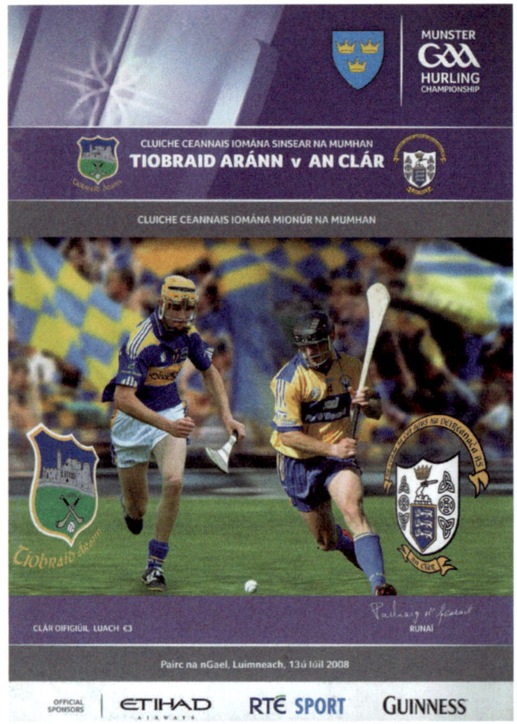

MUNSTER
GAA
HURLING
CHAMPIONSHIP
CLUICHE CEANNAIS IOMÁNA SINSEAR NA MUMHAN
TIOBRAID ÁRANN v AN CLÁR
CLUICHE CEANNAIS IOMÁNA MIONÚR NA MUMHAN
CLÁR OIFIGIÚIL LUACH €3
RÚNAÍ
Páirc na nGael, Luimneach, 13ú Iúil 2008
OFFICIAL SPONSORS
ETIHAD
RTÉ SPORT
GUINNESS

9

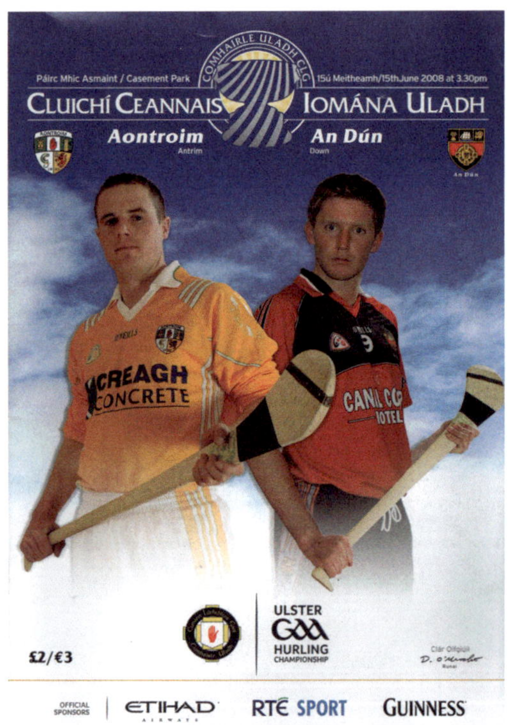

COMHAIRLE ULADH CLG
Páirc Mhic Asmaint / Casement Park
15ú Meitheamh/15th June 2008 at 3.30pm
CLUICHÍ CEANNAIS IOMÁNA ULADH
Aontroim
Antrim
An Dún
Down
ULSTER
GAA
HURLING
CHAMPIONSHIP
£2/€3
Clár Oifigiúil
Rúnaí
OFFICIAL SPONSORS
ETIHAD
RTÉ SPORT
GUINNESS

10

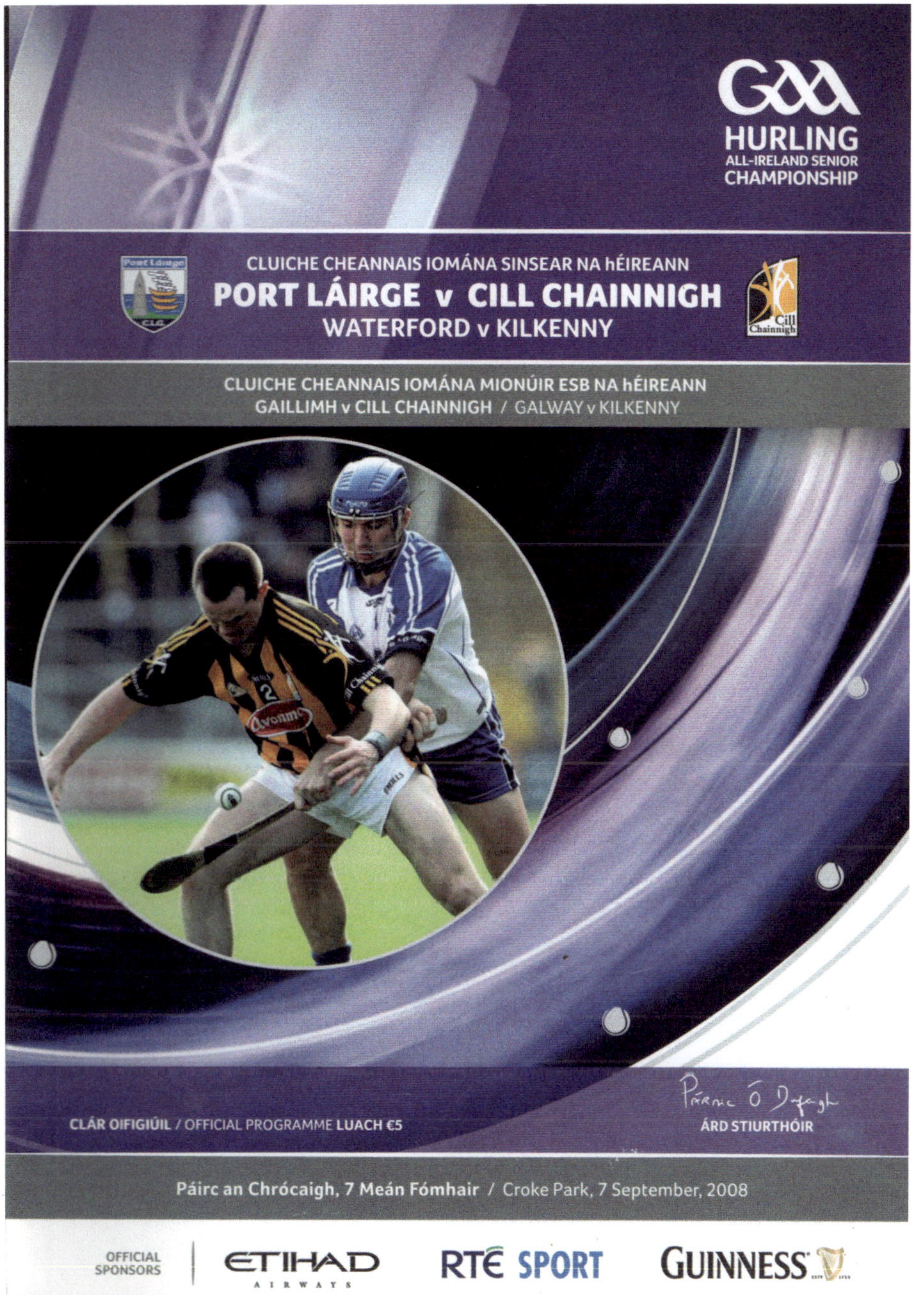

6 All-Ireland Football Final
Tyrone 1-15 Kerry 0-14
Attendance – 82,204

7 Leinster Hurling Final
Kilkenny 5-21 Wexford 0-17

8 Munster Hurling Final
Tipperary 2-21 Clare 0-19

9 Ulster Hurling Final
Antrim 3-18 Down 2-16

10 All-Ireland Hurling Final
Kilkenny 3-30 Waterford 1-13.
Attendance – 82,186

2009

The GAA celebrated its 125th anniversary in 2009, and during the year, programme covers sported the 'Ceiliúradh 125 Bliain' logo. Celebration was not on the minds of the Cork hurlers, however, as they went on strike again, this time over the reappointment of manager Gerald McCarthy. While Cork's travails continued in Munster, Kilkenny were thriving in Leinster. This year Kilkenny completed the twelfth of 14 consecutive Leinster championship wins to underline their absolute dominance of the province, which now included Galway for the first time.

In 2009, they won their fourth All-Ireland hurling title in a row, just the second team to do so and the first to do so when winning their provincial title in each of those years.* Kilkenny's wing back Tommy Walsh was named Hurler of the Year, while Henry Shefflin won a record-equalling ninth All-Star award for his contribution to the winning season.

* *Cork's four in a row in the 1940s included a defeat to Tipperary in the 1941 Munster final, delayed because of foot-and-mouth disease.*

1

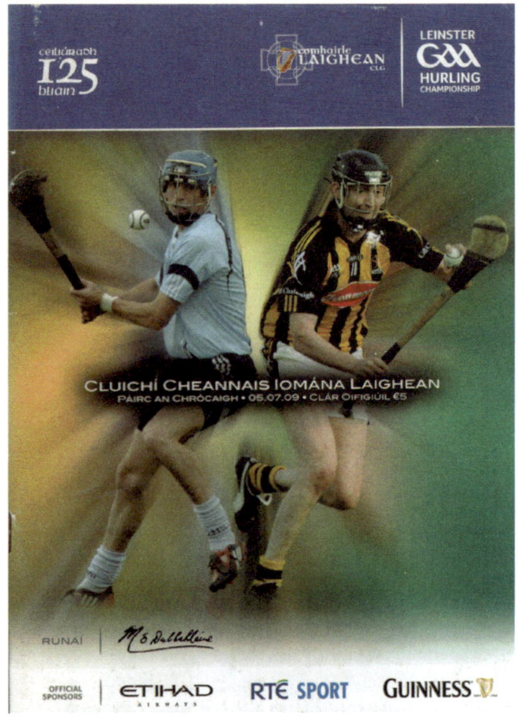

2

1 Leinster Hurling Final
Kilkenny 2-18 Dublin 0-18

2 Munster Hurling Final
Tipperary 4-14 Waterford 2-16

3 Ulster Hurling Final
Antrim 3-20 Down 4-15

CEILIÚRADH 125

GAA

3

Cluichí Ceannais Iomana Uladh

Ulster Senior Hurling Championship Final 2009

28Ú MEITHEAMH 2009

AONTROIM V AN DÚN

PÁIRC MHÍC ÁSMÁINT, BEAL FÉIRSTE

CLÁR OIFGIÚIL

D. O'Murchú

RUNAI

£2/€3

4

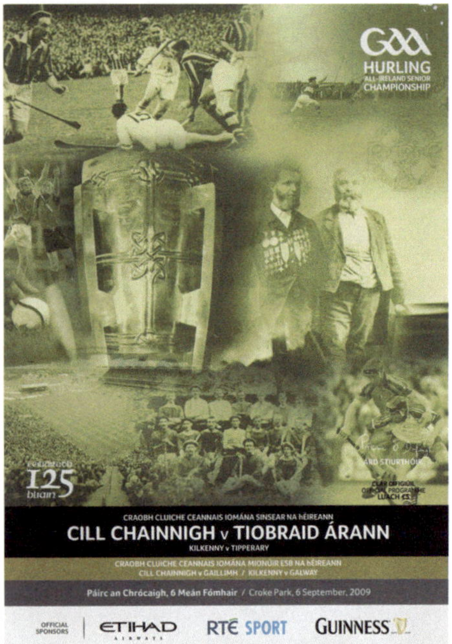

5

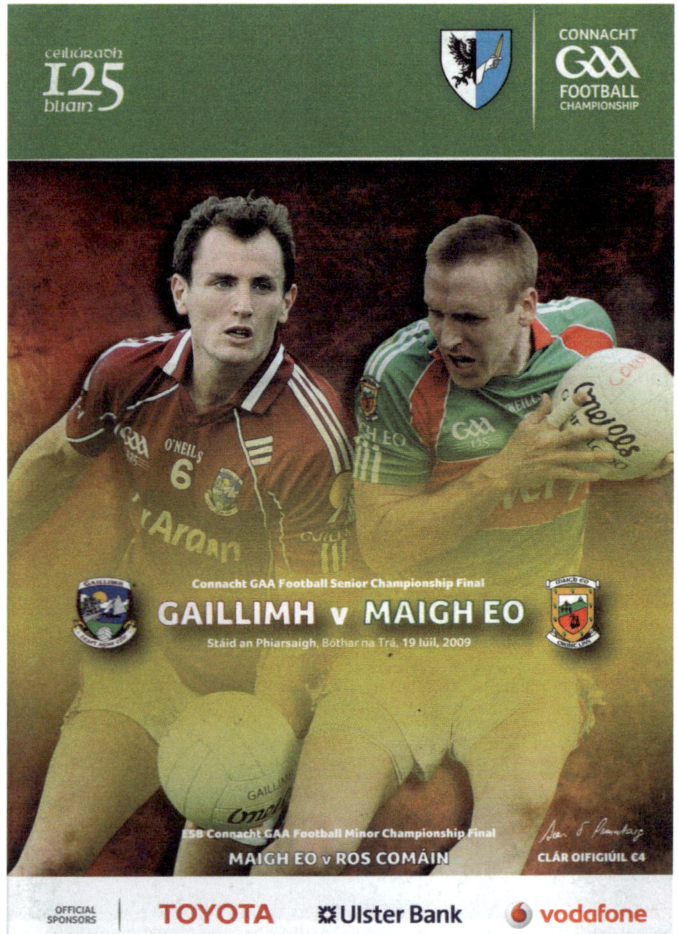

4 All-Ireland Hurling Final
Kilkenny 2-22 Tipperary 0-23.
Attendance – 82,104

5 Connacht Football Final
Mayo 2-12 Galway 1-14

6 Leinster Football Final
Dublin 2-15 Kildare 0-18

7 Munster Football Final
Cork 2-6 Limerick 0-11

8 Ulster Football Final
Tyrone 1-18 Antrim 0-15

9 All-Ireland Football Final
Kerry 0-16 Cork 1-09
Attendance – 82,286

6

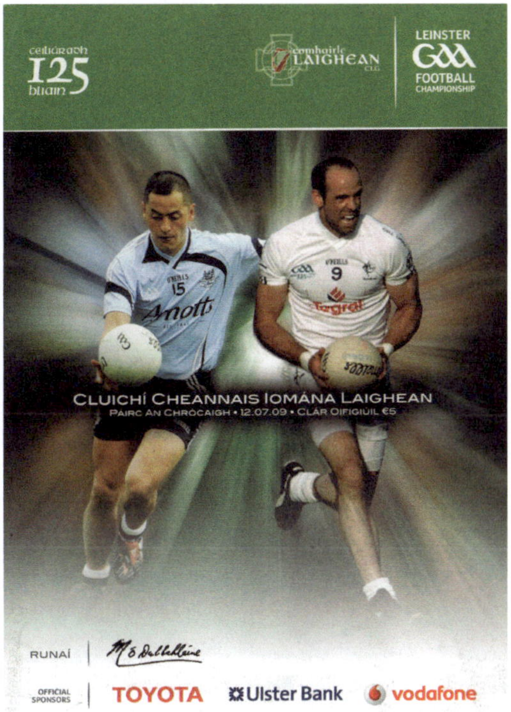
ceiliúradh 125 bliain
Comhairle Laighean CLG
LEINSTER GAA FOOTBALL CHAMPIONSHIP
CLUICHÍ CHEANNAIS IOMÁNA LAIGHEAN
PÁIRC AN CHRÓCAIGH • 12.07.09 • CLÁR OIFIGIÚIL €5
RUNAÍ
OFFICIAL SPONSORS
TOYOTA
Ulster Bank
vodafone

7

ceiliúradh 125 bliain
MUNSTER GAA FOOTBALL CHAMPIONSHIP
Cluichí Ceannais Peile na Mumhan 2009
(SINSEAR agus MIONÚR)
Páirc Uí Chaoimh, Corcaigh
Dé Domhnaigh, 5ú Iúil
Luach: €4
www.munster.gaa.ie
Clár Oifigiúil
Runaí
OFFICIAL SPONSORS
TOYOTA
Ulster Bank
vodafone

8

CEILIÚRADH 125 GAA
CLUICHÍ CEANNAIS PEILE ULADH
ULSTER GAA SENIOR FOOTBALL CHAMPIONSHIP FINAL 2009
19Ú IÚIL 2009
ULSTER GAA SENIOR FOOTBALL CHAMPIONSHIP FINAL
AONTROIM V TÍR EOGHAIN
ESB ULSTER GAA MINOR FOOTBALL CHAMPIONSHIP FINAL
ARD MHACHA V AN DÚN
PÁIRC TIARNAIGH NAOFA, CLUAIN EOIS
£4/€5
OFFICIAL SPONSORS
TOYOTA
Ulster Bank
vodafone

9

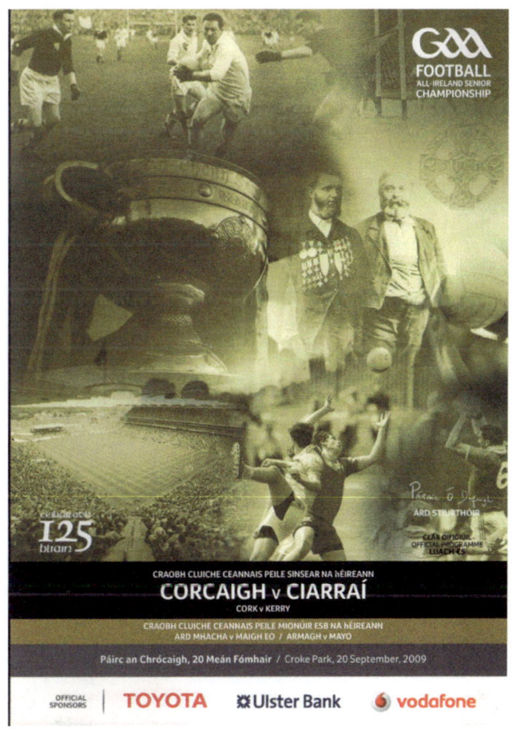
GAA FOOTBALL ALL-IRELAND SENIOR CHAMPIONSHIP
ceiliúradh 125 bliain
ARD STIÚRTHÓIR
CLÁR OIFIGIÚIL OFFICIAL PROGRAMME LUACH €5
CRAOBH CLUICHE CEANNAIS PEILE SINSEAR NA hÉIREANN
CORCAIGH v CIARRAÍ
CORK v KERRY
CRAOBH CLUICHE CEANNAIS PEILE MIONÚIR ESB NA hÉIREANN
ARD MHACHA v MAIGH EO / ARMAGH v MAYO
Páirc an Chrócaigh, 20 Meán Fómhair / Croke Park, 20 September, 2009
OFFICIAL SPONSORS
TOYOTA
Ulster Bank
vodafone

eircom
Liberty
ETIHAD

2010–19

ETIHAD
ETIHAD
ETIHAD
Centra
Centra
SuperValu
SuperValu
GAA MUSEUM
Liberty
SuperValu
Liberty Liberty Liberty Libert
Centra Centra Centra

2010

In 2010, the wearing of helmets became mandatory for adult hurling grades. Kilkenny entered the All-Ireland hurling final, hoping to become the first team to win five titles in a row. However, they struggled without the influence of Henry Shefflin, who, despite a serious knee injury, started the final, only to be withdrawn after 13 minutes. Lar Corbett scored three goals as Tipperary atoned for the previous year's defeat in the final to become All-Ireland champions.

Louth and Meath met in the 2010 Leinster football final. The match ended acrimoniously, after Joe Sheridan scored a highly controversial goal to give Meath the victory. With Louth winning by two points, and added time elapsed, the ball appeared to be thrown to the net and a first Louth victory since 1957 was denied. Cork eventually made the breakthrough to win the All-Ireland football final and, in the process, inflicted on Down their first defeat in an All-Ireland final.

1

1 Leinster Hurling Final
Kilkenny 1-19 Galway 1-12

2 Munster Hurling Final
Waterford 2-15 Cork 2-15

3 Replay
Waterford 1-16 Cork 1-13 (aet)

4 Ulster Hurling Final
Antrim 4-22 Down 1-12

5 All-Ireland Hurling Final
Tipperary 4-17 Kilkenny 1-18
Attendance – 81,765

2

Cluichí Ceannais Iomána na Mumhan
(SINSEAR AGUS MIONÚR)
Stáid Semple, Dúrlas Éile
11ú Iúil 2010
Clár Oifigiúil
www.munster.gaa.ie
Luach €4
MUNSTER
HURLING CHAMPIONSHIP
ETIHAD
Centra
GUINNESS
OFFICIAL SPONSORS

3

Cluiche Ceannais Iomána Sinsear na Mumhan
(ATH-IMIRT)
Stáid Semple, Dúrlas Éile
Dé Sathairn, 17ú Iúil 2010
(Extra time if necessary)
Clár Oifigiúil
www.munster.gaa.ie
Luach €3
MUNSTER
HURLING CHAMPIONSHIP
ETIHAD
Centra
GUINNESS
OFFICIAL SPONSORS

4

CLUICHÍ CEANNAIS IOMÁNA ULADH 2010
ULSTER SENIOR HURLING CHAMPIONSHIP FINAL
ESB ULSTER GAA HURLING MINOR CHAMPIONSHIP FINAL
27ú Meitheamh 2010 | Aontroim v An Dún | Páirc Mhic Ásmaint
H & W
LAND OF THE GIANTS
ULSTER SENIOR CHAMPIONSHIPS 2010
£2/€2
OFFICIAL SPONSORS
ETIHAD
Centra
GUINNESS

5

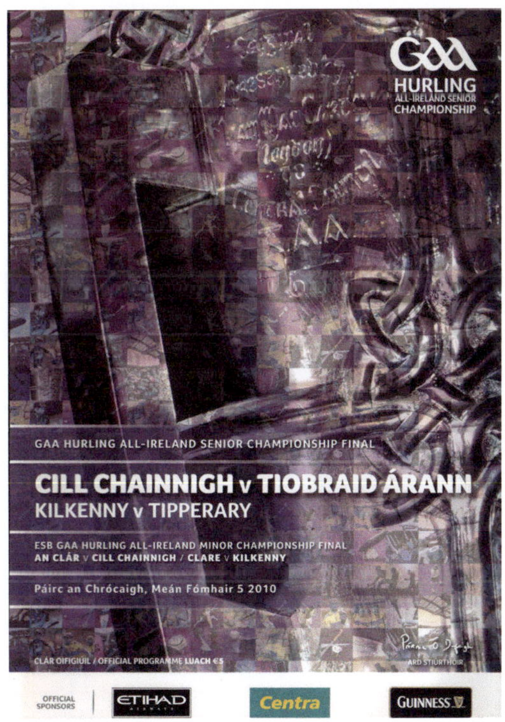

HURLING
ALL-IRELAND SENIOR CHAMPIONSHIP
GAA HURLING ALL-IRELAND SENIOR CHAMPIONSHIP FINAL
CILL CHAINNIGH v TIOBRAID ÁRANN
KILKENNY v TIPPERARY
ESB GAA HURLING ALL-IRELAND MINOR CHAMPIONSHIP FINAL
AN CLÁR v CILL CHAINNIGH / CLARE v KILKENNY
Páirc an Chrócaigh, Meán Fómhair 5 2010
CLÁR OIFIGIÚIL / OFFICIAL PROGRAMME LUACH €5
ARD STIÚRTHÓIR
OFFICIAL SPONSORS
ETIHAD
Centra
GUINNESS

6

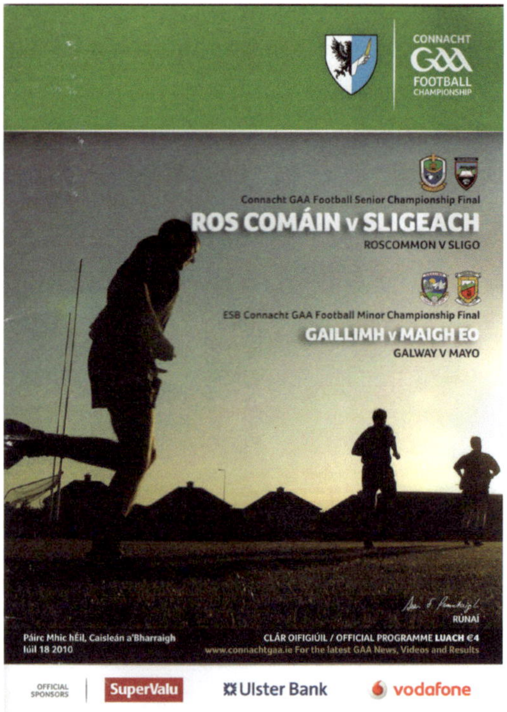
CONNACHT
GAA
FOOTBALL
CHAMPIONSHIP
Connacht GAA Football Senior Championship Final
ROS COMÁIN v SLIGEACH
ROSCOMMON V SLIGO
ESB Connacht GAA Football Minor Championship Final
GAILLIMH v MAIGH EO
GALWAY V MAYO
RÚNAÍ
Páirc Mhic hÉil, Caisleán a'Bharraigh
Iúil 18 2010
CLÁR OIFIGIÚIL / OFFICIAL PROGRAMME LUACH €4
OFFICIAL SPONSORS
SuperValu
Ulster Bank
vodafone

7

LEINSTER
LEINSTER
GAA
FOOTBALL
CHAMPIONSHIP
RÚNAÍ
2010
OFFICIAL SPONSORS
SuperValu
Ulster Bank
vodafone

8

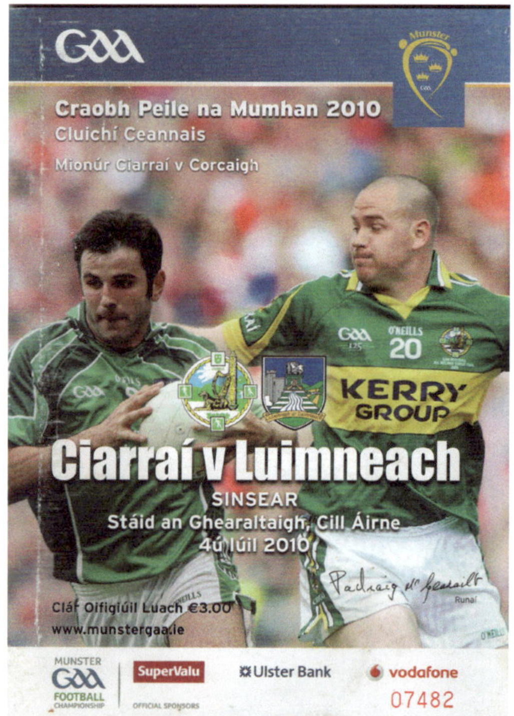
GAA
Craobh Peile na Mumhan 2010
Cluichí Ceannais
Mionúr Ciarraí v Corcaigh
Ciarraí v Luimneach
SINSEAR
Stáid an Ghearaltaigh, Cill Áirne
4ú Iúil 2010
Clár Oifigiúil Luach €3.00
www.munstergaa.ie
Rúnaí
MUNSTER
GAA
FOOTBALL
CHAMPIONSHIP
OFFICIAL SPONSORS
SuperValu
Ulster Bank
vodafone
07482

9

CLUICHÍ CEANNAIS PEILE ULADH
ULSTER GAA SENIOR FOOTBALL CHAMPIONSHIP FINAL 2010
ESB ULSTER GAA MINOR FOOTBALL CHAMPIONSHIP FINAL
18ú Iúil 2010 | Muineachán V Tír Eoghain | Páirc Tiarnaigh Naofa, Cluain Eois | 2.00pm
LAND OF THE GIANTS
ULSTER SENIOR CHAMPIONSHIPS 2010
€5/£4
ULSTER
GAA
FOOTBALL
CHAMPIONSHIP
OFFICIAL SPONSORS
SuperValu
Ulster Bank
vodafone

10

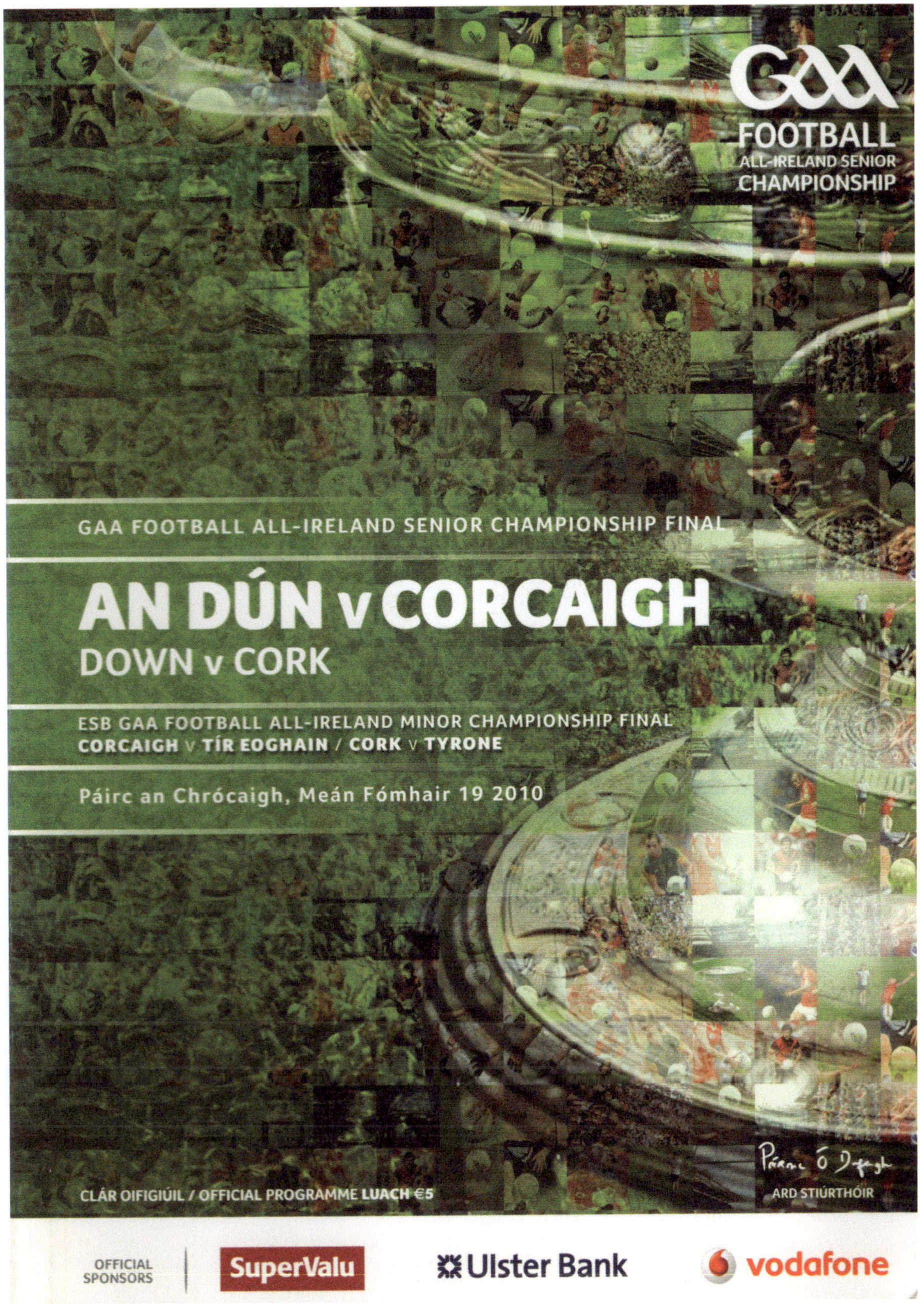

6 Connacht Football Final
Roscommon 0-14 Sligo 0-13

7 Leinster Football Final
Meath 1-12 Louth 1-10

8 Munster Football Final
Kerry 1-17 Limerick 1-14

9 Ulster Football Final
Tyrone 1-14 Monaghan 0-07

10 All-Ireland Football Final
Cork 0-16 Down 0-15
Attendance – 81,604

2011

Tipperary entered the 2011 All-Ireland hurling final as favourites to retain the title for the first time in 46 years. However, twelve months after their five-in-a-row dream had been crushed, Kilkenny exacted their retribution by inflicting a four-point defeat on their neighbours. A Man of the Match performance by Tommy Walsh, and 1-01 from Richie Hogan, were central to Kilkenny's victory.

In the All-Ireland football final, Kerry and Dublin opened a new chapter in their storied rivalry. With time running out and Kerry seemingly cruising to their thirty-seventh title, Dublin scored a goal and three points in the last seven minutes of the match to deny Kerry victory. Goalkeeper Stephen Cluxton's late free into the Hill 16 end clinched the win as Pat Gilroy managed Dublin to a first win since 1995.

1

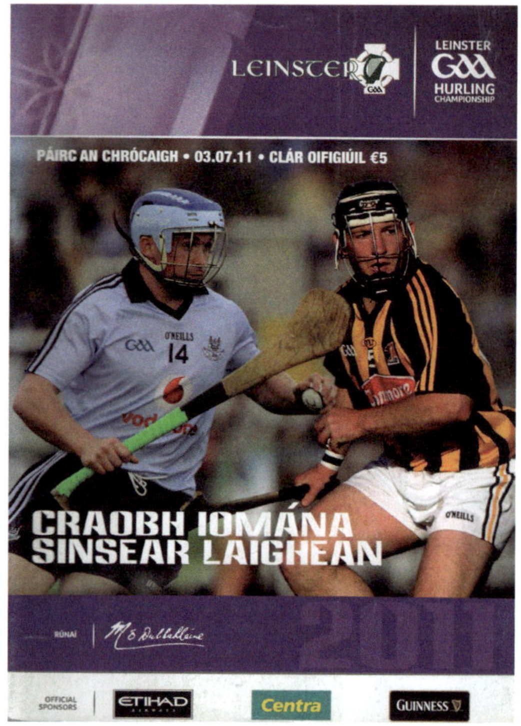

2

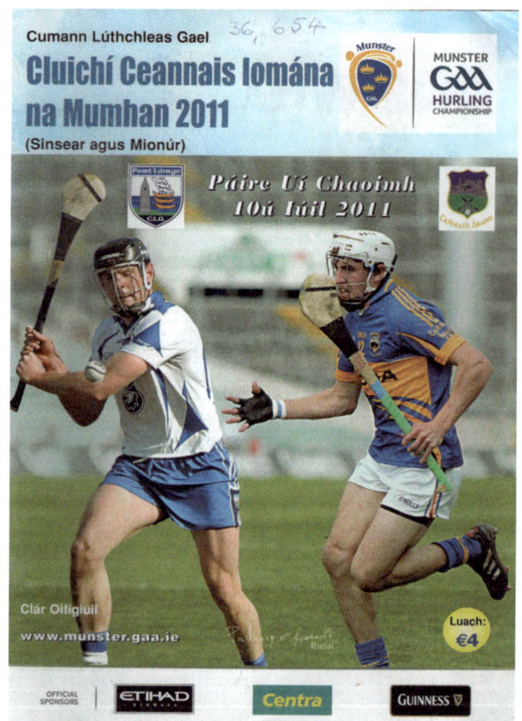

1 Leinster Hurling Final
Kilkenny 4-17 Dublin 1-15

2 Munster Hurling Final
Tipperary 7-19 Waterford 0-19

3 Ulster Hurling Final
Antrim 2-20 Armagh 2-12

Cluichí Ceannais Iomána Uladh

Ulster GAA Senior Hurling Championship Final 2011

3ú Iúil 2011 | Aontroim v Ard Mhacha | Pairc Mhic Ásmaint

4

5

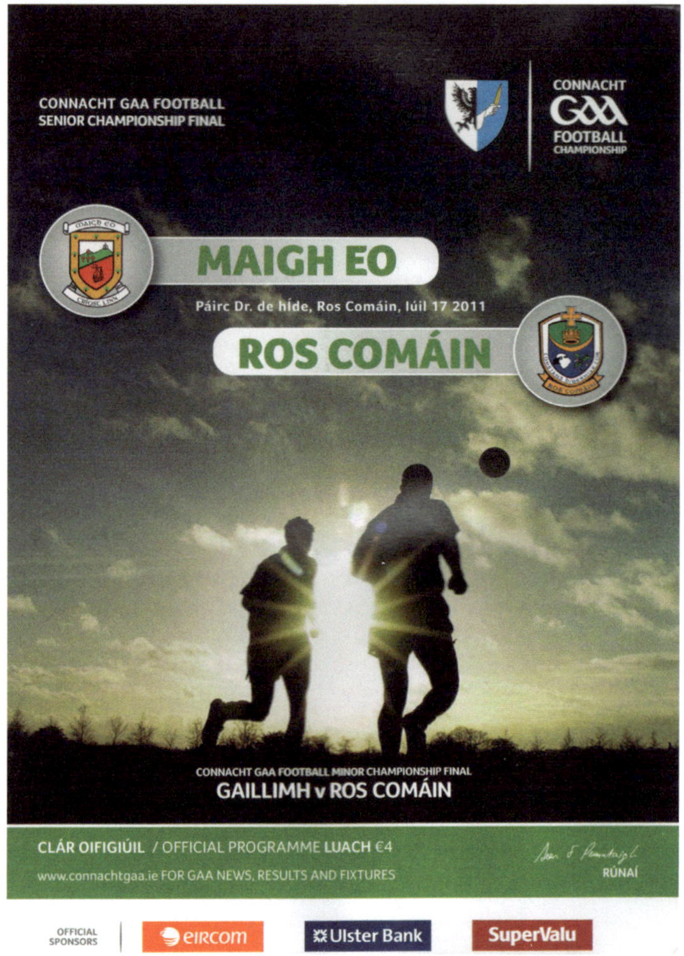

4 All-Ireland Hurling Final
Kilkenny 2-17 Tipperary 1-16
Attendance – 81,214

5 Connacht Football Final
Mayo 0-13 Roscommon 0-11

6 Leinster Football Final
Dublin 2-12 Wexford 1-12

7 Munster Football Final
Kerry 1-15 Cork 1-12

8 Ulster Football Final
Donegal 1-11 Derry 0-08

9 All-Ireland Football Final
Dublin 1-12 Kerry 1-11
Attendance – 82,300

6

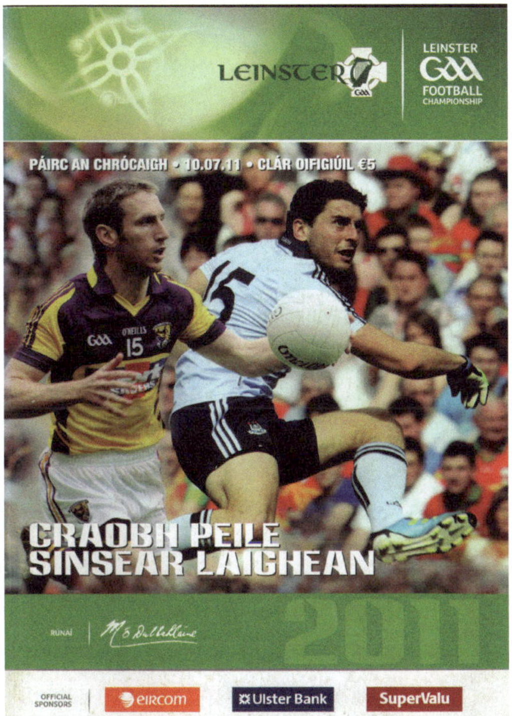
LEINSTER
LEINSTER GAA FOOTBALL CHAMPIONSHIP
PÁIRC AN CHRÓCAIGH • 10.07.11 • CLÁR OIFIGIÚIL €5
CRAOBH PEILE SINSEAR LAIGHEAN
2011
OFFICIAL SPONSORS
eircom
Ulster Bank
SuperValu

7

GAA
Craobh Peil na Mumhan 2011 Cluiche Ceannais Mionúir
Corcaigh v Tiobráid Arann
Craobh Peil na Mumhan 2011 Cluiche Ceannais
Ciarraí v Corcaigh
SINSEAR
Stáid an Ghearaltaigh, Cill Áirne
3ú Iúil 2011
Clár Oifigiúil Luach €3.00
www.munster.gaa.ie
MUNSTER GAA FOOTBALL CHAMPIONSHIP
eircom
Ulster Bank
SuperValu
OFFICIAL SPONSORS

8

CLUICHE CEANNAIS PEILE ULADH
ULSTER GAA SENIOR FOOTBALL CHAMPIONSHIP FINAL 2011
ULSTER GAA MINOR FOOTBALL CHAMPIONSHIP FINAL
DÚN NA NGALL
LAND OF THE GIANTS
€5/£4
OFFICIAL SPONSORS
eircom
Ulster Bank
SuperValu

9

GAA FOOTBALL ALL-IRELAND SENIOR CHAMPIONSHIP
GAA FOOTBALL ALL-IRELAND SENIOR CHAMPIONSHIP FINAL
ÁTH CLIATH
v
CIARRAÍ
DUBLIN v KERRY
GAA FOOTBALL ALL-IRELAND MINOR CHAMPIONSHIP FINAL
ÁTH CLIATH v TIOBRAID ÁRANN / DUBLIN v TIPPERARY
Páirc an Chrócaigh, Meán Fómhair 18 2011
CLÁR OIFIGIÚIL / OFFICIAL PROGRAMME LUACH €5
ARD STIÚRTHÓIR
OFFICIAL SPONSORS
eircom
Ulster Bank
SuperValu

2012

Dublin, the reigning All-Ireland football champions, surrendered their crown at the semi-final stage of the All-Ireland series as Mayo claimed a famous victory. Jim McGuinness was now in his second year as manager of Donegal. He guided his team to consecutive Ulster titles en route to qualifying for the All-Ireland final, after beating Cork in the semi-final. In the All-Ireland final, early goals from the Donegal captain, Michael Murphy, and Colm McFadden, left Mayo struggling to regain parity. Ultimately it proved too much, and Donegal won their second All-Ireland championship.

The All-Ireland hurling final ended in a draw for the first time since 1959, with controversy surrounding a Kilkenny point and a late Galway free. In the replay, Kilkenny's experience showed, and they had 11 points to spare at the end. Galway's Joe Canning and Kilkenny's Henry Shefflin both scored nine points, and Shefflin entered the record books as the first hurler to win nine All-Ireland medals on the field of play.

1

1 Connacht Football Final
Mayo 0-12 Sligo 0-10

2 Leinster Football Final
Dublin 2-13 Meath 1-13

3 Munster Football Final
Cork 3-16 Clare 0-13

4 Ulster Football Final
Donegal 2-18 Down 0-13

5 All-Ireland Football Final
Donegal 2-11 Mayo 0-13
Attendance – 82,269

2

LEINSTER
LEINSTER GAA FOOTBALL CHAMPIONSHIP
PÁIRC AN CHRÓCAIGH • 22.07.12 • CLÁR OIFIGIÚIL €5
CLUICHÍ CHEANNAIS PEILE LAIGHEAN
RÚNAÍ
2012
OFFICIAL SPONSORS
eircom
Ulster Bank
SuperValu

3

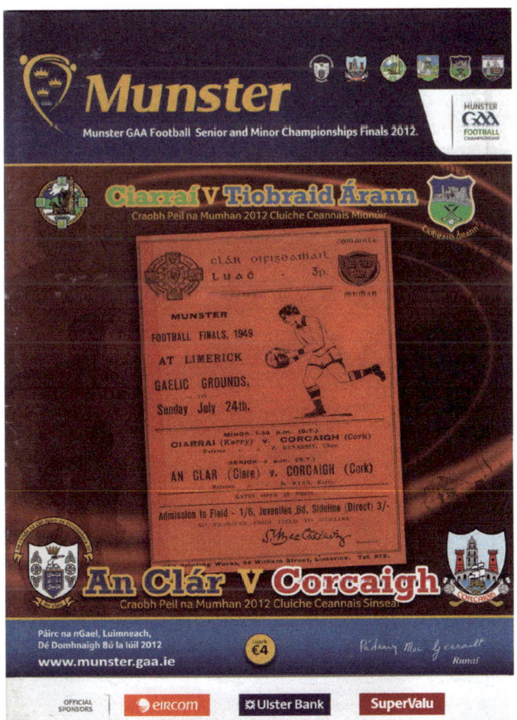
Munster
Munster GAA Football Senior and Minor Championships Finals 2012.
MUNSTER GAA FOOTBALL CHAMPIONSHIP
Ciarraí V Tiobraid Árann
Craobh Peil na Mumhan 2012 Cluiche Ceannais Mionúir
CLÁR OIFIGEAMAIL
LUAĊ - 3p.
MUNSTER
FOOTBALL FINALS, 1949
AT LIMERICK
GAELIC GROUNDS,
Sunday July 24th.
CIARRAÍ (Kerry) v. CORCAIGH (Cork)
AN CLÁR (Clare) v. CORCAIGH (Cork)
Admission to Field - 1/6, Juveniles 6d, Sideline (Direct) 3/-
An Clár V Corcaigh
Craobh Peil na Mumhan 2012 Cluiche Ceannais Sinsear
Páirc na nGael, Luimneach,
Dé Domhnaigh 8ú la Iúil 2012
www.munster.gaa.ie
€4
Rúnaí
OFFICIAL SPONSORS
eircom
Ulster Bank
SuperValu

4

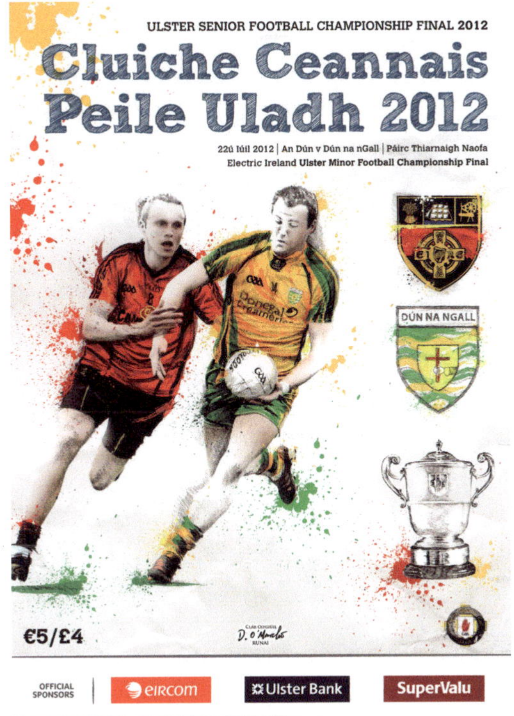
ULSTER SENIOR FOOTBALL CHAMPIONSHIP FINAL 2012
Cluiche Ceannais
Peile Uladh 2012
22ú Iúil 2012 | An Dún v Dún na nGall | Páirc Thiarnaigh Naofa
Electric Ireland Ulster Minor Football Championship Final
DÚN NA NGALL
€5/£4
RÚNAÍ
OFFICIAL SPONSORS
eircom
Ulster Bank
SuperValu

5

GAA FOOTBALL ALL-IRELAND SENIOR CHAMPIONSHIP
GAA FOOTBALL ALL-IRELAND SENIOR CHAMPIONSHIP FINAL
DÚN NA NGALL v MAIGH EO
DONEGAL v MAYO
ELECTRIC IRELAND GAA FOOTBALL ALL-IRELAND MINOR CHAMPIONSHIP FINAL
AN MHÍ v ÁTH CLIATH / MEATH v DUBLIN
Páirc an Chrócaigh, Meán Fómhair 23 2012
CLÁR OIFIGIÚIL / OFFICIAL PROGRAMME LUACH €5
www.gaa.ie FOR GAA NEWS, VIDEOS AND FIXTURES
ARD STIÚRTHÓIR
OFFICIAL SPONSORS
eircom
Ulster Bank
SuperValu

6

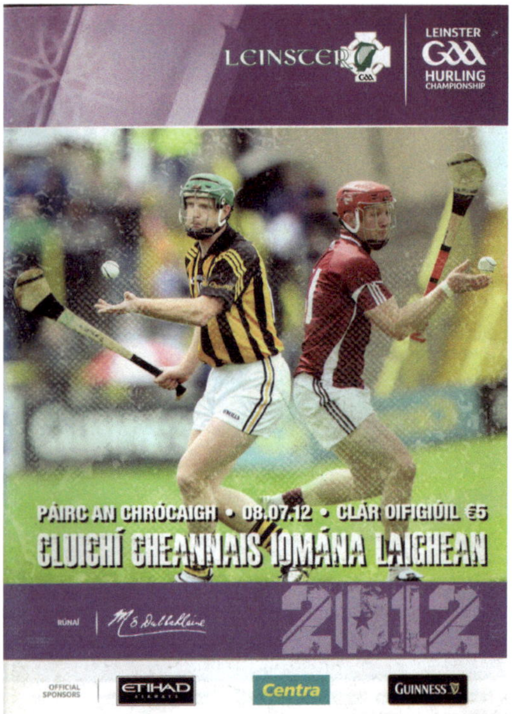
LEINSTER
LEINSTER GAA HURLING CHAMPIONSHIP
PÁIRC AN CHRÓCAIGH • 08.07.12 • CLÁR OIFIGIÚIL €5
CLUICHÍ CHEANNAIS IOMÁNA LAIGHEAN
2012
OFFICIAL SPONSORS
ETIHAD
Centra
GUINNESS

8

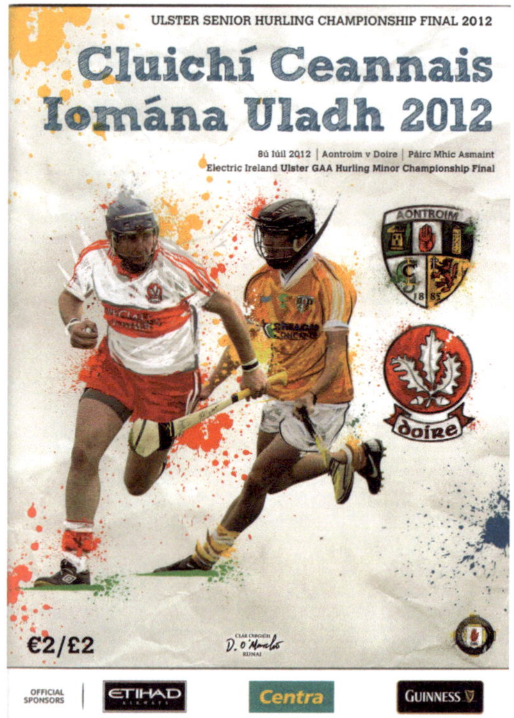
ULSTER SENIOR HURLING CHAMPIONSHIP FINAL 2012
Cluichí Ceannais Iomána Uladh 2012
8ú Iúil 2012 | Aontroim v Doire | Páirc Mhic Asmaint
Electric Ireland Ulster GAA Hurling Minor Championship Final
AONTROIM
Doire
€2/£2
OFFICIAL SPONSORS
ETIHAD
Centra
GUINNESS

7

Cumann Lúthchleas Gael
Cluichí Ceannais Iomána na Mumhan 2012
(Sinsir agus Mionúir)
Munster
MUNSTER GAA HURLING CHAMPIONSHIP
Páirc Uí Chaoimh, Corcaigh
15ú Iúil
Rúnaí
Clár Oifigiúil
www.munster.gaa.ie
Luach: €4
OFFICIAL SPONSORS
ETIHAD
Centra
GUINNESS

9

GAA HURLING ALL-IRELAND SENIOR CHAMPIONSHIP
GAA HURLING ALL-IRELAND SENIOR CHAMPIONSHIP FINAL
CILL CHAINNIGH v GAILLIMH
KILKENNY v GALWAY
ELECTRIC IRELAND GAA HURLING ALL-IRELAND MINOR CHAMPIONSHIP FINAL
ÁTH CLIATH v TIOBRAID ÁRANN / DUBLIN v TIPPERARY
Páirc an Chrócaigh, Meán Fómhair 9 2012
CLÁR OIFIGIÚIL / OFFICIAL PROGRAMME LUACH €5
www.gaa.ie FOR GAA NEWS, VIDEOS AND FIXTURES
ARD STIÚRTHÓIR
OFFICIAL SPONSORS
ETIHAD
Centra
GUINNESS

10

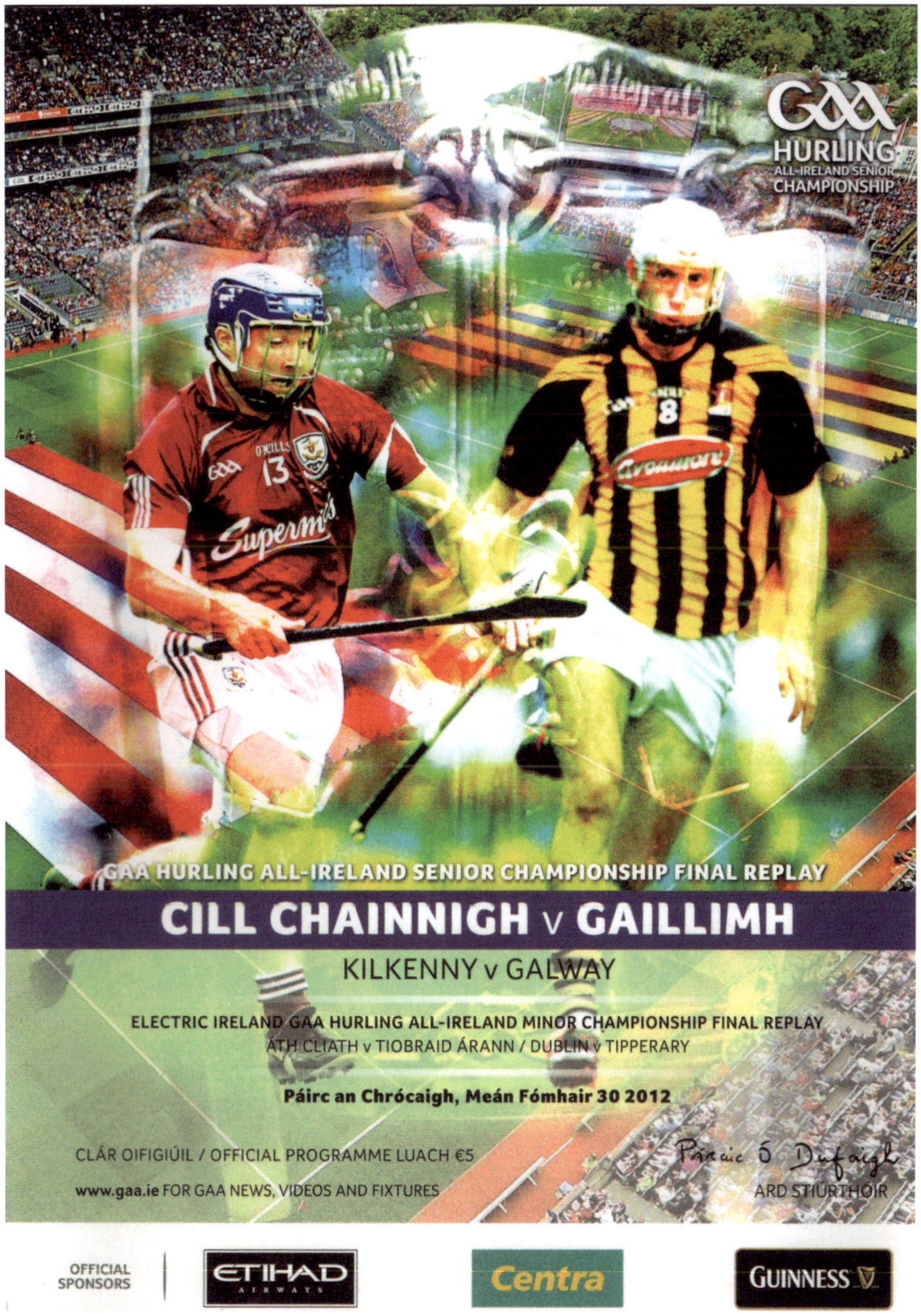

6 Leinster Hurling Final
Galway 2-21 Kilkenny 2-11

7 Munster Hurling Final
Tipperary 2-17 Waterford 0-16

8 Ulster Hurling Final
Antrim 3-18 Derry 0-09

9 All-Ireland Hurling Final
Kilkenny 0-19 Galway 2-13
Attendance – 81,932

10 Replay
Kilkenny 3-22 Galway 3-11
Attendance – 82,274

2013

In 2013, Hawkeye began to be used in Croke Park to assist match officials with accurate score detection. It was first used during the Kildare v Offaly Leinster football championship match when Offaly's Peter Cunningham had his attempt at a point deemed to be a 'Miss'. Later, 'Níl' became the term used to describe a wide. This year also saw the first Friday night championship match when Carlow played Laois in a football qualifier in Dr Cullen Park.

The Ulster football championship match between Monaghan and Antrim in June was the last time that Casement Park in Belfast hosted Gaelic games. The ground was due to be redeveloped into a more modern stadium but, over a decade later, work on the site has yet to begin. In the Connacht football championship, London defeated Sligo in the quarter-final, and Leitrim in the semi-final, to reach their first-ever Connacht final. They were outclassed in the final as Mayo recorded their third of five provincial titles in a row.

1

1 Connacht Football Final
Mayo 5-11 London 0-10

2 Leinster Football Final
Dublin 2-15 Meath 0-14

3 Munster Football Final
Kerry 1-16 Cork 0-17

4 Ulster Football Final
Monaghan 0-13 Donegal 0-07

5 All-Ireland Football Final
Dublin 2-12 Mayo 1-14
Attendance – 82,274

2

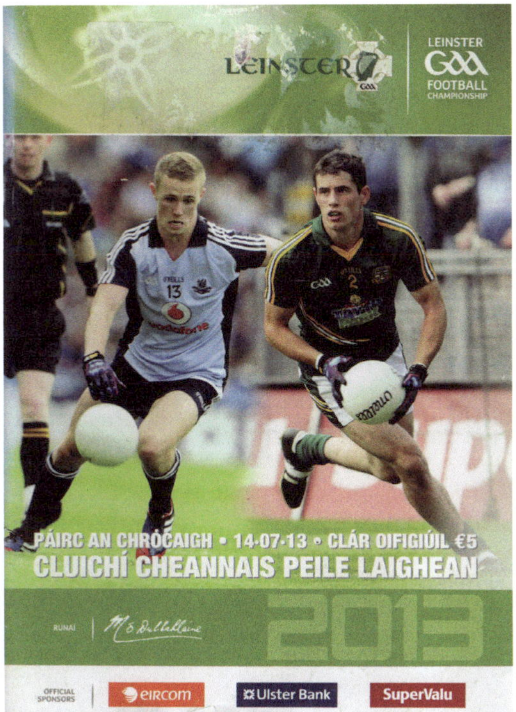
LEINSTER GAA FOOTBALL CHAMPIONSHIP
PÁIRC AN CHRÓCAIGH • 14-07-13 • CLÁR OIFIGIÚIL €5
CLUICHÍ CHEANNAIS PEILE LAIGHEAN
2013
OFFICIAL SPONSORS
eircom
Ulster Bank
SuperValu

3

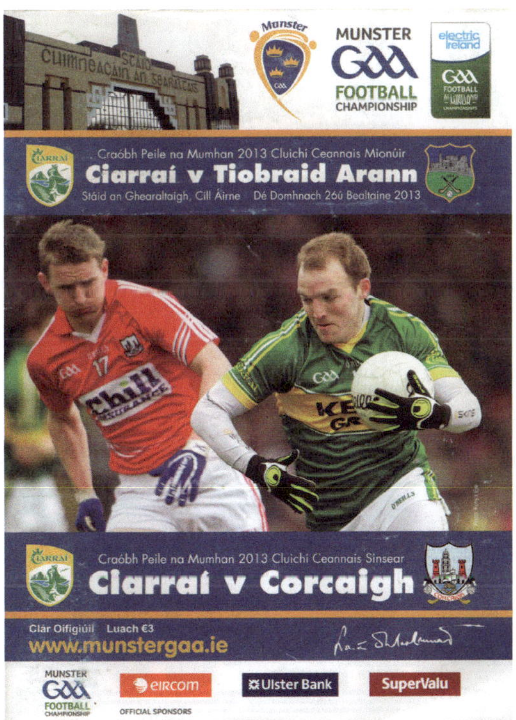
MUNSTER GAA FOOTBALL CHAMPIONSHIP
Craobh Peile na Mumhan 2013 Cluichí Ceannais Mionúir
Ciarraí v Tiobraid Árann
Stáid an Ghearaltaigh, Cill Áirne Dé Domhnach 26ú Bealtaine 2013
Craobh Peile na Mumhan 2013 Cluichí Ceannais Sinsear
Ciarraí v Corcaigh
Clár Oifigiúil Luach €3
www.munstergaa.ie
eircom
Ulster Bank
SuperValu
OFFICIAL SPONSORS

4

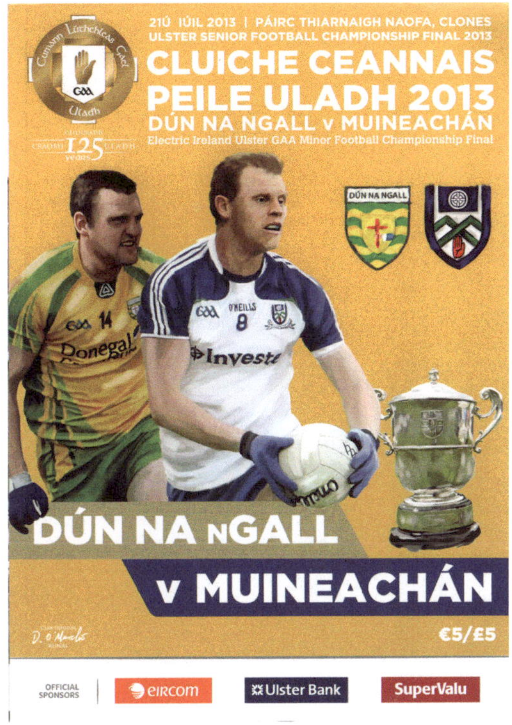
21Ú IÚIL 2013 | PÁIRC THIARNAIGH NAOFA, CLONES
ULSTER SENIOR FOOTBALL CHAMPIONSHIP FINAL 2013
CLUICHE CEANNAIS PEILE ULADH 2013
DÚN NA NGALL v MUINEACHÁN
Electric Ireland Ulster GAA Minor Football Championship Final
DÚN NA nGALL
v MUINEACHÁN
€5/£5
OFFICIAL SPONSORS
eircom
Ulster Bank
SuperValu

5

GAA
FOOTBALL
ALL-IRELAND SENIOR CHAMPIONSHIP
Electric Ireland GAA Football All-Ireland Minor Championship
Finals 2013
Páirc an Chrócaigh
Meán Fómhair 22

6

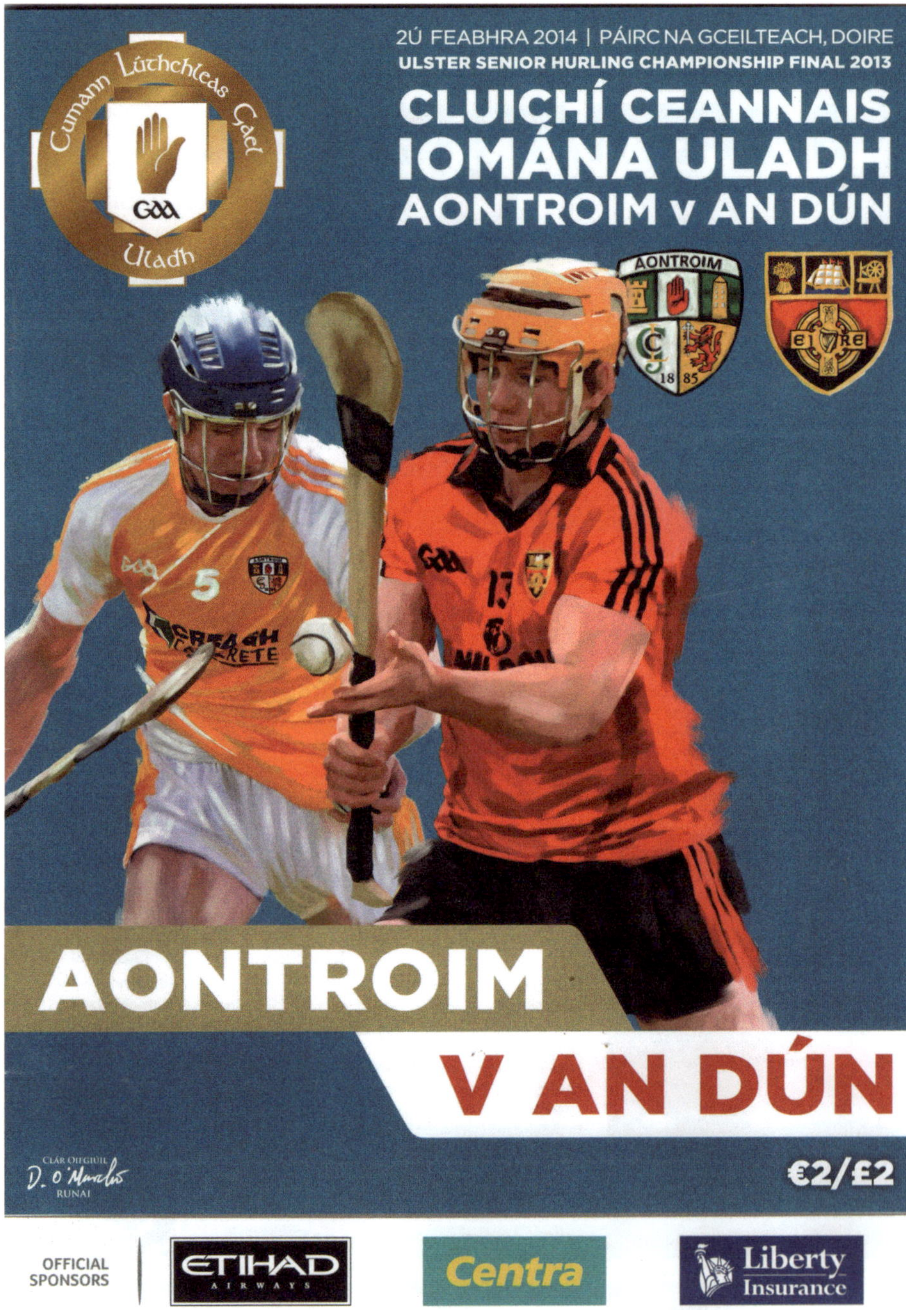

6 Ulster Hurling Final
Antrim 4-21 Down 1-17

7 Munster Hurling Final
Limerick 0-24 Cork 0-15

8 Leinster Hurling Final
Dublin 2-25 Galway 2-13

9 All-Ireland Hurling Final
Clare 0-25 Cork 3-16
Attendance – 81,651

10 Replay
Clare 5-16 Cork 3-16
Attendance – 82,276

7

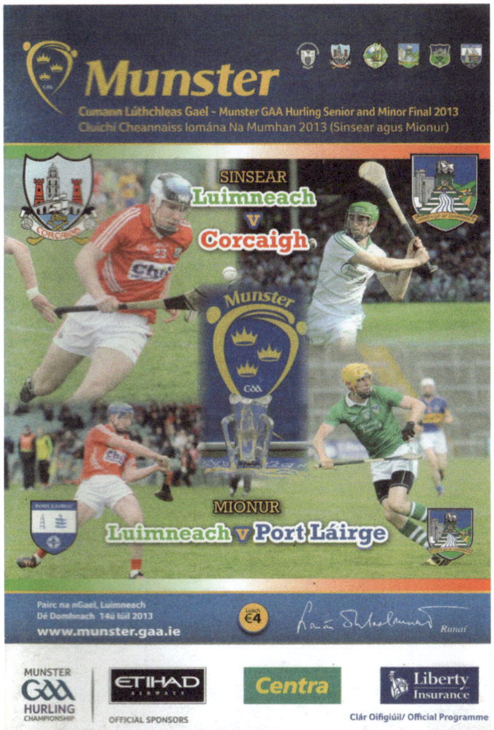
Munster
Cumann Lúthchleas Gael - Munster GAA Hurling Senior and Minor Final 2013
Cluichí Cheannaiss Iomána Na Mumhan 2013 (Sinsear agus Mionur)
SINSEAR
Luimneach
v
Corcaigh
MIONUR
Luimneach v Port Láirge
www.munster.gaa.ie
€4
Rúnaí
MUNSTER
GAA
HURLING
CHAMPIONSHIP
ETIHAD
OFFICIAL SPONSORS
Centra
Liberty Insurance
Clár Oifigiúil/ Official Programme

8

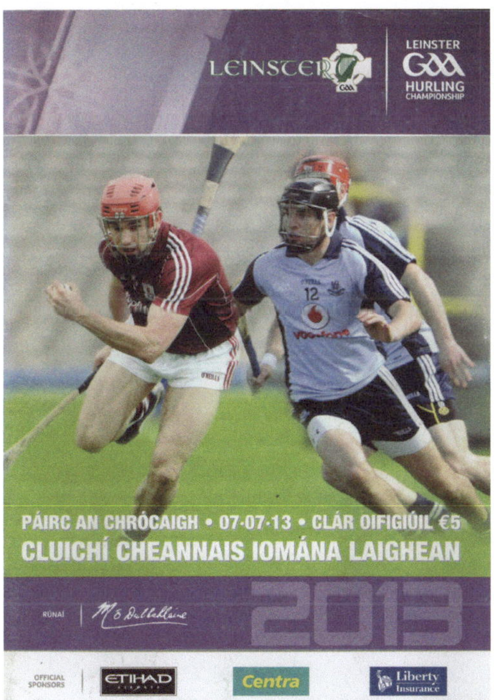
LEINSTER
LEINSTER
GAA
HURLING
CHAMPIONSHIP
PÁIRC AN CHRÓCAIGH • 07-07-13 • CLÁR OIFIGIÚIL €5
CLUICHÍ CHEANNAIS IOMÁNA LAIGHEAN
RÚNAÍ
2013
OFFICIAL SPONSORS
ETIHAD
Centra
Liberty Insurance

9

GAA
HURLING
ALL-IRELAND SENIOR
CHAMPIONSHIP
Electric Ireland GAA Hurling
All-Ireland Minor Championship
Finals 2013
Páirc an Chrócaigh
Meán Fómhair 8

10

GAA
HURLING
ALL-IRELAND SENIOR
CHAMPIONSHIP
Final 2013
REPLAY
Páirc an Chrócaigh
Meán Fómhair 28
OFFICIAL SPONSORS
ETIHAD
Centra
Liberty Insurance

2014

The All-Ireland hurling final had a familiar look to it in 2014 as Kilkenny and Tipperary faced each other for the fourth time since 2009. A high-scoring game saw the teams level as the match entered added time. Tipperary were then awarded a long-range free, which was taken by John 'Bubbles' O'Dwyer. His shot looked to have gone over the bar, but the umpire signalled for Hawkeye, which showed that the sliotar had gone fractionally wide. Referee Barry Kelly blew the final whistle, ensuring a replay would be needed to determine the All-Ireland hurling champions for the third consecutive year. Kilkenny had the edge three weeks later, as Brian Cody managed Kilkenny to the tenth title of his tenure.

The 2014 football championship saw the black card introduced for the first time to combat the cynical fouling which had crept into the sport. Donegal returned to the All-Ireland final, only to come up short against Kerry, who won their thirty-seventh title.

1

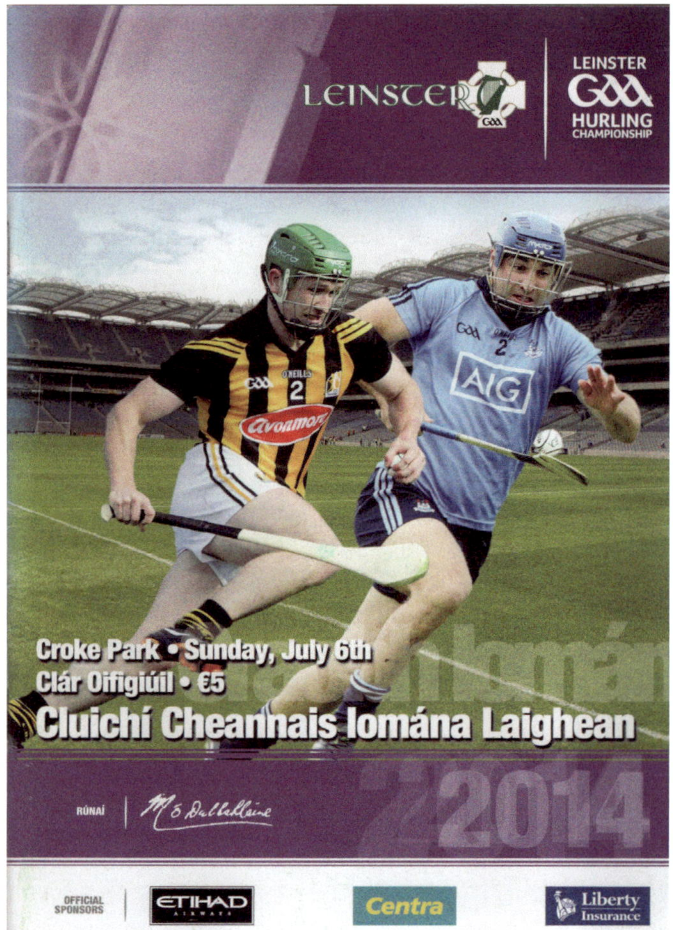

1 Leinster Hurling Final
Kilkenny 0-24 Dublin 1-09

2 Munster Hurling Final
Cork 2-24 Limerick 0-24

3 Ulster Hurling Final
Antrim 2-17 Derry 2-16

4 All-Ireland Hurling Final
Kilkenny 3-22 Tipperary 1-28
Attendance – 82,179

5 Replay
Kilkenny 2-17 Tipperary 2-14
Attendance – 81,753

2

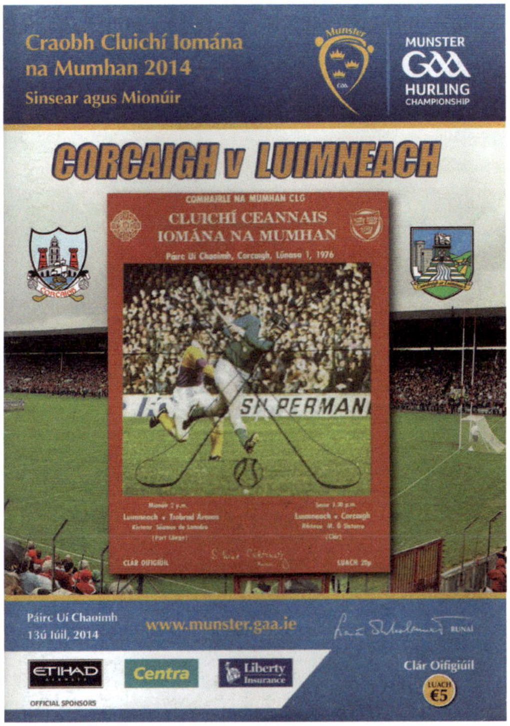
Craobh Cluichí Iomána
na Mumhan 2014
Sinsear agus Mionúir
MUNSTER
GAA
HURLING
CHAMPIONSHIP
CORCAIGH v LUIMNEACH
CLUICHÍ CEANNAIS
IOMÁNA NA MUMHAN
Páirc Uí Chaoimh
13ú Iúil, 2014
www.munster.gaa.ie
ETIHAD
Centra
Liberty Insurance
Clár Oifigiúil
LUACH €5
OFFICIAL SPONSORS

3

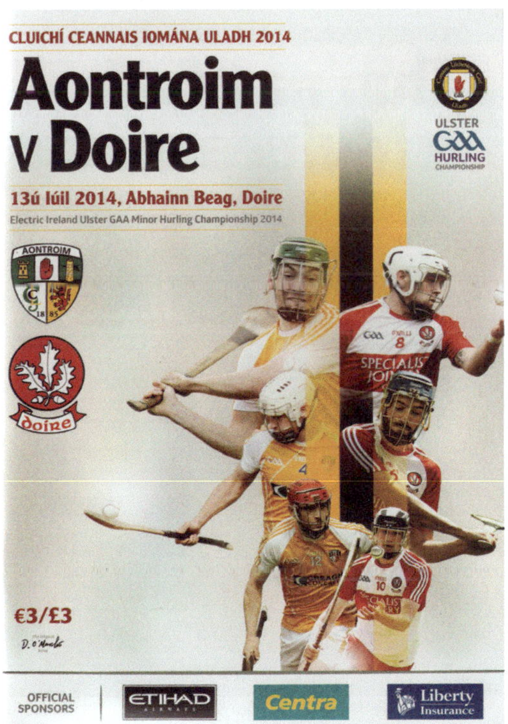
CLUICHÍ CEANNAIS IOMÁNA ULADH 2014
Aontroim
v Doire
ULSTER
GAA
HURLING
CHAMPIONSHIP
13ú Iúil 2014, Abhainn Beag, Doire
Electric Ireland Ulster GAA Minor Hurling Championship 2014
AONTROIM
Doire
€3/£3
OFFICIAL SPONSORS
ETIHAD
Centra
Liberty Insurance

4

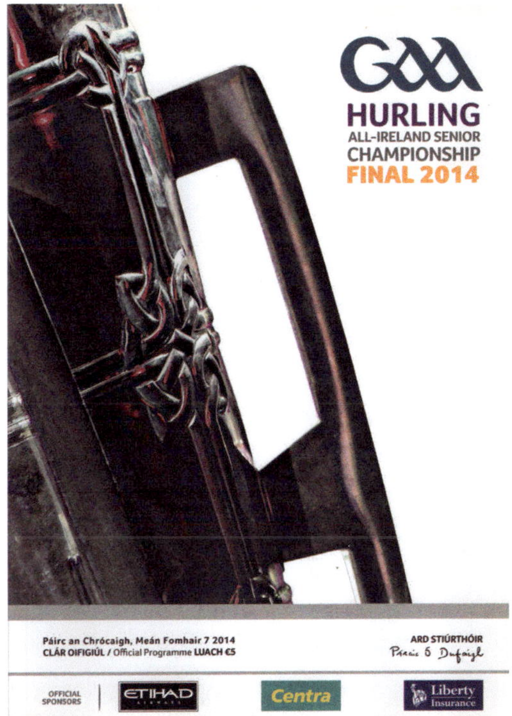
GAA
HURLING
ALL-IRELAND SENIOR
CHAMPIONSHIP
FINAL 2014
Páirc an Chrócaigh, Meán Fómhair 7 2014
CLÁR OIFIGIÚL / Official Programme LUACH €5
ARD STIÚRTHÓIR
OFFICIAL SPONSORS
ETIHAD
Centra
Liberty Insurance

5

GAA
HURLING
ALL-IRELAND SENIOR
CHAMPIONSHIP
FINAL 2014
Athimirt
Páirc an Chrócaigh, Meán Fómhair 27 2014
CLÁR OIFIGIÚL / Official Programme LUACH €5
ARD STIÚRTHÓIR
OFFICIAL SPONSORS
ETIHAD
Centra
Liberty Insurance

6

CONNACHT
GAA
FOOTBALL CHAMPIONSHIP
CONNACHT GAA FOOTBALL SENIOR CHAMPIONSHIP FINAL
GAILLIMH
v MAIGH EO
Páirc Mhic hÉil, Caisleán a'Bharraigh, Iúil 13 2014
ELECTRIC IRELAND CONNACHT GAA FOOTBALL MINOR CHAMPIONSHIP 2014 FINAL
MAIGH EO v ROS COMÁIN
Clár Oifigiúil / Official Programme LUACH €4
RÚNAÍ
OFFICIAL SPONSORS
eircom
GAAGO
SuperValu

7

LEINSTER
LEINSTER
GAA
FOOTBALL CHAMPIONSHIP
Croke Park • July 20th • Clár Oifigiúil • €5
Cluichí Cheannais Peile Laighean
RÚNAÍ
2014
OFFICIAL SPONSORS
eircom
GAAGO
SuperValu

8

Craobh Cluichí Peile
na Mumhan 2014
Sinsear agus Mionúr
MUNSTER
GAA
FOOTBALL CHAMPIONSHIP
SINSEAR: 14.00
CORCAIGH V CIARRAÍ
REFEREE: CORMAC REILLY (AN MHÍ)
MIONÚR: 12.00
CORCAIGH V CIARRAÍ
REFEREE: RICHARD MOLONEY (LUIMNEACH)
Páirc Uí Chaoimh
6ú Iúil 2014
www.munster.gaa.ie
Luach
€5
Rúnaí
Clár Oifigiúil
OFFICIAL SPONSORS
eircom
GAAGO
SuperValu

9

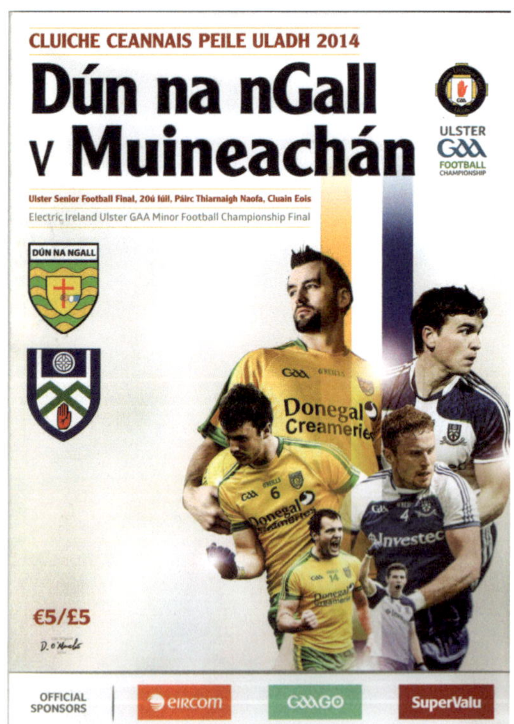

CLUICHE CEANNAIS PEILE ULADH 2014
Dún na nGall
v Muineachán
ULSTER
GAA
FOOTBALL CHAMPIONSHIP
Ulster Senior Football Final, 20ú Iúil, Páirc Thiarnaigh Naofa, Cluain Eois
Electric Ireland Ulster GAA Minor Football Championship Final
DÚN NA NGALL
€5/£5
OFFICIAL SPONSORS
eircom
GAAGO
SuperValu

10

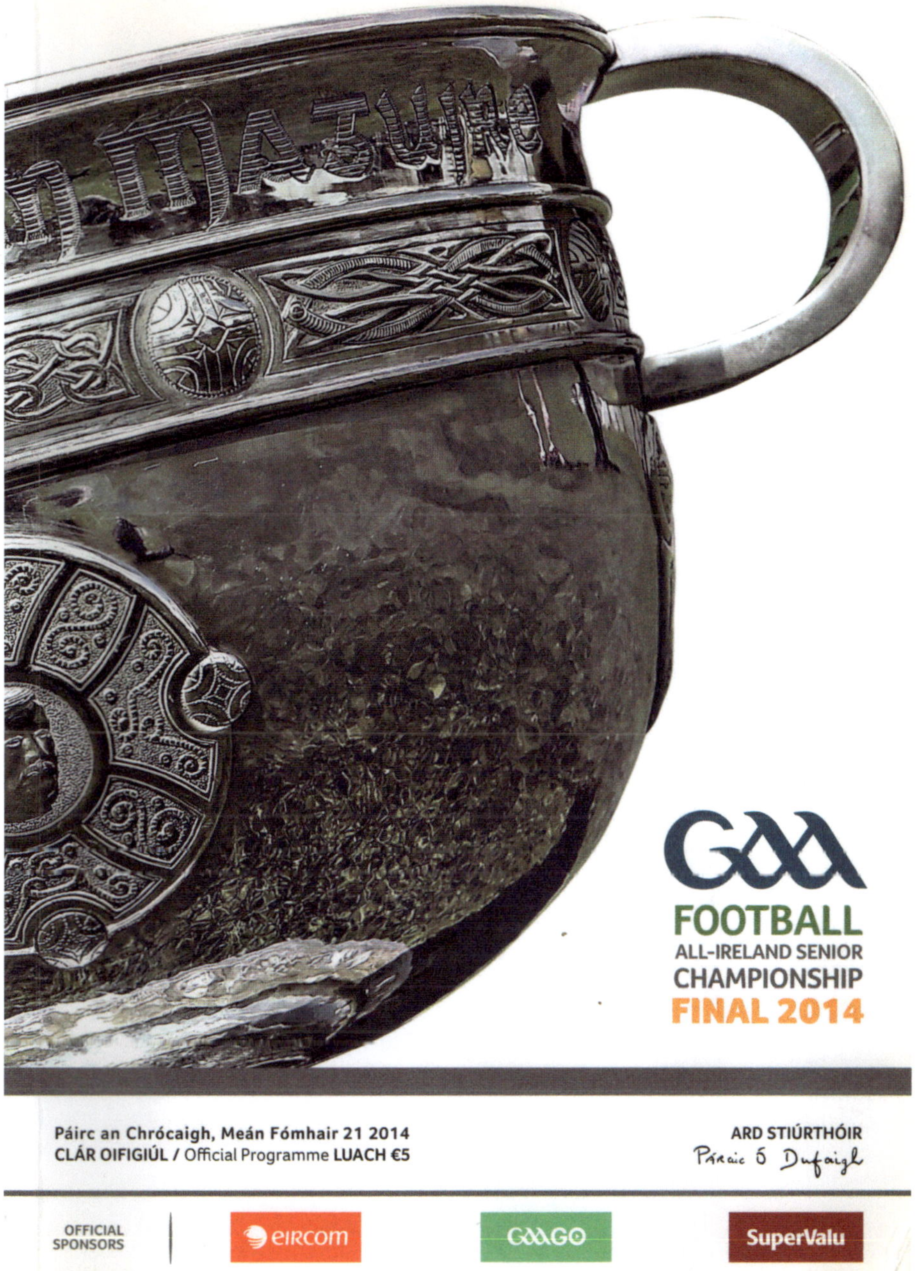

6 Connacht Football Final
Mayo 3-14 Galway 0-16

7 Leinster Football Final
Dublin 3-20 Meath 1-10

8 Munster Football Final
Kerry 0-24 Cork 0-12

9 Ulster Football Final
Donegal 0-15 Monaghan 1-09

10 All-Ireland Football Final
Kerry 2-09 Donegal 0-12
Attendance – 82,184

2015

If the Dublin and Kerry rivalry defined Gaelic football in the 1970s, another rivalry involving Dublin came to be synonymous with the 2010s. Late-season Dublin and Mayo matches became an almost annual event throughout the decade. Jim Gavin was appointed Dublin manager in late 2012 and, in his first season in charge, led Dublin to the All-Ireland title with a victory over Mayo in the 2013 final. This was the first of seven meetings between Gavin's Dublin and Mayo over the coming years. In 2015, Dublin and Mayo clashed again, this time in the All-Ireland semi-final, and a replay was required to see Dublin advance to the final, where Kerry awaited. In a low-scoring final against their old enemy, Dublin overcame the Kerry challenge by three points to take home the Sam Maguire Cup for the second time in three years.

1

1 Connacht Football Final
Mayo 6-25 Sligo 2-11

2 Leinster Football Final
Dublin 2-13 Westmeath 0-06

3 Munster Football Final
Kerry 2-15 Cork 3-12

4 Replay
Kerry 1-11 Cork 1-06

5 Ulster Football Final
Monaghan 0-11 Donegal 0-10

2

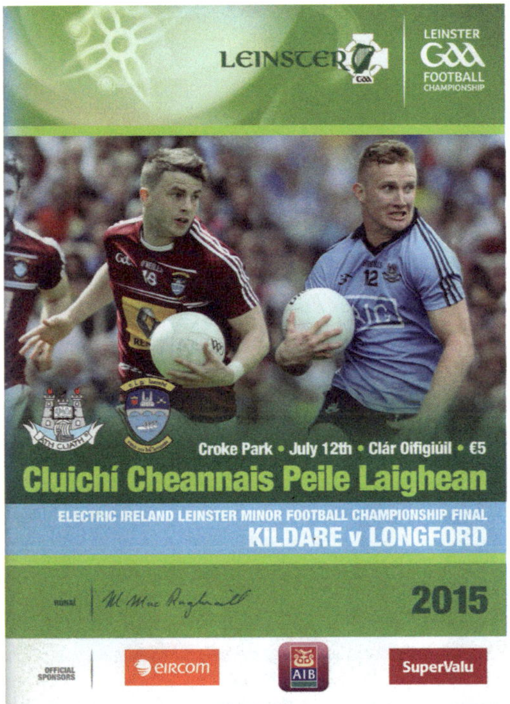
LEINSTER GAA FOOTBALL CHAMPIONSHIP
Croke Park • July 12th • Clár Oifigiúil • €5
Cluichí Cheannais Peile Laighean
ELECTRIC IRELAND LEINSTER MINOR FOOTBALL CHAMPIONSHIP FINAL
KILDARE v LONGFORD
2015
eircom
AIB
SuperValu

3

CLUICHÍ CHEANNAIS PEILE NA MUMHAN 2015
MUNSTER GAA FOOTBALL CHAMPIONSHIP
SENIOR CIARRAÍ v CORCAIGH
MINOR CIARRAÍ v TIOBRAID ÁRANN
Fitzgerald Stadium, Killarney
5ú Iúil 2015
www.munster.gaa.ie
CLÁR OIFIGIÚIL
LUACH €5
#munstergaa15
eircom
SuperValu

4

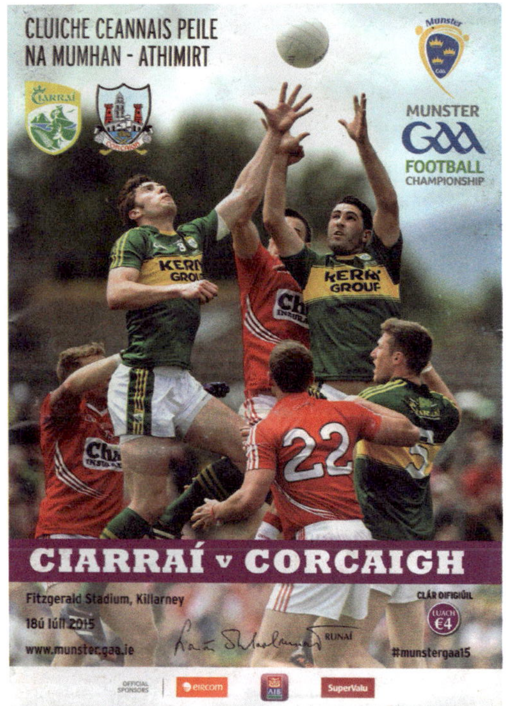
CLUICHE CEANNAIS PEILE NA MUMHAN - ATHIMIRT
MUNSTER GAA FOOTBALL CHAMPIONSHIP
CIARRAÍ v CORCAIGH
Fitzgerald Stadium, Killarney
18ú Iúil 2015
www.munster.gaa.ie
CLÁR OIFIGIÚIL
LUACH €4
#munstergaa15

5

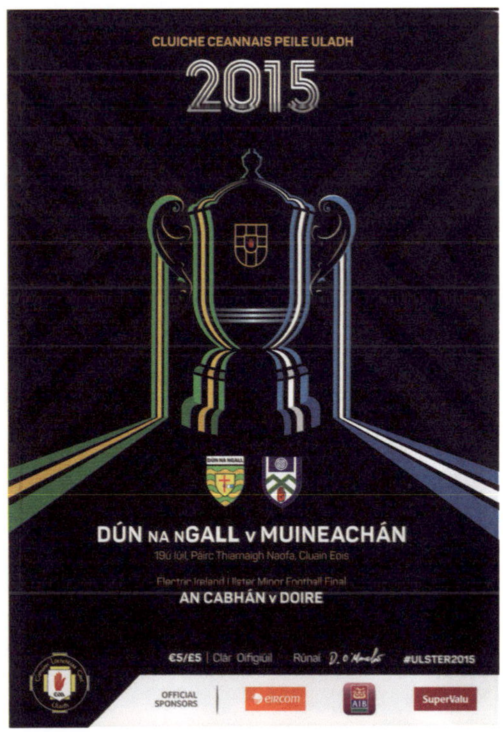
CLUICHE CEANNAIS PEILE ULADH
2015
DÚN NA NGALL v MUINEACHÁN
AN CABHÁN v DOIRE
€5/£5 | Clár Oifigiúil
Rúnaí
#ULSTER2015
OFFICIAL SPONSORS
eircom
AIB
SuperValu

6

GAA
FOOTBALL
ALL-IRELAND SENIOR
CHAMPIONSHIP
CLUICHE CEANNAIS SINSEAR PEILE NA hÉIREANN
Páirc an Chrócaigh, Meán Fómhair 20 2015
ARD STIÚRTHÓIR
SuperValu

8

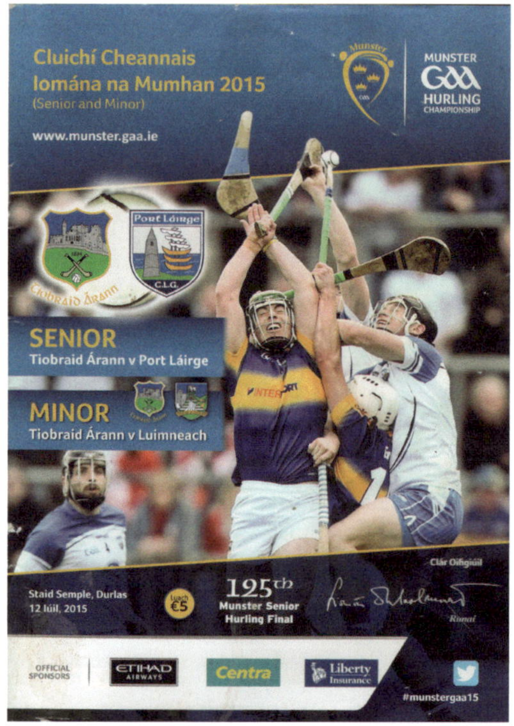
Cluichí Cheannais
Iomána na Mumhan 2015
(Senior and Minor)
www.munster.gaa.ie
MUNSTER
GAA
HURLING
CHAMPIONSHIP
SENIOR
Tiobraid Árann v Port Láirge
MINOR
Tiobraid Árann v Luimneach
Clár Oifigiúil
Staid Semple, Durlas
12 Iúil, 2015
€5
125th
Munster Senior
Hurling Final
Rúnaí
OFFICIAL SPONSORS
ETIHAD AIRWAYS
Centra
Liberty Insurance
#munstergaa15

7

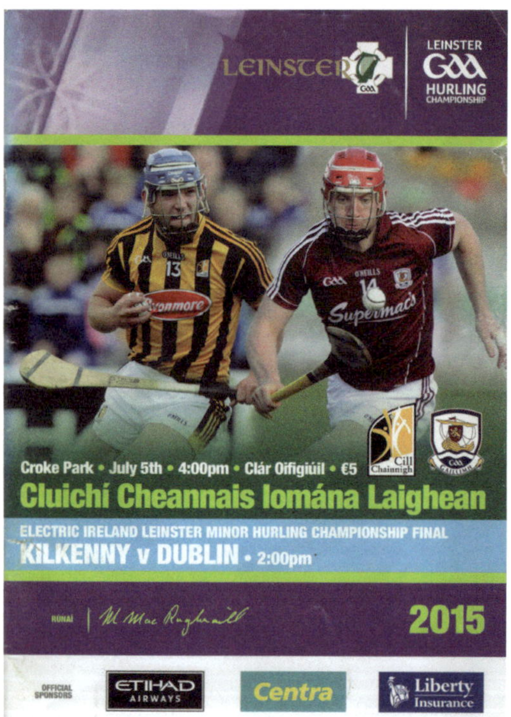
LEINSTER
LEINSTER
GAA
HURLING
CHAMPIONSHIP
Croke Park • July 5th • 4:00pm • Clár Oifigiúil • €5
Cluichí Cheannais Iomána Laighean
ELECTRIC IRELAND LEINSTER MINOR HURLING CHAMPIONSHIP FINAL
KILKENNY v DUBLIN • 2:00pm
RÚNAÍ
2015
OFFICIAL SPONSORS
ETIHAD AIRWAYS
Centra
Liberty Insurance

9

CLUICHE CEANNAIS IOMÁNA ULADH 2015
#ULSTER2015
AONTROIM
v AN DÚN
FINAL | 12Ú IÚIL | OWENBEG, DERRY | ELECTRIC IRELAND MINOR 1.30PM SENIOR 3.30PM
€3/£3 | Clár Oifigiúil Rúnaí
OFFICIAL SPONSORS
ETIHAD AIRWAYS
Centra
Liberty Insurance

10

6 All-Ireland Football Final
Dublin 0-12 Kerry 0-09
Attendance – 82,300

7 Leinster Hurling Final
Kilkenny 1-25 Galway 2-15

8 Munster Hurling Final
Tipperary 0-21 Waterford 0-16

9 Ulster Hurling Final
Antrim 1-15 Down 1-14

10 All-Ireland Hurling Final
Kilkenny 1-22 Galway 1-18
Attendance – 82,300

2016

In 2016, the covers of the All-Ireland finals programmes commemorated the centenary of the 1916 Easter Rising. The national flag occupied a central position on the cover, and the old Celtic font was reminiscent of the stye of print on the front covers of 1950s and 1960s programmes.

In the football championships, Kerry extended their dominance in Munster, defeating Tipperary in the final. Dublin racked up their sixth consecutive Leinster title, while Galway ended a period of Mayo superiority in Connacht by beating Roscommon after a replay. In Ulster, Mickey Harte guided Tyrone to their fifth title as county manager. After a replay with Mayo, Dublin retained the Sam Maguire Cup for the first time since 1977. In the hurling championships, the provincial finals were a repeat of the previous year. Tipperary eased past Waterford in the Munster final, while Kilkenny proved too strong for Galway in Leinster. In the All-Ireland final, Tipperary prevented a Kilkenny three in a row with a nine-point win.

1

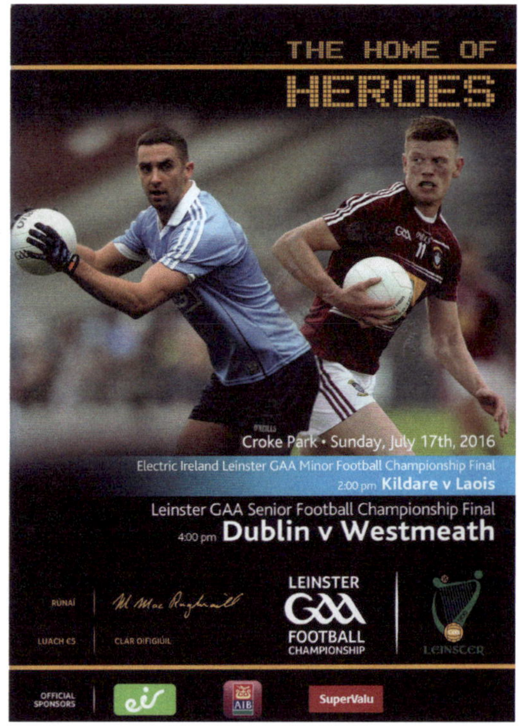

2

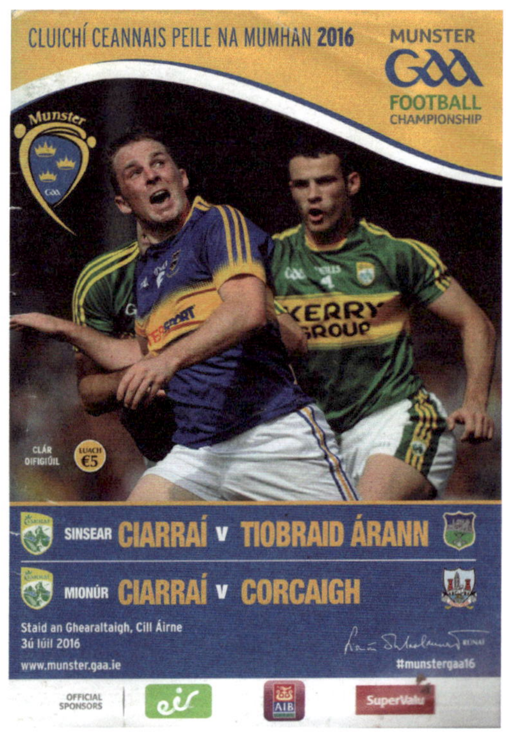

1 Leinster Football Final
Dublin 2-19 Westmeath 0-10

2 Munster Football Final
Kerry 3-17 Tipperary 2-10

3 Ulster Football Final
Tyrone 0-13 Donegal 0-11

4 All-Ireland Football Final
Dublin 2-09 Mayo 0-15
Attendance – 82,257

5 Replay
Dublin 1-15 Mayo 1-14
Attendance – 82,249

6 Leinster Hurling Final
Kilkenny 1-26 Galway 0-22

3

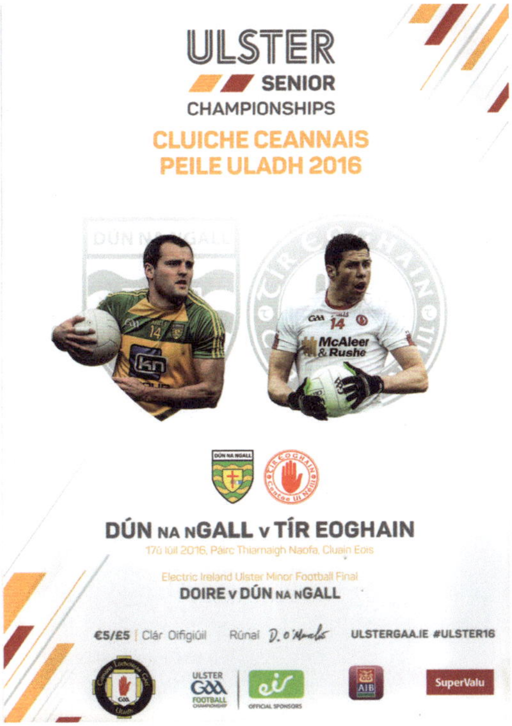
ULSTER
SENIOR
CHAMPIONSHIPS
CLUICHE CEANNAIS
PEILE ULADH 2016
DÚN NA nGALL v TÍR EOGHAIN
Electric Ireland Ulster Minor Football Final
DOIRE v DÚN NA nGALL
€5/£5 | Clár Oifigiúil
Rúnaí
ULSTERGAA.IE #ULSTER16
SuperValu

5

FOOTBALL
ALL-IRELAND SENIOR
CHAMPIONSHIP
Cluiche Ceannais
Peile na hÉireann
Athimirt
GAA FOOTBALL ALL-IRELAND
SENIOR CHAMPIONSHIP
FINAL REPLAY
Áth Cliath
v
Maigh Eo
Páirc an Chrócaigh
Deireadh Fómhair 1, 2016
CLÁR OIFIGIÚIL / OFFICIAL PROGRAMME LUACH €5
ARD STIÚRTHÓIR
OFFICIAL SPONSORS
AIB
SuperValu

4

FOOTBALL
ALL-IRELAND SENIOR
CHAMPIONSHIP
Cluiche Ceannais
Peile na hÉireann
GAA FOOTBALL ALL-IRELAND
SENIOR CHAMPIONSHIP FINAL
Áth Cliath v Maigh Eo
ELECTRIC IRELAND GAA FOOTBALL ALL-IRELAND MINOR CHAMPIONSHIP FINAL
CIARRAÍ v GAILLIMH
Páirc an Chrócaigh
Meán Fómhair 18, 2016
CLÁR OIFIGIÚIL / OFFICIAL PROGRAMME LUACH €5
ARD STIÚRTHÓIR
AIB
SuperValu

6

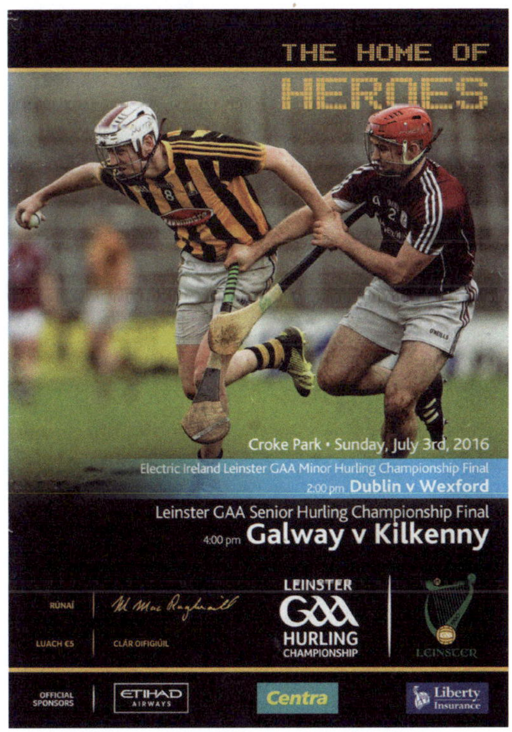
THE HOME OF
HEROES
Croke Park • Sunday, July 3rd, 2016
Electric Ireland Leinster GAA Minor Hurling Championship Final
2:00 pm Dublin v Wexford
Leinster GAA Senior Hurling Championship Final
4:00 pm Galway v Kilkenny
RÚNAÍ
LUACH €5
CLÁR OIFIGIÚIL
LEINSTER
HURLING
CHAMPIONSHIP
OFFICIAL SPONSORS
ETIHAD AIRWAYS
Centra
Liberty Insurance

7

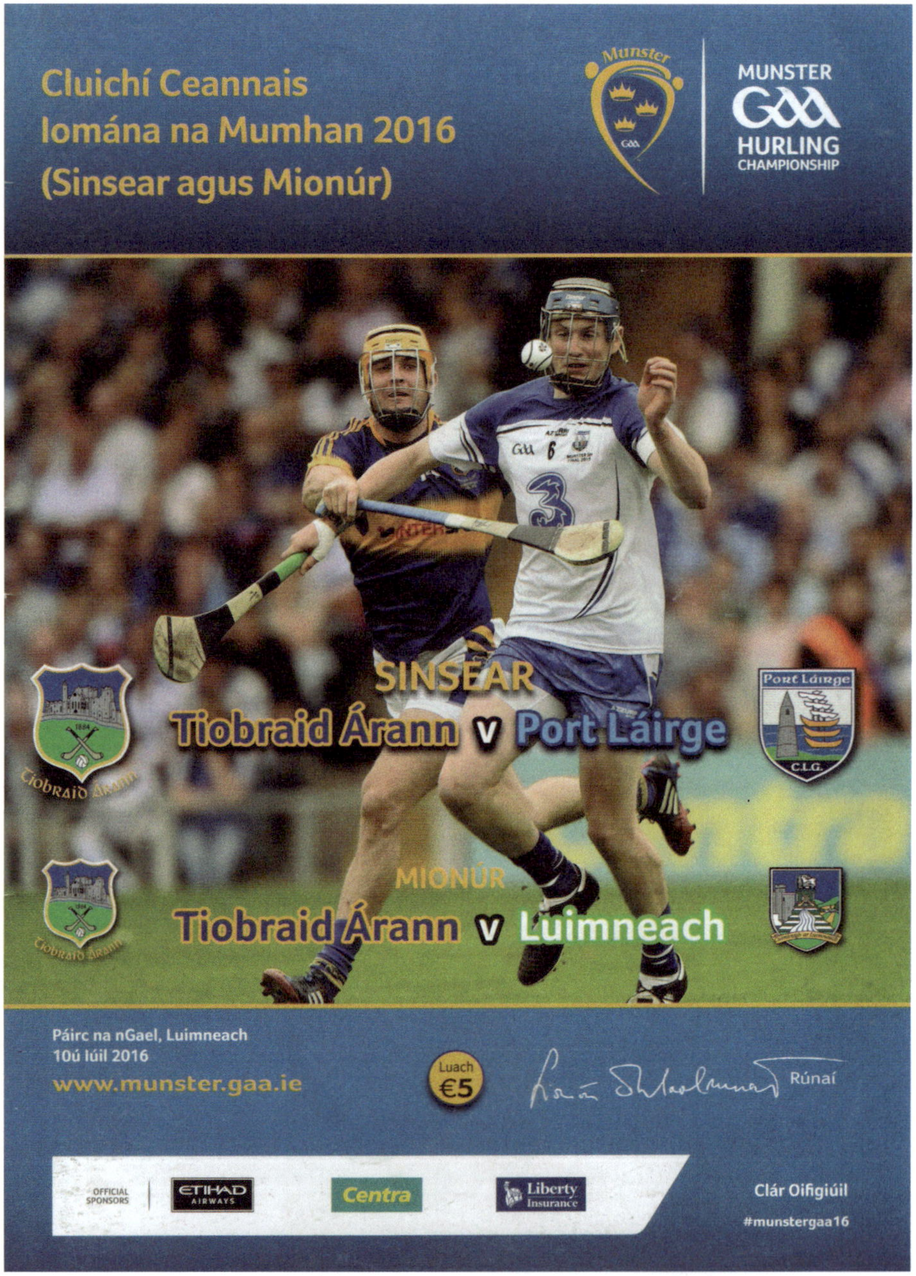

7 Munster Hurling Final
Tipperary 5-19 Waterford 0-13

8 Ulster Hurling Final
Antrim 6-21 Armagh 4-14

9 All-Ireland Hurling Final
Tipperary 2-29 Kilkenny 2-20
Attendance – 82,106

10 Connacht Football Final
Galway 0-13 Roscommon 1-10

11 Replay
Galway 3-16 Roscommon 0-14

8

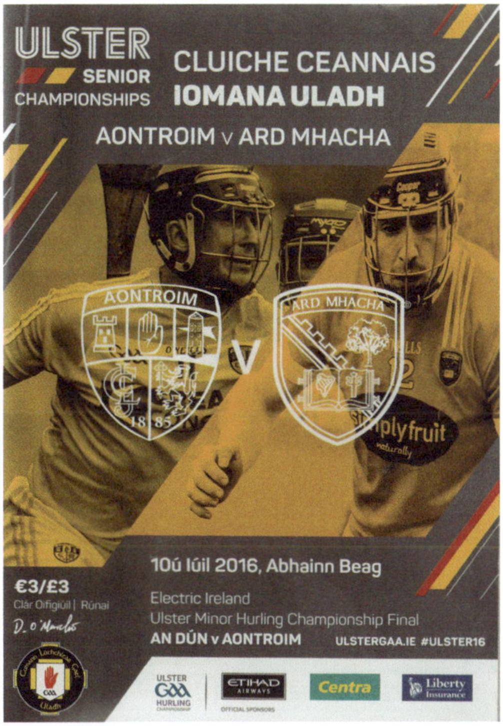
ULSTER
SENIOR
CHAMPIONSHIPS
CLUICHE CEANNAIS
IOMANA ULADH
AONTROIM v ARD MHACHA
AONTROIM
ARD MHACHA
10ú Iúil 2016, Abhainn Beag
€3/£3
Clár Oifigiúil | Rúnaí
Electric Ireland
Ulster Minor Hurling Championship Final
AN DÚN v AONTROIM
ULSTERGAA.IE #ULSTER16
Centra
Liberty Insurance

9

HURLING
CHAMPIONSHIP
Cluiche Ceannais
Iomána na hÉireann
GAA HURLING ALL-IRELAND
SENIOR CHAMPIONSHIP FINAL
Cill Chainnigh v Tiobraid Árann
ELECTRIC IRELAND GAA HURLING ALL-IRELAND MINOR CHAMPIONSHIP FINAL
LUIMNEACH v TIOBRAID ÁRANN
Páirc an Chrócaigh
Meán Fómhair 4, 2016
CLÁR OIFIGIÚIL / OFFICIAL PROGRAMME LUACH €5
ARD STIÚRTHÓIR
Centra
Liberty Insurance

10

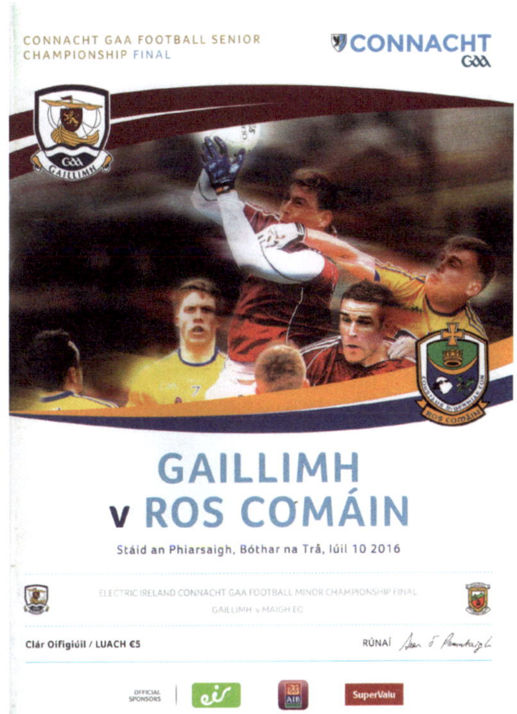
CONNACHT GAA FOOTBALL SENIOR
CHAMPIONSHIP FINAL
CONNACHT
GAILLIMH
v ROS COMÁIN
Stáid an Phiarsaigh, Bóthar na Trá, Iúil 10 2016
Clár Oifigiúil / LUACH €5
RÚNAÍ
SuperValu

11

CONNACHT GAA FOOTBALL SENIOR
CHAMPIONSHIP FINAL REPLAY
CONNACHT
GAILLIMH
v ROS COMÁIN
Páirc Elverys Mhic hÉil, Caisléan a'Bharraigh, Iúil 17 2016
Clár Oifigiúil / LUACH €5
RÚNAÍ
SuperValu

2017

Galway's Joe Canning had long been one of hurling's great players. With his club Portumna, and as an underage county hurler, he had won every honour the game had to offer apart from one – an All-Ireland senior intercounty medal. Canning suffered losses on All-Ireland final day in 2012 and 2015, but this year he finally got his hands on the coveted medal as Galway defeated Waterford in the final. Canning scored nine points in the final and was later named Hurler of the Year.

Armagh and Antrim contested the Ulster hurling final, played in Owenbeg, Co. Derry. Antrim had an easy victory in what was the last senior Ulster championship final to date. Dublin and Mayo contested one of the great All-Ireland football finals. In a nail-biting finish, Dean Rock's late free gave Dublin their third title in a row by the narrowest of margins.

1

2

1 Leinster Hurling Final
Galway 0-29 Wexford 1-17

2 Munster Hurling Final
Cork 1-25 Clare 1-20

3 Ulster Hurling Final
Antrim 5-22 Armagh 1-12

3

ULSTER GAA HURLING
FINAL 2017
Cluiche Ceannais Iomána Uladh
SENIOR HURLING CHAMPIONSHIP FINAL:
AONTROIM
18 85
ARD MHACHA
Aontroim v Ard Mhacha
SENIOR HURLING SHIELD FINAL:
doire
Tír Eoghain
Contae Uí Néill
Doire v Tír Eoghain
16ú Aibrean 2017
€2/£2 | Clár Oiguiiúil
Rúnai: Brian Mac Fhiodhai
#ULSTER2017
WWW.ULSTERGAA.IE
Bord Gáis Energy
OFFICIAL SPONSORS
Centra
Littlewoods Ireland

4

GAA
HURLING
ALL-IRELAND SENIOR
CHAMPIONSHIP
cluiche ceannais
iomána na héireann
GAA Hurling All-Ireland
Senior Championship Final
Electric Ireland GAA Hurling All-Ireland
Minor Championship Final
Meán Fómhair 3 2017
Páirc an Chrócaigh, Áth Cliath
LUACH €5
Ard Stiúrthóir
OFFICIAL SPONSORS
Bord Gáis Energy
Centra
Littlewoods Ireland

5

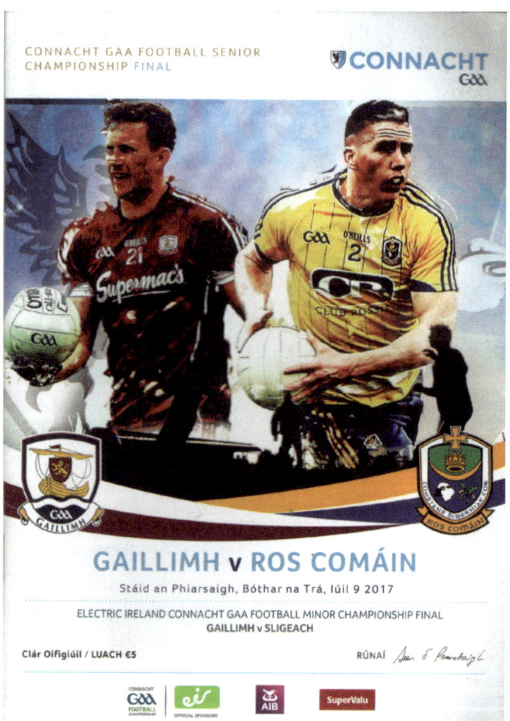
CONNACHT GAA FOOTBALL SENIOR
CHAMPIONSHIP FINAL
CONNACHT
GAA
Supermac's
GAILLIMH
ROS COMÁIN
GAILLIMH v ROS COMÁIN
Stáid an Phiarsaigh, Bóthar na Trá, Iúil 9 2017
ELECTRIC IRELAND CONNACHT GAA FOOTBALL MINOR CHAMPIONSHIP FINAL
GAILLIMH v SLIGEACH
Clár Oifigiúil / LUACH €5
RÚNAÍ
AIB
SuperValu

6

Páirc An Chrócaigh,
Áth Cliath
Leinster
LEINSTER
GAA
FOOTBALL
CHAMPIONSHIP
BRADY FAMILY
Leinster GAA Football
Senior Championship Final
Áth cliath
v
cill dara
Electric Ireland Leinster GAA Football Minor Championship Final
AN LÚ v ÁTH CLIATH
Clár Oifigiúil
LUACH €5
Iúil 16
2017
Rúnaí
OFFICIAL SPONSORS
AIB
SuperValu

7

CLUICHÍ CEANNAIS
PEILE NA MUMHAN 2017
CORCAIGH
CIARRAÍ
SINSEAR 2PM
CIARRAÍ v CORCAIGH
MIONÚR 12 NOON
CIARRAÍ v AN CLÁR
Staid an Ghearaltaigh, Cill Áirne
2ú Iúil 2017
CLÁR OIFIGIÚIL
#munstergaa17
Luach: €5
www.munster.gaa.ie
OFFICIAL SPONSORS
AIB
SuperValu

8

9

4 All-Ireland Hurling Final
Galway 0-26 Waterford 2-17
Attendance – 82,300

5 Connacht Football Final
Roscommon 2-15 Galway 0-12

6 Leinster Football Final
Dublin 2-23 Kildare 1-17

7 Munster Football Final
Kerry 1-23 Cork 0-15

8 Ulster Football Final
Tyrone 2-17 Down 0-15

9 All-Ireland Football Final
Dublin 1-17 Mayo 1-16
Attendance – 82,300

2018

Following the retirement of Páraic Duffy, Tom Ryan from Carlow was appointed to the role of Ard Stiúrthóir. He was the first Carlow man to hold the position, and his signature first appeared on the All-Ireland final match programme for the 2018 hurling final between Galway and Limerick. A new provincial hurling championship system was introduced in Munster and Leinster, with teams playing each other on a league basis and the top two qualifying for the provincial final.

Galway defeated Kilkenny in a Leinster final that required a replay to decide a winner. In the replay – a unique 'Leinster' final – a team from Connacht played a team from Leinster, in Munster, as the match took place in Thurles. Limerick, on the other hand, plotted their route to the All-Ireland final through the qualifiers, having failed to reach the Munster final. In the All-Ireland final, however, Limerick bridged a gap of 45 years to allow Declan Hannon to lift the Liam MacCarthy Cup on behalf of his team.

1

2

1 Leinster Hurling Final
Galway 0-18 Kilkenny 0-18

2 Replay
Galway 1-28 3-15 Kilkenny

3 Munster Hurling Final
Cork 2-24 Clare 3-19

CLUICHÍ CEANNAIS IOMÁNA
NA MUMHAN 2018
MUNSTER
GAA
HURLING
CHAMPIONSHIP
SINSEAR 2PM
Corcaigh -v-
An Clár
MIONÚR 11:30AM
Luimneach -v- Tiobraid Árann
Staid Semple, Dúrlas Éile
Dé Domhnaigh,
1 Iúil 2018
www.munster.gaa.ie
Clár Oifigiúil | #munstergaa18 | Luach: €5
OFFICIAL SPONSORS
Bord Gáis Energy
Centra
Littlewoods Ireland

4

5

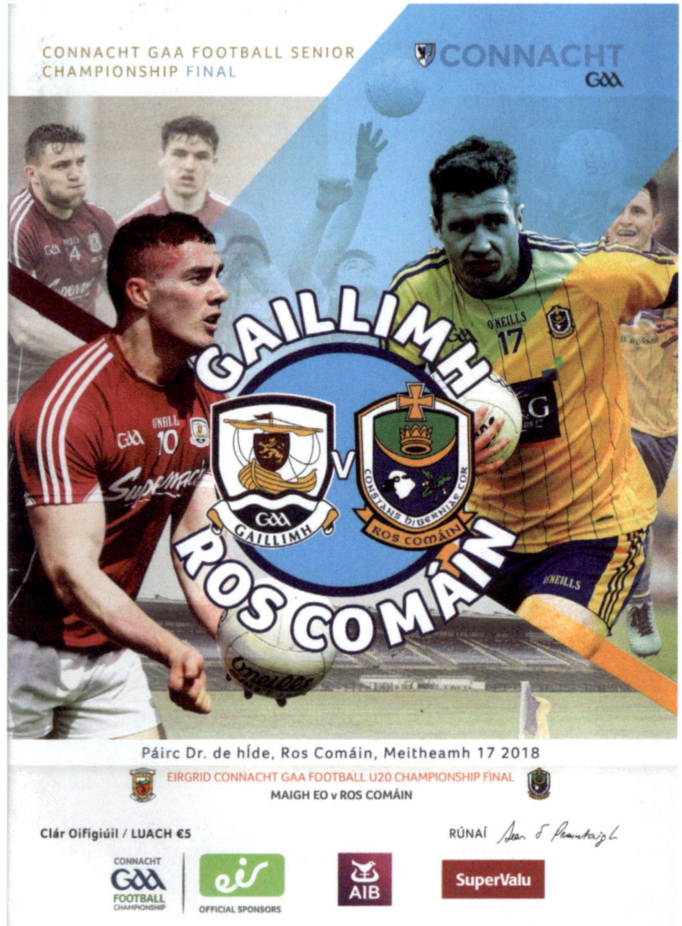

4 All-Ireland Hurling Final
Limerick 3-16 Galway 2-18
Attendance – 82,300

5 Connacht Football Final
Galway 0-16 Roscommon 2-06

6 Leinster Football Final
Dublin 1-25 Laois 0-10

7 Munster Football Final
Kerry 3-18 Cork 2-04

8 Ulster Football Final
Donegal 2-18 Fermanagh 0-12

9 All-Ireland Football Final
Dublin 2-17 Tyrone 1-14
Attendance – 82,300

6

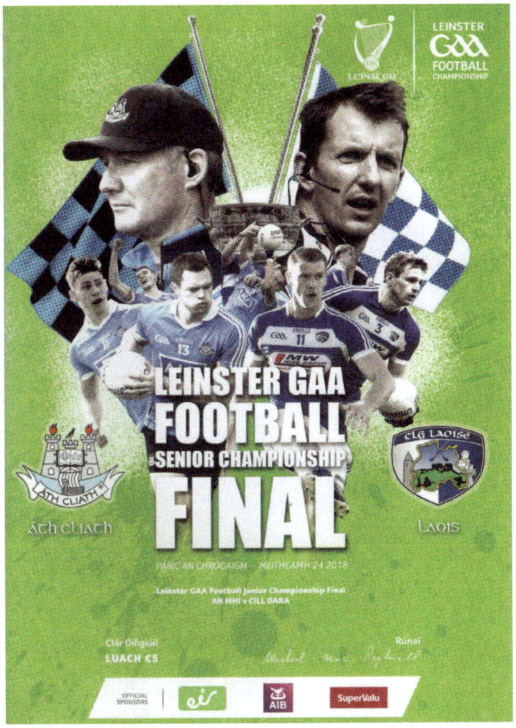
LEINSTER
GAA
FOOTBALL
CHAMPIONSHIP
LEINSTER GAA
FOOTBALL
SENIOR CHAMPIONSHIP
FINAL
ÁTH CLIATH
LAOIS
PÁIRC AN CHRÓCAIGH · MEITHEAMH 24 2018
Leinster GAA Football Junior Championship Final
AN MHI v CILL DARA
Clár Oifigiúil
LUACH €5
Rúnaí
OFFICIAL SPONSORS
AIB
SuperValu

7

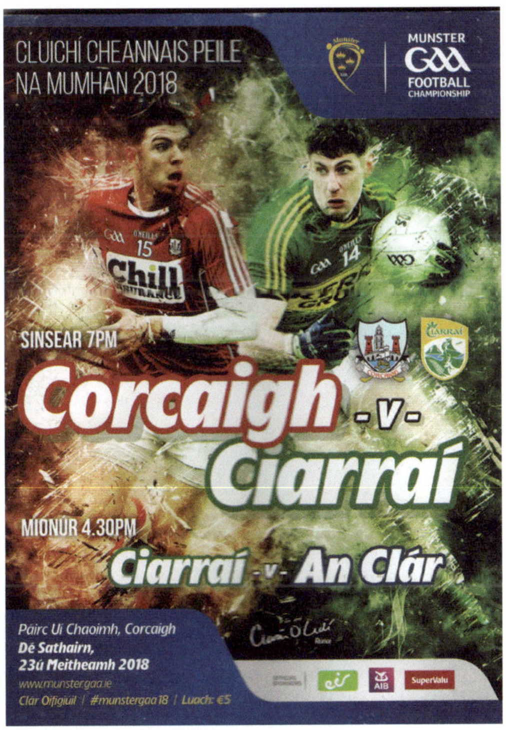
CLUICHÍ CHEANNAIS PEILE
NA MUMHAN 2018
MUNSTER
GAA
FOOTBALL
CHAMPIONSHIP
SINSEAR 7PM
Corcaigh -V-
Ciarraí
MIONÚR 4.30PM
Ciarraí -V- An Clár
Páirc Uí Chaoimh, Corcaigh
Dé Sathairn,
23ú Meitheamh 2018
www.munstergaa.ie
Clár Oifigiúil | #munstergaa18 | Luach: €5
OFFICIAL SPONSORS
AIB
SuperValu

8

ULSTER
2018
SENIOR FOOTBALL
CHAMPIONSHIP
FINAL
CLUICHE CEANNAIS PEILE ULADH
DÚN NA NGALL
V
FEAR MANACH
PÁIRC THIARNAIGH NAOFA, CLUAIN EOIS
24Ú MEITHEAMH 2018
EIRGRID ULSTER
UNDER 20 FOOTBALL FINAL
ARD MHACHA v DOIRE
€5/£5 | CLÁR OIFIGIÚIL
RÚNAÍ:
WWW.ULSTERGAA.IE
FIND US ON:
#BEPARTOFIT
OFFICIAL SPONSORS
AIB
SuperValu

9

GAA
FOOTBALL
ALL-IRELAND SENIOR
CHAMPIONSHIP
FINAL
Cluiche Ceannais Peile na hÉireann
Áth Cliath
Tír Eoghain
Electric Ireland GAA Football All-Ireland Minor Championship Final
Ciarraí v Gaillimh
CLÁR OIFIGIÚIL LUACH €5
Páirc an Chrócaigh, Meán Fómhair 2 2018
ARD STIÚRTHÓIR
OFFICIAL SPONSORS
AIB
SuperValu

2019

Prior to 2019, no senior intercounty team in either code had managed to win five All-Ireland titles in a row. Several had come close by winning four – Cork (1941–4) and Kilkenny (2006–9) in hurling and Wexford (1915–18) and Kerry (1929–32 & 1978–81) in football. However, the fifth consecutive title proved elusive until this year. Dublin had dominated the Leinster football championship, winning every title since 2011. They won the All-Ireland finals in 2011 and 2013, and now Jim Gavin's team had completed four wins in a row from 2015 to 2018. Standing in their way of the fifth were their old rivals from Kerry who, ironically, were the last football team to have had a shot at five-in-a-row immortality in 1982.

The final finished level at 1-16 each, and the teams met again a fortnight later. This time, Dublin made no mistake as they clinched the title, winning by six points. Stephen Cluxton, the Dublin goalkeeper and captain for all five wins, was also named Footballer of the Year.

1

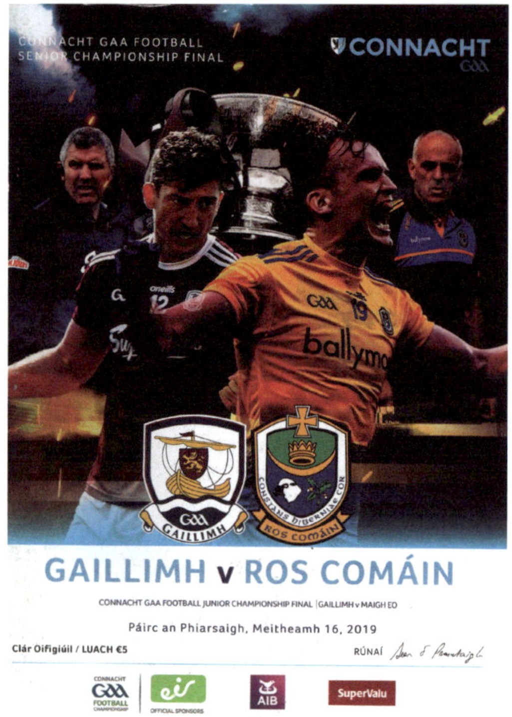

2

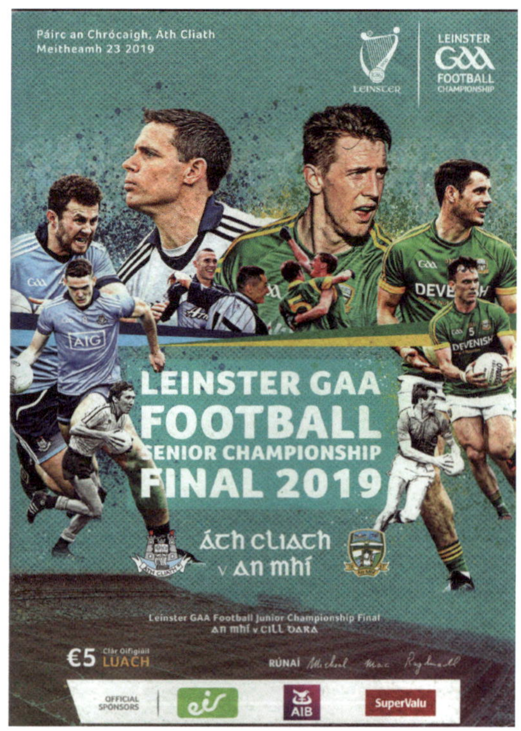

1 Connacht Football Final
Roscommon 1-13 Galway 0-12

2 Leinster Football Final
Dublin 1-17 Meath 0-04

3 All-Ireland Football Final
Dublin 1-16 Kerry 1-16
Attendance – 82,300

3

GAA
FOOTBALL
ALL-IRELAND SENIOR
CHAMPIONSHIP
ÁTH CLIATH
CIARRAÍ
Cluiche Ceannais Peile na hÉireann
2019
Áth Cliath V Ciarraí
Electric Ireland GAA Football All-Ireland Minor Championship Final
Corcaigh v Gaillimh
Clár Oifigiúil Luach €7
Páirc an Chrócaigh, Meán Fómhair 1 2019
Ard Stiúrthóir
OFFICIAL SPONSORS
eir
AIB
SuperValu

4

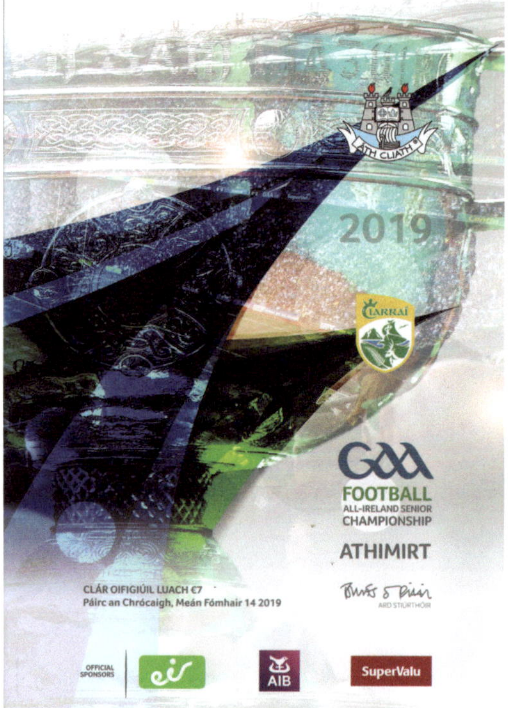

ÁTH CLIATH
2019
CIARRAÍ
GAA
FOOTBALL
ALL-IRELAND SENIOR CHAMPIONSHIP
ATHIMIRT
CLÁR OIFIGIÚIL LUACH €7
Páirc an Chrócaigh, Meán Fómhair 14 2019
ARD STIÚRTHÓIR
OFFICIAL SPONSORS
AIB
SuperValu

5

CLUICHÍ CEANNAIS PEILE NA MUMHAN 2019
MUNSTER GAA
FOOTBALL CHAMPIONSHIP
CIARRAÍ
GAA WHERE WE ALL BELONG
KERRY GROUP
SINSEAR 7PM
CORCAIGH V CIARRAÍ
MIONÚR 4:30PM
CORCAIGH V CIARRAÍ
Páirc Uí Chaoimh, Corcaigh
Dé Sathairn, 22ú Meitheamh 2019
RÚNAÍ
www.munster.gaa.ie
Clár Oifigiúil | #munstergaa19 | LUACH: €5
OFFICIAL SPONSORS
AIB
SuperValu

6

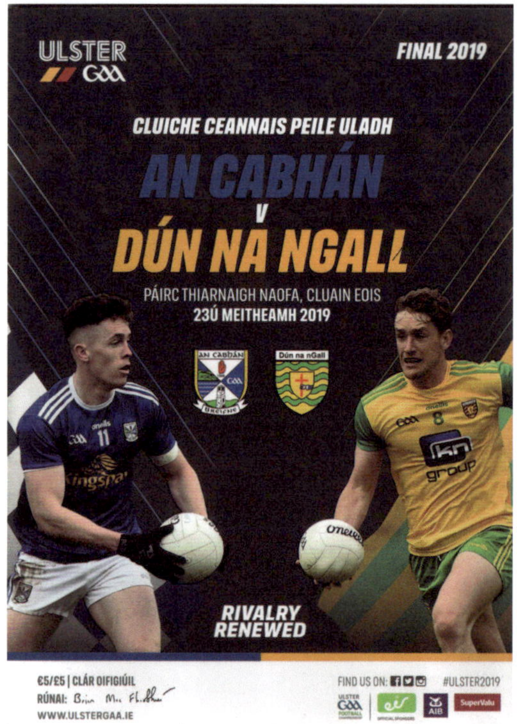

ULSTER GAA
FINAL 2019
CLUICHE CEANNAIS PEILE ULADH
AN CABHÁN
V
DÚN NA NGALL
PÁIRC THIARNAIGH NAOFA, CLUAIN EOIS
23Ú MEITHEAMH 2019
AN CABHÁN
Dún na nGall
RIVALRY RENEWED
€5/£5 | CLÁR OIFIGIÚIL
RÚNAÍ:
WWW.ULSTERGAA.IE
FIND US ON:
#ULSTER2019
AIB
SuperValu

7

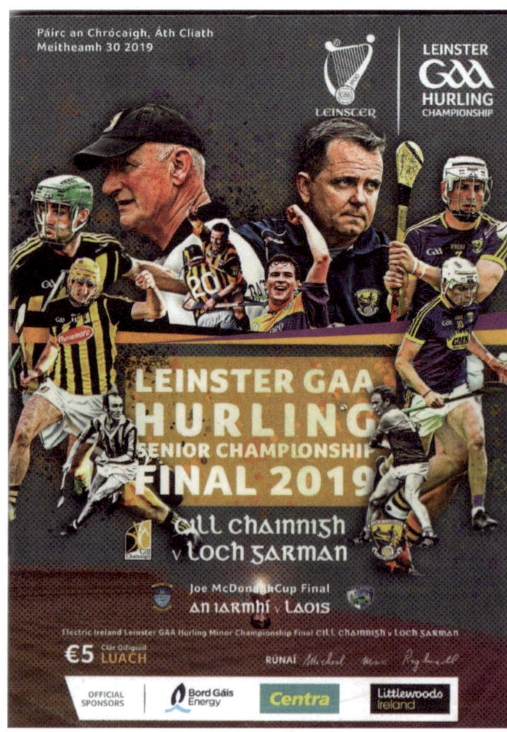

Páirc an Chrócaigh, Áth Cliath
Meitheamh 30 2019
LEINSTER
LEINSTER GAA
HURLING CHAMPIONSHIP
LEINSTER GAA HURLING SENIOR CHAMPIONSHIP FINAL 2019
Cill Chainnigh v Loch Garman
Joe McDonagh Cup Final
An Iarmhí v Laois
€5 Clár Oifigiúil LUACH
RÚNAÍ
OFFICIAL SPONSORS
Bord Gáis Energy
Centra
Littlewoods Ireland

8

9

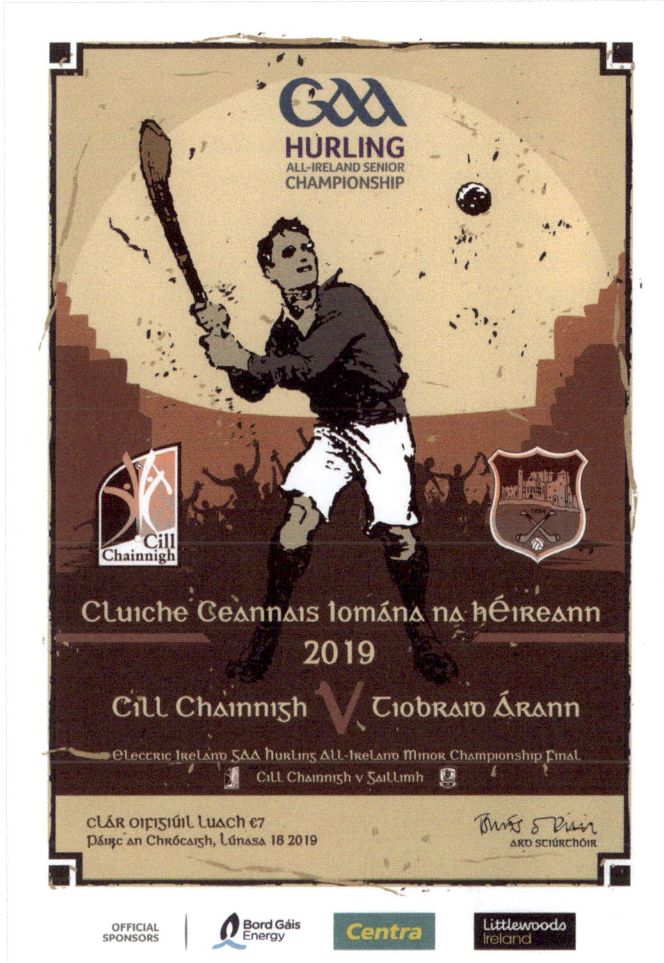

4 Replay
Dublin 1-18 Kerry 0-15
Attendance – 82,300

5 Munster Football Final
Kerry 1-19 Cork 3-10

6 Ulster Football Final
Donegal 1-24 Cavan 2-16

7 Leinster Hurling Final
Wexford 1-23 Kilkenny 0-23

8 Munster Hurling Final
Limerick 2-26 Tipperary 2-14

9 All-Ireland Hurling Final
Tipperary 3-25 Kilkenny 0-20
Attendance – 82,300

MHACHA
Chorn

2020–24

2020

Gaelic games, like most activities, fell victim to Covid-19 pandemic restrictions regarding the movement and gatherings of groups of people. The GAA reduced the number of matches in its football championship season by reverting to a knockout competition, producing surprise provincial winners in Cavan and Tipperary. Due to an outbreak of Covid-19, Sligo were unable to fulfil their Connacht semi-final with Galway, and the Connacht championship consisted of only three matches, with Mayo winning all three. To help prevent the spread of the virus, matches were played behind closed doors and while some programmes were printed, it was nothing like the number required for a typical match day. Virtual programmes were, however, made available for download on GAA websites and through social media. The eventual winners, Dublin and Limerick, celebrated their All-Ireland victories in an eerily quiet and deserted Croke Park, and returned home without either the Sam Maguire or Liam MacCarthy Cup.

1

2

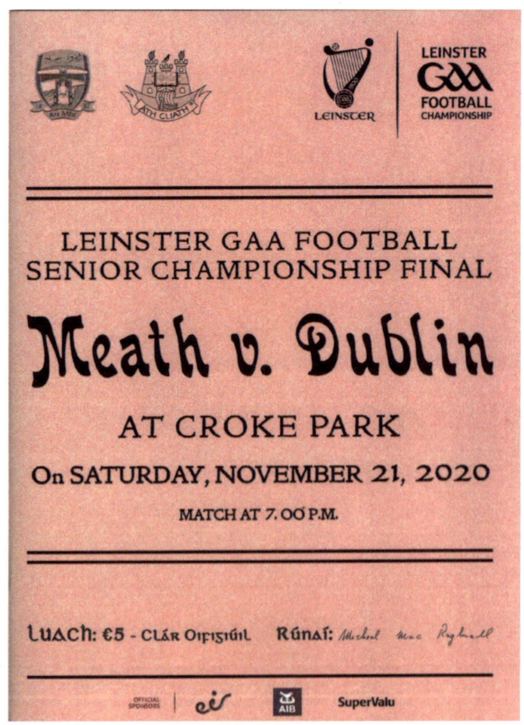

1 Connacht Football Final
Mayo 0-14 Galway 0-13

2 Leinster Football Final
Dublin 3-21 Meath 0-09

3 Munster Football Final
Tipperary 0-17 Cork 0-14

3

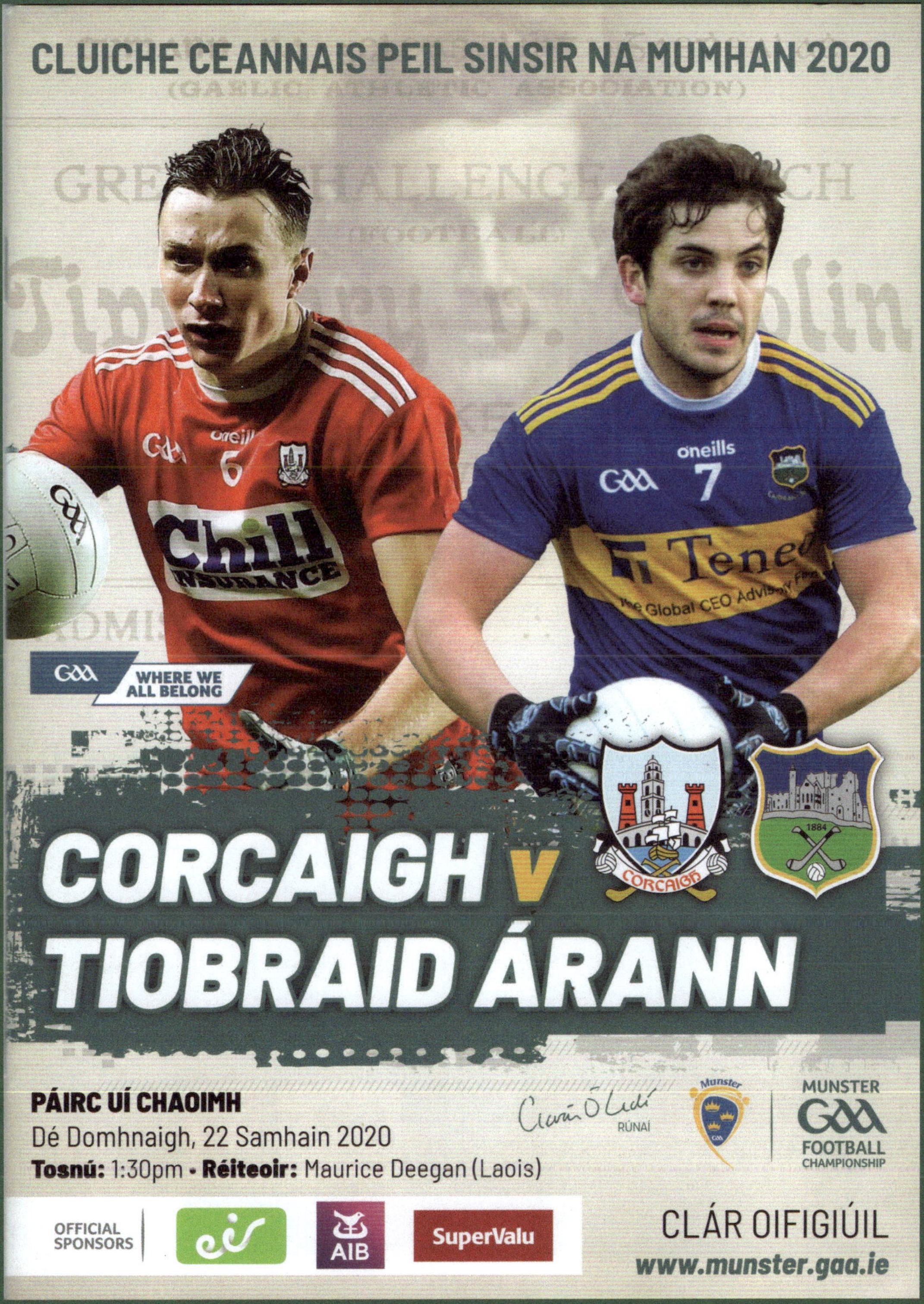

CLUICHE CEANNAIS PEIL SINSIR NA MUMHAN 2020
WHERE WE ALL BELONG
CORCAIGH v
TIOBRAID ÁRANN
CORCAIGH
1884
PÁIRC UÍ CHAOIMH
Dé Domhnaigh, 22 Samhain 2020
Tosnú: 1:30pm • Réiteoir: Maurice Deegan (Laois)
RÚNAÍ
Munster
MUNSTER
FOOTBALL
CHAMPIONSHIP
OFFICIAL SPONSORS
AIB
SuperValu
CLÁR OIFIGIÚIL
www.munster.gaa.ie

4

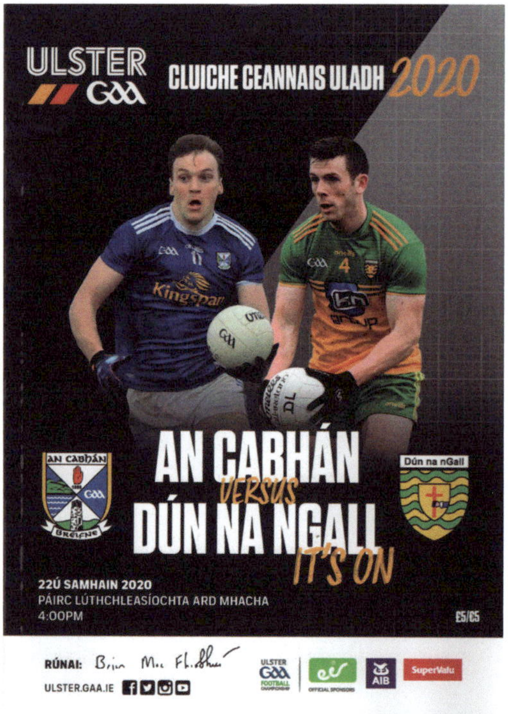
ULSTER GAA
CLUICHE CEANNAIS ULADH 2020
AN CABHÁN
VERSUS
DÚN NA NGALL
IT'S ON
Dún na nGall
22Ú SAMHAIN 2020
PÁIRC LÚTHCHLEASÍOCHTA ARD MHACHA
4:00PM
£5/€5
RÚNAÍ:
ULSTER.GAA.IE
SuperValu
AIB

6

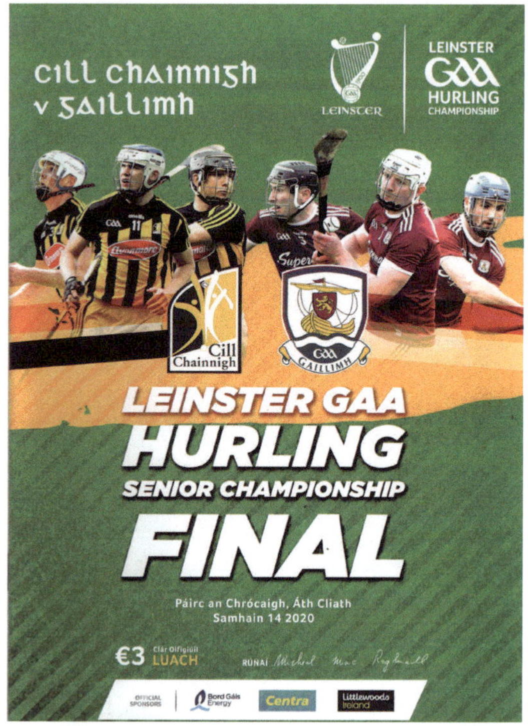
cill chainnigh
v gaillimh
LEINSTER GAA HURLING CHAMPIONSHIP
Cill Chainnigh
LEINSTER GAA
HURLING
SENIOR CHAMPIONSHIP
FINAL
Páirc an Chrócaigh, Áth Cliath
Samhain 14 2020
€3 Clár Oifigiúil LUACH
RÚNAÍ
OFFICIAL SPONSORS
Bord Gáis Energy
Centra
Littlewoods Ireland

5

Páirc an Chrócaigh
Nollaig 19 2020
GAA
FOOTBALL
ALL-IRELAND SENIOR
CHAMPIONSHIP
cluiche ceannais sinsear peile na héireann
áth cliath
Vs
maigh eo
EirGrid GAA Football All-Ireland U20 Championship Final - Áth Cliath v Gaillimh
GAA WHERE WE ALL BELONG
€7 Clár Oifigiúil LUACH
ARD STIÚRTHÓIR
OFFICIAL SPONSORS
AIB
SuperValu

7

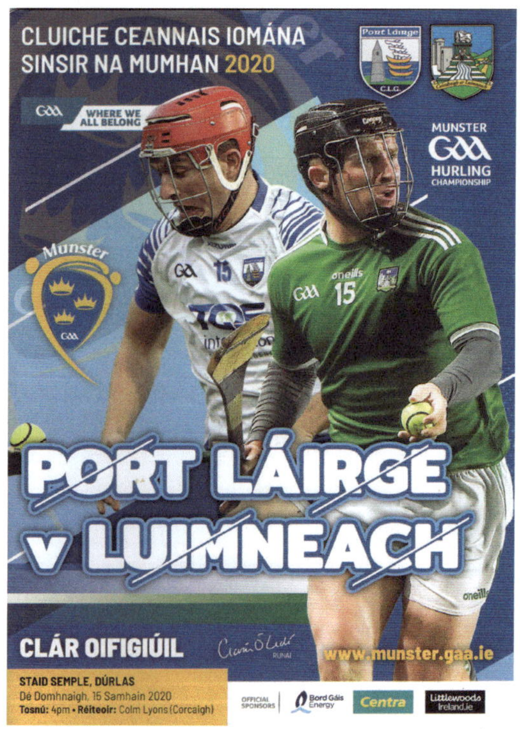
CLUICHE CEANNAIS IOMÁNA
SINSIR NA MUMHAN 2020
Port Láirge
GAA WHERE WE ALL BELONG
MUNSTER GAA HURLING CHAMPIONSHIP
Munster
PORT LÁIRGE
v LUIMNEACH
CLÁR OIFIGIÚIL
RÚNAÍ
www.munster.gaa.ie
STAID SEMPLE, DÚRLAS
Dé Domhnaigh, 15 Samhain 2020
Tosnú: 4pm • Réiteoir: Colm Lyons (Corcaigh)
OFFICIAL SPONSORS
Bord Gáis Energy
Centra
Littlewoods Ireland.ie

8

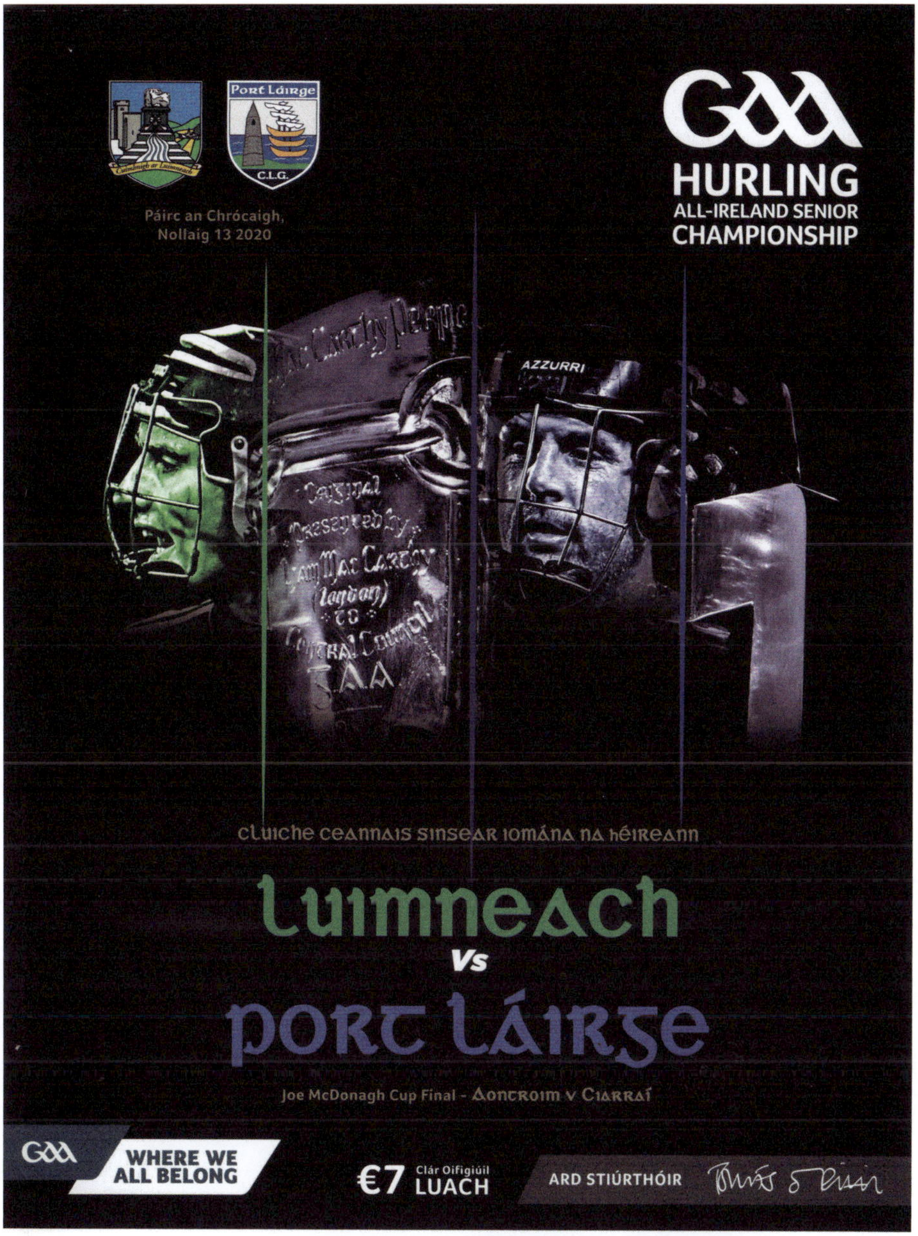

OFFICIAL SPONSORS | Bord Gáis Energy | Centra | Littlewoods Ireland

4 Ulster Football Final
Cavan 1-13 Donegal 0-12

5 All-Ireland Football Final
Dublin 2-14 Mayo 0-15
Attendance – 0

6 Leinster Hurling Final
Kilkenny 2-20 Galway 0-24

7 Munster Hurling Final
Limerick 0-25 Waterford 0-21

8 All-Ireland Hurling Final
Limerick 0-30 Waterford 0-19
Attendance – 0

2021

With the Covid-19 pandemic still causing disruption to daily life, the GAA operated its championships in a similar way to the 2020 season. The football championship went ahead on a knockout basis without Kilkenny, London or New York participating. The quarter-final stage was dispensed with, and provincial winners progressed to the All-Ireland semi-final. Controversy surrounded the postponement of the semi-final between Kerry and Tyrone following an outbreak of Covid-19 in the Tyrone team. An all-too-familiar scenario played out in the All-Ireland final when Mayo, having eventually beaten Dublin in the semi-final, lost to Tyrone.

The provincial hurling championships were similarly played with the old knockout system. While spectators were allowed back into stadia, attendances at matches were restricted throughout the season. Just over 40,000 people (half of the capacity) were permitted to attend each All-Ireland final.

1

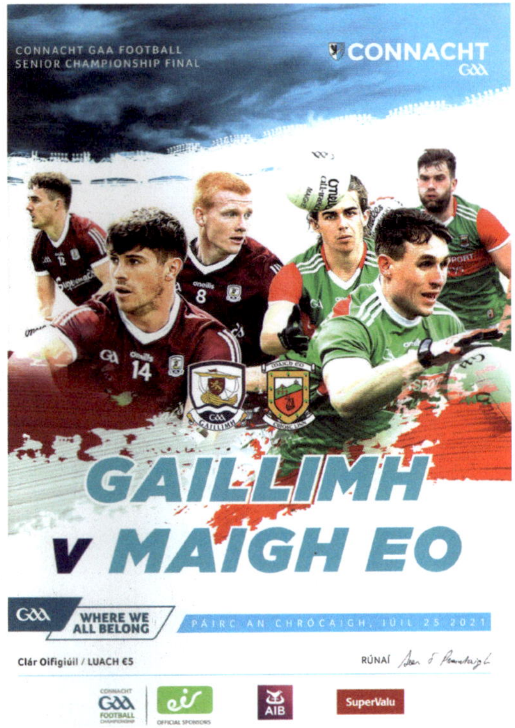

2

1 Connacht Football Final
Mayo 2-14 Galway 2-08

2 Leinster Football Final
Dublin 0-20 Kildare 1-09

3 Munster Football Final
Kerry 4-22 Cork 1-09

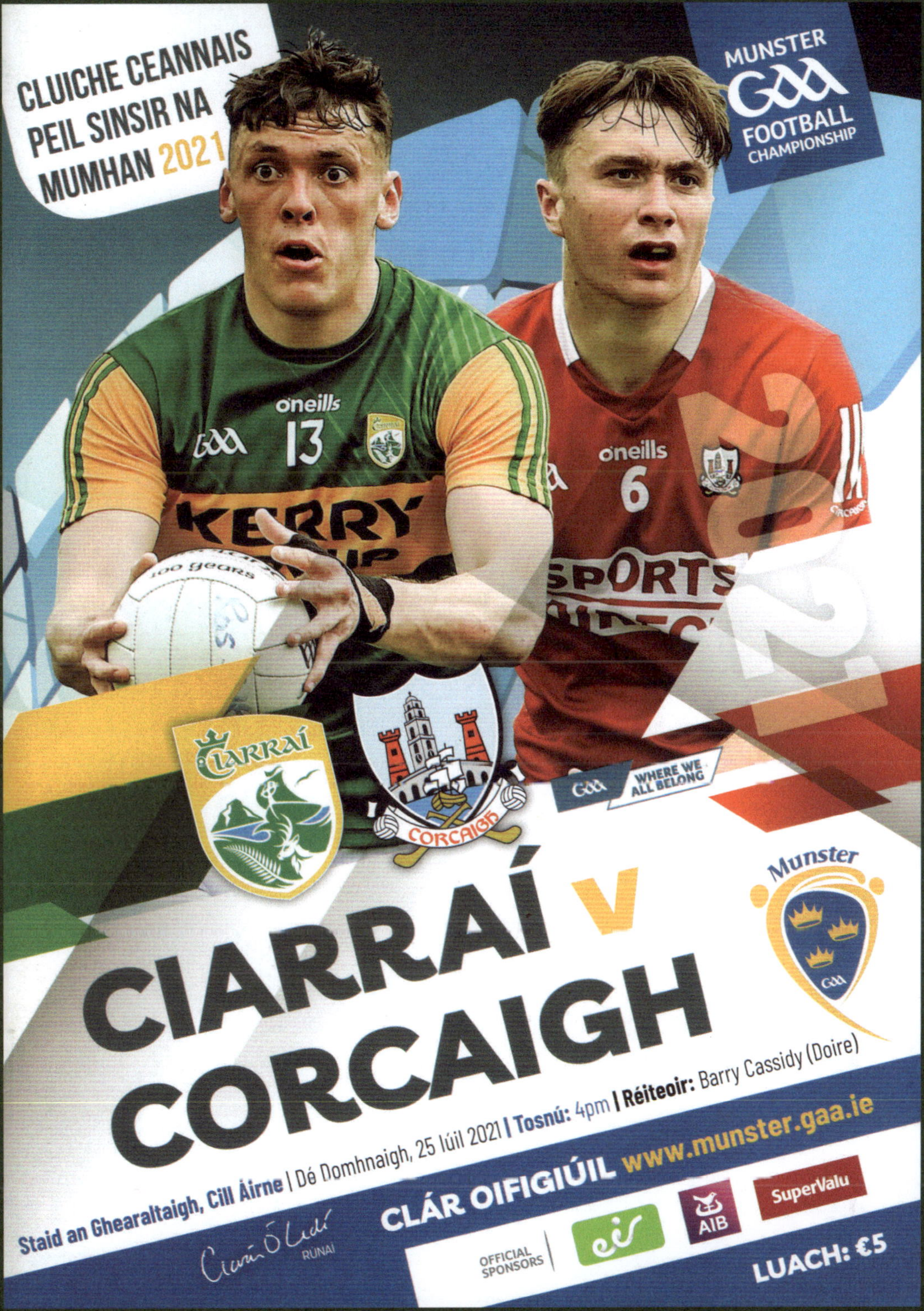
CLUICHE CEANNAIS
PEIL SINSIR NA
MUMHAN 2021
MUNSTER
FOOTBALL
CHAMPIONSHIP
WHERE WE ALL BELONG
Munster
CIARRAÍ v
CORCAIGH
Staid an Ghearaltaigh, Cill Áirne | Dé Domhnaigh, 25 Iúil 2021 | Tosnú: 4pm | Réiteoir: Barry Cassidy (Doire)
CLÁR OIFIGIÚIL www.munster.gaa.ie
RUNAÍ
OFFICIAL SPONSORS
AIB
SuperValu
LUACH: €5

4

4 Ulster Football Final
Tyrone 0-16 Monaghan 0-15

5 All-Ireland Football Final
Tyrone 2-14 Mayo 0-15
Attendance – 41,150

6 Leinster Hurling Final
Kilkenny 1-25 Dublin 0-19

7 Munster Hurling Final
Limerick 2-29 Tipperary 3-21

8 All-Ireland Hurling Final
Limerick 3-32 Cork 1-22
Attendance – 40,000

5

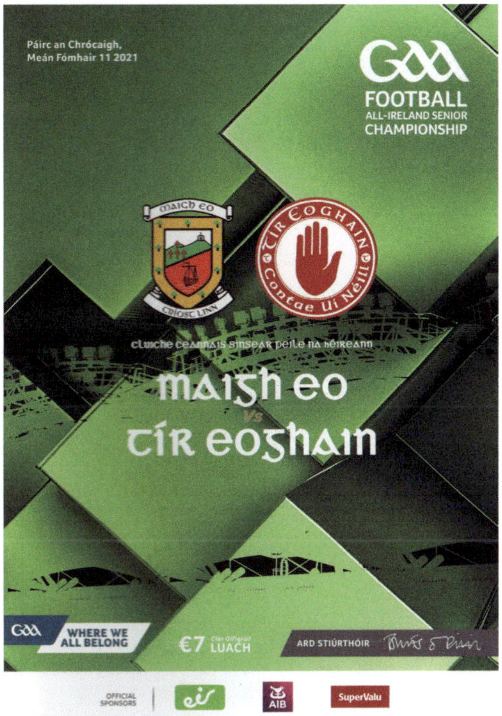
Páirc an Chrócaigh,
Meán Fómhair 11 2021
FOOTBALL
ALL-IRELAND SENIOR
CHAMPIONSHIP
cluiche ceannais sinsear peile na héireann
maigh eo
Vs
tír eoghain
WHERE WE ALL BELONG
€7 LUACH
ARD STIÚRTHÓIR
OFFICIAL SPONSORS
AIB
SuperValu

6

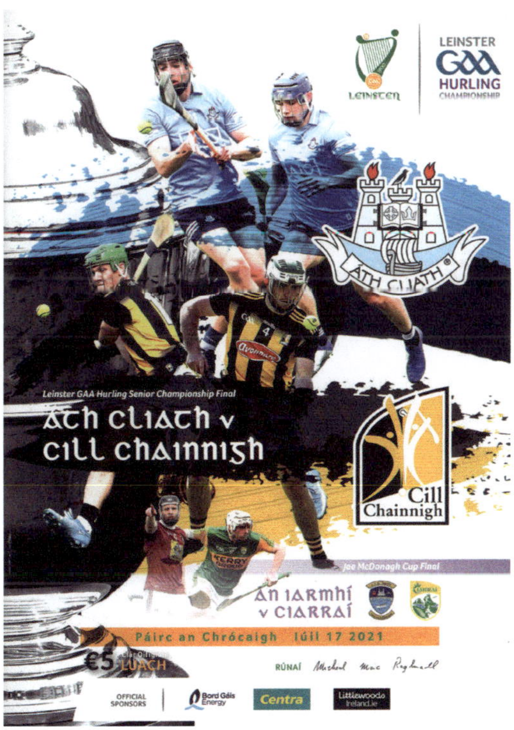
LEINSTER
HURLING
CHAMPIONSHIP
ÁTH CLIATH
Leinster GAA Hurling Senior Championship Final
áth cliath v
cill chainnigh
Cill Chainnigh
Joe McDonagh Cup Final
an iarmhí
v ciarraí
Páirc an Chrócaigh Iúil 17 2021
€5 LUACH
RÚNAÍ
OFFICIAL SPONSORS
Bord Gáis Energy
Centra
Littlewoods Ireland.ie

7

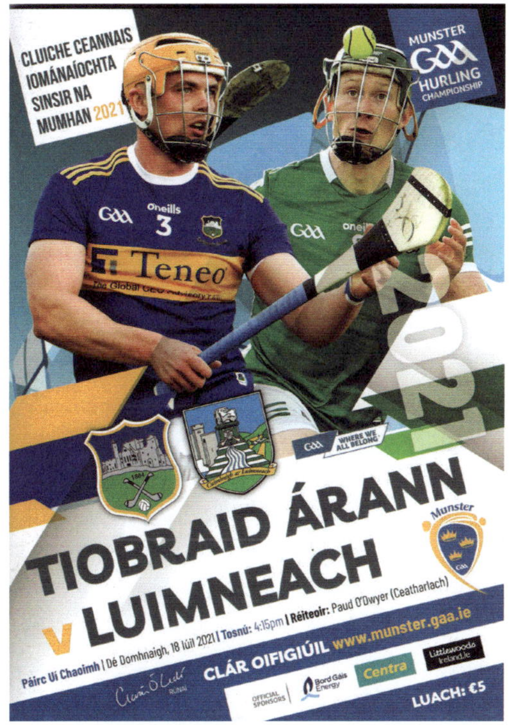
CLUICHE CEANNAIS
IOMÁNAÍOCHTA
SINSIR NA
MUMHAN 2021
MUNSTER
HURLING
CHAMPIONSHIP
Teneo
2021
WHERE WE ALL BELONG
TIOBRAID ÁRANN
v LUIMNEACH
Munster
Páirc Uí Chaoimh | Dé Domhnaigh, 18 Iúil 2021 | Tosnú: 4:15pm | Réiteoir: Paud O'Dwyer (Ceatharlach)
CLÁR OIFIGIÚIL www.munster.gaa.ie
RÚNAÍ
OFFICIAL SPONSORS
Bord Gáis Energy
Centra
Littlewoods Ireland.ie
LUACH: €5

8

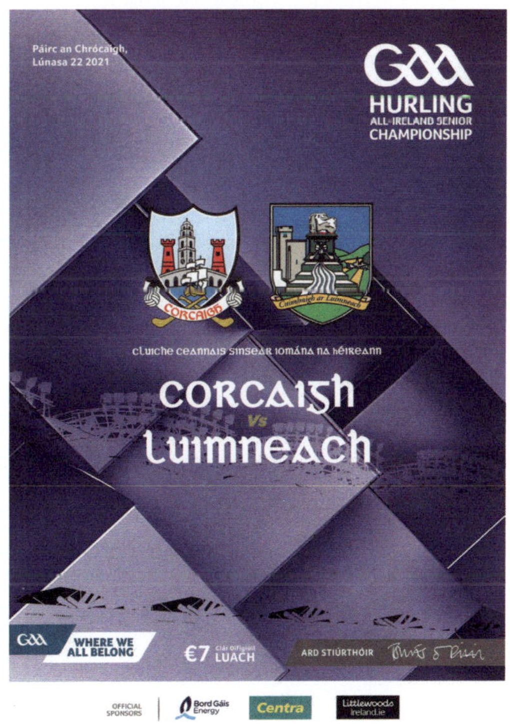
Páirc an Chrócaigh,
Lúnasa 22 2021
HURLING
ALL-IRELAND SENIOR
CHAMPIONSHIP
CORCAIGH
cluiche ceannais sinsear iomána na héireann
corcaigh
Vs
luimneach
WHERE WE ALL BELONG
€7 LUACH
ARD STIÚRTHÓIR
OFFICIAL SPONSORS
Bord Gáis Energy
Centra
Littlewoods Ireland.ie

2022

The covers of GAA match programmes can sometimes accurately predict the narrative of the matches. On the cover of the 2022 Leinster hurling final, Henry Shefflin, former Kilkenny player and then manager of Galway, and his former Kilkenny manager, Brian Cody, are facing in opposite directions. Having shared a fraught and much-analysed handshake after Galway's single-point win in the group stage at Pearse Stadium, all eyes were on the pair after Kilkenny defeated Galway in the Leinster final. The resultant handshake was the most dramatic incident of the afternoon after a lacklustre final which Kilkenny won.

The 2022 All-Ireland football final between Kerry and Galway will be remembered for the wonderful shootout that materialised between two of the game's marquee forwards. Kerry's David Clifford and Shane Walsh of Galway scored 17 points between them. Both players featured on the cover of the All-Ireland final match programme.

1

2

1 Leinster Hurling Final
Kilkenny 0-22 Galway 0-17

2 Munster Hurling Final
Limerick 1-29 Clare 0-29 (aet)

3 All-Ireland Hurling Final
Limerick 1-31 Kilkenny 2-26
Attendance – 82,300

Cluiche Ceannais Sinsear Iomána na hÉireann

3 Páirc an Chrócaigh,
Iúil 17 2022

GAA
HURLING
ALL-IRELAND SENIOR
CHAMPIONSHIP

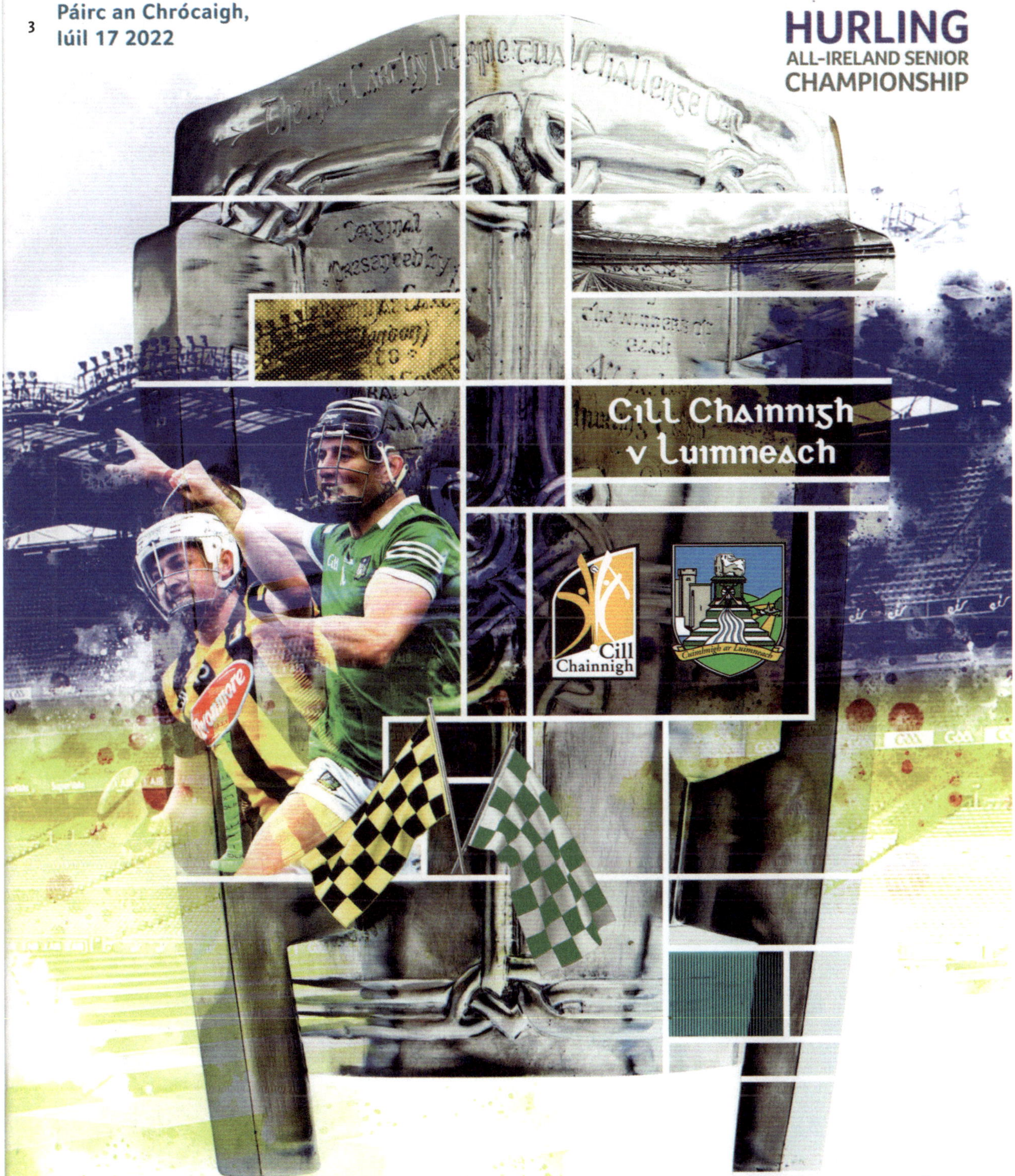

€7 Clár Oifigiúil LUACH

ARD STIÚRTHÓIR

4

CONNACHT GAA FOOTBALL
SENIOR CHAMPIONSHIP FINAL
CONNACHT GAA
GAILLIMH
v ROS COMÁIN
WHERE WE ALL BELONG
STÁID AN PHIARSAIGH
BEALTAINE 29 2022
Clár Oifigiúil / LUACH €5
RÚNAÍ
SuperValu

5

Bealtaine 28 2022
LEINSTER GAA FOOTBALL CHAMPIONSHIP
Áth Cliath v Cill Dara
LEINSTER GAA FOOTBALL SENIOR CHAMPIONSHIP FINAL 2022
TG4 LEINSTER SENIOR FOOTBALL FINAL
AN MHÍ v ÁTH CLIATH
€5 Clár Oifigiúil LUACH
RÚNAÍ
SuperValu

6

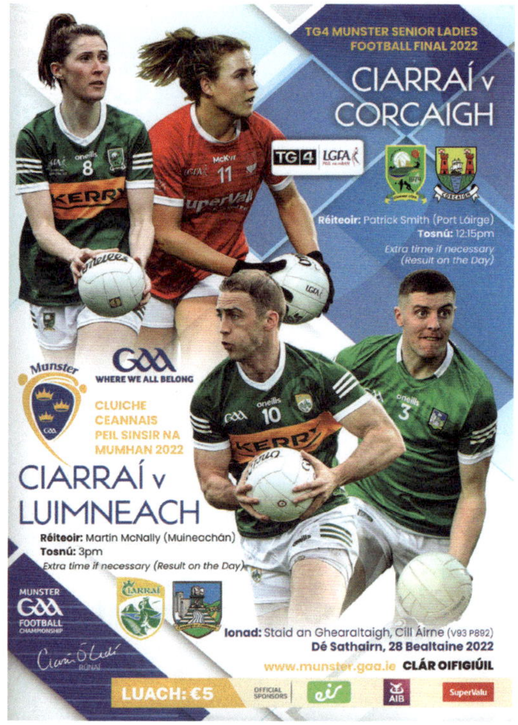
TG4 MUNSTER SENIOR LADIES FOOTBALL FINAL 2022
CIARRAÍ v CORCAIGH
Réiteoir: Patrick Smith (Port Láirge)
Tosnú: 12:15pm
Extra time if necessary (Result on the Day)
GAA WHERE WE ALL BELONG
CLUICHE CEANNAIS PEIL SINSIR NA MUMHAN 2022
CIARRAÍ v LUIMNEACH
Réiteoir: Martin McNally (Muineachán)
Tosnú: 3pm
Extra time if necessary (Result on the Day)
MUNSTER GAA FOOTBALL CHAMPIONSHIP
Ionad: Staid an Ghearaltaigh, Cill Áirne (V93 P892)
Dé Sathairn, 28 Bealtaine 2022
www.munster.gaa.ie CLÁR OIFIGIÚIL
LUACH: €5
OFFICIAL SPONSORS
SuperValu

7

ULSTER GAA FOOTBALL CHAMPIONSHIP
DOIRE
DÚN NA NGALL
CLUICHE CEANNAIS SINSIR ULADH SA PHEIL 2022
PÁIRC NAOMH TIGHEARNACH
29Ú BEALTAINE
CLUICHE CEANNAIS MIONÚR ULADH SA PHEIL 2022
DOIRE V TÍR EOGHAIN
€5/£5 | CLÁR OIFIGIÚIL
RÚNAÍ:
WHERE WE ALL BELONG

8

4 Connacht Football Final
Galway 2–19 Roscommon 2–16

5 Leinster Football Final
Dublin 5-17 Kildare 1-15

6 Munster Football Final
Kerry 1–28 Limerick 0–08

7 Ulster Football Final
Derry 1-16 Donegal 1-14

8 All-Ireland Football Final
Kerry 0-20 Galway 0-16
Attendance – 82,300

2023

In 2023, the Limerick hurlers continued their dominance of the Munster and All-Ireland championships. By defeating Clare in the Munster hurling final, they became just the second county to win five consecutive Munster titles. They followed this with a win over Kilkenny in the All-Ireland final to take the championship for the fourth year in a row.

Gaelic Park, in the Bronx, New York, was the scene of this year's biggest shock in the championship when New York finally won a Connacht championship football match at the twenty-third time of asking. Having finished level after extra time, a penalty shootout was required to decide a winner. US native Mikey Brosnan scored the decisive goal to give New York a famous victory over Leitrim. The All-Ireland football final featured a familiar rivalry as Dublin faced Kerry for the seventeenth* time in the decider, with Dublin winning their thirty-first title.

* *Includes 1908 home final and 2019 replay.*

1

2

1 Leinster Hurling Final
Kilkenny 4-21 Galway 2-26

2 Munster Hurling Final
Limerick 1-23 Clare 1-22

3 All-Ireland Hurling Final
Limerick 0-30 Kilkenny 2-15
Attendance – 82,300

GAA
HURLING
ALL-IRELAND SENIOR
CHAMPIONSHIP

CILL CHAINNIGH V LUIMNEACH | PÁIRC AN CHRÓCAIGH | IÚIL 23 2023

Cill Chainnigh

Cuimhnigh ar Luimneach

CLUICHE CEANNAIS SINSEAR IOMÁNA NA hÉIREANN

€8 Clár Oifigiúil **LUACH**

ARD-STIÚRTHÓIR

4

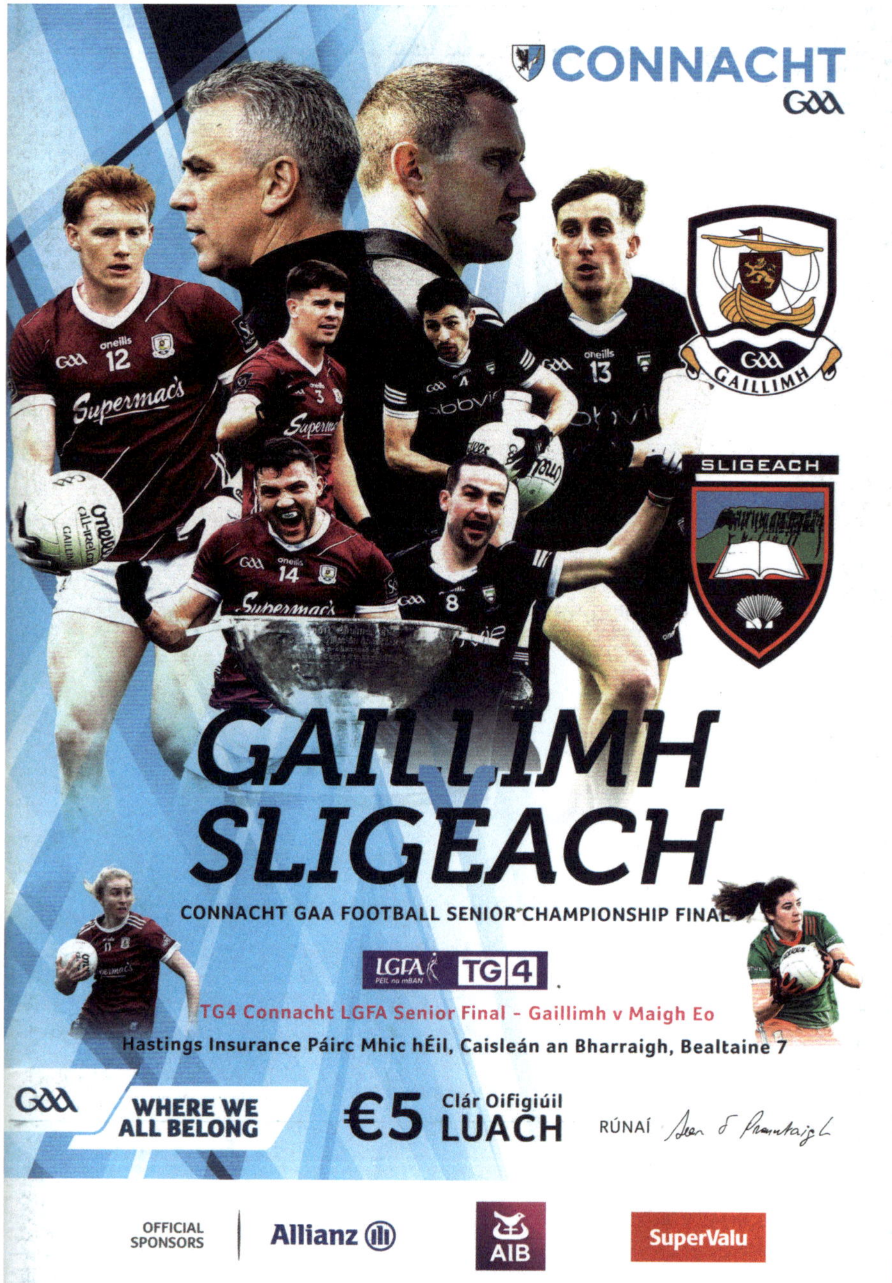

4 Connacht Football Final
Galway 2-20 Sligo 0-12

5 Leinster Football Final
Dublin 5-21 Louth 0-15

6 Munster Football Final
Kerry 5-14 Clare 0-15

7 Ulster Football Final
Derry 1-15 Armagh 0-18 aet
(Derry won 3-1 on penalties)

8 All-Ireland Football Final
Dublin 1-15 Kerry 1-13
Attendance – 82,300

5

LEINSTER GAA FOOTBALL CHAMPIONSHIP
LEINSTER GAA
FOOTBALL SENIOR
CHAMPIONSHIP FINAL
An Lú v Áth Cliath | Páirc an Chrócaigh | Bealtaine 14 2023
€5 Clár Oifigiúil LUACH
RÚNAÍ
OFFICIAL SPONSORS Allianz AIB SuperValu

6

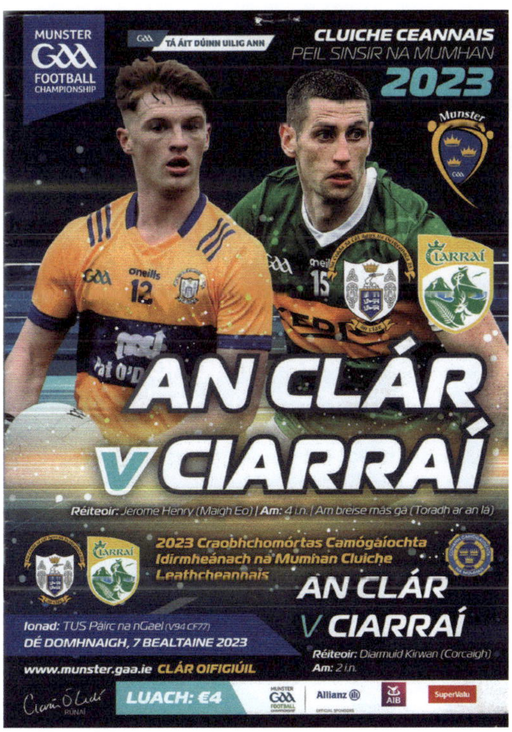
MUNSTER GAA FOOTBALL CHAMPIONSHIP
TÁ ÁIT DÚINN UILIG ANN
CLUICHE CEANNAIS
PEIL SINSIR NA MUMHAN
2023
AN CLÁR
V CIARRAÍ
Réiteoir: Jerome Henry (Maigh Eo) | Am: 4 i.n. | Am breise más gá (Toradh ar an lá)
2023 Craobhchomórtas Camógaíochta Idirmheánach na Mumhan Cluiche Leathcheannais
AN CLÁR
V CIARRAÍ
Ionad: TUS Páirc na nGael (V94 CF77)
DÉ DOMHNAIGH, 7 BEALTAINE 2023
Réiteoir: Diarmuid Kirwan (Corcaigh)
Am: 2 i.n.
www.munster.gaa.ie CLÁR OIFIGIÚIL
RÚNAÍ
LUACH: €4
Allianz AIB SuperValu

7

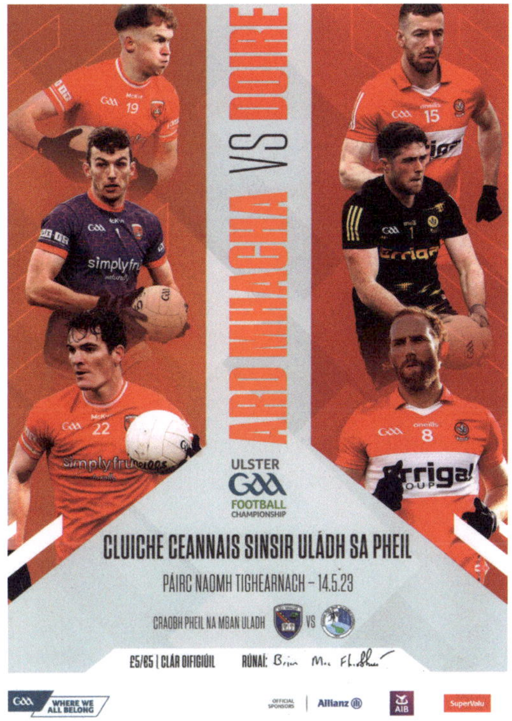
ARD MHACHA VS DOIRE
ULSTER GAA FOOTBALL CHAMPIONSHIP
CLUICHE CEANNAIS SINSIR ULADH SA PHEIL
PÁIRC NAOMH TIGHEARNACH – 14.5.23
CRAOBH PHEIL NA MBAN ULADH VS
£5/€5 | CLÁR OIFIGIÚIL RÚNAÍ:
GAA WHERE WE ALL BELONG
OFFICIAL SPONSORS Allianz AIB SuperValu

8

GAA FOOTBALL ALL-IRELAND SENIOR CHAMPIONSHIP
ÁTH CLIATH V CIARRAÍ | PÁIRC AN CHRÓCAIGH | IÚIL 30 2023
CLUICHE
CEANNAIS
SINSEAR
PEILE
NA hÉIREANN
€8 Clár Oifigiúil LUACH
ARD-STIÚRTHÓIR
OFFICIAL SPONSORS Allianz AIB SuperValu

2024

In addition to this year's official All-Ireland final match programmes, special limited-edition programmes were issued, which featured the participating counties on the covers. These programmes were only available for purchase inside Croke Park on final day. In 2024, the All-Ireland final match programme cost €8 and a ticket for the final cost €100. Clare and Cork met in the All-Ireland hurling final for the first time since 2013, and a thrilling match required extra time before Clare emerged as winners. Armagh and Galway met in the All-Ireland football final for the first time, but the match was a tedious affair. Armagh won their second All-Ireland with former captain Kieran McGeeney now managing the team. The contrasting excitement of the hurling championship, and the final in particular, highlighted the growing frustration with the indifferent state of Gaelic football at the present time. The inter-provincial football series was reintroduced in October to trial new rules in an attempt to rectify the malaise.

1

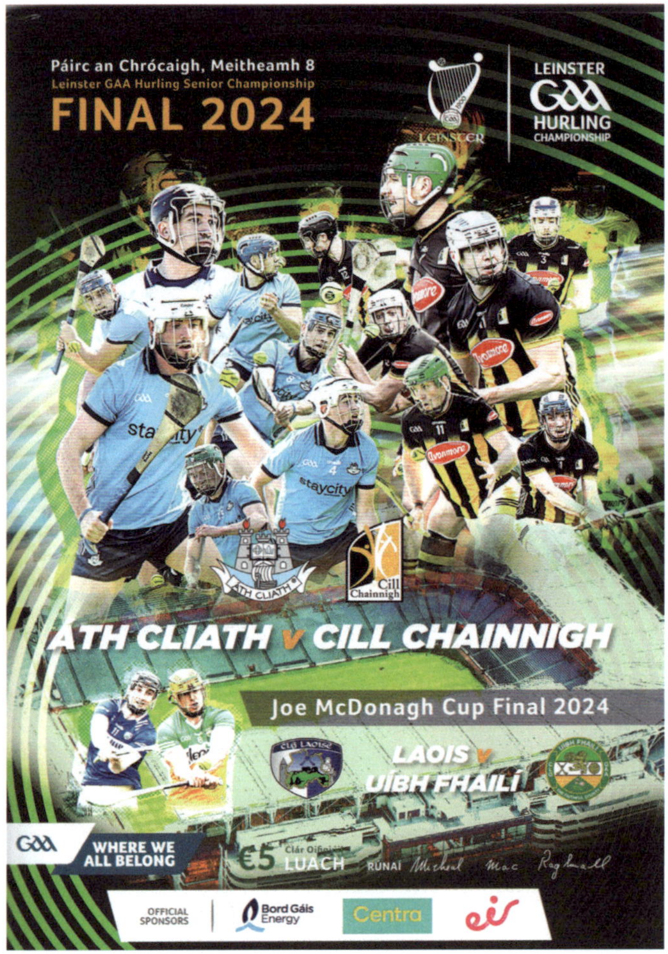

1 Leinster Hurling Final
Kilkenny 3-28 Dublin 1-18

2 Munster Hurling Final
Limerick 1-26 Clare 1-20

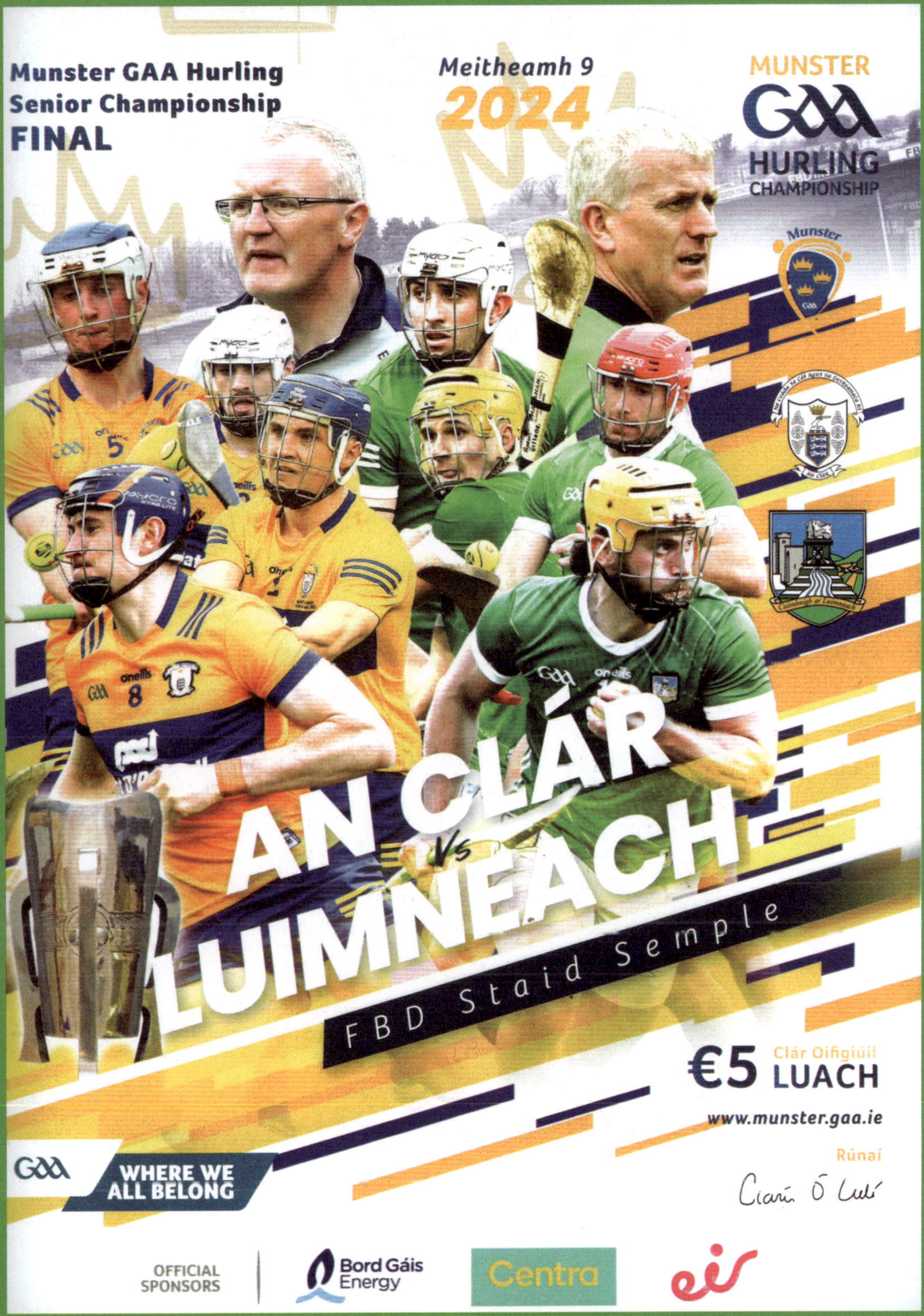
Munster GAA Hurling
Senior Championship
FINAL
Meitheamh 9
2024
MUNSTER
GAA
HURLING
CHAMPIONSHIP
AN CLÁR
Vs
LUIMNEACH
FBD Staid Semple
€5 Clár Oifigiúil
LUACH
www.munster.gaa.ie
Rúnaí
GAA
WHERE WE
ALL BELONG
OFFICIAL
SPONSORS
Bord Gáis
Energy
Centra
eir

3

3 All-Ireland Hurling Final
Clare 3-29 Cork 1-34 (aet)
Attendance – 82,300

4 All-Ireland Hurling Final (Cork edition)

5 All-Ireland Hurling Final (Clare edition)

6 Leinster Football Final
Dublin 1-19 Louth 2-12

7 Munster Football Final
Kerry 0-23 Clare 1-13

4

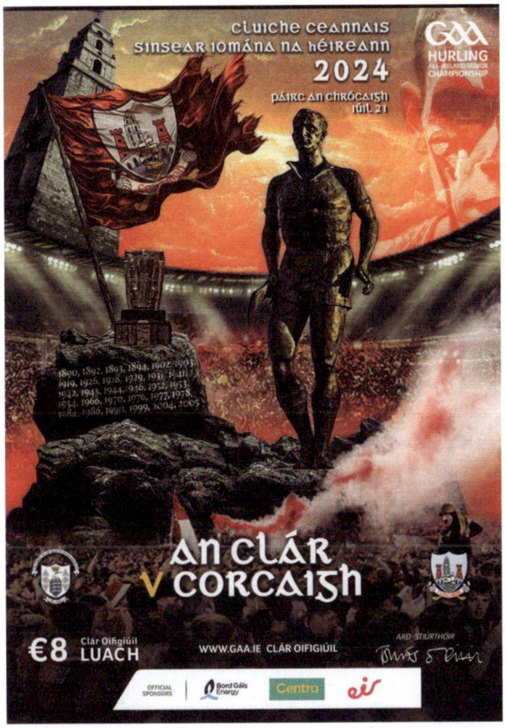

cluiche ceannais
sinsear iomána na héireann
2024
páirc an chrócaigh
iúil 21
GAA
HURLING
ALL-IRELAND SENIOR CHAMPIONSHIP
an clár
v corcaigh
€8 Clár Oifigiúil LUACH
WWW.GAA.IE CLÁR OIFIGIÚIL
ARD-STIÚRTHÓIR
OFFICIAL SPONSORS
Bord Gáis Energy
Centra
eir

6

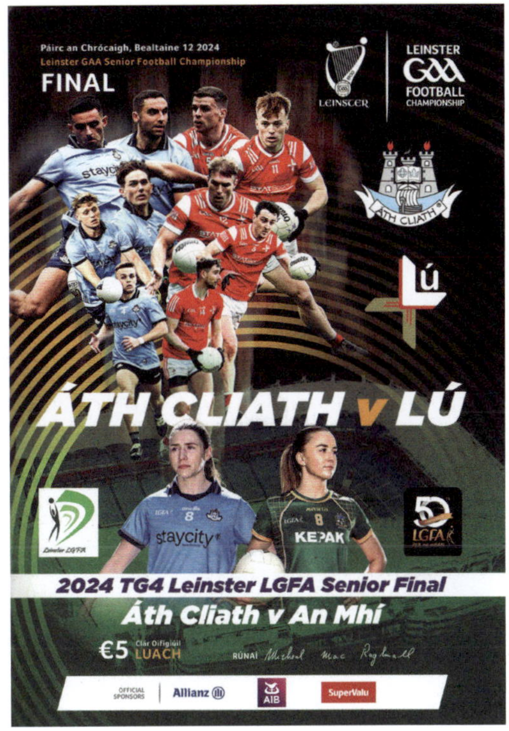

Páirc an Chrócaigh, Bealtaine 12 2024
Leinster GAA Senior Football Championship
FINAL
LEINSTER
GAA
FOOTBALL
CHAMPIONSHIP
ÁTH CLIATH v LÚ
2024 TG4 Leinster LGFA Senior Final
Áth Cliath v An Mhí
€5 Clár Oifigiúil LUACH
RÚNAÍ
OFFICIAL SPONSORS
Allianz
AIB
SuperValu

5

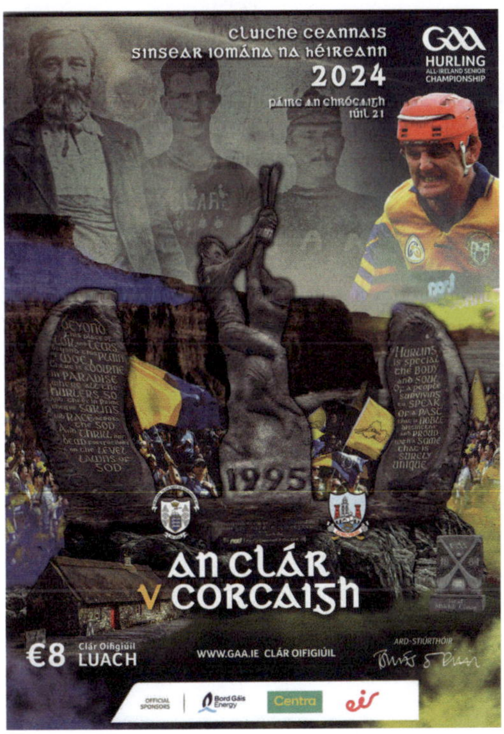

cluiche ceannais
sinsear iomána na héireann
2024
páirc an chrócaigh
iúil 21
GAA
HURLING
ALL-IRELAND SENIOR CHAMPIONSHIP
1995
an clár
v corcaigh
€8 Clár Oifigiúil LUACH
WWW.GAA.IE CLÁR OIFIGIÚIL
ARD-STIÚRTHÓIR
OFFICIAL SPONSORS
Bord Gáis Energy
Centra
eir

7

Munster GAA Football
Senior Championship
FINAL
Bealtaine 5
2024
MUNSTER
GAA
FOOTBALL
CHAMPIONSHIP
AN CLÁR
VS
CIARRAÍ
Páirc Uí Chíosóig, Inis
€5 Clár Oifigiúil LUACH
www.munster.gaa.ie
Rúnaí
GAA WHERE WE ALL BELONG
OFFICIAL SPONSORS
Allianz
AIB
SuperValu

8

ULSTER
GAA
FOOTBALL
CHAMPIONSHIP
ARD MHACHA
Dún na nGa
ARD MHACHA
VS
DÚN NA nGALL
CLUICHE CEANNAIS SINSIR ULADH SA PHEIL
BEALTAINE 12 2024
€5/£5 | CLÁR OIFIGIÚIL
RÚNAÍ:
WHERE WE ALL BELONG
Allianz
AIB
SuperValu

9

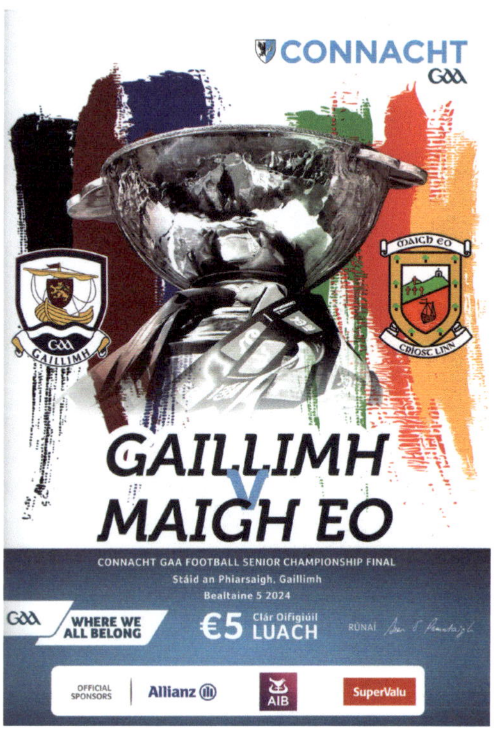

CONNACHT
GAA
MAIGH EO
CRIOST LINN
GAILLIMH
GAILLIMH
V
MAIGH EO
CONNACHT GAA FOOTBALL SENIOR CHAMPIONSHIP FINAL
Stáid an Phiarsaigh, Gaillimh
Bealtaine 5 2024
WHERE WE ALL BELONG
€5 Clár Oifigiúil LUACH
RÚNAÍ
OFFICIAL SPONSORS
Allianz
AIB
SuperValu

10

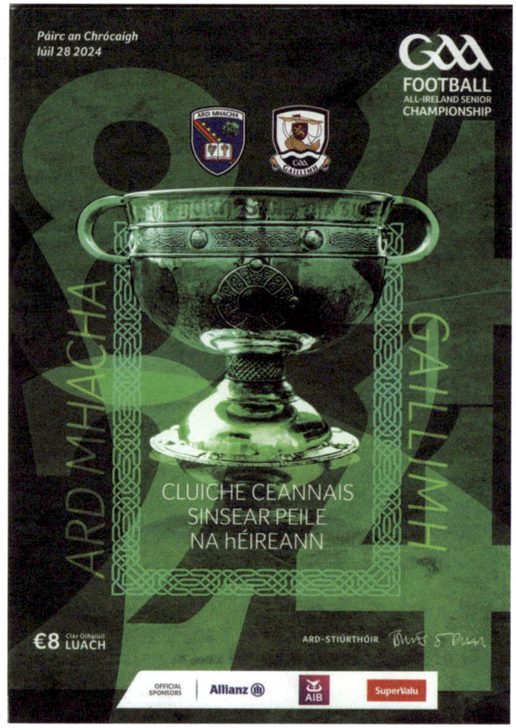

Páirc an Chrócaigh
Iúil 28 2024
GAA
FOOTBALL
ALL-IRELAND SENIOR
CHAMPIONSHIP
ARD MHACHA
GAILLIMH
ARD MHACHA
GAILLIMH
CLUICHE CEANNAIS
SINSEAR PEILE
NA hÉIREANN
€8 Clár Oifigiúil LUACH
ARD-STIÚRTHÓIR
OFFICIAL SPONSORS
Allianz
AIB
SuperValu

11

páirc an chrócaigh
iúil 28
GAA
FOOTBALL
ALL-IRELAND SENIOR
CHAMPIONSHIP
cluiche ceannais
sinsear peile na héireann
2024
ard mhacha
v gaillimh
€8 Clár Oifigiúil LUACH
WWW.GAA.IE CLÁR OIFIGIÚIL
OFFICIAL SPONSORS
Allianz
AIB
SuperValu

12

8 Ulster Football Final
Donegal 0-20 Armagh 0-20 aet
(Donegal won 6-5 on penalties)

9 Connacht Football Final
Galway 0-16 Mayo 0-15

10 All-Ireland Football Final
Armagh 1-11 Galway 0-13
Attendance – 82,300

11 All-Ireland Football Final (Armagh edition)

12 All-Ireland Football Final (Galway edition)

ACKNOWLEDGEMENTS

While writing this book I have been very fortunate to have had the support of many wonderful people, all of whom contributed to bringing this project to fruition.

I would like to acknowledge the help, support and encouragement I received from Tom Ryan, Ard Stiúrthóir Cumann Lúthchleas Gael, and Tadhg Cowhig, DBA Publishers, before the project got off the ground.

I would like to thank the private collectors who allowed me into their homes to scan the programmes. Some of them did not know me but were nonetheless willing to share their knowledge and collections with me. For that I will always be grateful to: John Clarke, Frank Coyne, Pádraig Duke, Eoin Fanning, John Ferris, Keith Heffernan, James Lundon, Pat Lynch, PJ Maxwell, Séamus O'Reilly, Jim Whelan, Dominic Williams, Paddy Quill and Liam Rabbitte.

Particular thanks are due to the following archives, which contributed images to this book:

» **Cardinal Tomás Ó Fiaich Library & Archive, Armagh.**
» **Croke Park GAA Museum and Archive, Dublin.**
» **Muckross House Research Library, Courtesy of the Trustees of Muckross House CLG, Killarney.**

The staff at these archives were extremely helpful, especially Roddy Hegarty in the Cardinal Tomás Ó Fiaich Library & Archive, Patricia O'Hare in the Muckross House Research Library, and Adam Staunton in the Croke Park GAA Museum and Archive.

The 1914 All-Ireland Hurling Final Programme image is courtesy of Whytes.ie auctioneers.

For their help with sources, fact-checking, proofreading and advice, special mention is due to Alan Aherne, Mary Brennan, Eoghan Corry, Vera Doyle, Lynn Fletcher, George Fonsie Mealy, Brian Kearney, Brian Kelly (Waterford), Mark Kelly, Kieron Kenny, Maria Kinsella, Leo McGough, Bobby McIlhatton, John McKenna, Liam Rabbitte, Cormac Walshe and Jim Whelan. I am particularly grateful to James Lundon for the time, interest, encouragement and advice he offered at several stages of writing this book.

I will be forever indebted to Patrick O'Donoghue at Gill Books for recognising the merit in this project and for taking a chance on it. Having taken that chance, a huge thank you goes to all the team at Gill particularly Margaret Farrelly, Charlie Lawlor and Deborah Marsh who turned my efforts into something special.

I would also like to thank my parents, Gus and Maureen, for instilling a love of Gaelic games in me and for the opportunities their sacrifices created for me. My brothers, Mark and Brian, and my sister, Áine, are a constant source of support and encouragement.

Finally, I would like to thank my wife Maria and my two sons, Pádraic and Lorcan, for their love, support, patience and input during the writing of this book.

BIBLIOGRAPHY

Breheny, Martin and Keenan, Dónal, *The Ultimate Encyclopedia of Gaelic Football and Hurling* (Kildare, 2001).

Carey, Tim, *Croke Park: A History* (updated edition) (Cork, 2013).

Cartwright, George, *The Gallant John Joe: Cavan's Millennium Man* (Bray, 2020).

Corry, Eoghan, *An Illustrated History of the GAA* (Dublin, 2005).

Corry, Eoghan, *The History of Gaelic Football* (Dublin, 2010).

Donegan, Des, *The Complete Handbook of Gaelic Games* (Dublin, 2021).

Doyle, Siobhán, *A History of the GAA in 100 Objects* (Newbridge, 2022).

Dunne, Eileen & Dunne, Moira, *All-Star Gazing: 50 Years of the GAA All-Stars* (Dublin, 2021).

Fitzpatrick, Paul, *The Fairytale in New York: The Story Behind Cavan's Greatest Victory* (Bray, 2013).

Kelleher, Humphrey, *GAA Family Silver: The People and Stories behind 101 Cups and Trophies* (Dublin, 2013).

Kelleher, Humphrey, *A Place to Play: The People and Stories Behind 101 GAA Grounds* (Newbridge, 2023).

Keys, Colm and Reilly, Dermot, *Chasing Sam Maguire: The All-Ireland Football Championship 1928–1977* (Dublin, 2023).

King, Seamus J., *A History of Hurling* (second edition) (Dublin, 2005).

Ó Ceallacháin, Seán Óg and McCann, Owen, *The Liam MacCarthy Cup* (Dublin, 2009).